*H*istorians usually look for the o
of American political culture amor
English-speaking people and Britis
stitutional and legal sources. Yet G
immigrants to the colonies also cor
tributed to—and developed for themselves—an American political
consciousness.

In *Palatines, Liberty, and Property* A. G.
Roeber focuses on this neglected subject
and explains why so many Germans,
when they faced critical choices in 1776,
became active supporters of the patriot
cause. Employing a variety of German-language sources, Roeber explores German
conceptions of personal and public property in the context of cultural and religious
beliefs, village life, and family concerns.
He follows all the major German migration streams, beginning with the Palatines
in New York and including Germans who
settled in Pennsylvania, Virginia, South
Carolina, and Georgia. Roeber's study of
German-American ideas about liberty and
property provides a unique perspective
within a growing historiography on the
transfer of culture and beliefs from Europe
and Africa to America.

A. G. ROEBER is professor of early American history at the University of Illinois at
Chicago and adjunct professor of law at
Chicago-Kent College of Law. He is the
author of *Faithful Magistrates and Republican
Lawyers: Creators of Virginia Legal Culture,
1680–1810.*

Palatines, Liberty, and Property

EARLY AMERICA:
History, Context, Culture

Jack P. Greene and J. R. Pole,
Series Editors

Palatines, Liberty, and Property

German Lutherans
in Colonial British America

A. G. Roeber

THE JOHNS HOPKINS UNIVERSITY PRESS

Baltimore and London

This volume has been published with the generous assistance of the Max Kade Foundation.

The Johns Hopkins University Press
2715 North Charles Street
Baltimore, Maryland 21218-4319
The Johns Hopkins Press Ltd., London

Library of Congress Cataloging-in-Publication Data

Roeber, A. G., 1949–
  Palatines, liberty, and property : German Lutherans in colonial
British America / A. G. Roeber.
     p.   cm. — (Early America)
  Includes bibliographical references (p.   ) and index.
  ISBN 0-8018-4459-2
  1. Palatine Americans—History—18th century. 2. Political
culture—United States—History—18th century. 3. Property rights—
United States—History—18th century. 4. Property rights—Germany—
History—18th century. 5. Liberty of conscience—Germany—
History—18th century. 6. Liberty of conscience—United States—
History—18th century. 7. Lutheran Church—Doctrines. I. Title.
II. Series.
E184.P3R64   1993
323.1'131073—dc20   92-25647

For Pat

CONTENTS

PREFACE and ACKNOWLEDGMENTS

THIS BOOK began when I grew curious about Willi Paul Adams's view of the German-language press in the age of the American Revolution. In 1976 Professor Adams responded to a query by Bernard Bailyn about the German-language newspapers published by Henry Miller and the Christopher Saurs, Sr. and Jr.: how did German speakers handle the political, legal, and constitutional terminology of the Revolutionary era? Adams found that Miller, especially, had reproduced revolutionary arguments and made a few translations of terms such as *direct representation* and *virtual representation,* and that was that. German speakers had no trouble understanding what the political fuss was about, Adams concluded, because "their political culture, as reflected in their press, was Anglo-American, if only because there were no German models to be transplanted that had any relevance to life in British America." Reading Miller's published works again, I wondered if Adams could be right. I doubted that the process had been so simple or so easy.[1]

The reasons for my doubts rested in the richness of German-American culture, especially in Pennsylvania, which even today is not simply a microcosm of English-language America. German-speaking Lutherans made up the majority of the 120,000 emigrants from the Holy Roman Empire who settled in British North America between 1683 and 1783. Unwittingly, however, other Americans tend to identify the "Pennsylvania Dutch" and their descendants as Amish, Mennonites, or Moravians. Studies of Pennsylvania folklore document the delights to ear, eye, and palate known to travelers in that state's southern counties. The scholarly literature devoted to the "folk" culture of the German speakers has tended to concentrate on the Plain Dutch, whose domestic customs and religious beliefs still deserve attention. The Pennsylvania Dutch culture of the eighteenth century seems, in the rich detail of its material and religious culture, to reveal cultural transfer and cultural retention belying Miller's easy translations. Yet only occasionally do the customs and behavior of the self-conscious separatists among German speakers reveal the thoughts

ix

and values of the majority of German-American colonists, who appear in general to have harbored considerable enthusiasm for British colonial life.[2]

Ethnographers and anthropologists have spent considerable time and effort reconstructing the contours of everyday life to shed light on how early modern rural and village people reacted to the rise of a political state and became politically conscious. I wondered how that process happened in British North America among the German speakers' Lutheran majority, and began looking into the backgrounds of the emigrants. In the early 1980s I had some reason to wonder whether my curiosity was justified. The most influential and accessible book in English on a German-speaking settlement had suggested that not many folklore aspects of German culture survived transfer and settlement. Its author labored hard with others in the 1960s and 1970s to correct overenthusiastic claims for ethnic uniqueness among the Pennsylvania Dutch. The German speakers of Germantown, Pennsylvania, turned out not to be better farmers; did not seek out limestone soils; and did not all cling to kin, the "home place," and religious conservatism. Those German speakers had "assimilated," "anglicized," or "Americanized" very rapidly indeed. They behaved no differently than did their English-speaking neighbors. Hence, they had no trouble with the terms and issues surrounding the Revolution. They fought for their "freedom," and provided their Anglo-American neighbors with the models around which stereotypes were formed: the Germans were hard working, industrious, thrifty, religious, and family and property-oriented—like their English neighbors. They were also apolitical, clannish, and a bit dull; they were at one and the same time sturdy Teutons and the "dumb Dutch."[3] And even as my own labors were coming to an end, a massive study appeared suggesting that aside from the dominant English-speaking settlers of North America, only the true Dutch, not German speakers, brought real "folkways" to North America.[4]

Fortunately, as early as 1982, I had the good fortune of meeting Hermann Wellenreuther and Marie-Luise Frings in Cologne. They encouraged me to pursue my doubts. In the past ten years, they have introduced me to other colleagues and have turned research trips to Göttingen into joyful, productive visits, including lively explorations of Lower Saxony, the Harz Mountains, and Thuringia. Hans Medick of the Max Planck Institute, Göttingen, has been especially generous in discussing our mutual interests in Swabian village culture. Kurt Aland and his associates at the Mühlenberg Vorschungsvorhaben, Münster, kindly provided me with page proofs of a forthcoming volume of Heinrich Melchior Mühlenberg's correspondence and advised me about the right people to consult at Halle. To Jürgen Storz, the archivist at the Francke Foundations in Halle, I am especially grateful for hospitality and extraordinary access, especially under the difficult conditions before 1989, to both working space and materials. Other colleagues discussed the project in detail, offered opportunities for seminar presentations, and forced me to clarify what it was I was finding.

The initial stages of research and the first chapters of the book began at the John F. Kennedy Institute for North American Studies in Berlin. To Willi Paul Adams and Knud Krakau, I extend profound thanks for two stimulating years with them and their colleagues; the institute librarian, Hans Kolligs, was especially helpful in providing office space and responding to inquiries about books and film.

I was not in Berlin for too many months when I discovered that I had no choice but to collect for myself village archival materials in the German southwest. Dietmar Willoweit of Würzburg, who was then in Tübingen, had just left Berlin, and he played a critical role in this enterprise by allowing me seminar space in Tübingen and the use of his assistants. Among the latter, Norbert Machheit was especially helpful in smoothing the first contacts with many skeptical village authorities who wondered what an American was up to snooping in dated, but possibly valuable, tax, land, and inheritance records. Gerhard Dilcher in Frankfurt, Wilhelm Brauneder in Vienna, Hartmut Lehmann in Kiel, and the German Historical Institute in Washington, D.C., all helped the project along in ways too numerous to detail.

Because of the complicated way in which village relationships and concepts of liberty and property were transferred in fragments to North America, I have divided this study into three parts. Readers will see my indebtedness to German colleagues at every turn in the first part of the book, which explicates German-language sources, terms, and cultural meanings. That my debts are no less profound in the United States, is revealed in the second section, which deals with cultural transfer, and transitional language and ideas. I thank my good friend of many years Lee Shepherd, chief archivist of the Virginia Historical Society, for generous and kind help in assembling many of the materials used for this section, and for his readiness to work as my research associate, checking materials in Virginia while I worked simultaneously in Germany. Bob Weir, of the University of South Carolina, Columbia, made an extended summer stay in South Carolina possible, after which I dashed back to Germany to check further discoveries and repair erroneous judgments. The third section of the book, which explores the final definition of the concepts liberty and property, focuses, not surprisingly, on Lutheran German speakers in Philadelphia and their shaping of these concepts. To

Jim Green and John van Horne at the Library Company of Philadelphia, Linda Stanley at the Historical Society of Pennsylvania, and John Peterson at the Lutheran Theological Seminary Archives I remain indebted for support during repeated Philadelphia stays. Billy G. Smith generously supplied me with printouts of his computerized breakdowns of the Philadelphia tax lists for 1756 and 1770 which enormously speeded up my prosopography of German-speaking Lutherans in that city.

Marianne Wokeck has been an unusually important and supportive colleague to me. She has generously devoted much time to repeated conversations and arguments about the process of settlement and cultural transfer, speaking from her unique perspective as a German seeing this process from her adopted country, while I as an American struggled to see the business from the vantage point of her native language and culture. Other colleagues, especially Tim Breen, Richard Dunn, John McCusker, and Leo Schelbert, have made important comments and offered suggestions at crucial junctures. I benefited especially from Bernard Bailyn and Phil Morgan's insistent prodding to clarify the argument of the book, as a truncated version became an extended work over which we all three despaired from time to time.

The book comes full circle in Chicago. It began here in 1981 thanks to a Midwest Faculty Fellowship at the University of Chicago, where Mark Kishlansky, Kathy Conzen, John Langbein, Gerhard Casper, and Ted Cook helped me to formulate the initial application to the Humboldt Foundation. To former colleagues at Lawrence University in Appleton, Wisconsin, —Dorrit Friedlander, Hartmut Gerlach, and Hans Ternes—I owe special thanks for allowing me to begin learning German under the tutelage of three native speakers. Their patience, and that of my instructor at the Goethe Institut, Berlin, Hans-Jürgen Rein, is complimented by the Europeans who today insist that I speak German like someone from Holland or north Germany. Leonard Thompson, Peter Fritzell, and Bert Goldgar of Lawrence heard more about this project as it evolved than they could possibly have wanted to know; their perspectives—based in the fields of religious studies, early American literature, and eighteenth-century English literature—helped me to sharpen key parts of the argument.

I have been especially blessed by the herculean efforts of two readers, David Sabean and John Murrin. David has offered sage advice repeatedly in Stuttgart and Göttingen, particularly his close reading of my conclusions. John continues to amaze me with the acuity of his judgments and the gentle wit with which he corrects the blunders of colleagues. To these two men, especially, the reader owes gratitude that an already long book is not even longer. In Robert J. Brugger I have also found a rare combination: a patient, judicious, and encouraging editor; Miriam Kleiger's expert copyediting saved me from several embarrassments. Win Thrall has provided the mapwork for this book, as for my previous one, to my great satisfaction and admiration. Jack Greene and J. R. Pole found the book significant enough to accept it for their series; I hope they will be rewarded for their act of faith. Pole in particular provided a final, meticulous reading of the manuscript, which improved its argument considerably.

The Alexander von Humboldt Foundation, Bonn–Bad Godesburg, made this book possible through a fellowship that allowed two years of residence and additional shorter stays both in the Federal Republic of Germany and in what was then the German Democratic Republic. I cannot adequately express my continued gratitude for the support and ongoing confidence the Humboldt Foundation places in its Fellows. The German Academic Exchange Program, the Alfred Beveridge Grant Program of the American Historical Association, the American Council of Learned Societies Travel Program, and the American Bar Foundation Fellowship Program — all supported research in Europe and the United States. Lawrence University's faculty research grants, the University of Illinois's Campus Research Board, and the summer fellowships provided by the Historical Society of Pennsylvania and the Library Company of Philadelphia helped me to complete my research in American repositories. I am grateful to the Humanities Institute at the University of Illinois at Chicago for awarding me in 1989–90 a fellowship that allowed me time to write, and I especially thank its director, Gene Ruoff, and his administrative assistant, Linda Vavra.

My oldest daughter, Maria, was thoughtful enough to be born a few weeks after the original proposal was complete in 1981; our second daughter, Grete, could not raise many objections when whisked off to Berlin at three months; our son, Christian, was born in Berlin but has expressed his impatience only in English as his sisters have hinted broadly in two languages that "the big book" more than warranted a conclusion. Through it all, Pat has proven that her Swiss-Palatine village ancestors were right: at the center of domestic economy, even in households where fathers shop, cook, clean, do music lessons, and try to write, the mother holds it all together. Such debts, deeper than any incurred in the realm of worldly goods, one can only accept on faith, with gratitude for what pietists knew was a graced life.

Palatines, Liberty, and Property

1

New York: Theme and Variations

I N 1729, at the dawn of the second George's reign, subscribers to Giles
Jacob's *A New Law-Dictionary* understood that according to Jacob's
definition, *liberty* was "a privilege held by grant or prescription, by which
men may enjoy some benefit beyond the ordinary subject." Exactly what
this privilege consisted of, Britons debated fiercely during the next half
century. The stream of denunciations and responses that greeted Richard
Price's explication of this term in February 1776 laid bare the boundaries
of debate surrounding the term. Price's *Observations on the Nature of Civil
Liberty* . . . extended the privilege or benefit to actual representation in
government, for the simplest of reasons: the exercising of power over
property—in the form of taxation—could not be justified without prior
consent of the property owners. To some Britons, those satisfied with
the notion of "virtual" representation of the entire nation, regardless of
actual participation, Price's idea seemed radical. Yet the simplicity of this
equation explains why, to British North Americans, "the sanctity of
private property and the benefits of commercial expansion, within customary boundaries, were simply assumed—the Revolution was fought
in part to protect the individual's right to private property" and the liberty
to choose one's representatives.[1]

German speakers in the colonies never said whether they understood
this equation. An English-speaking Pennsylvania lawyer, however, believed they did. Opposition to Frederick Lord North's ministry, and
support for the Revolution, opined Alexander Graydon, came down to
money and "very forceably appealed to the pocket." Since "the great
body of German farmers, [were] extremely tenacious of property," they
rebelled.[2]

I

By the 1770s, then, the authoritative power of the terms *liberty* and *property* appears to have been universal throughout British North America's shared political culture. But no historian writing on German speakers, political culture, and the authority bestowed on words such as *liberty* and *property* can elude the long shadows of the German past. To write of a "political culture" among German speakers in Europe before 1871 was nearly impossible. The evolution of political culture in Germany thereafter became a nightmare. Unless one subscribes to a theory of migration by which travel to a distant place miraculously leached out the memory and identity of German speakers in North America, the problematic nature of these terms in the emigrants' homeland must have survived the crossing. Leonard Krieger's classic essay *The German Idea of Freedom* laid out in stark and pessimistic terms German speakers' proclivity for a "positive" and "internal" liberty that led the later nation-state down the dark and pernicious road toward a "special way" *(Sonderweg)* in European history different from that of Western Europe. In this scenario, German speakers inherited from their religious and geographical past a tendency to idealize authority and "the state" as entities "above politics" and to define liberty as the working out of the "good life" in a rationally ordered, prosperous society to whose authority the individual owed allegiance and obedience. There is something to this analysis, and one strain of this kind of thinking did survive the transatlantic crossing to British North America in the eighteenth century. But this was never the whole story, on either side of the Atlantic.[3]

Others have suggested that a healthier, more "libertarian" tradition that defined freedom as an absence of constraints (a "negative" definition) flourished in the Swiss cantons and in the German states bordering the Helvetic Confederation. There, townsfolk and peasants used political organization and conscious cultivation of collective memory to protect privileges against the pretensions of ambitious lords. This "Swiss" tradition among German speakers also survived transfer to North America in the eighteenth century. It did so because an inordinately large number of immigrants, indiscriminately called "Palatines" by the British, came from families who had already emigrated from Switzerland to the Electoral Palatinate and the neighboring Kraichgau between 1648 and 1700.[4]

For carriers of both traditions among the German speakers in British North America, vocabulary had to be integrated into British-American concepts in a process that accepted some parts of each tradition and rejected others, as ideas were "brokered" by articulate representatives who defended aspects of German "liberty." The first group of representatives, or "brokers," were the Lutheran pastors and teachers who served in North America, most of whom came from central and northern German states; a disproportionate number had been educated at, and worked as missionaries from, the Francke Foundations, established by the Lutheran pietist August Hermann Francke at Halle, in Prussia. They retained a reverence for state authority, and cherished a definition of liberty that placed great emphasis on how freedom could be positively realized by meeting one's obligations and performing civic and religious duties. Their discussions and expositions of these concepts occurred in correspondence, sermons, and debates with ambitious lay leaders. Most of the latter—successful entrepreneurs, tavern keepers, booksellers, and agents involved in recruiting emigrants and doing business on both sides of the Atlantic—came from the Kraichgau and the Palatinate. This second group of brokers continued to interpret "liberty" by emphasizing choice and personal interest, just as they, their fathers, and their relatives had done in the villages they revisited and with which they stayed in contact.

Yet the confrontation between these two definitions did not occur immediately. Indeed, liberty was not regarded purely in political terms. Because of the influence of the religious renewal movement known as Pietism, German speakers tended to think of liberty more in terms of matters of conscience and faith than in terms of the concept's political and social dimensions.

The word *Freiheit* was rarely used in German-speaking North America before 1750; its plural form, *Freiheiten*—privileges—was used more often. But "privileges," or what some Britons called "rights," do not automatically translate into "liberty" and the accompanying concept of the autonomous, politically conscious individual. To fashion that connection took time—in part because of difficulties German speakers encountered in translating between two languages, as the early New York experience demonstrated, but also in part because the emergence of a German-American idea of "liberty" tied to "property"—and, hence, the emergence of a genuine political culture—could not occur in North America before midcentury because of the settlement process itself. Only when a German-American language began to emerge, created by social exchanges among German speakers, could debate begin over what these concepts meant. That language evolved because of practical adjustments to spiritual, material, and economic needs and possibilities. However, German speakers' adjustment to practical issues of emotional and physical survival—and their caution in dealing with common-law institutions and practices surrounding real property and its inheritance—only gradually permitted acquisition of associations surrounding the other "key word" of the day, *property*.[5]

Historians of central Europe have been struck by the extent to which controversy over and concern for property and its inheritance dominated village life. Relationships among individuals and groups received definition and meaning as property determined alliances and exclusions. Property was not understood communally in the villages, and people certainly knew what belonged to them, as individuals. But its defense was usually engaged in collectively, by means of grievances (*Gravamina*) drawn up by those with *Bürgerrecht,* or full privileges as taxpayers in village or town. As German speakers arrived in large numbers in British North America after 1727, they brought their concern over familial alliances and domestic relationships with them. But their own uncertainty both about the British colonial common law of property, and about the complications of resettlement in a land where each colony's inheritance law differed from that of the others, as well as from the German private-law system, postponed reflection on property and inheritance.

These German speakers arrived in North America at a a time when English speakers did not unequivocally equate material possessions with liberty. But Anglo-Americans *did* insist that *security* in one's property really did define liberty. This equation was a British constitutional construct, and one that depended upon a person's ability to understand representation and the long common-law tradition in which property was understood to be the bulwark of liberty against tyranny. This common-law tradition sprang from a concern with inheritance and ancestral custom, and from arrangements commonly arrived at on the basis of experience and practicality. It emphasized certainty and security in the enjoyment of personal possessions, or "vested interests." Yet these were just the associations and understandings German speakers could not come by automatically, and did not have until midcentury.[6] The even more complicated sets of associations springing from British opposition literature that spoke of "court" and "country" made no impression on German speakers at all.[7]

Even as late as the early 1900s, when American law professors struggled to convey to their students exactly what the term *Vermögen* meant, they had to confess to a frustration that German speakers in the colonies must have also felt. "We have no English word so definite and concise as this," lamented Richard Ely, concluding that "net assets" perhaps conveyed what the German term meant, but that the term *net assets* does not speak to political culture or privileges.[8]

The problematic nature of the term *property* in either language, and the question of whether one could connect it to *liberty,* became for German speakers more difficult still. This was so because of a profound challenge to village property relationships issued by the religious renewal movement known as Pietism. Especially in the hands of clerics and the married women of the villages, this movement fashioned a critique of "worldly goods" and of irresponsible male behavior exhibited by governmental authorities or by village fathers. Behavior that threatened the marginal economy of the household provoked a response demanding accountability from those charged with power in the state, the village, and the household. The pietist challenge—to live out in practical terms what the teachings of evangelical Christianity demanded of believers—encouraged among ordinary persons the development of reflection, criticism, and a language capable of conceiving of an "inner core self." The implications such reflection had for the creation of a political culture became considerable when transferred to the British North American context. Halle's pastors, as part of their pedagogical scheme to make of their parishioners good Christian and loyal subjects, made a valiant effort to instruct them in the obligations of individual stewardship and philanthropy in dealing with "worldly goods." Yet most parishioners remained chary of giving and deeply suspicious of how lay or clerical authority handled alms and other forms of church property. By the 1760s, German Lutheran churches from Pennsylvania to Georgia provided the arena where disagreements over the definitions of property and privileges were fought out. This confrontation, which took place after the settlement process and concern for securing domestic economy and religious faith, had created an adequate German-American language and produced a German-American reflection on liberty and property. It was not until 1738, when Christopher Saur began operating his press in Germantown, that the German-American language received printed form and became influential.[9]

Few of these eighteenth-century German speakers or their English-speaking neighbors made a careful distinction between "public" or "political" culture and "private" life. People understood the "personal" dimension of life, which could be threatened by other individuals, family, or public authority. But the pietist movement had a hand in creating the further distinction between public and private, and hence, in forcing reflection on the problem of property and its relationship to obligations to both church and state, and on its role as protector of the personal. Among political commentators and theorists, "privacy" meant a condition different from official, state authority.[10] It was also distinctly inferior, identified with money making and trade, the *commercium,* and secondary to the great affairs of the state, the *res publica.* As writers identified property and religious belief (soon to be described as "personal opinion") as key areas in need of protection against power, they distinguished "private society" from "public affairs."[11]

Neither in Britain nor in its colonies had people thought through this distinction as the first German speakers arrived in New York.[12] State power was simply another part of the general social order.[13] Commenting on how funds for military defense could be raised, writers in England and on the continent created the notion of the public order sustained by taxation. The concept of *Privatrecht* existed in German law, and university faculties had developed a literature on the nature of the person and the *Rechtssubjekt;* little of this mattered at the level of daily life.[14]

A great deal of effort has been expended by Jürgen Habermas to elucidate exactly how the "public" order could be distinguished from the "private social" realm as a European urban class emerged. Leisured contemplation by bourgeois, literate clubs and societies employing discussion and criticism helped to create a "public use" of reasoned discourse. French historians have explored this phenomenon from a number of perspectives.[15] But this literature does not say very much about rural and village life. Only recently has newer scholarship admitted that the formation of a political or civic culture in the eighteenth century depended on many forms of sociability, not only the discourse of the enlightened bourgeoisie. Pietism created a more wide-ranging network for circulating thought and encouraging reflection on public and private worlds than did Masonic lodges, reading clubs, and more familiar forms of bourgeois "private sociability."[16] Pietist literature and terms dictated, among ordinary villagers of central Europe, the definition of which norms were to be thought authoritative, and what social cement held together relationships.[17] Pietist households in the Reich, and in North America, still maintained a marginal existence, and unwelcome innovation or disruption could mean ruin, and death. Christopher Saur grasped this fact, and in so doing he began the broader process of reflection in print about what implications lay behind the key English words.

Coming to terms with "liberty" and "property" depended for German speakers on a sequence of necessary adjustments. The emigrants brought with them disparate, inherited definitions dependent on both region and specific religious-political history within the Reich. Those ideas were then brokered and translated by early arrivals, both clergy and secular traders, who tended to establish a kind of "cultural crystallization" among themselves, setting the terms under which later arrivals had to adjust to the German-American community. That process was not identical, however, nor was the outcome the same, in all the colonies where German speakers settled.[18] The New York experience demonstrated that settlement involved the new arrivals in harsh, practical affairs; no reflection upon the potential meanings of liberty and property circulated broadly before the 1740s. The influence of Pietism and the domestic concerns of village life continued to override in North American settlements any engagement with broader "public" issues that German speakers might have found worthy of their attention. The language German speakers evolved up to the 1740s reflected this "inward" quality. Scholars of the Pennsylvania Germans have documented the use of High German or Dutch in church services and formal documents, the spoken use of German or Dutch regional dialects, and the gradual adoption of English. The fusion between the spoken German and English (initially the English vocabulary of trade and economic exchange) occurred in print and was circulated via print distribution networks before German-American political concepts were given printed form. The German speakers of British North America, eventually trilingual, could only conceive of the New World in which they found themselves by referring to associations and meanings that still reflected the village and religious landscape from which they had emigrated. When German emigration peaked and declined after 1753, a deep cultural transfer had taken place. Engagement with British-American political culture occurred using terms that well-established networks of communication and trade brokers had developed in the preceding half century.[19]

By the 1760s German speakers apparently felt sufficient unity among themselves and with others to claim a place as members of "the people."[20] This happened not only among the numerically small groups of German speakers in New York. In early rural settlements of the 1730s such as Robinson Run, Virginia, and the Salzburger settlement on the Savannah River in Georgia, and in later, more urban groups in Philadelphia and Charleston, both group identity and agreement on the authoritative and normative meanings of liberty and property, and hence, participation in political culture, had became possible by the 1760s and 70s. German speakers thought they understood Price, Paine, and Jefferson. Whether they grasped the consequences of accepting the libertarian definitions of liberty and property, however, is a question one can safely postpone asking.[21] In 1711 observers of the Palatines in New York could not have imagined anything less probable than such definitions leading German speakers into a revolution.

II

If an observant German chronicler had been able to identify an *annus mirabilis* for his compatriots in British North America in the eighteenth century, he would have chosen 1727. Great Britain's first German king, George I, elector of Hanover, died; to the relief of many Britons worried about political stability, the new monarch retained Charles, Viscount

Townshend as secretary of state. Fewer rejoiced that Robert Walpole remained in office. George II secured both the Protestant Succession and the political status quo. Britons could respect him; German-born subjects pointed to him with pride.[22]

The Georges' predecessor, Queen Anne, had laid the groundwork for the encounter with British liberty and property by aiding "distressed Palatines" driven from the Rhineland by war, bad weather, and crop failure in 1709. Britons and "Palatines" alike regarded "liberty" in this context to mean freedom of conscience. Later, as the ranks of the immigrants swelled alarmingly, support had turned to suspicion and hostility, until the Catholic emigrés were sent home, a stop was put to further arrivals, and eventually some twenty-five hundred of the migrants were sent on their way to the American colonies. Britons had neglected to mull over what notions of liberty the Palatines had smuggled aboard.[23]

Those were alerted, however, who purchased the pamphlet *The Palatines Catechism . . . in a pleasant Dialogue between an English Tradesman and a High Dutchman . . .* The anonymous author, less interested in the description of the Palatinate than in that of its departed people, found little reason to be pleasant about an incompetent ally and his impoverished population. The strain upon the property of Britons, in the form of increased taxation and probable competition for jobs, filled the honest tradesman with alarm. To the High German's objection that after the war Britain would receive financial compensation and that "in the meantime, necessity has no law," the Briton responded with indignation. "This is High German doctrine with a vengeance[:] when the sky falls we catch larks."[24] The imagery of this old sixteenth-century proverb spoke to the opportunism of which the English believed German speakers capable. The Palatine also could not allay British alarm at hordes of impoverished continentals by citing allegories from the Protestant tradition. The German speaker noted the Old Testament example of the Gibeonites living in Canaan among the Israelites. To this, the tradesman responded with prophetic insight: "Yes; but then they were made hewers of wood and drawers of water to the people and not equal in freedom, trade, liberty and property as our strangers are like to be." The exchange ended with a recitation of how different social customs necessarily divided peoples. The tradesman wished the Germans out of Britain into "this imaginary English America." There, they could work out the intricacies of competing with Britons for "freedom, trade, liberty and property."[25]

The pamphleteer suggested that "freedom" meant freedom from constraint—most probably from interference in religious belief; but possibly from ruinous taxes, since "trade" follows next in the line of privileges. Yet "liberty and property" bespoke the bundle of rights and privileges granted by the British constitution, the peculiar blessing that Giles Jacob by 1729 suggested bestowed a "benefit beyond the ordinary subject." The Palatines expected such benefits, and this worried the tradesman. The language, customs, and values of the German speakers proved to him that they could never be true Britons.[26]

Had the Palatines' claims to privileges been defined and acknowledged before they reached New York, Governor Robert Hunter would have been a happier man. Yet the "severall poor Lutherans come hither from the Lower Palatinat . . . where they lost all they had," as the Board of Trade described them to the Privy Council on their arrival in London in 1709, brought misunderstanding and trouble in their wake. The intention of the Privy Council and the queen included granting them land and temporary assistance "till they can reap the fruit of their Labour (which will not be till after one years Time)."[27] Where and how they were to labor was not spelled out. The original settlers, led by Pastor Josua Harrsch, (also known as Kocherthal), enjoyed the promise of a settlement and a glebe for the pastor's support. Kocherthal's small group settled on Quassaic Creek (Newburgh), their number dwarfed by another influx in October 1710. From this latter migration came the families who later settled one hundred miles northwest of Newburgh, on Schoharie Creek or in the Mohawk Valley, with an initial detour onto Livingston Manor, where they were to make their living by producing naval stores. That attempt to employ the Palatines provoked the first dispute over liberty and property.

Hunter's difficulties with the Palatines, according to Edward Hyde, earl of Clarendon, were his own fault. To William Legge, earl of Darmouth, Clarendon opined that Livingston "has been known many years in that Province for a very ill man[;] he formerly Victualled the forces at Albany in which he was guilty of the most notorious frauds by which he greatly improv'd his Estate, he has a Mill and a Brew house upon his land, and if he can get the Victualling of those Palatines who are so conveniently posted for his purpose, he will make a very good addition to his Estate." Clarendon dismissed the notion that the Palatines could produce naval stores. Everyone knew that this land was "not the best Place for Pine Trees"; "Levingston and some others will get Estates, [and] the Palatines will not be the richer."[28]

Clarendon need not have worried. The "Palatines," originating in villages in the Rhineland; in the Neckar Valley, in Württemberg and in the Kraichgau knew nothing about producing naval stores. Faced with a financial squeeze, but still legally obligated to victual people who were grumbling about working like hired hands instead of being treated like landowners, Livingston consulted Hunter. Hunter bound out many chil-

dren to neighboring English farmers, a move that evoked memories of
the day laborers, the *Söldner* and *Tagelöhner,* who eked out an existence
on rented plots and in tiny cottages by working for others. Then, in a
cost-cutting move, Hunter instructed his compatriot, "Make the Expence
for the Palatins as little as possible, and . . . take beer only for the men
that work and not for their familys." In the next breath Hunter acknowledged the presence of a "great many widows and Orphans among the
people"; about these, his only worry was that he wished to know how
"they might be turned to some use, or be no longer a burthen . "[29] By
cutting the beer supply of the women and children, binding them out,
and preventing them from settling on lands they regarded as theirs,
Hunter violated German villagers' most deeply held convictions about
the sanctity of diet and household.

A nervous interview with the Palatines reported to Hunter by Johannes Cast, the Straßburger who operated as German commissioner,
revealed growing hostility. A few were reported to be content with the
settlement on the Livingston lands. These, the obedient Germans Livingston had thought he was getting, acknowledged that "it is our duty,
and we must absolutely work for the Queen, it cannot be otherwise than
that her majesty will put us in a position to earn our bread for she will
not keep us always in this way." But the guiding spirits among the settlers
pointed to what Hunter contemptuously dismissed as "pretended rights";
they scorned the idea that they had come to America merely to "earn
our bread." "We came to America to establish our families—to secure
lands for our children on which they will be able to support themselves
after we die." To the timorous who counseled patience, the sharp-tongued
quoted the *Sprüchwort* "Patience and hope make fools of those who fill
their hands with them." Hunter rightly feared that the Palatines would
not "conform to the intentions of those above them."[30] In response to
repeated pleas that they be allowed to leave for their lands, Hunter "in
a passion stamped upon the ground and said, here is your land (meaning
the almost baren Rocks,) where you must live and die."[31]

By September 1712 several Palatine families decided to abscond in
secret for the Schoharie, where promised property still awaited them.
During the winter some 150 families departed, followed by even more
the next spring. Ignoring Hunter's proclamation that they were rebels,
these settlers had by 1713 constructed a series of villages after securing
permission from the Mohawks to remain in the valley. According to the
Palatine version, the chiefs remembered what had been promised in 1710,
"saying they had formarly given that said land to Queen Anne for them
[i.e., the Palatines] to possess, and that no body else should hinder them
of it."[32]

In response, Hunter approved in early 1714 the land patent of Adam Vrooman, a wealthy Dutch merchant from Schenectady, for the land at Schoharie Vrooman had purchased from the Indians in 1711. Vrooman and his son Peter soon found their fields torn up by horses and their house and fences taken down by night. Peter was finally dragged from his wagon and severely beaten. Just before Vrooman's arrival, the Palatines had mistaken Nicholas Bayard for Hunter's henchman, as Bayard pretended to give deeds to the householders who could tell him the exact boundaries of their land. Whatever Bayard's intentions, the Palatine reaction was clear: they besieged him in a house, fired upon it, and just missed capturing him. He decamped at night for Schenectady.[33]

The governor cared little for what had happened to Bayard, but he did respond to Adam Vrooman's insistence that the "Ring Leader of all factions" among the Germans was Johann Conrad Weiser. A warrant for Weiser's arrest was issued, to be served by an undersheriff known only as "Adams." Arriving in July at "Weisersdorf," Adams flourished his warrant for the arrest of Weiser, the son of a Württemberg village *Schultheiß*.[34]

As Adams laid his hand on the troublemaker's shoulder to take him into custody, he touched off an exchange of symbolic gestures in which he was to play the role of the *Prügelknabe,* the knave beaten for the offenses of his better, who could not be touched. An entire complex of attitudes toward authority, the liberties surrounding household integrity and property, and the limits placed on authority that had rendered itself illegitimate sprang into action. Adams was set upon by the village wives, led by Magdalena Zeh. The women threw him to the ground, dragged him into a sow's wallow, bound him to a fence rail, and rode him out to the bridge, where he was thrashed. After breaking two of his ribs and putting out an eye, the women subjected him to a final indignity by urinating on his upturned face before returning to the villages, leaving him to crawl back to Albany.[35]

The assault upon Adams seemed to the governor the ultimate proof of Palatine vulgarity and insubordination. From the German villagers' perspective, an elaborate theater of justice had been played out by very specific actors. That the women took matters in hand was no accident: Hunter had separated women and children from their households in 1711, and Livingston's ill-conceived economy measure had denied them the promised ration of beer. Mothers had lost children who had been bound out to English farmers, no particular care being taken to distinguish orphans from the children of poor parents. Unable to reach Hunter and Livingston, the women seized these men's symbolic underling instead. The physical assault on Adams, and his being ridden on a rail, publicly humiliated this bearer of a compromised authority who had attempted assault upon the real figure in the village who enjoyed trust and confidence: the Schultheiß's son, Weiser. The women dragged Adams through a sow's wallow, smearing him with the most shameful substance in the German villager's scale of values. Adams was dragged through a degraded property, to remind the governor that he had tried to keep them from occupying what was rightly theirs. The final indignity—urinating on the poor deputy—completed the mirror image: urine for the denied beer, a form of *Nahrung*—sustenance.[36]

The governor decided not to pursue these dreadful folk during 1716. Other political concerns involving delicate negotiations with the colonial assembly over a naturalization bill and a measure disallowing all debt claims prior to 1714 prevented his taking action. Only in early 1717 did Hunter call Weiser to appear before him and explain the Palatines' relationship to property and rightful authority. To Hunter's threats that he would hang the truculent Swabian, and to the question as to why the Palatines had gone to Schoharie, Weiser responded that he was loyal to the monarch of Great Britain, but that the governor had failed in his obligation to sustain them and had told them to shift for themselves. Infuriated at the Palatines' refusal to knuckle under, Hunter "in a great passion" yelled, "What Great Britain?" Livingston, standing nearby, added, "Here is your King!", and pointed to the governor. Weiser then dissimulated, asking pardon for "Ignorance and Inadvertency." The governor next questioned why the Germans would not come to an agreement with the Albany group of landowners (which included Robert Livingston, Jr.) who since 1715 had held the lawful patents over the Schoharie lands. Weiser explained that the Palatines had invested labor in the lands that had been given to the Crown for their use. If they had a master, it was King George, "and not a private person."[37]

A *Privatperson* lacked authority, and both Hunter and Livingston recognized the insinuation behind Weiser's seemingly innocent declaration of loyalty to the Crown. Some years later, Weiser's fellow emigrant from Reutlingen, the Reformed pamphleteer Ulrich Simmendinger, justified the Palatines' actions in identical terms. Like his fellow Swabian Weiser, Simmendinger pointed out that the Palatines had come to New York with the expectation of getting land, and had been promised temporary support from the governor. Yet, he wrote, in a veiled reference to the claim that the Palatines felt betrayed and abandoned, "each one received his freedom to the extent that he might seek his own piece of bread in his own way." They were "free" to sustain themselves, but freedom from constraint had not been the point of Weiser's argument with the governor. The Palatines acknowledged their duty to the Crown, and in exchange for exercising positive freedom, they expected from an officer of the king defense of their privileges as German subjects of the Crown. Instead, Hunter had chosen to act as a mere "private person," forfeiting his claim to authority.[38]

The Schoharie settlers, convinced that Hunter meant to destroy them, sent Weiser and two other men with letters of power of attorney to London. Unfortunately, the ship was captured by pirates, and all of the messengers' money was stolen. They landed in debtor's prison; and two of them died, one on the return trip, the other shortly after his return. Not until 1723 did Weiser reach New York. By then, the Palatines' formal protest against the governor had been drafted and sent to London.[39]

This protest was not the work of Weiser, still in England when the document appeared in August 1722. The writer repeated the German speakers' claims that the Schoharie was theirs because of the "vast expense and labour" invested in the land. Crown authorities recognized this as one of two competing theories regarding the right to property. The Palatine argument cited the second argument also, that is, that ultimate title had been vested by the Native Americans in the British monarch. But the Palatine version ignored what would have been interesting to English theorists: whether the Indians had been the original possessors or merely the occupiers of the land. Instead, it was the Mohawks' prior use of the land that the Germans emphasized, and not the notion of first possession, the grounds upon which Hunter repeatedly ignored their claims.[40]

Years later, after a settlement had been reached, the Palatines clung to this notion that their right to the land was based both on use and on the Mohawks' gift of the land to the monarch for their enjoyment. They embellished their story with a legend according to which Mohawk chieftains had been in London *before* the Palatines arrived in New York, and had explicitly granted the land to Queen Anne for the Palatines' use. Though exploded by later historians, the legend is revealing. It casts into relief the Germans' underlying claims about "use," now given mythic form. It also shows their dawning realization that to win their argument they had to demonstrate prior title, that is, possession, an alien concept that they struggled to appropriate.[41]

Confrontations over liberty and property did not end with Hunter's removal in 1719. German-speaking religious leaders also complained about English land law and its deleterious effects on religious liberty. Kocherthal's small group, originally granted a glebe to support the Lutheran pastor, eventually dwindled and nearly died out. In the 1720s, just as the Schoharie controversy was being settled, the religious condition of the Lutherans became precarious and gave rise to another extended debate over the nature of liberty in a new land.

Kocherthal died in 1719, and the only other active Lutheran minister

in New York, Justus Falckner, died in 1723. The Society for the Propagation of the Gospel in Foreign Parts had sustained the Palatines and
attempted to win their affection for the Church of England. Johann
Frederic Haeger, ordained by the bishop of London, accompanied his
fellow countrymen to New York and tried to prevent a separation between Lutheran and Reformed worshipers and to attach both groups to
the Book of Common Prayer, receiving one hundred copies in German
for their use in 1711. He failed in both attempts. Bereft of pastoral care,
the Lutherans and Reformed settlers fell back on singing from their
hymnbooks and listening in household gatherings to sermons read from
collections appointed for the Sundays of the church year. Conrad Weiser
was one of those who acted as a lay reader (*Vorleser*). A young tailor's
apprentice named Johann Bernhard van Dieren, from Königsberg, in
East Prussia, arrived in New York in August 1721 after attracting the
attention in London of the German court chaplain Anton Wilhelm
Böhme, who sent him on to America. Though not ordained, van Dieren
apparently served with considerable success among the Lutheran settlers
for about four years. Since Böhme, too, had never formally received
orders, he remained unconcerned about van Dieren's dubious status.[42]
News of the spiritual plight of these Lutherans filtered back to the Reich,
where interested parties arranged to send books to sustain spiritual life
in the settlements.

In 1725, Wilhelm Christoph Berkenmeyer arrived in New York City
from the orthodox Lutheran city of Hamburg. Joined by a few other
pastors sent by the Holy Trinity Lutheran Church in London, a daughter
church of the Hamburg Consistory, Berkenmeyer became the dominant
force among New York Lutherans for the next thirty years. His influence
was strengthened by the fact that after 1746 no European pastors arrived
in New York at all. Berkenmeyer first drove out the unordained van
Dieren (who retired to Hackensack, New Jersey, as a miller); and in 1735
he drew up a formal church order for German Lutherans in New York,
one of the earliest reflections on the nature of liberty in the New World
by a Lutheran German speaker.[43]

Berkenmeyer began by reviewing the grievous state of affairs in which
he had found the church in 1725. Most of the problem originated in an
erroneous notion that "every congregation is permitted to defend its own
doctrine and views, and they assert that any individual is free to expose
the truth to ridicule, or to oppose or to defend false doctrine, and so
they make round what is square." Such licentiousness occurred because
"freedom easily degenerates into abuse of liberty, because freedom does
not lend itself to sharply defined bounds of right and justice, or to any
propping up by any one order whereby all things are established and

sustained." Berkenmeyer's German text singled out subjective, individual opinion as a defective concept, one that neglected to heed the objective norms by which "right and justice" were established. Public authority must shape the definition of *Freiheit*. Insisting that all clerics coming into New York subscribe to his church order, Berkenmeyer ignored the role of leading laymen and warned against those who "unwisely misuse their freedom by upsetting the Church and ruining its order." Such abuses stemmed from people who pretended that order was the work of the "free decision of human beings." Oddly enough, Berkenmeyer either ironically or unwittingly fought his battle on his putative opponents' ground by concluding that, in his opinion, order, and hence a proper liberty, is "based on divine justice."[44]

The 1735 document reaffirmed what Dutch and German Lutherans in the colony had acknowledged—loyalty to the Lutheran confessional symbols. Berkenmeyer attacked private conventicles and "secret assemblies" ("geheime Versammlungen"), a pointed reference to the pietist cells widespread in the Lutheran church in the German southwest and sustained by a movement one of whose major centers was the university at Halle. No sooner had Berkenmeyer defined the nature of liberty and its abuses than a dispute of ten years' duration broke out on the Raritan River in New Jersey,[45] a conflict that further sharpened debate over liberty and property.[46]

Lutheran services in New York had historically been held in Dutch, not German; the worship service was modeled on the 1689 version of the Lutheran consistory at Amsterdam and was barely distinguishable from Reformed liturgy. For the first forty years of the eighteenth century, New York's Lutheran church provided no locus for German-language culture or values, for it had been a multilingual and multinational confession since the days of New Netherland. Relatively bereft of pastoral care, the Lutherans had run into difficulties with the English over their church property, and Berkenmeyer had to resolve these difficulties. Their Reformed cousins, even fewer in number, were even worse off, and did not succeed until 1758 in establishing congregations at Albany and New York City.[47]

By 1747, as Lutherans moved away or died out in the old Quassaic community, their trustees were replaced by Anglicans, led by Alexander Colden and Richard Albertson, representing the dominant English and Dutch. German Lutherans struggled to retain this property. Meanwhile, language purity within the mixed German-Dutch Lutheran churches emerged as a new issue as Anglicans successfully took over the Quassaic glebe land. The New York City Lutherans twice unsuccessfully asked Governor George Clinton to preserve the glebe lands for the use of their own Lutheran pastor, but in 1751 the governor approved the petition to transfer the property to the Church of England. Trying to preserve the glebe lands, the German Lutherans approached two English attorneys, who advised them to establish first possession. The best way to do this was to "buy, secretly, a few acres near the church land and see to it that at least seven German Lutheran families build houses thereon; then they [the jurists] would help these Germans to recover *possession* of the church and glebe."[48] Incensed over English-Dutch collaboration to confiscate property that had been in their pastor's use for twenty years, New York German speakers rebelled.

Although German migration to New York had slowed to a trickle by comparison with the waves of immigration that repeatedly swept Philadelphia, Germans in New York City, at least since the 1720s, had enjoyed Lutheran pastoral care and developed a sense of German Lutheran identity. Influenced by the doctrinal orthodoxy of the Hamburg ministers, these urban Lutherans cared little for the denunciations of *Gemütlichkeit* that characterized eighteenth-century German Pietism. An enterprising group insisted on gathering contributions both in Europe and in the province to build a brewery and a second church. Then, to the extreme annoyance of the Dutch Lutherans, whose language had long been the one in liturgical use, they demanded that services be held in High German. Pastor Heinrich Melchior Mühlenberg, serving three Pennsylvania congregations, tried to explain to his superiors at Halle what had happened. He could find no German equivalent for *possession*, leaving it untranslated. He also could not explain why this term was significant. The German New Yorkers, slow to take the lawyers' advice, had lost the battle. Their English opponents, knowing both the law and the need for speed, successfully pressed their petition; the Quassaic glebe passed to the Anglican church in March 1752. Settlement had been too thin, networks of information and collaboration too weak, to fend off challenges from clever Dutch or English neighbors. There were as yet no linguistic connections between German definitions of key terms and North American political realities. What the early arrivals in New York had at their disposal to read in their own language on "political" topics turned them even more inward, even as they changed their language of worship from Dutch to High German.[49]

III

Awareness of German speakers' alien political lexicon prompted one pastor to doubt their ability to "bear the noble English freedom. They are like the fat horses and oxen who have gone to rich pasture for a long time and then refuse to take the bit or bear the yoke. It takes strong legs to bear prosperity. The liberty, peace, wealth and abundance which they enjoy cause them to be uncivil, wanton, proud and violent."⁵⁰

The imagery of wild animals came directly from the political literature in the Reich. Pastor Mühlenberg, too, showed the same awareness when answering New York chief justice James DeLancey's queries as to why German speakers behaved "in such a disorderly manner." The pastor explained that they "are poor, ignorant people who have no guardian or supervisor, who abuse the freedom they have by reason of the English privileges." A year earlier, Mühlenberg had already identified the English conquest of the Dutch colony as the root of Lutherans' difficulties, for "they not only received liberty"—a liberty they could not handle—"but also privileges from all the succeeding governors."⁵¹

That Muhlenberg would distinguish "liberty" from "privileges" makes one ask where the difference lay. The term *Freiheiten* (privileges) referred to those guarantees of the protection of the law which all British subjects enjoyed, whereas *Freiheitin* the singular implied the exercise of choice by self-conscious, disciplined individuals—the kind of people who were rare among Mühlenberg's flocks. The Anglican cleric Alexander Murray sniffed at the German Lutherans in Reading, Pennsylvania, who "are ever & anon quarrelling at their Preachers, whom of humour & Caprice they Change much oftener than they renew their Cloaths." The Germans, he thought, were determined to keep their pastors impoverished, to withhold their salaries, and "in their Language they *Hire* a Minister generally for no longer than a year, which renders his Office as Contemptible as Poor. Their Elections are like Polish Diets; they meet again & again, & as often dissolve in Confusion, till at last tired out, they submit to any Measure or any Minister for a Time, which makes the Settlements short lived & Unsatisfying & vacancies long."⁵² Murray saw German speakers using the liberty of choice, albeit in an awkward and uncivilized manner, within the walls of their churches as they chose to give as little of their property as possible to religious authorities. He accurately described a late step in the Germans' process of redefining liberty but had little understanding of its significance.

The clerics and judges who suspected that recently arrived German speakers clung to definitions that equated freedom with absence of constraint were right. An early correspondent from Pennsylvania informed his relatives that this was not Germany, where theft, murder, swearing, and other scandals abounded. Despite the need to work off one's passage, Mathias Otte reported in 1725 that High German was spoken everywhere and "this is a right good free land," where one could do as one pleased.

Johannes Schlessman, originally of Wertheim, reiterated the definition years later. To kinsmen in the Main Valley he wrote, "This is a free country; one is not required to give anything to any authority."[53]

The late seventeenth-century titles in the last collection of "mostly German books" sold before the Revolution reveals why the New York Palatines reacted with a mixture of demands and suspicions when confronted with key terms such as *authority, liberty, property, obedience,* and *political association.*[54] German speakers continually purchased and read religious treatises, Bibles, catechisms, and moral tales, reflecting their concern for domestic economy and religious norms. But at least a dozen titles circulated which touched on what might broadly be called political and legal culture.[55]

Some of the works in the collection expressed radical pietist criticism of secular authorities who meddled with "true religion." Johann Caspar Schade's *Bedencks Berlin . . .* (1696) warned impious rulers of God's judgment if they refused to listen to the gospel renewal that pietists were bringing to a dissipated society and an enervated state church.[56] North American readers could purchase a similar indictment in *Warnung an die Obrigkeiten um sich vor aller Alienation geistlicher Güter zu hüten,* which condemned the abuse of church property by unscrupulous princes who diverted the profits made from selling church lands to the purposes of show and display.[57] The collection also included treatises explaining political terms and the histories of the Holy Roman Empire, or of all existing monarchies and republics and their antecedents. These included a genre current in the empire: accounts of curious cases settled in Reich courts. Authorities on "uncertain laws" and a handbook of oaths accompanied two or three small pamphlets warning officials to respect church property and to refrain from violating liberty of conscience.

This seventeenth-century literature summarized the wisdom, cynicism, and caution of central Europeans familiar with religious warfare, chronic political instability, and difficult social conditions. The histories provided sweeping summaries of ancient and modern kingdoms and cities; the court cases redounded with bizarre crimes, odd local customs, and hair-raising punishments. Nicholas Vigelius's treatise on uncertain law would have been of no help in a common-law context, although its purchasers would have nodded in recognition at the 143 cases out of 300 that dealt with the various complexities of inheritance law.[58] But definitions could be looked up in the lexicons of "key words," revealing both the complexity of the world left behind, and the open-ended quality of definitions that offered positive and negative readings of terms such as *liberty, property,* and *authority.*

Freiheit, Johann Hübner said in his *Kurze Fragen aus der politischen*

Historia, meant "privilege." But no privilege was a "wall against an armed enemy." At the time of the Peasants' War (1524–26), freedom had meant liberty of conscience, interpreted by peasants as incompatible with the "unbearable feudal obligations" they had resisted as destructive of their ancient rights. But that catastrophic war had abused true liberty and destroyed society and authority.[59] Christoph Lehman concurred. His collection of sayings (Sprüchwörter) offered the libertarian definition, the definition of freedom as absence of constraint.[60] Here was the source of the analogy to animals repeated by the New York pastor: the ox resists the yoke, the bird springs forth from its cage, the dog kept on a leash bites more often. But the same collection pointed out that "the sheep that wanders free is eaten by the wolf," and that following one's own will was the sure sign of the devil's work and a contradiction both of God's will and of social authority and order. Positive freedom implied following the lead of authority. "Obrigkeit" (authority) and "Gehorsamkeit" (obedience) received lengthy treatment. Yet when discussing the practical expression of authority, under the heading "Office" (*Amt*), the sayings were quite cynical. Officers of the land were the guarantors of order. Yet everyone knew that "officials are like the fox playing at gooseherd and like wolves guarding sheep." The local official held the key to the peasant's money, and every officer lived from the fees extracted from the people by his office. Corruption through bribery — *Schmieren* — characterized those in office. But authority had to be exercised by the few, for "too many cooks spoil the broth" ("Viel Koch verfälßen den Brey"). If authority did not do its duty, each would do what he wanted, and destroy all.

The lexicons dismissed the possibility that people could cooperate in political associations. Everyone knew that unity (*Einigkeit*) was the "strongest band that held people and land together." But associations (*Bündnisse*) to defend common interests almost always failed. Only those who shared unity in religious belief had a chance at common associations. The history of Germany had shown how doomed most associations were. "Religion and German Liberty are the state ornaments of associations." But such unions always ended in disarray, with parties quarreling and destroying one another, as shown by the Thirty Years' War, and by alliances with the Turks or against coreligionists. "German Liberty" meant precisely the formula of the Peace of Augsburg: *cujus regio, ejus religio.*

The distinction between public and private life involved equally subtle distinctions. Although liberty of conscience emerged as the definition of freedom most often cited among early Palatines, the reader of these treatises would have found the treatment of conscience heavy going. On the one hand, freedom meant, thought Lehman, that man should live according to healthy reason (*gesunde Vernunft*), distinguishing what is true from what is false, not holding for certain that which was questionable. But the entry on conscience included a wickedly witty summary of two contending theological and jurisprudential schools of thought.

One school held that conscience was unitary, known only to God, and that it could not be forced. Others argued for a casuist distinction: there were two aspects of conscience. One was enjoyed as a private person: no court should invade a person's thoughts. But as a public person owing obedience to authority, every individual also possessed a second facet of conscience. Presumably, then, one might lie to a figure in authority who was seeking to discover what he had no right to know, but still be secure in one's "private" conscience. We know, wrote Lehman, that an official is never allowed to let "private" considerations influence him. Should we imagine then that at the Last Judgment God will bind the devil, as scripture says, but nonetheless, being just, allow Lucifer's "private conscience" a place in heaven?

This skepticism about the privileges surrounding "private" concerns showed itself in the conviction that when authority does its job of defending the common good, private judgment and thought must take second place. That the categories of private and public were anything but certain was proven by the 1585 investigation of Heinrich von Nassau by imperial assessors. Refused access, the imperial council and visitors invaded his household, declaring him no longer a private person (*privatus in loco*) but *persona publica*. The judicial handbooks agreed. A Privatperson "should not punish, decide, condemn [others], but instead the ruler, preacher, parents, and preceptors should, and must do so." Further, it was "impossible for a private person to make an uncertain right certain." A judge, in seeking ways to determine what was right, had to think through a controversial case in order to seek out a known principle of right, by applying the rule that mandates looking at the intent of the law.[61]

Well into the eighteenth century, the notion of "freedom" (Freiheit) continued, according to commentators, to be tied to the word *Recht* (law, or right) and was taken to mean protection before the law against arbitrary power (*Willkür*). Legal commentators even spoke of the "freedom of the unfree." The concept of the *Rechtssubjekt*, or *Person*, operated as a function (dependent on city or other region) of particular status: rank in the peasantry, the nobility, or the clergy. The honesty of the compilers of the lexicons demanded that they acknowledge the libertarian definition of freedom as freedom from constraint, but this definition was, on balance, rejected.[62]

English observers in the colonies continued to repeat the shrewd insight of the tradesman in the *Palatines Catechism* who insisted that definitions acquired meaning only in context. A dismal German political history did not bode well for immigrant Palatines' understanding of English liberties. As late as 1756 the Reverend William Smith wrote to the Right Reverend Dr. Secker in London of the continued dangers of "our disaffected Germans" in New York. Both the English language and the Anglican church, Smith opined, made for loyal subjects. "In short, till we can succeed in making our Germans speak English and become good Protestants, I doubt we shall never have a firm hold of them."[63]

New Yorkers did not have to concern themselves with the problem of the Palatines to any great degree. The colonial historian William Smith, Jr., explained in his 1757 *History of the Province of New-York* that the Palatines had labored quietly, but they were now Pennsylvania's problem not New York's. Few descendants of the original Palatines remained in New York, most having left for Pennsylvania; fewer still emerged as significant political leaders in New York or left wills or instruments revealing what they intended to do with the property that finally came to them, or how they regarded liberty and property in a practical sense. But in Pennsylvania, Smith warned, "they are too numerous, to be soon assimilated to a new constitution. They retain all the manners and principles which prevail in their native country."[64]

Smith's judgments reflected those of other New York officials, who first showed alarm at the Palatines' truculence and then strongly asserted that English speech and culture would triumph. Justice DeLancey encouraged preaching in English because, according to Mühlenberg, he believed that "in a few years all foreign languages will go out and English will prevail, as it can be observed among the youth of foreign nationalities that they are forgetting their mother tongue and learning English without any compulsion."[65] In neighboring Pennsylvania and other colonies where the Germans now arrived in increasing numbers, such confidence was hard to sustain. Thomas Penn's governor wrote in 1727 that the proprietor would "soon have a German colony here." His successor in 1753 reported that if only they would learn English and master English law, all would be in order. "But," wrote Governor James Hamilton, "these people do neither, nor will they for some time to come. . . . The Germans, from being the most abject Slaves at home are upon their coming hither more licentious and impatient of a just government than any others, in consequence thereof we may always see the most turbulent and seditious of the people chosen into the assembly."[66]

Only much later did authorities see evidence of German speakers' understanding of the connection between liberty and property. In 1771

Peter Miercken, a member of Saint Michael's Lutheran Church and a prominent sugar refiner of Philadelphia, petitioned the Pennsylvania Board of Property for local naturalization, reciting his past as a Hamburg Lutheran who had lived for ten years in Philadelphia and acquired "some real and personal Estate or Property." He intended to pursue his profession and hold land, "transmitting the Possession and Inheritance thereof to his Posterity," with the same "Rights and Privileges of natural born Subjects of his Majesty."[67]

Pastor Mühlenberg by 1751 saw too much libertarian freedom of choice in New York and neighboring Pennsylvania. The predominance of subjective opinion, and a riot of choice that could only be described as licentious, prompted him to seek retirement in Georgia. Deeply disappointed after enormous struggles, and illness, the Halle missionary wrote to his confrères on the Savannah. The New York Lutherans in particular, he wrote to another correspondent, should be allowed to suffer "their Choice and liberty" and "be tossed to and fro." Mühlenberg remained committed to the idea that "it is not the Multitude of disorderly people that maketh a good state, but the law and the Rulers." To Pastor Johann Martin Boltzius he rejoiced that "Eben Ezer has so many advantages over Pennsylvania. There, religion, church, and government are at one! There shepherds and sheep unite with one another. . . .there justice and righteousness are supported, wickedness punished, and goodness rewarded."[68]

Yet the same conflicting mix of ideas about liberty and property would vex the Salzburgers in Georgia, and the settlement process would create a language capable of connecting these concepts to political culture among German speakers in the southern British provinces, too. The subtle regional differences in this language depended on which networks of trade, communication, and ideas, established by competing sets of brokers, successfully penetrated a given region. As late as midcentury, far from New York, an anonymous South Carolinian copied into his commonplace book an English traveler's judgment about the Germans. He spoke for many Anglo-Americans: "An Unhappy effect of an attachment to hereditary traditions . . . must be confided as a national foible of the Germans."[69] Exactly *which* set of hereditary traditions German speakers would choose to cling to, the Carolinian did not venture to say. South Carolina's governor William Bull, however, was confident that the latest group of German speakers to arrive at Londonborough, South Carolina, in the late 1760s would serve as a bulwark on the frontier and would quickly be anglicized. He had made one of them "to be a Justice of Peace with a Book compiled for the Instruction of the Justices of this Province. This I hope will preserve good order amongst them, & prevent those jealousies which strangers are apt to conceive, of their being improperly treated by the English, until they understand our language & Laws. To encourage a military spirit & attachment to the English, I gave them a set of silk-colours, with the name of their Township wrought thereon."[70] The formula was precise, and telling: fluency in the language and the laws secured an ordered liberty and put German speakers on the road to a rightful understanding of what the English meant by that term.

Perhaps Bull was aware of the parallels between this latest group of *Auswanderer* and that of 1709. These German speakers, like the original New York Palatines, first camped in London, and were the recipients of popular and official philanthropy, and then were shipped to the colonies in hopes that they would help sustain the empire. Like the New York Germans, these new South Carolinians would also fight for the empire. The Londonborough settlers remained staunch loyalists and later resettled in Nova Scotia, their original planned destination.

Private letters and comments by German speakers reflected this same desire for a unified world, but in a different language. The *Amerikabriefe* all centered upon household, family, food and drink, and land. The earliest Swiss and Palatine letters repeatedly make ritual requests to be remembered to village authorities and all their relatives, and list recent marriages and deaths, and news of neighbors. They describe the land and its particular products, and compare and contrast these to those of the home village. This obsession with household, family, property, and liberty of conscience survived transfer. But this same set of concerns did not easily translate into political consciousness, or into notions that "private" property defended liberty against power.[71] A clue that family and household concerns might become politicized, however, lay in the terms Anglo-Americans used most often in defending their liberty and property—*birthright* and *inheritance*.[72]

In 1771 Frederick Wilhelm Hecht and five other New Yorkers proposed to the royal governor, John Murray, earl of Dunmore, that a German militia of 120 men and officers be established at the Germans' own expense. Governor Dunmore wrote to Secretary Henry Hill, earl of Hillsborough, that he supported the idea, certain that "your lordship will think it right to give encouragement to their zeal and spirit; the emulation which is observed to actuate all national bodies of men serving with others never fails to produce good effects, and there cannot be the same objection made which is common to auxiliaries, these being established in the country and their interest concerned in its safety."[73] The "Palatines" in New York had come full circle, voluntarily serving the king, as had their ancestors who had marched off with Hunter in 1711 to combat the French in Canada. By 1770, as Johannes Cruger, the former mayor of New York City, decided to stand for election to the colonial assembly, a small pamphlet revealed that New York German speakers referred to themselves proudly as members "of the German Nation" and insisted that any intelligent Lutheran or Reformed Christian knew that the Lutheran and Reformed Creeds were "Original Religions" that agreed with the English church in its principles; their members were not "Dissenters." The British were understandably puzzled when so many of these German speakers, like their "dissenter" fellow colonists, turned out to be revolutionaries.[74]

PART I

The Origins of German Ideas of Liberty and Property

2

Liberties and Households: The Village

THE BELL continued to toll on a sunny May morning in 1740 as Elisabeth Hausmann of Reudern, in Württemberg, made her painful way to the village square to lay down a public burden. Aged and infirm, mourning the death of her husband Johannes, Elisabeth had notified the pastor and the village Schultheiß a few days before that she could no longer continue as head midwife. As prescribed by ducal law, the village bell summoned all the married women who were members of the families possessing Bürgerrecht (full civic rights) to a public debate and an election for a chief midwife. As she expected, Dorothea Andrea Hausmann, the younger of the two midwives, received 11 of the 23 votes. Four came from the influential Hausmann family and those who had married into it.[1]

A month later, in Oberboihingen, the larger town whose pastor also cared for Reudern, a similar vote took place. Here, too, the village midwife, Matheas Schneider's wife, was so ill that she could no longer carry out her duties. Of the thirty votes, Johannes Schumacher's wife received thirteen, and she was declared the new midwife. But this election was not final. Several women had been unable to be at the *Rathaus* for the public debate and contested the election on well-established grounds. Schumacher, they argued, knew nothing about being a midwife. She was known to suffer from a bad back and could hardly go shopping, much less make her way in the dark of night to help with birthing a child. When all opinions had been voiced this time, the Hausmann family, influential in Oberboihingen as well as Reudern, backed their sister-in-law Schumacher, but to no avail. Instead, Hans Jerg Mayer's wife claimed twenty-one of the forty-five votes. The displaced and embittered Elisabeth Schumacher decided to carry out her own idea of justice. On the

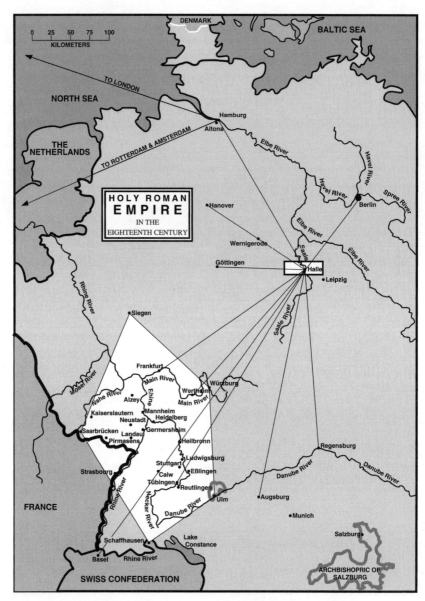

The Holy Roman Empire in the eighteenth century. Original map by
Win Thrall, 1992.

feast of Saints Philip and Jacob one year later, she was publicly repri-
manded for having spread malicious calumny for months about her successful rival, Catherine Mayer. Schumacher's husband confirmed that at
Plochingen, the large market town nearby, stories circulated in hilarious
detail about how much wine Catherine Mayer could put away at a sitting.
Not content with spreading malicious stories, Frau Schumacher had written to the superior district (*Oberamt*) officials at Nürtingen demanding
that they order an investigation of the election. Village authorities in
Oberoihingen complied, only to find against the disappointed midwife.[2]

The social relationships dictated by influence and authority among
leading families in Oberboihingen remained clear after this unpleasantness. In nearby Reudern, however, Elisabeth Hausmann's successor
Dorothea no longer wanted the job. The women of the village assembled
in bitter weather in January 1743 to elect her successor. The young
Dorothea explained that her predecessor had taken a blow on the head
that made her incompetent (*untüchtig*) and had convinced the younger
woman to accept the election. But to ensure getting out of the job,
Dorothea had also allowed the accusation to spread that she was revolting
(*eckelhaft*) to many women, could not wash her clients properly, and was
deficient on other, similar grounds. The younger women argued for the
schoolmaster's wife, who received seventeen of the twenty-four votes.
Others countered that she was too young and that an older, more experienced person had to take charge of village births. Unanimously they
chose Ursula Hausmann, wife of Andreas.[3] Andreas, the *Heiligenpfleger*,
acted as elected administrator, helping the pastor care for the church
building and lands, and the rents due on them. The hierarchy of village
values regarding custom, family ranks, and public debate was reconfirmed. Their midwife crisis resolved, these villages on the Neckar could
turn their attention to more pressing problems: bad weather, crop failure,
sickness, and their consequences.

Ducal law had adapted itself to, and confirmed, the folk wisdom that
had solved the midwife dispute. The village worthies who sifted through
the options knew from long experience what to do. By 1750, a handbook
issued in Ludwigsburg revealed in its language how official law codified
and gave further force to such practices. The handbook reflected the
speech of accumulated custom and behavior. In an early section dealing
with midwives and their election, it warned village authorities that a
midwife should be chosen who was "neither too young nor too old"
(repeated twice), and that she should have borne some children herself
and should suffer from no loathsome disease "seye mit keiner ansteck-
enden, oder sonst eckelhaften, und ihre Verrichtung verhinderenden,
Kranckheit behaftet"). In bigger towns, midwives chosen from God-

fearing, reputable families should be sent to Stuttgart or Tübingen to study with experienced midwives at the expense of the *Bürgermeister*. In all towns, big or small, midwives were to be given a modest allowance. More particularly, the local court (*Gericht*) and town meeting (*Rat*) were to defend the husbands of midwives from all personal feudal obligations, such as supporting hunts, feeding hounds and horses, and working on hedges. Such privileges (Freiheiten) were to be protected at all times.[4]

The world of the Hausmanns, the midwives, and their neighbors extended a few miles beyond the escarpments and hills on the middle Neckar. They could walk the distance easily between Oberboihingen and Reudern to Nürtingen; the trip down the river to where the Neckar bends in a large bow to the west before sweeping down into Stuttgart brought them to Plochingen. Village officials were annoyed when the local drunk was caught again after carousing all day and an entire night in the ducal capital,[5] but his debauches and willingness to travel were common only among traders, the young, and the shadowy figures who existed on the fringes of village life—the deserters, charcoal burners, day laborers, and other unwanted vagrants who perpetually wandered through the lives and consciousnesses of settled villagers. With them, this malefactor shared a careless religious life, demonstrated by his habit of mowing hay on the sabbath. More commonly, relatives, acquaintances, and laborers from across the river—from Schlaitdorf, Neckartailfingen, or Neckarhausen, or from downriver, from the imperial city of Eßlingen, showed up to visit, or to do business. If a village enjoyed market privileges and was designated a *Fleck,* or market town, contact within a broader region was more common. And villagers saw both regional church officials and district civil officials from the Oberamt in nearby Nürtingen, who came to the village to make their biannual visitation in spring and fall at the two pivotal points of the year, the feasts of Saint George (24 April) and Saint Martin (11 November).

Wherever they might have looked among the villages, visitors would soon have discovered what these residents along the Neckar knew about the Hausmanns: the family was part of the multiple hierarchies, created by wealth and length of residence, that shaped the contours of public exchange. Villagers were never precise in spelling out these relationships, yet one can reconstruct these hierarchies in part whose changing status in the villages may have contributed to the decision to see a new life in the British colonies.

Larger district towns such as Nürtingen shared with cities a political and bureaucratic elite made up of nobles, officers, clergy, and city officials. A second group, made up of large merchants, bankers, factory owners, and tradesmen, were less likely to live outside the bounds of large towns. In villages, however, a third group, made up of smaller tradesmen, the village pastor, the schoolmaster, and wealthier peasants who also sat on the village council and court, dominated most affairs. Next came the artisans and smaller peasants, and last the day laborers and the genuinely poor, the widows, and—at the very fringe of existence—the military deserters, charcoal burners, and old unmarried women.[6]

Geography and crops, religious confession, and the multitude of accumulated legal customs dictated by family, old tribal laws, and newer, written law helped bind together subregions within the bewildering patchwork of political entities.

I

If one could construct an imaginary *Turm,* a tower on the border between modern Germany and the Swiss canton Schaffhausen, one might with the mind's eye survey to the north, east, and west the homelands of the Reformed and the Lutheran migrants to North America. The choice of perspective is not arbitrary. From Huldrich Zwingli and the Swiss Reformation to post-1945 Europe, many observers of the German speakers of Europe have from this vantage point imagined and urged a Rhenish state in the German southwest. Within this corner of German-speaking middle Europe, rulers and ruled made fundamental political choices, or were forced to accept them, owing to tribal, geographic, agricultural, and religious realities. These choices continued to bear directly on the issues of liberty and property in both the Old World and the New.

Three realistic political options lay open before Swiss, Swabian, and Franconian towns and principalities at the time of the Reformation. First, the free cities of the Reich might have "turned Swiss" and federated with rural communes both to preserve local autonomy and to bolster economic cooperation, with resulting political clout within the Holy Roman Empire. Second, with cities leading the way, a German monarchy might have evolved, allowing leading families in large cities and market towns to exercise dominance, with only a distant king as a reminder of larger sovereignty. Third, the region could have turned to particularism, with local princes dominating the patchwork quilt of lands and towns. This is what actually happened, because life was dominated not only by the cities but also—as the scholars interested in "protoindustrialization" have emphasized—by the multitude of small villages that clustered along river bottoms or hugged the wooded outcroppings, where sheepfold, paper mill, and spinning *Stube* controlled the destinies of regional and individual life.[7]

The people of the German southwest managed, despite the region's princes, to preserve among variegated political entities a measure of popular will in public life. Precisely because no political, economic, or religious center dominated the entire region, the traditions of subregional and local autonomy survived, even in the face of the eighteenth-century trend toward absolutism. This pattern held true in the lands of the Palatinate, on either side of the Rhine; in the Baden territories; in the Kraichgau, southeast of Heidelberg; in Württemberg; and farther east, in the villages of the imperial city of Ulm; but less so in the Austrian territories of the Breisgau.

Across this vast territory seen from the imaginary vantage point at Schaffhausen, there existed a "bewildering variety of geographic formations . . . no single concentration of population . . . a linear landscape."[8] Yet that landscape had borders shaped by geography and crops, by religious controversy, and by accumulated customs regarding property. A more focused scrutiny from the tower reveals distinct geographic, economic, and institutional contours that explain both differences and commonalities among the villagers who in the eighteenth century left this area in droves for Russia, Hungary, Prussia, and less often, North America. A wanderer notices immediately the escarpments of the *Schwäbische Alb,* the rough mountains that sweep across the southwest, harboring tiny villages on the flat tops of forested mountains that then fall sharply to the many valleys that crisscross the land. This range begins just to the east of Schaffhausen, at the northwest corner of the *Bodensee* (Lake Constance), and sweeps north and east toward Ulm, finally bending even further east along the northern banks of the Danube and fading off into the distance, where a similar range, the *Fränkische Alb,* begins below Nuremberg. These hills marked the eastern and northern boundaries of the German southwest.

If one descended from the tower at Schaffhausen to journey into this region, one could start at the sources of the Neckar at Villingen, with the Black Forest on one's left, and march northward over Rottweil. To the northeast, leaving the river valley, one comes to Bodelshausen, near Mößlingen, on the southern border of the old duchy of Württemberg. Standing in the churchyard at the top of the hill in the center of town and looking down on the old Rathaus and the surrounding fields, one confronts the Schwäbische Alb; across the valley, rising in majestic outcroppings of rock and fir. On stormy days or during winter, clouds scud across the valley and hide the crags and jutting peaks that dominate the hills and the fields of the valley. This area, far south of Stuttgart and Tübingen, was border country, and hence poor and politically uninfluential. The real power in the region lies some twenty-seven kilometers further west, atop the hill where the enormous castle, the Hohenzollernburg, broods over Hechingen. The contours of hill and valley are sharper here than in the northerly, sunnier, wine regions. Life in these hill country villages was difficult under any circumstances; weather, and relatively poorer soil, restricted sheep raising and its ancillary spinning and weaving industries to marginal levels in the eighteenth century.

Villagers scratched out a living on this terrain, which rapidly rises into foothills and rugged mountains. By 1726 there were twenty-four weavers in Bodelshausen; the other five hundred residents tried to raise sheep and farm on the very small area fit for cultivation, hoping to avoid the periodic hailstorms that destroyed crops on a depressingly regular basis. The rare good fortune of local worthies such as Johannes Hauser was not shared by many. An expert at firing the furnace at the ducal porcelain factory in Ludwigsburg, Johannes left his wife Maria of Bodelshausen well provided for; his assets were so considerable that he left a written will, an exceptional step in which his wife's poorer relatives and friends rarely indulged.[9]

Yet the mean conditions of life produced little popular resentment that took the form of outright revolt. A dim memory survived that the town had in 1409 been handed over to Duke Eberhard von Württemberg after a protest against the Zollern lords down the valley; since that time, there had been no uprising. By 1750 another form of protest occurred instead: 150 people left the village for the Siebenbürgen, in Habsburg territory, or for North America.[10]

Not very far away, in the poor district (Amt) of Balingen, residents in Lauffen an der Eyach labored under similar conditions. By the 1740s the wooded hills were more jealously guarded than ever, since a paper mill had recently been constructed. The general shabbiness of this poorer regional center struck eighteenth-century visitors journeying from Hechingen, near the Hohenzollernburg, to Balingen, the latter place not much more than one long alley. All buildings in that town were poorly constructed of wood, increasing the danger of fire. The stench of the paper mills was so great that it pursued travelers well downwind.[11]

Local residents appeared before the local court (*Ruggericht*) with increasing regularity for having felled wood to create fencing for their gardens against the predations of sheep. Authorities tried to staunch the pilferage by insisting that by the Feast of the Beheading of Saint John the Baptist (29 August) each resident had to present the Bürgermeister with a receipt, to be notarized, indicating that he had taken only his

quota from the common woodlands. Attempts to escape from the subsistence economy of this region predictably led to abuse of the lands.
The court in 1762 forbade residents to allow the increasingly large herds
of *Geiß* (young nanny goats) to wander over the hillsides. Only under
the watchful eye of the village herder could residents send one of every
two animals out to pasture; the other was to be kept in the stalls or sold.
Neighboring towns such as Meßstetten, Hofingen, Balingen itself, and
Dürrwangen, with which the Lauffen villagers shared a pastor, suffered
the same hard times.[12]

The sheep and goats marched to a rhythm dictated by the hills, the
weather, and the church calendar. on Saint George's day (*Jörgentag*), the
same day the semiannual dues on rented properties were collected, sheep
were driven out to summer pasture. Until 1724 in old Württemberg only
one market day existed: it was held on Saint Bartholomew's Day (24
August) at Markgröningen. This, the occasion for the famous *Schäferlauf*,
became an excuse for dancing, drinking, and general amusement,
frowned on by religious reformers for its excesses. In 1724 Duke Eberhard
Ludwig granted Urach, Wildberg, and Heidenheim similar privileges—
Freiheiten—to hold market, but not on the traditional day. In Urach
market day was the Feast of Saints Peter and Paul (29 June), in Wildberg
Saint Lawrence Day (10 August), and in Heidenheim the Beheading of
Saint John the Baptist (29 August), a date that the poorer in Lauffen
observed as the deadline submitting one's receipts for the use of wood.
On such market days, the village bell tolled a procession into the church,
where a special sermon was preached; a second procession led the herders
back to the Rathaus. There they took their oaths of office before ad-
journing to a rare evening of dancing in the street, wine, and general
merriment.[13]

Sheepherding had long been regarded as a dishonorable calling, connected in the popular mind with magical knowledge of the weather, and
of the herbs, soils, water, and wood that the herders gathered to make
medicines—and poisons. Persons suspected of witchcraft were often
asked if they had had contact with herders. Perhaps because Saint John's
Day (24 June) celebrated the old Germanic Midsummer's Day, still associated with magical powers and rituals, so too the herders were often
associated with this date, even though their patron was Saint James. In
addition to joining celebrations at midsummer and in August, the herders
appeared at Pentecost. By the eighteenth century herders were more
prosperous and more respectable, but old suspicions died hard. By the
nature of their calling, herders like day laborers, were wanderers at the
edges of the concentric circles of social power and ritual that held village
life together.[14]

Social tensions in these marginal villages sometimes spilled over on festivals such as Pentecost, when multilayered rituals and incidents revealed economic and religious components of a bare-subsistence, "minimalist," culture. Anything untoward, hidden, or secret that might jeopardize delicate relationships was interpreted in the worst possible light.[15] At Lauffen, on Ascension Day in 1762, Elisabeth, née Öhrle, wife of the cowherd Hans Gompper, accused her stepson Hans Martin and his wife Anna Maria of saying she had laced her gift of clabbered milk with mercury before giving it to the younger couple. Her stepson had contemptuously derided her as barren ("Du bist nichts nuz"), and had said that her children were whoresons. He had attacked Elisabeth with a club when his wife fell ill. Though the parties were reconciled and the stepson forced to apologize, the incident revealed more than the usual intrafamilial and intergenerational tensions of a village. Since quicksilver was a substance identified with witchcraft and magic powers and the woman was identified with herders who knew of such things, the stepson seized upon mercury as the substance responsible for the supposed poisoning. That Elisabeth was also sharp tongued, and involved with another neighbor, Adam Britz, over stealing eggs and chickens, explains why, as a perceived troublemaker, she was fined and set in the town jail briefly. Her detractors were also punished.[16]

Some seventy kilometers to the northeast, villagers at Seißen, a village perched on the flat hill above the cloister Blaubeuren, struggled with similar tensions and difficulties. The Seißener also experienced bad weather, flooding, and an increase in the number of transient and marginal day laborers who swelled the population on the edges of the village. These workers grew increasingly desperate for access to land on which they could raise enough to support themselves and their families. Like the other villages, Seißen numbered perhaps 450 persons by the mid-eighteenth century, and contained eight *Höfe,* or hereditary farmsteads; seven split *Höfe;* and nine *Lehen,* smaller plots of land, each of which would still support a family that rented it. Like other villagers, Seißeners gathered at Saint George's Day and Saint Martin's Day to pay their money tax, the tax on grains; the *Naturalien* (dues in poultry, eggs, and cheese), a tax on the land (*Grundsteuer*). The village lands (the *Heiligenstiftung*) belonging to the cloister at Blaubeuren evolved into smaller and smaller parcels of land, on which the day laborers lived. In 1725 there were sixteen day laborers and their families supplementing their incomes by working small plots they rented from land-owning Bauern; by 1752, there were twenty-six. Visitors were struck by the region's pastoral beauty, rarely rising above superficial impressions to note straitened social and economic conditions.[17]

Marginal conditions did not end in the hill and forest areas of Württemberg. Neighboring villages on the plain just north of Seißen belonging to the imperial city of Ulm struggled, too. This series of hamlets, stretching up the plain from Ulm into the hill country toward Stuttgart, had become chronically impoverished by the 1740s. Spinning and weaving industries attracted the laborers, so much so that both towns and small villages counted a sharp increase in handworkers, day laborers, and small farmers. Those villages along major roads, those obligated to pay rents or dues to cloisters, and those places where day laborers could obtain work from nonagricultural sources saw the largest increase. The harshness of the obligations laid on those who rented from cloistered lands had long passed into wisdom: "Church lands have iron teeth." Protestant ownership of the cloisters did not change the villagers' estimations. These villages included in unaltered condition the large Höfe (enclosed farms) that had been handed down intact from father to son for the past two centuries. They also were home to smaller Bauern who rented parcels of older Höfe that had been partitioned in earlier times or when families died out. But it was the growth in the numbers of the day laborers in the small alleys, on the main thoroughfares, and in outlying cottages that brought increasing pressure to bear on the land needed to sustain all sectors of village life.[18]

Arriving again at Schaffhausen, one could ascend the tower once more to see on the far western edges of the southwest a geographic and social pattern remarkably similar to that prevailing in the villages of the Schwäbische Alb and of Ulm. Nassau-Saarbrücken and the Pfalz-Zweibrücken shared with the more rugged terrain far to the east a dependence on sheep grazing, spinning, and skilled handicrafts. But a determined set of government officials in these western territories labored to break the power of local villages, the traditional guilds, and old privileges, so as to bring the economy under central control.

Like so many locales in the southwest, Saarbrücken and Zweibrücken villages had experienced slow but steady population growth that by the 1720s had stretched resources. In a classic downward spiral, alarmed officials watched as customs relating to land, crops, and inheritance threatened to destroy the fragile balance between land and people. As the need for food grew, large numbers of cattle and sheep were raised, and their products—milk, cheese, and wool—helped feed, clothe, and provide work for villagers. But as herds grew ever larger, they wandered over wider areas. As long as every family demanded access to grazing land and ownership of a herd, only relatively small operations were possible. But not enough cattle or sheep could be sustained on the land to manure it sufficiently to plant desperately needed crops, such as wheat and the more common peasant grains, barley and rye. More land was needed for these essential grains, even though the lands were inadequately manured. But putting the land into production meant shrinking herd size, and hence, the quantity of manure available.

Authorities broke this vicious cycle in the 1740s by drastic measures never successfully implemented elsewhere in the southwest. In 1742 the old local courts were shorn of their authority and brought under the control of new, professional, administrative bodies ordered to carry out the decrees of a government inspired by the two-pronged ideals of cameralism. Government officials were determined to bring city, land, and household economy under a rationalized system of control and at the same time to institute an administrative state to guarantee both order and financial policy through the use of trained civil servants—what contemporaries referred to as *Polizei*. In Zweibrücken the 1742 court reform preceded by only two years a new law forbidding the marriage of young men unable to prove that they had planted six new fruit trees on their property. Equal partitioning of realty among all of a testator's children was now also forbidden.[19]

Had these regulations touched only the peasant population, they would have been striking enough. But Zweibrücken also diminished the independence of the handworkers' guilds. In 1731 an imperial law, the *Reichszunftordnung,* called for the subjugation of the guilds to local state authorities. No longer could guilds police conditions in the shops, regulating strife between masters and apprentices, contentions between members, or disputes between guilds over privileges granted by regional authorities. The 1731 law had little effect in most places, because the territories of the Reich were free to promulgate it or not. Zweibrücken did, in 1732, and then moved by 1742 to regulate the wages of workers and forbid coalitions of *Gesinde* (domestic servants) as well. Three years later, in 1745, Zweibrücken passed its own, tougher laws, which destroyed the independence of the old guilds. Local courts could render no decisions on disputes without the express prior permission and approval of the regional authority, or *Amtsmann*. For the widows of master craftsmen, the law meant the end of older customs that allowed a widow to continue running her late husband's shop—even taking on apprentices (if her husband had been a guild member)—until she sold the shop, or remarried.[20]

The very rarity of such rationalized planning and reform in the agricultural and social life of the eighteenth-century southwest reveals how relatively unchanged much village and rural life remained. But the changes that did occur seemed ominous to those jealous of older Freiheiten (privileges). By 1787 one of the first urban engineers of the age, Rudolf

Eickemeyer, reflected on the entrenched patterns of unplanned settlement and irrational village growth. Both had to be combated if the villages of the southwest were to prosper. Most villages were simply accidents— unsanitary, dangerous firetraps that were ill suited to provide fresh air and water to residents. In their places, Eickemeyer envisioned planned communities and for 100 families apiece, each complete with church, parsonage, Rathaus, and school, with no more than 16 large holdings, 32 middling Höfe, and 32 small ones. In particular, he argued, the marginalized dwellings at the edges of the village, where the day laborers lived with no access to grazing, woodland, or arable plots, had to be eliminated.[21] These prescriptions for reform came in the second half of the eighteenth century, by which time both the villages' traditional customs and more recent crisis conditions had left a permanent imprint on the memories of those who had left for North America. The emigrants also remembered innovators' enlightened schemes that threatened to disrupt already precarious domestic existences even further.

From the imaginary tower in Schaffhausen one could also see evidence of viticulture, which, more than any other material reality, distinguished some areas of the southwest from others. Another long walk from Schaffhausen due north would keep the Black Forest on one's left as the Neckar River begins to broaden. The contours of the land soften as the Neckar flows northeast, eventually past the university town of Tübingen. Along this broader plain and on the southern slopes of the hills, one would see small vineyards, which become larger and more opulent as the river flows northward through Stuttgart, joining the Enz below Heilbronn and finally passing Heidelberg before it joins the Rhine above Ludwigshafen and Mannheim. The Württembergers who lived on the middle and lower Neckar shared the cultivation, harvesting, and production of the fruits of viticulture with their Palatine and Baden cousins to the north and west. Wine-growing areas—those of Württemberg, Baden-Durlach, and Hesse-Darmstadt; as well as the Palatinate villages scattered north to south along the *Weinstraße,* near the base of the rolling Palatine hills; some towns of the Kraichgau, southeast of Heidelberg; and the valleys of the Mosel, the Nahe, the Aar, and the Rhine—produced the largest numbers of Reformed and Lutheran emigrants to America. This appears at first to be one all-inclusive region. The speech, the customs, the values, and the rhythms of life centered around the vine, the gift of the Romans to the Germanic lands.[22]

Contemporary travelers recorded their impressions of the wealth of the wine-producing areas, and of cities with particular crops or commodities that could be shipped via the rivers for profit. An occasional center that lay outside a wine-producing area, might prosper—as did

Calw, in Württemberg, for example, because of its wood. The gardens that dotted its hillsides, the good clothing worn by its one thousand citizens, sprang from the factories and shops that depended on the wood market. The merchants dealing in forest products here traded downriver to Holland, and their estates were valued at between 20,000 and 40,000 Gulden, at a time when 70 Gulden was a worker's yearly wage in the region, and cattle sold for about 20 Gulden per head.[23]

It was, however, cities such as Mainz and Speyer, in the midst of the Rheinland, or Schwaigern, in the Kraichgau, famed for their wines or fruit trees and brandies, that cast the greatest aura of wealth over the landscape they controlled. Travelers marveled at the speed with which Speyer had been rebuilt after its destruction by the French in 1689. The property destruction, in the amount of three million Gulden, had been reclaimed by the merchants, tavern keepers, and butchers, those controlling access to Nahrung, (food and drink), who restored to the city a small degree of its former glory. However, Speyer never again became the transregional marketplace it had been before 1689. In most of the imperial cities such as Speyer, heavy indebtedness from the previous century's catastrophes still retarded full recovery.

Handworkers and people situated at the lower end of these cities' social scales struggled to maintain their positions, often unsuccessfully. Of the five hundred Bürger in Speyer, nearly all the prominent ones were Lutherans, who owned the massive orchards, the fields of tobacco and madder, and the rape that was harvested and brought into the city for grinding in the mills. Such prosperity enabled Speyer to supply the surrounding Palatine towns such as Landau with surpluses in wheat, rye, and fruit, in exchange for wines, which were mixed with brandy in the city for preservation. But the Rhine and other rivers like it fostered prosperity, and the proximity of the vineyards gave the lucky inhabitants just enough fluid capital to allow these marketing networks to rebuild, even after the seventeenth century's disastrous wars, and later, repeated cold snaps, periodically wreaked havoc.[24]

As eighteenth-century travelers summed up impressions of landscape and society in the southwest, they concluded that the towns and cities from Württemberg west to Straßburg were dominated by merchants and tavern keepers who prospered even in the midst of the warfare that repeatedly swept the area. Württemberg itself was, as one put it, nothing but a great accumulation (*Haufen*) "of fortified mountains that piled upon one another, with fruitful valleys lying among them." In surveying the landscape, the crops, and the inhabitants, many judged the Palatines the best gardeners and peasants; the villages and villagers of the Kraichgau, between Württemberg and the Palatinate, and the region from Stuttgart westward to Karlsruhe, in Baden, boasted prosperity and cleanliness. But as one traveled further west from Baden through the Palatinate to Straßburg, both beauty and productivity declined measurably. That fact suggests why Zweibrücken's authorities successfully intervened in the faltering agricultural and artisanal life of their subjects.[25]

The ownership of small plots of vineyard, however, could not indefinitely sustain the smallholder in a village pressed by increasing population. Just as day laborers, herders, and woodcutters in the more mountainous regions grew desperate when bad weather, crop failure, or a sudden tax increase threatened, so too by the 1730s did the villagers in the wine valleys experience similar pressures.[26]

Geography and agriculture enabled Württembergers, Badeners, and Palatines to converse about some norms they held in common. But the prosperity of the Palatinate, due in no small part to its lush vineyards, had led to repeated warfare and devastation. The wars had been motivated both by desire to control the wealth of the region, and later, by France's intention to destroy the region's strategic value to the Reich. The immediate justification for warfare, however, often took the shape of religious differences. Surveying the political results that these religious differences had at the local level, one can see how differently public life evolved in the ravaged Palatinate and the Kraichgau than in Württemberg, which was more tranquil. The early-arriving Palatines and Kraichgauers in North America brought with them different expectations than did later arrivals from villages of the more closed, uniform duchy of Württemberg, as well as experiences with religiously pluralist village life and busier trade patterns. Bitterly anti-French, Kraichgauers and Palatines of Swiss ancestry identified quickly with the political and commercial values they associated with the Protestant power Great Britain.

II

The imaginary tower at Schaffhausen does not reveal any geographic explanation of why few residents of the Rhine valley from Basel north to Straßburg emigrated to North America. Religion does. The Catholic-Austrian Breisgau, centered around Freiburg and the Catholic Baden territories to the north, produced significant migration to the Habsburg lands in the eighteenth century, but imperial prohibition kept Catholic peasants from emigrating to North America, where a variety of strictures discouraged the open practice of their faith. Only in Lutheran Baden-Durlach, some forty kilometers northwest of Stuttgart, did subjects join the streams of Württemberg and Palatine groups who took the Rhine northward to Amsterdam, and America. The general designation of the migrants as "Protestant" by the British or by Catholics obscured the differences between the Lutheran and Reformed confessions, which were sharpened in the Palatinate by political decisions affecting the use of church property.

Lutheran subjects of the Württemberg dukes could tell immediately in 1726 that the Reformed religion would be tolerated, not welcomed. In that year, Reformed subjects began worshipping in Holy Trinity, on the market square of Ludwigsburg, one of the towns where the duke resided. A simple, small building, the church was used until 1781, when it became the garrison church for the region. Directly across the square, however, the duke had already built in 1718 a spectacular *Stadtkirche,* the only baroque Lutheran church constructed in Württemberg in the eighteenth century. Its double-towered spires in gold and rose colors, and the enormous cartouche of angels supporting the ducal coat of arms, looked directly across the square to face the statue of Duke Eberhard Ludwig erected in 1723. Württemberg would remain what it had been since the 1530s: a Lutheran bastion boasting the foremost university of that confession in the southwest, at Tübingen. Surrounded by powerful Catholic foes in Bavaria, the Palatinate, Mainz, Baden, and the Austrian territories, the Swabian Lutheran consciousness developed and sharpened. It withstood assaults from ducal families who became Catholic; it would not vanish during migration to another land. Reinforced by a pietist renewal movement that had been domesticated and incorporated in large part into the state church by the 1720s Württemberg's Swabians marked the Lutheran experience in all of the North American colonies with the stamp of Swabian dialect, piety, and suspicion of both local and distant officials who abused church property. As Pastor Mühlenberg himself later said in Pennsylvania, the Swabians were the best-catechized and the most dedicated Lutherans among his flocks.[27]

A day's horseback ride west from Ludwigsburg brought an eighteenth-century courier across the frontier into lands that typified the confused religious and secular loyalties of the Palatinate and its subsidiary territories on Württemberg's western border. Well into the eighteenth century, cartographers continued to show the Kraichgau as an independent region. A rich territory reaching from the southern border of the Odenwald, in the Neckartal, to the Rhine, the area had been repeatedly used as a highway for armies. This hilly land of some sixteen hundred square kilometers boasted a loam and limestone soil and was full of small streams along which villages and vineyards sprang up amid the red marl hills. During the Thirty Years' War, Tilly, the French, and later the Austrians crossed it repeatedly. Technically, the Kraichgau's towns formed part of the *Reichsritterschaft,* the coalition of imperial knights whose privileges the knightly families defended fiercely because the Palatine elector was not on friendly terms with the emperor, or with them.[28]

Since the 1480s the knights had been caught between the Schwäbischer Bund, the alliance dominated by the Württemberg power to their east, and the Palatine and Bavarian families who controlled the Electoral Palatinate to their north and west. The emperor had protected the Reichsritterschaft from the Palatinate during the Thirty Years' War as well as he could, ordering the Calvinist Palatine elector Maximilian not to meddle in the traditional rights of government exercised by the knights over courts and taxation. This strange conglomerate of knightly towns and territories was bound together in various Cantons, each of which in turn recognized a *Hauptmann* in charge of a council. The councils together answered to the Directorate of the Cantons at the imperial city of Heilbronn, some fifty kilometers north of Stuttgart, halfway down the Neckar to Heidelberg. Despite their independence, the cantons enjoyed special relationships both to the nearby bishopric of Speyer and to the Palatinate. Most of them completed treaties with the Palatinate recognizing the elector as protector (*Schirmherr*). The elector remained a powerful presence after the Thirty Years' War and fought to maintain his rights and dues against the pretensions of bishops in Worms and Speyer who also coveted the rich territories. Even the conversion to Catholicism of the Neuburg line of the Simmern family in 1612 and its acquisition of the Lower Palatinate in 1685 did not end these conflicts.[29]

Repeated changes in religious confession in the Palatinate meant that some Kraichgau villages were predominantly Reformed, while others were predominantly Catholic or even predominantly Lutheran, or had Catholic or Lutheran majorities but substantial minorities of other confessions. In Ittlingen, for example, the knightly von Gemmingen family and the village engaged in a long struggle over the appointment of a pastor. The village refused the man nominated notwithstanding the von Gemmingens' claim of a *jus patronatus* legally recognized since 1666.[30] Catholic villages owed allegiance to the bishopric of Speyer; the villages bordering Württemberg and members of the Swabian League were predominantly Lutheran. For the many Calvinist villages that were attached to the Palatinate, religious divisions were inseparable from those caused by the rise and fall of the electoral family's political and religious fortunes.

Lutheran in 1556, the Palatinate became Reformed in 1563; in 1685 it again became Catholic. After evicting Reformed pastors from about one hundred parishes, the new rulers succumbed to pressure from Prussia, Holland, England, and Sweden to accommodate Protestants within their territory. The resulting *Religionsdeklaration* of 1705–7 prescribed that five out of every seven parishes should be Reformed and two out of every seven Catholic, and that no Lutheran parishes should exist at all, even though some Lutheran villages received two-sevenths of Reformed church lands and came under Reformed protection. Reformed pastors could still collect fees for performing pastoral acts for Lutherans. Considerable strife arose from such cases, as they did in the more obvious instances involving Catholic pastors.[31]

The dispute in Ittlingen echoed in other towns in the Kraichgau and farther afield in the Palatinate proper. In the larger and more prosperous town Sinsheim, only a few kilometers distant, the Reformed city council petitioned the electoral district court at Mosbach that they be allowed to discontinue providing the feudal service due to religious authorities. These included inspection of the parsonage. The claim that more wood and materials were needed to repair the building was acknowledged by electoral officials, but they warned that these costs could only be paid by raising the small tithe due the pastor, upon which Catholic, Lutheran, and Reformed townsfolk would have to agree. All parties had to come to terms on sharing the use of the building.[32]

Such complicated shared uses of buildings (*Simultankirche*) were typical throughout the Palatinate and led to long, embittered fights. In Dossenheim, a town of perhaps five hundred persons in the Palatinate northwest of Heidelberg, during the eighteenth century one-third of the population was Reformed and perhaps one-half Catholic. Of the some ninety families, more than forty-four were headed by day laborers and vineyard workers; some eighteen by tradesmen, and nineteen by landowning peasants. By 1752, when several Reformed families left Dossenheim for South Carolina, a fight still raged which would continue for years.[33] Lutherans had been excluded from the church buildings but needed pastoral care. The Catholic pastor decided that he would provide spiritual ministry to the Lutherans, much to their dislike. In a petition signed by the Lutheran pastor from neighboring Schriesheim, the Lutherans pointed out that under the religious agreement in force in the Palatinate, where no resident Lutheran pastor could be found pastoral acts were to be performed by a pastor under whom Lutherans gathered as a filial congregation. The Lutheran Consistory at Heidelberg had protested against the Catholic pastor in Dossenheim a year earlier, and a process had been initiated to enjoin the priest from ministering to Lutherans.[34]

By 1769 ecclesiastical visitors interviewed the priest, inquiring how often he distributed the catechism and rosaries among the youth of Dossenheim. He answered that he left that to the Jesuits who came during the summer. More to the point, he was also asked whether "he was not still living in strife and lawsuits with some protestants and children of their pastors?" Unruffled, he answered that he "knew of nothing extraordinary; such things happened to him as happened to all pastors in a two-bit parish."[35]

III

Just as religious divisions complicated life in the Kraichgau and the Palatinate, so too did patterns of secular authority, as well as the legal customs governing property. Ittlingen's pastor and congregation squabbled with the knightly family of Schmidtburg from 1737 to 1740 over the pretended rights of the Schmidtburg assessors to one *Morgen* of pasture in the village. The disputed land had been plowed and now produced grain; the assessors demanded that they be allowed the tithe from the natural products, and they refused the ritual payment of one penny. Ittlingen had its own Schultheiß, who claimed authority over land, rents, and privileges, and protested the Schmidtburg pretensions.[36]

In many of the towns of the Kraichgau and the Palatinate, overlapping feudal claims pitted two or more Schultheißen against each other, sometimes with a church body claiming certain dues while a knightly family, or the elector, or an intermediate body demanded theirs. No systematic study of the local courts and villages exists for the Palatinate. But newer courts at the district and central level seem to have overshadowed older, local bodies. Villagers had an intense interest in knowing precisely to whom dues were owed, and whether a claim was legitimate, for upon such knowledge hung their relatively weak grip on the little property they called their own.

Traditionally, the local authority in the Palatinate had been the *Zentgericht.* An old Frankish institution, nearly identical to the English hundred courts, it was governed by ancient collections of oral wisdom handed down by the local elders, the *Schöffen,* whose main job it was to "speak the law" by remembering the multiple dues, obligations, rights, and relationships perpetuated in "sayings," or *Weistümer.* Though the Zentgerichte were originally quite autonomous, by the early eighteenth century their powers had been sharply curtailed. The elector now appointed the Schultheiß directly. In order to win the acquiescence of conservative and suspicious peasants, officials tampered with the actual language of the Weistümer, rewriting them to fit desired political results. Newer appellate structures dominated the older hundred courts. The *Hofgericht* at Heidelberg settled final questions of succession and inheritance, sales, and personal dues on individual parcels of land. By the 1740s, when the villagers of Hockenheim passed their own regulation for policing the village, higher authorities nullified it and dictated a new one. Local worthies still sat four times per year, settling petty misdemeanors (*Frevel*) on the district court (Ruggericht), but neither serious crime nor complex civil matters could be settled locally.[37]

As the Palatinate suffered internal political and religious upheaval, much accumulated local power evaporated, leaving this part of the southwest open to incursions of absolutism that were partially resisted in neighboring Württemberg. Moreover, the population of the Palatinate, like that of the Kraichgau, was highly diverse, and a large proportion of its residents had recently moved there, primarily from Switzerland. Mennonite and Amish Swiss, as well as Reformed and Lutherans, had moved into the Palatinate in large numbers, distinguishing the area from the more settled Lutheran territories of Württemberg or Ulm.[38]

In Württemberg, the experience of families such as Johann Conrad Weiser's in local government led to a consciousness of modest local autonomy in the duchy, albeit autonomy not immune to corruption from above. The Württemberg Parliament (*Landtag*) successfully resisted the absolutist pretensions of the duke, partly because for much of the eighteenth century the Lutheran worthies tilted with a Catholic lord when the duchy's estates met in Stuttgart. The Gravamina (grievances) of villagers in most Württemberg villages and towns have been lost. Some petitions from the Nürtingen district survive, fewer from other districts. Even though active resistance to ducal demands for money and services did not develop in the eighteenth-century duchy, criticism of the central regime's attack on traditional privileges did. By 1737 a group of tradesmen in Stuttgart, going over the heads of the *Magistrat* (city council), petitioned the Landtag to bring before the estates the proposal that persons serving in the military swear loyalty to the Landtag and the duchy, not to the person of the duke. The outraged city officials protested the attempt to circumvent their authority, and the petition died without further comment. But the surviving outlines of the Gravamina even from small villages or from distant districts such as Balingen are sometimes tantalizing. There are petition headings such as "Strife with Duke Karl"; and— more significant to the story of liberty and property—from Ebingen, there are protests against the duke's attempt in 1714–22 to wring taxes from religious charitable organizations.[39]

Despite real geographic and religious differences among these territories of the German southwest, in the region extending from the Pfalz-Zweibrücken to the right bank of the Rhine all knew the *Fauth*, or *Vogt*, who recorded land transactions, intestate inheritance cases, and administrations of estates in the *Ausfautheiakten*—roughly the equivalent of the

Realteilungen in Württemberg. Practices there paralleled those in Württemberg, Baden-Durlach, and Ulm.[40] Württembergers still determined locally who became Schultheiß, resisting ducal pressures toward centralization. The Palatine and Zweibrücken governments drastically curtailed local autonomy and institutions. The Kraichgauers, playing knights off against other patrons, also resisted attempts to impose a rational system of administration and law from above.

The world in which German villagers and peasants of the southwest lived was one in which everyday routine was linked to the long-term rhythms of life by imagined continuities. The written language that shaped these ideas of continuity could be found in village court records of property, the Bible, pietist tracts, and hymnody, all of which defined and sustained village norms. The nature of those writings and the language they used blurred the particularity of the here and now and encouraged a sense that one could both stay in one place and still be a part of a larger, continuing community, which did not seem very distant because nothing in village life contributed to the sense that the past was different than the present and sharply cut off from it by time.

Villagers knew and used the language of the law, and demanded that it be carefully recorded in written form to assure them of their property rights. What had been handed down from the past, in terms of oral wisdom and tangible goods, continued to affect relationships in village life through many events, especially marriage, childbirth, and preparing for death.[41]

Above all, these hamlets and towns continued to be guided by at least four distinct sources of law: family and clan tradition, local custom, princely legal codes, and church prescription. The threads of these codes wove a tight skein around the entirety of life. That these villagers seemed intensely litigious and held tenaciously to rights to property in subsistence villages is hardly surprising. Yet such behavior like that of other villagers in Toulouse, Andalusia, or England, reflected something else: the need for certainty of results. For by the eighteenth century, nearly everywhere in Europe the customs and practices of an older law had fallen before systematic inquiry by legal experts learned in written, codified law. To the old village feuds and disputes, and to the need for charity to care for the indigent, the scribe brought law that represented the state, which had its own interests, often resisted by hostile villagers. Often enough as well, these villages lived in an uncompleted state of transition, in which both older disputes that had been settled by the common opinion of the village court, and newer, more complex cases reflecting the growth of a centralizing, acquisitive state, existed side by side. Those who could mediate such disputes and navigate between the shoals of novelty and custom included pastors, and persons engaged in trade who by necessity had to deal with both worlds. Those adept at handling both local and cosmopolitan concepts would be just as significant to transplanted German speakers in British North America.[42]

The four sources of law that prevailed in village life could not survive migration to a new private-law system. Instead, remnants having to do with law and inheritance customs would have to be reassembled and, via a process of intermediation, be assimilated to the colonial common law that was dominant in the regions where various groups settled in North America. And the intermediaries, both clergy and others, had to reinterpret select aspects of these legal sources in that strange new context. But these sources for law provided villagers—both in memory and in active use of newer instruments—with broad participation in settling property matters. Public, formal, and written law—what one might call manifest law—existed side by side with latent sources. Villagers regarded property both as something that had come down from one's mother's and father's families and as something that one genuinely owned and controlled during one's lifetime. Villagers did not see themselves as "trustees" of an "estate" passed on intact. Yet the constraints imposed by the four sources of the law made certain that a rough equality of claims was respected when property was divided or brought together.[43]

The first source of law, the rights and wishes of clans, constituted customary law as it had existed since the early Middle Ages. Both Alemannic and Frankish customs dictated that property be controlled by their clans (*Sippen*). Distribution of goods, especially through alliances in marriage, was carefully thought out and negotiated. Focused around intestate law, this tradition continued to favor blood relations. Spouses were originally excluded from succession, and if the deceased person had no children, property that was seen as intrinsically linked to the spouses' individual families and brought together temporarily by marriage "fell" back to the respective families.

This community property system (*Gütergemeinschaftssystem*) distinguished the real property of each partner entering a marriage, as well as the chattels of each. Property acquired during the union enjoyed a separate status and was mixed together with the original property in a kind of suspended solution, death or divorce acting as a catalyst to precipitate various kinds of property out again. If the deceased had no living kin, a surviving spouse was given the entire marital property for life. A wife could bequeath only jointly with her husband, which was one way that the old system protected a wife's rights. At his death, the law of poor widows, borrowing from ancient custom fused with Christian teaching, also gave her limited support. Children were protected under a law of obligation (*Pflichtteil*) that dictated that each receive a portion of the residue of the deceased (*Nachlaß*).[44]

This "Germanic common law" had weakened by the eighteenth century. Tribal customs had since evolved around local agricultural practice. The second source of law, local village practices, modified further by feudal obligations to various overlapping authorities, evolved in oral, and eventually written, form. Oral tradition about the proper disposition of property was protected by the elders, or Schöffen, who "spoke" the law. The Weistümer, those spoken declarations of what law "showed," or "declared" (the word is derived from the verb *weisen* [to show]) had been recorded by the fourteenth century. To these were added the *Urbarien*, documents that clarified the rights of various authorities to rents, dues, and the control over uses of real property.

The verbal wisdom of local worthies found its way also into Sprüchwörter, first collected systematically in the eighteenth century, which also reflected the workings of the law in specific localities and regions. One compilation of about 330 sayings details rights of occupancy of certain types of land, reveals relationships within marriage, and shows how inheritance rights had developed. Generally, the sayings of peasants living under papal or episcopal jurisdiction were positive: "It is good to live under the bishop's staff" ("Unter dem krummen Stab ist gut wohnen"), or "One can deal with Saint Peter" ("Mit St. Petrus ist gut handeln"). Older residents recognized "Nourishment is no inheritance" ("Nahrung ist kein Erbe"), a double-edged saying reflecting their anxiety about their future treatment once they relinquished control over property, and their obligation to pass on property to their children in addition to simply giving them nourishment.[45]

Property had been tightly guarded by family groups to such an extent that it was difficult to disinherit an heir, or to sell property without providing advance notice and allowing time for the seller to reconsider. Villagers intent on disinheriting had been required to ponder for six weeks and two days, and only if the local court were given wine—the most valued local commodity, to prove serious intent—would the court agree. To sell acreage or establish life tenancy in property (*Leibgeding*), the seller had to appear in the market for three consecutive Thursdays and, by the ringing of the evening bell in the church, offer the property to the highest bidder. In some villages the selling occurred with candles burning before the church door and was cried out three times, a practice immortalized in the saying "A field comes by burning light" ("Der Acker kommt zum brennenden Licht"). Yet by the eighteenth century the expanded land market in the southwest, and a burgeoning population, challenged these customs. Contractual relationships were regulated by the cultural institution of giving wine to the court, and public selling or bidding of lands with the burning candle was regulated by 1756 in Württemberg. The public sale of land was still not deemed final until a ritual glass of wine was drunk by both parties. By the 1740s more people were competing for land in the market than had done so in 1700, but what they were able to buy was smaller and generally, at least in Württemberg, probably at higher prices; and the buyers were slightly younger.[46]

In areas of the German southwest characterized by partible inheritance both the propertied peasantry and the day laborers shared in the rituals described above. The 1514 *Tübinger Vertrag,* a kind of Swabian Magna Carta, had laid the foundations for the few remaining feudal obligations still in force in the eighteenth century. In practice, most Württemberg peasants became the same as free citizens, with dues largely restricted to contributions in grains.[47]

Yet the variety of local custom had been further reduced by the third source of law, princely legal codes, in the course of the sixteenth century. University jurists, at the behest of their lords, initiated the official reception of Roman law, imposing this law on the older inheritance and property customs. The key difference centered on freedom of testation (*Testierfreiheit*), which received its definitive exposition in the Württemberg revisal of the laws of 1555. Copied by the Palatinate in 1582 and 1700, this revisal also provided imperial cities from Eßlingen to Ulm with the model developed by the Tübingen law faculty.[48]

Modeling their efforts on the 1493 city law of Tübingen, the jurists first sent commissioners to collect the Urbarien, descriptions of various pieces of property in a village stating to whom taxes on each were due. Overlapping claims on the same piece of ground were settled, with the renter assuming new obligations. Farmsteads with outlying lands had separate designations: the *Widdumhof* had originally been a plot set aside for the care of widows. Its rents were paid to the local pastor, the local church, or the administrator of cloistered lands often belonging to the Lutheran university. The *Almosenwiese,* which had originally belonged to a cloister, were rented grounds, the dues on which went to relieve the local poor. The poor lands were worked communally or rented out. The common village lands, the *Allmend,* were avoided by villagers, who squeezed what they could from them if forced to rent. Yet as population grew in the eighteenth century, communal land was divided up for widows, and those men enjoying citizenship (Bürgerrecht) who planted flax, hemp, cabbage, or root crops. Population pressure and land scarcity began challenging the old wisdom "Communal land is accursed land" ("Gesamt Gut, verdammt Gut"). But those without access to such common lands often rebelled at having to care for them. In Fellbach between

1720 and 1724, villagers suspended their labors on those church-owned fields whose working was a shared village obligation.[49]

By the eighteenth century, as a result of the reformers' efforts, property lay in the hands of male heads of households; women were represented by legal guardians authorized to speak in court (*Kriegsvogte,* or *curatores ad litem*). Marital property law had evolved from three customary systems. Under *Fallrecht,* the spouse enjoyed a lifetime occupancy of estate, but in the absence of an heir the property "fell" back to the relatives of the deceased spouse. Under *Teilrecht,* in the absence of an heir the property went to the surviving spouse in perpetuity; if children survived, however, the property was divided by quotas determined by the number of heirs. The widow could not take her share of property into a second family at remarriage. Almost impossible to enforce and manage as the number of children increased, the formulas of division inspired communities to encourage specific contracts to sort out these difficulties. Under *Verfangenschaftsrecht,* realty was reserved for direct heirs and movables went to the surviving spouse, who was given lifetime use of all property even after remarriage. In essence, this law operated much like the English law of waste, forbidding sale, damage, or reduction of realty by the surviving spouse which might damage the interest of the heir. When the second parent died, the heirs of the first marriage inherited the realty. By the eighteenth century, villages mixed the last two systems.

But the changes and streamlining encouraged by the jurists in 1555 had encountered stiff resistance. Protests had led in 1572 to a clarification of inheritance practices, and revisers strongly advocated, without success, that villagers begin writing wills. Throughout the Reich, all subjects who were not minor, mentally incompetent, or in a condition of servitude were encouraged to adopt this novel practice. Southwestern villagers clung to older practices, and even in the eighteenth century intestate law controlled how property was passed on.[50]

Old Württemberg law and the new Roman law had compromised eventually: a surviving spouse inherited the entire estate if no children had been born of the marriage and if the deceased had no living relatives. If relatives did survive, one-half of the acquest property (*Errungenschaft*) went to them, the rest to the spouse. In the case of a previous marriage with children, one-third of the residue (Nachlaß) of the deceased fell to the surviving partner and two-thirds to the children by the previous marriage. If the marriage just dissolved by death had produced children (and there were no children from a previous marriage to consider), they had rights to one-half the residue, and the other half went to the surviving parent; if more than four children survived, they got two-thirds of the residue. Spouses retained lifetime occupancy of house and realty. The law was vague about the surviving parent's obligation to supply children with modest provisioning for their households at the time of their marriage (*Ausstatungen*). For the most part, these provisionings from the childrens' portions and were deducted from the children's inheritance when the parents' estate was divided for the last time.

The revisers refined older customs into a system of community property in which goods brought into marriage by either partner, whether chattel property or realty, constituted one body of property; property acquired during marriage was another. Yet the older distinction between moveables and realty belonging to each spouse survived in actual inventories, since at the time of a marriage village authorities still listed under the separate categories of moveables and realty the properties that were brought together. Although one can only speculate, it may have been the Protestant allowance for divorce for infidelity or desertion that dictated prudence in distinguishing what belonged to each partner, in case (as did happen) the marriage ended before the death of one or both parties.

German-speaking families who left the southwest also remembered that their laws favored the widow with surviving children. Remarriage could not damage her right to lifelong occupancy on an estate. In sharp contrast, a childless widow had her percentage rights to property reduced by the sixteenth-century revisals. The preference for lineal descent pioneered in the 1500s stood as a fixed part of the legal landscape two centuries later.[51]

Beginning in 1567, all transactions involving property were recorded by village scribes and kept for future reference. Upon marriage, divorce, death, renunciation of the accepted faith, or emigration, the law demanded a meticulous inventory of all moveables and realty. These *Realteilungen und Inventuren,* copied onto good-quality paper about thirteen by nine-and-one-half inches in size, had like the sixteenth-century revisal originated in Tübingen's city law; ironically, if the revisers' wishes had been followed and wills written, these voluminous documents would not have been so necessary. Their form and composition were also carefully spelled out. The local Schultheiß and two lesser members of the village Gericht presided over the report. Trusted appointees of the court, or its own members, took inventory and submitted the results to the members, who sat in session with hats on, cockades indicating village rank. Most commonly it was marriage or death that dictated the taking of an inventory; in the latter case, inventory had to be taken within sixty days of death.[52]

The internal structure of the inventories deserves brief attention, for it revealed the perceptions of property which villagers absorbed as they heard the documents assembled and debated. The introductory salutation

(*Exordia*) listed the deceased's name, occupation, marital status, and date of death. The wealthier and the titled were described in glowing terms; one scribe revealed some annoyance over having to inventory a poor widow in the scribbled words "Being the worldly goods, of not much value, of the late widow."[53] The names of heirs; their marital status, ages, and occupations; and their status as minors or adults followed; women, minors, mental incompetents, or absent heirs were given guardians or representatives to protect their interests. Real property was listed first, with primacy of place to vineyards. Pasture, meadowland, and tilled grounds came next. Moveables were divided, with coins enumerated according to place of origin. Jewels, gold, and silver followed—scarce items in village inventories. But books, the next type of item to be listed, appeared in nearly all inventories—most often in Württemberg, less so in the Kraichgau, and least in the Palatinate. Listed by title, author, and size, hymnals, Bibles, pietist tracts, and treatises on household care were all identified and priced. The clothing of the deceased, as well as bed linens, preceded general linens and tools of trade. Household tools and kitchen implements followed, together with furniture. Tools, implements, and furniture were not listed by room; rather, they were grouped according to function or association with the domestic economy, both bed and food-preparation items occupying a special place. Finally, the total value assigned to all these sundry bits of property was entered against debts and outstanding credits owed by or to the deceased.[54]

The inventory's attention to survivor's ages, occupations, marital status, and legal capacity defined the survivors in the wake of family death: a surviving spouse enjoyed place of precedence, with children following in birth order, regardless of gender. This order of precedence reflected the succession of property, although not excluding ad hoc arrangements. Here another of the legal codes or systems emerges, half-hidden in the phrase local officials never excluded regarding absent heirs. Military service took some heirs away; others had emigrated and were unaccounted for. Falling back on religious norms that had achieved the status of custom, officials described absent folk as those "concerning whose place of living or death we have heard not the slightest word," the biblical law of three score and ten defining their life span, and hence their legal rights as heirs. A commentator explained that "in the Roman and common German law, this phrase does not exist, but still it is established in practice." The unwritten but observed biblical law dictated that "when someone is departed into a strange country and one can learn nothing of his life or death—he is therefore presumed dead [*ein Verschollener*]—and can be so regarded if he would have already turned seventy, and his property may be passed on to his nearest relations." But until that time (the *annum decretorium*), such property had to be held under administration pending the unlikely possibility of the absent heir's return or the appearance of someone bearing a letter of power of attorney (*Vollmachtsbrief*).[55]

Church prescription, or biblical teachings, provided an additional source of law. By 1610 a final revision in Württemberg formally incorporated an aspect of canon law into property law, stipulating that property could be given for charitable purposes (*mildtätige Vermächtnisse*), and excusing privileged testaments from the usual required witnesses if property were donated to the church—even if the testaments were written by women, and even if they were found after the donor's death. Married women were restricted to willing small amounts of personalty to the church or to charity. Villagers were reminded of religious teaching by the introductory words of the inventories when the deceased was identified as "[X], who some [Y] weeks ago changed this worldly for an other-worldly existence." By the eighteenth century the elaborate and pietistic euphemisms for "died" included "changed this unholy for the true life"; "has fallen asleep in the Savior Jesus Christ"; "has given up the spirit and gone into eternity"; "was called by the Creator of all out of this temporal world and to Himself in the happiness of a God-given eternity."[56]

Yet such reminders yielded few tangible fruits; bequests to church and charity remained rare in the German southwest. Population pressures, straitened economic circumstances, and a subsistence economy continued to block the urgings of pietist preachers, just as older customs frustrated jurists who wanted villagers to use written testaments. Württemberg inventories included these religious introductions until the 1790s, when they abruptly vanished; also somewhat common in the Kraichgau, they were rare in the Palatinate and seem to reflect the Swabian Lutheran religious consciousness, at least that of village scribes.

IV

A close examination of the disputes that swirled around these inventories provides a glimpse of villagers' notions of property and rights. The reordering of relationships within the village and family received written form as each person got his or her individual list (*Looß-Zettel*) of what was to pass into new hands. Within this process, the multiplicity of legal codes gave room for maneuvering. By the eighteenth century, village disputes seem to hint that securing a patrilineal succession was a deeply held value often at odds with another, equally cherished norm: that all persons receive equal treatment. As long as these disputes were settled in the German southwest, women, minors, and those not necessarily the primary heirs stood a good chance of preserving their privileges (Freiheiten). Emigration to North America, however, would tilt the balance decisively over time, in favor of the first value.

A surviving spouse received what he or she had brought into the marriage and any property acquired by inheritance or specifically designated as a gift by the deceased. Burial costs were deducted, the remaining estate totaled, and acquest property listed and divided; the surviving spouse got half. The spouse also acquired a percentage of the deceased's residue equal to that which went to the children. The oldest child obtained both real and movable property, although prior arrangements sometimes required that a child's portion be cut down. A sharper attention to eventual claims often surfaced among children when a surviving parent continued to exercise tight control over some parts of the property despite an agreement granting the parent lifetime use of the house and provisions for diet. This familiar devolution of property lying outside the strict definition of "inheritance" was relatively common. The Palatinate mother who insisted that her children receive no wine at settlement time "because the mother has reserved this all for herself" controlled the most lucrative property but sharpened her children's determination to have what was theirs from the less valuable residue.[57]

Johann Dietrich Kirsch decided to turn over his property for equal division among his sons because of failing health. The predeath agreement (freiwillige Vermögensübergab) specified that he receive candles, wood, grain, peas, salt, lard, pork, and wine for his sustenance (zu seiner Nahrung). As long as the domestic economy provided such essentials, families remained intact and political loyalties were also secure; disruption of that economy, however, brought protest, revolt, emigration, and—within families—bitter disputes.[58] The determination to retain control over the most profitable crop—a market-driven decision—coincided with a culturally shaped equation of well-being with nourishment. Both values would survive transfer to the New World. Repeated references to the right kind of food, especially wine and warm food (Speise), and to the importance of nourishment (Nahrung) occur in village property disputes. Control over the very substances that provided life identified the powerful, and sometimes made them targets of resentment. This, too, would survive transatlantic migration.

Children whom their parents had already favored by giving them advances for some significant undertaking such as entering a trade, marrying, or emigrating, received reduced sums. When certain types of land or movables were valued and produced too much for an heir, assessors wrote, "Thus, he has received too much," deducting the appropriate sum and giving it to another sibling, or subtracting the amount against an outstanding debt and the cost of writing up the inventory. Each portion had to equal the others, down to the smallest local coin (*Heller*). Ritual words ended the evaluation: "Everyone [was] satisfied and contented with this" ("und Alle damit zufrieden und contentirt"). A many-layered phrase, this endorsement of village values also offered local scribes protection against reprimands from the district officials if protests were made.

The death of the head of a household normally produced the types of documents and disputes discussed above. Yet inventory at marriage, divorce, or emigration also provided occasions for reexamining property and rights. In Seißen, Anna Magdalena Braun petitioned church authorities for, and was granted, a divorce because her husband Mattes had deserted the family and decamped to the bright lights of Blaubeuren, where he now lived with another woman. Anna intended to use the marital property to educate her children; in extreme necessity, she would tap it for sustenance (Nahrung). Another woman, Christina, a member of the locally prominent Pfetsch family, lost her mother in 1726. Receiving some money then, she moved away to work; her interest in the realty was put under guardianship by the court. By 1734 her father had died and she returned but was frustrated in her attempts to claim what was lawfully hers. The disapproval of the village speaks in the excited strokes of the scribe's pen describing how "the said Christina Pfetsch, having fallen away from the true evangelical faith, and having married herself to a papist named Johann Freymann from Jungenau . . . has thereby forfeited her civic rights in Seißen." After paying the costs of renouncing her rights as subject in both town and duchy, Christina and Johann left, later returning to Seißen, where Johann served as night watchman from 1746 until 1752, when the couple left for Pennsylvania.[59]

Disputes over property and succession had the capacity to bring back into village life customs and symbols that were largely in disuse by the eighteenth century. The written records kept by the village scribe had long become the villagers' preferred source of information when they needed to know what the law was. Courts now met inside the Rathaus, usually on the ground floor, and by the 1720s they had dispensed with the use of crucifix and candles on the table and the sword of justice laid across it. Some villages retained the court staff (*Gerichtsstab*), originally a willow branch with three buds at the top, representing the Trinity as the source of law. Oaths were sworn to reflect this symbol, the thumb and first two fingers raised in trinitarian form. By the eighteenth century, however, family members' testimony that the inventory was true and accurate took the form of an oral promise: "instead of an oath, this person promised faithfully" that the inventory was correct. Yet the words for "promised faithfully" ("Handtreue gelübt, versprochen") implied the formal raising of the hand.

In Grötzingen, Württemberg, the 1738 will of Jacob Raisch illustrated how the modern, written document could be combined with older forms and used by both court and family to set aside what they regarded as injustice. Married twice in his seventy-three years, first to Anna Elisabetha Gräniger of the village, later to a widow from the imperial city of Eßlingen, Raisch antagonized his families by leaving more than one thousand Gulden almost exclusively to his second family. The inventory began, but the scribe noted suddenly that "the entire body of heirs was sharply reminded to give true witness concerning the property, and to that end had actually to be sworn on the Oath Staff." Since Germanic private law did not allow for private wills but prescribed witnesses and scribe and also barred disinheritance, the family members probably knew in advance what the document contained, although perhaps not the details. After their initial squabbling ended, the scribe noted that "the widow, and the children of both marriages, to quash all hatred, unrest and strife, knowingly and with deliberate, considered agreement, independently have decided (having obtained during the lifetime of their twice-married husband and father his own permission) that this testamentary disposition, whatever it contains or intends, should be completely set aside and remain null and void, without power and capacity." Since Württemberg law allowed heirs to set aside a will if they could prove that someone had been unfairly disadvantaged, and since an heir could challenge a will, and the burden of proof justifying exclusions lay with heirs who had been favored, one wonders why Raisch's permission had been sought. Equality of treatment, however, won out in Grötzingen; overriding the modern use of a will, the court invoked ancient ritual to prevent a dispute.[60]

Such disputes were not confined to Württemberg. Konrad Hildenbrand lived in Weiler am Steinberg, in the northern Kraichgau. The local customs of the Weistümer in this area included the belief that a man could dispose of his owned and rented realties, his personalty and the properties of his spouse as long as he could sit his horse. Once he had taken to his deathbed, he could give away only what he could grasp and lift with his hand. This wisdom was summed up in the saying "One hand must maintain the other" ("Hand muß Hand wahren"). Predeceased by two wives, Hildenbrand disposed of his property by will but on his deathbed extracted a verbal promise from his son to make the stepmother a pair of shoes. No longer able to write, the dying man dictated his will, hoping, as he said, to avoid future strife; in case of quarreling, he enjoined "strict justice." He reminded everyone of a marriage contract that gave his third wife, Catharina, a marriage bed, lifelong occupancy of the house, and a child's portion of the estate. In a subsequent suit, Catharina accused her stepson of refusing to make the shoes, absconding with the bed, and—while his father was still alive—threatening her with a stick. She petitioned first the local and finally the regional court. Catharina's Catholic faith may have set her at odds with her Reformed stepson, as did her recent marriage into a family now run by the eldest stepson. The marriage contract and the will both gave her written authority for grounding her accusations against the eldest son. Her willingness to appeal above the village level illustrated how disputes could spill over local boundaries.[61]

Clever women in the southwest also knew the law well enough to put a will beyond the reach of heirs by invoking their privilege to give to charity. Anna Class of Seißen, the sole daughter of the deceased Hans Jürgen, left property to her nephews and nieces. A sister-in-law had received one hundred Gulden for care given while Anna was ill, but two months before her death the deceased had donated a substantial sum to the ducal orphanage at Stuttgart. Her sister-in-law and nephews broke into a chorus of anguish, threatened to appeal to the Amt, and protested that the witnesses to the disposition had not signed in the presence of the village legal advisor (*Anwalt*) who represented the cloister at Blaubeuren. The relatives accused designing outsiders of hoodwinking a sick old woman into making a charitable donation without the family's knowledge. Irresponsible local officials who should have prevented this invasion of familial rights were now threatened with district court review. But the local authorities were not to be bullied. A warning about the costs of appeal, and a sharp word about greed—the family had already received one hundred Gulden—brought the complainants to heel. The scribe then recorded the village norm these disputes cast into relief: "finally this business was concluded, without quarreling and wrangling, and in peace."[62]

The desire for equal treatment which seems to underlie so many of these disputes could be deceptive. In Bodelshausen, Württemberg, the Eitel brothers in 1747 seemed to exercise concern for their sole unmarried sister in that they voluntarily renounced their rights to various items of personalty in order to do what was "right," as they explained—to secure her future. Yet debts on the property left by a father could also be avoided in this manner, and the ultimate motivation and intent behind such declarations was seldom obvious. The conflict between ensuring equal treatment and securing an unencumbered property to be passed on in a stem family remained.[63]

These select cases drawn from a variety of villages suggest that by the eighteenth century customary attempts to provide equal treatment for family heirs have become increasingly difficult to sustain. The disputes illustrate how population increases and anxieties about the household economy made it unlikely that charitable giving would be a widespread practice, and showed how easily siblings could be alarmed over potential injustices. Paternal wills might be challenged and stepparents threatened; and elderly parents' control of lucrative crops reflected a society in the throes of difficulty. The southwest was slow to adapt to novel ideas of production. Market towns existed, but the entire region was characterized by local, and at best districtwide, exchanges of goods. The farming techniques in use lagged behind those advanced in Britain before mid-century. Not until 1769 did the pastor Johann Friedrich Mayer publish a tract suggesting ways of expanding beyond the medieval three-field system.

V

For most residents of the entire area visible from the imaginary tower at Schaffhausen, the wisdom and cynicism of old sayings remained intact: One should not break with old customs; they are stronger than letters and seals; and what is regarded as custom in the land is worth the greatest honor. Yet some southwestern traders were intensely interested in commerce, especially around the market towns located on rivers or blessed with access to wine. They could not, however, have conceived of a genuinely capitalist world, nor was the economy or social structure of the eighteenth-century German southwest capable of the flexibility that economic vision presupposes. But the migration of people in and out of the Palatinate and the Kraichgau seems to have created an openness to patterns of opportunity, as well as a tendency toward adaptation that also survived transit to the British colonies. It was from precisely these areas that, by the 1740s, some of the emigrants to the New World who were most open to change and adaptation emerged. Later-arriving Swabians would be excluded from that easy adaptation in Pennsylvania, while in Georgia they quickly showed a willingness to adapt to the lure of land. They would retain, however, their village disinclination to engage in philanthropy.[64]

Records of prices and income among handworkers and poorer peasants suggest that food prices rose sharply across the German southwest between 1737 and 1741, whereas wages remained relatively stagnant. Travelers distinguished between the more prosperous wine-producing areas and the marginal sheep-raising regions and wooded areas. Those in the most marginal areas were hit hardest, while access to the rivers and to the region's wine trade made a critical difference in enabling at least some to think about moving elsewhere in the Reich, or overseas. That workers in the hayfields in Bavarian Augsburg needed to work three times as long as did similar workers at Speyer to earn a given wage illustrated the limitations placed on residents of the eastern borders of the southwest.[65] As day laborers and smaller peasants were reduced to beggary, theft, or starvation, even if they rented and could farm a small bit of land in the southwest, they began to calculate with precision that they could not hold out. As one Wertheimer informed his former lord—writing from Worms, where he had removed—he wanted formal manumission because he "could not hope to receive the slightest aid from his still living mother who must seek her bread from door to door, but rather would have to sustain himself, his wife, and child wretchedly in day labor."[66]

These villagers still harbored notions of marital property that depended on intestate practices. In this context, Palatines, Swabians, and Kraichgauers shared a lively awareness of their privileges, or Freiheiten, which fostered vigorous, often acrimonious disputes pitting the pursuit of equal rights against the desire to pass on a viable holding to at least one heir.

Only fragments of this private-law system concerned primarily with the inheritance of village property survived transit. Equally important, the "sociability" of the villagers, among whom married women played a key, participatory role in defending privileges (Freiheiten) surrounding the domestic economy, also failed to survive intact. And yet German speakers' confrontation with a new law of property in North America was informed by the sources of law that had provided villagers with collective memory and options from which to choose in determining how to defend their privileges. Likewise, although no village ever was transferred intact from the southwest to the British colonies, ways could be found to give voice to some of the social concerns regarding domesticity and the privileges that had defended it. Cultural brokers had to find a language capable of explaining British law regarding property, and of conveying how privileges that defended emotional interests touching the household could be reconstituted, too. The institutional arena that provided space, time, and social exchange to ponder and argue these difficult matters in the British colonies was the Lutheran congregation. The language within which the adjustments would be couched was that of Pietism.

When young Dorothea Hausmann quit her job as midwife to her fellows in Reudern, she wanted time to raise her own family. In most villages, the midwife was also the *Leichensagerin*. As soon as a death occurred in the village, she donned mourning attire to make the rounds through the village bringing the news of death, announcing the day and time of burial. To her fell the task of washing and binding the corpse and of accompanying it, as a professional mourner, with suitable lamentations to its final resting place. Perhaps Dorothea would have been spared the task, since it was the oldest midwife in the village who enjoyed this privilege, for which she was given a traditional allotment of bread by the bereaved. Like the other women, Hausmann could eventually have claimed this privilege, one of many that village women enjoyed.

That world of privileges affecting household economies transcended both geographic and religious boundaries in the southwest. Not only Lutheran married women in Swabia but also Catholic and Reformed ones in Baden and the Kraichgau observed Ash Wednesday as women's day, on which they gathered to drink wine. In some locales either the church or the town paid the costs for such gatherings. Near Tübingen in the eighteenth century, Swabian women during February enjoyed the Freiheit of selling wood from the oaks that were cut down at that time of the year, and then using the proceeds for a common wine drinking.[67]

Neither these privileges nor the sociability of village life survived uprooting and resettlement. Whatever *liberty* and *property* would mean in that new context, they could not contain the exact memories, nor could the mere words *Freiheit, Eigentum,* or *Vermögen* convey the emotional associations, that had accrued over centuries. New associations, couched in a language capable of binding familiar emotions to novel relationships, could only be created in a context of shared confidences, of a kind of "private sociability" that for most married women meant religious association.

Many years after the German-speaking families had arrived in North America, Thomas Jefferson, in his journey through the Rhineland, was "continually amused by seeing here the origin of whatever is not English among us. I have fancied myself," he wrote, in "the upper parts of Maryland and Pennsylvania." Here, from the "palatinate on this part of the Rhine [came] those swarms of Germans . . . who, next to the descendants of the English form the greatest body of our people." Yet Jefferson also confessed disapproval: "The women do everything here. They dig the earth, plough, saw, cut, and split wood, row, tow the batteaux, &c."[68] German-speaking women seemed to Jefferson, and before him, to Benjamin Franklin, to be valued for their capacity for hard labor, through which they built their households. What alarmed both Franklin and Jefferson was these continentals' attachment to a profoundly inward piety that seemed to keep them separate from participation in the broader contours of public life. Yet out of German Lutheran Pietism would come the German speakers' eventual encounter with political culture in British North America.

3

Pietism, Christian Liberty, and the Problem of "Worldly Goods"

The household could not long be maintained as it had once functioned; the house was demanded of the aged mother by her son-in-law Simon and his wife Elizabeth. They had rented another house and farmstead as long as Elizabeth's father lived. They came now with their children and utensils and took over the paternal homestead. Suddenly, everything was strange—they broke a hole in the *Stube* and extended it into the yard. Simon had room enough—he just was no Stilling. The old oaken table full of hospitality and plenty was exchanged for a yellow one of maple, full of locked drawers.

The soft tone of the Stilling spirit was now transformed into the boisterousness of fretful craving for money and possessions. Both Margarete and her children felt this; she retreated to a corner behind the tile stove, and lived out her remaining years there. She was now completely blind, although this did not prevent her from devoting her time to spinning.[1]"

HEINRICH JUNG-STILLING captured in this scene much of the essence of southwest German Pietism, its understanding of inner freedom, and its critique of village social relationships defined by inherited property. Taken from his novel, the first in the German language to treat Pietism, this still life portrays the tension between the emphasis on "worldly goods," and the pietist emphasis on inward rebirth, biblicism, and the daily experience of faith in devotion to mundane, domestic duties. Jung-Stilling centers his scene around the blind, aged mother taking refuge and finding spiritual liberty in her personal space behind the symbol of familial sustenance—the tiled stove in the room that served as both kitchen and parlor: the Stube. The supposed generosity and openness of pietist believers he juxtaposes to the reality of village life—everything was kept locked up; there was a key to every door, every cupboard, every trunk, every box. The homely, solid, village oak he elevates above the cheap, urbane, maple veneers of the new in-laws; he implies that the proper place for spinning is the solitary, contemplative Stube, not the boisterous and sexually questionable atmosphere of "spinning evenings" that drew village youth together, to the alarm of southwestern village pastors and parents. Yet southwest German Pietism depended on a shrewd manipulation of the worldly goods, trading routes, and networks of communication that the regional economy of the villages had created, even as the movement, and Jung-Stilling, professed to disdain them.[2]

No other phenomenon so dominated eighteenth-century German Protestant life as Pietism did. No simple definition adequately sums up the complex theological origins, the socioeconomic and cultural impact, of the movement. It survived, flourished, and shaped German speakers' lives in Europe and beyond. The internal, the separate, the conscious personal sphere of life emerged—especially among southwest German pietists—as the chosen arena of struggle and true Christian liberty.

Pietism's influence on later literary and political movements in Germany has long been debated. Romantic German literature's fascination with the domestic, the homely, received considerable impetus from Pietism's emphasis on the "conversion" of the individual, the scrutinizing of conscience and behavior, the focus on duty in one's calling, and the scorn for external show and consumption. When the Swabian Friedrich Schiller began writing domestic tragedies, he took his domestic and religious models from the forms pioneered in Jung-Stilling's 1777 novel and Karl Philip Mortiz's *Anton Reiser* (1785).[3]

German-speaking women from the southwest territories of the Reich, especially, holding to their faith like the mother of Jung-Stilling's piece, continued in North America to read certain types of literature, seek out a certain kind of pastor, and demand support for both schooling and worship in the language redolent of Pietism's "inward" values.[4] In its developed critique of village culture, this variant of Pietism also transferred to North America a "negative" definition of freedom, which equated it with separation from the corrupting influences of the world. The pietist conventicle, the unsanctioned, extralegal gathering of villagers and their spiritual leaders, created a kind of "private sociability" among members that linked them beyond their individual villages to like-minded believers elsewhere. Members of these conventicles saw themselves as truly reborn, and as self-consciously superior critics of village life and the scandalous behavior of Ludwigsburg and Stuttgart courtiers. Most intense in Württemberg, this version of Pietism created echoes in neighboring areas of the southwest and in the domestic culture of German-speaking settlements in North America. If its idea of liberty survived transit, its understanding of property did too, redolent of the suspicion directed against those in charge of church property who abused its care. In addition, property remained a domestic and familial concern around which "privileges" circulated, and the defense of which often poisoned relationships in families and broader social circles.[5]

The shepherds of the pietist movement arrived from the Prussian institutions at the Francke Foundations in the new university city of Halle. They shared with congregants from the Reich's southwest many values, including the conviction that Christian liberty was an inward virtue and that the conventicle contained the seeds of renewal for the church. But the Prussian variety of Pietism also envisioned broad social reform originating from educated, trained subjects, under state auspices and with state support. In Halle's view, both liberty and property had positive dimensions that connected the believer to broader public obligations.

The version of public, institutionalized, missionary Pietism that grew out of August Hermann Francke's labors eventually provoked North American German speakers, even though they lacked state support for their faith, to consider this more positive definition of liberty, which included responsibility for the broader public weal. Pedagogy in practical as well as theological matters remained the key to philanthropy and social transformation for the Hallenser. Therefore an individual's liberty implied obligation toward others. The same concept applied to property. In North America, pastors and schoolteachers educated at Halle criticized too much involvement in "worldly goods," of course. But Halle's own aggressive missionary activities were based on shrewd business judgments that reflected a developing doctrine of stewardship over property which tied personal concerns to the public, political culture.

Both variants of German Pietism—the Prussian and the southwestern—developed communication and support networks composed of distant conventicle members, booksellers, pastors, and patrons interested in supporting the renewal movement through philanthropic donations. These networks existed alongside the more worldly center of exchange, the village tavern, or *Wirtshaus*. The tavern represented much of what many pietists thought was wrong with public life in the eighteenth-century southwest. The two versions of Pietism, with their networks of information and support, were transferred to British North America. But so too, to the pietists' dismay, were the tavern and its commercial networks. Pietists sought to sustain, in networks of like-minded persons, the qualities of individual spiritual discipline, literacy, order, and certainty. Those virtues turned out to be not unlike those that a successful entrepreneur needed. In the settlement process, successful cultural brokers emerged, among them Prussian pietists who contributed to developing a language capable of integrating the competing definitions of liberty and property from within the Reich into North American political culture.

I

One of the major shapers of Prussian and central German Pietism was Philipp Jacob Spener (1635–1705). His renewal efforts within the Lutheran church began during his student days in the imperial city of Straßburg and continued during pastorates and university work in the imperial city of Frankfurt am Main; the Saxon capital, Dresden; and the rising center of Brandenburg-Prussia, Berlin. Spener rarely overstepped the bounds of orthodox Lutheranism in his preaching and writing, unlike more radical denouncers of the orthodox Lutheran emphasis on the baptismal font, the pulpit, the communion table, and the confessional. Spener devoted some writing to the issue of individual "rebirth" and "conversion," but rejected a wholly subjective or mystical interpretation of the believer's relationship to God and the problem of salvation. The objective presence of God in the preached Word and received Sacraments of the church continued to bind the "awakened" believer to the state churches. Spener's real interest lay in rekindling Lutherans' confident belief in the Reformation teaching on the priesthood of all believers. He held that a transforming personal and social behavior ought to flow from lives spent unfolding that conviction.

Spener reaffirmed with Luther that the true church was invisible, known only to God, and neither ascertainable to humans nor outlined in structural detail in the New Testament. But he envisioned a renewal of the state church through education which would create self-sufficient productive subjects and resultant social welfare for the poor, as well as enabling pastors to preach more imaginatively and stirringly on a range of scriptural texts that went beyond prescribed Sunday gospel. To aid renewal, the conventicles, *ecclesiolae in ecclesia* (little churches within the church) would act like fermenting yeast. But separatism, "private" assemblies, and spiritual superiority—all sins laid at the door of Pietism by critics—Spener struggled to avoid.[6]

The conventional wisdom about the church Spener criticized holds that a generation of academic theological debate had stifled piety. This "dead" church bore some responsibility for the lawlessness and libertine behavior of the Reich that crept from beneath the ruins of the Thirty Years' War. Penned by the spiritual descendants of the pietists, the picture is badly overdrawn. Pietist visitors to the orthodox center Leipzig, for example, were stunned to discover that by the 1720s, during Johann Sebastian Bach's tenure as cantor at Saint Thomas's Church, the city fathers, to accommodate popular sacramental piety, had to reopen one of the churches closed during the Reformation. Bach, like many other Leipzigers, went to auricular confession and received the Lord's Supper on Thursdays and Sundays weekly, not four times a year as was common among the pietists. During Sunday worship, chains were drawn across the city entrances and around the churches to stop traffic; pietist critics admitted that in this bastion of orthodoxy, genuine moral improvement seemed to flow from the sacramental piety sustained by the Leipzig high church liturgy for which Bach wrote his cantatas.[7]

Even though orthodoxy was not as "dead" in its preaching and worship as pietists claimed, pietists and orthodox believers did disagree fiercely on three related issues: the theological implications of certain pietist emphases; economic protests levied by groups threatened by pietist privilege; and the political implications of the success of Pietism's patrons, the absolutist princes.

The most significant emphasis among early pietists which separated them from Lutheran "orthodoxy" involved the movement's relationship to the state. Spener at first had no inclination to link his reform proposals to the power of princes. Like his orthodox Lutheran opponents, he believed that the prince should operate as head of the church in his land, but have no direct, administrative role. Pietist circles in the imperial cities such as Straßburg and Frankfurt were tolerated, even encouraged, by some civic leaders. Hence, Pietism's relationship to public authority rarely caused trouble there. But Spener's 1691 removal from Dresden (after criticizing the elector of Saxony's debauched court life) to the oldest, most prestigious Berlin church, the Nicholaikirche, signaled a dramatic turn. Three years later, in July 1694, the elector Frederick founded the new university in Halle.[8]

The French invasion of the Rhineland in 1688, which lasted until the Peace of Ryswick in 1697, catapulted the elector of Brandenburg, Frederick III, to unprecedented popularity and importance. As the German prince who threw back the French near Bonn, forcing their retreat beyond Mainz in the midst of the war, Frederick won plaudits and prestige for himself and his scattered principalities. While the war raged, he founded a new university, which was deliberately and publicly proclaimed to be the successor to the beloved Heidelberg, recently reduced to ashes by the French invaders.

At festivities marking Halle's founding, students sang for the assembled estates from Magdeburg, in whose territory Halle lay, "As we bathe ourselves in tears / a rejuvenated Phoenix rises / from the collapsed seat of learning, out of Heidelberg's ashes." Hailed as the conqueror of the French (*victor Gallorum*), the elector and his new university seized this identity for themselves. The Hohenzollerns took seriously their role as protectors of the university that was the logical successor to the older center of German Calvinism. Equally significant, they meant to use Halle as an alternative university to combat the nearby orthodox Lutheran bastions in Saxony at Wittenberg and Leipzig, which soon produced Halle's severest critics.[9]

By 1613 both the Rhineland and Brandenburg houses had formally adopted Calvinism, the former as a territorial confession, the latter as its personal one. The political consequences enabled the respective princes to achieve greater central control over their churches than older Lutheran beliefs and practices had allowed. Lutherans had preached submission to the princes. In practical terms, however, this had meant loyalty to the local feudal authority. Lutherans did not envisage a prince actively engaged in administrative reform or control of the church. The use of Calvinism in both the Rhineland and Brandenburg for just such a purpose portended a substantial innovation in defining how church and prince were to shape public life.[10]

A particular novelty lay in the coupling of the Calvinist investment of a moral quality in the state with the belief in the prince's right and obligation to intervene directly in church doctrine and discipline. Territorial Calvinism gave political reformers in Germany a theological basis on which to construct the centralization of power that the Palatinate and Pfalz-Zweibrücken's rulers used later to reform local courts and guilds. In both instances, the adoption of Calvinism allowed those territories to distance themselves from both Catholicism and Lutheranism, the two confessions recognized since the Peace of Augsburg in 1548. In practical terms, the new Protestantism officially recognized after the Peace of Westphalia in 1648 could be used to bind together the diverse religious and territorial splinters comprising these states. In Brandenburg especially, Frederick William, the Great Elector, intervened in the administration of the church, demanding a cessation of strife between Reformed and Lutherans and forbidding Lutheran preachers to subscribe to the Formula of Concord, the document that had ended a generation of internal doctrinal strife within that confession. Frederick III in 1698 further forbade Lutheran preachers to insist on private confession before individuals received the Lord's Supper. At the same time, he forbade Reformed preachers to teach predestination or practice ritual exorcism at baptism.

One social and demographic difference continued to separate the Rhenish version of Calvinism from the Prussian one. In Prussia the new religion remained that of the court and some of the nobility; the population—with the exception of Dutch and Huguenot minorities—remained stubbornly, hostilely Lutheran. As late as 1700, only one in every four Berliners was Reformed. Huguenot and Dutch refugees of the 1680s were deliberately settled not merely at Potsdam and Berlin but also in Halle, to improve the economic and social conditions in the town, which had been badly damaged in the Thirty Years' War. Between 1685 and 1713, Reformed migrants from Holland, the Palatinate, and Switzerland swelled the congregation at Halle and introduced new techniques in weaving, hatmaking, and other industries, rejuvenating a ruined economy. Relationships between Lutheran pietists and the Reformed were cordial and congenial. Yet the social and economic consequences of cooperation between the two groups disturbed many.

The tension between religious conviction and the mores of public, state-controlled society had a long and troubled history in Prussia even before the founding of the university at Halle. Strife broke out in 1692 between pietist preachers and the orthodox Lutheran pastors at Sankt Ulrich's over how to reform the tavern culture and the overt sinners who kept showing up for communion in the churches on Sundays with no apparent qualms of conscience and no signs of repentance. The pietist prescription smacked of Geneva: use the confessional, and bar obdurate sinners from the communion rail to bring them to heel. August Hermann Francke's tenure as pastor in the wretched village of Glaucha, just outside Halle's walls, showed him the filth, despair, drunkenness, and ignorance that pietists were determined to combat. The thirty-seven taverns that operated among the two hundred houses were among his first targets; so too, was the village *Kantor,* whom he refused the sacrament because of the man's conspicuous consumption of tobacco and frequent enjoyment of card games, and liquid refreshment. Soon, many fled the strict pastor for refuge within the walls of Halle at Sankt Ulrich's, the *Pfarrkirche.* [11]

Tavern owners feared the collapse of business. Orthodox Lutheran preachers questioned pietists' manipulation of the sacraments as a means of social control. Indigenous druggists, guild members, and book dealers resented the electoral privilege granted in 1698 to the new pietist orphanage at Halle. That jealousy accompanied envy directed at the Reformed immigrants' economic and social advancement, which threatened guild privileges and social relationships. A peculiar connection thus emerged between Halle Pietism and Prussian public life. Officially Lutheran in doctrine, Halle pietists behaved more like Reformed, with whom they enjoyed cordial relations while insisting on barring the latter from university posts and chaplaincies. Stewardship of worldly goods caused pietists considerable discomfort; the question of how to avoid entanglements in very worldly affairs—in which Hermann August Francke operated as a consummate businessman—forced reflection on the question of law and state authority. In an age when public culture seemed indistinguishable from the quality of society, Halle's answer tilted sharply away from orthodox Lutheranism.

The electors in Brandenburg demonstrated considerable interest in bequests and projects to improve their territories. They encouraged patronage of improvements among wealthy aristocrats and *Bürgertum,* without which Halle Pietism could never have existed. Despite the Great Elector's spending, which nearly bankrupted Brandenburg, his successor, Frederick III, maintained a glittering court but began by formal intervention in court proceedings to encourage and sustain inheritance claims and bequests that would aid the hospitals, orphanages, and schools.

In 1696, two years after opening the new university at Halle, the elector established the Mons Pietatis foundation (the name means "mountain of piety") in the Kleve-Mark, Münden, and Ravensberg territories, specifically "for the support of the Reformed churches and clergy." The elector's awareness of the benevolent foundations and orphanages in the Netherlands lay behind his decision, and when Francke decided to erect the orphanage at Halle, his associate Georg Heinrich Neubauer traveled west to see a functioning orphanage firsthand. Reformed models for building social and charitable institutions in Prussia found their expression not in the tiny Reformed minority's churches, however, but in Hallensian Lutheran Pietism.[12]

Frederick III and (after 1713) his successor, Frederick Wilhelm I, showed an interest in such enterprises; their directions to the *Kammergericht* in Berlin suggest as much. Of a list of fifty cases brought to the attention of the court between 1685 and 1739, some fifteen dealt with inheritances and bequests. In early 1713 Frederick Wilhelm, known for the thrift by which he tried to save the nearly bankrupt state, also ordered the court to hand down a decree compelling a foundation to pay money owed the *Parochialkirche* in Berlin as required by the terms of an endowment. The king curbed excessive philanthropy resulting from his own encouragement of benevolent activities. In one instance he ordered an investigation into an overzealous (and probably illicit) attempt by the widow of a Prussian officer to hand over the deceased's mines and iron and alum works in Züllich to an orphanage there.[13]

In a famous incident Francke later related, he found in a tin can at his house the four Taler sixteen Groschen with which he opened the first paupers' school at Halle during Easter 1695. He took this providential sign for an omen of later support from benefactors. Nor was he disappointed. By the mid-eighteenth century the Francke Foundations comprised the largest public concern in Prussia. Pietists operated schools, an orphanage, a pharmacy, a printery, and bookstores, and oversaw foreign missions scattered from Siberia and Moscow to India and North America. Over eighteen hundred persons were employed in this enterprise, which began in earnest in 1695 with a gift of five hundred Taler from Freiherr Georg Rudolf von Schweinitz.[14]

Three years later, one hundred orphans had been taken in under Francke's care, and his pleas for support had brought between 18,000 and 19,000 Taler into his hands. Special privileges ordered directly by the elector released the Halle work from the indirect tax on consumer goods (*Akzise*); privileges for the erection of the printery and bindery; baking and brewing rights; and privileges for building the linen cloth factory and the pharmacy followed in succession. As the buildings at Halle went up, the first of many public collections of funds began in all the churches of each province. The elector set the example by promising 1,000 Taler; his wife Sophie Charlotte donated 300, and Prince Frederick Wilhelm, 125. The pharmacy and bookstore in particular supported Halle's public efforts. Perhaps between 2,000 and 3,000 Taler per year flowed into Halle from the book sales, and an electoral threat to punish plagiarists by confiscation, imprisonment, and a 1,000-Taler fine secured copyright for Halle publications. Christian Richter, the pharmacist who developed the famous collections of recipes and prescriptions packaged and sent with missionaries the world over, guaranteed the enterprise 9,000 Taler per year by 1720, and that sum soared to an average of 30,500 Taler annually by 1760–70.[15]

In 1737 the king reconfirmed the old privileges and promised to keep members of Reformed churches off the university faculty. Between 1713 and 1740, Lutheran Pietism had become the new orthodoxy in Prussia, bound to the state by the privileges granted to it and the donations of the aristocracy which made its missionary work possible. The privileges protected the pedagogical ideas of the Francke Foundations. Technical and vocational training, including empirical scientific study of flora and fauna, accompanied scriptural piety in Francke's plan to eradicate ignorance and poverty. By 1695 Francke envisioned a complete system comprising an orphanage, a poor children's school, a German school, a Latin school, a *Gymnasium,* and a teachers' training institute. His objectives were realized by 1710, and the reconfirmation of privileges three years later ratified the connection between philanthropy and education. Halle's reforms helped Prussia reach the goal of compulsory general education, at least west of the Oder. Francke and his colleagues, Prussian state servants, reveled after 1713 in their success and their undisputed role as the leaders of a new political-religious orthodoxy in Prussia.

Halle's success shaped its ideas of public life. The guiding inspiration for Francke's enterprises remained the rhetorical question put in Isaiah 58:7–8: "Is it not [your duty] to share your bread with the hungry and bring the homeless poor into your house; when you see the naked, to cover him, and not to hide yourself from your own flesh? Then shall your light break forth like the dawn, and your healing shall spring up speedily; your righteousness shall go before you, the glory of the Lord shall be your rear guard. Then you shall call, and the Lord will answer; you shall cry, and he will say, Here I am."

This, Francke's favorite scripture, brought to mind the apocalyptic use of the passage by Christ: "As you did it not to one of the least of these, you did it not to me" (Matt. 25:31–46). At least initially, an apocalyptic vision drove Halle's efforts. The desire for certainty of salvation lay behind this fear of terrible judgment. Once certain of both salvation and one's calling in life, the devotee of Halle Pietism possessed an enabling power and labored under the obligation to direct his or her daily activities toward both personal and social salvation—which, nonetheless, could only come through grace grasped by faith. If one examines closely the sermons and pamphlets produced by Halle's pietist writers throughout the eighteenth century, the concern for certainty and power—certainty of one's own salvation, and the power to help effect social reform, without which personal salvation seemed unlikely—dominate the literature.[16]

The pietists' relationship to state power and public life included their almost total silence about how deep involvement in work, business, state enterprises, and other "worldly" matters—in short, property—could be reconciled with spiritual, internal values—that is, a true Christian liberty. Pietists such as Francke preached a work ethic that implied that those who could turn a profit should donate to the Francke Foundations. Work was a positive aspect of one's calling in life, good for keeping people out of mischief; but more than that, it was a part of God's justice, his law, by which one discovered one's obligations and potential. Pietists did not envision a society without various orders and hierarchies, but they did encourage a closer cooperation between rich and poor, symbolically shown in their insistence that wealthy Prussian Junkers' sons work along-side orphan students at Halle, and in their proscription of the insignia of aristocratic rank. Though the Hallensers did not attempt to justify profits for profit's sake, neither did they envision a reordering of property and public power.[17]

It might logically seem that the problem of property and public power would create an elaborate doctrine of "stewardship," yet this did not happen quickly. Opportunities existed during the church year when obvious texts practically begged for this exegesis. Instead, they were turned

to other uses. Thus, in parables from the gospel that directly dealt with
the wise and foolish use of property, or counseled stewardship, pietist
comments opted for allegorical and purely spiritual conclusions and
avoided the hard questions such passages raised.[18]

The simplest explanation for the silence lies in the supreme confidence
many pietists possessed that their use of donations springing from the
labor or surplus of others would benefit the poor, and the realm. They
believed firmly that self-sufficiency and technical training would eradicate
the need for any philanthropic works but those run by the state. The
objections of individual tavern owners, book dealers, or property owners
injured by Halle's enterprises could be met: Halle's power and property
benefited state and society, whereas the injured were mere private persons.

Halle pietists saw nothing wrong with the way the *Polizeiordnung,*
the administrative, coercive arm of a centralized state, supported their
understanding of public life, even at the expense of older local privileges
or liberties.[19] In sharp contrast to the village inheritance disputes over
property in the southwest, where local custom and written law resisted
central authority, in Prussia absolutism and Halle Pietism worked together in triumph. The potential for explosive conflict between the vision
brought to the New World by Halle-trained missionaries—a vision of
positive liberty and the use of property for broader religious and social
ends—and the ideas of congregations in North America composed of
southwesterners, inheritors of dramatically different definitions of both
liberty and property, could hardly have been greater.

Not all pietist notions of public obligation for philanthropy originated
in Halle. In Frankfurt, where Spener had begun his career, magistrates
approved a number of institutions administered by the city council. But
Spener and Francke remained suspicious of "private" institutions and
insisted that the Francke Foundations enjoy state protection. They then
worked hard to keep Prussian administrators from interfering directly
in Halle's affairs. For smaller princes, examples of social experiments in
Wetzlar or the area of Solms-Laubach seemed promising, although most
experiments attempting to combine orphanages and poorhouses with
some form of work and training failed. Halle's succeeded.[20]

Halle Pietism's relationship to public life and its rather vague treatment
of "property" or "worldly goods" were in part borrowed from traditional
Lutheran and Calvinist notions of property and public order. The assessment of public authority and the law developed by Luther in the
sixteenth century owed much of its pessimistic outlook to the reformer's
reading of Augustine. The development of the famous doctrine of the
Two Kingdoms provided distinct areas of work for state and church.

The first use of law was civil or political, to strike terror into sinners and keep them in order. Thus, law revealed the role of the state in human affairs. Luther shared with Augustine the conviction that Adam's desire for "liberty" (in this case, prideful self-will consciously set against an explicit command of a loving God) had made Adam sin, and hence made him responsible for the need for law. God's will, as represented in state power, disciplined rebellious human beings and prevented the tendency toward self-will from degenerating into social disorder and anarchy.[21]

For Luther, however, the second use of law, its theological use, emerged as the more important. Thus, law accurately describes what human beings are truly like, since in nature all people know what they should do to others by simply asking themselves what they would like done to them. They also always fail to act accordingly. All are condemned to fail because of the Fall in the garden. Luther saw law as a mirror that reveals the true misery of the human condition and the hopeless sinfulness of each individual and of all humanity by contrasting God's original will and plan, and his commandments, with actual human behavior. The pessimistic view of human nature and history which Luther inherited from Augustine and developed further had direct consequences for his assessment of property and worldly goods. Social reform did not interest Luther because his major concern was the individual's relationship to the question of justification—how do I find favor with God? To the extent that property had to be considered, Luther conceded that it was useful for Christian communities. But he denounced usurers and speculators such as the Fuggers of Augsburg. Property was defensible if it supported Christian communities. Theft was forbidden by the eighth commandment, but property was "good" only if one held it with a sense of duty and worked to justify one's right of title. For Luther, property was in the realm of law and had nothing to do with the gospel as such. Though Luther conceded that the Sermon on the Mount assumed that property existed—how else could one "give to the poor"?—early church communalism had been voluntary and not normative. In any event, the New Testament provided no blueprint for contemporary society. Luther's assessment of the threats posed by the Turks and an aggressive emperor and papacy prompted him to pay little attention to developing an extended social ethic around property and its stewardship.[22]

Lutherans and Calvinists broke, however, in their famous disagreement over the third use of law. For Calvin and other Reformed thinkers, the gospel and the message of love summarized law and were not antithetical to it, and law provided a comprehensive image of creation and redemption. The New Testament must, indeed, in their view, be used as the model for building church and state on earth. For Luther, this approach sneaked in by the back door the notion that law—that praise-worthy human works in general—could function as a form of self-sal-vation. Ironically, Calvinists viewed the state, law, and history more positively than did Lutherans. Luther and his followers condemned and rejected the doctrine of absolute predestination, election, and reprobation, but it was precisely this concept that gave the Calvinist elect a sense of certainty and power in their vision of worldly affairs which the Lutheran theologians could never share. Lutherans, like their Roman Catholic, Anglican, and Eastern Orthodox counterparts, found ample scriptural basis for a doctrine of God's election by grace to salvation. Jean Calvin's lawyerlike logic developed the doctrine of an election of wrath, to dam-nation, as well, alarming Lutherans who saw here a way to excuse humans from the consequences of their own faults, sins, and unbelief. For the Reformed, however, the symmetry of the doctrine provided a kind of positive liberty that was ideal for building a Christian state and society.[23]

Halle Pietism tended toward the endorsement of this "third use of the law"—one more closely related to Calvin than to Luther, as Lutheran critics pointed out. True, the Halle pietists continued to subscribe to the Augsburg Confession, and never openly deviated from the formal con-fessional symbols of Lutheranism. But in practical terms, their confident certainty and their willingness to harness a vision of spiritual power to the engine of state absolutism that bestowed on them special commercial, institutional privileges, looked very un-Lutheran, indeed. Many of the aristocrats who gave lavishly to the Halle projects were not giving of their surplus. Instead, some members of the aristocracy were granted special licenses to open enterprises whose profits were specifically ear-marked for Francke's purposes. Orthodox critics denounced the "busy Martha of Halle," consumed by interest in worldly affairs, who could not stop to listen to the gospel itself; meanwhile, the mercantilist engines of Francke's enterprises spun more dynamically than ever.[24]

Spener's vision of the human condition had brought him close to repudiating the doctrine of the Two Kingdoms. The notion of original sin which Luther developed from Augustine "was not shared by Spener. . . . Spener valued primitive Christianity as a historical possibility for the future. Spener prepared the way for an optimistic view of history. 'He serves [as an example of those whose thinking led to] . . . the reduction of the Gospel to Christian ethics.'" Francke, too, had no use for Luther's insight that weak faith is characteristic of human life; for Francke, "power" and concrete institutions, such as money and patronage, could conquer the social and personal accident of weak faith.[25]

As one orphanage student said, Halle theologians needed no study of the law of nature outside the Bible, "for their law of nature was the Decalogue and their law of nations the command, 'go therefore to all peoples and teach all the pagans.'" Eventually, these attitudes built for Halle pietists and their students a bridge to Enlightenment rationalism, for the church as institution faded in comparison to individual conscience; pastoral office easily succumbed to a cult of personality; and dogma inexorably was displaced by a concern for ethics. Supreme confidence in a rational, planned use of charitable bequests; public patronage; and the dismissal of older Lutheran doubts about the glory of princes gave Halle "certainty" and "power" that provided an impetus for global energy. By the 1730s Halle's efforts extended to the British colonial world.[26]

A seed of interest in North America had been planted in the 1680s. Pietist connections to Frankfurt am Main, Württemberg, and the Rhineland had been well tended during Spener's work in the imperial city. As the first organized group of German speakers left for Pennsylvania in 1683, the group of radical separatist pietists at Frankfurt which produced Francis Daniel Pastorius appreciated Spener's conventicle and conversion themes, not his Lutheran doctrine. Pietists followed New World developments also because Spener's close associate August Hermann Francke, and his son Gotthilf August Francke, were personal friends of the Erfurt merchant Hiob Ludolff. Ludolff, by 1675 *Kammerdirektor* for Altenburg-Thuringia, pursued his obsession with building a coalition between the Holy Roman Empire, Holland, England, and Coptic Ethiopia to oppose the Turks. By 1678 Ludolff had moved to Frankfurt and become acquainted with the pietist movement; in 1683 he journeyed to Holland and England just as William Penn's German-speaking colonists embarked for North America. The younger Francke resided briefly in Erfurt with Ludolff, and both the settlement of the Pastorius group at Germantown, Pennsylvania, in 1683, and the war that swept over the Rhineland beginning in 1688 eventually drew Halle's attention to the North American settlements. The Halle pietists knew the brothers Justus and Daniel Falckner, for in 1697 one of Justus's compositions was published in the Halle hymnal. Both Falckners' mystical inclinations led them briefly to the Wissahickon Brethren in Pennsylvania, led by Johannes Kelpius. By 1700 Halle's connections with North America were fragile, but in place.[27] But Daniel Falckner's first task, performed for the Halle fathers, would be to address the Württemberg pietists led to New York by Josua Harrsch. To that strain of Pietism, one must also devote close attention.

II

In 1734 the Württemberg pietist and jurist Johann Jacob Moser published a seminal essay on "private" conventicles and Pietism in Württemberg. His *Rechtliches Bedencken von Privat-Versammlungen der Kinder*

Gottes . . .[28] attempted to close the gap between the conventicles' critics and the pious who conducted meetings in homes throughout the duchy. Moser claimed to be inspired by recent events in Hanover and in the imperial city Reutlingen (a few kilometers northeast of Tübingen), where the debates and conventicle activity had been particularly tense. But he may also have been spurred into action by reading, one year before, the definition of *conventicle* in Johann Heinrich Zedler's *Großes Vollständiges Universal-Lexikon:* "a secret meeting, an impermissible congregation, which in every time has been understood as having an evil meaning."[29]

The essay's title could nearly serve as a guide through the southwest German pietist's ideas about liberty, always understood in a domestic, familial context. Moser's words could be interpreted to mean "legal considerations" about the "private meetings of God's children." But he could also have meant to convey the notion of "second thoughts" about the correct understanding of the conventicles.[30] In either reading, the title encouraged inward reflection on meetings deliberately described in familial domestic terms. Moser himself hardly fit his own description of the movement. He belonged to a small group of "activist" pietists who were atypical of the movement in Württemberg. Stemming from an old Württemberg family, he had been educated a Lutheran, and sometime between his father's death in 1716 and a professed conversion experience in 1728 he turned away from an earlier fascination with Deism to read Spener's *Theologische Bedencken*—almost certainly the inspiration for the title of his own pamphlet. Moser's own Pietism emphasized pragmatic work in the world, not withdrawal into the circle defined by the family of true believers. Studies at Tübingen were followed by more cosmopolitan exposure, at the Prussian university of Frankfurt an der Oder, to cameralist theory that shaped his pragmatism and interest in the use of state institutions to promote a Christian society.[31]

Other activists at work in the German southwest shared the Prussian version of Pietism. Friedrich Nicolai eventually came from Berlin to help plan a Württemberg academy modeled on Prussian discipline. When financial difficulties threatened the project, Nicolai suggested that income be taken from church funds, the *Kirchenkasten,* regardless of the Landtag's wishes. What had worked in Berlin, however, or in Halle, where by the king's orders no chaplains were to serve in the Prussian army unless they had been trained at Halle, did not work in Württemberg.[32]

Later institutional reforms, such as the foundation of the first *Realschule* within a traditional *Gymnasium* at Nürtingen in 1783, were carried out by people such as Jacob Friedrich Klemm, a former student of August Hermann Francke. Christoph Carl Ludwig von Pfeil, the son of Quirin Heinrich von Pfeil, the *Obergerichts-Assessor* for the duchy, was sent by his uncle Justus for education at Halle. He began a notable career in political service to the Reich. A devout pietist, von Pfeil later wrote a number of devotional tracts, remaining active in political and institutional reforms such as the promotion of orphanages and (in his role as imperial knight at Denkstetten) the extending of protection to his Jewish subjects. But these pietists who understood both Christian liberty and the use of property in the positive sense of obligation and connection to state interests remained the exception. On the whole, the judgment on the Württemberg movement offered by one of its premier historians stands: "Pietism with its striving toward concrete reforms did not grow in Württemberg." Reforms were carried out by individual pastors within the state church, but by the 1740s whatever radical implications early pietist conventicles threatened had vanished.[33]

Due in part to Moser's labors, Württemberg's duke issued in 1743 the famous *Pietistenrescript* that laid down the conditions under which pietist associations and projects would be permitted. The edict in effect reduced Pietism to a part of the public, state church, defusing the radical, antisocial, and antigovernmental potential the pietist movement had had between 1684 and the 1730s.[34] By 1800, hardly anyone remembered the earlier times when such radicalism seemed genuine. The common Württemberg definition of a pietist offered by F. A. Weckherlin in 1787 seemed accurate enough: "merely devout people, earnest in Luther's service, quiet enthusiasts in public and common worship, penitent sighers in their private religious exercises. Only lack of charity, or more loosely, dissatisfaction with this people's search for singular reputation, bestows on them the name headhangers, which is more of a concept than a name."[35] But it was a concept that spoke volumes of the characteristics of the Movement—inwardness, and the detachment from the broader culture.

Pietism in Württemberg exhibited these two curious characteristics, which informed its concepts of liberty and property. *Freiheit* (liberty) remained largely interior, and connected to its plural form *Freiheiten* (privileges), which meant, essentially, freedom from state interference with the conventicles. Property, when referred to at all, was suspect, especially in the form of wealth obtained by taxes used to support ungodly behavior by the duke and his courtiers. Otherwise, property functioned to protect the domestic hearth, even though bitter disputes swirled around the relationships it defined. Pietism in Württemberg could never resolve this fundamental tension: was property a trap, responsible for the corruption of spirit Jung-Stilling's kitchen scene described, or was it a good, provided that true believers rather than rapacious state officials had charge of it? This ambivalence, too, survived the Atlantic crossing.

Württemberg's church authorities, most of whom pietist critics suspected of abuses, presided over twenty four cloisters (still populated by Lutheran clerics) as well as other properties, and more than four hundred villages and other jurisdictions. Not only did the leading prelates possess considerable influence, exercised through the *Kirchenrat,* but they also sat with other deputies in the Diet and on the Small Committee (*Engerer Ausschuß*) that protected the Diet's privileges when the larger body was in recess.

The Württemberg state church's relationship to worldly goods and economic power became by the 1700s increasingly problematic. The Kirchenrat oversaw more than 198 officials administering lands comprising one-third of the duchy's reality. More than seven hundred pastors and ninety teachers who worked in parishes and Latin schools were supported in part by the Great Tithe that went straight to the Kirchenrat, but more importantly by the small tithe guaranteeing fixed salaries in the form of small grains and crops (barley, rye, cabbage), wood, wine, and small bits of cash. Between 1654 and 1738, a 10 to 14 percent increase in the cost of food was not matched by a rise in the value of these crops and products. Though never suffering as much as the poorer peasants, artisans, and tradesmen, over half the duchy's pastors slid from modest middling status into poverty. Bitter letters from pastors complaining of their inability to feed, clothe, and educate their children provoked conflict with parishioners, who resented the loss of village status represented by the presence of poor pastors but resisted their duty to provide the contributions in kind collected by administrators. Recriminations before local courts and threats to turn out greedy pastors by boycotting services became commonplace.[36]

Nonetheless, the economic and social difficulties that brought the church into conflict with the absolutist aspirations of the Württemberg dukes did not initially provide the context for Pietism. Although Spener himself visited Württemberg in 1662, church renewal in Württemberg was indigenous and assumed a character different from that of the renewal Halle created in Prussia. An institutionalized form of social control peculiar to the Lutheran church in Württemberg was introduced by Johann Valentin Andreae in the early seventeenth century. The *Kirchenkonvent* (church consistory), a local inquisitorial body presided over by the local pastor and members of the Rat and Gericht of the town, reflected the influence of Calvinist Geneva, and attempts to discipline common people.[37]

This attempt to link doctrine to daily practice preceded an even lengthier debate on the need for education and social control in the years following the Thirty Years' War. Reeling from demographic catastrophe, the remaining 98,000 inhabitants of a duchy that had numbered 445,000 in 1622 had barely begun to recover when the French Wars of the 1670s, 80s, and 90s again ravaged the province, culminating with the 1693 invasion. The social and political consequences of these disasters took two forms: on the part of the few, excessive hedonism and indulgence in luxury; and on the part of the many who predicted imminent apocalypse, retreat from sociopolitical hardship into apocalyptically minded cells, superstition, and magic practices. Faced with potential social and political quietism from some quarters and radicalism from others, pietist leaders such as Johann Andreas Hochstetter, a friend and correspondent of Spener, in 1692 proposed unsuccessfully the *collegium pietatis* to stimulate piety and religious education.[38]

Between 1693 and the incorporation of Württemberg's pietists into the state church, quarrels arose over "private" religious assemblies. One concern that emerged at the village level and in pietist writings in Württemberg stimulated the growth of such assemblies: officials' corruption, and their abuse of church properties and charities. The conclusion of one scholar about the nature of Württemberg Pietism seems correct: by the 1740s pietists were quietistic, disconnected politically, passive, and tolerated. But the reason for this posture lay in the abuse villagers increasingly resented but could not reform: the pilfering of church properties and the collusion of local magistrates and worthies who fixed the price of the tithes that amounted to one-fifth of village produce. By auctioning off to the highest bidder the job of collecting the tithes at harvest, magistrates, and by association, pastors, participated in the pilfering by the state and religious leaders of property due the church. From such developments, in part, came the withdrawal that disconnected pietists from the mainstream of village life in Württemberg and nurtured a profound skepticism about requests to give of their meager property for charitable purposes. This posture would have stranger consequences in the novel context of the British colonies, when such people were confronted with the need to recruit and pay for their own pastors, and to build their own churches and schools.[39]

Pietist preachers rarely confronted head on the scandals surrounding church property. By 1718 Samuel Urlsperger, who would soon emerge as the major supporter of the settlement of Salzburgers in Georgia, lost his post as court preacher in Stuttgart after attacking the mores of the courtiers. Four years later, when Duke Eberhard Ludwig redirected the larger part of the Great Tithe from the pastorates, claiming to be equalizing salaries, he used these funds to build the new ducal *Residenzes*. Open protest, however, remained rare. A generation later, Friedrich Carl von Moser, son of the famous jurist Johann Jacob, published in Frankfurt his essay "On the Use of Wealth." Moser, like the Halle pietists, claimed to review the duties of the rich to the state and to the poor. Like the Halle pietists, Moser believed that England's example should be followed in directing charity to those willing to work. In too many parts of the Reich, the rich would sooner endow a professorship in Greek than train an apprentice for trade. "Work is the death of beggary," Moser concluded.[40] Street beggars cluster like flies around the richest charitable institutes. The noblewoman who founded a cotton-spinning mill to provide work for the poor provided the correct example. Obliquely, Moser reflected the distaste that many eminent pietists felt for the peculation of Würt-temberg's duke, who by the 1700s made increasing use of a loophole in the original laws erected to protect church goods. Monies left from local projects no longer went to the central treasury in Stuttgart but had been used to finance palaces, cultural institutes, and a military academy. Such abuses, coupled with the manner in which local administrators guaranteed the flow of grains into the duchy's economy by auctioning off the privilege of doing the assessments, represented flagrant corruption.

Georg Conrad Rieger, a pietist preacher in Stuttgart, echoed Moser's criticism. Low attendance at church and extravagant worldly show characterized his city. Denouncing the misuse of funds intended for the church, Rieger intoned, "Church property is that which is dedicated to the maintenance of God's worship; when it is turned to any other end, this constitutes abuse, and abuse of this sort will finally kindle a fire in the soul." Not only churches but also other charitable institutions were neglected, torn down, or left in "worse condition than stables," in favor of pleasure and hunting lodges. The support of the poor and of orphanages and poorhouses, which people grumbled at, remained a basic obligation. In addition to supporting orphans with food and clothing, true Christians had to "extract them out of conditions of laziness, idleness, blindness, ignorance, godlessness, in short, out of the power of hell and raise them up for heaven."[41]

III

Pietist conventicle activity emerged in certain Württemberg locales where critiques such as Rieger's received enthusiastic affirmation. In those villages and towns, one also notes how villagers' personal space in the houses, as well as the crimes committed against the household, and the offenses brought before the Ruggericht and the Kirchenkonvent, revealed that intrusive public authority coexisted with a developed sense of personal space and personal consciousness among villagers. From the villagers' reading material and the works spread by distribution networks, one glimpses the outlines of an individual pietist identity that valued personal space but was also apolitical, an identity in which the notion of "private property" conceived as a bulwark against "state" power could not exist. Indeed, by 1743 the cooptation of Pietism by the state church rendered social or political criticism increasingly powerless. Private sociability in the context of conventicles existed, but in muted form. Liberty, in this setting, also remained largely internal: freedom from the state church's interference with the conventicles rather than a positive liberty that envisoned engagement with the broader contours of public life and society.

If the observer from the imaginary tower at Schaffhausen had possessed the capacity of identifying "hot spots" of pietist ferment in Württemberg, conventicles would have been seen to cluster together on the landscape. Authorities recognized by the 1680s that major cities located on the rivers and avenues of trade had produced conventicles. Wine-market towns such as Vaihingen, on the Enz; the capital, Stuttgart; the university town of Tübingen on the Neckar; and the imperial cities, Reutlingen and Eßlingen, all became pietist centers. Further to the west, Calw, the wood-shipping entrepôt on the eastern slopes of the Black Forest; Freudenstadt, the planned town on the forest's western edge; Dürrmenz and Zaningen, in the forest proper; and towns (e.g., Herrenberg and Böblingen) that strung out along the roads connecting Calw with Stuttgart also alarmed officials. Near the university at Tübingen, ancillary parishes such as Mössingen and Altensteig, served by pastors with close connections to the university; or the exquisitely beautiful cloister town of Bebenhausen, just over the hill from Tübingen, provoked consternation among authorities worried that devotional circles threatened to lure the faithful away from normal Lutheran services.[42]

Smaller villages along the Neckar, such as Obereßlingen, and towns such as the poorer paper and wood center Balingen, or the weaving center Laichingen, on the eastern edges of the duchy, bordering Ulm's villages, produced patriarchal figures: schoolmasters, pastors, or wealthy merchants around whom ordinary pietists gathered, indulging an extremely subjective interpretation of biblical passages and held together by group loyalties and conformities bolstered by the certainty that membership in a self-consciously separate culture provided.[43]

Yet attempts to tie the rise of the conventicles to specific socioeconomic or political postures would frustrate the tower observer. No completely satisfactory explanation accounts for the fact that villages on one side of the Neckar in the Nürtingen district "got religion" (e.g., Obereßlingen), whereas villages only a few kilometers away, sharing the identical social, economic, and demographic conditions (e.g., Schlaitdorf, Grötzingen, Neckarhausen), remained untouched.[44]

The concept of liberty in these conventicles remained tied to a highly developed interior sense of the sufficient "self," defined in the sociability of fellow believers, the use of space for conventicle gatherings, and the literature read and discussed. Various notions of social disorganization, deprivation (socioeconomic or "relative"), psychological maladjustment, and social marginality have all been tried in an attempt to get at this renewal movement; none is convincing. Seen, however, as a vehicle of negotiation with prevailing village homes, in whose language deeply felt emotional values could be expressed in powerful terms, Pietism reassumes some of its proper importance.[45]

The activities and disputes brought before the village Kirchenconvent at least shed some light on a curious dimension of southwest village life: public authority regularly invaded personal space, rendering the creation of concepts of physical and mental privacy exceedingly unlikely. Yet at the same time, a highly developed sense of the integrity of the household, and of personal space within it, coexisted with regular intrusion by public figures, and even by other members of one's family.

How people in these villages actually lived, and what the houses looked like in which these conventicles took place, deserves some attention. Large, spacious houses in the imperial cities or larger towns provided ample space for conventicles. But in the eighteenth century Württemberg did not boast many large towns. The population density, forty eight per square mile in 1734, did not increase to sixty seven per square mile until 1790. At that date, the only towns of more than five thousand persons were Stuttgart, Tübingen, and Ludwigsburg. Another five towns contained perhaps three to four thousand persons apiece, but most people were spread over the landscape in some eighteen hundred villages, hamlets, farmsteads, and towns. Since most of those who eventually took their experiences to North America came from these smaller and more typical settlements, their housing is particularly interesting.[46]

Eighteenth-century travelers recorded with some care the houses of the larger towns such as Calw. The homes of the local eminences were remarkably simple. When a professor from Göttingen visited Calw in 1781 he was stunned to find the houses all badly built (*schlecht*) and too close together for comfort. The wealthy inhabitants were so provincial that as late as the 1740s no one even knew what a coach was. An earlier visitor who assured his readers that he "knew the richest men in the town" was astounded that his host wore the same simple dress as his poorer neighbors and that "his living area was the common room," indicating that the sleeping and cooking areas of the house had not yet been separated. A visitor to Stuttgart from Lower Saxony wondered at the houses with barns, stalls, and other structures built into them; even in the larger towns, such as Vaihingen, the manure piles stood in the streets before the houses; the capital itself held no balls or concerts, and had no clubs. The visiting academic wandered for months without being invited into the simple homes.[47]

Visitors had less reason to visit, and seldom described, peasants' and artisans' homes. One can supplement guesses about what travelers saw by more recent studies. From the seventeenth century until sometime around 1750, the so-called *Einhaus* dominated peasant villages from Saarbrücken and Lothringen into the Palatinate. Activities in the basic two-room-deep house centered around the stove, which was centrally located in the *Stube*. Not until the later eighteenth century were these areas separated from one another or another story added. In order to keep all rooms warm, the central stove in the Stube could not be blocked off from adjoining spaces where beds and spinning equipment stood.

The even simpler cottages of the day laborers which stood back from the streets of these villages were smaller. Lacking access to fields, they also lacked thatched straw roofs, settling for whatever twigs, branches, and other materials were at hand; not until 1767 did towns such as Oberlinxweiler or Ottweiler, in the Palatinate, acquire tile roofs for their dwellings. In both the day laborer's cottage and the more prosperous peasant's home, personal space was limited. The nearest one came to such a phenomenon as personal space was the marriage bed, which, at least in Württemberg villages, developed in the seventeenth and eighteenth centuries into a curtained four-poster. This curtained area of privacy was actually less private than its predecessor, for sixteenth-century houses had sometimes built into the wall of the Stube a kind of closet, complete with lock and key, into which one climbed to sleep. But only the married couple had access to such a bed; children, servants, and the unmarried slept on pallets or cots that often slipped under the main bed.[48] When the planned villages proposed by Rudolf Eickemeyer were drawn to scale in his 1787 pamphlet, he explicitly described as an innovation a floor plan dividing the parlor and the sleeping area from the kitchen to ensure personal space.[49]

Conventicle regulars understood and valued the notion of private conscience and a limited liberty of choice. Yet village living conditions continued to conspire against actual separate space, leaving the reflective or critical observer of village life with few options except, perhaps, like the aged mother in Jung-Stilling's novel, to retreat behind the tile stove — or to some similar space identified as theirs but not genuinely apart from the rest of the house — to exercise an interior freedom of judgment and reflection.[50]

The language used by ordinary people suggests a slowly developing idea of privacy. It was one thing for an educated legal expert such as Moser to speak of "private" assemblies, or for pastors to enter into their records that they had examined someone *privatissime*. But in the mouths of ordinary villagers, such words felt alien.

Certainly Palatines, like their Baden contemporaries, seldom heard the word *privat*. When they did use it, it was not with the modern meaning. *Privat* meant "not the usual, common custom." Thus "the children go privately to communion" meant that they went at a time other than Whitsunday, the normal date for taking the sacrament. It did not mean they went secretly, or outside the normal service.[51]

In Württemberg the term appeared first in the sixteenth century, but only among the educated. Its latinate quality kept it out of the common discourse and understanding. Only the pastor or official noted that someone had been examined *privatim*, usually meaning in the pastor's residence, about potentially scandalous sexual behavior.[52] When Jerg Ulrich From was called before the pastor and village officials as a common swearer ("ein gewesener Fluchmaul"), he may have understood that the mitigation of punishment came from his promise of improvement, or perhaps he really did appreciate the significance of the note that his offense had taken place "privatim."[53]

But the absence of a word meaning "private" in common speech was rendered far more significant by the manner in which society and authority intruded into personal space. Not only were village homes not divided into separate quarters, but the norms of religious and state control penetrated even into the supposedly "personal" area of behavior that took place behind closed doors.

Villagers in Württemberg experienced this most directly before the Kirchenkonvent.[54] These courts met every three months and investigated every aspect of daily life. Compulsory attendance at the Sunday morning service, the afternoon children's catechism, the Wednesday service, and Saturday vespers, as well as observance of the day of prayer and abstinence on the first Thursday of the month, were socially enforced. The *Umgänger*, or wandering inspector, worked the village alleys and lanes, peering through windows to check on nonattendance. Even people passing through town were sent to church; for instance, a group of gooseherds were ordered to show up for midweek service. By the eighteenth century, missing midweek service or failing to send children to catechism, especially during the summer months, led the lists of common offenses in nearly all villages. Though offenses mounted, Sunday attendance remained high, and by 1755 the Umgänger was instructed to be diligent in looking into houses.[55]

The struggle of the church against the atmosphere of the village tavern, or Wirtshaus, also came to light in these court proceedings. In Seißen, for instance, the village fathers were incensed to note that people were being called out of church, even by the Umgänger for the most frivolous of reasons. In 1729 a visiting butcher from Ulm, a particular friend of the Umgänger, was treated to a glass of wine during the service, for which purpose the innkeeper had been hauled out of church during the sermon by the overly friendly inspector. By the 1730s even Michael Mayer, one of the court judges, had been accused of drunkenness and setting a bad example by dancing, which was particularly scandalous in a seventy year old. In the same year Georg Strübel was threatened with a ten-Kreuzer fine for drunkenness, and if he failed to reform he faced the *Saufgulden,* or special penalty, of a full Florin (the cost of two pounds of meat or half a month's bread ration).[56]

Invasions of personal choice or behavior did not always go unchallenged. One Seißener objected indignantly that a relative's failure to wear the prescribed short jacket (*kurze Rock*) to church was not a sin; both ended up paying the fifteen-Kreuzer fine.[57] But the most common offense cited in these proceedings was holding *Lichtstuben,* gatherings in the evening around the common stove, with candles and conversation—and illicit pleasures such as dancing, cards, and, of course, alcohol and loose language. From Seißen to Derendingen, from Grötzingen to Oberboihingen, Reudern, and Lauffen an der Eyach, this offense and the failure to attend church or to send children to church and catechism outnumbered all others.[58]

The Lichtstube offense threatened the mores of the young, unmarried village youths, the apprentices, laborers, and maids. Permission had to be secured beforehand to hold a specific gathering. But matters often enough got out of hand, and the tavern, from which alcohol was sometimes illicitly taken to such evenings, lay at the bottom of altercations and violence. Broken windows in houses, loud laughing and swearing, sexual innuendo or dalliance, and fisticuffs on the way home from such frolics occupied the courts' time year in and year out. Young people sometimes slipped out of an authorized Lichtstube to congregate at a less savory person's dwelling for unsupervised revelry egged on by unscrupulous characters.

By 1727 a list of rules for regulating such "private" gatherings was drawn up in Seißen; it included stipulations that only previously approved heads of households were to preside at such gatherings; that no eating, drinking, or other consumption (*Zehren*) was allowed; that those allowed to hold such gatherings were not to leave their charges unattended; and that the young were not to engage in words or deeds that would lead to anger and uproar, especially since they were there to learn quiet and honorable behavior. No single male servants were permitted to attend these evenings, under penalty to be levied against the Hausvater as well as the unpermitted individuals; such evenings were to be over at ten-thirty or eleven; and no house with a confirmand under instruction qualified.[59]

Naturally, such attempts at social control over younger people, over the unmarried and lonely laborers of the village, revealed a larger social problem. The somewhat contradictory coexistence of personal space and public intrusion manifested itself in concerns over the youth. Court records reveal that young women often slept alone, either in attics, if the house had them, or in some sort of personal spaces, and received young male visitors at night, often becoming pregnant as a result. This fact seems to have been less a matter of concern for villagers than the possibility of undesirable alliances begun at the spinning evenings, where the parents could not control who came in contact with their daughters.[60] The Kirchenkonvent was used most often by married women complaining about disorder, or threats to the domestic economy of the households over which they presided. Actual marital conflicts appear rarely, but complaints about unruly children, day workers, neighbors, and occasionally husbands put married women and the Kirchenkonvent in alliance against irresponsible male heads of household. The courts preferred to believe that an "outsider" was at the bottom of most trouble. Vagabonds, soldiers who had deserted, Catholics from nearby "godless" territories, and desperate members of the robber bands who periodically stole through the villages to pilfer when most were gathered in church were commonly blamed for unrest. In more candid moments, the court and church authorities acknowledged that the misuse of wine and the culture surrounding the Wirtshaus were to blame, and that local residents were perfectly capable of making their own mischief.

Various incidents sometimes revealed the serious social tensions that threatened to tear apart the fabric of village relations. In March 1749, the pastor at Oberboihingen complained to the Stuttgart consistory, demanding satisfaction for having been called a sowherd by Jacob Kopple, a day laborer. Besides the obvious insult to the pastor, this was a challenge to the village hierarchy. But behind these factors lay a bigger scandal. Jacob's son, the furloughed grenadier Jung Jacob, had been romancing Commissary Grohsen's wife, a woman of ill repute whose carryings-on in Dettingen and Obereßlingen had preceded her activities in Oberboihingen. Determined to put a stop to scandalous behavior, the pastor excluded the guilty parties from the sacrament. The elder Kopple, incensed at the pastor's presumption, invaded the rectory and, being told the grounds for the ban, slammed "the door with such force the entire house shook," cursing the hapless pastor.[61] But two maidservants testified to the ex-soldier's naked presence in the house and bed of the accused, and reported that the pair had constantly kissed and cuddled ("*geküßet und geschleppelt*"). Although this behavior had taken place in personal space, it had become the source of public comment; thus it had to be routed out, and it was. What seemed to give added offensiveness to such goings-on was the disorder such dalliances brought into the household.[62]

Assaults on houses and gardens—breaking windows, defacing doors, cutting down fruit trees, damaging vines—were all regarded with the gravest alarm, almost more so than assaults on persons. The Manhardt family, who by 1755 would emigrate to Pennsylvania, became entangled in just such a dispute in Nürtingen two years before they left Württemberg. The city court heard Jerg Friedrich Braunlen, a cabinet maker, accuse one of the Manhardts, also a cabinet maker, of having trampled his seedlings. The case was complicated by Manhardt's attempt to claim that he had been put up to the deed by another resident, who had wanted him to break the windows of Braunlen's house by night; herbs in the garden were also destroyed. The bribe for keeping quiet about the assault was a quart of wine. The court found especially outrageous that this assault on a fellow tradesman had been made with no thought for the consequences for his wife and children. Manhardt was punished with a one-Kreuzer fine due the duke and another fine to the poor box; and for leading a younger confederate into such outrages, he was to spend eight days in the tower on bread and water. Such instances, which can be found in every village court record in the southwest, illustrate the centrality of the domestic household, the importance of foodstuffs (Nahrung), and the low tolerance for assaults on property. Although mob actions against property were still acceptable forms of constitutional protest in the English-speaking world in the eighteenth century, they had no place in the German-speaking villager's hierarchy of values.[63]

Such incidents confirmed pietists' distaste for ungodly concerns about "worldly goods." Their impressions were reinforced because until the 1720s the village tavern had functioned as the local courthouse in villages too poor to build a Rathaus. An edict forbade this practice, as well as the hallowed custom of bestowing the office of Schultheiß on the most popular and prosperous *Wirt*. Pietists also knew that the robber bands plaguing the villages and roads received cover and sustenance from unscrupulous tavern keepers, who in exchange for this service were given a part of the band's booty. While day laborers regarded the bands with either disinterest or admiration, the majority of small landowners, artisans, and village worthies cursed the robbers as a threat to household integrity. Such conniving by tavern keepers, coupled with discontent over the manner in which local worthies sometimes colluded with officials to set prices and seemed to disregard religious ideals, deepened pietists' withdrawal from, and criticism of, village life.[64]

The pietists were not alone in their criticism of village tavern culture. Ironically, just to their south, the Jesuits, who were instrumental in sending thousands of Lutheran pietists fleeing into exile from Salzburg in 1731–32, agreed completely with their Evangelical opponents on the baneful influence of village taverns. In a report submitted to authorities in 1733, the Jesuit fathers identified taverns and their owners as the places and persons most included to keep people out of church, to encourage servants to run away from household devotions, and to stimulate conversation insulting the saints, the mass, and godly behavior. More significant, these worldly tavern keepers were also deeply involved in the astounding illicit trade in books which continued to flourish even after the migration. More than 460 Lutheran and pietist tracts had been found in Sankt Veit initially, and another 200 during a later investigation.[65]

IV

Pietists sought to shun the worldliness of the tavern, but they could hardly do without the tavern entirely, because it was a center of communication. The developed sense of the pietist self as one among an embattled, but faithful, minority depended on the circulation of devotional books, hymns, and pamphlet essays for the reinforcement of this self-image. One pietist who became a village Schultheiß later recalled that when he was to be baptized his excited father sent for the aged pastor who had been responsible for his own "rebirth," and hurried down to the village tavern to order the pony-trap that would fetch the awakened patriarch from another village.[66]

Pietists in the German southwest operated within a network of booksellers, tavern keepers, and merchants who aided the distribution of literature and information that kept the pietist conventicles in touch with one another and with like-minded people in other lands. Within this circuit of information, in Württemberg, at least, the distinctions between town and country, wine growing and sheep raising, well-to-do and marginal made little difference in what devoted pietists read. For example, the townspeople of Tübingen had access to some of the greatest pietist writers of their age, scholars on the university faculty. The so-called *Kleinbürgertum*, however—not the relatives or families of the faculty, therefore, but shopkeepers, masters of guilds, and even some tavern keepers—did not read Spener, or even home-grown theologians such as Johannes Bengel or Friedrich Oetinger. The mainstream fathers of Lutheran Pietism were not purchased. Instead, out of the ten books, on average, in the inventories of these ducal subjects at midcentury, the most common were the Bible, the Württemberg hymnal (*Gesangbuch*), and one of the more popular, simple tracts. German religious tracts and Bibles comprised 80 percent of the reading material; about 6 percent was in a foreign language, and the balance consisted of household remedies, pharmacopoeias, calendars and almanacs.[67]

Far to the east of Tübingen, pietists in Feldstetten (near Laichingen), a spinning and weaving center dependent on the sheep and wood culture of the Schwäbische Alb, exhibited similar reading behavior. Most households had a Bible and a hymnal, and an additional ten to twelve volumes. At midcentury, these books, which cost one Gulden apiece, were worth about as much as a plow; a cow could have been bought by selling twenty of them. Although some villagers read Arndt's classic *Wahres Christentum,* or his *Paradiesgärtlein,* common in all pietist circles, local and less-known works predominated. Württemberg authors whose names today are nearly forgotten outside the area were as popular here as in Tübingen. Johannes Habermann's prayerbook competed for place with the equally popular devotions by Johannes Starck and the sermons of the popular preacher at Eßlingen, Immanuel Brastberger. Most of the books were worth between one and twenty-five Kreuzer. They were worth less than the books owned by Tübingen Bürger because the bindings were cheaper. But the substance remained the same.[68]

Other villages—Seißen and Bodelshausen, in the more wooded areas dependent on sheep and lumber; and the smaller villages along the middle Neckar—reveal the same pattern. In most households, the Bible, the Württemberg hymnal, and one devotional tract, either a book of sermons or a prayerbook, comprised the library. Wealthier villagers boasted Ulm, Tübingen, or Frankfurt Bibles bound in leather; other villagers had bought the Marburg hymnal, a Nuremberg devotional handbook, an aid to dying (*Sterbekunst*), or a household pharmacopoeia. Few possessed more than four or five titles, but rare indeed was the inventory that revealed no books at all.[69]

Inventories of books and printed materials from Kraichgau villagers, and even more so from Palatine villagers, reveal a less literate world. Generalizations are perilous because so many village records have been destroyed. But many inventories reveal no books, even when the total evaluation of property seems no different from comparable Württemberg summaries. For instance, some families from Mühlhofen, in the Billigheim Amt, left no books to relatives. Those who did commonly possessed the Palatine hymnal, the Marburg hymnal, or a prayerbook. A psalter or New Testament seems to have been common, and occasionally the popular "Habermann" from Württemberg appeared.[70]

Since both Reformed and Lutheran Protestants were people devoted to the Bible, this regional difference in ownership of books is difficult to account for except in terms of the networks developed by Lutheran pietists. Lack of access to the networks that supplied such tracts and books seems to explain more than do confessional or political differences. Inventories from Nassau-Dillenberg, further to the north of the Palatinate, show among both Reformed and Lutheran families a scarcity of books and pamphlets. Those who did own books seldom had more than a single Bible, psalm book, testament, or catechism. One misses both the Württemberg libraries' richness and diversity, and their size. The library of a wealthy merchant in Dietz, Philipp Wilhelm Bitzer, might not only boast nineteen titles but also include north and south German samples, from the *Lippstädter Gesangbuch* and Marburg's, to the Württemberg favorite, Starck's *Gebetbuch,* and the Nuremberg Bible. But such exceptions merely cast into sharper relief the general pattern. When the schoolmaster Johann Seybert of Camberg died, his wife took an unnumbered sum of books into a second marriage, since her husband "had never thought of giving them up, still less of selling them, or dividing them up; hence, they will remain for the time being in equal parts as found, and later divided."[71]

The destruction of Heidelberg by the French in 1693 eradicated what had previously been the learned center of German Reformed life, reinforcing the centrality of Frankfurt, an orthodox Lutheran city, as the center of the book trade in the southwest. This fact suggests why Lutheran Württemberg offerings enjoyed primacy of place in pietist reading matter, both in the Reich and, later, in the British colonies. In the 1680s, book dealers such as Andreas Luppius had helped to distribute Lutheran, Reformed, and radical pietist tracts throughout the lower Rhine areas, linking Netherlands pietist movements to German centers in Cleve, Duisburg, Detmold, and Herborn. In the early 1700s, Theodore Undereyck had been credited with spreading Reformed pietist conventicles even further, to Hesse-Kassel and Bremen. Reformed patrons such as the countess Hedwig Sophie of Hesse, the sister of the Great Elector of Brandenburg, took an active interest. These northern networks, however, had little impact upon Pietism's development in the southwest.[72]

Dutch Reformed pietist tracts also failed to penetrate the Reich markets in the late seventeenth century. The Reformed-Netherlands pietist movement did not enter the Rhineland—for example, the Reformed center at Herborn—at all. It is equally surprising that English Puritan literature did not travel up the Rhine from Holland as easily as one might imagine. From Basel, Switzerland, however, Reformed pietist materials, often translated there from Dutch or English, made their way into the Palatinate, and especially the Kraichgau, where so many Swiss families had settled between 1648 and 1700.

Frankfurt's Lutheran pietists seldom traveled to Holland, and Halle's faculty may have had the distinction, unique in the eighteenth century, of not having done the obligatory study and travel tour in Holland. The early contact between Spener and Labadist Dutch radicals at Hamburg or Altona apparently was not continued by others after Spener's death; by the eighteenth century, Lutheran pietist networks in the German southwest were dominated by Württemberg, and increasingly, by Halle's agent in Frankfurt.[73]

The Frankfurt newspaper the *Ordentliche wochentliche kaiserliche Reichs-Post-Amts-Zeitung* operated as a kind of a clearinghouse for general news of, and commercial advertisements for, such networks. (Hereafter, its title will be shortened to *Reichs-Post-Amts-Zeitung*.) It reveals the connection between merchants, book dealers, and pietist leaders. Halle was well represented. After securing his initial concession for a printery, bindery, and bookstore in Halle, Francke opened a subsidiary in Berlin. By 1715, he also secured a factor, or agent, to work at one of the bookshops in Frankfurt, which with Leipzig had long operated as one site of the biannual bookfairs in October and at Easter. Jacob Michael Gentzell, Halle's factor, operated from a store in the street called the Sandgaße, directly across from the Sand-Hof, just west of the Kornmarkt, and off the large Buchgaße. There, established shops had long crowded along the street that ran past the Römer, the site of imperial crownings, to the Main. Gentzell worked with Philipp Heinrich Hutter, who ran a second shop, the Waltherische Buchhandlung, on the Pfarreisen nearby. Both specialized in pietist literature, calendars, and almanacs, rounding out their list of attractions by periodically offering apothecary supplies from Halle, and "costly, delicate English chocolates."[74]

In his correspondence with Halle, Gentzell revealed the importance of connections to sympathetic booksellers and printers who would support Halle's objectives. Discussing a forthcoming visit of Francke to the southwest, Gentzell pointed out that the Halle father would receive an enthusiastic welcome from the Tübingen and Stuttgart dealer Christian Gottfried Cotta. If possible, Gentzell wanted Francke to make a stop in his own village, Ingelfingen.[75]

Among these Lutheran-pietist connections, the Eßlinger Buchhandlung represented that imperial city near Stuttgart and carried extensive offerings published by Christian Gottfried Cotta. Cotta advertised regularly in the imperial newspaper, as did Joseph Sigmund and Johann Heinrich Schramm, also from the university town on the Neckar. The

Bronnerische Buchhandlung also carried the Württemberg favorite, Habermann's *Kern-alter Morgen und Abend-Seegen*. More distant Lutheran book dealers, such as Johann Conrad Wohler, in Ulm, and Johann Michael Funcke, of Erfurt, advertised their wares to be had in their towns or in Frankfurt. Lorentz Reutlinger, a tradesman, offered various editions of Spener's work.

Pietists who adhered to the Moravian movement could purchase Count von Zinzendorf's works at Reinhard Eustachius Möller's store, but the fact that the public book fairs took place in Frankfurt and Leipzig meant that the two main confessions had the advantage in what was available for sale. And, as Gentzell reminded his readers, in the Frankfurt paper, he was glad to take advance orders and obtain catalogs of the upcoming Leipzig and Frankfurt fairs.

Two types of pietist comprised the readership for Lutheran–pietist materials during the early eighteenth century: first, the more extreme, who would join a conventicle, place themselves under the tutelage of a patriarch and an exclusive group, and conform to the behavior and teachings of fellow members; and second, the minority who, like Moser and other Halle-inspired leaders, became more deeply involved in worldly affairs. Both types remained mostly within the bounds of the orthodox teaching and practice of Lutheranism, and most were at least somewhat in touch with the world of the tavern and the Lichtstube, and the common affairs of village life, and were disturbed by the human frailty they witnessed there. Both types also depended on the networks that circulated the printed forms of thought which sustained the sociability of quasi-private pietist gatherings.[76]

As these networks expanded in the 1730s to include British North America, they carried the southwestern variant of Pietism to those shores in printed form as emigrants themselves packed their trunks. One volume the travelers brought along came from the sermons of the popular Nürtingen preacher Immanuel Gottlob Brastberger. Those sermons, printed by 1758, survive in many a village inventory.[77] Brastberger begins with an acknowledgement of Halle's Spener and Francke, and Württemberg leaders such as Rieger and Bengel. He not only attempted to link two variants of the movement in his preaching but denied that he wrote for learned people alone, stating that he intended ordinary Christians to profit from his preaching.

Overindulgence in wine and food, and concern for one's business, stood out as common vices. The imagery of the inward struggle (*Kampf*) appears repeatedly as Brastberger returns to the image of the village tavern, the drunkards in the cities, and the dependence (*Abhängigkeit*) which destroys the capacity for faith. The devil appears in many forms:

the "village devil, who leads people on the land into stupidity, lack of awareness and superstition; the city devil who knows how to trap citizens in their middle-class respectability [*bürgerliche Ehrbarkeit*]"; then there is "the devil who works at court, filling all with envy, falseness, the lust for worldly goods, trash, and shame."[78]

Brastberger was no separatist; Word and Sacrament and his insistence that only God knows the true member of the church warned conventicle habitués against seeing themselves as "visible saints." Yet he passed over reconciling Christian liberty to public authority or village relationships poisoned by strife over property. Commenting on the admonition "Render to Caesar that which is Caesar's and to God that which is God's," Brastberger spoke of hypocrisy, not of practical difficulties. Texts on the clever steward, or on the need to concern oneself first with the things of God, he glossed over. Stewardship themes he reduced to statements of the value of having a good conscience, or suggestions that avoiding excess in food, drink, and concern for goods did not signify true spirituality. Those who gave to the poor begrudged the gift because the rich never had enough; under the appearance of responsible householders and Christian thrift, they hid their lust for gain.

Brastberger gave little practical advice. Making a will or testament appears allegorically, in the context of the Last Supper, suggesting that "one makes a Testament for the benefit of friends; here however, were those who at the time belonged to the enemies of Jesus and they were not excluded from his Testament." Social criticism Brastberger aimed at types of sinners, not at particular dilemmas involving property relationships.[79]

The pastor filled his preachings with allusions to the vineyards, the beauty of the landscape, and the sheepfolds and village scenes that brought his lessons home to the village readers who treasured his efforts. But after Urlsperger's dismissal, pietists such as Rieger, Moser, and Brastberger trod warily around the issue of property in the village, or the abuse of church property by ducal authorities and local worthies. By the 1770s, Brastberger's emphasis on struggle, the fight to persevere in the heat of the day, had been modified even further. Preaching on the identical text Brastberger had also addressed—the story of the laborers who entered the vineyard later in the day and who got exactly the same reward— Philipp Matthäus Hahn completely spiritualized the message: not those who worked for pay but, rather, those who contemplate the mysteries of the gospel are the ones pleasing to God. The passive, interior quality of Christian liberty dominated Hahn's reflections completely. Though Hahn could also argue that each person had his job to do in the vineyard, he was even vaguer in grappling with property, labor, stewardship, and justice. A public sense of either liberty or property, connecting individuals to the political realm, would have to come from other sources, along other networks.[80]

Yet even as Brastberger preached in Nürtingen and in Obereßlingen, along the middle Neckar, thousands of his neighbors streamed downriver, some taking his works with them, to a landscape barren of vineyards, alien in speech, different in traditions of public life, and strange in customs and traditions surrounding property and liberties. He never mentioned them. What had been created in his own lifetime, however, contributed directly to the redefining of the concepts of liberty and property in British North America. The southwestern networks among pietists had arisen around bookfairs, taverns, traders, and the ungodly, and had been based on the devoted efforts of those who had experienced rebirth. That network intersected with Halle's own, which extended via Frankfurt and Hamburg-Altona to reach former Reich subjects from the southwestern territories who were now in North America.

Equally important, Brastberger's readers carried away, albeit in fragmented memories and emotional longing, the conviction that true Christian liberty remained tied to the sociability of the conventicle and the domestic economy defended by the married women of the village. The critique leveled by pietist women against irresponsible or conniving authority had placed the women in alliance with pietist pastors in using the Kirchenkonvent as the forum where such protests were legitimately voiced. That institution did not survive transit. But the memories, the emotional needs, and the conviction that privileges protecting the household demanded stout defending did survive. So did the suspicions southwestern pietists nurtured about peculation and the abuse of church property. Settlement in the New World, and association within the context of Lutheran churches in the British colonies, would reawaken these convictions. Where Halle's networks, its pastors, and its definitions of positive liberty and property devoted to philanthropy prevailed, the German speakers engaged in cultural transfer and adjustment to North America celebrated the advantages of British liberty and privileges. The majority of southwesterners from the Reich, however, were not so sure. Settlement in a land of minimal government, and the early language of their brokers, continued to define liberty as freedom from constraint, and property as a purely domestic, familial preserve, now liberated from taxation and from meddling state functionaries. Until settlement created a language capable of adapting such variant traditions to North American conditions, German speakers' political culture remained as chimerical in the "imaginary English America" as it did in the Reich.

4

Marginal Property-Holders, Brokers of Liberty

IN DECEMBER 1685 a Palatine magistrate of Alsheim reported to Heidelberg about Swiss immigrants. The free-church settlers who repopulated the Kraichgau and the Palatinate after the Thirty Years' War were generally well liked. "They have all demonstrated a Neighborly attitude, and industry in their work just as their forefathers . . . as they are good housekeepers, they turn everything into money . . . [but] they bring nothing into the country, and are swindled from the time they escape."[1]

The description might have applied a half century later to Pennsylvania. British-American assessments of continental immigrants emphasized that they owned little but were family-centered "housekeepers": frugal, industrious, and religious. Even though the Kraichgau and the Palatinate had been the scenes of early migrations between the 1640s and 1709, eighteenth-century migration from the Reich would be different. From 1727 through 1753, the ruinous effects of equal partition of family property in conjunction with population growth encouraged family groups to leave for North America. These migrants and those who guided them brought the competing definitions of liberty and property from the Reich with them. Over three-quarters of some five thousand emigrants from the Palatinate, Baden, and the Kraichgau represented related family groups, but they came from regions that differed significantly in terms of what property claims the emigrants still had on their ancestral villages.

The migration that began in earnest in 1727 also differed from the earlier arrival of German speakers because of developing support networks. Halle pioneered one such network in Georgia in the 1730s, which was to shape ideas of liberty and property along lines laid down by the pastors there. But the Pietism of the German southwest, as we have seen, possessed no great missionary impulse, nor did it enjoy Halle's ties to London. By default, then, secular traders, many of them Kraichgau emigrants with Swiss family ties, developed a secular network, especially in Pennsylvania. These ambitious entrepreneurs encouraged German speakers in their inherited suspicion of political authority, reinforced the definition of liberty as freedom from taxation and religious dogma, and cheerfully informed arrivals that property could be not only acquired but also aggrandized by careful, if cautious, use of British colonial common law.

It would be tempting to move at once to see in detail in specific settlements how these competing networks and ideas began to evolve. But settlement itself cannot be understood apart from a comprehension of the subtle regional differences that dictated who among the German-speaking Lutherans would arrive with more advantages than others. Some were among the truly marginal of the villages. Others who left the Reich still claimed rights to inheritances. These naturally became more aggressive in seeking out the brokers and agents who were only too eager to offer aid in making good those claims. But such claims had to be made now in the face of an alien language and inheritance law. As one German visitor to London put it, English—"the desperately hard language, and, above all, [its] pronunciation, of which every foreigner complains, even if he imagines he is far advanced in the language and can read every-thing"—guaranteed a role for the agile, if not always honest, agent and broker.[2] Advantage would go to the early arrivals who set the terms of settlement and adjustment for others. Most of the secular agents, many of them from the Kraichgau, were firmly in place in 1740. The complex puzzle of regional variation in the networks and the brokers who defined liberty for arrivals must be reassembled before one can properly penetrate what happened in specific German-speaking settlements.

I

The act of leaving kin, as well as familiar physical surroundings and linguistic associations, for a strange country characterized much of eighteenth-century Germany. Villages of the German southwest changed their social structure slowly; but Palatines and Kraichgauers were very much on the move. All migrations, as "rites of passage," force participants to reassess their self-image and their values. Among seventeenth-century New Englanders, the metaphors of the sea crossing permanently marked the sermon literature and the consciousness of those who had gone down to the sea in ships. The German-speaking passage and later accounts of it created no such tradition. Letters warned the interested at home about the costs and dangers of the passage, about the unscrupulous who preyed upon the unwary, and about the privations that attended the initial days in North America.[3]

But the majority of Lutheran and Reformed Germans came from inland territories, settled in places far from the sea (with two exceptions: Philadelphia and Charleston), and wasted no time ruminating about the passage or the ocean. Perhaps the familiar phenomenon of internal migration in the Reich made the overseas trek so alien that participants could find no analogies for it. Perhaps the images and metaphors of sheepfold and vineyard which were characteristic of sermons and devotional literature among southwestern villagers transferred easily to the rural environments and small hamlets of the American settlements. Even as an old man, Pastor Heinrich Melchier Mühlenberg, making a sea journey from Philadelphia to Charleston in 1774, tried to forget an attack of "fiendish seasickness," concentrating instead on the "chickens, rooster, geese, and ducks" brought aboard for the passengers' meals. Drawing comfort from these reminders of his past, he mused that "with their crowing and constant cackling they awaken distant associated ideas and pleasant feelings, so that one imagines that one is in some noble court or village."[4]

From 1727 until 1753, German speakers emigrating to British colonial America traveled in family groups of about four persons each.[5] They moved through Rotterdam aided by a select group of Dutch companies, originally Mennonites who had obtained privileges to help transport the 1709 Palatines through Britain to New York. As the interest in moving German speakers to North America grew, so did the demands that a near monopoly on this trade be broken. Isaac and Zacharias Hope and Company may have controlled the emigrant trade until 1738, but competitors, including John and Charles Stedman and, by the 1740s, interested British merchants such as John Hunt challenged them. These entrepreneurs consigned emigrants to sea captains. Some captains made repeated voyages, trading in immigrants. But most made such voyages only once or twice. By the 1730s Philadelphia had replaced New York as German speakers' preferred destination. Once ships arrived in Philadelphia, immigrants found themselves bound out to masters by a diverse group of large and small merchants, especially Benjamin Shoemaker, the firm of Willing and Morris, the Stedmans, and Daniel Beneset.[6]

Not everyone hailed the connection between Rotterdam and Philadelphia. In 1749 one German speaker suggested that for eighty-four Gulden one could go to London, ship one's luggage via Amsterdam to New York, take ship for America, and then pick up one's belongings, "and this route is far more advantageous than the one over Rotterdam."[7] Yet most secular Dutch connections avoided New York, as did Halle, which, after transporting materials and ministers via Hamburg-Altona, used either its London connections or its Netherlands connections to Georgia and Pennsylvania. When Gotthilf August Francke wrote to Pastor Brunnholtz and Pastor Mühlenberg in 1746, he advised them to consign their letters for him to the firm of List and Feiler in Amsterdam, who owed Halle money for pharmaceuticals and would forward North American post. In Altona itself, Halle enjoyed the services of van den Smithen Söhne, who shipped books for Halle to Rotterdam on consignment to Johann Heinrich Keppele via the ship *Sally*.[8]

In response to the trade in immigrants, other entrepreneurs, the so-called newlanders (Neuländer) plied the routes, often free of charge, emerging as key figures in the creative attempt to get cash-poor migrants passage to the colonies. Securing in North America a future purchaser for the price of passage, the newlanders helped invent redemptioner contracts. Merchants offered contracts in Rotterdam on credit. If migrants could not "redeem" this contract in two weeks after arrival among the small but successful German-speaking population already living in Pennsylvania, the contracts were put out for general bid. Humane and workable in its early stages, the system degenerated as the number of migrants swelled; delays occurred in redeeming contracts, sometimes separating family members permanently, and confining the newcomers to unsanitary ships swept periodically by "Dutch fever," the uncomplimentary name attributed to various contagious diseases of German speakers, especially typhus. At least 5 percent of German speakers perished in the crossing; even more failed to survive the first-year adjustment to a new climate. Among small children and debarking arrivals in Georgia and South Carolina, mortality rates nearing 50 percent decimated former Reich subjects through the 1740s.[9]

After 1763 single young men and poorer families less well-connected than those who funneled into the Rotterdam-Philadelphia route arrived in Norfolk, Baltimore, Charleston, and Savannah. From the end of the Seven Years' War to 1783, perhaps another twenty thousand Germans joined the one hundred thousand previous arrivals. By 1773, after interruptions caused by the efforts of worried authorities concerned about the loss of wealth and potentially valuable labor, transports arriving in Baltimore and Philadelphia brought one thousand persons per year. As recruiters proliferated, authorities in the Palatinate, in Mainz, and in Württemberg impeded movement on the Neckar and the Rhine; Prussia, Hanover, and Saxony obstructed emigrants on the Elbe.[10]

By 1768 Joseph II's imperial edict forbade all emigration to lands not connected with the Reich. Despite all obstacles, in 1750 Pennsylvania's

German speakers may well have comprised 50 percent of the total population; by 1775 every third Pennsylvanian spoke German; New York and New Jersey together counted 14 percent German speakers; Maryland and Virginia together 17 percent, South Carolina and Georgia together, 9 percent.[11] Some 10 percent of Britain's mainland colonial population now spoke German, provoking Benjamin Franklin to xenophobic jitters.[12]

Regional variations in the laws affecting emigration rights also affected the property of migrants differently. Württemberg, for example, had pioneered a liberal guarantee of unrestricted migration under its 1514 Tübinger Vertrag. A declaration of 1520 elaborated these rights to include unrestricted emigration for those under feudal obligation as long as they paid their debts or made arrangements with creditors. In fact, ducal fees conspired against the supposed rights. In the seventeenth century, Württemberg imposed a fee on those securing freedom from feudal status and took a percentage of the property owned by, or eventually coming to, a prospective heir. In 1628 the duke demanded that all subjects wishing to leave renounce their allegiance and right of return. The upheavals of the Thirty Years' War interrupted a debate between proponents of the freedoms guarded by the Stuttgart Landtag, and the centralizing, absolutist desires of the duke. When the *Amerikaauswanderung* began in earnest in 1709, Württemberg watched with concern, no doubt because Stuttgart officials knew Josua Kocherthal, leader of the 1709 Auswanderung to New York, to be Josua Harrsch of Eschelbronn, in the neighboring Kraichgau. Born their subject in Fachsenfeld im Kocherthal (hence his pseudonym), Harrsch was a Württemberger. In 1717 Württemberg authorities dictated that no emigrant would be allowed to sell moveable property, that contracts entered into would be declared null and void if persons attempted migration, and that local authorities risked stiff fines for aiding migration. These restrictions intensified by 1749 as migration increased.[13]

An alarmed fiscal authority that year reported the worth of property that had been taken out of the duchy by some 4,049 persons. Conservatively reckoned at approximately 34,190 gulden, the sum misled the complacent into concluding that riffraff were taking a paltry 8 Gulden apiece. District officials in the *Ämter* warned that the estimates had been intentionally scaled down: the real figures revealed 45,000 Gulden in losses. If the truer figure were used, the average individual worth came to 11 Gulden. Even this figure deceived. Many emigrants possessed no more than this. But at least one-third of the departing subjects were industrious, propertied people hopeful of a better future in North America.[14]

Moreover, authorities knew that these figures did not include property smuggled out by crafty tax dodgers on the way to North America. The *Leibfreie* (free subjects) and especially the *Leibeigene* (women bound by feudal status, and the children of such women) continued to be pressured by taxes and fees on their property. Leibfreie, despite the Tübinger Vertrag, had to obtain permission to emigrate (*Emigrationsconsens*) and renounce their rights (*Bürgerrechtsverzicht*). These persons were freed from the obligation to pay the *Abzug,* or *Nachsteuer,* the departure tax of 10 percent on the remaining value of property (real and personal) they took with them. After the freedom tax (*Manumissionsgebühr*) had been paid, the Leibeigene paid the Abzug as well. If property remaining in the duchy would later be due to emigrants from their families, the Nachsteuer was imposed at the time of emigration. Because of these attempts by the central authority in Stuttgart to control property and the flow of money, crafty Leibeigene sought to sell property or arrange deals with family members to convert their future rights to immediate cash, and then present themselves as propertyless people petitioning for emigration. By the 1740s Württemberg, like most other southwest territories, forbade such practices, warning of confiscation of the proceeds from private sales. Prospective emigrants became obsessed with what happened to their trunks, for in those chests they hid tools, clothing, and articles they might sell in America from the probing inquiry of village authorities commanded to inventory departing subjects. The actual value of property taken out of Württemberg and the southwest in general, and what was still due the emigrants, therefore, remained higher than official records ever revealed.

The Palatinate, the Pfalz-Zweibrücken, and the Kraichgau's imperial knights guaranteed their subjects no rights to emigrate. An arm of the privy council, the *Hofrat,* gave permission for the lifting of feudal obligations. In these territories the *Oberamt,* or regional district center, acted as the intermediary between localities and the central regime. Most of the district officials were members of the Hofrat in any case. Unlike Baden, where not only the Hofrat but also the *Hofkammer,* or ministry of finance, had to approve of manumission or, for free citizens, permission to emigrate, the Palatinate did not involve its finance ministry. Like Württemberg, Palatine territories began restricting migration in the early seventeenth century through financial manipulations of property. A 1724 prohibition on emigration to Hungary evolved on religious grounds— that is, it was to avoid Protestants' leaving for a Catholic, Habsburg territory. But in 1737 a prohibition against the emigration of propertied people took direct aim at North America. The Zweibrücken authorities demanded that property worth over two hundred Gulden be taxed not at the usual 10 percent (the *Abzug*) but at 16 percent. Two years later, handworkers, some of whom had sought to emigrate under the pretext of going on the traditional journey to gain experience (*Wanderschaft*), were ordered to show what property they intended to take with them; if they failed to return, their parents or guardians would be assessed both the manumission tax and the Nachsteuer. Palatine emigrants from the right side of the Rhine had to request permission not only from the reigning prince or duke (*Landesherr*), but also from the *Grundherr*, or immediate owner of the lands they rented. By 1750 the Palatinate had ordered that no attestation of property, no birth certificates, and no official recording of private sale of properties would be allowed until the three-Kreuzer *Abzugsgebühr* was paid and proof of manumission presented. The usual tenth part of the net worth of property was due until 1764, when authorities doubled the rates of both the Abzug and the manumission tax to 20 percent.

II

Regional authorities controlled migration rights by manipulating taxes on property. Their actions explain in part why some German-speaking Lutherans enjoyed advantages over others after arriving in North America. The socioeconomic conditions of certain regions produced emigrants who can be traced to settlements in various British colonies. The degree of poverty, and the proximity of villages or towns to trade and communication routes, would also dictate who eventually had a chance to use the agents and brokers in North America who plied these routes seeking inheritance claims for the departed and dispersing news from America.

Nassau-Siegen, Nassau-Oranien, and the Kraichgau:
Emigration to Virginia, 1717–1730

It was not only failures in New York that by the 1730s had made Pennsylvania the colony of choice for Reich migrants. In the 1710s and 1720s mixed groups of German speakers had settled in Virginia, and their experience there had been less than ideal. Lieutenant Governor Alexander Spotswood's interest in mining ventures had created the Germanna colony, which drew its first settlers both from Nassau-Siegen and Nassau-Oranien, and from the Kraichgau. Appropriately, given the migration of the Swiss into the Kraichgau, Spotswood's interest had been piqued by a Swiss proposal made by Franz Louis Michel and Christopher von

Graffenried, both from Bern, to mine silver ore. The settlement of
Siegeners in 1714 at the Germanna tract developed from this proposal.
By 1717 Kraichgauers joined the group. They were part of four transports, three of which ended up in Pennsylvania. By 1725, accusing Spotswood of denying them property and initiating a court suit against him,
the Kraichgauers removed to Robinson Run, founding the Hebron Lutheran settlement. Two of the emigrants returned to the Kraichgau and
Württemberg in 1725; Nassauers also maintained an interest in this settlement.[15]

The miners of Nassau–Siegen, as well as later Nassau–Oranien arrivals,
appear to have been slightly wealthier than most early settlers. The later
migration of 1749–54 from Nassau–Oranien's Dillenburg Amt reveals an
average wealth that seems higher than that in the Palatinate, the Kraichgau, and Württemberg. Some 20 percent of the inhabitants made their
living in handwork, especially in leather and textiles. By the 1740s the
cultivation of land was restricted to about eight Morgen (about 6.1 acres)
per household. Nearly 100 percent of the members of both the 1709 and
1749–53 migrations came from interrelated family groups.[16]

Fear of falling from propertied status motivated the departures. One
man acknowledged that "he feared he would shortly be pulled down into
the most abject poverty." Although surviving inventories for the early
migration are rare, twenty Gulden—the market price of a cow in the
southwest—comprised the officially recorded worth of property that each
of these families had after they had sold their belongings and gone through
the process of manumission and payment of the tithe.

Of the 344 persons from Ebersbach, Nassau–Oranien, who left for
Pennsylvania, Virginia, and New York, about 88 percent came from the
western high Westerwald. About 53 percent of this group still owned
property worth about six hundred Gulden after paying their debts. Typical of peasants who owned their own land, 9 percent owned less than
thirty Morgen of land, and 13 percent only four Morgen.

The arrivals in Virginia from the Kraichgau, Württemberg, and the
Palatinate were poorer. In 1779 Karl Theodor von Dalberg described the
impoverishment of the archbishopric of Würzburg, on the Main River,
attributing it to the practice of equal partition of vineyards, a practice,
he concluded, that revealed that "there are too many peasants, and hence
their children will become beggars."[17] The analysis of their original property status is, however, impeded by the fact that British officials, in
transcribing places of origin during naturalization procedures, misun-
derstood the new arrivals, obscuring their home places. When a group
of Virginia German speakers sought naturalization in Williamsburg in
1745, Zachariah Blankenbecker and Johann Tomas were thought to be

from the "Bishoprick of Spire" in "Nieuberg," while Johann Zimmermann came from "Saltzfeld in Germany." Closer inspection reveals that Zimmermann came from Sulzfeld bei Eppingen, in the Kraichgau. "Nieuberg" (Neuenbürg) was a town of the Rhine under Austrian lordship, not far from Karlsruhe.[18]

These Kraichgau emigrants had maintained holdings by paying fees— a kind of rent—to landlords or to the imperial knights or the distant archbishopric. As scholars have attempted to compare this system to British and North American concepts and terms, most conclude that except under unusual circumstances, "the peasant could not be expelled . . . and his tenure was heritable . . . approach[ing] what we mean by private property, real estate, despite the name landlordship."[19] Yet "private property" did not exist, if by this term one means to attribute political significance to ownership. Villagers understood individual ownership. But they spoke of neither "family property" nor "private property" as a basis of political rights or activity.

In Würzburg, agricultural patterns and inheritance practices pushed marginal people into migration. As the population grew, the living standard fell, and dues increased. By midcentury an estimate of the conditions under which most people lived revealed that the majority were *Söldner,* or renters, living in straw-roofed earth huts. The amount of cultivable land available had shrunk owing to hunting privileges; only about 10 percent of available meadow, vineyard, and farmland was being used for food production. A bad harvest or an outbreak of disease among the farm animals tipped marginal peasants over the edge into real property. In a part of the southwest where a typical family needed four to eight hectares of land to raise the grains that composed the typical diet, less than 10 percent of the population in the Solms-Braunfels district could boast such holdings. By 1720 conditions had worsened in places such as Tauberretersheim, where 956 Morgen of land supported 531 residents— each was supported by about 1.8 Morgen. By 1764, while the amount of land remained at 956 Morgen, the population had risen to 655 persons, each now relying on only 1.45 Morgen, and this despite a steady outflow of migrants.[20]

In the 1760s, Würzburg and other southwest territories sent away younger, single males who had less claim on property. Of 306 emigration petitions processed in that decade, 117 were from single males or widows. Of 305 persons whose total worth was estimated at 13,200 Gulden, most had 24 Gulden left after paying the manumission tax and the tithe.[21]

Würzburg represented the extreme in the marginalization process. In the Kraichgau proper, from which some of the early Virginia arrivals emigrated, fragmentary evidence confirms a similar, if not quite as harrowing, pattern. Michael and Dieter Danner of Walldorf, near Wiesloch, in the Kraichgau, were completely impoverished at the time of their decision a decade later to leave for the Virginia settlement; the Zimmermann family of Sulzfeld were propertied artisans before leaving for Virginia. The absence of complete inventories in these places invites the comparison of records from neighboring villages.[22]

Zuzenhausen, Reihen, and Weiler present a handful of surviving inventories from 1730–49, which suggest that heirs were left with an average of between 100 and 200 Gulden apiece in inherited property before their decision to emigrate to the New World. In the wealthier town of Schwaigern, where many of the confirmed emigrants appear neither on the taxation lists nor regularly in the estate partitions, another group of ten emigrants were worth an average of 137 Gulden apiece. But wealthier families in general characterized Schwaigern, a center for vintners in the northern Kraichgau. More residents there wrote wills and left estates worth over 700 Gulden. A few later emigrants to North America benefited from membership in these wealthier families. They represent the upper range of emigrant wealth from the southwest.[23] Although no estate partitions for the town of Sinsheim survive, records of sales suggest that out of the dozen families who left for Pennsylvania between 1730 and 1746, the Beyerles and Brenneisens may have been typical. Both managed to sell between 180 Gulden and 200 Gulden worth of property before leaving the Kraichgau.[24]

Between 1749 and 1754 the town of Dossenheim, lying just northwest of Heidelberg, on the right bank of the Rhine, sent about eighty persons to South Carolina and Pennsylvania. No partitions of estate survive, but tax lists drawn up for reviewing vacant or unused lands in 1728 point to the gradual marginalization of later emigrants. By the 1720s Dossenheim counted nineteen propertied peasants and forty four day laborers and vineyard workers in addition to eighteen persons involved in trade. Of ninety families, thirty six owned property worth less than 50 Gulden. A two-field system of agriculture and its failure to produce sufficient food may have contributed to the outbreak in 1731 of various diseases, including dysentery, consumptions, and fever—disorders that, like sweating fever or scarlatina (*weiße Frieseln*), characterized malnourished populations.[25]

Dossenheim's entire court, led by the Schultheiß, was ordered to appear by 7:00 A.M. on 17 April 1728 to examine the vacant and hidden property (*verschwiegene Güter*) that indicated the declining fortunes of the village. The lists from the 1703 ledger of inhabitants (*Lagerbuch*) indicated 75 heads of families, 9 children cared for by village charity, 7 widows, and 9 residents of other towns currently residing in Dossenheim. By 1717 the number of persons listed had risen from 100 to 123. The 1728 reassessment showed that 147 Gulden was due the electoral government. Town officials swore they could only pay half of what was due by Christmas and would pay the balance a year later. The special commissioner sent from Mannheim ordered not only that the old lists be made available but also that "all documents necessary [be] in hand for forwarding in order that the same not hinder a collating of evidence to bring this work of revision completely to an end." In January the court at Mannheim agreed to delay payment but insisted that a special commissioner named Wachter continue to monitor Dossenheim in order that the monies be paid on time.[26]

The Kraichgau village of Ittlingen, some forty miles southwest of Dossenheim, may give the best impression of the poorer early emigrants, since most of its emigrants left in the 1730s for Virginia and Pennsylvania. Ittlingen is also important because it produced one of the most important agents operating the secular network between British North America and the Reich, Jacob Geiger. In 1718 Ittlingen was already involved in litigation with the von Gemmingen knights because of tax increases, loss of access to the cattle pasture and the woods, and the usurpation of the bakehouse and the cellar of the Rathaus. At that time, its population, who rented parts of the five large Bauernhöfe, numbered approximately 630. At the time of the 1759 assessment, 40 families (out of a total of 640 residents, including 140 heads of families) had already emigrated to North America. The 40 counted as neighbors a dozen Jewish residents, 4 Mennonites, and 21 widows. Most who left had come to the village only recently or were too poor to qualify for town citizenship; few had possessed Bürgerrecht in 1718. Nonetheless, even these people left traces of their marginal property status. The incomplete register of citizens records that Rudolph Conrad, whose son Johann Martin emigrated in 1740, paid 38 Gulden in taxes on various small pieces of property. Johann Michel Hoffman's father Johann Georg, one of the innkeepers in the village, was assessed on property worth four hundred Gulden; Johannes Grob, more typically, was assessed on only eighty five. The surviving data on the more than 50 emigrants, who mostly settled in Lancaster County, suggests that their average assessed property value never exceeded one hundred Gulden before the payment of manumission and emigration fees. In fact, most who emigrated had property worth no more than fifty Gulden. Although no complete price series for these villages exist, and no estate inventories, a surviving 1738 evaluation schedule, certified again in 1752 by an imperial notary at Heilbronn,[27] reveals what land was "worth" in the village, as well as how rates originally stated in terms of money were expressed in terms of village land, produce, and livestock:

LAND

Vineyard

1 Morgen of good land:	12 Gulden
1 Morgen of "fair" land:	10 Gulden
1 Morgen of poor land:	8 Gulden

Meadowland

1 Morgen of good land:	30 Gulden
1 Morgen of "fair" land:	24 Gulden
1 Morgen of poor land:	20 Gulden

Arable Land

1 Morgen of good land:	8 Gulden
1 Morgen of "fair" land:	6 Gulden
1 Morgen of poor land:	4 Gulden

LIVESTOCK

Geese

1 goose:	2 Gulden
$\frac{1}{2}$ goose:	1 Gulden
$\frac{1}{4}$ goose:	30 Kreuzer
$\frac{1}{6}$ goose:	15 Kreuzer

Hens

1 hen:	1 Gulden
$\frac{1}{2}$ hen:	30 Kreuzer
$\frac{1}{4}$ hen:	15 Kreuzer
$\frac{1}{6}$ hen:	10 Kreuzer
$\frac{1}{8}$ hen:	7 Kreuzer 2 Heller (half-penny)

Roosters

1 rooster:	30 Kreuzer
$\frac{1}{2}$ rooster:	15 Kreuzer
$\frac{1}{4}$ rooster:	7 Kreuzer 2 Heller
$\frac{1}{6}$ rooster:	5 Kreuzer
$\frac{1}{8}$ rooster:	3 Kreuzer 3 Heller

Capons

1 capon:	1 Gulden 30 Kreuzer
$\frac{1}{2}$ capon:	45 Kreuzer

$^1/_4$ capon: 22 Kreuzer 2 Heller
$^1/_6$ capon: 15 Kreuzer
$^1/_8$ capon: 11 Kreuzer 1 Heller

PRODUCE

Wine

1 Maß (4 quarts):	15 Kreuzer
3 quarts:	11 Kreuzer 1 Heller
2 quarts:	7 Kreuzer 2 Heller
1 quart:	3 Kreuzer 3 Heller
$^1/_4$ quart:	2 Kreuzer
$^1/_4$ quart:	1 Kreuzer

Eggs

100 eggs:	2 Gulden 40 Kreuzer
12.5 [!] eggs:	4 Kreuzer

This rate of evaluation reveals that the values of land in Ittlingen were below the values of lands held in Baden by emigrants to Lancaster. There, in Söllingen, for instance, 0.25 Morgen (0.08 Hektar; 0.19 acre) of good vineyard was rated at forty Gulden; 0.25 Morgan of good meadowland at thirty Gulden; 0.25 Morgen of good arable land at twenty Gulden—considerably more than the value of comparable properties in Ittlingen. Yet 80 percent of Baden emigrants to Lancaster owned property worth less than two hundred Gulden, living in modest circumstances in a region where one hundred Gulden was worth 0.5 Hektar of arable land or 0.3 Hektar of vineyard described as "fair."[28]

Ittlingen's tax records reveal an even grimmer picture, suggesting that Kraichgau villages not located in prime wine-growing areas may have been in even more straitened circumstances. The 1759 taxes on properties included the major holdings of the Geigers, who soon emerged as major cultural brokers in North American and holders of property in Sippingen, Berwangen, and other locations outside Ittlingen. But more typical was Rudolph Conrad, whose son Johann Martin left by 1740, and who paid his thirty eight Gulden on 1 Morgen of middling arable land and 2 quarter-Morgen of vineyard. Johannes Grob's total property, assessed at eighty five Gulden fifteen Kreuzer two Heller, totaled only a modest 1.5 quarters of arable land, vineyard, and herb garden. The payment of one Gulden per year for those with Bürgerrecht, or thirty Kreuzer for widows and those merely resident, allowed for little margin of error in running a household. Yet those of middling circumstances who arrived early in North America, and survived, emerged as the cultural brokers, provided they hailed from places lying within networks of communication, or had wealthy connections back home, as did the Geigers.[29]

*Ulm and Eastern Württemberg: Emigration to
Ebenezer, Georgia, and to Charleston, South
Carolina, 1737–1753*

In the winter of 1731–32, Archbishop Prince Leopold Anton Eleutherius von Firmian expelled Lutheran Salzburgers, scandalizing a Europe grown used to the religious tolerance that had been secured by treaties signed after 1648. The Treaty of Westphalia and subsequent agreements in the 1690s had made the sudden, forced emigration of religious dissidents illegal in the Reich. Firmian's decision to rid Salzburg of religious dissenters had financial roots. His advisors disappointed him, nonetheless. When confiscated Protestant properties came on the market for Catholic peasants, they languished for most of a generation. The propertied Protestant settlers among the twenty thousand emigrants secured a future in the lands near Gumbinnen, in the Lithuanian part of East Prussia. Sweden, Great Britain, the Netherlands, and Prussia had all protested the forced emigration, and the emigrants instituted legal processes to force compensation for the losses suffered in deportation. After years of wrangling and enforced compensation, the value of their lands had fallen 50 to 77 percent.[30]

The mostly landless day laborers who journeyed through Augsburg, Ulm, and eastern Swabia, and down the Rhine to the Netherlands, Britain, and Georgia, had almost no ties left with their homeland. In passing through Württemberg, the Salzburgers left a permanent mark on the consciousness of later emigrants, who in applying to leave consistently identified "Ebenezer," "Georgia," or "Carolina" as their goal. These later emigrants came from the hilly, marginal lands, where villages depended on weaving, wood cutting, and cereal production. Although the practice of equal partition of property characterized many of these villages, some also observed, like the Salzburgers, the practice of closed inheritance (*Anerbenrecht*): settling property upon one heir, who then compensated other siblings.[31]

Families from this general region used marriage contracts more often than did families further west. Among poorer couples in Salzburg a mutual covenant, the *testamentum mutuum,* ensured that if one spouse died and there were no children, the partner would inherit everything. If children came of the marriage they would be specified as heirs, but normally only after the death of the second parent. The tendency among marginal property holders to look after one's immediate family at the expense of extended kin, legally sanctioned in the Salzburg and eastern Swabian area, nonetheless characterized most eighteenth-century areas of the German-speaking southwest. Coupled with the additional factor of forced migration of the Salzburg Protestants, such tendencies meant that emigrants' ties to their original villages and families often became minimal.[32]

Between 1731 and 1752, the Salzburger migration brought approximately 1,000 German speakers to colonial Georgia. But after 1741 actual Salzburgers rapidly became a minority in the transports. The first transports of 1734, 1737, and 1741 included Swabians; Palatines arrived after 1739. By 1754, some 650 persons had arrived, comprising about 12 percent of the colony's population. The 1750 and 1753 arrivals, overwhelmingly Swabian, challenged with Württemberg customs, attitudes, and practices the original Halle-Salzburg network of the settlement.[33]

The towns belonging to the imperial city Ulm (i.e., Langenau, Lonsee, Nerenstetten, Altheim, and Weidenstetten), produced small numbers of emigrants whose property averaged roughly the same fifty to two hundred Gulden common in the Kraichgau. Lonsee, a settlement of 250 people, was by the early 1740s having increasing difficulty collecting taxes. Emigrants such as Hans Geywitz, a weaver, and Jacob Junginger were assessed twenty Kreuzer for their meager holdings. The village, which collected between 274 Gulden and 358 Gulden in taxes per year, barely met its obligations by 1745, with one Gulden left after the books were closed. The migration that began in the late 1740s and lasted till 1753 improved conditions slightly; in 1754, two Gulden thirty two Kreuzer remained when the accounts were balanced.[34] By 1750 Altheim taxed its weavers and day laborers one to four Gulden per year, in an economy where day laborers earned twenty Gulden per month and spent about that much per year on bread. Gingen-an-Fils, larger, and on a major trade route, sent emigrants whose properties were, on average, valued at about two hundred Gulden; Weidenstetten emigrants were generally poorer, except for the exceptional family like the Sailers, who arrived in South Carolina by the 1760s.[35] Württemberg border towns such as Seißen, near Ulm; and Bodelshausen and Freudenstadt, on the southern and western borders, respectively, shared similar economies, for they were all in forested, hilly areas where grazing, lumber, weaving, and agricultural day labor provided subsistence.

In 1752 Freudenstadt and villages in its environs contributed to the migration 111 persons, comprising 18 households worth a total of 2,180 Gulden—approximately 19.6 Gulden per person. These villages displayed a mixed pattern of closed inheritance and equal partition that sometimes divided parts of villages from one another. Regardless of the prevailing legal customs, small property owners with artisanal skills made up the emigrating contingent.[36] Bodelshausen and the Balingen-district town Lauffen an der Eyach, in southern Württemberg, also contributed to the Swabian transports sending settlers to Georgia and later to South Carolina and Pennsylvania. Here, too, two hundred Gulden represented the upper range of total assessed worth of real and moveable property. In Lauffen, the description of the property held in the village in 1714 reveals that a cow could still be purchased for twenty Gulden, and the average holding consisted of arable property of 21 Morgen (about 5.5 hectares, or 13 acres). The Stotzes, Bitzers, Konigs, and Wolfers who would leave the village for the New World in the 1740s were all comfortable, though not well-to-do. Their small plots of land, averaging about 10 Morgen, meant that they were able—barely—to sustain families. By 1737, however, the increase in population, rising taxes, and resultant impoverishment affected members of these families as they intermarried. The reevaluation of property done that year revealed townspeople with holdings of less than 2 Morgen. When Mathes Bitzer married Esther Treuck in 1731, she brought only sixteen Gulden to the marriage, he three Gulden worth of clothing and no realty; Philip Rominger's death in 1734 left his wife and two daughters with about one hundred Gulden each, which perhaps explains why Christina Rominger left for North America along with twenty one others between 1746 and 1750. Sixty villagers from Ebingen, Erzingen, Dürrwangen, Tailfingen, Heselwangen, and Oberdigesheim left for North America by midcentury.[37] Seißen's estate partitions for the sixty emigrants also suggest the two-hundred-Gulden average ceiling for property evaluation in the eighteenth century. Only Michel Mayer, son of the village Schultheiß, was a wealthier emigrant; he died intestate in Pennsylvania, never reestablishing contact with Seißen.[38]

Württemberg and the Palatinate: Emigration to
Pennsylvania, 1727–1753

In the Neckar Valley of Württemberg between 1700 and 1730, an average household worked about thirteen acres of mixed agricultural land, meadow, and vineyard. But towns such as Grötzingen, along the Neckar, and its nearby neighbor Neckartenzlingen, averaging between 300 and 600 inhabitants by midcentury, each lost 100 persons to the North American migration by the middle to late 1740s. Oberboihingen, Reudern, Neuffen, and Schlaitdorf today hold only fragmentary records of partitions of estate before 1754. Records of partitions and taxation from nearby Grötzingen and Neckartenzlingen reconfirm the average property worth of 100 to 200 Gulden. Tax books and parish records also chart a rapid decline in the status of formerly prosperous villagers.[39]

In the present-day valley of the Aich, which flows into the Neckar, one can see the undulating hills that in the eighteenth century harbored small vineyards, pasturages, and small crops, especially spelt (winter grain). As the Aich winds its way through hills with outcroppings of forest and stone, it passes Grötzingen; Aich; and Neuenhausen, some twenty kilometers south of Stuttgart. In the eighteenth century, Grötzingen still boasted its medieval status as a market town, with a large Rathaus and an impressive church topped by a massive, spired belfry. The pastoral beauty of the villages today, only slightly damaged by newer low-income housing and small industries, has erased the memory of the poverty that stalked this valley in the eighteenth century. After 1706, funds assessed according to the tax rate and collected on the monthly fast days went to the orphanage. Grötzingen began a Sunday collection of offerings for the poor and a quarterly collection for indigent persons in the 1720s. By 1734 widows and orphans received eight to ten Kreuzer per week; by 1748, to prevent begging in the street, ten poor people each got one Gulden worth of baked bread, which was to last fourteen days. By 1746, the *Bettelvogt* (beedle) had become a permanent fixture in Württemberg villages.[40]

Between 1746 and 1754, one hundred persons fled Grötzingen for Pennsylvania, among them Johann Christoph Jäcklen, one of the clever emigrants. Dodging evaluation, Jäcklen left his wife Elizabeth behind to shoulder an indebtedness of 173 Gulden which the assessed value of his property (124 Gulden) could not cover. He had brought 81 Gulden in moveables into his marriage; leaving, he took 150 Gulden in cash and bought a new suit of clothing and new woodworking tools, which he hid from the assessors until after he had decamped.[41]

Neckartenzlingen in 1722 had 106 houses and 110 persons enjoying Bürgerrecht. Taxes totaled 72,288 Gulden. The population of 570 persons boasted three taverns, including the Stag, housed in one of the best structures in the village. Hans Siglin operated the tavern, which was assessed at 700 Gulden. At his marriage in 1740 he had brought 500 Gulden into the marriage and his wife another 406. But bad times touched the Siglins as they did poorer folk. On 27 April 1753, the description of the indebtedness of Siglin and his wife which was compiled before they and their five children were allowed to leave for Pennsylvania showed creditors claiming over 1,800 Gulden. Like the weaver Jacob Thumm, their much poorer fellow traveler from nearby Neckarhausen, the Siglins experienced increased taxes and declining income. And, just like the Thumms, who had at their marriage in 1746 only brought into their combined estate land and chattels worth 277 Gulden, the Siglins calculated the risk of converting what money they had into moveables that could be stored in trunks or traded on the journey; and they left.[42]

When questioned about their reasons for leaving, emigrants listed first the lack of food—*Nahrungsmittel*—and insufficient acreage outside of the vineyard to sustain them in a year of crop failure. Crop damage by wild game, the increasing cost and general scarcity of wood, obligations to be performed for the hunt, annual road work and forest upkeep, and the prohibition against cutting grass or allowing animals to graze in woods and meadows angered them. They particularly noted that forest damage was often blamed on their cattle when local officials knew that wild animals were responsible. The quartering of soldiers, and ever-increasing taxes and obligations, joined the list of reasons inspiring people in Protestant territories north of the Danube to risk the journey.[43]

Such complaints reveal again how the idea of property remained firmly linked to the subsistence household economy. Liberty, to the extent the concept surfaced at all, continued to be seen in terms of privileges that guaranteed protection against obligatory services or other demands on scarce time and resources.

Some began their journey grateful for the charity of local officials. The Neckar Valley district of Nürtingen voted a small donation to one woman and her seven children to help pay her way from Obereßlingen to Nürtingen, where she would renounce her rights as a subject before journeying onward. Such charity was motivated in part by the desire to keep such people from becoming public charges. Other authorities knew what had occurred in neighboring villages in the winter and spring of 1751. The pastor's entries in nearby Oberboihingen's church records present a chilling description of child deaths from whooping cough, measles, and inflammation of the limbs brought on by malnutrition. When John Philipp and David Manhardt of nearby Nürtingen departed for Pennsylvania, leaving their wives temporarily behind, authorities exempted them from paying the fees for renunciation of subject rights "because of their great poverty," and sent them on their way.[44]

In the Palatinate, towns west of the Rhine on the eastern skirts of the western hill country—Bergzabern, Dörrenbach, Heuchelheim, and Mörzheim—faced similar conditions. Towns and villages on the borders of the mountain country—such as Weyher, Endenkoben, and Burrweiler—stretched north to Diedesfeld, Deidesheim, and Bad Dürkheim. Clusters of villages northwest of Worms, around Mölsheim and Westofen, produced immigrants. Towns further west, like Ginsweiler and Katzenbach, where the mountains thinned out, boasted slopes running north and west into the Nahe Valley which also produced wine and the attendant commerce that spelled travel and communication—and the fatal pattern of equal partition that reduced the probability of individuals' maintaining their propertied status.

The even more straitened agricultural circumstances in the middle of the Palatinate—in the Pfälzer Wald, for instance, the hills (*Haardtgebirge*) south of Kaiserslautern to Pirmasens—did not produce many emigrants. Neither did the Reichswald, the Oberhaimgeraide, or the Limburger Stifswald. The regional centers at Simmern, or at Veldenz did not commonly deal with emigration to North America. The meager economic possibilities provided by wooded areas and the growing of *Hackfrucht* (root crops) dictated the customs of impartible inheritance here. What holdings there were tended to be kept intact, and the designated heir paid off younger siblings in the same pattern of Anerbenrecht that prevailed in the Black Forest of Württemberg. Some migrants from villages such as Gerhardsbrunn, in the hills southwest of Kaiserslautern, did come to America; they were the exception.[45]

The valleys along which lay the communication, trade, and wine routes not only produced the emigrants but also encouraged movement along reasonably good roads and streams. In the Palatinate as in the Kraichgau, many towns included numerous Swiss families who had only settled in the area a generation of two earlier. Rieschweiler, east of Zweibrücken and north of Pirmasens, was a Swiss town from which twenty-eight emigrants left for Pennsylvania in the eighteenth century. In the neighboring parish of Ulmet, composed of eleven villages, sixty-two emigrants left for the New World. The major post road from Meisenheim to Kusel and Zweibrücken aided repeated migration from the towns.[46] Lutheran villages such as Thaleischweiler sent fifty family members to Lancaster, York, and Philadelphia in the same pattern. Inventories for Mühlhofen and Billigheim, further to the east, reveal the same final average property worth, ranging from fifty Gulden to two-hundred Gulden over the course of the century, in a period when agricultural prices either stagnated, or fell.[47]

III

Halle's missionary network first emerged in the 1730s in Georgia before extending to Pennsylvania in 1742. Pastor Johann Martin Boltzius and his assistants operated as self-conscious cultural brokers, shapers of the "charter group" of German speakers who were creating a new society in Georgia. But Halle relied heavily on Samuel Urlsperger of Augsburg, the former Stuttgart court preacher who had also served in London, for regular correspondence with Georgia and for keeping alive a network of support in the German southwest towns. Urlsperger edited (and bowd-lerized) Boltzius's reports, but saw no reason to disguise the role of Superintendent Bonaventura Riesch, at Lindau, who also acted on the Salzburgers' behalf, even recovering an inheritance from Salzburg for one of the Georgia settlers in 1740. Other members of this network included the Augsburg banker Christian von Münch, who sent money to America via a contact with a Savannah merchant; and when Bartho-lemew Nübling of Langenau attempted to recover some 435 Gulden in 1768, von Münch was authorized to secure its passage. The Mak children of Ebenezer, whose property had been sequestered for them until their parents proved safe arrival, secured its release in 1752 for disbursement in cash to Ebenezer, again via Urlsperger and the church authorities in Augsburg. A bookbinder named Scheraus in Ulm, well-inclined patrons in the pietist centers of Calw and Canstatt, and church officials in Stuttgart all materially aided the struggling settlement.[48]

Ebenezer's reputation was such that when von Münch wanted to forward an inheritance for a Pennsylvanian in 1740 and donations for Germantown's church eight years later, Boltzius and his contacts in Sa-vannah provided the means. William Hopton in Charleston forwarded letters to Ebenezer and acted from time to time as agent in South Carolina, as did the firm of Harris and Habersham. Boltzius and his colleagues received shipments from Halle that were sent via London to Charleston, and then forwarded. Shipments including "infallible Berlin fever powder" bought in Stuttgart went down the Rhine via Rotterdam for Savannah.[49]

Religious authorities controlled all aspects of this network. No en-terprising merchants, traders, agents, or speculators emerged in the Geor-gia settlement before the 1750s. Until then, German-speaking Swiss re-sidents in Purrysburg, Orangeburg, and Charleston, South Carolina, obtained through the Halle network medicine, books, donations from Switzerland intended for their churches, and eventually the opportunity to grind meal at Ebenezer on European stones. Carefully cultivated through the Lutheran chapel at the court of Saint James in London, the network of the Halle fathers relied on Hiob Ludolff's nephew Heinrich Wilhelm, a member of the British privy council; on chaplain Anton Wilhelm Böhme; and after 1723, on Friedrich Michael Ziegenhagen. The Society for the Promoting of Christian Knowledge (SPCK) founded by Dr. Thomas Bray elected Francke and two Halle associates to member-ship. In 1731, about the time James Oglethorpe and other philanthropists began contemplating a colony to provide an example of social reform, with a population of skilled artisan-farmers, Halle took an interest in the plight of the Salzburgers.[50]

Already in the 1730s, however, Halle's missionary network coexisted

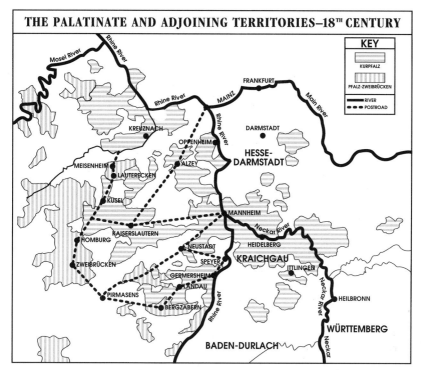

THE PALATINATE AND ADJOINING TERRITORIES–18TH CENTURY

Original map by Win Thrall, 1992. Political boundaries and post road information taken from comparisons with Willi Alter, ed., *Pfalzatlas: im Auftrag der pfälzischen Gesellschaft zur Förderung der Wissenschaften* (Speyer, 1963), maps 9, 58, 86; and Fritz Trautz, *Die pfälzische Auswanderung nach Nordamerika im 18. Jahrhundert* (Heidelberg, 1959). Unless otherwise noted, "Palatinate" in the text of this book refers to the Electoral Palatinate, emigrants, and not to the Zweibrücken territories under the lordship of a different family but still considered "Palatine."

alongside a growing group of secular traders, mostly Kraichgauers with Swiss connections. Palatines, for example, recognized that Bergzabern, Dörrenbach, Heuchelheim, and Mörzheim were connected by trade routes. A main post road in the Palatinate linked Meisenheim with Kusel to the south and with Homburg and Zweibrücken before swinging to Pirmasens, Anweiler, and Landau, and thence over Neustadt to Mannheim. North of Homburg, another road veered off toward Kaiserslautern to Dürkheim; a third ran from Kaiserslautern north over Kircheim-Bolanden to Alzey and thence to Mainz. Traders and recruiting agents penetrated the Ämter of Neustadt, on the Weinstraße; Alzey and Oppenheim — centers that combined, included some ninety villages or more under their jurisdiction.

Frankfurt's role as book center, second only to Leipzig, guaranteed both Halle's and the secular traders' connections at taverns, bookshops, newspapers, and publishing houses. Factors and contacts for Britain and its colonies consulted the *Frankfurter Mercantil-Schema,* the city directory, to find the seven post locations, including the *Churpfälzische Postwagen,* and another for Hesse-Darmstadt. Württemberg was not represented in the city, nor was its newspaper, although the Stuttgart and Tübingen publisher Christian Gottfried Cotta advertised his wares in the *Reichs-Post-Amts-Zeitung,* as did Tübingen's Joseph Sigmund. Samuel Wohler, bookseller and publisher in Ulm, also used the Frankfurt newspaper to advertise. Visitors wishing to obtain other newspapers, such as the Stuttgart, Karlsruhe, or Mannheim papers, could do so via the office of the Reichs-Post-Amts-Zeitung, which also offered nine British newspapers and five monthly or weekly magazines from Great Britain.[51]

The sole successful attempt by the German Lutheran congregation in Virginia to exploit the Halle network used the Frankfurt connection. Johann Caspar Stoever's journey via London to the Hanseatic cities in 1734 obtained for his congregation in Orange County a substantial collection of money and books. Many of the books he obtained from booksellers in Leipzig and in Straßburg were, he found, "of no service to the congregation"; in Frankfurt he exchanged the Leipzig titles with a bookseller for two-hundred copies of the Frankfurt hymnal and service book. The Straßburg books he exchanged in Darmstadt with his relative Johann Philip Fresenius for "long books with great letters."[52]

Halle's patrons or friends knew where to find the pietist factor in the Sandgaße. But access to such powerful friends ended for early Virginia Lutherans with Stoever's death. They, like free-church groups, remained excluded. Mennonites in Virginia or Pennsylvania had to contact a book dealer in Frankenthal, near Mannheim, on more than one occasion in an attempt to recover small familial estates for members in North America. Isolation from powerful agents and networks explains why officials rejected a request from the book dealers Hermann and Carl of Frankfurt to pursue a legacy for Catharine Stumer of Lachen.[53]

Those who emigrated from more distant villages and to colonies in North America less familiar to the agents and centers around the Main-Rhine center encountered more trouble. In 1766 Hans Jacob Sailer of Weidenstetten returned to this village. (Following common usage, he will henceforth be referred to as "Jacob Sailer.") A successful emigrant himself, he took his brothers with him to Charleston, although Christoph and Johannes died upon arrival, leaving only David as a trader in Charleston. Sailer's own emigration in 1753 had involved him in a dispute with a bookbinder and dealer in Reutlingen from whom he had purchased 249 books or pamphlets. He had paid the bookbinder Gottfried Mack fifty Gulden and had taken the books with him to Heidelberg, promising to pay the fifty-Gulden balance. Sailer sold the books in Heidelberg, and the tavern keeper at the *Kleiner Viehhof* wrote out a receipt for him, as he informed his father by letter in 1770 when the latter was being dunned by the Reutlingen man for the balance. Calling the Reutlinger, "an old thief" and "dog's ass" (*Hundesfutterei*), Jacob suggested that if the bookbinder were in America, he would be thrown into prison or would have his ears cut off for trying to extract the money from Jacob's father.[54] Even after Jacob's death the bookbinder's son continued to dun the estate, suggesting the perils of individual deals not conducted within a well-established network.

The circulation of printed matter, and agents' activities, were concentrated in the valleys of the Neckar, Main, and the Rhine, and their immediate tributaries. In the Kraichgau, recoveries were more likely in the key towns of Sinsheim and Wiesloch, or areas close to the Rhine. Proximity to Heilbronn; to Eppingen, for people in Schwaigern; to Ittlingen, where the network of the Geigers and Schuchmanns had connections; and to the Keppeles (part of the Gensel-Beyerle network), in Sinsheim, made a difference.

In the Palatinate, along the Weinstraße or well-traveled post routes, villages such as Mutterstadt, Eberbach, Lachen, and Edenkoben witnessed repeated attempts at recovering property. These were also villages where outmigration was a common phenomenon: Edenkoben, for instance, had produced over fifty emigrants to Pennsylvania, and its authorities had had repeated contacts with former villagers.[55] Agents recovered property for clients in the neighborhood of Worms or near Mainz, in the county of Erbach, within easy reach of the Rhine. Yet north of this area, agents rarely operated. If one positions oneself in the imaginary tower at Schaffhausen looking northward, one sees that remote villages in upper Swabia, and—with the one exception noted—the Ulm villages, remained isolated. Similarly, almost no recoveries can be found in Baden-Durlach or in areas further to the south. Although network contours are irretrievably lost for Hesse-Darmstadt, contextual evidence from Halle's correspondence with lively pietist groups in this area suggests that agents often penetrated this region as well.[56] Württemberg agents operated mainly in the Neckar Valley, or on the major roads leading southward out of Stuttgart to the imperial cities of Eßlingen and Reutlingen, and further south, to Balingen. Major towns outside this area—such as Calw, the noted pietist center, or Freudenstadt and its

environs, in the Black Forest—were rarely touched. Nor did agents find
their way back to Seißen and the eastern Swabian villages.

Sifting the local and regional records of the German southwestern
communities, one can identify some eighty persons operating with powers of attorney to recover village property for emigrants. The agents and
their field of operation rarely included Baden. The Palatinate, Württemberg, and the Kraichgau defined the boundaries of their activities, largely
shaped by the pattern of outmigration and by preexisting networks of
trade and communication. Two hundred recovery attempts (out of some
forty-three hundred emigrants' names) provide the basis for some analysis. Alzey's, Mannheim's, Darmstadt's and much of Stuttgart's prewar
archives do not survive; figures are not precise. The recovery attempts
are not evenly distributed between 1712 and 1792. One of the earliest
attempts was undertaken by an illegal emigrant of 1712. Henrich Eibach
of Armsheim, in the Palatinate, asked that proceeds from the auction of
his father's estate, confiscated after Henrich's illegal migration, be sent
him in Pennsylvania. The authorities agreed, as long as the sum came
to ninety-five Gulden. Although illicit migration was sufficient grounds
for denying any claims on property in the homeland, the authorities in
this instance relented; however, they identified the minimum amount
they thought worth their while to administer once fees and conversion
of the property into cash were deducted.[57]

Early Swiss- and German-Reformed agents emerged in the mid-
1740s. Swiss authorities eventually arrested Jacob Joner for enticement
of potential emigrants. But Joner, who had emigrated in 1719, began his
career as an agent in the mid-1730s and ended it in 1752 by collecting
twelve separate commissions, offering to pay clients in advance if they
would sign over to him all rights to their inheritances, which he would
then claim in the Reich.[58] Prior to the 1740s, only a half dozen cases of
attempted recovery survive for areas in the Reich. In the 1740s one finds
about a dozen; in the 1750s, in spite of the disruption of the Seven Years'
War, more than thirty. But in the 1760s, 37 individuals sent powers of
attorney back to their villages, and in the early 1770s, before the imperial
crisis disrupted contact once more, another 50 did so. After the peace in
1783, twenty-nine more recoveries were attempted, and in the 1790s,
another twenty-eight.[59] But if some two-hundred cases can be drawn
from among 4,300 emigrants, one cannot extrapolate that there were the
same proportion of recovery attempts in the total of 120,000 German
speakers who emigrated to America between 1683 and 1783. The printing
and distribution of power-of-attorney forms in German and English in
Philadelphia by 1756 suggests that sufficient demand existed to justify
such expense.[60] German speakers from the marginalized villages claimed

inheritances of between one hundred Gulden and two hundred Gulden. Given the costs involved in hiring agents and pursuing cases that could easily take between three and seven years to complete, recovery lay beyond the resources of many ordinary settlers on the lower end of the social scale, even if they owned modest property in the New World. Occasional examples from such ordinary folk do surface in the records. The survey of regions above suggests why many emigrants from the most marginal areas would have had either no claims, or insufficient resources to seek inheritances through agents.

The timing of recovery attempts among the more successful, however, is significant. About twenty years elapsed between the date of emigration and the time of attempted recovery. The pattern of attempts fits the arrival and subsequent success of the family groups who dominated the German-speaking emigration to North America that peaked in the 1750s. The amounts pursued by emigrants sending powers of attorney suggests that both authorities and emigrants understood one-hundred Gulden to be the minimum amount worth claiming. Of the cases summarized, only nine fell slightly lower. Most involved one hundred to seven hundred Gulden, suggesting that those persons making recovery attempts were emigrants from the middle level of village society. Not surprisingly, most attempts came out of Pennsylvania using the secular network and its broker-agents. Attempts originating in Georgia and South Carolina usually relied on Halle, as did some Lutherans in Philadelphia.

The success rate of the attempts remains uncertain. At the end of the proceedings, whether simple or lengthy, the agent bearing power of attorney signed the *Quittung* acknowledging receipt of the money—always both given in figures and written out. This document formally renounced all future claims on village property by the claimant and his or her heirs. The chief district official or a member of the central government often ordered that monies be disbursed, although in some of these cases one cannot now find the receipt in the records. Depending on how one chooses to interpret such fragmentary data, perhaps half the claimants enjoyed success.

Agents rarely took cash back to the colonies. Instead, after perusing the published lists of exchange rates in the Frankfurt paper, they would sell the money on the market in exchange for bills of credit used on their clients' behalf. Because such exchanges were private, no surviving records track these transactions. Since by the 1750s the *Reichs-Post-Amts-Zeitung* was broadly distributed and exchange rates were common knowledge, peculation by unscrupulous agents became riskier. Ignorance could still favor those attempting fraud. In 1777 the Göttingen publicist A. L.

Schlözer published in his *Briefwechsel* the news that Heinrich Fretter of Horchheim, near Worms, had left via a testament 124 Gulden to Caspar Schönebrugh in North America, to settle a debt. Yet the episcopal vicariate advertising in the Frankfurt paper to notify Schönebrugh could only hope he would respond within the requisite nine-month period. Schlözer noted that German newspaper readers and justice officials needed a precise and accurate map of North America "so that no one thinks it means North Holland . . . and therefore so much greater must be the news for the German public that three such world maps are to appear where before not one existed."[61]

IV

Agents' activities on behalf of the propertied recreated the social conditions that had originally stimulated emigration. Someone well enough established in North America to reclaim property in a Reich village excited both interest and envy in those towns and valleys where repeated recovery attempts occurred.[62] A select profile of a few agents suggests how they operated and the importance of their networks in areas they regularly visited.

Three particularly significant networks will be discussed in greater detail because they provide further insight—and not only into how, where, and for whom property was recovered. The entrepreneurial behavior of these early arrivals also suggested how in North America the definition of freedom as the absence of constraint could be linked to broader social and perhaps even political ambitions that ran counter to pietist visions.

The Gensel-Beyerle connection linked emigrants from Württemberg and the Kraichgau to the powerful Keppele and Hilegas families from the Kraichgau towns of Treschklingen, Sinsheim, and Eppingen. The Geiger network centered at Ittlingen, also in the Kraichgau, and was accessible to German speakers in both Pennsylvania and South Carolina. Ernst Ludwig Baisch's network connected Philadelphia to his hometown of Pforzheim, to Mannheim, and to towns and villages along trade routes in the adjoining Palatinate, in Baden, in the Kraichgau, and in Württemberg.

Typical of the lesser agents was Johann Christian Schmitt—formerly owner of the White Stag, an inn in Leiman—who, between the 1750s and 1770s, served as an agent in the Palatinate and the Kraichgau.[63] Zacharias Endreß, a relatively late (1766) arrival from Wertheim, on the Main, also came from a prominent innkeeping family, members of the local court. Endreß opened a brew- and malthouse on Vine and Callowhill between Second and Third streets, in Philadelphia, acting for other Wertheimers. In 1770 he asked his "cousin Kraft, the bookbinder" to keep him informed, and noted that another emigrant, the baker Daniel Frischmuth, had recovered his 155 Gulden.[64] Another agent was a converted London Jew named Mayer, who operated at the Three Kings Inn in Heilbronn, where he prepared transports from the Kraichgau to London with the city.[65]

In the spring of 1749 Stuttgart officials compiled a report against Johann Georg Koch of New York for luring away not just "people of no good reputation" but also propertied subjects. The Württemberg official, anticipating potential legal objections, argued that Koch's activity did not fall under the privileges of the Tübinger Vertrag but constituted attempts at ensnaring the unwary. Koch's success might lead men to desert their wives and children, reducing these families to widowed and orphaned status at the expense of public charity and of the pious foundations. Scarcely a month later, Balingen authorities reported the suspicious activities of three men, Matthias Gensel, Johannes Hummel, and Jürg Landenberger, who appeared annually around Saint Martin's Day (11 November) at the slaughtering feast under the pretext of bringing letters from Pennsylvania. Some forty families had been lured away from Balingen and Lauffen, and their vicinity, another supposedly from Rosenfeld.[66]

Landenberger, a stocking weaver by profession, presided over an elaborate and sophisticated trading network that turned him into a transatlantic magnate. Arriving in America around 1746, he led emigrants possessing between five hundred and one thousand Gulden apiece in property to Pennsylvania. Investing eight hundred Gulden of their money with a promise to pay 10 percent interest from his profits, Landenberger bought mirrors, brandy kettles, porcelain tableware, cupping glasses, bed coverlets, and sickles in Pennsylvania—trading in the domestic household implements and goods he knew would be in great demand. Using connections in Europe, he traded porcelain in Holland and silk in Switzerland, secured Bavarian items out of Nuremberg at the Frankfurt fair, and turned his eight-hundred-Gulden loan into one thousand five hundred Gulden, repaying handily, with interest. A second set of loans, adding up to one thousand Gulden, he turned into two thousand Gulden. He could afford regular crossings with Gensel (from neighboring Lauffen) and still maintain a house and family in Ebingen. Threatened with imprisonment at Hohenneuffen, Landenberger settled down in Württemberg in the 1750s a wealthy Bürger.[67]

The Gensels, who, with the Beyerles, built the first of the major networks on Landenberger's example, settled in Pennsylvania. Their knowledge of prevailing exchange rates and their ability to skim off the top the difference in exchanges between currencies, about which most of their clients knew nothing, guaranteed them success. The dubious quality of Württemberg currency on the international market enabled these agents to claim prejudice against the duchy when they returned less than the expected amount to clients. As German-Americans caught on to this dodge, they turned to Halle's network.[68] Halle pietist leader Gotthilf August Francke commented on Württemberg money to Mühlenberg in 1756. Recovering an inheritance of four hundred Gulden by using his connection to the prelate Weißensee in Denckendorf, Francke complained that "because of the very bad money which circulates in Württemberg's territory, one must reckon with at the least ten if not twelve percent loss of the Louis'd or—at the least 8 Gulden and 15 Kreuzer, and on the Carolinen, which here bring 6 or 8 percent, outside 10 Gulden 40 Kreuzer. In the meantime I give you this information with the object that you should take care of the interested parties there, that they not suffer loss."[69]

Württemberg officials knew only a small part of Landenberger's connections. He involved himself in Halle's network, securing for Saint Michael's Lutheran Church an organ built at Heilbronn and personally escorted by him and Gottlieb Mittelberger to Philadelphia in 1751. Nor was Landenberger alone in recognizing the possibilities Halle's network presented.[70] His colleague Matthias Gensel would act as agent for the Nova Scotia and New York colonization scheme beginning in 1751, having been recommended by the Heilbronn official Heerbrand to his cousin, Jakob Heerbrand, in Balingen. Jakob, the Balingen shopkeeper, may not have been as impressed as was his Heilbronn cousin with Gensel's knowledge of the Schwäbische Alb villages and the routes running east toward Ulm. Matthias Gensel and two Jacob Gensels settled in Germantown and Philadelphia in the mid-1740s; by 1748 Jacob had acted as agent for the recovery of an inheritance for Heinrich Valentin Bernhard of Unkenbach, in the Palatinate, and Matthias Gensel had witnessed the letter of power of attorney. As Lutheran presence grew in the 1750s, so did the Gensels'.[71]

Matthias Gensel had already made Pastor Brunnholtz suspicious in 1746 when he volunteered to obtain in Stuttgart a bell for Saint Michael's church. If a gift from Württemberg were forthcoming, Brunnholtz reported, Halle should ask that the money he sent to him directly. Brunnholtz would only allow Gensel to pick up a bell, not money. In 1769 Jacob Gensel presented himself under dubious circumstances as the agent representing the Sonntags, emigrants from Selchenbach, in Zweibrücken, although he was unsuccessful in pressing the claims of his supposed client.

Although nearly as ubiquitous as Baisch would later be, the Gensels developed an unsavory reputation for milking property to their own financial advantage.[72]

In Württemberg's Balingen Amt, the Gensels' powerful network could sometimes operate, but rarely, and only in competition with the smaller but well-organized Moravian system. The Bitzer and Stotz families and their relatives the Klingles and Wolfers were among the one-hundred or more families from the Balingen region who eventually settled in Bethlehem, Pennsylvania. In 1762 the Stotz family sent Simon Keppele, a merchant in Sinsheim and brother to the Philadelphia merchant Johann Heinrich, to collect their inheritance. But the Wolfer family, named as heirs to a deceased unmarried uncle who died an infantry soldier in 1764, claimed property with Moravian help in Bethlehem. Ludwig Wolfer, a smith at Neuwied on the Rhine, delegated his power of attorney to Johann Jacob Rossern, a Moravian tanner of Stuttgart. This same tanner, Rossern, appeared in 1763 in Steinenbronn, on the Neckar, as the designated representative of Abraham Dürrtinger and Company, merchants at Herrnhut, the Moravian center in Lusatia. Rossern assumed for these merchants the task of recovering the estate of Ludwig Dani and his wife Catherine.[73]

One glimpses the other end of the secular network in Pennsylvania beginning in the 1740s. In 1744 John Potts, trader and later justice of the peace, decided to engage in a risk venture by shipping rum, tobacco, molasses, nails, and assorted small goods among the German speakers of Pennsylvania's Berks and Lebanon counties, along the Susquehanna River. Potts chose as his agent the printer Christopher Saur, who had begun publishing his *Hoch-Deutsch Pennsylvanischer Geschichts-Schreiber* in 1739. Saur proved a poor agent; by 1746 Potts found a collector in Conrad Weiser, the son of the New York leader on the Schoharie. Weiser began visiting Potts's debtors and upon collection paid off Potts's creditor William Gilmore, as well as Jacob Dester, another Potts employee. Weiser sometimes resorted to legal action, paying "Peter Urban Constable for John Potts in an action against Caspar Dorst wherein plaintiff was none Suited [*sic*]." Most of the debts ran from fifteen shillings to one pound, and by his own handling of affairs Weiser not only satisfied Potts but also extended his own influence over settlers in the area.[74]

Weiser numbered among his own clients the young Johann Heinrich Keppele, who arrived in Pennsylvania as a teenager in 1738. (Because Keppele is most often referred to as "Henrich Keppele," that name will be used hereafter.) Keppele's family came from Treschklingen, northwest of Heilbronn. Within the triangulated area of the Kraichgau towns Heilbronn, Sinsheim, and Eppingen grew powerful family connections, from which Keppele benefited, as did the intrepid Jacob Geiger of Ittlingen, whose village also lay within this charmed region. Keppele apparently worked for a time as a butcher but branched into trade, by 1748 consigning a shipment of linseed oil to John Yeates. By 1751 land was surveyed for him, and his account with Conrad Weiser in the 1750s reveals that Weiser in 1756 bought 115 gallons of rum. Keppele by then operated a store in Lancaster, Pennsylvania, supplying tradesmen in that emerging entrepôt. When Keppele's son Jürg Christopher was baptised at Saint Michael's in 1747, Jürg Christopher in Heilbronn was his sponsor by proxy, the proxy being Jürg Landenberger of Ebingen. Keppele knew Michael Hillegas, as well. This Anglican member of the German-Americans in Philadelphia came from Sinsheim and had an extensive family branch in Eppingen, with further connections in Heilbronn. Michael, Jr., born in 1729 in Philadelphia, son of Georg Michel, who died in 1749, enjoyed the presence of extended family who had been in the New World since 1722. Appearing in the Philadelphia Orphan's Court in February 1750, he and his sisters Susanna and Mary asked for guardians, and William Clymer became the young man's patron. A year later Michael was appointed appraiser of the estate of Philip Fohl, thereafter appearing in the 1750s with Heinrich Keppele and Christian Lehmann as appraisers and guardians of German speakers.[75]

Keppele eventually began receiving consignments of immigrants, although probably his share in the trade with the Pennsylvania-West Indies trading family the Steinmetzes never exceeded five hundred adult males. By 1751 he was prosecuting debtors in the Court of Common Pleas, one of a small number of Germans using the court to resolve issues of debt.[76] Despite his later activities in helping to found the Deutsche Gesellschaft zu Pennsylvania in 1764, ostensibly to prevent abuses in the shipping of Germans to Pennsylvania, Keppele was involved in the trade himself and invested his profits to become part owner of the ship *Britannia* by 1761, venturing into the Barbados and Jamaica trade. By 1771 his network of clients extended to Baltimore, as he informed Jaspar Yeates, who acted as Keppele's attorney not only in Pennsylvania courts but also against "some persons at Baltemore Town Largely indebted to me."[77]

Aggressive arrivals such as Keppele had the advantage of Kraichgau connections already pioneered by Hillegas and a handful of Swiss entrepreneurs in the 1730s. Now the sheer numbers of German speakers arriving in North America, as well as their need for patrons and for intermediaries with the broader culture, guaranteed the success of well-connected entrepreneurs. Lutherans depended on both Swiss and Moravian early arrivals for the construction of their own North American networks. The Lehmanns of Germantown were a respected family from

Saxony who had joined the Moravian movement. Christian Lehmann's father Gottfried, who had learned the craft of a woodworker, emigrated to America in 1731, having built his own house in Herrnhut and helped construct an organ. Gottfried married again in 1735 and by the 1750s saw his sons established in lucrative careers.[78]

Christian, arguably the most eminent member of the family, mastered the skills of a surveyor and by the 1740s was executing exquisitely drawn and colored surveys indicating a mastery of the art and meticulous attention to legal detail. Called on by German speakers to execute surveys and indentures, Christian also learned to trace titles. His submission of a brief of title on Anna Kauffmann's land in Germantown showed how he followed the property back through eight deeds to the original patent given by William Penn to Jacob Tetner while the latter was still in the Reich in the 1680s. This expertise and dependability explain why on the backs of some draft surveys he sketched the last wills and testaments of German speakers, including the 1748 will of Baltes Barth, which Lehmann translated; and that of Paul Knipner, who bequeathed four hundred pounds to his brother in Marienwerder, Polish Prussia, with the proviso that if he or a child or grandchild did not appear within ten years, the deceased's wife and executrix Susannah was to receive this sum in addition to the residue of estate already provided her.[79] In 1752 Lehmann appeared for the first time as an assessor for the Orphans' Court of Philadelphia. By the 1770s both he and his wife Elisabeth signed many of the powers of attorney which Lehmann, now a notary, also attested to or translated for prospective agents such as the young Ernst Ludwig Baisch of Pforzheim, who first arrived in the 1750s. Only Lehmann's authority could allow Baisch to recover at Worms for his client Adam Schweigert, a Philadelphia tailor. Schweigert's father had died, leaving an estate that Baisch was to recover within seven years. Miller advanced thirteen pounds in current Pennsylvania money to have the power of attorney sworn before Lehmann, who also witnessed the mutual bond of fifty pounds each party took out to seal the agreement. Lehmann had made himself indispensible to many in the German-speaking community by the 1760s, surveying Lutheran church lands in Germantown in 1761, and giving legal advice to Mühlenberg as well.[80]

In May 1760, Michael Hillegas informed Peter Clopper that he was to invest "Mrs. Gensells Money hence as I directed." Hillegas oversaw the interests of Jacob Gensel's widow, whose husband had operated the tavern in Philadelphia and whose relative owned the land on Creesam Road to the west of the Great Road leading to Germantown, which Christian Lehmann would examine in 1770. Gensel had arrived in the mid-1740s. His Pennsylvania business suggested the wisdom of taking out a tavern license in Philadelphia; he operated his tavern until his death in March 1759. On his death, his widow Katherine sold the moveables at auction and married Christopher Minge of Germantown. Jacob Winney, on behalf of Gensel's children Charlotte and John, petitioned the Philadelphia Orphans' Court in March 1761 to force Minge and his new wife to render an account of their handling of the estate, which seemed to contradict the terms of Gensel's will. To secure the future of Gensel's son John, the court appointed Heinrich Keppele his guardian, cementing network alliances among the Gensels and Keppele. Not surprisingly, Jacob Winney, a trader like Keppele, helped to found the German Society of Pennsylvania with the aid of Ludwig Weiss, a Moravian attorney and Lehmann's friend.[81]

Gensel's career in Pennsylvania intersected with that of another Kraichgauer, Hans Jacob Beyerle (referred to henceforth as Jacob Beyerle, as that is how he was generally known). Beyerle emigrated from Sinsheim to Pennsylvania in 1730, after learning the trade of a baker. In November 1729 Beyerle had arranged with his father, Johann Daniel, also a baker, to purchase half of a small house, garden, and land his father owned in a suburb of Sinsheim. Jacob was to pay 180 Gulden for the transaction, but only 65 Gulden went to Johann Daniel, who professed himself "truly contented." The young Beyerle invested the 115-Gulden difference in his own business. Three years later, he emigrated with his wife of seven years, and four children. His brother Hans Michael had preceded him in 1730, settling in Lancaster. The two brothers had stayed in touch; Jacob also settled at Lancaster, baptizing a son there in 1735. Cousin Andreas, from Rohrbach, arrived in 1738, joining his skills as a baker to the role of tavern keeper.[82]

In 1737 these ambitious men used their contacts back in the Kraichgau to bring 610 Gulden in inheritance money to Lancaster on behalf of Michael Pfautz and his wife Anna Margarete. Over the protests of Frau Pfautz's relatives, the baker at Sinsheim, Johann Daniel, father to Hans Michael and Jacob, was authorized by a power of attorney to bring the money to Lancaster, where Hans Michael was sworn to see that the Pfautz family would receive it. The court officials described Hans Michael as a *Wechselsteller* (arranger of money exchanges), though whether the Lancaster man regularly engaged in these transactions remains uncertain. Unfamiliar with British common-law terms and officials, Sinsheim authorities described the notarized documents as authorized by "Herr Justus," interpreting "justice" as the given name of the officer they designated as *Staabshalter* (authority, or holder of the court staff upon which oaths were sworn).[83]

Hans Michael Beyerle established himself as a patron of the Lutheran church, donating a copy of the Baden-Durlach liturgy and sponsoring his cousin Andreas's children for baptism.[84] Jacob Beyerle, after his arrival in Lancaster, did not stay long, but began looking for opportunities elsewhere. Sometime in the 1740s he moved to Philadelphia and opened a tavern.[85] In Lancaster, he had become fast friends with the pastor Laurentius Nyberg, who by 1745 had shown tendencies toward Moravianism that split the congregation in half and resulted in a court suit for control of the building. Beyerle's role in the controversy remains unclear, but sometime in the late 1740s he left Lancaster.[86] By 1751 he entered the dispute for control of the Germantown Lutheran church, joining forces with Matthias Gensel and bringing himself to the attention of Pastor Mühlenberg, who regarded him as a meddling and contentious person. Further attempting to expand his opportunities, Beyerle appeared at Shamokin, fifty miles northwest of Reading, in February 1755 to warn the Moravians in the region that the Penns had given the entire region to him, and that he intended to settle some forty families there. When Conrad Weiser's sons heard of this, they reported to their father that the local Native Americans were upset to learn of Beyerle's claim, "and complained of the inJustice of the proprietors to give away their land which he never as yet had purchased." Even more distraught by the "little log houses on the Nordwest Branch of Susquettana," the Indians expected Weiser to take action, which he did in writing to provincial secretary Richard Peters in March: "I hope notice will be taken of that Impudent Rascal Jacob Beyerly."[87]

Although Gensel and Beyerle collaborated in the attempt to take over the Lutheran church in Germantown, their ambitions eventually collided. In February 1756 a team of arbitrators assigned by the Philadelphia Court of Common Pleas reported on the case *Mathias Gensell v. Jacob Beyerle.* The auditors found for Gensel, ordering Beyerle to pay fifty-five "Spanish Milld Dollars, or pieces of Eight, and three shillings now justly due and owing from the above Defendant."[88]

This secular Pennsylvania network of the 1740s found its equal in the Geiger network, which centered on Ittlingen and extended both to South Carolina and to Penn's province. In 1711 Johann Heinrich Schuchmann, village smith of Ittlingen, married Maria Elizabeth Schleif. No inventory of estate was made when Schuchmann's wife died in 1727, leaving three daughters: Maria Margarete, who later married Jacob Geiger; Anna Magdalena, who married Joseph Geiger; and Maria Elizabeth, wife of Ludwig Keller. Schuchmann married a second time, and his second wife, Anna Maria Fried, died in 1730, leaving a daughter, Maria Juliana, who married Josef Seitz. Finally, after marrying a third wife, who died in 1749, Schuchmann himself died in 1761. The exact partitioning of property among these half sisters grew increasingly complex; in 1754 the property was divided into four equal parts, and Jacob Geiger oversaw the partition, which involved a house and farmstead worth over twenty-four hundred Gulden.[89]

The families involved in the dispute were among the local worthies: Johann Martin Schuchmann became Schultheiß in 1756, and Johann Jacob Schuchmann became administrator of the von Gemmingen village interests. Ludwig Keller was also a member of the local court. By the 1760s, Johannes Geiger joined the local court, and this august company.[90] The Geiger connection to the Schuchmann family apparently began with Johann Jacob's marriage to Maria Margarete. The thirteen Ittlingen men possessing Bürgerrecht and involved in the dispute with the Gemmingen knights in 1718 had included the Schuchmanns but not the Geigers. The marriage of the latter family tied them later to a place and social caste extending far beyond the village. These ties extended by 1751 to Georg Leonhard Keppele of Treschklingen, the cousin of Johann Henrich Keppele of Philadelphia. The Keppeles were tied to the Schuchmanns, and both Halle and Philadelphia pietists recognized this connection in securing the organ for Saint Michael's. The Schuchmanns and the Keppeles selected Jürg Landenberger and Gottfried Mittelberger to make the trip.[91]

The Jacob Geiger born in 1722 who married Maria Margarete Schuchmann in 1750 had been in Pennsylvania with his father Jacob and his uncle Valentin in 1744. But both Jacob and his brother Johann Valentin returned in 1749 to Ittlingen, and Jacob seems to have traveled back and forth on various errands. His experience in his in-laws' inheritance dispute was part of the training that enabled him to handle the details of inheritance recovery.[92]

Geiger's powerful connections emerged by 1748 as he became involved in two exceedingly complex inheritance cases. In 1727 Hans Martin Liebenstein and his siblings Bernhard and Maria Magdalena left Dühren in the Kraichgau and settled in Pennsylvania. After their mother's death in 1737, their property, worth some 506 Gulden, fell under administration until 1748, when Jakob Hillegas of Sinsheim, the brother of the elder Michael of Philadelphia, came forward to recover it. The administrators challenged the power of attorney and cast aspersions upon the character of Hans Martin, calling him untrustworthy; they suspected him of having fled Pennsylvania. Since the authorities could find no fault with Hillegas's power of attorney, however, the money had to be paid within two weeks, with the proviso that it could remain for one year under guardianship until confirmation from the three Liebenstein siblings arrived.

But Hillegas's brother Michael had apparently already bought the inheritance and paid the Liebensteins, only to die himself in 1749. Jakob Hillegas demanded that the property be given to him; his brother had already paid 500 Gulden for it. But in December 1751 Johann Georg Kies of Manchester township, in Pennsylvania, appeared with another power of attorney on behalf of Maria Magdalena, who had married Peter Gärrn of York County. The court decided that Hillegas would have to recover from Martin Liebenstein; Magdalena's part was to be readied for extradition, but not for two months; and the inheritance due her brother Bernhard was to remain under administration.

Suddenly the schoolmaster of Michelfeld, Philipp Hartung, appeared, demanding part of Magdalena's estate. Hartung also taught in Ittlingen, although he was not assessed for a house there and did not hold Bürgerrecht. Some vineyard, herb garden, and plowed field worth 17 Gulden gave him propertied standing. Just as he made his claim, Jacob Geiger of Ittlingen and Pennsylvania now appeared, testifying that he had taken a letter from Dühren to Pennsylvania for Martin Breunigheim. There in Pennsylvania, he learned that Breunigheim had left for Virginia, or to join Maria Magdalena Liebenstein—who could not very well have authorized a power of attorney, objected her administrators.

Geiger's return to Ittlingen in the 1750s placed him immediately in the midst of the dispute over his in-laws' property, a dispute during which he rose to become an official for the *Kellerei,* or village wine cellars. His ties to America extended eventually beyond Pennsylvania, for a son, Heinrich, was a merchant and a member of the vestry for Saint John's Lutheran Church in Charleston, South Carolina, shortly after the Revolution. By this date Jacob had become Schultheiß in Ittlingen, and even before this date he had invested heavily in South Carolina property, and in a mill in Germantown, Pennsylvania.

A collateral branch of this originally Swiss family had settled in Beihingen, Württemberg, not far from Ittlingen. From Beihingen, the two brothers Johann Michael and Jacob had emigrated to South Carolina in the 1750s.[93] By 1771, Jacob Geiger of Ittlingen moved to buy the property due the orphans of these two men. Their uncle Johann Friederich in Beihingen apparently arranged the sale to the Ittlingen member of the family, and Jacob authorized Jacob Williman, his close friend in Charleston, to secure the property for him. By July 1772 a bond of indemnity was sworn out, repairing the defective conveyance of 2 November 1771. By this date, the Ittlingen Geiger was therefore not only involved in recovering property for Pennsylvania Germans but also deeply enmeshed in a complex property matter in South Carolina, which did not end with this purchase.[94]

For Jacob Geiger, his involvement with the Liebenstein case came full circle when his son Heinrich, acting at the request of the widow and children of Philipp Hartung of Charleston, asked his father in 1789 to secure the Hartung children's inheritance against the claims of other persons in neighboring Michelfeld. Philipp Hartung, apparently the son of the schoolmaster Geiger had encountered in the Lienbenstein case, had emigrated to Philadelphia and then to Charleston, South Carolina, where he worked as the organist at Saint John's. An estate was still due him and lay under administration in Michelfeld. Hartung died in the early 1780s, and his widow followed him in 1785, leaving the three children destitute and dependent on the charity of the congregation. Jacob Geiger informed his son that collateral kin of the deceased mother were attempting to "steal the Hartung children's inheritance." Geiger reminded his son that "Americans don't have the best reputation in this country, even if they may be the most honest people in the world. If someone authorized by a written warrant wants to realize an inheritance here, he is considered to be a thief." Germans, Geiger went on, generally "act most fraudulently" in such cases. Geiger predicted considerable costs, including hiring an attorney and probably approaching a university faculty for a *Gutachten* (expert opinion), and noted that he had already spent 130 Gulden of his own to initiate recovery. He believed that he could cover expenses from his real property, and perhaps "I may even realize my fortune which I own in Carolina." Indicating that he might come again to Charleston, Geiger promised to do all that he could, and particularly mentioned his friend Williman, with whom he had purchased the Geiger inheritance in 1771.[95]

The third and latest of the major secular networks was the creation of Ernst Ludwig Baisch, son of a linen weaver, who in 1752, at the age of fifteen, emigrated with his parents from Brötzingen, in Baden-Durlach's Pforzheim Amt. By the 1760s Baisch had begun to trade both in books and in various agricultural and household implements. Like the earlier arrivals the Gensels and the Geigers, he accepted commissions to act as an agent recovering property. The actual amounts which he received, he sold on the exchange for bills of credit in Frankfurt and Mannheim; he then invested in the books and household goods he imported, sold these at a profit, and reimbursed his clients, probably again in goods or credit, not in cash. By 1773 he was pursuing fifteen cases simultaneously; and he may have represented more than fifty clients in his career, which lasted into the 1790s. When in Philadelphia, he was a member of Saint Michael's Lutheran Church and associated with Jacob Bertsch, another Pforzheim trader, who operated the inn the White Lamb. Unlike the members of the other two major networks, Baisch appears to have worked largely alone, to have had relatively few contacts, and to have made few trips back to Baden-Durlach itself, staying resolutely out of both secular and church politics in Pennsylvania.[96]

V

The reputation of some of these agents left much to be desired, and the fate of socially marginal emigrants varied not only according to their region of origin but also according to which agents, in which networks, they depended on. Somewhat plaintively, and to avoid having to support a resident now an object of public charity, officials in the county (*Grafschaft*) of Erbach, near Frankfurt, asked Philadelphia officials for help in 1774. Johann Wilhelm Müller, a potter who had emigrated to Pennsylvania in 1754, had returned to Erbach, intent on making a place for himself in the network of trade and immigration. Buying 140 Gulden worth of goods, Müller had agreed to take his brother and several others to North America. City officials noted that for many years "others who have produced Powers under the proper Solemnities of Office, for taking considerable Estates out of this County, have from Time to Time been assisted." Instead of fulfilling his agreement, Müller abandoned his brother and the others not far from Mainz, and they returned, destitute, to Erbach. According to the original letter, but not the English translation, Müller's brother was *blödsinnig* (feeble-minded) and thus unable to fend for himself. Such episodes mounted as the number of attempts to claim inheritances climbed between 1750 and 1775, intensifying suspicions about the agents who plied the secular networks between the Reich and North America.[97]

Aside from Halle's missionary network, connections among emigrants from the southwestern Reich came to be created by default by the early-arriving secular traders from the Kraichgau or from the major commercial and trading centers of Württemberg or Baden. These entrepreneurs' raw ambition did not merely focus on securing more immigrants for the importing companies of Holland and Britain. Immigrants clamoring after inherited property in the villages of the southwest constituted too alluring a possibility for profit to be overlooked. Yet the machinations of the self-conscious cultural brokers who confidently shuttled between two continents, two languages, and two private-law systems did more than advance their own stature. On the one hand, their success undoubtedly helped German speakers to grasp how to use, cautiously at first, colonial courts, notaries, and documents, and how to reach beyond the boundaries of an immigrant group.

On the other hand, their behavior also showed German speakers how freedom in the libertarian, "negative" sense—freedom from traditional restrictions such as taxation, labor, and scarcity of land—might lead to unparalleled accumulations of wealth for the bold. But these entrepreneurs did not enjoy an entirely free field in which to link transferred cultural definitions of liberty and property to novel conditions. Their very success awakened resentments and suspicion, nowhere more so than among Halle's clergy, with its own positive notions of the stewardship of property, and of Christian liberty to be exercised for the common good. The clerics' natural allies were the married women, who saw in the worldly ambition of the entrepreneurs threats to the security of their households and churches.

When Thomas Jefferson made his first trips into the Rhineland after the Revolution, he noted John Dick's establishment in Frankfurt. Of Scottish ancestry, agent for the firm of Dick and Gavin at Rotterdam, John Dick had played a central role in gathering prospective migrants for Nova Scotia. He recruited from shipper Johann Adam Ohlenschläger at the Sachsenhausen Bridge, where his clerk G. T. Köhler answered inquiries and acted as intermediary with Count von Atzenheim, the British monarch's Frankfurt representative.[98] Dick himself, like Jefferson, knew what Johann Georg Keyßler had already noted in 1741: that the biggest and best tavern in Frankfurt was the Rotes Haus, where for fifty Kreuzer a room and board could be had, and where one was in touch with all the goings on in town.[99] By the time Jefferson visited Frankfurt, he was gratified to see Dick "keeper of the Rothen-house tavern at Francfort, a great wine merchant," and to note with relief, "the son of the Tavern keeper speaks English and French."[100] The critical importance of being located in the right place, with access to networks whose agents were fluent in the language of the dominant culture, became obvious to the first settlers in North America by the 1730s.

Part II

*Cultural Transfer and
Redefinition*

5

Liberty and Property in the Early Lutheran Settlements

I N DECEMBER 1769 the Virginia House of Burgesses received from the governor's council a report on petitions and orders that had been demanding attention since 1752. Most of these were from persons requesting grants for lands west of the Allegheny Mountains. Some of the Burgesses, themselves investors in the Ohio Company (founded in 1749) paid close attention. Among the petitioners in 1752 and again in 1754 had been those seeking a grant of thirty thousand acres "to the Revd. Geo[rge] Sam[ue]l Klug & others . . . lying between Green Briars to the South and Youghyougany to the North bearing [text missing] of Monangelie, upon a river called Goose River beginning at a run, known by the name of Muddy Run, up the River upon a white walnut tree marked M.T."[1]

The grant symbolically revealed how, within a generation, some members of the oldest German Lutheran congregation in Virginia had gathered together the shards of their cultural transferred notions of liberty and property to seize upon the British colonial possibilities. The Reverend George Samuel Klug was the Lutheran pastor at Hebron Evangelical Church in Culpeper County. Mühlenberg noted his robust constitution and overbearing physical presence, which dominated his congregation from his arrival in 1739 until death silenced his preaching in 1764. A native of Elbing, in Prussia, Klug had studied at Helmstedt with the famous church historian and theologian Johann Lorenz von Mosheim. Ordained in 1736 at Danzig, he had been recruited for the Virginia congregation by the pastor Johann Caspar Stoever, Sr., who had come to Hebron in 1733, and by Stoever's lay companions. Not a pietist by training or inclination, Klug cultivated close relations with the Anglican establishment; in 1752 he pleaded for a "small Allowance" for his "indigent Circumstances" and was voted twenty-five pounds by the governor and council for his "services for many years past to the neighbouring English Inhabitants of the said place, and his good character." Attempting to augment his income and cement his relationships to the established church, Klug assumed some of the duties of John Thompson, pastor of Saint Mark's, who spent much of his time successfully wooing the widow of Lieutenant Governor Alexander Spotswood.[2]

Klug's son Samuel followed his father's example; after study at the College of William and Mary, he took Anglican orders. Yet when the crisis with Great Britain broke, Samuel would become chairman of the Middlesex County Committee of Safety, for he was a member of a generation of German speakers able to reconcile traditional concepts of obedience to lawful authority with revolution in defense of liberty and property. Both father and son served German speakers as translators and scribes, copying and translating wills and other documents. In short, the Elbing native acted as the major religious and cultural broker and intermediary between his German-speaking congregation and the wider world of Virginia's planting society—of which he, a slaveholder on a glebe, wished to be counted as a member. Yet language ability was not enough. Pastor Klug and his Lutheran congregation remained isolated from the networks of communication and trade, cut off both from the Pennsylvania German settlements and from Halle's Georgia outpost. The Hebron settlement lacked communication and access to printed sources for reflection. The partial reconstruction of village sociability in this settlement pointed briefly toward extensive cultural transfer in the initial pattern of settlement, in wills, in building a German church and school. Yet that initial pattern had changed by the time of the speculators' petition.[3]

Hebron's isolation explains why only bits and pieces from transferred definitions of property and liberty eventually survived in that settlement. Klug intentionally cut himself off from Halle and its conceptions of stewardship; he yearned for recognition from the Anglican establishment. Yet Klug was not alone in his land speculations. The "others" named in the report to the House of Burgesses included seventeen persons drawn from the Hebron Valley settlement: these German speakers who emerged as well-to-do but culturally isolated worthies included members of the Wayland, Broyle, Aylor, and Tomas families. By the time the speculators began looking westward for new land, both the Seven Years' War and the success of other families may have provided reasons for their restlessness. Their definition of liberty apparently remained freedom from economic frustration; their view of property was one that favored personal risk, speculation, and aggrandizement. Yet neither that view of property, nor that "negative" conception of liberty would have correctly described the settlement in its early years, between 1725 and 1750.

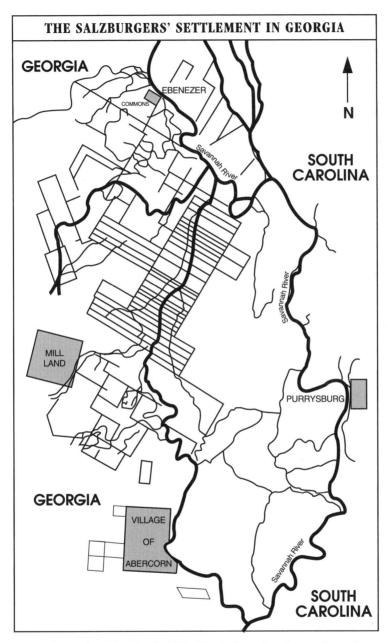

THE SALZBURGERS' SETTLEMENT IN GEORGIA

GEORGIA

EBENEZER

COMMONS

N

Savannah River

SOUTH CAROLINA

Savannah River

MILL LAND

PURRYSBURG

GEORGIA

VILLAGE OF ABERCORN

Savannah River

SOUTH CAROLINA

Original map by Win Thrall, 1992. Plat information drawn from "A Map of First Patents of Land in Madison County Virginia as of the Year 1740," by D. R. Carpenter, included in *Germanna Record No. 6* (Culpeper, Va., 1965). Keys to plats by area of origin drawn from author's archival work in German archives, from genealogies in various numbers of the *Germanna Record,* and from information supplied by Klaus Wust.

Transpose maps on pages 137 and 159. Legends to the maps are correctly placed.

I

Halle knew of Pastor Johann Caspar Stoever, Sr., and the laymen Michael Schmidt and Michael Holt, who came to the Reich in 1734 seeking financial support for this Virginia Lutheran group. That trip had been endorsed by Lieutenant Governor William Gooch, and the crucial connection had been made in London with Friedrich Michael Ziegenhagen and Heinrich Alard Butjenter, Halle-trained chaplains at the court chapel of Saint James, and with Heinrich Walther Gerdes and Heinrich Werner Palm, pastors of the Lutheren church in the Savoy. The tour of Hanseatic cities netted Hebron the future pastor, Georg Samuel Klug, as well as a substantial library and funds. An especially successful appeal in Hamburg allowed Virginians to change their money—3,000 pounds—through merchants; and Holt returned to Virginia. Stoever collected Klug and the library, especially Luther's works, and sent both back to Virginia, too. Stoever, a native of Frankenberg, in Hesse-Darmstadt, went on to Darmstadt to study theology with his distant relative Johann Philipp Fresenius, later a preacher in Frankfurt, and after 1748 *Senior,* or leader, of the city's Lutheran clerical body, the Frankfurt Ministerium. Fresenius promised to provide a conduit for monies to Virginia. Halle was aware of Virginia not only through Fresenius; the Halle fathers also knew of the Hebron congregation because Samuel Urlsperger, Augsburg patron of the Salzburgers at Ebenezer, Georgia, corresponded regularly with Fresenius about the need for charitable bequests to support these struggling North American missions. In 1737, in Hanover, Stoever published his account of the congregation, whose mission included not only the "awakening of the souls of your poor fellow believers, [but also] the conversion of the Heathen." On his return journey to Virginia with Schmidt, the elder Stoever died at sea.[4]

Hebron's connections to Halle started to decay. The pietists in Halle and London deplored the irregularity of the elder Stoever's pastoral training and service and his son's ordination in 1733 in a Pennsylvania barn by Christian Schulz, a recently arrived Lutheran pastor from Ansbach. But these difficulties had not prevented Halle in 1735 from collecting 12 Reichstaler from the Haupman de Rohly "for the poor evangelical congregation in Virginia." As late as 1748, Halle designated £8.14.0 for Pastor Klug's Virginia congregation, although £320 went to Pennsylvania and another £21 to Ebenezer.[5]

By 1742, Halle's representative Heinrich Melchior Mühlenberg had arrived in Philadelphia. He took an instant dislike to Johann Caspar Stoever, Jr., and had nothing good to report about Pastor Klug, in Virginia, either. The connection with Fresenius died with the elder

Stoever, for although Hesse-Darmstadt gave impressive amounts to the Philadelphia missions via Halle, nothing further was collected for Virginia. Klug, complaining of loneliness and isolation, visited Pennsylvania in the summer of 1749, but never again.[6] Mühlenberg's reports to Halle were cool and somewhat disapproving. He took offense at Klug's physical heartiness. The large and imposing Prussian enjoyed a regular income from his glebe land and slaves, while the diminutive Mühlenberg and his Halle companions struggled to survive on European charity and the insufficient salaries gleaned from congregational contributions in Penn's colony. Mühlenberg was not to blame for Halle's lack of interest in the Virginia congregation, but his descriptions cannot have helped. He noted on more than one occasion the three thousand pounds the Virginia German speakers had collected in the Reich and mentioned that they had a library, a church and a school. In 1753, Mühlenberg even questioned whether a love of books and the Word of God characterized Klug's ministry, since ("if the tale is true") he had heard that Klug had collected a large number of pamphlets and tracts and burned them. The Philadelphian suspected that the tracts were Halle's, but perhaps they were Moravian products, against which Klug informed Mühlenberg he labored hard.[7]

Mühlenberg thought that Klug's fondness for the Anglican church and Virginia society showed in the Prussian's having adapted himself to "innocent and allowable *adiaphora* [and being] on good terms with the English *county rector.*" Too much for Mühlenberg's taste, Klug lived "according to refined and sensuous taste"; he "was well liked by the established clergy. . . . because he was not careful about observing the proper *balance* with respect to *adiaphora* and probably went to extremes, he fell out with his congregation, but not with the established clergy."[8] Moravian travelers to Hebron told a slightly different tale, but one that also reflected the isolation Klug felt from Halle pietists, who nonetheless continued to influence him. In 1748, the Moravian pastor Mathias Gottlieb Gottschalk, a Brandenburger from Arnswalde, visited the Virginia Lutheran settlement. He was undoubtedly nervous because he met with hostility at the outset from Mathias Selzer, a wealthy trader and a son-in-law of Jacob Beyerle, the Lancaster trader and agent, who maintained close ties to the Moravians. Selzer did not share his father-in-law's fondness for the Herrnhuter. According to Gottschalk, Selzer warned him that if he presumed to preach at Hebron, "the [High] Germans . . . would take me by the neck. . . . they had such an excellent minister, that if the people were not converted by his sermons, they would certainly not be converted by my teaching." Arriving at Hebron, Gottschalk met Klug, who "received me with much love and courtesy." Learning that Gottschalk was Moravian, Klug appeared to be persuaded by his guest's explanation that the act of parliament recognizing the Moravians as an "ancient apostolic church" exempted them from the strictures leveled by Governor Gooch's proclamation of 3 April 1747 against "several Itinerant Preachers."[9]

Gottschalk expected a fellow Prussian, educated under von Mosheim, to boast a more impressive preaching style and to have retained his own regional dialect. After hearing Klug preach upon "the sufferings of Christ before the civil authorities, in just the same manner as the Hallensians," Gottschalk was shocked. Privately, Klug derided Mühlenberg and his cohorts. "Do you know what I think about them? I regard them as Pharisees, who impose unbearable burdens upon the people, which they are not willing to touch with a single finger." Yet, Gottschalk reported, Klug used Pietist rhetoric and "their forms of speech, partly because of his acquaintance with them, but mostly because during the ten or eleven years of his ministry his own stock has been exhausted and he now uses their writings for his sermons. Thus he has unconsciously adopted the principles and language of the Hallensians." Gottschalk concluded, his disappointment at Klug's preaching style palpable: "Probably he himself does not know how it happened. He studied in Helmstadt under the abbot Mosheim. He was born in Danzig."[10]

The Moravian visitor confirmed the pastor's isolation and gradual disintegration, relating that Klug had once drunk too much and on the way from Selzer's to the parsonage "lost his saddle, coat, and everything else from the back of the horse." Some of the congregation, Gottschalk believed, "are not satisfied with him . . . they object to him especially because, as they claim, he drinks too much." Inadvertently, the Moravian revealed why Klug used pietist rhetoric. Besides having run out of sermon material, Klug served in an area where "within a circle of a few miles, eighty families live . . . together, Lutherans, mostly from Württemberg." Klug's largely Swabian flock responded to Halle's materials and its rhetorical emphasis on "inwardness" and "rebirth," themes the north German orthodox Lutheran minister regarded with distaste. Klug's gradual disassociation from the Halle connections, his ties with his Anglican planter neighbors, his good relations with Governor Gooch, and his land speculation—all revealed not merely social climbing or ambition but also his cultural background and, increasingly, his isolation and depression. This Baltic-born, university-educated man accustomed to the intellectual and mercantile stimulation of Danzig or Helmstedt barely managed in the poor, rural community, albeit in beautiful surroundings. Klug had no apparent difficulty adjusting to the novelty of chattel slavery, which might have appeared to him to provide the North American answer to pastoral poverty Stoever had prescribed. (Stoever had come to this conclusion after observing the institution in a brief visit to North Carolina in the late 1720s.) Klug extended his horizons to Virginia's public life in the only way he knew, by cultivating associations he believed would help his family and his church.[11]

By the 1750s his ambitions reflected those of his parishioners who yearned for broader horizons. The speculators had patented land not at the center of the valley but at a greater distance from the church and the glebe. Klug's connections to Halle had nearly vanished, but ties to the planting and speculating society beyond the settlement on Robinson Run attracted others like himself who looked for possibilities wider than those offered by the isolated German settlement in the Virginia Piedmont. Originally, few arrivals on Robinson's Run had looked for wide horizons.

The Lutheran part of the Germanna group, disgruntled with Lieutenant Governor Spotswood's treatment of them, had in 1725 participated in the suit against him after he accused them of nonperformance of their obligations. Although an attorney, Henry Conyers, was appointed to represent the German-speaking settlers, the suit was dismissed. The early years of settlement—between 1725 and 1734—passed without pastoral care; Stoever did not arrive until 1733. A glebe house was built the following year on 193 acres bought from Wilhelm Zimmermann whose family quickly anglicized the name to "Carpenter."[12] The struggling community disbursed some.monies for drinks to celebrate the raising of the pastor's house and to seal the agreement with Carpenter. Both John Miller and Michael Clore gave unspecified gifts to the church the settlers named Hoffnungsvolle Kirche (church full of hope). After Stoever's arrival, Benjamin Borden and Jost Hite both became justices of the peace for Orange County. The selection of these merchant–land speculators, one an agent of Thomas Lord Fairfax, seemed to point to rapid rise of European worthies via the county court bench, the acknowledged institution of public influence in Virginia.[13]

The relationship of German speakers to county government and Virginia's Anglican culture assumed a more complex form than this early success suggested. Both Borden and Hite relocated quickly to the far side of the Shenandoah River; and from the more western counties of Frederick and Augusta, created in 1738 (including the territory that later became Rockingham County) came German speakers such as the Hites, the Bordens, and Peter Scholl, who would speak for their countrymen. Although some German speakers in the Shenandoah Valley were direct immigrants from Europe, most were second-generation migrants from

Pennsylvania or New Jersey, already secure in both the English language and English laws. Williamsburg authorities appointed them willingly to the bench.[14]

Orange County's German speakers, living in that area that became Culpeper County in 1748, never ascended the county bench, never served as sheriff, and never learned the duties of court clerk before the American Revolution. Two men did serve as officers in the county militia. One, the 1717 arrival Christopher Zimmermann, accumulated more than thirteen hundred acres between 1726 and 1749, marking him as one of the greatest landowners before his death. His rank as lieutenant in the Orange County Militia in 1735 was matched only by that of Johann Michael, the possible brother or son of Francis Michael, who served in 1739. Francis, probably Franz Ludwig Michel, counted as his friend de Graffenried, Swiss leader of the New Bern, North Carolina, settlement, perhaps explaining Johann's position. In neither case did the offices pass to the next generation.[15]

Spotsylvania and Orange County court records reveal glimpses of the emerging German-speaking leaders. Between 1725 and 1740 the settlers appeared infrequently before the county courts, but some names seemed to promise eminence. Michael Holt and his wife Elizabeth sued Friedrich Kabler in the Spotsylvania County court for debt in 1725. Holt, who accompanied Stoever on the 1734 voyage to Europe, seemed likely to emerge as one of the cross-cultural brokers. But his landholdings remained small—never more than 600 acres. His potential leadership role had been compromised by bad behavior on the trip. Even as he lay dying, Stoever sought to chastise Holt, rehearsing again "what wicked knaveries he hath raised there [in Danzig] against us and what damage in our collecting affairs by the ministry in London on his return he hath caused." By 1755 Holt and his sons removed to Orange County, North Carolina, where Michael, Jr., became a figure of great importance and power, as J. D. F. Smyth found him to be during the Revolution—a former justice of the peace, a Regulator, a staunch Loyalist, and a committed Lutheran.[16]

Even in this fledgling community, certain people transferred to the Virginia courts a litigious spirit nurtured in the villages' associations and tensions. After Stoever's death, both Michael Clore and George Utz, as elders of the congregation, sued the younger Stoever on 24 May 1740 for monies due the congregation out of the deceased pastor's estate. In 1736 George Moyer was presented by the grand jury for having "at the German Chappel insulted and abused Michael Cook and divers other persons there assembled together for celebration of divine worship." Moyer's son Christopher was sued in 1738 on two occasions, and George and his wife Barbara sued Friedrich and Catherine Baumgardner on 23

March 1743. Yet these were exceptional cases, for most German speakers' contact with the county court amounted to registering deeds, probating wills, and simple confession of debt. They avoided more elaborate actions calling for full command of the language—actions for slander, trespass, assault and battery, and pleas of trover and conversion, or assumpsit. Christopher Zimmermann, complaining "that he lives in a very publick place and is very much opprest by Travellers," petitioned for a license to open a tavern, giving German speakers access to familiar institution and securing his own central role in the settlement. The county agreed to the petition of Nicholas Yaeger, who had asked to be excused because of his age from working on the roads and mustering with the militia, but ordered "that he pay levy according to the Law." William Carpenter, likewise, was not fined by the justices for his presentment for failing to keep up the road "whereof he is overseer" in 1739. Otherwise, court day in Culpeper evolved before the Revolution without German speakers.[17]

One of the greatest landowners was the Reformed settler John Hoffmann, who moved to Robinson Run and contributed to the Lutheran pastor's salary. After arriving in 1729, Hoffmann built a gristmill and sawmill near the Great Mountains on the Run, securing the Spotsylvania County court's approval by petition. By 1764 his holdings were immense—over 3,525 acres—yet he never held a significant public office, confining himself to personal affairs, except for his aid to the Lutheran chapel, and later to a German Reformed chapel. Hoffmann cannily built his gristmill just to the southeast of Hebron's church, making his business the focal point of German life in what became Culpeper County. From this point, the Germanna Road, or Kirtley's Road, ran directly northeast, eventually skirting the new courthouse on the south at what became the town of Fairfax before ending at old Germanna.[18]

Hoffmann's Mill and the Lutheran church nearly marked the center of German settlement that ranged west against Garr's Mountain, and the even more rugged German Ridge beyond it. Settlers further east and to the south of the Germanna Road took their grains to Frey's Mill, off Frey's Road; those further east on Meander Run relied on Wayland's Mill, on Zimmermann's Road. Few German speakers lived further north than Uhl's (Yowell's) Mill on Fleischmann Run; Garr's Mill, on the Deep Run; and Crigler's Mill, on the South Fork of Gourdvine Run, all five to ten miles upstream from church and glebe. Clore's Mill, on Robinson Run northwest of the church, by Clore's Road, bespoke the wealth and power of its owner.

In 1735 Michael Clore, elder of the Lutheran congregation, sought the county court's permission to build a gristmill on Clore's Run. Since he had signed the bond for Susanna Crigler enabling her to act as administratrix of her deceased husband Jacob in April 1734, he expected her to sell him an acre of land on the opposite bank. She refused, and as late as 1741 Clore still sought an acre of Philip Roote's land for his mill. Clore had served a a road surveyor, taking over this position from Michael Holt in Spotsylvania County in 1727, and continuing in 1734 as the surveyor from Potato Run to the foot of the mountains. No stranger to litigation, he submitted a complaint to obtain the gristmill, suing for the church to recover the £11.3.0 due it from Stoever's estate; and on 24 November 1739 he sued Zachary Martin successfully for a small debt in the Orange County court. Clore's will and inventory testified to his influence by 1763. Family members, Pastor Klug, and neighbors were in debt to Clore's estate. An informal broker and the rural version of a village worthy, he had extended notes and bonds reflecting holdings in tobacco, corn, wheat, horses, hogs, and slaves.[19]

The landowner Christopher Zimmermann, also a tavern keeper, was sued in 1738 by Roger Oxford. In the action of trespass on the case, Oxford recovered a debt of £4.0.0 sterling, including damages. The jury included no German speakers. One of the county's first juries, empaneled to try the charge of assault and battery brought by James Porteus against Jonathan Fennell, included William Carpenter and Mark Finks, both German-speaking residents.[20]

Zimmermann and the other German speakers lacked the linguistic and legal skills their clever Scots-Irish counterparts employed. In 1748 Governor William Gooch sent his observations to the Board of Trade regarding a recent revisal of the colony's laws. He noted an item regarding a local court practice that had been altered, precisely because of new-comers in the Piedmont. "Numbers of Scotch Irish have removed from Pennsylvania into the upper Countys in this Colony leaving Debts behind him [sic] on Bonds," Gooch explained. "Their Creditors would transmit the Bonds after them and when Sued the Debtor sheltered himself under this Plea [non est Tactum] and thereby put the Plaintif to the choice of either loosing his Debt or bringing his Witnesses from other Colonys at great Expences to prove a Thing which generally was given up at the Witnesses Appearance. This Amendment is not consonant with the English Practice but necessary for the above Reason."[21]

The success of the Clores, Hoffmanns, Zimmermanns, Michels, Moyers, Carpenters, and Utzes reflected early settlement in the fertile valley bottoms. These families did not join Klug in the western land speculation of the 1750s. The group of families who did join in the speculation shared two attributes: they were all either original 1717 settlers or immediate sons of that charter group; and their properties lay not in the favored bottom along Robinson Run, but further back up the wooded slopes surrounding the stream. Not "marginal" people in the way that day laborers had been in the villages, their geographic location and associations with the pastor nonetheless bespeak outward orientation.

Michel Tomas, son of the 1717 settler of the same name, took over 156 acres by 1769, after which he disappeared from the records; perhaps he took up residence in the western lands confirmed in his name. Adam Broyle, son of the 1717 immigrant John Broyle, another of the speculators, was allied by the marriage of his brothers Michael and Mathew Broyle to Eva and Elizabeth Klug. Adam Broyle's sister Catherine married John Wayland; Adam Wayland, western speculator and son of an original settler, was Catherine's brother-in-law. Nor did the connections end there. Before his death, the original settler Thomas Wayland deeded some of his land to Michael Smith, the man who had accompanied Klug to Virginia. Smith's brother Mathew, also a 1717 immigrant, deeded his sons Nicholas and Mathew one hundred acres each in 1750 and 1753, but both brothers must have envied their cousin, young Michael. By 1772 he owned over one thousand acres. Both Nicholas and Mathew joined the western speculation after acquiring paternal lands.[22]

The Smith family had from the beginning been connected with the Barlers, whose progenitor Christopher arrived in 1717. Mathias Barler patented four hundred acres jointly with Mathias Smith in 1726. When Smith died without issue in 1747, he deeded his half of the patent back to Jacob Barler. When Adam Barler the speculator married, he chose Margarete, the daughter of Michael Smith, Jr., and received another one hundred acres from his father-in-law. Henry Aylor, son of the 1730 arrival Johann Pieter Aylor, could not claim direct descent from a 1717 family, but he married into one. Anna Margarete Crigler's father Jacob came from the original group. When Henry's mother married a second time, she chose a 1717 arrival, Henry Snider, who died in 1747, leaving his estate to stepson Henry Aylor.[23]

The German speakers joining Klug in speculation included Aylors, Waylands, and Broyles—all of whom were Württembergers—and Tomas, whose father had come from Nuenbürg, the Austrian town further up the Rhine from the Kraichgau. The outlying location of speculators' properties did not preclude intermarriage with the Clores, Holts, Hoffmanns, Utzes, Blankenbeckers, Fleischmans, and Criglers: those people who settled in the valley along the run itself. But the Württembergers, like Klug, seemed more willing to gamble on lands far removed from the safer horizons of the Virginia Piedmont.[24]

Settlement patterns among the first arrivals at Germantown promised to transplant Nassau-Siegen village customs. The *Straßendorf,* or one-street village, of many Reich hamlets was what the Moravian Gottschalk had in mind when in 1748 he described houses along Licking Run as "like a village in Germany, in which the houses are far apart."[25] On Robinson Run, a southwestern village pattern of long land strips running back from a central spine—the "fishbone" settlement—replicated itself. The earliest patentees guaranteed themselves pasture with access to water, and woods at the back of their lands. Nonetheless, the house built by Tilman Weaver in 1721 indicated immediate adaptation to North American conditions. Built of logs and incorporating double chimneys at each end rather than a central stove, it stood until 1924. Two floors were divided into two rooms each, and there was a spring under one of the separate rooms on the main floor, suggesting a desire for an amount of personal space that had been available only to the more well-to-do in the Reich villages.[26]

Although Gottschalk came from northern Germany, he clearly did not mean to imply that the settlements he visited were like the North German detached farms (*Einzelhöfe,* or *Einodhöfe*) of his childhood. Rather, he may have seen in his travels the three sorts of villages German-speaking settlers would have remembered. The nineteenth-century English clergyman Stephen Baring-Gould described one type, the "street of houses," as typical of Baden and much of the Rhineland. On strips of land behind the house, villagers kept an orchard and a vegetable garden; farther from the house, they tilled the arable fields, then grazed a meadow, then used woods. A second type of village stood near the most available water and the best soil. Houses stood apart from one another; orchards or well-manured vegetable gardens surrounded the village. Different kinds of property held by each owner or tenant could be widely scattered. Small villages of no more than fifty people and perhaps ten houses with church and Rathaus were a third type, which could be found in the Palatinate; and as hamlets grew, the practice of equal partition caused the patchwork quilt of properties to subdivide in bewildering variety.[27]

The "farm village" did not typify German-speaking settlement for long. Access to relatively cheap land militated against old patterns. The Robinson Run settlers of 1724 included the Blankenbecker, Utz, Scheible, Fleischmann, and Schnidow families. The properties of each paralleled those of the others, straddling Robinson Run, and averaging 156 acres. These first settlers came from villages along the Rhine or from the Kraichgau. The Fleischmann, Scheible, and Blankenbühler families departed from Neuenbürg am Rhein, originally an Austrian city near Karlsruhe; the Blankenbühlers (who in Virginia adopted the name Blankenbecker) originated from Gresten in Lower Austria. Michael Clore, who patented land both farther up the Run from, and just to the south of, these Rhinelanders, came from Gemmingen, the town named for the imperial knights of the Kraichgau who controlled Ittlingen. Clores, Schmidts, Zimmermanns, and Motz's from Bonfeld and Sulzfeld swelled the ranks of Kraichgauers. The Utz family and the Wilheits, the former from the Palatinate, the latter from a village under the archbishopric of Mainz, expanded the Rhenish character of the settlement.

This series of farms sprang up along Robinson Run as the stream wandered in a southeasterly direction down from the nearby mountains. By 1734, the glebe and by 1740 the Hebron church sat about one-half mile away to the west. The original contours of settlement and speech would change dramatically, by the 1740s: new arrivals swamped the original settlers. William Carpenter, for example, had patented four hundred acres in 1726 and added another 193 two years later. So too, did Matthias Crisler, who patented three hundred acres in 1728; fellow Württembergers Jacob Broyle and Thomas Wayland did the same. The Yaegers and Folgs came from Hesse-Darmstadt. The Silesians Michael Cook and Jacob Crigler joined them in acquiring holdings dwarfing the original farms. The Öhler, Schneider, and Käffer families from Botenheim and Zaberfeld, in the Neckarkreis, also patented lands further away from the Run. Between 1734 and 1747, when the Moravians noted the dominance of the Swabian, or Württemberg, dialect, these larger holdings belonged to Württembergers or Kraichgauers, and not to the Baden–Palatine settlers from west of the Rhine. The larger holdings of the Württembergers and further acquisitions by the Clores, Hoffmanns and Schmidts altered completely the original pattern of settlement and landholding.[28]

Gottschalk counted 80 families in 1747; by 1775 176 people took communion at Hebron Church, and the list of 133 family names suggests the growth of the German-speaking community. But the tide of English speakers and their African slaves dwarfed this increase. When Culpeper County was created in 1748, the list of tithable numbered 3,111. By 1750 the population grew to 5,078, of whom 3,508 were British or European, and 1,570 African. But in 1755, the number of whites increased to 4,884; while the slave population held steady. Between 1755 and 1773, the population grew 69.7 percent. In this growth spurt, the number of German speakers remained small. Members of various families did see military service during the Seven Years' War. In 1756 Adam Wayland, John Relsbach, Andreas Carpenter, Mathias Weber, Christopher Barler, Mathias Rouse and Michael Yaeger were each paid for seven to ten days of military service.[29] Yet neither in Gooch's comments about the developing Piedmont nor in the lists of county officers, especially justice of the peace or sheriff, did these German speakers figure.

Between 1749 and 1762, land patents for the area remained modest; only nine revealed 1,000 acres or more confirmed or transferred. Modest acreages—between 100 and 400 acres—remained the norm. The mixed economy depended on a combination of tobacco, fruit trees, corn, and wheat, and modest raising of live stock, largely cattle and sheep. Good bottom land that could be had for £10 per 100 acres in 1730 increased to £1.18 per acre in the 1760s. More commonly, poorer lands could be had for £0.18 the acre. As late as the 1760s, when seven hundred landowners had settled in the county, almost all owned between 100 and 400 acres. The powerful sixty-three owning over 1,000 acres included John Hoffmann, with 3,525; but this Reformed German was atypical. The modest life with which the German-speaking Lutherans remained content showed in the 1782 tax assessment. German speakers owned no "wheels," and the Carpenters, Wilheits, Yaegers, Waylands, Broyles, Fleischmanns, and other Hebron members paid an average tax of only £1; none owned more than six slaves and none more than five horses; most boasted fewer than a dozen head of cattle.[30]

The settlement pattern of German speakers in this Piedmont County reflected property acquisition, adaptation to North American conditions, and use of realty on a modest scale. These people did cultivate Catawba grapes in the lower-lying acres; German crops, including wheat, rye, and barley, were planted. But the most common Württemberg grain, *Dinkel* (spelt, German wheat); rape, for oil processing; and groats (*Grütze*) failed to be transferred. Flax was cultivated, as it had been in villages such as Neckarhausen (in Württemberg) and other spinning centers; but so were the *Amerikaner* crops tobacco and maize. The domestic economy of the southwest German villages never completely revived on these farmsteads. No record survives of the actual appearance of the homes; estate inventories remain cryptic, noting only on occasion the odd "parcel of Dutch books," suggesting that outside the church library there was little access to the German pietist works that had been common in Württemberg. One inventory at least notes a "Dutch stove"; the occasional brandy still appears in the listing of personalty, and bills paid to a "Dutch doctor," suggests a German-speaking expert in physic. The presence of pewter eating ware and the absence of English tinware or (in wills) references to silver family seals reveal modest retention of domestic items. But these German-speaking households quickly became indistinguishable from others in the county, save that they rarely exceeded four hundred acres in size. No contemporary comment remarked on peculiarities of crops, agricultural methods, or building appearances.

Both the German language and the settlement's location conspired together to ensure isolation not merely from English speakers by also from the Reich itself. No agents returned from the settlement claiming inheritances before the Revolution. Neither do village inventories mention the Virginia settlement, or potential heirs known or rumored to be living there.[31]

One Hebron settler indicated an interest in recovering his estate from the Reich. In 1773 Ludwig Fischer, a resident since 1739, ordered that "if my German Estate Should be Recovered, it Should be equally divided amongst all my Children."[32] A single connection using a network of trade did find its way from property settlements in Europe far into the back country at a remarkably late date. In 1784 Ralph Landenberg, a wealthy wine merchant, died at Salisbury, England, after a long life in Castle Street, Westminster, in the parish of Saint Martin in the Fields. Originally from Frankenthal, northwest of Mannheim, Landenberg left £27.16.8 to each of the six children of his deceased sister Catharina Elizabetha Wilhemina Lotspeich. In 1795 two of those children, Joanna Frederica Lotspeich Jacoby and John Christopher Lotspeich, recovered their shares in Virginia and in Bourbon County, Kentucky, respectively.[33] Their brother, Johann Wilhelm Lotspeich, son of the tailor Johann Conrad Lotspeich and Catharina Landenberg, had arrived in Virginia from Philadelphia in 1772, apparently bringing his brother and sister. His sister married a late arrival in Virginia, Lucas Jacoby, who had come to Virginia with his father, John Daniel Jacoby, in about 1760. The father of the Lotspeichs died in 1778. Despite Frankenthal's advantageous location on a major trade route through which many German-American agents regularly passed, no recovery attempt had been made. Instead, only the connection to their wealthy uncle in London secured the property.[34]

II

The devisal of property upon heirs by these German speakers mixed southwestern village preferences for the equal treatment of children with concern for the security of a homestead. Of the 133 families who comprised the Hebron settlement up to the Revolution, 36 heads of family left last wills and testaments—an unusual number, given the reliance upon intestate procedures in the German southwest. The earliest will, that of Johann Just Broyle, made when the community was still in Spotsylvania County, was brief and to the point. In labored English, Broyle announced his intention "to setel my affairs." Everything went to his wife; and after her death, "my land, Goods, and Catel to be so equally Divided amongst all my Children mail [sic] and female."[35]

The "charter group" of founding families from 1725 to 1736 numbered fifty-six, of whom half chose to write wills protecting their families and properties. Many wills were written in German, the clerk noting that only the translated version could be admitted to record. The forms used to compose the wills reveal both the role of Pastor Klug and of pietist sentiments in the settlement. A half dozen of the twenty-eight wills set apart in parentheses redemptive language common in German Lutheran pietist wills of the eighteenth century. Most refer to the trust "for perfect Remission and Pardon of my Past Sins & follies and through the Merits and Mediation of my Blessed Saviour and Redeemer Jesus Christ." The more usual trinitarian salutation common in the Reich may have been in the originals, especially if Klug wrote, and not merely translated, a will. Klug and his son provided English translations of wills "being wrote in an unknown language," and learned to omit peculiarities that clerks obliged to make fair copies dismissed as irrelevant details. The structure of these documents in their original language suggests a partial transferral of religious sentiment. The German-speaking pastor would have leaned how to draft such documents from handbooks that instructed all educated persons, not merely court clerks.[36]

Of the "charter group" of fifty-six, twenty-nine men with daughters left deeds and wills. Fifteen of the latter group provided their daughters with land, not just personalty.[37] Occasionally later testators continued this practice—for instance, Johannes Hirsch (Deer), who in 1781 ordered that his daughters Mary and Elizabeth each be given seven pounds, and that his married daughters Dorothy Fleischmann and Eve Bohannon each be given three pounds "in the old way to be raised out of my Estate."[38] Since he gave dower and courtesy, the usual one-third of estate and lifelong occupancy, to his wife in both realty and personalty, and his home place to his youngest son, Moses, upon the mother's death, "the old way" seems to refer to the southwest German practice of providing equally for daughters and sons.

The earliest settlers also intended to keep the initial "home place" within the family while devising lands in the vicinity to sons and daughters equally. Forty of the fifty-six provided by deed or will for the retention of the original homestead. German speakers devised these home places upon sons, daughters, middle children, and in a few cases, the youngest child.

The practice of settling upon the youngest, "Borough English" customs or *Minoratsuccessionrecht,* was not exclusive to any one area of the German southwest, or any particular religious or economic pattern. It was more common in Alpine or heavily wooded areas such as the Black Forest; or the Upper Palatinate, in Bavaria. But instances occurred elsewhere, often a matter of family preference. Michael Clore settled his home place upon his youngest son; his son Peter did the same when he wrote his will. In the Wilheit family, Johann Michael left his property in 1746 to Philip; Philip's son Tobias in 1761 followed custom by dividing the home place between his youngest sons Jesse and Wilhelm. Peter Weber in 1763 had already by deeds settled 200 acres of land upon his sons before giving his home plantation to his two youngest daughters in his will in 1763. Weber harbored plans for the future, for he received patents on 1,295 acres in 1762, but his death within the year frustrated his ambitions. Other members of the community, including Nicholas Blankenbecker, Friedrich Kepler, and Christopher Zimmermann, also settled their home estates either upon middle sons or upon grandsons.[39]

The German speakers who wrote wills did not always display a mastery or understanding of the common law. Provisions that in the Reich would have been placed in inter vivos agreements (the *freiwillige Vermögensübergabe*) made their way into wills. Such trust provisions were not enforceable, for only upon the probate of the will could they become binding. Heinrich Schneider's 1742 will devised lands and chattels in exchange for an oral agreement from his grandson, who promised both "to honour and respect me and my dear wife Dorothea during our lives and to find us due food and clothing and other necessarys of life," as well as to care for a widowed aunt, Anna Magdalena Aylor. Michael Schmidt willed everything to his son in February 1760, reserving its use "as long as I live"; a provision one would have expected in a deed or indenture. Later, in 1779, Jacob Manspeil correctly drew up an indenture with James Shearer and his wife, handing over his property upon a promise and condition of maintenance for himself and his wife in old age.[40]

The German-language wills reveal indifference to, or positive avoidance of, primogeniture. In devolving both realty and personalty upon daughters and sons, the founders of the Hebron settlement did little to enhance the potentially precarious state of their wives. Virginia's laws of dower and courtesy were, in comparison with those of some other colonies to the north, comparatively generous, as they were in other planting provinces, Maryland and South Carolina. Both the scarcity of women and the desire to keep land and slaves within the family contributed until 1705 to women getting dower in a combination of realty and personalty. Rarely did one of the German testators allow a wife more than the normal dower and courtesy by specifying that she have the ability to sell or otherwise alienate property as she saw fit. Nor did these testators make their wives executrices. Between five and seven of the fifty-six — depending on how one reads their intentions — gave legal powers or status to their widows. In this, the Hebron settlers conformed to the customs of the German southwest which gave women relatively little real power over any property except that which they had brought into the marriage. In the case of these immigrant families, lands were patented in the husbands' names; German-speaking wives exercised no formal powers over them. Contrary to German private-law practices, the wives' personal effects brought into the marriage were not handled separately in these wills. A provision of Virginia's laws may explain this oversight. Unlike Pennsylvania, where creditors had to be paid before dower was given to widows, Virginia gave primacy to the widow's rights; only then were creditors allowed to press claims. In such a context, German speakers felt relatively secure that widows could be provided for by giving them their "seat" for life as well as the household furnishings—the nearly universal provision in all the surviving wills. The net effect of such practices, however, was that married German women had fewer privileges and less power under a common-law system. Nor could a wife, given the language barriers, use the public sanction of the court against a wastrel, spendthrift, or adulterous husband as she had in the village.[41]

Deeds and wills should not be read too literally. Informal agreements between German-speaking husbands and wives controlled reality differently than did the formal face of the law. When Johann Leonard Ziegler died in 1757, his will divided property among sons and daughters, specifying as coexecutors his wife, Barbara Zimmermann, and Frederick Zimmermann. The will and previous deeds are silent concerning 200 acres which Barbara by deed of gift granted to her daughter Elizabeth on 15 November 1758.[42] Similar puzzles surround John Hoffmann's will, probated in 1772. Hoffmann made sure that his sons and daughters both received land, although the sons received 290 acres each and the daughters 150. For unexplained reasons, the eldest son, John, later issued a series of deeds in exchange for the symbolic consideration of one dollar, vesting in his brothers and sisters title to the land left him.[43] Such arrangements suggest that settlers of the founding generation used British-American legal procedures with some confidence, but informal arrangements regulated relations and testified to the persistence of "the old ways."

In 1776, Catherine Wayman deeded a slave to her daughter at marriage as a gift, but the full deed for her property was committed to her son-in-law only upon his promising Catherine maintenance: thus Adam Utz, grandson of Georg Utz, was bound to the customs of his homeland through the American institution of chattel slavery, in a unique use of a common-law mechanism by a German-speaking woman.[44]

Hebron's relative isolation from Pietist networks, however, conspired further to undercut married women's power over property in support of household integrity. When William Carpenter died in 1745 he had lived in the community since 1726, even deeding land in 1733 to the trustees of the church for its glebe. But his will specified that after his wife Elizabeth's death, Catherine Proctor would inherit everything except for two slaves reserved for nephews John and William, and half of the dying man's mill to nephew Andrew. He reserved one slave for his brother John.[45]

His brother contested the will; the document had been made under duress and "by the Persuasion of one Catherine Proctor the Devisee in remainder in the sd Will." Further, John asserted, his brother had not been of "Disposing mind and Memory"; moreover, he had never published the document as his last will. In his deposition, Richard Burdyne refuted John's objections, stating that he had been called by John himself to come to William's house when William lay dying after being kicked by a horse. The dying man, "in Great Pain as appeared by his Sighs and Groanes . . . could not rest long in one Place and was supported by his wife who was some times in the House & some times out but chiefly out of the Room but chiefly by one Cath. Proctor who lived in the sd William Carpenters Family and was reputed his Whore by Sevl Persons." Burdyne believed William Carpenter to be fully in his senses. Burdyne noticed in the will he witnessed that nothing was being left to John Carpenter and remonstrated with the dying man, saying, "Wm you must take notice as you are going to appear before the God of all soules, do Justice to your own Flesh and Blood." Moved by his neighbor's words, the dying man remembered "my poor Brother John who has been with me in my Travels & Distresses & came unto this Country with me, I will give him a Young Negro." Catherine Proctor demanded to know which slave, but Burdyne objected that if the name were specified, John Carpenter would get nothing if the slave died before the will was probated. Demanding to know which slave John Carpenter should have, Proctor was rebuffed by the dying man, who "seemed to be Angry with her."

The other witness, John Floyd, was called into the room, and Carpenter told him that the paper was his last will. Asking what the will contained, Floyd was told, "It was no Occasion to hear what was in it," and he signed. Carpenter told Burdyne to add the names of Nicholas Yaeger and Andrew Garr as his executors, although Floyd could not recall if he was in the room when this was done, and both witnesses admitted that after the executors' names were added Carpenter did not again indicate or "publish" that the document was his will. Catherine Proctor then put both the document and William Carpenter's purse, from which he had paid Floyd "the heaviest Pistercen" (1 silver pistercen = £0.05 sterling), into a chest "which she Locked and put the Key in her Pockett and . . . at the same time Eliz. the wife of the sd Wm Carpenter was sometimes in the Room with them and some times out but . . . she was very seldom in the Room." Floyd concluded that the mark on the will next to his name "is not the Mark he Usually makes use of and that he does not know whether the Paper Produced was the same he signed and that he had Drunk Cyder at the House but was not Drunk norther (sic) does he Use to get Drunk and that this Deponent Cant Write." Both deponents were English speakers; one unable to write. Their depositions were lengthy, Carpenter's complaint short; no depositions were taken from Elizabeth Carpenter or Catherine Proctor.

By the time John Carpenter made his own will in 1782, he had already, in 1762, deeded lands, including the original patent of 1728 made to Andrew Kirker, to his sons. It appears that John took over his brother's neighboring tract; Catherine Proctor was unable to sustain her claims under the will. But William Carpenter's wife Elizabeth vanishes completely from all records. Her control over property and the household had apparently been nonexistent. One wonders if the dying William Carpenter recalled that according to German law, what he was attempting was illegal. As long as a blood relative lived, German private law forbade the alienation of property to an outsider. Such proscriptions reflected the old Sprüchwort "He who would die a holy death must leave his property to the rightful heir" ("*Wer will gut und selig sterben, läßt sein Gut zum rechten Erben*").[46]

One German-speaking wife felt similar restrictions placed on her liberties by her husband, Heinrich Hoffmann, a later arrival and the younger brother of Johann Hoffmann, one of the original 1714 Siegeners. Arriving from Siegen in the early 1740s, by profession a carpenter, Hoffmann brought with him a flask inscribed with the date of his acceptance into the guild and the saying "Vivat dass Lehrbarhandwerck der Zimmerleuth" ("Long live the skilled handicraft of carpenters"). He patented land in 1746 and by 1764 owned two hundred acres. At some point during his twenty years in Virginia, he returned to Siegen, for on 14 August 1765 he wrote, without regard to form, a German-language will. "I find my Self Sick, and Dont now [sic] when it shall please god to call for me, and . . . I have not made any will since my Return from Germany," he wrote, noting the document's informality; he explained that he was uncertain he would "be able either to make it or Cause it to be written in another Form." His wife Catherine was to live on his plantation "that She may get her Livelyhood thereon, and She Shall bring up the Children (that are as yet helpless) in the Fear of God, that they may not only labour but Come to the Knowledge of God and the Holy Scriptures." His three eldest children were each to be given five pounds cash or equivalent goods; they would divide equally the balance, "land, Stock, Household furniture, working Tools, Cloaths, Books, Money, &c and I Desire that no one Shall endeavour to cheat the other for Fear there Should arise Quarrels amongst them." The eldest children were charged to raise the younger should their mother die, to "provide For them instead of parents that they may be brought up a[s] Christians, that they my [*sic*] deal Faithfully one with another." Hoffmann ordered: "I Don't allow my wife to marry again upon my Land: I leave the Right of the Land to the Boys and they shall not Sell it unless they sell it to one another; also I leave them my Tools for I hope they will learn to make use of them." By 21 December, Pastor Klug had translated the will, and on 19 June 1766 both documents were proven in court and the English version recorded.[47]

Hoffmann's restrictions on his wife's control of property illustrate the gradual shift among German speakers away from one of the two objectives German private law had supported in the Reich. The liberties and privileges of both parties to a marriage came into increasing conflict with the need to pass on two viable streams of properties—maternal and paternal—to heirs. In the case of German speakers in Virginia, the latter objective won out. Hoffmann's is an unusual will, almost singular in mentioning education and religion. An almost total absence of and provisions for education, and of bequests left for the church, characterizes the wills and deeds of the earliest German Lutheran settlement. Despite German speakers' need to provide their own pastors and churches, and schools in their own language, the founding generation clung to older habits. Family property did not support such institutions in the German southwest, save among the very wealthy; Virginia Germans retained those habits. Except for the late-arriving Hoffmann, only Peter Clore specifically set aside twelve pounds that "shall be Kept out of my Estate for the Schooling of my Children."[48]

By the 1740s, Hebron boasted pastor, church, parsonage, glebe, and a school. Yet even the incidence of will writing in the settlement highlighted a dissolution of an initially promising cultural cohesion. The twenty-eight wills of the fifty-six founders were probated over the entire period between the 1730s and 1790. But thirteen of the twenty-eight were probated between 1760 and 1779. During the 1760s, ten of the founders passed from the scene; and Pastor Klug died—intestate—in 1764. His inventory of estate, taken by his non–German-speaking friends Elliott Bohannon, Benjamin Powell, and Ephraim Rucker, totaled £361.13.6, including six slaves with a total value of £260. His speculative ventures, perhaps interrupted by Pontiac's Rebellion, had proved unsuccessful.[49] With the passing of Klug and many charter members, Hebron Lutherans contacted Halle's network at Philadelphia for spiritual support. They secured the European-educated Johannes Schwarbach and his wife, Anna

Margarete Roemer, both from the Baden towns of Seelbach and Koeppl-stein. A schoolmaster by profession, Schwarbach had arrived in Penn-sylvania in 1751 and served in York County until 1763. (He had been authorized to preach and catechize there by Mühlenberg's Ministerium of Pennsylvania, organized in 1748.) Ironically, although the Hebron congregation secured him for the purposes of education, the German school, one of the few operating in colonial Virginia, remained closed for lack of support during Schwarbach's tenure.[50]

Anglican neighbors and their priest, the Reverend William Meldrum, queried Schwarbach for his ordination credentials, since he apparently began administering the sacraments. Fearing intervention from Williams-burg and bereft of the close relations Klug had cultivated with the es-tablished church, two delegates from Hebron journeyed with Schwarbach to Philadelphia, where he was ordained in June 1766. At ordination, Schwarbach took an oath acknowledging the authority of the Ministerium of Pennsylvania, formally linking Hebron to Pennsylvania and the Halle network. Within two years, Adam Garr and Adam Wayland—the one Bavarian, the other a Württemberger—reported to Philadelphia that they were delighted with Schwarbach but could not pay him adequately. Forced to contribute to the "English Parish Levee" to support the An-glican pastor, they acknowledged that the church building was in a dilapi-dated and inadequate state due to "our predecessors [who] ought not to have squandered the collections so foolishly, but we cannot alter what has already been done. The little that remains is now administered prop-erly."[51]

By the mid-1760s, this German Lutheran settlement, some three hun-dred miles from Philadelphia, was drawing closer to the orbit of Halle's missionary network, over which Mühlenberg presided. How Hebron's monies and library of the 1730s were mismanaged remains obscure; the earliest church records before 1754 have disappeared. Even records of the names of baptismal sponsors, which show the linkages in property relationships that traditionally bind interested families to one another, are absent.

Restrictions on naturalization and denization had never been used to discourage settlement in Virginia or to harass German speakers. Thomas Lord Culpeper's pioneering act of 1680 served as a model for all the colonies; and Virginia developed the system by which the governor technically controlled naturalization. The Hebron settlers were natural-ized without difficulty—many of them simultaneously in February 1743. Those who were not naturalized, however, were not kept from acquiring property or devising it to their heirs or to church or school.[52] Governor Spotswood's removal in the 1720s, and Governor Gooch's laconic style of leadership, which put a premium on good relations with the county leadership and the House of Burgesses, contributed to Hebron's liberty to do as it pleased.[53]

Initial cultural transfer of the German private-law system revealed what people valued and held dear as they settled in the fishbone pattern on Robinson Run. Parents' awkward misuse of wills rather than indentures to secure care showed how difficult connection between the two private-law systems could be, especially in the absence of open discussion of how "old ways" could be preserved, and what objectives were being sought. The initial pattern of devolving land equally, even at times upon daughters, suggested further a close tie to village norms of equal treatment of children. Yet the notion of property as intimately tied to domestic happiness and as a mechanism for making alliances solidifying village relationships did not survive intact. Wives in Hebron seldom were empowered to act as executrices; the will provisions tended rather quickly to favor sons over surviving widows; and the Catherine Proctor incident revealed in shocking fashion not only the irrelevance of Pietism's moral sanctions in one of the leading families but also the powerlessness of a wife, who was not even consulted as her husband's mistress controlled the deathbed scene in the absence of a pastor. As the settlement spread out further from the Run, speculators turned their eyes even further westward, not towards sustaining the church or school, or securing contact with other German speakers.

The physical isolation of these German Lutherans, their inability to obtain access to news—not only news from home but also information about how other German speakers dealt with the novelties of North America—explains much. The fragmentary evidence regarding domestic life at Hebron suggests the relative weakness of Pietism as an enforcer of domestic virtues. The wives of Hebron could not successfully demand that the school remain open; they never challenged the mores of their husbands or other males in the settlement; and if moral qualms ever existed about the rapid adaptation to slavery, no such evidence survives. Only belatedly did a succeeding generation, alarmed after Pastor Klug's death, move to revive the school, obtain a pastor, and admit that the congregation's considerable resources had been squandered. No one, certainly not Mühlenberg, would have predicted such outcomes in 1740. What happened at Hebron illustrated why, given the privileges of liberty of British North America, Halle and its missionaries became alarmed. Property, in the form of slaves, and land speculation; and liberty, in the guise of movement outward, and away from close-knit settlements and churches, lured people away from the sociability and exchange that could encourage a stewardship of, and a sense of responsibility for, the common weal. Liberty, in this context, could only mean freedom from any form of restraint—whether of movement, aggrandizement, association, or belief. Yet Hebron's early years did not point inevitably in this direction. Its contemporary settlement on the Savannah River in Georgia showed why—given closer ties to a network of information and support—other transferred definitions of property and liberty were also possible for German-speaking Lutherans.

III

Lutherans in Georgia never confronted British authorities like Alexander Spotswood. As Pastor Johann Martin Boltzius observed, settlers delighted at the absence of "difficulty, oppression and violence, which is exactly the famous English liberty."[54] Despite Boltzius's apparent definition of liberty as the absence of constraint, Halle's carefully cultivated connection to Britain demanded the transfer of more positive definitions of both liberty and property than German speakers from the Reich's southwest brought to North America. The tractable Salzburger exiles put into Halle's hands the malleable instruments with which to construct those definitions. And they knew the wrong definitions, too. After all, it had been Halle's own Anton Wilhelm Böhme who had unerringly identified the libertarian, wrong-headed visions of the Reich's emigrants in 1711. It was exactly their false hopes of "good days" and "Liberty," driving German speakers "in hopes of possessing goods and lands, houses and gardens, to tear them away from the burdens of authority in Germany," that Böhme warned against. These people had been promised "much freedom," but it was a "false freedom," namely that of "self-willed" licentiousness. True Chistians of the new order would not act like these people, who resembled Old Testament Israelites who "wanted to possess lands, goods, and acres to divide them among themselves."[55]

The expulsion of the Salzburgers in the winter of 1731 had followed secret meetings and ritual oath-takings binding clandestine Lutherans together in mutual covenants of protection that perhaps predisposed them to a more positive definition of both liberty and property. The most famous of these ceremonies occurred at Schwarzach on 13 July 1731 and at a later convening of a *Salzbund* in August. At Schwarzach, a blacksmith from Hüttau urged a concrete sign that participants affirm their statement of faith. He suggested that each put his finger into a salt cellar. That many of the assembled interpreted this ritual differently they later attested, some believing that they affirmed Jesus's command that his followers be the "salt of the earth," and others that the ritual was to remind them

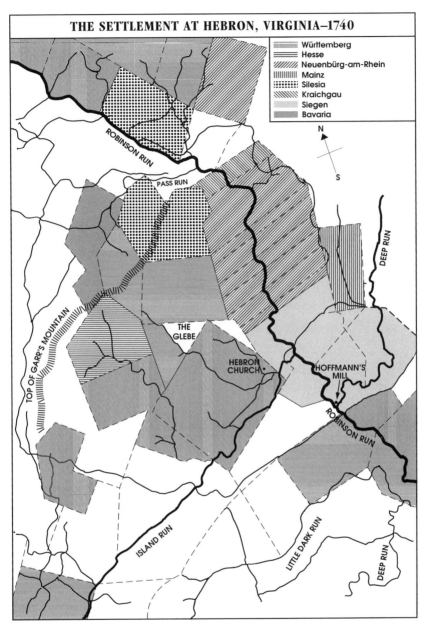

THE SETTLEMENT AT HEBRON, VIRGINIA–1740

Württemberg
Hesse
Neuenbürg-am-Rhein
Mainz
Silesia
Kraichgau
Siegen
Bavaria

ROBINSON RUN

PASS RUN

N

S

DEEP RUN

TOP OF GARR'S MOUNTAIN

THE GLEBE

HEBRON CHURCH

HOFFMANN'S MILL

ROBINSON RUN

ISLAND RUN

LITTLE DARK RUN

DEEP RUN

Original map by Win Thrall, 1992. Plats and dimensions drawn from
reproductions of the original map "The Saltzburger's Settlement in Georgia,"
by John Gerard William De Brahm, *History of the Province of Georgia*
(Wormsloe, Ga., 1849).

that, like sheep, they were bound by a common source of nourishment. By August, the salt ceremony assumed the meaning of an oath of loyalty to one another, and to a religious confession.[56]

This ceremony, drawn from the local traditions of the *Handwerker* of the Pongau Valley, became part of the collective memory of emigrants in Prussia, Holland, and North America. The Georgia-bound emigrants encountered a similar ceremony, reminiscent of medieval oaths of fealty and homage, in Britain. Despite the Georgia trustees' intentions to ensure foreign Protestants English liberties, and property rights identical to those enjoyed by subjects of the realm, nothing in the charter of 1732 made this clear. British supporters assured the Salzburgers and Pastor Boltius that denization would bring with it all the rights and privileges of Englishmen. But on 21 December 1733 Captain Thomas Coram, as deputy of the trustees, came aboard ship and read aloud to the Salzburgers their rights and duties. After affirming in chorus that they would carry out their duties, each person had to come forward, touch the paper, and shake the hand of the deputy. The parallel with the salt ceremonies in Salzburg struck the departing emigrants forcibly.[57]

Naturalization, denization, and property law at first remained vague in colonial Georgia and initially threatened to complicate property devolution in the Ebenezer settlement. In 1751 Boltzius—mistakenly—informed his Augsburg correspondent Samuel Urlsperger that the settlers enjoyed all the rights of the English just as if they had been in the realm. By 1761 a colonial statute allowed every free white male of at least twenty-one years of age who could prove six years' residence and ownership of fifty acres of land to vote in local elections. However, only a naturalized subject or a free-born subject could hold elective office. In 1765 a second statute in the now-royal colony authorized the naturalization of all male and female persons, of any nation and color, "born of free parents." Neither clarification disturbed Ebenezer or its environs.[58]

Instead, accident cleared up notions of property and its importance. Henry Newman, writing for the SPCK, which also supported the Salzburger resettlement in Georgia, informed Urlsperger that settlers would be given lands in perpetuity "free from all Vassalage and Servitude, liable to no Rent for the first Ten Years, and then only to the small acknowledgement of Ten Shillings per Annum, for every hundred Acres." But settlers demanded information about inheritance and succession rights. A year later, Newman reluctantly admitted that the lands allotted the settlers were held in freehold tenure, but only "to themselves and their Heirs male for Ever."[59]

British officials doubted the wisdom of settling the lands in male tail; Governor Jonathan Belcher of Massachusetts correctly predicted problems. James Oglethorpe, the colony's philanthopic founder, remained adamant. Oglethorpe believed, correctly, that only by keeping the farmsteads small, free of chattel slavery, and settled upon male heirs could Georgia prevent the growth of large plantations sustained by slavery. South Carolina's inventive reading of the law of dower as well as other forms of property, proved him correct. But as news of Georgia's restriction spread, protests erupted. The initial transports of 1734 and 1735 had settled at "Old Ebenezer." This unproductive area they abandoned in 1736, partly because of more fruitful lands along Ebenezer Creek. But abandonment of the colony also stemmed from the colony's land policy. Boltzius informed Urlsperger that a widow from nearby Purrysburg, South Carolina, had wanted to join Ebenezer but changed her mind upon learning of the restriction. In addition, Ebenezer's schoolmaster left for Pennsylvania or New York for the sake of his wife and daughters.[60]

Despite Oglethorpe's obstinacy, during his absence in the spring of 1739 the trustees abolished male tail succession. Ebenezer evolved in the 1740s into a fee-simple tenure settlement similar to those in the New England provinces. The small size of farms, partly explained by terrible mortality rates and resulting labor shortages, continued to keep the Salzburger settlement an insignificant threat to the native population, and one matching the ideals of the trustees, patrons like von Münch and Urlsperger in Augsburg; and the Halle fathers.[61] Boltzius condemned settlers who wished to exterminate the Indians, "the first and legitimate inhabitants and hence . . . the rightful owners of this land."[62] Trustees discouraged contact with the native peoples; neither Halle not Augsburg intended conversion as a prime objective. Their reluctance sprang from skepticism about Moravian claims regarding progress among Native Americans. But mostly, opposition to missionary outreach flowed from Halle's commitment to the notion that property had first to be worked by trained, educated, self-sufficient subjects who would promote the good of both the Crown and the gospel.

The creator of Halle's Francke Foundations had struggled to avoid status as a *Privatanstalt* and had secured royal recognition as a public foundation. So too, the SPCK in London, Halle, and Augsburg assumed from the beginning that Ebenezer would mix the private industry of its farmers and artisans with the objectives of a public, mercantile economy, providing an example of how a pietist German social experiment worked. An orphanage and old folks' home stood at the settlement's center, supporting education and training in ancillary industries and contributing to the self-support mission. Ebenezer's founders never presumed to exclude public patronage from their mix of the public and private realms, a mix unremarkable for the early eighteenth century.

Gotthilf August Francke described Ebenezer to the two Georgia ministers Boltzius and Gotthilf Israel Gronau as a "city upon a hill" and a "fortress of all refugees" in a 1743 letter written at a time when the settlement seemed capable of sustaining its orphanage by means of agricultural success plus milling, sericulture, and the contributions from Halle and Britain. Ironically, in the very next year, 1744, the orphanage had to give up its residents, who were farmed out to families in need of labor. The 250-odd members of the settlement in 1743 had used the orphanage building not only to shelter genuine orphans and widows but also as a boarding house for children of impoverished settlers, and the aged. Until 1744, the experiment successfully prevented the allure of hiring their labor out to other private owners from distracting people from community works. Throughout the 1740s, after an initial 27 persons applied in 1742 for fifty-acre allotments, the number of applications remained modest—two or three a year. Applications peaked at eight in 1745 before falling back again.[63] But the arrival of the Swabian transports in the 1750s transformed this pattern, the dialect spoken at the settlement, and definitions of both liberty and property.

Private farming attracted the Salzburgers; moral suasion accomplished voluntary communal work. These early settlers found even a hint of forced public labor (*Frondienst*) intolerable. In 1738 Boltzius was already noting his congregation's "desire to move to their plantations and live there, as necessity demands. For many plantations lie at a distance of four to six English miles from our place, and it will not be possible to come here every evening . . . However, since they emigrated from their homeland not for the sake of land but for the sake of the word of God, they should well deliberate together as how they could arrange to retain the diligent public practice of God's word and prayer without hindrance from their external occupations."[64] Boltzius and other pietists struggled continually with their dependence on "worldly goods" and their concerns with the "external occupations" needed for the sustenance of a spiritual community. Halle's vision provided the theoretical understanding of how to use material goods to accomplish the ends of a spiritual community, but practical tensions sharpened in the 1750s as the physical settlement pattern of Ebenezer altered suddenly. Just as the Virginia settlement on Robinson Run failed to remain a miniature version of a Straßendorf, so too did Ebenezer.

Initially, the "fishbone" pattern had characterized Ebenezer. Settlers occupied town lots sixty feet by ninety feet; garden plots abutted onto the village in parallel columns, with forty-five additional acres per settler nearby—running parallel to and straddling Ebenezer creek as it flowed into the Savannah. The initial transports of 1734, 1735, 1739, and 1741 had brought a small number of "Palatines"—in reality not only genuine Pfälzers but also Kraichgauers—into predominantly Salzburger Ebenezer. The town heard no dramatic alteration in speech, saw no change in settlement pattern.

Both the mortality rate, however, and the dogged attempts of Boltzius and his brother-in-law Pastor Gronau to root out folk customs they thought incompatible with Halle's version of Pietism conspired against the emergence of a "charter group" of founders. Halle's very success in this regard ironically weakened the emergence of secular allies who might have reinforced Halle's definitions of the concepts of property and liberty against the challenge issued by the passengers on the Swabian transports, whose arrival coincided with Georgia's change in status to a royal colony, and the introduction of chattel slavery. Early families such as the Flörls, and subsequesntly, the Kieffers, Wertschs, Treutlens, Meyers, and Holtz-endorffs, emerged as local worthies. But from the start, the pastors controlled the legal as well as spiritual institutions. As English observers reported, the pastors and one or two laymen—described by Boltzius as Schöffen, village elders learned in the law—presided over the court, settling disputes in ways that replicated the combined clerical-legal functions of the Kirchenkonvent. No settlement scribe kept records for these courts, and only Boltzius's letters to Augsburg relate how he attempted to eliminate village baptismal and confirmation customs that families employed to link property interests together. In 1736 he wrote to Augsburg, "With respect to godparents, the Salzburgers have some customs that do not please me and which will be dropped gradually after I have given them instructions, E.g., that the child must always receive the name of the godfather whether it means anything or not."[65]

Urlsperger attributed the custom to the Catholic cultural influence out of which the Salzburgers came, where the "spiritual kinship" created by such bonds forbade intermarriage, hence favoring the repeated use of the same godfather for all children in a family, and keeping open the possibilities of marriage and property alliances with other, more prosperous, neighbors. Had Urlsperger bothered to look at the villages around Stuttgart where he had once preached, he would have seen identical customs among Swabian villagers. Boltzius claimed, perhaps too assertively to be quite believable, that his Salzburgers were immune from elaborate baptismal celebrations "at which the godparents, neighbors, and friends gather as soon as the baptism is finished, or else after the six-week period for eating, drinking, and worldly merriment." In fact, material conditions prohibited such revelry, although what may have gone on despite the pastor's confident report, one can only surmise.[66]

The Swabian transport of 1748 brought people to Ebenezer in spite of Boltzius's pleas to his European superiors to prohibit anyone not committed to the settlement's experiments. Circumstantial evidence suggests that some members of the SPCK and Christian von Münch, the Augsburg banker, together with one of the Georgia trustees, favored expanded population, larger farms, and abandonment of Halle's goal of self-sufficient community. Active competition with the agricultural capitalism of neighboring South Carolina implied a radically different future. But such competition could only be sustained by continuing to use transatlantic support and planning built on Augsburg's part of the Halle network of information and financial patronage. The Halle fathers remained ignorant of this substantive shift in their allies' objectives.[67]

Swabian arrivals refused all forms of communal labor, even when offered wages. Most were artisans and day laborers but not experienced farmers; some ran away to South Carolina, and the older Salzburgers who were successful artisans, craftsmen and farmers now endured challenges from aspiring newcomers. Boltzius urged immediate curtailment of immigration. The pastor, who still functioned as a de facto justice of the peace, remained displeased with Johann Ludwig Meyer. This Augsburg emissary had arrived in 1743. Active as an herbal gardener, he supplemented the medical expertise of Halle-trained physician Christian Ernst Thilo. Meyer enjoyed a house and four hundred fenced acres, and neglected his duties as justice when the trustees of the colony approved him in office with a yearly salary of twenty pounds. By 1750, after only nominal service, he resigned to pursue his commercial and medical interests. Boltzius resumed legal duties, and translated for himself William Wilson's *The Office and Authority of a Justice of the Peace*. When the orphanage was repaired in 1750, Halle intended Meyer to use this central building, the symbol of its enterprises, as his courtroom. Meyer was persuaded to resume his office nominally, but Boltzius did the work. Within two years the Swabians, settling south of Ebenezer along the Savannah River and around Goshen, demanded their own teachers of German and English, and eyed a glebe that had been set aside as a future retirement home for Halle's missionaries. The crystallization of a "Swabian party" whose ideas about property were very different from those of the rest of the settlement became more marked in 1752 with the arrival of Pastor Christian Rabenhorst.[68]

Rabenhorst, a Pomeranian, had studied in Silesia with the family of the Count von Bogatsky, finishing his training at Halle as a charity student after the funds obtained from his father were stolen. In Ebenezer, perhaps stung by this misfortune, Rabenhorst married the widow of David Kraft, the commercial agent for Christian von Münch. Kraft had died shortly after arriving in Georgia and patenting lands that now became Rabenhorst's. Rabenhorst's new wife soon showed her mettle by guarding his financial affairs so closely that he could give alms to the poor only in secret. Malicious stories whispered after his death reported her at night digging by lantern in search of money he had hidden from her.[69] Rabenhorst soon became the darling of the Swabian arrivals. After the death of Gronau in 1745, Augsburg's Urlsperger demanded and obtained the right to nominate a replacement for Ebenezer's third pastor. (The other two were Boltzius and the Reverend Heinrich Lemke.) He secured Rabenhorst's appointment without consulting Boltzius. Unlike the two earlier pastors, Rabenhorst arrived without SPCK support, drawing his salary from a capital trust fund that had been established at Halle for the pastors' retirement home. These events suggest Halle's declining control of the settlement and the rise of Urlsperger and the Augsburg investors. Rabenhorst saw this plantation as his private property, rather than a property held in public trust.[70]

The Swabian arrival that challenged these notions coincided closely with the arrival of royal government in Georgia. Between 1754 and 1757, Governor John Reynolds reviewed all grants, promoting the clearing and use of new lands. On the first Tuesday of the month, "Land Day" gave applicants an opportunity to deliver petitions in the council chamber. Heads of household were entitled to a minimum of 100 acres, with 50 acres more for each dependent, white or black. A demonstrated ability to cultivate land made additional land, not to exceed 1,000 acres, available at one shilling per 10 acres. At least 3 out of each 50 acres had to be cultivated. The land warrant, once issued to the surveyor general, was returned to the attorney general's office, where the colony secretary prepared the plat. The governor signed, the clerk and the council countersigned, the registrar recorded, the secretary sealed, and the settler paid the dues. Even before Reynolds encouraged the resurvey of old allotments and the exchange of traditional plots in Ebenezer for more rationally planned plats, Ebenezer had lost population to outlying areas. Original settlers had swapped lots across boundary lines, rendering impossible the crown surveyor's job of establishing title. Older people kept old plots. New arrivals and the young had to settle at Bethany and Goshen.[71]

Proper stewardship of property involved more than proving titles, however. Moveable property entered the settlement because of the Halle network Boltzius assiduously built up. Making a trip to Charleston, South Carolina, he recognized the value of Peter Timothaeus, whom he identified (erroneously) as a "German printer" of potential use to his settlement. Timothaeus, of Huguenot parentage, born in the Netherlands, had trained in Philadelphia under Franklin and had recently arrived in Charleston to begin a distinguished career as printer to the royal government. Boltzius was disappointed that Timothaeus did not promote a network for printed German materials. However, Boltzius found instead a merchant in the city, William Hopton, who agreed to take wares shipped from von Münch in Augsburg and forward them to Savannah and Ebenezer. In Savannah, Hopton's contact with the firm of Harris and Habersham facilitated the shipment of books and materials back to the Reich via London, or in reverse, upriver to Ebenezer.[72]

Boltzius and Halle preferred Charleston to Savannah despite the difficult overland trek or added coastal voyage. Georgia's weaker economy and exposure to Spanish attack meant that the value of Spanish silver money was more inflated in Georgia than in neighboring South Carolina. Boltzius explained that the Savannah merchants "do business only by going into debt and because they pay people who are entitled to something for their work, crops, etc., with a written order or note, which the merchants accept instead of money, these issued orders or notes are paid with the trustees' so-called 'sola bills' and sent to London instead of drafts, Hence none of their money stays in this country." Savannah merchants found that in taking drafts they lost money in the exchange: "In one pound, they would lose forty pence or three shillings four pence, or almost one-and-a-half florins. If they wished to exchange their small, hard-earned reserves, that would be impossible because there is no other money in the country. Little or no paper money from Carolina gets here." Alarmed by indebtedness that was exacerbated by Virginia and Carolina planters whose arrival was transforming Georgia into a plantation society, Boltzius concluded, "I cannot understand why the money in a king's country cannot have the same value, regardless of whether it is made of silver, paper, or leather." Boltzius found the fluctuations in colonial currency which undermined self-sufficiency at Ebenezer a sign of disorder.[73]

IV

Surviving fragments of German-language wills, deeds, indentures, and land records provide hints that Georgia's Salzburgers valued an ordered society, and that they defined property and liberty along lines suggested by Halle's pastors. Unlike contemporary German speakers in Virginia, these early Salzburg emigrants, especially women deeply committed to pietist teaching, could envision property as a good held in trust, and often took care to exercise stewardship over it for the less fortunate. Their opposition to male tail succession indicated that they were as capable of understanding personal property and inheritance as anyone from Württemberg. But their early use of property, and a reflective and essentially passive understanding of liberty, seemed to augur well for a sense of responsibility to the ordered society Halle hoped they labored to construct. Halle's network linked Ebenezer to the Salzburgers' relatives in Prussia and sometimes secured inheritances from Salzburg itself for the early Georgia settlers. In 1740 the contact at Lindau, Pastor Bonaventura Riesch, forwarded news of inheritance to Boltzius for a man now in Philadelphia. Until the arrival of Mühlenberg two years later, Ebenezer functioned as the sole North American end of Halle's network. In Georgia, a shoemaker, Solomon Adde, apologized to his Tübingen mother for departing, asked for his inheritance, and offered to pay his mother's passage to Ebenezer. The settlement's Swabians, especially those of the fourth transport, enjoyed support given by one of the privy councillors at Canstatt, a pietist center; using this conduit, patrons in Straßburg invented a novel and useful gift: designating that twenty-five Gulden for a cow be given to the poorest member of the Ebenezer community. Riesch successfully secured the inheritance of Mathias Brander of Werffen in 1747; in 1743 Johannes Schmidt had received his legacy and, in gratitude, gave a small bequest to the Ebenezer church.[74]

As was the case in Europe, those who gave to charity came from the very wealthy, or the very poor. Boltzius reported that one Gulden for pious giving was made up of four hundred separate contributions from the poor boxes of six Augsburg Lutheran churches. In 1748 Prussian Salzburgers used the Halle-London-Ebenezer route not only to send letters to Stephen Rottenberger and other artisans but also to send three Reichstaler (£0.3.½ current money) for the relief of Ebenezer's poor widows.[75] Deacons and pastor at the Merchants' Church in Erfurt, a monument to the success of the traders of Thüringen, contributed to Halle's mission in North America.[76] No slackers themselves, Ebenezer Salzburgers contributed £4 sterling toward Mühlenberg's building of Saint Michael's in Philadelphia. Boltzius had to dissuade his congregation in 1741 from sending money to Halle's East Indian mission at Malabar when they learned that a poor student at Halle had contributed for Ebenezer, an example they wished to follow.[77]

The use of property for philanthropic purposes among such a formerly marginalized population of servants and day laborers contrasts sharply with the contemporary Lutheran group in Virginia. If anything, despite similar village cultural roots, the Hebron Lutherans were probably better off materially. They were freer, in the sense that Halle's missionary network did not reach them; neither did pastoral and European mercantilist control. At Ebenezer, profit-oriented commercial enterprises, such as lumber, grain and corn mills had been initiated under a 1745 recommendation from Gotthilf August Francke. Outsiders paid user fees not only to free the mills from subsidies but also to create a fund for poor relief—the classic Halle model of self-sufficiency and philanthropy.[78]

Boltzius reported unusual evidence of this Halle-directed mentality in 1748. He took the oral will of a twelve-year-old servant boy who eventually left his few possessions to a thirteen-year-old sister. Boltzius noted that the boy's parents had died in Spain, where they had been imprisoned en route to North America. But the pastor had to redirect the boy's wishes. In gratitude, he had originally left his belongings to his Salzburger master, who refused them, granting instead the boy's wish that his sister leave the plantation near Savannah where she labored and join the boy's master at Ebenezer.[79]

Between the 1730s and 1800, some eighty-nine Georgia German speakers wrote wills. Many of these have not survived. But from those that do and from Boltzius's journal comes evidence that small bequests *ad pias causas* occurred more often than the poverty of the settlement would have predicted. However, as the settlement increased in wealth, and newer arrivals who did not share Halle's moral vision of property and the public weal predominated, the practice collapsed. Boltzius noted in 1742 the locksmith Ruprecht Schrempf's intention to donate four pounds sterling to the orphanage; Maria Maurer née Wemmer, originally of Sankt Johann, in Salzburg, died after orally dictating a will. Sworn in front of the congregation to speak the truth regarding what German speakers knew as a *bäuerliches Testament,* or scholars called a *testamentum rusticum* (nuncupative will) her neighbors revealed her bequest of plantation, cow, and calf, and one-third of the household goods to the orphanage. She pleaded that Urlsperger in Augsburg look after her mother in Memmingen, Württemberg. Boltzius noted another Ebenezer woman donating to the orphanage seven shillings sterling received via London. Christian Riedelsperger asked Boltzius's help in writing his will, donating his clothing to the poor of the orphanage and freeing his wife, upon her remarriage, to arrange her portion "to satisfy her." Bernhard Glocker, another Salzburger, thanked Pastor Riesch of Lindau for acting as his contact with his home village in 1742; a year later, Hans Flörl, Glocker's administrator, turned over a legacy to be distributed by Boltzius, who cited Jonah 2:9 approvingly: "They who cling to their vanities (as is accustomed to happen in the division of legacies) forsake their own mercy." Neither Simon Riser, in his will, nor Catherine Scheffler forgot mercy. Riser supported the orphanage; Frau Scheffler left her clothes for the poor.[80]

Of eighty-nine wills that were written, forty-one survive. The majority were written and probated in the 1760s or 1770s, at a time when Ebenezer and Bethany had at least 1,041 communicants, and the smaller German Lutheran groups at Goshen and Savannah had 128 and 203, respectively. Reformed communities at Vernonburgh, Abercorn, and Acton had small, undetermined numbers of German speakers. Four surviving wills contain provisions ad pias causas, as legacies to the church or the poor. With Boltzius's record, the wills suggest that one-tenth of German speakers made philanthropic provisions in the stewardship of their property.[81]

Significantly, most of the provisions as pias causas came from women. The cultural memory of widowhood and of dependency on village charitable institutions operated in tandem with Halle's pastoral teaching. In the Reich, alms in the villages and the state-supported *Stiftungen* (foundations) helped to sustain widows and orphans; some German-speaking women in Georgia recognized that dependence on European charity was unwise. Pietism's appeal to women and its public support for the integrity of the household in the German southwest had provided a small degree of power and control over threats to domestic economy. In Georgia, a cultural transfer sustained by Halle's missionary network, pastoral preaching, and control of the public institution of the courts brought the same tendencies to bear. Like the alms sent to the New World by the marginal or the wealthy, philanthropic provisions in Georgia came from well-to-do or poor women. Amelia Alther, a Swiss resident of Savannah, suffering from palsy after working for years in Bartholemew Zouberbühler's home, received a legacy guaranteeing residence on his plantation; the services of a black servant, Peg; and a yearly stipend of ten pounds sterling. Alther, widowed since 1755, had retained fifty pounds according to her marriage contract with Johannes Alther; Zouberbühler had been her husband's executor. In 1759 Pastor Johann Joachim Zubly had acquired a town lot owned by another widow. He deeded it to Alther, who sold it to George Winkler in 1760. Not forgetting these kindnesses, Alther instructed Zubly to see if her relatives in Kempten still lived; if not, her estate should support pious and philanthropic uses.[82]

The Swiss Reformed example demonstrates that Halle pietists held no monopoly on using property for philanthropic purposes. But the eastern Swabian and Salzburger women from modest economic backgrounds who predominated in the Ebenezer settlement seem all the more remarkable by contrast. Altheim, Weidenstetten, and other Ulm villages produced some of these women. Barbara Groner received from her father in 1752 an undisclosed settlement and was excluded from the final partition of estate; the portions, however, came to little more than fifty Gulden for each heir, and she could not have received much more than this sum before leaving for Ebenezer. Magdalena Staudenmeyer née Bader emigrated in 1752; her mother had left her fifty-eight Gulden upon her death in 1745. Her brother Martin, dying in 1755, left her another ten

Gulden, By 1767, when she passed the annum decretorium, the family asked authorities in the *Pflegsschaftsamt* to declare her dead so that the small bits of property could be claimed by her two sons, one legitimate and one illegitimate; the stepfather of one, Niclaus Bunz declared himself ready to reimburse his stepson if, unexpectedly, Magdalena returned to demand her inheritance. Another inheritance of thirty-seven Gulden, according to the relatives of the young daughter of emigrant Johannes Braunmüller, was so small that a power of attorney and court costs far outstripped its worth; Ulm authorities agreed but insisted that the siblings of Johannes invest it to ensure interest accrual before permitting its use.[83]

German-speaking women in Georgia exercised stewardship for philanthropy and controlled domestic economy to an extent unknown in the Virginia settlement because of what their husbands did, too. Fourteen of the surviving forty-one wills provide wives with more than the usual thirds; several make explicit reference to premarital contracts and to what the wife had brought into the marriage (the German *Allatum*). For instance, when Ursula Unseld, a spinster, married the carpenter Christopher Peters in or before 1765, she insisted on the premarital contract common in her native Gingen, near Ulm, where she had been confirmed in 1754 before arriving in Georgia.[84] In addition, fourteen German speakers—though not in every instance the identical persons—allotted realty to daughters or nieces as well as to sons. Eleven of the forty-one wills contained inter vivos provisions in the form of trusts for the future education, maintenance, or nourishment of children or spouses; fifteen of the forty-one named the wife as executrix or coexecutrix.

The twelve surviving wills by German speakers of unknown origin bequeath artisan property in Savannah, Halifax, or Vernonburgh. Seven were certainly written by Swiss or "Palatine" settlers. But twenty-two of the forty-one Swabians and Salzburgers dictated their wills; even more of the Ebenezer community wrote wills that no longer survive. Probably fifty-six persons in Ebenezer wrote wills, only some of which survive. The Georgia German speakers neglected inter vivos bequests in conveyances, indentures, or bonds, apparently in favor of wills. Conveyances among English speakers regularly devise property "out of love" between the 1730s and 1776; only six German conveyances or bonds survive for the entire period. The Virginia wills that mistakenly tried to set up trust provisions reserving the use of a plantation after the writing of the will but before its probate find no corresponding examples in Georgia. Carefully constructed trust provisions underscore the advice of pastors familiar with trusteeships from their training at Halle, which urged the right use of property for philanthropic purposes.[85]

Ebenezer pastors influenced many such decisions and provided practical aid. When in 1767, Pastor Rabenhorst went over Theobald Kieffer's last will in darker ink making improvements in language for clarity, he continued a practice that Boltzius had pioneered. Poor or nonexistent penmanship required that "we often guide their hands and pens when they write."[86] Even the physical appearance of some of the wills revealed a livelier cultural transfer because of the Halle network. When Anna, Christian Steinhebel's widow, wrote her will at Vernonburgh in 1748, a German model complete with black-letter calligraphy lay at hand. A Trinitarian invocation, a pietist redemptive passage relying upon "my Dear Redeemer Jesus Christ with fervent prayers to pardon my Sins for his high Merits Sake to Grant me a happy Departure from this World into his Kingdom," and required signatures and seals mark this example. By the 1760s Ebenezer wills reflected the rapid anglicization of justice Johann Treutlen, transplanted Württemberger of the 1750s. Phonetically spelled formulaic words in labored English proclaim George Mauer's 1775 will "Sined Seled Bronounsed in the brasend of us hous nms ar unter written": Christopher Cramer, John Mauer, and John Glanir. The few surviving German originals reveal specific provisions for bequeathing and devising meticulously translated.[87]

Pietist redemptive language vanished in translation. Thus, Thomas Schwieghofer's will spoke in German of his reliance upon God, "the Almighty, my Creator and Redeemer," who would through Christ save his "dearly bought soul" as it was demanded from this valley of sorrows, eventually to be brought to an eternal joy, though his body was to be given to a gentle rest ("sanfter Ruhe") until the joyous resurrection. The English translation was: "My body I give unto the earth nothing doubting but that I shall receive the same at the great and general Resurrection." When the will was proven on 10 December, Frederick Rosenberg attested that this was a true translation.[88]

Halle's familiarity with trusts shaped the dealings in the court of conscience or equity (*Billigkeit*) conducted in German at Ebenezer, before which annoyed Irish and Scots settlers had to plead in German. Those records do not survive, nor can one reconstruct what Boltzius, and later Meyer and Treutlen, or Theobold Kieffer, advised informally out of court or during the sessions held for Effingham County.[89] But Boltzius knew he was charged with holding the gristmills, and rice stamping mill in trust, along with the retirement property for Halle's American missionaries. In 1757 he conveyed this trust to Herman Heinrich Lemke, his junior colleague, reviewing the 1740s trust. The mills had been constructed to provide a perpetual source of revenue for the self-sustaining Salzburger experiment. Their profits built the churches and schools, and salaried the pastors and schoolteachers. The training and education of the future secured, the trust should also sustain widows, orphans, and the aged. The Georgia trustees, the SPCK, Augsburg, and Halle's supporters contributed to the money Boltzius borrowed for construction. Boltzius managed to pay off the loan, at the same time erecting a trading house where lumber products were sold to West Indian buyers.[90]

The trust eventually provoked the dispute that destroyed Ebenezer; it also guaranteed the emergence of late arrivals who led the dispute. Johann Georg Mayer, who ran the shop next to the lumber mill, and Johann Treutlen, a Palatine servant who would quickly rise to become a major landowner and a justice of the peace, got their start because of the mills begun in public trust. Johann Caspar Wertsch, a 1740s indentured servant, served, like Treutlen, as a storekeeper. By the 1760s he rivaled Treutlen as the major property owner in Ebenezer. He counted as allies Johannes Flörl and Boltzius's friends Theobald Kieffer and Johann Holtzendorff, arrivals from Purrysburg in the 1750s.[91] All of these worthies made additional acquisitions that seemed to ratify their own success. Urban Buntz, a Swabian arrival, patented 650 acres between 1759 and 1761 and another 150 before dying in 1774. The Salzburger Johannes Flörl owned more than 800 acres; to three smaller 100-acre plots on the Savannah he added 500 acres owned jointly with Johann Ludwig Meyer and Christian Rabenhorst in 1759. With Meyer and Theobald Kieffer in 1756 he co-owned the 125 acres where the mills were located. By 1771 he acquired two more lots in Ebenezer. Johann Ludwig Meyer acquired 300 acres outright and another 800 jointly with Flörl and Rabenhorst in 1759.[92] Johann Treutlen outstripped them with his 1,540 acres. Johann Caspar Wertsch, from his vantage point as storekeeper, added to his 1,000-plus acres by trading in land at his store. In 1766 he was party to an indenture with Benjamin Williamson of Saint George Parish. Henry Overstreet, bound to Wertsch since 1765 for securing payment of a bond for eighty-seven pounds sterling, had to pay forty-three pounds with interest by 1766. Wertsch obtained 300 acres of land, trading again to Williamson in exchange for the forty-eight pounds he preferred.[93] By the time he died in 1766, Pastor Boltzius provided for his children through the discretion of his wife, relying on Lemke and Rabenhorst to see her housed. His witnesses were John Flörl, Wertsch, and Theobald Kieffer. His son Gotthilf Israel decided to stay in Europe and sent a power of attorney from Halle in 1770, asking for his inheritance. He chose Wertsch as his agent.[94]

Inventories of the worthies mentioned "some Dutch books," coffee and chocolate pots, coffee mills, china tea sets, delft china, wine cruets, tumblers, beer and wine glasses, and pewterware. But inventories and wills also revealed a new form of property wholly at odds with Halle's original objectives. Benjamin Stirk had china services served on mahogany tea boards by twelve slaves. Michael Birkhalter owned six slaves; Theobold Kieffer, sixteen.[95] The late-arriving German speakers traded in slaves with no second thoughts; at Savannah in 1754. Solomon Shad traded "a Negroe Girl named Nanny" to Jacob Helvenstein for "a Negroe Boy Sampson." Johann Peter Schlechtermann, who had arrived on a Palatine transport, used a trust provision in an indenture with Joseph Parker "in Consideration of the natural Love and affection which he hath for Eleonore Sliterman his Wife." Parker was to have three slaves and their increase; the profits from this labor would support Johann Peter's widow.[96] These German speakers bequeathed slaves without comment. Only Theobald Kieffer ordered in 1767 that "the Young Negroes who were born in my House Namely Peter Ernst Martha Catherina, Adam Rudy who were all baptized shall be kept in my Family and be brought up in the Christian Knowledge and Shall not be lyable to be given away in mortgage or Execution but Shall be only Sold or Changed to one or other of the Family or to Such as will take care that the Ends of Baptisms Grace may be obtained." The Swiss Reformed immigrant Bartholemew Zouberbühler, having become an Anglican priest, wanted his inheritance in Appenzell used for the Swiss poor, and asked someone "qualified for teaching and Instructing Negroes in the principles of the Christian Religion as held by the Church of England" to instruct his slaves. A male slave wishing to minister to his own people would be manumitted; all slave children were to be baptized and taught to read.[97]

The Halle fathers pondered the problem of slavery when their English colleague George Whitefield, admiring both the orphanage and the other enterprises at Halle, informed Gotthilf August Francke in 1746 of the founding of his orphanage in Georgia. Six years later, Francke was shaken as Whitefield told him that four hundred acres received as a gift to the evangelist would be worked by slaves. Boltzius dismissed Whitefield's hope that through an orphanage worked by slaves, black children would be brought to Christ. Francke responded, "If the decision were to be ours, it would be our wish that such [i.e., slaves] had never been brought into Georgia." The Two Kingdom teaching of Luther put the question in secular hands; wishing to offend neither Whitefield and his powerful patrons, nor his British allies, Francke hoped that "what we fear, God through the strength of his great wisdom not only can defend against, but [he can] turn what could lead to harm for his kingdom to his own advantage." We must constantly pray and, "insofar as it lies with us, support his [acts] with great care."[98]

Settlement in Georgia under Halle's auspices had revealed that the idea of property, used and defined in the positive sense that connected it to a public purpose, could survive transfer from the Reich. Halle's network to London facilitated the construction of trusts intended to secure that purpose, although later events would prove these defective, revealing again how difficult it was to move from one private-law system to another.

What eased the Salzburgers' adjustments—if they survived the horrible climate—was their own lack of commitment to the notion of privileges and social relationships defined by property so common in the German southwest. Moreover, unlike Swabian pietists, they also brought no tradition of hostility to pastors and secular authorities of their own faith—no sense of the need for freedom from their own coreligionists. Coming from a land not dominated by the custom of equal partition, most of them had also not been landowners before, and they were grateful for the privilege of acquiring any property and of practicing their Lutheran faith. These early Lutherans came close to personifying exactly what Halle wanted. The networks that sustained them were dominated by Halle's own pastors; no competitive secular brokers emerged in the Georgia settlement before midcentury. The Salzburgers, and even the Palatines with them, embodied the positive definition of a true, interior, spiritual liberty; their initial behavior in dealing with property showed the capacity to think in terms of providing responsible stewardship and caring for others even more indigent than they.

Yet in neither Georgia nor Virginia could anyone have discerned the existence of a "political" culture before 1750. In neither colony did transferred definitions of liberty and property connect individual ownership and choice in matters of conscience and worldly goods, to a broader notion of a political liberty for which one was responsible. For this last, crucial step to occur, a sociability similar to that created in the conventicles had to be reestablished so that a public, shared debate and exchange of views could develop. The language necessary for such a debate had to be capable of melding both positive and negative possibilities of the terms *liberty* and *property* to British colonial terms and conditions. The emergence of this language, and with it, a private sociability capable of engaging political issues, began in 1738, in Pennsylvania.

6

The Early Language of Liberty and Property in Pennsylvania

B Y THE 1740s secular trader-agent networks had begun to span the Atlantic, linking German speakers and recovering inheritances destined for Pennsylvania households. Halle's network, already established in Georgia since the 1730s, had included Penn's colony since the arrival in 1742 of Heinrich Melchior Mühlenberg. The struggle to re-define both the negative and positive meanings of the terms *liberty* and *property* unfolded in this context, partly because of tensions between the two kinds of networks, each with its brokers who interpreted the English-speaking world for German speakers. But an even more fundamental reason dictated immigrant engagement with these authoritative terms: the separatist pietist Christopher Saur began publishing an almanac in 1738, a newspaper a year later.

The convergence of networks and printed word created a transitional language apt for constructing the "private sociability" often attributed by scholars to eighteenth-century clubs, reading societies, Masonic lodges, and literary groups. Among German speakers, Saur's almanac and newspaper, along with the other printed offerings available through the Germantown printer, provided news about scattered family, as well as pietist tracts and essays. Saur presented in dialogue form familiar themes: freedom of conscience, privileges granted to the German speakers, and concern for inheritance of property. Despite "public" access to this printed material, English speakers rarely knew, or cared about, what the Germans were up to. Because of this, a semiprivate sociability emerged among German speakers across the scattered farmsteads and townships. Within this context, Saur would eventually encourage engagement with—and criticism of—the English-language public, political culture.

175

Since language, like all aspects of culture, not only is socially created in exchanges but is communicated differently once it is disseminated in print, one can hardly exaggerate the significance of Saur's accomplishment. By giving printed and semipermanent form to the concerns of German speakers, he made possible reflection on, and scrutiny and abstraction of, the meaning of terms such as *liberty* and *property*. Having laid the groundwork for this pivotal advance, Saur inadvertently erased some memories of village life—especially the fractious, combative nature of relationships—even as he invoked them in printed form and urged the defense of village values in an English-speaking culture. He also moved from a completely inward definition of liberty to a definition that hinted cautiously at responsibility—the freedom to engage and create. His ability to express pietist concerns for, and criticisms of, property relationships and privileges prepared the way for the overtly political printer and publisher Henry Miller. Miller, who scorned Saur's concern with the domestic, the homely, and the religious, profited immensely from Saur's efforts, for by the late 1750s Saur had provided his readers with a full-fledged discussion of the terms *liberty* (in both the positive and negative senses) and *property*, both with reference to North American conditions.[1]

I

By 1743 Saur was selling advertisements in a monthly paper; three years later, it had at least two thousand subscribers. By 1755, as the German-speaking population continued to swell, the paper was increasingly in demand as a means of locating people. To his long essays on religious liberty, Saur also now added reflections on property, publishing notices of inheritances, and the advertisements of those offering to make trips back to Europe. He also began charging for the notices.[2] Saur perused the German newspapers himself and, using his newspaper, he alerted North Americans to the legal notices, the *Edictal-Citationen*, which, according to German law, were required to be posted over a period of weeks, allowing interested parties in a settlement to respond. By the 1730s, the *Reichskammergericht* had determined that as long as notice was given in three different places, it could be posted on the walls of a Rathaus, read from the pulpit, or proclaimed with trumpet and drum. These procedures could not reach potential heirs who had emigrated overseas, but the newspaper ads did. Palatinate authorities chose to use the imperial paper, the *Reichs-Post-Amts-Zeitung* at Frankfurt, for its advertisements; Württemberg officials never did.[3]

Yet the heightened interest in both religious liberty and family inheritances could not have developed among German speakers in the British colonies had the family groups not shared one extraordinary characteristic. From signature rates on naturalization oaths, it appears that German-speaking families boasted a literacy rate as high as 71 percent for the early years, 1727–50. The rate rose to nearly 80 percent by 1770 and to nearly 100 percent by the Revolution.[4]

To understand the treatment of "liberty" which Saur propagated among these highly literate readers, one must appreciate the particular religious perspective from which he came. Precisely where Saur's religious loyalties lay remains a topic of debate. For a time, at least, he was a Dunker, and he was certainly connected by his background to radical separatist Pietism in the Rhineland. Saur did not begin his discussion of the nature of liberty by citing Luther's famous essay on Christian liberty. That text and its implications would have to wait for Lutheran engagement in the 1760s. What is most important in understanding Saur's own perspective on the term *liberty* is the conviction he shared with all free-church radicals.

The free-church Protestants who in 1527 subscribed to the Schleitheim Confession, which rejected the prevailing notion of the *Corpus Christianum*, under whose terms the Two Kingdoms teaching on authority and liberty had developed, refused to affirm the legitimacy of secular authority's duty to uphold true religion. These free-church people also severed their allegiance to the broadly accepted definition of Christian liberty. By this move, radicals such as Saur identified the term *liberty* with the story of Exodus, and shaped their own self-image or typology as a persecuted people. Yet they could also connect the definition of liberty as freedom from persecution for conscience's sake to the positive definition of liberty as interior freedom *for* obedience to God—that is, the freedom of a faithful remnant of the chosen still obedient to the Holy Spirit's gift of grace.[5]

For the Reformed tradition, rejection of the link between state and church was just as unacceptable as it was for Lutherans. And yet, because of Reformed teaching on the relation between law and gospel, as we have already seen, Calvinists found it possible to interpret liberty so that they, too, identified closely with the Exodus story. The sense of mission that drove them to apply New Testament "gospel liberty" directly to models of the godly society created its own ironies, but it was an enormously "liberating" and powerful solution to the double-edged meaning of the term *liberty*.[6]

Neither solution worked easily for Lutherans who remained committed to the Two Kingdoms doctrine and the conviction that secular authorities exercised legitimate authority of the sword (*potestas*) while the authority of the gospel (*auctoritas*) was protected by the state to do its own work. Liberty in its negative (and secular) sense might well have meant escaping from taxes and forced labor for southwestern villagers; but for Lutheran pietists, it was harder to suggest that they had been persecuted for the sake of conscience, especially since Pietism had achieved official recognition in Württemberg by 1743. Nor could Lutherans easily see how a positive, interior definition of liberty, meaning obedience to God's grace and law, held any particular ramifications for their connection to political authority, especially in North America. Little or nothing had been demanded of them upon arrival in North America by British authorities, and they saw no reason to be concerned with the dire warnings that issued from Saur's press, especially since he delighted in attacking Lutherans, clergy and lay alike.

Saur's difficult relationship with his own wife, who abandoned the family to join the Ephrata monastic experiment in the 1730s, suggests why he not only chose in his paper and almanac to concentrate on liberty of conscience but also built his paper around advice protecting the sanctity and centrality of the domestic hearth. It was his reflections on the importance of defending the home that probably touched Lutherans most directly. Moreover, German-speaking women used to the village Kirchenkonvent, that public forum where they had made a reflective pietist critique of worldly affairs, found their concerns identified in Saur's suspicion of taxes, militia service, lawyers, conniving clerics, and threats to the German language, which married women had little reason to abandon. These concerns were common to all German speaking families, regardless of confessional loyalty.

From 1739 until Saur's death in 1758, *Der Hoch-Deutsch Pennsylvanische Geschichts-Schreiber*, focused German speakers' attention on the "Collection of Credible News, from the Realm of Nature and the Churches; and also Useful Knowledge for the Common Good."[7] The interests of a familial, agricultural, religious readership determined what Saur chose to define as useful for the common weal. He addressed the issue of "liberty" strictly in terms of freedom from constraint upon conscience, and from taxation foisted upon property to promote the worldly ambitions of the ungodly at the expense of the Christian household.

Saur understood that in order to achieve acceptance among the welter of conflicting faiths of German-speaking Protestants in Pennsylvania, his definitions had to be presented authoritatively. He accomplished this not only by concentrating on liberty of conscience in his essays but also by shrewdly copying the appearance of authoritative religious texts for his newspaper. Benjamin Franklin's failure in 1730 to create a readership for his *Philadelphische Zeitung* rested both on his poor German grammar and on his use of roman fonts, which produced an alien-looking paper. But Franklin also mistakenly thought that German readers were interested in public affairs. Saur knew better. He had ordered gothic Fraktur type from Frankfurt to guarantee an authoritative appearance for his printed offerings. The physical presentation of his paper thus also did little to encourage in his readers the development of a critical sense of reflective judgment or of the autonomous self that had to precede the emergence of political consciousness.

The English language literature of the day had already developed this sense among its readers. The layout of printed texts could convey different messages to readers depending upon the associations triggered by seeing regularly arranged blocks of print. Thus, in Great Britain, an alteration in the stamp tax law after 1725 levied new charges on six-sided weeklies that had previously only been required to pay the pamphlet tax. The new tax drove some marginal papers from the market, and altered the appearance of others. Double-columned, regular blocks of texts, readily identified in the popular mind with the Bible, religious pamphlets, and officially sanctioned political pamphlets, conveyed a different sense of "truth" than more hastily assembled papers, struggling for financial survival and unable to command a battery of typesetters and printers. Cautious, conservative presses flourished by avoiding censorship and potential financial ruin.[8]

The need for modest profit explains why Saur avoided complex typesetting, not putting editorial remarks or commentary on news reports and texts in italics. He also dropped the doubling of German consonants. Instead, his paper presented to the reader as a seamless whole news from Europe, provincial and local developments, and his own comments. The uninterrupted double columns closely resembled the printing of Bibles, religious pamphlets, and other forms of officially sanctioned, authoritative printed truth.

German speakers and readers in North America purchased volumes of religious verse and hymnody produced at Ephrata and by Saur's press more than any other form of literature. Nearly all the poetic efforts of the Pennsylvania-based culture reflected the writers' pietist inclinations, the tradition of inwardness (*Innerlichkeit*) that encouraged cultivation of self-awareness judged against the commandments and demands of scripture. But the Moravian, Ephratan, and thirty Schwenkfelder poets whose 350 efforts survive for the period before 1830, when taken in conjunction with the broadsides and leaflets of various German printers, created little in the way of a critical, public language capable of dealing with the complexities of legal, commercial, and political life in the colonies. Nor did this literature make what was meant by "liberty" in a British context

more specific than the absence of coercion of conscience, and inner obedience to God's grace.[9]

During the early 1740s, Saur never ventured beyond a definition of
liberty as freedom of conscience and inwardness. His essays on war and
peace, his excerpts from the Lutheran pietist Johann Arndt's *Wahres
Christentum*, and his advertisements promoting the pamphlet containing
the profession of faith by Ernst Christoph Hochman von Hochenau all
reflected this definition. If Christians were truly free of worldly ambition, they would need no priests, no lawyers, and no physicians, and
would rejoice in the inner liberty of God's grace. The poem "Ich armer
Mensch . . ." ("I, a Poor Human Being") Saur reprinted regularly; in it,
the sentence "O Jesus, make me free" refers to inner liberty. Yet it occurs
in the midst of condemnation of those who lust after worldly goods,
reflecting the pietist critique of property and its corrosive effect on all
human relationships.[10]

Saur's 1747 offering of an essay, entitled "A Thorough Instruction
toward a Holy Life" continued in this tradition of inwardness, identifying
terms such as *freedom* and *righteousness* solely with the "inward retreat"
toward the kingdom of God found only within the believer's soul. Even
authors who did not share Saur's free-church loyalty tended to identify
liberty with a purely subjective, inward life. Mühlenberg's own poem
written for the dedication of Germantown's Saint Michael's Lutheran
Church as late as 1752 suggested the inappropriateness of God's subjects
wanting "more Liberty than is allowed to a subject, thereby robbing
Him of his Lordship."[11] Even secular Lutheran leaders such as Conrad
Weiser, in their poetic efforts, paid little attention to the positive obligations of freedom obtained by material success in the absence of feudal
lords. Weiser, in lines declaimed at Reading, Pennsylvania, in 1753 at
another church dedication, was one of the first Lutherans to use the
concept of a covenant. Weiser used the image of the Lutherans as God's
Bundesvolk—a curiously non-Lutheran image, because Luther's own theology had rejected any active, creative role for human beings in shaping
their salvation, even substituting systematically in his New Testament
translations the term *testament* for *covenant*. The possibility of a "covenant"
(*Bund*) defining the relationship among people in a public, political association, other than the narrowest association of religious confession,
had been scorned inside the Reich. Weiser's use of the term in the North
American context reflected the original usage, which occurred only within
the context of a church dedication by people of one confession. Still, by
midcentury German speakers in Pennsylvania had been exposed to the
idea and the possibility of political covenants whose bounds could be
expanded beyond this transferred meaning.[12]

This early tendency to identify liberty with an absence of government and with inner liberty of conscience, or with freedom from coercion, found its way into private letters, too. Writers from diverse parts of the Reich described Pennsylvania as "ein recht gutes freyes Land," by which universally they meant only that one paid no taxes and enjoyed liberty of conscience.[13] Various emigrants, writing back home to boast of their success (in part to take revenge on authorities, and perhaps neighbors who had never thought highly of them) showed a remarkable unity in their enthusiastic descriptions of Pennsylvania and North America before the Seven Years' War. When Peter Lohrman in 1739 wrote to Schwaigern from Pennsylvania, he repeated the standard report that all were "fresh and healthy" ("frisch und gesund") and that they lived in a land that was much better than Germany. "I pay no tithe," he boasted, and he was free of the frustrations of Schwaigern relatives who suffered forced labor (*Frondienst*), sickness, and taxes. In Pennsylvania "we live very pleasantly, and I live every day as good as a usurer." Another Schwaigern resident had married well. Martin Schwartz had bought 150 Morgen of land for fifty pounds; "that is the equivalent of three hundred Gulden," Lohrman noted carefully. One could not only have property but regular church attendance as well, although schools were rarer except in Germantown and Philadelphia. Moreover, "from what one accomplishes, one can feed oneself well" ("Wann man aber schafft kan man sich wol Nehren"). To those wanting to come to Pennsylvania Lohrman recommended the best captain with whom to sign a contract ("ein guten akcort") but cautioned against signing with a newlander. "Liberty" for Lohrman meant getting oneself free from service, or coming of one's own will to North America. Liberty in the New World was linked to the fruits of one's labor, as well as to the important domestic value of Nahrung (nourishment), the term that occurs repeatedly in the predeath care provisions villagers established with their heirs.[14]

The most popular printed texts that circulated in early Pennsylvania among German-speaking Lutherans continued to focus their concerns about freedom upon domestic imagery and the value of "inward" liberty. Although no definitive lists of books and pamphlets read by German-speaking Lutherans survive, booksellers continued in the 1760s and 1770s to supplement almanacs and newspapers with Bibles, and especially with the prayerbooks of Johannes Habermann and Johannes Starck. In these beloved works, brought to the New World in emigrants' chests, imported by booksellers, and eventually offered by German-American printers, one can divine the emigrants' primary concerns, and the utility of what was read. Such indices at least suggest what kind of response these texts created.[15] The prayerbooks kept alive transferred images of what pietists had meant by "liberty" and "property" even as the North American conditions in which they were read demanded reflection on how to apply the lessons of these favorite devotional sources.[16]

These pietist devotional manuals became so popular that copies were given as bridal gifts, and the books were sometimes slipped under pillows to ensure fertility and the safety of the household. Redolent with pietist images of "inwardness," the sermons, prayers, and meditations focused almost exclusively on the crises of childbirth, death, disease, drought, famine, and warfare—the narrow passages of life and death.[17] Prayers for the spirit of "rebirth" and for the strength to resist "bad company" accompanied encouragement to love one's neighbor. But the latter exhortations centered purely on the avoidance of envy or tale-bearing. Halle's insight—that love of neighbor might mean stewardship of worldly goods by educated, self-reliant subjects in accordance with a broader state and social purpose—never surfaces. Those who carried these books to North America or bought them there from importers found resonance in prayers "in a foreign land," as their parents in the village could find solace for those who had "left my house," praying that God would still be with them.[18]

Such collections transcended the purely personal, for they reminded readers not only of their village pasts but also of the private sociability that had bound pietists together throughout the German southwest and continued to do so in North America. Both Starck and Habermann, orthodox Lutherans who encouraged reception of the sacrament as a means of grace among their readers, demanded fidelity to the public, state-supported church. But the center of both prayerbooks remained unmistakably the household and its distress. The prayers against various forms of evil provided a handy catalog of potential horrors. Books other than these safe companions, the prayerbooks and the Bible, were viewed with suspicion: German speakers in Pennsylvania clung to the folk belief that too much reading was unsafe. The perils of being drawn deep into a text by the devil could only be negated by reverse reading and the help of a skilled practitioner of magic (*Braucher*) invoking the proper charm.[19]

Despite such beliefs, the most widely read story among German speakers in Pennsylvania (still in print today) incorporated the ambivalence they felt about worldly goods and ambition, as well as powerful imagery that underscored the centrality of domestic fidelity and piety. The story of the holy "Genovefa," reprinted by Christopher Saur, emerged before 1763 as a central motif for German speakers in North America. During its tortuous oral history, the character of Countess Geneviève of Brabant had been inserted into a French tale based on classical models. In German-language circles, the tale was spun further at the monastery of Maria Laach; by 1400 it identified the heroine with the wife of the cloister's founder, Pfalzgraf Siegfried von Ballenstädt. By the seventeenth century the story, in the form of a play, was disseminated principally by Jesuit missionaries who concentrated on the martyred quality of the heroine. But in German Protestant circles, the story took on a distinctly different meaning. Genovefa, pregnant and faithful in the absence of the count, emerges in this reading as an idealized figure of a mother and protector of the domestic hearth. Rejecting the sexual advances of her husband's steward, she is unjustly cast off by her husband and survives miraculously in a forest cave sustained by the roots of herbs; the milk of a doe nourishes her son Schmerzenreich, named for the many carvings of Christ as the Man of Sorrows (*Schmerzensmann*) who stood at the center of much late-medieval German Catholic piety. Her husband's awakening to his gross injustice comes too late to save her life, but in solitude and reflection she saves both her own soul and the future of the family in her son's person. The story ends with her death and the bitter self-condemnation of both her husband and even her son, aware of their unworthiness in the face of such fidelity and devotion.[20]

The popularity of this tale among German speakers of all religious hues serves as a reminder that Saur shrewdly knew the sentiments and reading preferences of his German-American readership. The married woman's central role in the domestic hearth of this tale, her resistance to sexual allures, and her endurance of her husband's unjust suspicions reinforced the sense of solidarity among German-speaking wives, particularly in a land whose language they did not understand. The tale can be read as both a story of married women's power and importance, and as a moral lesson in interior liberty—that is, a statement that passivity and long suffering create a soul purified of worldly concerns and free for its ultimate union with God. Certainly one should be skeptical of those commentators whose understanding of the household has overlooked the relationships of power which German-speaking women were able to construct.[21] But the Genovefa tale also serves as a timely reminder that moving German-speaking women into an alien linguistic and legal system may well have forced them to redefine the arena of control over domestic matters they were now allowed. In Georgia, fragmentary evidence from the period of transition between cultures suggests attempts by women to remember philanthropy and the poor in devising their property, influenced by Halle's preaching. In Virginia's Lutheran settlement, however, even though the occasional married woman rose to the challenge of settling property—even slaves—upon descendants, married women's rights over the domestic economy seem to have diminished in the new legal system. Rural Pennsylvania German-speaking women, too, clearly voiced concerns over their privileges and property, as witnessed now in Saur's essays on the latter topic beginning in the 1750s.

II

Saur's reflections on liberty of conscience and domestic concerns forced him to address the Anglo–American concept of property. In the process of doing so, he began, perhaps without even recognizing it, to alter his treatment not only of worldly goods but of *Freiheit*, as well. The very material success of the early arrivals who were now busily shuttling between German and English speakers helped transform the inward-looking definition of liberty by forcing a discussion about property. German speakers' contacts with legal and business affairs created a hybrid language for whose terms German equivalents could not always be found.

In 1741 the German-speaker Conrad Weiser, now a justice of the peace in Pennsylvania, issued a circular letter urging German support for a tax to be levied for defense funds. Saur attacked him openly. Yet even Weiser himself, like Saur a wanderer in religious opinions who dabbled at Ephrata and tried on many religious vestures before returning to Lutheran practice, only reminded the German speakers that their possession "of temporal goods" could enjoy protection under the "priviledges & liberties" secured by British law. Weiser invoked the biblical metaphor "a house divided in itself cannot stand" to urge German-speaking people to "trust" the English, more "jealous and Carefull of their Laws" than any other nation. But even Weiser had apparently not contemplated long-term involvement. It was "their" laws, not "our" laws, he admired; he supported a short-term, necessary defense measure. Weiser's own pragmatism, honed by his years of cross-cultural mediating between Pennsylvania and the Native Americans among whom he had spent his youth, probably inspired his writing more than deep reflection on German speakers' civic role in Pennsylvania.[22] Yet by raising the issue of "privileges" (Freiheiten), Weiser reminded German speakers that their enjoyment of liberty (Freiheit) might depend on their willingness to support actively those who had granted them privileges. That support had to take the form of taxes on property (Vermögen).[23]

In 1747, as Saur's press continued to offer advice regarding inward freedom, Benjamin Franklin's publication of a London wag's response to the classic 1678 essay of Quaker Robert Barclay, *An Apology for the True Christian Divinity*, suggested how material realism would shape even German pietist definitions of liberty and property. To Barclay's claim that Quakers did not object to self-defense, his respondent replied acidly

Eighteenth-century Philadelphia's Lutheran and Reformed Churches. Original map by Win Thrall, 1992. Modeled on map by Peter E. Daniels that appeared in Billy G. Smith, *The "Lower Sorts": Philadelphia's Laboring People, 1750–1800* (Ithaca, N.Y., 1990), 10. Used with permission.

that this position of criticism and suggestion of how civil society should be governed seemed quite dependent on social rank and largesse. It was, the respondent noted, well and good of those "who with Lands and safe Bank Stock / Have Faith so grounded on a Rock" to interpret Scripture to please themselves. Most ordinary people, however, less well off materially, would read the story of the starving Old Testament prophet Elijah differently, agreeing that "the honour'd Prophet that of old / Us'd Heav'n's high counsel to unfold / Did, more than *Courier-Angels*, greet / the *Crow*, that brought him Bread and Meat."[24]

The material prosperity that came to vex and embarass Quaker dominance of Pennsylvania also forced a discussion among German speakers of how "worldly goods" acquired under the "privileges" granted them might also imply taking another look at what "property" meant. A belief that liberty was freedom from taxation, and a narrow, domestic view of property, Weiser knew, would not be enough to defend Pennsylvania in the event of a general war with France and its Native American allies, with whom Weiser had spent his own youth. As pressure mounted in the 1740s to tax Pennsylvanians to protect the prosperity European settlement had created, Weiser's critic Christopher Saur was obliged to respond to the issue of how worldly goods could be passed on to the next generation, even as he was dismayed at the prospect of militia laws and those who promoted them.

Saur's newspaper first recorded in the 1740s the novel language created by German speakers' encounter with English commercial and legal affairs. Saur never borrowed domestic and religious terms from English.[25] But from the start his almanac and newspaper referred to the fairs that had begun at Germantown in 1701 as "die Fairen" instead of "Märkte"; and the terms for exchanges surrounding bargaining and selling he took over wholesale from English after carefully listening to Pennsylvania German speech and usage. Money was loaned "auf Intres" (instead of "durch eine Hypotheke" or "mit Zinsen"); a bond was simply "ein Band" (not "eine Schuldverschreibung"); an accord was "ein Accort" (not "eine Vereinbarung"; although the German term *Akkordarbeit*, which could mean piecework or jobbing, perhaps lay behind this easy adaptation). Saur's publication of a religious alphabet to instruct his readers in proper free-church doctrine and warn them away from lawyers and disputes reflected the earliest emphasis of his publications.[26] But a year later his *Nützliche Anweisung . . .* , an aid for Germans learning English, gave the proper terms in each language, not those in common use. Thus, for *lawyer*, the dictionary correctly provides "ein Advocat," although Saur commonly used "ein Layer" in his newspaper. Legal terms in particular were not readily translated and tended to be adopted directly into German (e.g., *freeholder* became *Freihalter*, just as *ein Trusteeschaft* described the trusteeships used in indentures and, erroneously, in wills that had provisions intended to go into effect with the testator still alive). Heinrich Melchior Mühlenberg, like Saur, struggled to convey to authorities in Europe what some of these terms meant and noted that German speakers swarmed like bees into the commercial areas of life, retreating into cultural hives for dialect use of German in church and family matters. For example, Mühlenberg used the meaningless term *Freihalter* for *freeholder*, a term that English speakers associated with "freehold," "freedom," and the like. But associative significances only develop slowly, over time, and many such terms had no German equivalents. Explaining the possession of lands in fee simple, for instance, Mühlenberg told Halle that this meant that Germans would have liked to obtain from the "proper owners" the rights as heirs and absolute owners and not mere possessors; he used the key words of inheritance and absolute property ownership (*Erbe* and *Eigentum*) to convey what "freeholder" meant.[27]

The concern with property among German speakers remained focused on inheritance. By the 1740s, agents such as the Gensels, Jürg Landenberger, Jacob Geiger, and others actively pursued Pennsylvania German speakers' inheritances for them in their ancestral villages. Notices in the Reich papers and in Saur's paper told German speakers where agents could be found—at Beyerle's or Gensel's taverns, for example. The agents circulated throughout the areas of German settlement but were concentrated in Philadelphia and Germantown. Most of the agents who were merchants and shopkeepers in Philadelphia lived between Second and Fourth streets, knew each other, relied on Christian Lehmann as notary, and also used the services of Peter Müller (a Nassauer who had arrived in the 1750s and, though he had land surveyed for himself in 1766 in Cumberland County, resided in Second Street) as notary and justice of the peace. By 1771 Müller had built such a reputation that letters from the Reich arrived regularly addressed to "Peter Müller, in der 2te Strass."[28]

Many agents resided in the homes or had rooms above the businesses of German-speaking shopkeepers and traders. Germantown residents contacted such agents at Turk's Keyser (an inn founded by the de Turck family, Huguenots who had emigrated to New York and relocated in 1718 to Pennsylvania), or used Johann Michael Weckesser, a former Schultheiß in Horb, Württemberg, who used the home of the stocking weaver Lorenz Riess as his base of operations. Lancaster residents who did not use the Beyerles sent messages and obtained inheritances from the storekeeper Jacob Schaffner in Hitestown, who had contacts in Essen. The Klein family of Kusel, in the Pfalz-Zweibrücken, some of whom had settled near Albany, New York, sent letters to Europe asking for their property through their cousin Heinrich in Lancaster. Georg Börstler, born at Assenheim, in the Palatinate, and active for some years as a blacksmith, served many clients from the Pennsylvania towns of Oley, Amity township, Elizabethtown, Nazareth, and Bethelehem between 1734 and the late 1760s.[29]

Johannes Sautter of Dürrwangen, who owned a dry goods store at Second Street near the German auction house, used auction day and the taverns of Philadelphia as opportunities to advertise his trips back to Germany for clients, and inserted notices in Saur's paper. David Lumbeck, a bookbinder by trade, used Heinrich Keppele's house to store and sell his books before returning to Mannheim to retrieve his family, carrying letters with him. Simon Keppler, also a trader in the same part of town, returned to his home village, Aidlingen, in the Böblingen area, just southwest of Stuttgart. He represented clients on his many visits to the Reich, touching base at Darmstadt; Frankfurt; and Nordheim, near Heilbronn, in the Kraichgau. When Jacob Geiger of Ittlingen was in town, clients knew they could ask for him in the same neighborhood, when he stayed with Nicholas Weber. The presence of such agents in the homes of German speakers also brought interested parties, and the curious, together for discussion about how to use the common-law mechanisms of the colonies to secure inheritances at home in the Reich. And out of such discussions and puzzles came Saur's printed expositions on property in the 1750s.

German speakers at greater distances from Philadelphia—for example, in upstate New York; far western Pennsylvania; Virginia; or Frederick County, Maryland—benefited more rarely from agent networks and information. Saur found distributor-agents for his almanacs and newspaper as far north as Stone Arabia, on the Mohawk River. Yet it was German speakers' geographical access—or lack of access—to the network, that controlled their relationship to the recovery of property and their role in discussions of the problems surrounding the term *property* in the German language. A former resident of Edenkoben, in the Palatinate, Maria Catharine Andrein, wanted to recover an inheritance from her mother totaling about seventy Gulden. Although she lived in New York, through Saur's paper she contacted the Philadelphia merchant Heinrich Mensch, who successfully recovered for her.[30]

Between 1739 and 1750 the three shillings' cost for a year's subscription to Saur's newspaper had to sustain the operation, because Saur had not yet charged for advertisements. Neither did many of his "subscribers" actually pay what they owed, as he complained to his readers. Perhaps reflecting the rapidly expanding circulation created by German immigration, Saur finally began charging his readership of between four thousand and ten thousand persons for advertisements. Not too surprisingly, eminent brokers and agents such as Heinrich Keppele, and other Philadelphia worshippers at Saint Michael's Lutheran Church, such as David Schäffer and Ernst Ludwig Baisch, used the paper to remind people to pay what they owed. Since all mortals must die, debts should be paid so that heirs will not have to be troubled by creditors, Keppele warned; irresponsible people had already cost him much money. Saur heartily recommended the avoidance of courts and indebtedness. And this topic seemed to spur him into active consideration of the problem of property, couched in pietist terms as "worldly goods."[31]

Saur's almanac reached even more German speakers than did his paper. *Der Hoch-Deutsch Americanische Calender . . .* , begun in 1738, announced to purchasers that it would concentrate on "various needful and edifying theological topics, and also household remedies." Saur's habit of interlacing theology with household remedies also provided the printer with a context in which to begin advising his readers on the issue of property and its security in an English-language legal culture. He attempted to clarify these matters after about ten years spent putting out a straightforward set of astrological tables and listings of court days, and indulging himself in essays on agricultural problems. He reached beyond his essays on liberty of conscience, exemplified in the acts of heroic religious dissenters, and his attacks on Catholics, Lutherans, greedy lawyers, clergymen, and unscrupulous physicians. In 1749 Saur began to disregard his early heading of "Courten oder Gerichts-Tage" and settled instead for a simpler heading, "Courten," as he opened an essay on how unworthy it was for Christians to go to law. But two years later, he hit upon a novel technique, the use of the "political conversation" to encourage public discussion among German speakers about difficult and obscure areas of colonial property law.[32]

Saur's introduction of the conceit "Ein Gespräch" or "A Conversation between a Newcomer and an Inhabitant of Pennsylvania," produced consequences far beyond what he probably intended.[33] Between 1751 and 1756 Saur regularly used the Gespräch to instruct his readers, and by 1755 he had introduced the same technique into his newspaper as he printed in argumentative form a discussion of Franklin's proposed bill for the introduction of a militia, which this time Saur did not oppose as vigorously as he had Weiser's advocacy of a similar act in 1741.[34]

British literary and political writers had begun using the "political conversation," or "discourse," to encourage the "culture of conversation" in the early years of the eighteenth century. Writers used this conceit to present choices and provide open access to topics formerly the sole province of government ministers. As a result, the judgment of the individual, and the sovereignty of that judgment over the entire spectrum of social and political topics, increased apace. The juxtaposition of ideas and possibilities, and the underlying dualism and rationality suggested by these conversations, not only encouraged the use of subjective judgment, already common among English speakers as well as German-speaking pietists, but also provoked a more active engagement in public, cultivated political life.[35]

The conversation as a literary conceit had a long history in the German almanacs or calendars whose content and style were familiar to Saur. The focus of the conversation had never been primarily political. In the 1500s the yearly almanac emerged as an intimate part of daily German life, containing not just information on astrological signs, weather, court days, and medical topics but also tales or stories. In fact, a tale or story became a central feature of the almanac. But in the eighteenth century, the stories in German-language almanacs—in sharp contrast to the picaresque tales of *Der abenteuerliche Simplicissimus* (1669), by Hans Jakob Christopher von Grimmelshausen—concentrated on political events. The telling of actual historical events in the form of a fictitious conversation aided the construction of a genuine self-consciousness tying the reader's personal life and story not to a fable, or to "stories" in general, but to present politics. The "miracle stories" or fabulous events of the earlier almanacs fell into disuse. Now dialogue, either between two fictive persons or between a storyteller and the reader, increasingly characterized the almanacs and their stories; and the stories, no longer direct carryovers from a "folk" tradition, were literary and didactic efforts. By the time the *Curfürstlich badischer gnädigst privilegierter Landkalender* of 1750 was replaced in popularity by Johann Hebel's *Rheinländischer Hausfreund* in 1808, this transformation had been completed. Saur participated in this process on his side of the Atlantic.[36]

Since in the 1750s Saur still held a near monopoly on the German-language publishing in the New World, commercial or competitive pressure seems an unlikely explanation for his introduction of the "conversation" in his almanac and newspaper. As a non-Lutheran, however, he may have been responding on confessional grounds to the pioneering effort of the brothers Armbrüsters, Lutheran arrivals from Mannheim. Gotthard Armbrüster's almanac for 1750 represents the earliest surviving example of the German-language political conversation.[37] The upsurge in immigration, coupled with the rising interest in property recoveries and security for lands and chattels in the new land under English law, probably spurred both Saur and Armbrüster to adopt this didactic approach. The passage of a naturalization act (13 Geo. 2, c. 7) by Parliament in 1740 had prompted two years later a bill enabling non-Quaker aliens to affirm allegiance without swearing an oath, as well as providing that estates of aliens who died prior to naturalization would not escheat to the Crown. Governor George Thomas rejected the provisions regarding property rights, separated from the affirmation proposals into a separate bill. But Saur, alerted to the potential dangers to property rights, urged his readers to be naturalized. During 1742, some three hundred followed his advice. His reprinting in his almanacs of 1743 and following years of selected laws regarding inheritance and property foreshadowed his discussion at the end of the decade, of the complex issue of English laws surrounding inheritance.[38]

Some of his readers objected, claiming that they found the presentations difficult. They preferred a simple, straightforward retailing of information and comment. Saur, undeterred, pursued the issues of property inheritance, will making, and avoidance of lawyers and courts, as well as German fathers' moral obligations to provide through English legal mechanisms for their wives and families.

Saur—typically—never admitted in print that the Lutheran challenge posed by Gotthard Armbrüster's almanac had spurred him to launch a discussion of property issues in the early 1750s. The requests for help in obtaining inheritances from abroad, the requests from the Reich from authorities trying to contact legitimate heirs in the colonies, and perhaps also the increasing number of immigrants asking local worthies such as the pastors and Saur for help in writing wills—all remain plausible additional motives. No shift in Pennsylvania's laws regarding naturalization and denization occurred to explain an upsurge in 1751 in German-speaking people's anxiety about protecting their property through mastery of the law. Nor can one find a believable controversy in the politics of the late 1740s that accounts for Saur's attention to the issue. Saur may have been alarmed at Lutheran successes symbolized by the creation of the Ministerium of Pennsylvania in 1748, Saint Michael's dedication that year, and the Armbrüster almanac. But he seems also to have been motivated by genuine concern that the German speakers who had successfully reestablished themselves as property holders in North America did not know how to secure their property for posterity. Perhaps without completely acknowledging to himself his own internal shift, Saur began to perceive the intimate link that connected the concept of interior liberty to the rights and obligations surrounding property, the "worldly goods" that increasingly marked German speakers' success in the New World.

His interest was nearly matched by Mühlenberg's. By 1749, in a letter to a Hanoverian friend, Mühlenberg suggested that the kind of liberty exercised in North America led, in the absence of guild restrictions, to extraordinary riches not only among the English but also among "right roguish shopkeepers among the Germans who could teach the subtlest Jews somewhat concerning bargains." Mühlenberg rarely specified who he meant in these comments, but he later suggested that the "godless prattling storekeepers who move about all over the country" included precisely cultural brokers on the make, such as the entrepreneurial Gensels, Beyerles, and their ilk, who plagued congregational life while acting as sometimes unscrupulous agents in inheritance cases.[39] Saur, showing a similar attitude, warned his readers in 1755 that they should under no circumstances sign *ein Accord* with a newlander regarding their inheritances. Instead, they should choose "a propertied citizen of fixed residence . . . who intends to do business faithfully." Everyone should have such accords written by someone who understood how to execute such documents, before a justice and a notary. If this were done, then even a "Newlander [is] compelled to do business honorably" ("so ist der Neuländer genöthiget redlich zu handeln").[40]

The general context that produced Saur's Gespräche can be inferred. Their contents were remarkable. They began with the now-customary praise of Pennsylvania as a land of no taxes, little government, and material plenty. But the heart of Saur's contribution lay in his tutorials in English legal procedures, and in the language he employed to explain these technicalities, as he cleverly interlarded such technical discussions with the domestic concerns his readers had come to expect.

The newcomer's natural anxiety to find a good place to work, and to put his affairs in order so as to enjoy an undisturbed old age, seems an unremarkable set of concerns common to local life in Europe or North America. Saur felt compelled to insert into the mouth of his experienced settler a long, moralistic discourse on the danger to the Christian life posed by the lust for worldly goods. To the newcomer's lament about the great distances, the loneliness, the absence of churches and schools, and the probability of dying without pastoral comfort, Saur responded by noting the deplorable state of the Reich. Were the people there any better off for all their churches, preachers, and schools? And if one were to criticize the bad conduct of clergy and their families, he would likely be saddled with a suit, brought forward by the lawyers who always managed to twist words to their own ends.

Saur cannily spread out his conversation over the next two years (to 1753), first answering anxieties about the lack of sourdough for good rye bread, the dreaded rattlesnakes, and the vexations of cows wandering off in the absence of good cowherds. But these domestic exchanges bracketed a steadily more substantive discussion of public issues. Saur's response to the worried newcomer consisted of instruction in how to use the apothecaries of Pennsylvania and how to secure home remedies against diseases and accidents, as well as an explanation, in 1752, of how schoolmasters and educational opportunities actually existed within various religious groups.[41]

In his 1753 almanac, after beginning the conversation again on the care of animals, Saur moved into the issue of buying and selling lands, with the experienced settler warning the newcomer to consult God before buying a *Plantasche*, which was best done without a lawyer but not without a bill of sale—which Saur carefully referred to for newcomers' sake as a "Kaufbrief," not a "Bill of Sääl," as he often termed it. At this juncture the newcomer introduces the issue of inheritance, commenting, "I hear that in this country there is much strife over inheritances, which occurs because the English law is different from that in Germany in many respects. How is it here if one should die and has no testament? Who are the heirs, and what happens?"[42]

The experienced settler responds by first reminding the newcomer that many spend their entire lives ignoring their souls and whether they lived a godly and orderly life, thinking only of worldly affairs. Yet it was true that many had worries about their worldly goods and what would occur after their death. Sadly, many did not understand English law "and write either too much or too little, so that their testament is challenged." In a long and detailed description, Saur explained Pennsylvania intestate law, the favoring of eldest sons with a double portion. But Saur gave primacy of place to widows' rights to their thirds of rent or income and of the moveables until remarriage. To the newcomer's observation that in Pennsylvania everyone could do with property as he wished, Saur warned that the widow's thirds were protected absolutely but that an ungodly eldest son had to be set aside with the ritual English shilling, "otherwise the Testament is invalid, and just such a malicious eldest son will take two parts as soon as the testament is declared invalid." Saur came back time and again to a barely disguised acknowledgement of the wife's central role in the German-American household and farm, and the dangers to her status posed by an unscrupulous, Americanized eldest son.

Saur felt compelled to remind the newcomer that the best way to look upon worldly goods was to follow Christ, who let Judas care for the common purse and whose own garments the soldiers divided among themselves. People of this world ("natürliche Menschen") tend on the other hand to strive with one another and end up suing in the courts with lawyers. To avoid this latter possibility, Saur's inhabitant lays down a series of steps for the newcomer. The Germantown publisher knew that the ideal way of following Christ, the communal option regarding worldly goods, would find few followers among his readership. His construction of a middle ground between idealism and worldliness subtly but significantly began shifting the manner in which he was willing to treat the issue of property, and the obligations that English liberty brought with it.

In a North American testament, Saur noted, the precise inventory of what was to be passed on to heirs came first followed by the exact designation of children as heirs forever, and careful specifications for philanthropy—to a hospital, or to the poor or the sick. (These last-named types of property devisal, he knew, largely belonged to married women in the Reich.) Both executors and two witnesses needed to be mentioned by name, and the signature of the testator and the signature of the witnesses were needed to finish the properly executed document. Saur's care in pointing out the need for an inventory of the estate reflected more than colonial procedures. He here tied the alien practice of writing a will to the familiar village routine of inventory which estate partition demanded throughout the entire southwestern Reich. Saur also encouraged philanthropy and largesse by suggesting that provisions ad pias causas should be made carefully, reflecting his suspicion of the clergy among the welter of confessions among German speakers in Pennsylvania.

But the newcomer—and Saur—devote the balance of the conversation to the status of married women and the role of public authorities in settling complex questions—for instance, what would happen if the testator's son or heir predeceased the testator. Here Saur reflected a particularly sensitive concern. His newcomer becomes quite agitated to hear that despite the hard physical labor German women commonly contributed to bring a "plantation" into order, they would be treated no different from English women, who commonly (according to Saur) worked less diligently. No Christian man of understanding would leave his pious and faithful widow to the mercy of English law and its thirds. As the experienced settler observes, "a true Christian love and fidelity will not go unrewarded, either in this life or in eternity."

Outraged once again, the newcomer protests the fact that if his son has already been named the father's heir and dies, the son's property will not automatically fall back to the father as would have happened in the German southwest. Instead, his next oldest son, or that son's heirs will receive the property: "That is an astonishing Law! especially if I gave this out of my own poverty and now should be even more needy than before." Counseling the newcomer that one cannot change the ways of the world—but clearly implying his distaste for the law—Saur concluded by warning against going to law, despite the newcomer's admiration of the fact that in Pennsylvania legal suits and complaints are public and everyone seems to have the right to hear and see, or even to speak his mind if he believes that right is not being done. The importance of a public arena in which property could be protected Saur reemphasized by proudly explaining through the experienced settler that under British law one can give affirmation instead of taking an oath. This freedom of conscience is precisely the best evidence that subjects have not only the wisdom of Solomon to recognize what is vain, but also the "spirit and mind of Christ in full measure."

Saur cleverly closed this tutorial with domestic concerns: religious customs, household recipes, and instructions for cleaning spots from clothing and ridding plants of pests. But an extension of the conversation in the 1754 almanac elaborated on definitions of legal and political terms, describing in detail how one should deal with bonds, indentures, and warrants (*Bürgen*).[43] For the most part, Saur pointed out, English law was such that when subjects were quiet, authority had no right to interfere with their lives—precisely the definition of freedom so cherished by German immigrants. Yet there were cases where authority itself could not resolve difficulties, and where the newcomer had to be on guard. Asked to explain, the longtime inhabitant pointed to four troublesome problems: that of someone who had bought land where no valid warrant had been issued; that of a dying person leaving an affair unsettled which could be fought over in court; that of a person wishing to open an inn where strong drinks are sold; and that of a man found dead under circumstances in which no one can say how he died.

The experienced settler takes pains to encourage the newcomer to come to a peaceful arrangement with his neighbor ("mit seinem Nachbar friedlich ausmachen"), and through patient suffering as a Christian, or through the mediation of neighbors, to avoid becoming entangled with the courts. As if to drive home the message of genuine equality, which should make legal disputes unnecessary, the newcomer notes with astonishment that the law against debtors is so severe that even the poorest man can bring the governor to justice. But, he queries, what is this term that I hear of so often, *Freyhalter*, or *Freieholder*? Saur defined the term elegantly: a citizen with fifty pounds in land or chattels, or with at least fifty acres, and twelve of which are in cultivation. In addition, he had to have been a resident for two years and to be naturalized. Saur's experienced settler then explains the notions of representation and property holding, suggesting that those who had a permanent interest in the country had rights to vote, unlike those not owning property. Yet the poor had equal rights before the law and could summon others to collect debts of under forty shillings just as freeholders could. Saur suggested that the severity of laws against debt worked to maintain order and protect Pennsylvania's inhabitants. Still, Saur warned his readers, "protect yourself from debt!"[44] In Saur's mind, the dreaded condition of indebtedness undercut and nullified liberty and property to such a degree that he could not discuss the merits and liberties of Pennsylvania without charging his readers with a central obligation to remain solvent, a charge freighted with moral as well as pragmatic qualities. Indebtedness threw the entire economy of the household into question, threatening ruin, especially for people insufficiently fluent to defend themselves before English-language courts. Although Saur could not have known that debt was the most common cause to bring German speakers before the courts, either as defendants against other Germans or English, or—far more rarely—as plaintiffs against English speakers, he did know that indebtedness was a common and worrisome condition.

In the 1755 almanac, Saur interrupted the conversation, instead catechizing his readers on what the term *Eigentumsherr* meant, explaining that the proprietors of Pennsylvania "owned" all property in the province but that this did not interfere with freeholders' rights. In this discussion he defined an assemblyman; urged his readers to get a receipt (*Quittung*) upon payment of debts; and noted that the words "more or less" ought always to be included in any land survey. This briefer conversation rounded out a 1754 reminder to German speakers to avoid debt and to be especially careful in the acquisition of lands, since clear title to realty would qualify a man to vote for assemblymen, a significant turn toward the public arena.

In 1756 Saur resumed the political conversation, demanding that the reader comprehend the legal process so as to avoid losing property to sharp Englishmen. Here the newcomer's major complaint centers on the problem of invalid warrants that could lead to confiscation of improved land. The experienced settler repeats again that even though the law seems harsh and unchristian, no judge can set aside the law of the land. German speakers under eighteen, for instance, might mistakenly sign bills of sale, but those documents are invalid, and later buyers who take up such lands unwittingly are simply out of luck. By contrast, in the Reich, "common and important sales and purchases are made in the presence of the court and council [*Gerichtsmänner*], who understand the law and can serve the uninformed; they do this gladly, because it is customary." Let the English settle their affairs according to their laws in their own language; German speakers, as long as they are peaceful and no judge is involved, can also arrange things for themselves, more or less as in the Reich ("dürffen ihre Sachen untereinander auch selbst machen nach ihren Gedäncken"). Yet knowledge of how the laws regarding property worked in Pennsylvania was indispensable.

By 1758, the year of his death, Saur conceded that some readers objected to the complicated conversations. Others believed that the device made useful lessons and counsel more accessible to the unlearned. To satisfy both, he included a long essay on a large snake and the description of the horrors of the current war in the Reich, but also a "small conversation." Saur could not resist a lengthy personal observation that in Pennsylvania alone more than ten thousand pounds per year could be saved if people avoided suing each other in the courts. But, as he noted wryly, ending his remarks above the table of court days, since there are people who prefer the way of wrath to the path of peace, "they will find here a description, when and on what days the quarrelsome can sue one another."

III

After Saur's death, his son, Christopher, returned from time to time to the warnings against going to law, admitting in 1763 that he had nearly lost all hope of deterring German speakers from suing one another. Indeed, so contentious had the Germans become that lawyers in Pennsylvania were commonly heard to say, "If we did not have the Germans, two lawyers would have to ride on one horse." Yet, Saur concluded, he believed that no purpose would be served by continuing the essays on the law, since many Germans followed the advice of the almanac and settled their differences among themselves. He repeated the strictures against debt, and above all, against settling such indebtedness by hiring attorneys.[45] In fact, the last conversation in the Saur almanac had appeared in 1760. It was a dialogue on authority and freedom, which concluded that Pennsylvania, in contrast to Europe, enjoyed the mildness of its authorities and because of its freedom had unheard of privileges. The younger Saur abandoned the political conversation permanently with the 1760 almanac.[46]

The Seven Years' War, whose end the elder Saur did not live to see, also worked subtly on the language the German speakers came to use in their descriptions of Pennsylvania. Whereas earlier writers had boasted of the absence of government in Pennsylvania, and its people's liberty of conscience, writers of the 1760s were more sober. Nicholas Bach, writing home to the Palatinate in 1769, used the services of the Philadelphia agent Ernst Ludwig Baisch from Saint Michael's. To his family he reported himself "fresh and healthy" and asked them to care for the sale and investment of his inheritance, but no enthusiastic description of life in America finished his letter. Similarly, Adam Sontag, who wrote from Reading in June 1770 to his brother, reported that everyone was well and that the land was "good." But the "wild men" (Native Americans) had engaged the settlers of Pennsylvania "for many years in the bloodiest war . . . whose horrors no man who had not experienced them would believe. Only the arms of our King have through God's assurance finally overcome them and brought peace, or at least a truce."[47]

The conceit of the 1756 conversation in which the elder Saur juxtaposed English cunning and German virtue in a peaceable land probably fooled no one. Caution and the inability to master technical legal terms probably explain why relatively few German speakers used the courts for more than basic registering of deeds and recovery of simple debts. Christopher Saur, Sr., must have known what the court records suggest— by the time the immigration peaked and the war began in 1754, indebtedness was as common among German speakers as among English speakers. Saur, however, cleverly and deliberately constructed a contrast between godly German-speaking pietists and ungodly English law, to urge German speakers to master alien forms and find ways to further their cultural values. The war simply illustrated how real were the dangers to household and real property. The encouragement Saur provided evoked memories of village life, where public authorities oversaw buying and selling. Now, in North America, one would have to come to agreements (*ausmachen*) with neighbors in a common context and fix affairs according "to our own thinking" to avoid costly suits. At the same time, Saur insisted that the novelties of North American inheritance law, and the procedures for the warranting and selling of lands, could be mastered. Slowly but certainly, the linkage emerged that tied transferred cultural concerns for the household and faith to the idea that one who would enjoy liberty and property under British had law obligations to the public world.

The language that Saur helped to perpetuate, and to which he helped give authoritative stature, mixed German and English terms, creating a hybrid form that reflected where penetration of English into German daily life was most difficult: areas having to do with the law of property. The evolution of a kind of half-language was not unique to German speakers. Nor was "lexical interference," the misperception of the sounds of an unfamiliar language because of what the hearers think is being said, unique to German speakers' cultural adjustment. But Saur knew that this problem had to be addressed. In one of his attempts, he tried to explain what Germans thought they were hearing when they sometimes—with comical results—attempted to replicate the greeting "How d'ye do" (realized as "Hau di rhu" by Saur).[48] The purpose of this 1754 warning, however, was to suggest that English expressions should not be used unless one was absolutely certain of their meaning. Immediately thereafter, Saur reported that a lawyer had said that he would accept business from the Germans as gladly as from others, so long as documents were written and recorded properly.

Mühlenberg noted the similar difficulties which German speakers created by confusing what they thought they heard in English. In 1772 the pastor noted how Germans from the district of Mount Joy called the district *Mondschein* ("moonshine") "because the sound is somewhat similar. Even so, they call the agent of the king (in English the *King's Attorney*) the kings' *Saturnus* because they find the word in the calendar and the sound is almost identical with *attorney*. Consequently the German preachers, unless they make some acquaintance with the English language, very readily fall into the third language, and from saying *Mondschein* slip into the habit of saying *Saturnus* too."[49]

Shortly after the elder Saur's death, and just before Henry Miller began publication of his newspaper *Der Wöchentliche Philadelphische Staatsbote*, concerns similar to those of the younger Christopher Saur—concerns about German speakers' lack of comprehension of the proper definition of liberty, and how to secure their property—received new attention. A Berks County attorney, David Henderson, decided to publish a handbook of English legal terms in German. Henderson himself was not adept enough to translate his efforts, and he turned to Miller, who in 1761 issued *Des Landsmanns Advocat*, the only German-language legal handbook printed in America before the Revolution. Henderson had consulted with Conrad Weiser before the latter's untimely death in the summer of 1759; had contacted the Lancaster justice Emmanuel Zimmermann, to whom he dedicated the book; and had spoken with Mühlenberg and with Weiser's sons, as well. All encouraged the project. Explaining why he had written the book, Henderson encouraged the rapid acquisition of English and excused the book only as a stopgap measure. His purpose required a German-language edition, however, for he meant to instruct German speakers in the proper understanding of English liberty.[50]

That concept, Henderson wrote, Britons summed up in the ritual and privilege known as the jury trial. For what this important institution guaranteed was that "each is to possess the right to enjoy the fruits of his labor, and under the protection of certain, known, and publicly printed laws, to see the same enjoyment extended over his wife, his children, his good name, his person, and his life." The right of possession and the means of passing on the fruits of one's labor produced the longest entries in Henderson's book: "Concerning the Property of One Dying without a Will," and "Concerning Last Wills and Testaments." The only other section comparable in length dealt with a related subject, naturalization.[51]

Henderson's table of contents, as translated by Miller, reflected the hybrid mix of English and German terms that had been codified by Saur in his earlier grammars. Yet both Henderson and Miller seemed to sense that the analogies to the institutions of the German southwest local culture Saur had sometimes made were not correct, and omitted them. Significantly, they refused to attempt a translation of *jury trial*, precisely the institution that Henderson had argued provided the surety for both liberty and property. Saur, in his writings, had translated *jury* as "des Gerichts" (literally, "of the court," meaning the village members of the council and court, who were referred to either by the term *Gerichtsverwandten* or, more simply, in the partitions of estate, by the phrase *des Gerichts*).[52]

To equate a jury of one's peers, ordinary freeholders (another untranslatable term), with these village officials was misleading. But it did give German speakers appearing before courts at least some confidence to think that the juries had some official standing, and somehow provided the same kind of forum of collective advice and judgment they had known at home.

Henderson's treatise did not replicate Saur's approach. Instead, in his introduction, he put forth the notion, which came to characterize Miller's assumptions as well, that "there is a considerable agreement between their [i.e., English and German] languages, and the one-syllable words are nearly all alike. The old English came from Germany, and I am certain, that the greatest part of their present day descendents stand ready to greet with open arms a people with whom they stand in so close a degree of kinship [*in solcher nahen Verwandschaft stehen*]."[53]

Henderson and Miller nevertheless did incorporate other usages that had come to be universal, providing, for instance, under "Concerning Fences," both the correct German *Zäune* plus the German-American *Fensen*, the term used from Nova Scotia to Georgia by all German speakers. This borrowed term reflected the difficulty German speakers had experienced in transferring to rail fences the same qualities, and attendant rights and privileges, that in village life had belonged to stone boundaries.[54] While village markers indicated properties such as the *Allmend*, the bounds of the village itself, and stone field-markers certainly indicated property boundaries, fencing as such was a rarity in the German southwest, and the novelty of this English phenomenon prevented German speakers from making a simple translation of one word to the other. Miller rejected Saur's approach of equating English terms and German-American borrowings: for example, the term *zu Zinsen*, which had become in Saur's hands the grammatically different *auf Interesse* referring to interest paid on loans. He did not call contracts "Kontracten" (as one sometimes saw in Saur) but the correct "Kaufbriefe," explaining that this was actually a "Vertrag" (contract) between two or more parties. Henderson and Miller also carefully explained the issue of taxation by pointing out that excises (*Akzisen*) were taxes on liquors, or other items in use (*Verbrauchsteure*); these taxes they carefully distinguished from the county tax, using the correct German *Taxen* to designate this direct tax, which might also have been designated "direkte Steur."[55]

Henderson's volume contained more than a clarification of difficult terms, however. He related the purpose of sharpening German speakers' understanding of complex English legal language to the accepted wisdom that "it is a miserable form of slavery where the laws are unknown . . . the learned of the old Roman or imperial laws noted, that 'before subjects could be bound to a law, such had to be made public in sufficient manner . . . because it is impossible for a people who are not aware of a law, to observe it, or to be subject to it.' " Just as in Saur's writings, the public arena, in which an informed readership could openly debate issues that had formerly been the secret preserve only of princely officials, lay at the heart of British liberty. Yet this discussion was still taking place in German, and therefore constituted a kind of "private sociability"— not completely identified with the "public" realm but certainly not personal, or completely divorced from the public realm, either. Some, Henderson noted, had tried to discourage him from publishing the work, not so much because of its length and the difficulties of translation as because they were "mob leaders" (*Pöbelführer*) "would rather that their countrymen remain blind, as that they should suffer no longer to have the honor of being leaders." They had expressed the notion that "as soon as the Germans have the laws made clear to them, they will begin through legal process to bring us to ruin"—as if, Henderson sarcastically noted, "ignorance were the mother of liberty."[56] All intelligent people knew, to the contrary, that just as knowledge of sacred scripture saved people from error and superstition, so too, only knowledge could overcome that ignorance of the laws which could lead to errors, eventually tying one up in suits to the detriment of one's property. Liberty and property, conceived of in the closed, familial, and religious context of transferred cultural norms, could only flourish in North America when tied to responsibility for, and active involvement, in the public arena of legal and political discourse. This was the real message and meaning of Henderson's treatise, one that could not have created a response had Saur's work not already shaped the social discourse among German speakers and readers over the previous twenty years.

Henderson did not intend his book to make a learned legal expert out of a farmer. But if the current generation of German speakers were brought into full contact with English law, the succeeding generation would, Henderson concluded, make his work superfluous. That was his intent. The growing sense not only that a public political arena existed but also that German speakers were compelled, if only out of self-interest, to participate in it, Henderson insisted on even more directly than had Christopher Saur through his "political conversation."[57]

It remained, however, for Henry Miller to profit from Saur's labors in the 1760s and to engage British colonial politics fully in the German-American language. Miller was born in 1702 and baptized Johann Heinrich Möller in Rhoden, County Waldeck. His father was Swiss, a stonemason in Altstätten near Zürich, where the future printer lived as a boy. Miller served an apprenticeship in Basel before going to London; eventually he landed in New York, and in 1741 settled in Philadelphia. Beginning his career under Franklin's tutelage, Miller returned to Europe a year later converted from Lutheranism to the Moravian faith and instructed to set up a Moravian printing shop in the Hague. Wanderings in the late 1740s took him through Great Britain until in 1751 he came again to Pennsylvania and began publishing the *Lancastersche Zeitung*. Back in Europe again in 1754, he published a German-language paper for the Hanoverian and Hessian troops during the Seven Years' War in Britain. By 1760 he had returned to Philadelphia, where he translated Henderson's law book.[58]

Miller demonstrated from the start a deeply cosmopolitan, acculturated, pro-British posture. He unabashedly oriented his publishing toward politics and the shaping of public opinion. His flirtation with the Moravians temporarily over, he signaled his independence in the 1762 broadside *Geistlicher Irrgarten . . .* , a complex maze of biblical passages directing players from four different sides through a labyrinth. At the bottom of the page Miller added "Philadelphia, printed by Henrich Miller, in the year after his release out of the garden of errors and the opening up of heaven's gate, 1762."[59] The Swiss identity of his father's household, never completely absent from his self-consciousness, grew especially after 1765. By August 1770 Miller enthusiastically noted an essay by Christian Ziguerer, a preacher at Grüsch, in Graubunden. Comparing his reaction to this piece with his admiration for Gotthilf August Francke's *Heiliger und sicherer Glaubens-Weg*, Miller concluded that an American version in both English and German deserved publication. For those who had doubts about the essay's theological soundness, Miller triumphantly pointed out that a synod of pastors and professors in the Swiss Reformed church had already verified the work's orthodoxy.[60] Miller's independent posture and his many wanderings barely disguised the fact that his identity, and the one he chose to promote as a model for German speakers' understanding of their rights in America, sprang from his years in Switzerland and his cosmopolitan travels.

The self-concept of German speakers in Europe had been vague and ill-defined for centuries, largely because of the local privileges that territories within the Reich exercised under the theoretical supremacy of the emperor. Miller assumed that acculturated German speakers in the colonies could make easy analogies to other countries' experiences as he had done. By the mid-1700s, some German writers in Europe had begun to complain openly of the lack of a "German" identity and to cast about for appropriate models that might supply this lack. Most thought that, although some princes had regularly aped the French court at Versailles, the traditions of German local life suggested the republics of the Netherlands or Switzerland as apt models. Certainly, similarities of local institutional life had long suggested that the small republics might have something to offer, especially to the German southwest, which shared many affinities in population and religion with Switzerland.[61]

Miller, sensitive to his newcomer status before the German reading public, declared in the first issue of his paper that he intended to serve "the Germans in this part of the world, so far removed from their fatherland." His somewhat chauvinistic reporting of German overseas bravery sought to reassure both readers and himself that "the German people have never been inferior to any other in bravery, or any other virtues." Both Christian and civic (*bürgerliche*) virtues found room with him, although no one could miss the preference given to secular affairs even in the title of his newspaper, which can be rendered in English as *Weekly Philadelphia State Messenger: With the Newest Foreign and Local Political News, including the Remarkable Events Occurring from Time to Time in the Church and the World of Learning*. The title of Miller's almanac, the *Neueste, Verbessert-und Zuverlässige Amerikanische Calendar*, while admitting that the almanac was "newest and improved," also claimed that it was "reliable."[62]

For the first two years of the paper's existence, Miller faithfully reported on British and North American politics. He took for granted that his readers had a cosmopolitan interest in the world and the capacity to understand politics. By 1764, he began to use without comment the term *American* to describe his readers, and melded together English and North American political history in the German language. Yet Miller was disappointed by his readers' indifference to politics. He took to identifying in parentheses cities in the German Reich outside of the southwest from which so many German speakers came. Towns such as Speyer, Heilbronn, Stuttgart, or Landau were clear. But Regensburg had to be located in Bavaria on the Danube, and identified as where the *Reichstag* met, and Berlin had to be labeled as "a large and well populated city in the Central Mark of Brandenburg on the River Spree, the residence of the King of Prussia and Elector of Brandenburg."[63] Miller rarely drew upon historical images from the German past, sensing ignorance on the part of too many readers. His Swiss heritage remained unimportant until the crisis with the British Empire deepened with the passage of the Stamp Act and the campaign to secure a royal charter for Pennsylvania. He allowed himself only the observation in 1765 upon a letter from "*a German North American*" that the "*German Tongue* is the *Mother* of the *English Language*, so that . . . the laying a *Double Burden* on a good ancient *Parent* . . . [breaks] that divine Commandment, *Thou shalt honour thy Father and thy Mother.*" This was an obvious reference to the double tax laid upon foreign language newspapers by the hated Stamp Act that Miller vociferously opposed in his paper. In the aftermath of these controversies, Miller's allegiance to the Swiss struggles for liberty emerged and deepened between 1768 and 1775.[64]

At first glance, Miller's unencumbered translations of British parliamentary debates, ministerial decisions, and provincial politics do seem to demonstrate that German speakers had no trouble penetrating the mysteries of British legal and political culture, and hence, that they would have had little difficulty in understanding the debates over liberty and property. But Miller assumed a different audience, a different response, than did Saur, whom Miller never ceased to delight in attacking or belittling.

Miller had lived in England, worked for Franklin, and translated Henderson's essay on the law. He was deeply familiar with British political and legal terminology, and at first assumed that his readers were, too. He made no comments on and gave few explanations for his accounts of British politics. At first, he may well have thought that he would lure away Saur's readership, and that German speakers were fully conversant with, and interested in, political culture. Although he aimed at a pan-colonial distribution, with agents located from Halifax to Ebenezer, by 1776 his circulation may not have exceeded one thousand. He probably reached only half as many people as did Saur. The best explanation for his decision not to explain political terms seems to be that, after having to explain where German cities were, Miller gave up on reaching most of Saur's readership.

He remained consistently and aggressively proroyalization in Pennsylvania, and allied himself to the imperial perspective of Benjamin Franklin, whose politics he unswervingly supported. His list of correspondents included Daniel Jacobi, the planter in Little Fork, on Great Battle Run, in Culpeper, who received the *Staatsbote,* delivered via the Reformed schoolmaster Holzklau. (Perhaps this explains how in the 1760s the Hebron settlement, the oldest settlement of German speakers in Virginia, kept abreast of Miller's perspective.)[65] Judging from the content of his paper, he assumed that just such a smaller group of informed and acculturated readers constituted his audience—the cultural brokers who since the 1740s had run the taverns, owned the bakeries, breweries, and the plantations, engaged in coastal and overseas shipping, and comprised the leadership in German North American settlements.

Miller shared in the general adulation of Frederick the Great of Prussia, apparently oblivious to the combination of taxation and military expenditures on which the success of the Prussian state was grounded. The *Staatsbote* promulgated support for Britain's continental ally, reflecting the enthusiasm for Frederick engendered during the Seven Years' War.[66] Yet Miller avoided the German past, taking for granted readers' status as German-speaking British subjects in North America. He devoted none of his efforts toward their domestic concerns. Miller poked fun at the unease of the Quakers when confronted by demands for military defense of the frontier, and their fears engendered by Pontiac's Rebellion. He pointed out that as the elders of the colony had sown, so now the young would reap, not knowing how to defend province and city.

Miller may well have concentrated on reaching the influential and the acculturated among the German-Americans. Even so, he could not have drawn on their abilities to urge deeper engagement with the political culture of British North America without Saur's prior work. Despite his invocation of remembered village customs that had protected inherited property, Saur recognized the need for German speakers in North America to write wills, to register deeds properly, to be alert in using common-law instruments. Similarly, his definition of liberty purely along negative lines, as freedom from taxation or from the claims of a state church, gradually had to be modified to include at least the possibility of providing active support *for* a colony defense and voting to keep the proprietary charter privileges intact. Miller's attempt to reach those who needed no elaborate explanations of "representation," however, could only succeed because so many German speakers had begun to sense that privileges, liberty from oppression, and the enjoyment of property rights were connected to their mutual obligations within the German-language churches, and with obligations toward the larger, political culture. This sense had been incomplete in the 1750s, in no small part because the migration of German speakers had peaked in 1753, bringing enormous numbers of late arrivals who did not as yet perceive this connection.

In the 1760s, among German speakers from Georgia to New York, concepts of liberty and property (whether transferred or hybrid German-American) solidified with remarkable speed and became an integral part of German speakers' relationship to the political culture of North America. For Lutherans, the local congregation provided the forum in which this process took place, using the language that Saur and Miller had helped to fashion.

7

Carolina Liberty and Property, and "Such Monstrous Sins"

THE MISSIONARY network developed by the Halle fathers around their Georgia experiment naturally brought South Carolina to the attention of European Lutherans, increasingly so after midcentury. Both letters and goods bound for Ebenezer passed through the port of Charleston. But the initial impressions of South Carolina received by pietists in the Reich since the 1730s remained overwhelmingly negative. Pastor Boltzius wrote to Samuel Urlsperger of an Ebenezer resident who had traveled overland to Charleston in 1735 to observe the farms and plantations. Although Urlsperger suppressed Boltzius's observation in the published version of the edited reports, the Halle fathers noted Boltzius's conclusion in the original: "both the masters and the servants appear so miserable and live in such monstrous sins that one is horrified at it." Rather than endanger Ebenezer or spread missionary support too thin, Halle and Augsburg concurred with Boltzius that since "the people on the plantations in Carolina are like the nobility in Germany and have means enough to employ theological students, as is done in Germany, for their own benefit and for that of their children," this was not a field for Halle's work. The Salzburger, too, agreed, returning to say that "he could now understand what Ebenezer is and that he was now resolved to remain in Ebenezer with water and bread rather than to live well in a place where people walk the straight path to hell."[1]

A generation later, the extraordinary costs—in Halle's opinion—of using Charleston as the connecting port to Ebenezer reinforced the pietists' doubts about a colony nonetheless known to be filled with German speakers in need of spiritual care. In a letter to Francke in 1762, Friedrich Wilhelm Pasche in London explained why costs in Charleston were so high. British shippers told Pasche that the connection from Hamburg-

Altona to South Carolina far exceeded the 8 percent costs incurred if one shipped to the East Indies. "The ships to the East-Indies have good convoys for nearly the entire journey, those to America, however, were left more open to danger."[2] Even before Mühlenberg's successes in Pennsylvania by the 1750s dwarfed Halle's original missionary effort in Georgia, he too, weighed in against South Carolina.

Mühlenberg, who had originally wanted to serve in Halle's East Indies missions, shared Boltzius's extreme revulsion toward slavery, both because of how the institution brutalized the slaves and masters, and because of the threat slavery posed to Halle's objective of producing self-sufficient, skilled pietist subjects to live under Christian princes. In his first journal entries for 1742, made after witnessing the institution firsthand, Mühlenberg wrote of the mulatto children, "offspring of those white Sodomites who commit fornication with their black slave women. This goes on dreadfully and no one dares to say anything to the blacks concerning the true religion, because the so-called Christians object that the blacks would kill them all, and make themselves masters of Carolina, if they accepted the Christian religion." Contemptuously dismissing the whites' "absurd and contradictory opinion, resting on corrupt reason," Mühlenberg concluded that white Carolinians led more vicious lives than did their slaves. The Halle fathers must have taken special note of the Carolina conspiracy against pedagogy which Mühlenberg observed. By forbidding blacks to "acquire knowledge," the slaveholders attempted to avoid being "punished or disturbed in their sin. This is a horrible state of affairs, which will entail a severe judgment."[3]

One is tempted to conclude that British North American definitions of property and liberty prevailed very quickly among German speaking Lutherans in South Carolina. The absence of Halle's influence first of all meant that the definition of liberty that predominated among many German-speaking settlers was freedom from authority, taxes, and, for that matter, obedience to religious teaching. Likewise, to the consternation of Lutheran pastors and observers, property could neither be conceived nor spoken of apart from the American institution of slavery, which Halle had striven to keep out of its neighboring settlement at Ebenezer. Moreover, Lutheran settlement in South Carolina occurred late—only in the 1750s—and came largely from eastern Württemberg and Ulm, not from the Kraichgau, the Palatinate, Baden, or the vineyard valleys of Württemberg. Neither did a secular trading network emerge in South Carolina among German speaking Lutherans before the Seven Years' War. No "charter group," no cultural brokers, crystallized a set of references within which reflection on the meaning of key terms could develop. Yet events were to prove that more Lutheran pietist emotional expectations sur-

CHARLESTON'S GERMAN–LUTHERAN AREA, CA. 1770

Original map by Win Thrall, 1992. Modeled on information drawn from wills, deeds, and inventories in the South Carolina Department of Archives and History, Columbia, and compared with the map "Ichnography of Charleston, South Carolina" (London, 1788), in South Caroliniana Library, Map Collections, Columbia, S.C.; and Jeanne A. Calhoun et al., *A Survey of Economic Activity in Charleston, 1732–1770* (Charleston, 1982).

rounding property and liberty survived the Atlantic crossing than first appearances suggest.

In contemplating the South Carolina example, it helps to review the possible combinations and permutations of transferred definitions of liberty and property which might have found a home in this province. A positive, inner definition of liberty which encouraged political obedience or disengagement as well as a cultivation of passive spirituality did not flourish, if surviving evidence can be trusted. Early Swiss Reformed settlement in the backcountry of South Carolina left some remnants of both a concern for education and stewardship of property, yet showed no reflections upon the connection of either property or liberty to the broader contours of provincial political life, and established few institutional settings save for scattered and irregularly shepherded congregations. The notion of liberty as freedom from oppression and taxation did undoubtedly lure some German speakers to Carolina, as later inheritance recovery attempts suggest. Yet some fragments of transferred sentiments about property did survive. Among them one can barely discern—almost hidden in the few written records of land transactions and wills, and in the Charleston church order for Saint John's Lutheran congregation—Swabian women's conviction that threats to domestic stability lurked in the form of both pastors and lay elders who took ungodly liberties with alms and church property. Charleston provided the setting in which these suspicions were played out among late-arriving Lutherans from eastern Swabia, in a congregation shaped by their cultural background and customs.

Halle had to take note of Charleston by the 1770s, for finally a group of ambitious brokers, having arrived in the 1750s, were jockeying for position in the young congregation of Saint John's, threatening to destroy it. Perhaps the key to the problem lay in their wording of the congregation's *Kirchenordnung* (church order). The only mention of "liberty" had nothing to do either with "gospel liberty" or with freedom of conscience. Rather, "each member of our congregation who is able to give good advice for the betterment of our church life not only has the freedom, but is requested to do so."[4] Alarmed, Halle fathers read what Mühlenberg, called upon to mediate, believed lay behind the upheaval. The new worthies would not be content merely to exercise a questionable liberty that bordered on the confusion of opinion and anarchy. Rather, they intended to exercise authority within the narrow confines of a German- speaking parish, hoping "to break off their *connection* with their original patrons and benefactors in London and Halle and . . . they feign and flatter only until they are free from their debts." Liberty, in this context, meant "freedom from constraint" in alarming terms.[5] Yet whether these ambitious leaders actually spoke for—in short, represented—the congregation, also quickly became problematic. Even worse, the late-arriving Württembergers in Charleston were connected by family and property holdings to their ambitious relatives across the Savannah River at Ebenezer and Goshen. But the dispute centered first not upon a proper definition of liberty, but on the way, in the opinion of many, property was being misused within the church. To understand how German-speaking arrivals in South Carolina thought about property, one must first survey their behavior over the quarter-century leading up to the conflict of 1768–75 at Saint John's.

I

Neither Boltzius nor Halle ever acknowledged or gave much credit to the network, however weak, that had long tied South Carolina German speakers and their property to the Reformed cantons of Switzerland. The Lutherans who arrived in large numbers after midcentury found some Swiss settlers already in Charleston since the 1730s; others in the Orangeburg area, further up the Edisto River; and yet others at Purrysburg, on the Savannah. Figures for both Swiss- and German-Reformed migration to South Carolina remain guesses; perhaps the eight hundred Swiss who settled at Purrysburg counted another two hundred countrymen at Orangeburg, and another, smaller group in Charleston. The Reformed church in Switzerland harbored either antipathy or indifference toward emigrants, most of whom they (correctly) suspected of clinging to Pietism and a critical attitude toward the Reformed state churches.[6] The combined strength of the Reformed Swiss settlers and emigrants from the Palatinate and Pfalz-Zweibrücken in the 1730s totaled about 9,000 by the 1750s. The Lutheran German speakers at Saxe-Gotha, on the Congaree River, numbered only about 280.

Swiss and Palatine German speakers in South Carolina came from widely disparate cantons and parts of the southwestern Reich. Purrysburg, for instance, potentially a Swiss-Reformed version of its neighbor Ebenezer, failed both economically and culturally. The French- and German-speaking Swiss there mirrored the Helvetic Confederation's own diversity. To this original mixture were added Württembergers, as well as the Prussian nobleman Johann Friedrick Holtzendorf, practitioner of physic and later a friend and correspondent of Pastor Boltzius; and Theobold Kieffer, whose departure for Ebenezer symbolized German speakers in Purrysburg: they left, either for Ebenezer, or for Orangeburg and other Carolina settlements. French speakers on the Savannah River ran the biggest and most profitable plantations and, like the German speakers, at first intermarried among themselves. Artisanal culture disappeared with the triumph of chattel slavery; left in the position of dominance, the French speakers allied by marriage and business with the English. Debt collection emerged as the major concern of the Goudet, Vauchier, Vaigneur, Bourguin, Dupont, Pendarvis, and Buche families. No ties connected this settlement to Charleston or Savannah; religious differences kept German speakers from worshipping across the river at Ebenezer; use of the Anglican service in a quasi-Presbyterian form also solidified a tendency toward cultural adaptation and anglicization. After the death of a German-speaking schoolmaster in 1737, the German language and cultural forms withered.[7]

The bare outlines of a communications and trade network that German-speaking Lutherans would later build on emerged by the 1740s. As early as 1736 Durs Thommen, a Swiss emigrant who had chosen Pennsylvania over Carolina, informed a locksmith that "as far as Carolina is concerned, do not believe anything in the booklet of lies, because I myself have talked with honest Swiss people who told me that there was no other bread in that country except made from flour that had come from Pennsylvania to Carl Statt. They had travelled 150 miles inland, but had not been able to get any bread. . . . There is in Carolina quite rotten land, no good crop grows there, one must have wheat from Pensilvania [*sic*], otherwise they do not have decent bread save pumpernickel."[8]

The grain trade Durs Thommen cited also showed that Swiss-Reformed settlers in Charleston had ties to the Orangeburg community. Reformed pastors served Orangeburg after its founding in 1735, John Giessendanner's pastoral record for the community revealing Swiss and, later, Palatine families who either settled in no particular pattern in this area of South Carolina, or had their children baptized before moving on. Giessendanner's record of marriages confirms that German speakers tended to intermarry only with one another; the nineteen marriages with non-Germans over a period of twenty-three years posed no threat to the religious and cultural core of the community. Communication along the old Native American path that served eventually as a post road allowed families to keep in touch with Moncks Corner and Charleston. Johannes Tobler and Jeremiah Theus very early on served as justices of the peace, as traders with the Cherokee, and as translators of German for the colonial government. Theus, who ran a trading post at Monck's Corner, had some connections far into the backcountry, for he had a brother, Christian, at the Congarees, and another brother, Simon, at Amelia.[9]

Despite Swiss settlement in 1737 at Saxe-Gotha, both it and the entire area between the forks of the Broad and Saluda rivers remained isolated from the trading and communication that flowed out of Charleston. Migrants from Pennsylvania largely settled what later became known as the "Dutch Fork" area. Flowing down from the Shenandoah Valley, these arrivals brought house styles that still survive in buildings at Newberry and on some farms. In the 1790s, when a Pennsylvania folk artist made his way through the backcountry, his work in Pennsylvania German art forms on birth and marriage certificates excited eager patrons who had not forgotten their backgrounds in Pennsylvania. Most of these families arrived in the company of Adam Summer in 1750, and stayed to themselves. This area remained for the entire colonial period disconnected from Charleston, Orangeburg, and Saxe-Gotha. Other Carolinians quickly labeled the Forks Dutch "qu'ar."[10] Jeremiah Theus's shadowy brother Christian, although a pastor in the Saxe-Gotha area, remained unknown to the Ebenezer pastors, but his ministrations may have penetrated the Dutch Fork area. The equally elusive John Gasser labored there from 1754 until 1763, when John Adam Epting and Peter Deckert obtained the one hundred-acre royal grant for what became Saint John's Lutheran Church.

Two examples of group settlement—one, of Dossenheimers, in the Orangeburg country; the second, of Ulmers and Kraichgauers, in Sandy Run, at the forks of the Broad and Saluda, and in Charleston—suggest how German-speaking arrivals after the 1750s used already-extant connections in combination with attractive land policies promoted by the colonial government. In both instances, German speakers enjoyed a freedom from both onerous taxation and interference with religious conscience and practice. In both examples, the allure of property and the possibility of securing it for succeeding generations moved them quickly into conformity with their Anglo-American neighbors, leaving only minor traces of transferred cultural definitions of liberty and property.

In its encouragement of "foreign Protestants" the provincial government offered land to immigrant families: one hundred acres for the master or mistress, and fifty acres apiece for all other members, slaves included. Rent-free for two years, such grants supposedly produced a four-shilling quit rent that seems not to have been collected. By 1761 liberal policy extended the two-year freedom from quit rents to ten years, bestowing four pounds sterling to cover the costs of passage, with additional funding to cover the costs of provender for incoming foreign Protestants, mostly Scots-Irish, and German speakers. Artisans' tools specifically received protection from sale to cover transportation costs, an indirect testimony to colonial officials' awareness of how such personalty had been smuggled into baggage by German speakers leaving the Reich. The bounty lands were intentionally located in townships positioned at strategic locations in the backcountry to form the province's defensive perimeter. German-speaking settlers found themselves funneled toward these areas. By the time such liberality was reduced in 1768, German-speaking settlement reached in an arc from the Savannah across New Windsor, Saxe-Gotha, and Amelia townships, and into the Dutch Fork near the North Carolina border. Whether these foreign Protestants were permitted to vote was not clear. It is likely that they could, but did not. As early as 1704, South Carolina's naturalization procedures forbade naturalized foreign Protestants to sit in the colonial assembly, although they could vote; this prohibition went unenforced.[11]

Although no planned settlements followed the pattern initiated at Purrysburg, settlers from specific villages did tend to settle near one another and depended on their emerging leaders to help them adjust to an English-speaking colony.[12]

How the emigrants from Dossenheim came to know of Giessendanner's settlement at Orangeburg remains unclear. More than likely they were enticed by Johann Adam Riemensperger, who left Dossenheim in 1747 with his wife. As early as 1740 this Swiss entrepreneur from Toggenburg, after a short stay in Carolina, returned to Switzerland, Germany, and Holland to entice settlers to Saxe-Gotha. Amassing bounties for over six hundred persons he supposedly brought to the backcountry, Riemensperger advised the later Dutch Fork settlers to choose Crim's Creek as a possible site, and extended his counsel to his former townsmen from Dossenheim. By 1764 Riemensperger or a relative of the same name sent for his inheritance in Dossenheim, even though this came to a mere 38 Gulden.[13]

Arriving in South Carolina in 1752, the Dossenheimers made their way to the Orangeburg settlement. Among the mysteries surrounding many of the links between Reich and plantation, the most intriguing is the capacity of marginal people to not only pay their passage but also begin again in such a short time. Georg Wedel and his family had paid 15 Gulden on their property of 154 gulden before leaving Dossenheim with Georg Bär, Eva Catharina Wedel, and Johann Heinrich Möll and his wife Maria Catharina (neé Wedel). The widow Anna Maria Wedel and her small child also left. Although Anna Maria's land, worth 25 Gulden, was assessed 2 Gulden before she was permitted to leave, she reappeared as the owner of one hundred acres surveyed for her in 1757 in Orangeburg township, next to Bernard Ziegler. Quickly cementing an alliance with the Zieglers, Anna Maria Wedel married her neighbor in 1753 in Orangeburg.[14] Presumably the land was surveyed and paid for by one of the other members of the emigrant group, although no record survives of such a transaction. Eva Maria Wedel's husband Johann

Bär, or another Dossenheimer of the same name, settled in the Berkeley County area, where another Dossenheimer, Nicholas Fetterolf, signed an indenture to him. But the Fetterolfs, perhaps not finding sufficient land in Orangeburg, but more likely advised by Riemensperger, patented three hundred acres of land on the south side of the Santee River between Amelia and Saxe-Gotha townships. Like many of these later arrivals of the 1750s, Nicholas Fetterolf borrowed money from more established German speakers. Eberhard Ehney, one of the founders of Saint John's Lutheran Church in Charleston, prospered as a butcher by the early 1750s.[15] Fetterolf in 1767 bound himself for £448.9.6 with the understanding that if he were able to pay £224.4.9 by February of the same year, the debt would be cancelled. In fact, Ehney sued for nonpayment on this bond, and in the South Carolina Court of Common Pleas in April he obtained a judgment for debt, interest, and £40 in damages.[16]

Johann Konrad Hungerbieler and his wife Maria Elisabeth also arrived in 1752, obtaining land on Pope Spring Swamp in Orangeburg township, as did Margaret Hungerbieler, who must have accompanied this family. The family of Johann Fontius, which included Anna Catharine and eight other persons, also chose Orangeburg, where Sebastian Fontius (Funtjes) also settled. Hans Adam Fontius a decade later obtained another one hundred acres in Berkeley County at an undetermined location in Saint George Parish. English speakers clearly had difficulty with the names of these settlers and obscured the grant given in 1754 to Anna Catharine Fontius by designating her Anthony Catherine Frenchinson until the collector of quit rents noted the error.[17]

In the absence of full tax records and supporting information, the manner in which lands were acquired, traded, or sold by the German speakers who began arriving in ever greater numbers in the 1760s remains unclear, except for the occasional connections that one can laboriously reconstruct. Only about 140 inventories of estate survive for the backcountry area in the 1760s, inadequate to reveal acquisition of property among German speakers from 1750 to 1770. Yet newcomers from Kraichgau and Ulm also linked themselves to other Lutheran German speakers in the Saxe-Gotha region as the Dossenheimers arrived in Orangeburg.

Already in 1742 the Swiss settlers of Saxe-Gotha, led by members of the ubiquitous Geiger family (Johann Caspar, Abraham, and Hermann) petitioned the provincial governor and council for the bounty and warrant for lands. The Geigers, represented in both Beyhingen and Ittlingen, in the Kraichgau, may have circulated news of the Saxe-Gotha settlement at an early date. In any event, when members of the Kirsch and Hildenbrand families departed from the Kraichgau towns Zuzenhausen and Weiler, they headed for Saxe-Gotha. Generations later, Jacob Hildenbrand's great-grandson recalled that Jacob had settled on the road between Swansea and Saint Mathew's. The dispute over naming the area had been "intense." Johann Jacob Hildenbrand was a half brother involved in the unpleasant dispute between a stepmother and Conrad Hildenbrand's testament provisions which had reached the appellate courts. Close relatives had already emigrated to Pennsylvania in 1732, and a half brother, Hans Adam, arrived in Philadelphia in 1750, settling in Frederick County, Maryland, as did Johann Georg Koberstein of the same village. John Hildenbrand first obtained fifty acres on the Santee in 1756; another one hundred acres was surveyed in Saxe-Gotha for him, plus a second two hundred in the township itself, but these unrecorded plats indicate that the lands were not granted. However, two years later two hundred acres on the Santee appeared in a memorial under his name, and an additional fifty acres in 1761.[18]

Like Hildenbrand, three of the four Kirsch brothers of Zuzenhausen, Johann Jacob and two named Conrad, all chose South Carolina. The stimulus for emigration may have been village officials' judgment that Johann Georg, their father, was a poor steward of his property ("ein schlechter Haushalter"). He divided his property among his children in exchange for the typical annuity providing basic food and shelter (*Leibgeding*). The elder of the two Conrads, twenty-six when he left, accompanied his younger brothers Johann Jacob, twenty-two, and Conrad the younger, eighteen. The elder Conrad died within a year and a half of arriving in South Carolina. Johann Jacob apparently stayed in Carolina, but the younger Conrad returned to Zuzenhausen in 1755, bringing back both the death certificate of Conrad the elder, and an oral agreement with Johann Jacob that he, the young Conrad, should have Johann Jacob's inheritance portion, which was under administration in the village. Since no written proof of this agreement existed, however, and local officials could not find the proper record of administration (*Pflegschaftsrechnungen*), the village Schultheiß rejected the claim. A close relative of this family, Johann Georg, also settled in Carolina after his father, Johann Dietrich Kirsch, bestowed his estate on his children, the annuity specifying food, warmth, and clothing. The successful emigrant Johann Georg invested his paternal portion of 246 Gulden and patented land in South Carolina as early as 1749, expanding his holdings in 1768 and again in 1770. But the children of the "schlechter Haushalter" apparently, even after borrowing two hundred Gulden each for their journey to Carolina, never succeeded. Johann Jacob Kirsch's first appearance as a landowner occurs in 1770. These settlers near the Santee—Conrad on Cedar Creek, and Johann Georg by 1749 settling near Thomas Hodge at the fork of the Santee and Wateree rivers, may have typified thousands of German-speaking emigrants for most of whom the vagaries of climate undermined the hope for their investments of paternal property in a new land. Only Johann Georg, who by 1768 obtained 250 acres in Saxe-Gotha, seemed to prosper; Johann Jacob in 1770 signed an indenture that conveyed his 105 acres on the Congaree River to Baltasar Neze.[19]

These Kraichgauers were near neighbors to Ulm emigrants who had originally intended to settle among the Salzburgers at Ebenezer. By the time the Ulm emigrants had arrived with the Swabian transports in the 1750s, internal tensions at Ebenezer, and coolness on the part of Boltzius, who had not been consulted about their joining the settlement, motivated some Ulmers and Württembergers to try their luck elsewhere. The settlement of some 320 Württembergers at Bethany began with these Lutherans petitioning in London to go at their own expense to Ebenezer. But by 1767, for example, when Georg Heisler applied for a new grant after Georgia became a royal colony, his survey of one hundred acres near Blue Bluff turned out to be in South Carolina, and not among his fellow Ulmers who had arrived in 1750 on the *Charming Martha*. By 1752, in the wake of the Swabian transports, Blue Bluff emerged as a settlement predominantly of Ulmers, although Boltzius arranged to have some Salzburgers, who had so far not prospered on the lands adjacent to Ebenezer, settle there as well. The contingent, approximately forty-four families, remained in touch with the Saxe-Gotha settlement in Carolina. Sponsorship of these Swabian and Ulmer settlers by Christian von Münch of Augsburg put them in an awkward relationship to the controlled and disciplined environment Boltzius wanted to preserve among his flock.[20]

Most of the Ulmers, from Langenau and Altheim, had been able to put together the funds for passage, but little else. Unhappy with life in Ebenezer, Bartel Bozenhard wrote home in 1753 that there was no land to be had at this distance of forty miles from Ebenezer; there was no church, no school for children, no gristmill. He desperately wanted to come home, admitting that his pastor had been right to warn against emigration. There were, in fact, lands, gristmills, schooling, and churches, although not yet right in Blue Bluff. But Bozenhard wanted to secure permission for return by exaggerating the plight of the emigrants from Ulm. This weaver wrote a second time, via Mathias Neidlinger, who returned home, that their friend Henrich Junginger should thank God that he had not emigrated and that he had healthy, warm food and good water ("eine gesunde Speiß und ein guter Trunck Wasser"), which Georgians lacked. Bartel's brother Martin complained of similar problems, especially the lack of beer and good bread, in his June letter, mourning that only in Ebenezer or Savannah could one find a butcher.

The brothers' exaggerations—that there was no game; fish, but no boats; and nothing but snakes and crocodiles—revealed the projected expectations, the European norms, that could not come to grips with the North American context, from which property had to be wrested with great labor. The culturally transferred obsession with appropriate food (Nahrung), evidence of the properly constituted household, remained with these day laborers and artisans. Martin found America to be marked by a dangerous liberty: "a wild, desolate country, nothing more than wood and wilderness; each sojourns in the forest, removed from Christendom into the midst of pagans; everyman lives only as he wishes." In the end, the brothers fled, and in Langenau Bartel at least managed to obtain from Anna Ehrat, a widow, a small piece of land, a stall, and a garden, as a day laborer.[21]

A particularly enterprising Ulmer, Hans Lohrmann, emerged by 1752 as a slave overseer in Purrysburg, and appeared in Ebenezer before Pastor Boltzius to be married shortly thereafter. Lohrmann, originally of Nellingen, had intended to go to "Ebenezer, Carolina," only to find that his wife, Barbara (neé Mayer), of Bermaringen, refused. He went anyway, taking with him a birth certificate and thirty Gulden worth of his property. The marriage was annulled, thus accounting for his appearance before Boltzius seeking to be married in North America.[22] Lohrmann appeared by the 1780s as a petitioner seeking to have a Lutheran pastor sent to Saxe-Gotha, but his activities in the region remain mysterious. He was obviously a landowner, and his memorial for fifty acres on the Santee summarized a chain of title which in 1775 dated back to the 1760s; but Lohrmann, like several Weidenstetten arrivals, did not emerge as a key figure, as did his acquaintances and distant relatives by marriage, the Sailers of Weidenstetten, genuine cultural brokers linking Saxe-Gotha Lutherans to Charleston.[23]

The weaver's assistant Jacob Sailer and his brothers made such a mark in Carolina that they inspired others to try their fortunes there. Some of the Sailers' neighbors from Weidenstetten also did well. Their fellow former villager Jacob Löcher obtained 150 acres on Sandy Run in 1769.[24] The weaver's assistant Hans Staudenmayer, who took fifteen of his eighty Gulden with him on a Wanderschaft to Carolina, declaring that he would return, stayed; by 1762 he obtained 100 acres between the Broad and Saluda rivers. Johannes Kassberger was still more successful, obtaining 250 acres of property between Gilders and King Creek in Craven County in 1767. His success in Carolina enabled him by 1787 voluntarily to renounce claims on his inheritance in Weidenstetten.[25] Kassberger, a weaver's son, had emigrated in 1752 (as had Sailer himself) with his wife and two children. Kassberger's rise to propertied status apparently took longer, but Sailer, undoubtedly helped by his father's wealth, not only bought the large number of books in Reutlingen detailed above (see chapter 4) but after arriving in South Carolina received a 50-acre grant in Amelia Township by 1756 and another grant in 1758, and prospered.[26]

In 1765 Sailer returned to Weidenstetten, intending to take his three brothers, Christoph, Johannes, and David back to Carolina, leaving in Weidenstetten only his sister Barbara, who had married Georg Lohrmann, a weaver. Jacob Löcher, a weaver's assistant (*Weberknappe*), decided to go with the Sailers; and his settling on Sandy Run near the Sailers' own property proved the importance of having a patron who had mastered the adjustment to North America. Sailer's brothers were not so fortunate. Christoph died almost immediately upon arrival at Charleston in 1766, as did his pregnant wife. Johannes died only a few months later, as Sailer reported to his family in a letter in January 1770. David Sailer, however, survived the seasoning process. He stayed with his brother at Sandy Run for a time but finally established himself in Charleston as a cooper, eventually employing thirty workers in his packinghouse.[27]

In the 1770s, as David Sailer emerged as one of the successful Lutheran artisans of Charleston, his brother Jacob patented more land, this time three hundred acres at Little Bull Swamp in 1771 and another one thousand acres in Berkeley County in 1773. Jacob, along with Heinrich Felder and Christopher Zahn, served as collector and inquirer for taxes in the Saxe-Gotha area.[28] How often Jacob came to Charleston on business is unclear, although his 1770 letter was written from the town, not from his plantation on "Sandiris am Bach Sandiran," from which he and David both wrote in 1775. Travelers such as the Moravian missionary Johannes Ettwein of Freudenstadt, in Württemberg, however, noted the relative isolation of Württembergers, the dominant group around Saltcatchers, which he visited before coming to Orangeburg and the Edisto. Connections with Charleston did not apparently reach that far upcountry.[29]

The Sailers' successful transfer of wealth and connections—albeit at a tragic cost in familial lives—marked them as a rare example among German-speaking Carolina cultural brokers. Yet they arrived late, only in the 1750s, as did most of the Lutheran German speakers in South Carolina. Marginal emigrants from Weidenstetten and other Ulm villages depended all the more on the Sailers and their contacts.[30] Georg Fischer, a carpenter's assistant, sold his property for 130 Gulden before departing with his wife and one child for the New Mark of Brandenburg. His kinsman Johann Georg, also a carpenter's assistant, had already left Weidenstetten for South Carolina with his wife and child in 1752. Anna Barbara Bader angered her father by marrying the young Christoph Sailer and departing for America; he grudgingly gave 16 Gulden for the journey.

After news reached her family that she had died, pregnant, in Charleston a year later, her 31-Gulden inheritance was divided among her siblings.[31] With the Sailers, Bader, and Löcher, also went Christian Dorn of Holzkirch. Dorn put his two quarters of a *Juchert* of "debt-free" land under administration with Nicolaus Gugenhaben for 30 Gulden and left with his daughters Maria and Catharine.[32] Johannes Schick, a day laborer, completed the exodus headed by the Sailers; perhaps he wanted to join his unmarried sister Barbara, who had left for Carolina with an illegitimate child in 1752.[33]

II

By the time the Sailers emerged in the 1770s as major figures among the German speakers, some of whom they had sponsored and helped to bring to the colony, Charleston had emerged as the most visible German-speaking Lutheran settlement in South Carolina. There, from the ranks of the artisans and traders, a network arose in the 1760s tying Carolina German speakers to Pennsylvania as well as to the Reich, and defining the major issues for backcountry settlers who increasingly found that King Street, the major road into Charleston, along which they traded their agricultural goods, cut through what had come to be known by the 1760s as "Dutchtown."

The institutional base for Charleston's Lutherans was "The German Evangelical Lutheran Church of Saint John the Baptist." Neither the name, nor the timing of the congregation's founding, was accidental. By the 1750s, Charleston's social life had quickened as aspiring planters founded in 1754 the Charleston Library Society to avoid duplicating the purchase of imported books deemed essential for an anglicized culture. In January of that year, Friedrich Holtzendorf, a former Berliner, was buried in the first Masonic funeral held in Charleston. The Masons' celebration of the feasts of Saint John the Evangelist (on 27 December, near the winter solstice) and Saint John the Baptist (at the summer solstice, 24 June) lay at the heart of this alternative religious society, whose ceremonies had already attracted the condemnation of both Catholic and Lutheran traditions in Europe. In 1755 Pastor Johann Friedrichs of Hanover arrived in Charleston to found Saint John's congregation.[34]

No one among the large number of Ulm and Württemberg emigrants in the congregation missed the significance of founding a church on the day known throughout Swabia as the day when villagers lit the bonfires, the *Johannesfeuer*. As the sole saint's birthday—as opposed to a day of martyrdom or death—on the church calendar, Saint John's Day had provided Christian missionaries with a festival in honor of the cousin of Jesus to wean the pagan peoples of Europe away from the celebrations of the solstice. Lighting the fire and springing through it guaranteed protection from fire during the year—and, as the folksongs associated with the day promised, speedy marriage for young people. For Charleston's Lutherans, their congregation functioned as an alternative cultural center to the Masonic lodge. This sense of an alternative society deepened when, in 1762, the mechanics of the city founded the Fellowship Society, a mutual benefit society dedicated to educating and caring for its poor members.

Michael Kalteisen, a carter and drayman from Württemberg seems to have been nearly the only German speaker in the Fellowship Society when he left in 1766 to help found the German Friendly Society. Membership lists there mirrored the congregational roster of Saint John's. Alexander Gillon, the Dutch merchant and the Friendly Society's co-founder, securing money in Holland and England for the new German church, joined it in the late 1760s. His eminence may have aided a congregation composed of laborers and middling artisans, about whom Anglo-Americans entertained serious reservations.

To be sure, some Germans seemed enterprising and public-spirited enough. Johannes Schwertfeger served as constable for Charleston in the 1750s; and the Commons House of Assembly was enthusiastic (at first) about Heinrich Christoph Beudeker's promise to establish a brewery at Saxe-Gotha, with a loan of five hundred pounds from the township funds of the province. But when insufficient barley was harvested and Beudeker still complained of his "Want of a Copper, Hair-Cloth, and so forth," the members of the Commons House refused his petition for another loan. Another German speaker promised to be able to construct a more efficient rice-pounding machine, which also intrigued the provincial authorities. But German speakers remained largely isolated, retaining their speech and habits even after years in the colony. When Jacob Joseph Kogar pleaded indigency despite his invention of windmill sails to power rice-pounding mills, the Commons House attributed it to his being "without any Connections in the Country and speaking English but poorly." Kogar had been in the colonies for nearly twenty years. But such examples only served to make indispensable the role of the translator paid by the colony "as Linguister . . . to the German People who were in search of proper Lands for a Settlement."[35]

Far more troubling, German-speaking immigrants did not settle fast enough on western lands. By 1754, after a two-year wave of immigration, the new provisions that gave immigrants farming implements and provisions expired, and the assembly failed to respond to the governor's pleas for more money to honor the promised bounties. Crop failure in 1753 discouraged the proposal to mortgage the future proceeds of Carolina's township fund, the same monies out of which Beudeker had been paid. By March 1753 the council wrote to the Commons House reminding them of their obligations to provide a bounty, but to no avail. By February 1754 the church wardens and vestry of Saint Philip's parish in Charleston petitioned the Commons House for relief. Pointing out that "many poor Lame and Impotent persons were frequently sent in numbers by Carts or Waggons from the several Townships and Out Settlements of this Province . . . to Charles Town," the parish officials pleaded for help. These indigent German speakers were a plague upon the population, who were appalled by beggars, most of whom were "old and Impotent Palatines," going "from Door to Door."[36]

By the 1760s Charleston planters boasted the highest per capita wealth of any elite in the British mainland colonies. The town rapidly developed a hierarchical society. African-American slaves provided a broad base to the social pyramid, along whose slopes artisans and workers—and the newly arriving German speakers—found life increasingly uncertain. The city, which boasted one hundred tippling houses among its thirteen hundred dwellings and had a population of eleven thousand in 1770, paid a far higher share of taxes than the hinterland, where three-quarters of South Carolina's population then lived. Charlestonians paid 41 percent of the colony's taxes in 1760; they contributed 46 percent in 1767. Charleston residents reckoned that most of the province's wealth came from export trade, which by 1768 exceeded £500,000 per year. Any disruption in that trade threatened the £20 sterling in annual income which, on average, white inhabitants in the low country enjoyed. Estate inventories for the period 1763–88 demonstrated the vulnerability—as well as imbalance—of the white economic structure. During those years 26 percent of inventoried estates (truly impoverished decedents of course remained uninventoried) were valued at £100 sterling or less. While many (approximately seventy-nine) artisans and mechanics did leave wills, only thirty-seven owned slaves, a critical index of personal wealth. More worrisome, commodity prices for the late 1760s suggest that the cost of food increased, adding to the pressures on members of the city's lower orders.[37]

The physical changes Charleston underwent between 1750 and 1775 also directly affected the German Lutheran artisans and workers who founded Saint John's. The vortex of commercial and social life in Charleston had long spun on the streets running from east to west, centering on the open square or piazza that had by midcentury disappeared under the pressure for commercial building. Both Bay Street and Broad Street boasted jewelers, cabinetmakers, merchants, retail shops of factors, and the two-storied residences of the planter elite. Yet in the mid-1760s the city, twice the size it had been in the 1740s, shifted west and north along King Street. The area west of this artery and on the north side became the artisans' and laborers' quarter. After the middle of the century, squeezed by a burgeoning population bounded by two rivers, artisans and workers linked to the backcountry by trade settled here. The major merchants of the town sponsored storekeepers at ferry crossings and dispersed their wares at Moncks Corner, Cainhoy, or Childsbury, on the Wando and Cooper rivers. But these settlements' trade with Charleston flowed along King Street, which led out of the new town gate at Boundary Street which William Gerard de Brahm had helped to lay out in 1751, just beyond the new area of Ansonborough which opened up for development in 1746. Nearly under the shadow of de Brahm's new tabby wall of seashell, daub, and lime, highly reminiscent of the enclosed villages from which they had come, German speakers settled in. The commercial core of the city, although remaining important for the large merchants, shifted for artisans to the west and northern streets, to escape the higher rents in the center of town.[38]

The ties that bound German speakers in South Carolina to Pennsylvania wheat, noted by the Swiss commentator Thommen in the 1730s, bespoke the economically dependent quality of Charleston and its hinterland. Likewise, South Carolina's German-speaking Lutherans had initially emigrated to Pennsylvania, or had come to Charleston only after finding, as Mühlenberg noted in his letter to Pastor Krone, that artisans and farmers were not needed in Pennsylvania except on the far western frontier.[39]

Some Saint John's congregants—those from Neuffen, for instance—may have intended all along to move to South Carolina. At least, the Birckenmeyer, Nuffer, Kirchner, Dürchner, Eberlen, Muckenfuß and Schrade families who left that village in Württemberg in 1749 all reemerged at Saint John's.[40] Like Muckenfuß, many German speakers did not regard the Savannah as an impediment to investment in property in either colony. Johann Treutlen of Ebenezer appeared in Carolina, where he owned property; he and Jacob Cronberger, the registrar of deeds at Ebenezer, were suing Elijah and Richard Oglesbee in the South Carolina courts.[41]

But many of Charleston's German-speaking Lutherans, such as Michael Kalteisen the drayman and carter, immigrated via Philadelphia and only later chose Charleston. The successful butcher Melchior Wehrle, who vied with Kalteisen, his Swabian countryman, for eminence in the congregation, was one of these. Karl Florian May, a merchant of Danzig, had not intended to make Charleston his place of business. But on arriving at Philadelphia, May discovered that he could find no lucrative business in the competitive atmosphere there; he took the advice of the German merchant and ironworks owner Peter Hasenclever and his brother, the merchant Francis Hasenclever, who sent him south to Kalteisen, who in turn connected May with the Dutch merchant Alexander Gillon. Both Gillon and Francis Hasenclever were experts in the Dutch trade, and May soon became an accomplished transatlantic entrepreneur, specializing in the Amsterdam-to-Charleston route, with the occasional trip to Saint Eustatia. The shipping manifests for Charleston suggest that he, like many future worthies among the German-speaking population, devoted most of his time to trade and rarely risked entanglement in the internal disputes of the German-speaking congregations.[42]

So successful was May that he cultivated connections with Philadelphia's wealthy merchant elite, earning sufficient trust to be named coexecutor (with John S. Cripps) of the estate of the Philadelphia merchant George Nixon. Unable to attend at the Philadelphia probate in person, May employed Pierce Butler of Charleston to represent him in August 1791. Mühlenberg's journal entries revealed further Philadelphia connections of Charleston Lutherans. Many butchers, tailors, draymen, bakers, and turners, and the occasional merchant trader spent at least some time during the year in the northern German-speaking center.[43] Charleston Lutherans naturally turned to Philadelphia as Saint John's began to experience tensions about property and its control by congregational leaders.

Pfalz-Zweibrücken contributed early Lutherans to Charleston, but no institutional base and no network sprang up to create an early group of cultural brokers such as the one Mühlenberg found in Philadelphia in 1742. The former warrant officer for Zweibrücken, Johann Heinrich Degin, arrived in 1738, but his widow was threatened with expulsion from her chair in Saint John's for refusing to pay rent in 1773. Neither advertisements in the *South Carolina Gazette*, nor jury lists, nor the Court of Common Pleas volumes, nor surviving wills and inventories reveal an emergent charter group from the Reich and Switzerland among Lutherans. Remarkable careers shaped the family histories of the Theusses, Giessendanners and Toblers, and those of German-Jewish merchants such as Job Rothmaler, but not those of the early Palatines.[44]

By midcentury these same indexes showed German speakers in a different light. "We, the High-German [Evangelical Church] dedicated to the Augsburg Confession form, in America, a separate people," declared the founders of Saint John's. Jury lists suggest that Charleston German speakers—among them, Michael Muckenfuß, Johann Schmetterling, and Jacob and Johannes Boomer—began serving at midcentury, Lutherans now joining earlier Swiss settlers. How well these individuals understood their duties some doubted; John Meyer, empaneled in May 1759, through an interlocutor "informed the Court that he was a foreigner and did not understand the English Language and therefore prayed that he might be Excused from Serving."[45]

A survey of cases brought in the court through 1771 reveals the same general pattern seen in other provinces: German speakers were sued, or, more rarely, brought suit, for recovery of debt; they rarely took recourse to the courts in cases of slander, assault, or defamation, or domestic quarrels. In South Carolina, the absence of any courts outside Charleston further reduced the likelihood of immigrants using the courts unless they were longtime residents and living in the vicinity. But the selective use of the courts by some German-speaking Lutherans for securing property and recording wills provides a brief glimpse of their property and the values they invested in it.[46]

Before midcentury, few of South Carolina's German speakers left a testamentary record. The few wills that do survive come from Charleston, where, for instance, Johann Pachelbel's son Charles Theodor left all personal and real estate in the hands of his wife, Hannah, in 1749. Earlier emigrants (e.g., Johann Jacob Brücke, at Goose Creek, in 1745; and Johannes Shettig, at the Swiss settlement in Saxe-Gotha, in 1738) also left wills, which have survived not in the original German-language versions but only in translations by Christian Motte or Jeremiah Theus. These fragments tell us little, divorced as they are from a broader sample of testation patterns.

In general, South Carolinians disregarded the law of primogeniture but nonetheless chose, in devising their property, to ensure that the eldest son most often inherited the home plantation. In perhaps no other mainland British colony did married women exercise as much control over their property, either through the mechanism of a premarital contract, or through men's wills that recognized the importance of placing widows in control of both land and slaves and remembering kin orphaned or widowed in the lowland climate.[47] The inclination of the South Carolina planters to accept only those aspects of the common law regarding property which would support the evolving American institution of chattel slavery underscored their early adoption of the slave codes developed in

Barbados. The harshness of the black code in South Carolina matched the colony's draconian punishments against counterfeiters, and statutes allowing injured parties to pursue administrators of estates for damages. This overall Carolinian concern with controlling and perpetuating property, much of it in the form of human chattels, shaped the colony's handling of familial property and its devisal.[48]

Among German speakers, testation reflecting adaptation to these Carolinian legal practices stumbled over difficulties with the English language and unfamiliarity with English legal mechanisms and institutions. South Carolina's centralized court system, which forced all prospective testators to record wills in Charleston, acted as a further deterrent. By the 1770s Charleston's German speakers had learned to use premarital agreements that closely approximated Ulm and eastern Swabian custom. A tripartite indenture in January 1771 regulated the marriage of John Sayler, the baker of Charleston, and Jacobina Catarina Stoll, a shopkeeper of Charleston. Establishing a trust provision, Stoll ensured her independence by having the turner Abraham Speidel, a fellow of Saint John's, take possession of her three slaves and her shop goods, worth a total of five hundred pounds current money, in exchange for ten shillings, enabling her to continue to buy and sell independently and appear in court to recover debts owed her, as well as to protect her property from John Sayler's future indebtedness.[49]

To such occasional agreements, one can add gleanings from approximately one hundred wills dating from 1750 to 1783. As in Virginia, most of the wills were written and probated in the 1760s and 70s, reflecting the largely Lutheran immigration that continued into the 1760s. The combined Orangeburg-Saxe-Gotha area produced twenty-nine of these wills, while Charleston's artisan German speakers wrote twenty-seven. Another ten wills survive from the Berkeley County area just outside Charleston—at Goose Creek, in Saint Andrew's Parish, and in adjacent areas. A dozen German speakers left wills in the area along the Savannah in Saint Paul's Parish, Colleton County, and Saint Peter's. A scattering of wills from Georgetown, on the coast; from New Windsor; and from Saint Mark's Parish completed the picture. The Dutch Fork area, above the form of the Broad and Saluda rivers, produced few wills.[50]

The isolation of these German speakers from the Halle missionary network partly explains why little pietistic language or imagery marks South Carolina wills left by Lutheran German speakers. Of the seventy-six wills written outside Charleston, fifteen contained language expressing redemptive or pietistic sentiments. The Giessendanners' ministry, and Christian Theus's presence especially, explain this tendency in wills from the Orangeburgh area. The Reformed Swiss in Orangeburg, the Geiger families, Heinrich Gallmann, and Jacob Roth also left explicit trusts or provisions for contributions to the poor, or established educational provisions for their own children to be raised in the fear of God. Twenty-seven of the wills contain such provisions, endowing a schoolmaster at Townhole Swamp to read services, or remembering relatives in the Reich, but devising such remembrances upon the church if the relatives should not claim the gifts. Roth simply left money to the German Reformed Orphanage in Orangeburg and the congregation at Four Holes.

German speakers outside Charleston showed some inclination to favor eldest sons in their wills: fourteen wills bestow upon the eldest son the home place or otherwise favor him (e.g., Franz Erhardt of Saint Peter's gave his eldest son David his "accoutrements of war"); four among the Swiss unaccountably bestowed the home plantation upon the youngest son, just as some German speakers in Virginia did. Only eight gave their daughters land, but eighteen made their wives executrices, and nineteen made explicit provisions that gave their wives considerably more than the usual thirds of dower plus courtesy of living on the estate during widowhood. The ownership of slaves presented these testators with no profound moral dilemmas, nor were they inclined to manumit them or otherwise make provision for them. Only one, David Rumph, specified in a will written in 1774 that his slave children were not to be separated "from their Mother and Father, during all the Days of [his wife's] natural Life." Adapting to the prevailing mode of owning property in human chattels, German speakers made no comments and apparently had few scruples about the practice, just as Mühlenberg had feared. George Goette, a former subject of the county of Waldeck—the same area that produced printer Henry Miller—became overseer of Robert Phillips's plantation on the Combahee River, between Charleston and Ebenezer, also without second thoughts.[51]

German-speaking Lutherans outside Charleston left even fewer records than the Swiss and German Reformed, but the handful that survive suggest that as they prepared to pass on their property to heirs, some sought out acquaintances from their home villages to witness their wills and serve as executors. John Lorhmann, a planter in Craven County in 1775, designated his Ulm village compatriots Jacob Mayer and Jacob Sailer as executors, and turned to another Weidenstetten man, Jacob Löcher as witness, "hoping for Redemption through the mercy of my Blessed saviour and Redeemer Jesus Christ." The proceeds from land already sold, he ordered invested in the '96 District to provide an income for his widow and children. Jacob Geiger in 1769 left the children of his brothers George and Friedrich, in Beihingen, the estate of his only daughter Mary if she should die before her eighteenth birthday. When Mary did die, Jacob Geiger of Ittlingen bought the interests of the Beyhingen Geigers through a bond Jacob and Christopher Williman of Charleston executed in his name.[52]

These testamentary records and accompanying deeds suggest the networks that bound Charleston residents to the backcountry. The Geigers, like a handful of other notables such as the Lohrmanns and the Sailers, used the Charleston Lutheran church as part of a network that bound them not only to the town but also to events further afield. When Jacob Geiger, who died in 1769, paid five pounds for burial costs at Saint John's for his brother Michael, who had died in 1761, he was also asked for an additional fifty-nine pounds, a necessary surcharge, the church vestry noted, "for burial grounds of people who do not belong to our congregation . . . [which cost] shall not cover any fence or boundary for a grave, the construction of which, in order to prevent the neighboring grounds to the right and the left from being an obstacle for further burials, shall be performed at a later date."[53] Within a decade, Saint John's began defining access to burial plots on the basis of membership, making privileges formerly common to all villagers contingent upon support of the congregation.

Within two years of Saint John's founding, temporary German-speaking residents of Charleston sought privileges in the church. The vestry decreed that "people who maintain a chair in the church and want to continue this right when they move away shall contact the Vestry or Wardens and may maintain the chair as long as they continue to contribute to the salaries of our church employees."[54] Friedrich Hoff, an early member of the congregation who advertised himself as a keyboard tuner for a time in Charleston, died in 1774 and was inventoried in Orangeburg Township. George Keckle, also a member, owned 100 acres on Beaver Creek, which he patented in 1767; Nicholas Fittig, a baker, was related to the Swiss family that had begun under Jacob Fittig at Saxe-Gotha in the 1730s, and his relative Martin still operated a ferry on the Congaree; Heinrich Metzger, also a member, still owned 150 acres between the Broad and Saluda, as well as his house and lot on King Street, in Charleston, when he died in 1777. Daniel Birckenmeyer of Charleston left his house lot in town to his wife, but this former Neuffen resident left 400 acres on Turkey Creek to his son George Henry, using Pastor Friedrich Daser of Saint John's to write his will in April 1774. Jacob Werner's plantation in Saint Andrew's parish, where he died in 1782, apparently did not prevent him from continuing on as a member of Saint John's.[55]

Nearly all twenty-seven Charleston wills reflect the wishes of members of Saint John's. Like the Geigers, both Margaretha Claß, formerly of Pflugfeld, near Ludwigsburg, and Johann Ernst, of Ihringen, Baden-Durlach, hoped to use as executors fellow members of the church, such as Jacob Wirth and Johann Werner, either to recover property for the sake of their children, as Claß ordered, or to inform brothers, as did Ernst, of bequests.[56] Approximately sixty-five families comprised the congregation in 1770. Testators reflected its artisan-based membership, and its pastors helped in the writing and execution of wills. "Home places" figured very seldom in the bequeathals. Like most Charleston artisans, the German speakers leased or rented their properties, and in some cases devised the balance of a lease or rental upon heirs.

Blacksmiths, tavern keepers, turners, tradesmen, carters and draymen, bricklayers, tailors, and bakers, the German testators were not counted as the social equals of silversmiths, jewelers, cabinetmakers, and fine craftsmen. Both bequests and specific capital left to heirs rarely exceeded three hundred pounds in these estates, except in the case of testators who also owned plantations outside the city. Because of the tendency of urban artisans to move or to rent, acting upon the transferred cultural inclination to bestow upon daughters realty or its equivalent worth was not possible, even if it was a desideratum; only five testators did so. Nor did these Lutherans leave philanthropic bequests or gifts to the church. While six of the wills provided for educating the testator's own children, only one person—Johanna Christiana Evans—provided a bequest "towards the Foundation or Building of a German Lutheran church" in the amount of forty pounds.[57] A few gave the church something while still alive. John Paul Grimke in 1768 donated a silver dish that became a collection plate; Alexander Gillon the Dutch merchant gave the congregation two silver candlesticks that graced either side of the pulpit in 1769; Heinrich Diemroth, a skilled tailor who also made the pastor's gown, gave a silver ciborium in 1769; and Dr. Nicholas Schwarzkopf donated twenty-three pounds to the church in 1772. The German Friendly Society was thanked for the 1775 gift of a "graceful clock" to be used during services, apparently to prevent sermons from dragging on. When added to the anonymous gift in 1784 of a white altar cloth, these items describe the sum of donations ad pias causas.[58]

Surviving inventories are so rare for most of the German speakers that one suspects they did not use the courts and successfully avoided the inventory procedure.[59] This was not true for their descendants, who after the Revolution can sometimes be traced in the surviving inventories. But as with other colonial groups, only the successful tended to be inventoried. Thus it is nearly impossible to determine with precision what the social standing of Saint John's membership was. The extant evidence reveals some dimensions of the emerging leadership but leaves most of this German-speaking group in silent obscurity.[60]

Both the humble circumstances of most Charleston Lutherans and the absence of a Halle-inspired tradition of giving account for the absence of a concept of property that implied a positive obligation toward stewardship. The Society for the Promoting of Christian Knowledge, until 1756 instrumental not only in supplying funds to supplement Halle's missionary efforts but also in underwriting charitable ventures, now curtailed its activities. A model for emulation could, of course, have been found in the Anglicans' poor relief in Charleston, but the founding both of the German Friendly Society, which advanced modest sums for relief to its members, and of the artisan-dominated Fellowship Society suggest that a concept of property implying stewardship did not emerge early in Anglican or Lutheran congregations. Public relief in Charleston worked well enough to discourage that impulse. The relief allotment was three pounds per month by midcentury, provided to a population half the size of Philadelphia's; and authorities did not distribute relief at a poorhouse. Rather, those who preferred indoor to outdoor relief work usually got it, and were not required to live in the poorhouse. Moreover, by 1760 Charleston's overseers had stopped binding out poor youngsters in the town, despite higher food costs than those prevailing in Philadelphia. Such practices alleviated some of the psychic burden of being poor, among both German and English speakers.[61]

If one were to single out one characteristic of the Charleston Lutheran wills, however, it would be the manner in which husbands favored their wives. Ten of the 20 married, male testators chose their wives as executors—far above the rate in Hebron, and compared with 14 of the 41 surviving wills of early German-speaking testators in Georgia. Moreover, fourteen of these twenty provided for more than the normal "thirds" for their widows. But unlike the pietist-influenced Reformed wills of Orangeburg and Saxe-Gotha, the Charleston German wills contain nothing in the way of "redemptive" language, settling instead for the normal English introduction. The confidence that Lutheran men expressed in their wives, however, reflected more than rapid copying of similar patterns among English testators. It also testified to the influence the wives at Saint John's possessed, and exercised. Controversy suddenly erupted in the congregation around the misbehavior of a genuine Tübingen-educated Swabian pastor, Friedrich Wilhelm Augustus Daser, who arrived in 1768. German-speaking Lutherans in Charleston now took a vital interest in property; and an improper liberty exercised by a pastor and his wife demanded discussion of what was meant by liberty and property.

III

Since the term *liberty* never surfaced in the disputes at Saint John's, and since no written record of the wives' demands and criticisms survives, much must be inferred from the consistory records. The preamble to the congregation's church order notes that only "after many troubles and expenses" could German speakers build a church in which "our duty" (*Pflicht*) "to pass on to our descendants" the Lutheran faith be realized by the founders. The repeated admonition that "the transmission of our religion depends completely on our rising generation" reinforces one's sense that domestic concerns inspired the document and the search for a pastor. Württemberg villagers' inherited suspicion about the ways in which authorities abused taxes and church properties received implicit treatment. No fees could be charged for sacramental acts, lest the poor or servants be discouraged from seeking the means of grace. "Beyond that, it is up to the individual's love and discretion" to decide whether he or she wished to give anything for the pastor.[62]

The founding fathers of the congregation, however, recognized the importance of presenting a proper public face to English-speaking Charleston. In giving, the wealthier had to "carry the weak members" to insure "that a minister and his family may be able to lead a decent life." The concern that English speakers would continue to look down their noses at boorish Germans surfaced repeatedly in the document. In 1768, the German tradition of singing hymns at an interment ceremony had already been suppressed. So, too, did the elders erase the collective memory of the congregation as they banned the custom of reading aloud the *Lebenslauf*, or life-history, of the deceased. English speakers in attendance had expressed annoyance at such practices.[63]

The mixed composition of the congregation in Charleston, where artisans and laborers joined with planters and traders, apparently led to internal struggles over control of the proper image the pastor should present to the rest of society. That struggle over the public face Saint John's should present inevitably led to a discussion of who properly represented the congregation, and at what expense. Worldly goods lay at the heart of this debate, as did outrage over an improper liberty, and a demonstrated inability to run a pastoral household in an edifying manner.

Most of the membership came from either Württemberg or Ulm. From surviving references in the wills and deeds, one can discern that the congregation's places of business and residence stretched along King Street into Ansonborough, where Conrad Kysell kept tavern, and along Beresford Street, in "Dutch Town," just south of Dutch Church Alley, where Saint John's was built. Beresford itself connected Archdale, where several German artisans had their shops, to the major northwest thoroughfare King Street, the road to Charleston Neck, where Johann Köhle the baker lived.[64]

The dispute over a proper understanding of property and liberty began as seating arrangements in the congregation took final form. Like every other Lutheran German-speaking church in the colonies, Saint John's divided men from women, giving seats of prominence to married persons of both sexes, with single members, servants, and finally, slaves at the rear or in the balconies. To supplement income, some gallery chairs nearest to the altar and pulpit were auctioned off to bidders living in the northeastern, German-speaking part of Charleston in February 1768.

Michael Kalteisen, who had come to Charleston in 1762, enjoyed an unusually low rent, two pounds per year, for a closed chair on the left side of the pulpit. The place of honor on the righthand side belonged briefly to Jakob Wirzer before he disappeared from membership shortly thereafter, outraged because he was one of the few members of Saint John's to be denied membership in the German Friendly Society at its meeting of 29 January 1766 at Kalteisen's residence. "Mr Rippele" meanwhile bid twenty-four pounds for a chair, and "Mr. Lindauer" twenty-nine, reflecting the wealth of a master baker who dominated a small coterie of bakers—including Joseph Kimmel, Nicholas Fittig, Johannes Köhle, Johannes Baltz, and John Sailer—in the congregation.[65]

On the main floor, Jacob Wirth, the executor of the Claß will, who paid £10 per year for chair number 1 in the church, stood out as the leading power in the church, along with the butcher Melchior Wehrle, who paid £12 rent for chair number 2. Abraham Speidel the turner was noted by the visiting Mühlenberg as one of the oldest members of the congregation, and a leading member, and he and Johann Speidel occupied chairs 3 and 7, respectively, paying £13 and £14 per year. Eberhard Ehney, the successful butcher who had lent poor Dossenheimer Fetterolf ~~ney to~~ money to get started in Carolina, paid £18 for his seat in the congregation; Philip Mintzing, the wealthiest blacksmith, who counted as other members of his trade the congregants Michael Muckenfuß and Justinus Stoll, a relative of Jacobina the shopkeeper, paid £10. Most members, however, rented their pews or chairs for £8. The more well-to-do dominated the early vestry and, naturally, intermarried. Ulrich Ehney, who died in 1764, made certain that not only his son, Eberhard, but also his daughters, who were married to the Speidel and Hoff families of Saint John's, were provided for; and Jacob Wirth was his witness.[66]

Image and public honor meant much to these eminences, as they did to Anglicans. Establishing themselves now in a new world above their fellow worshipers, the members of the consistory noted that, since they presided over the growing German Lutheran church in the provincial capital, "honor and public esteem" required an exceptional person for the office of pastor.[67]

On the surface, Friedrich Augustus Wilhelm Daser should have been the model of what propertied, aspiring Swabians in Charleston desired. Born in 1740, Daser, a native of Schorndorf, was probably related distantly to the more eminent Paulus Achatius Daser who had emigrated to Pennsylvania in 1753 after being paid eight hundred Gulden for his services as *Vogt* (roughly the same as Amtsmann, or district magistrate) for Nagold.[68] Before Daser's arrival, a nonordained itinerant, Johann Nicholas Martin, served from 1763 to 1767, either leaving voluntarily for the backcountry or forced out by the aspiring leaders. Pastor Johannes Severin Hahnbaum came to Charleston through the mediation of Gustav Anton Wachsel of Saint George's Lutheran church in London, who may have been contacted by Alexander Gillon, the Dutch merchant member of Saint John's. Hahnbaum lived only three years after his arrival in Charleston, however, dying in 1770 after examining and ordaining the young Daser. Daser had been taken in by Michael Kalteisen after arriving, as Mühlenberg said, "without credentials, clothing, or money, because, as he said, his trunk containing the said valuables had been stolen from him in Holland." Daser married the ailing Hahnbaum's daughter and seemed to bode well for Saint John's members, many of whom were Swabian in origin.[69]

In a discussion of finances, Daser announced that his salary was wholly insufficient for an urban pastor because of both food costs and the expense of proper attire for a minister in Charleston. Daser undoubtedly knew that to avoid unpleasantness with Pastor Hahnbaum, the consistory had voted Hahnbaum a salary of six hundred pounds in 1769. The pastor could supplement this amount by charging fees for certain pastoral acts. To avoid charges of simony, no fees could be accepted for administering the sacraments; the consistory also noted that such fees might also discourage servants and the poor from seeking the means of grace. But the pastor could charge between five and ten pounds for marriages, depending on whether the service was performed privately or in church, with or without sermon. Three pounds was thought reasonable for a funeral sermon, and one pound each for writing birth, baptismal, marriage, or death certificates.

Daser noted, however, that in recent months such fees had almost completely dried up, and he was in danger of destitution. Given the downward trend of Charleston's economy during the nonimportation boycott of 1768–70, he was again correct. After some debate, the vestry voted to increase the new pastor's salary to £440 and extend to the young man a contract for two years, ending on 19 July 1773. Since the income of the church for 1772 came to £947 pounds, and only £250 was spent, the balance, £697, seemed to be sufficient to maintain Daser in his post. In fact, the congregation owed creditors so much that in the 1773 reckoning, although £1,431 was taken in, the £758 left after expenses could not cover the debts on purchased lands. Into the breach stepped Jacob Williman, the new warden, extending a loan of £1,000 to the church. With Williman's appearance, intense scrutiny of the pastor's financial and personal conduct began in earnest.

Between 1771 and 1774, disputes over Christian liberty—especially, what pastoral behavior was permissible under this heading—and stewardship of property threatened to tear apart Saint John's congregation. Mühlenberg journeyed south in 1774 to mediate this conflict on his way to settling a dispute over church property at Ebenezer. Daser's hopes for a salary to match Hahnbaum's were never met. Indeed, after Daser's dismissal and the temporary return of the autodidact Johann Nicholas Martin in 1775, the salary remained £520, not reaching £600 until after the Revolution. In light of the wages of the congregational membership, Daser's expectations had been reasonable. By the 1770s, blacksmiths, wheelwrights, and saddlers in Charleston could expect £1.4.0 to £1.10.0 plus four shillings rations as daily wages. A master carpenter by 1773 could make perhaps £930 per year in Charleston, and cabinetmakers' employees about £400. Thus, even blacksmiths and the other skilled members of the congregation might expect a minimum annual income of £300. The pastoral duties included preaching, visiting the sick, keeping all the congregational records and presenting them to the consistory, attending to the school and quizzing the children, catechizing, holding a prayer service on Friday, preaching two sermons on Sundays and holy days, and offering the Lord's Supper every other month.[70]

The coalition who were demanding Daser's removal but were willing to help him financially included Michael Kalteisen, who had first befriended him; Kalteisen's wealthy merchant allies Alexander Gillon and the Williman brothers, Jacob and Christoph; the baker Joseph Kimmel; and the increasingly influential and wealthy Charles Florian May, who did not attend Saint John's regularly but occasionally helped facilitate communications abroad for the congregation. The merchant Franz Copia joined the coalition. Connected to the Dutch merchant Gillon's trade, Copia consulted with Mühlenberg about the power of attorney given to Gillon by Copia's cousins Sigmund and Simon Copia in Philadelphia. Apparently an occasional attender, Georg Vielhaur of Heilbronn had prospered on his two plantations outside the city which Mühlenberg visited. A frequent correspondent with Friedrich Hagner (an elder of Saint Michael's in Philadelphia and originally a schoolmaster from Neckargartach in Württemberg, Vielhaur also had two sisters in Pennsylvania, and allied himself with Kalteisen's group.[71]

Heinrich Geiger, son of the Ittlingen entrepreneur Jacob, joined his father's friends the Willimans of Hoffenheim-Sinsheim. So did the newly arrived organist-clerk Philip Hartung, from Michelfeld, only a few kilometers from Ittlingen, who had landed first at Saint Michael's in Philadelphia, where he communed briefly before moving on to Charleston. Yet the land titles and important documents of the church regularly were committed not to this coterie of cosmopolitan Kraichgauers and Württembergers who enjoyed ties to Philadelphia and the Reich, but to the safekeeping of Philip Mintzing, the blacksmith; Abraham Speidel, turner; and Jacob Wehrle, saddler, brother of the wealthy and powerful butcher Melchior Wehrle.

Daser's creditors, by the time of his dismissal, were pursuing him for debts in excess of one thousand pounds. If Mühlenberg's admittedly pietist-inspired description can be trusted, Daser had earned the wrath of the more dignified members of Saint John's and of the German Friendly Society, who now believed he had betrayed their trust after being elected to membership. He retained the moral support of his own family and a few among the less powerful members of the congregation who either professed not to be offended by his behavior or—as Mühlenberg thought—were not risking much property in the way of contributions, anyway. Besides his wife, Daser's supporters included his brother-in-law Peter Meurset, and perhaps the sponsors of Meurset's children, the widowed Dorothea Schrad, formerly of Neuffen; Magdalena Schwarzkopf, the widow of a physician; and Peter Horlbeck. None of these were in the congregation's powerful inner circle. Mühlenberg queried rhetorically, in a pietist catalog of Daser's sins, how a congregation could respect and love a man who "indulges in . . . dancing at frolicsome weddings, studies the fine points of morality in the current comedies, runs the streets at night, bombards doors and shutters with sticks and stones, gets into debt, and even loses his reputation as a citizen, and practices his weighty office as a mere *parergon?*"[72]

At first glance one is puzzled that pietist judgments about unsavory pastoral behavior sprang not from the humble poor but from the ranks of aspiring worthies at Saint John's. No early coterie of Kraichgauers or Palatines had emerged in Charleston to set the agenda for Saint John's members. The late-arriving Württembergers and Ulmers yearned for social acceptance and at first hailed Daser as a fellow countryman apt to further their own, and the congregation's, welfare. Moreover, the eventual criticism did not focus solely on the pastor. These male worthies did not operate in a vacuum, immune from advice and demands emanating from their own households. Mühlenberg let slip in his report to Halle the origin of the charges: they came from outraged wives who believed that "[Daser's] young wife did not know how to run a household and lacked the true ornament of a woman." Mühlenberg did not simply mean that Frau Daser did not practice responsible stewardship of the household. In quoting 1 Peter 3:4 he also meant to convey the accusation that she attended too much to worldly appearances, clothing, and jewelry, and not enough to cultivating a spiritual life with a meek and quiet spirit ("mit sanftem und stillem Geist").[73]

The influence of the congregational women barely shows in the records of the church, which reflect more the activities of the consistory and pastors. Moreover, where mention of the women did appear, the overbearing behavior of consistory members toward them appears somewhat unsavory. Not only did widow Degin lose her pew rights. The first notice taken of women in the church recited Georg Hormeister's deserting his legal wife in Pennsylvania and bringing "another woman into this province, and, since she passed away, he is cohabiting again." Catharina Moody sold the congregation a house and some land next to it for future use in 1769; two years later the debt of £523 was retired, but the church apparently rented out its property, since it later ordered that the widow Mrs. Bader "be notified by the Wardens tomorrow . . . to move out of the house she occupies now and which belongs to the church. If she refuses to do so, the rent shall be increased in the future step by step to an extent that she can be forced to move out." During his visit, Mühlenberg met with several of the church women, many of whom (including the widow Bader, who had a sister in Philadelphia and another in New York) were asking for news of relatives in Pennsylvania.[74]

Concern for domestic order and dissatisfaction with the abuse of contributions given for the pastor's salary, factors barely visible in the official record of the dispute, surfaced in these notes, and in the consistory's own treatment of women seen as untrustworthy stewards of their own households. The hands that wrote the record might have been those of the men, but the voice is the voice of their wives. The Swabian women of the congregation still exercised considerable influence. A special sense of betrayal intensified their outrage at the indebtedness incurred by Daser, a fellow Württemberger. Mühlenberg symbolically patched up the quarrel by asking these alienated members of the congregation to come to confession before communion. Some forty people did so, and Mühlenberg especially noted hearing the confessions of two mothers unable to attend the scheduled confessions.[75] Many of the congregation's wives had avoided the sacrament during the dispute. Their nonattendance reflected village practice: avoidance of breaking bread with an enemy.

Although the women of the New World congregations could not meet to vote for midwives, did not drink wine together at ritual gatherings as in the German southwest, had no consistory court to enforce their wishes, and were excluded from voting in the election of the consistory and wardens, they nonetheless exercised indirect power. Daser enjoyed some support from poorer widows and humbler non-Württembergers in the congregation, and, despite his flamboyant lifestyle, was personally kind. At least, when collections were taken to speed him on his way to London for an Anglican ordination that never happened, the congregation still seemed genuinely to like him.

Mühlenberg noted the influence of the married women in these communities on several occasions, pointing out a growing tension. Pietist convictions held that liberty was an inward virtue that should show in proper behavior, and that property should be dealt with cautiously. To many German-speaking women, however, domestic economy and frugality seemed increasingly threatened by the ambitious male brokers' engagement with a public order and worldly show even within the congregation itself. Such a tension inadvertently, but inexorably, demanded discussion about what constituted a proper liberty, and whether the pastor and members of the consistory truly represented the sentiments of those who contributed, however modestly, to the congregation's support. Mühlenberg remained uncertain as to who his allies should be: the worldly-wise aspiring patrons desperately needed to further Halle's missionary goals, or the poorer and female congregants who shared his deepest convictions about behavior and values. In reporting to Halle, he reminded himself of the time of the Interim (1548–55) when pastors in the Reich were urged by their wives to sign a compromise document ordered by the emperor which many thought undercut the doctrines of the Reformation. The pastors' wives who urged, "sign, sign, that you may keep your parish," Mühlenberg mourned as all too typical of the narrow household mentality that obscured all other issues.[76]

If German-speaking women in North America perpetuated a tradition of anxiety, defensiveness, and insecurity about domestic life, marginal local life in the Reich and their own uncertain status in the new land surely explain why. Lutheran women in Charleston took the lead in insisting that a German-language school and an eloquent, European-trained pastor be secured for Saint John's. The indifference of some male members about the German language surfaced in the curious notes of the German Friendly Society itself. Although originally for German speakers, the society was quickly opened to non-Germans, and its records were kept in English from the outset. In 1769, the membership was assessed to pay for the society's rules to be translated (*from* English into German) and printed—in Philadelphia. During the occupation of Charleston, a German-speaking mercenary praised the quality of spoken German in the city. "In Charleston," he wrote, "one meets people of all nations of Europe. . . . The Germans are resident here in large numbers; and they speak their mother tongue better than I have ever heard Germans speak in America." Yet by 1810 a Scots observer chronicled the ethnic diversity of the town and missed a German presence altogether.[77]

The women of Charleston's German-speaking Lutheran congregation intended to preserve their language and, through it, a defense of pietist norms of behavior and domestic economy. Their posture toward property in their homes and in their inherited language was defensive and careful. They suffered under an additional handicap in that their sociability remained completely oral, in the absence of a press such as existed in Pennsylvania; and they lacked contact with Halle's network as well. They enjoyed sufficient confidence to be named executrices of their husbands wills, perhaps profiting somewhat from South Carolina's peculiar dower provisions, which sprang from statutes intended to bolster slavery, an institution Mühlenberg and Boltzius feared would destroy the integrity of any household. Daser, and the ambitious brokers who had at first defended him, valued the broader English-speaking life of Charleston and beyond. Their concern for the public dimensions of life sprang partly from the fact that ominous events had broken on Carolina just as the Germans arrived in great numbers in the 1750s.

During his visit, Mühlenberg discussed with Michael Kalteisen the fact that South Carolina Lutherans were bound to Pennsylvania by more than congregational family ties. They shared a common dread: the prospect of war with France and its Native American allies. In March 1753, Felix Schmidt was killed by a party of Indians, and a woman in his house was rumored to have been abducted. The South Carolina Commons House of Assembly offered a reward of one hundred pounds for the slaying or taking of any Indian from the areas of the province; yet upon receiving word in June of the expected incursion of the French into the Ohio Valley, Governor James Glen reacted with skepticism. As late as

1755, Governor Robert Dinwiddie complained of South Carolina's refusal to contribute to the military expedition against the French and their Indian allies.[78]

Glen's conservative reaction was reflected on a more modest scale among the German-speaking brokers at Saint John's. Slow to give money from their hard-won advances over previous marginal existences, these men nevertheless participated in the Cherokee War of the 1750s on the Carolina frontier. That experience helped to give men such as the Sailers, the Lohrmanns, and Kalteisen a broader awareness of the need to defend liberty and property. (Like Mühlenberg's father-in-law Conrad Weiser, Kalteisen knew the Cherokee well and served as a translator between them and the provincial government.) Peter Kolb's regiment, formed in 1759, had included in its ranks, under Johann Herrensperger's lieutenancy, Johann Lohrmann and Jacob Sailer; Dossenheimers Jacob Hungerbieler, Adam Fontius, Jacob Kirsch (from Zuzenhausen), and Johann and Jacob Geiger.

These men gradually emerged as the key figures who brokered the attitudes and perspectives of their fellow immigrants within British colonial society. Kalteisen informed Mühlenberg that "he had been acting as an envoy of the local government to the savage nations"; he also served the same function among fellow German speakers. Kalteisen believed that exposure to Europeans had corrupted the Cherokee, who possessed a more developed sense of charity than Europeans, since in every village they built houses "in which they kept their aged, sick, and helpless people, maintained by freewill gifts received weekly from the inhabitants. When those in the lazaretto suffer any lack, one of them who still has strength enough to do so climbs up on the inside and, standing on the top of the building, movingly sings out the song of need and admonishes the people to well-doing. The contributions in kind then begin to come in again." Mühlenberg and his superiors in Halle must have been especially impressed by a sense of stewardship and obligation which they found hard to build among the transplanted Europeans, though pastors depended on it for their survival. But disagreements among German speakers over how property and liberty were to be conceived of went deeper than Kalteisen's somewhat self-conscious reflections on the customs of the Cherokee.[79]

The late-arriving cultural brokers such as Kalteisen had moved with extraordinary speed to construct their own forms of "private sociability" in the German Friendly Society and in congregations like Saint John's. Almost immediately upon arriving they served in the German regiment in the Cherokee War, and their understanding of both property and liberty

perforce came to be tied—faster than was perhaps possible elsewhere—
to prevailing British-American definitions. To these experiences they
could add their own material success, and their liberty to worship in a
Lutheran church and to shape its social prestige in the face of English
speakers' condescension. They must have been exasperated and bewil-
dered at the challenge to their judgment that erupted in their own midst
by 1770. Indeed, some, such as Charles Florian May, or Jacob Williman,
Geiger's friend from Ittlingen, seem to have declined to take part in such
squabbles at all.

These leaders, having reestablished themselves in an urban setting in
North America, began to exhibit classic signs of the Bürger of the towns
and small cities in the Reich. They expected deference to their understanding of how propertied German speakers should relate to the British
world; they themselves had already fought actively in defense of both
property and British liberty against the French and their Native American
allies. They were the fathers of the Germans in Charleston society. They
adapted very quickly to British colonial standards of behavior and sociability. They hired Daser on the basis of his affable nature and reputed
academic achievement, not his pietist demeanor or theology. Their indifference to the retention of German-speaking culture was apparent in
the rapid disuse of the language within the German Friendly Society
itself.

Yet challenge to such worldly, libertarian understandings of how
property could be used for show and standing, and how liberty could
be managed for personal and group sociability and aggrandizement, came
from their own households. It was not from Halle or its pastors but from
the married women of the congregation that the challenge came. The
criticism of Daser's licentious behavior and his wife's indifference to
domestic stewardship, the repeated insistence in the church order that
the "rising generation" had to be provided for in a godly manner—these
signs pointed to the power married women exercised, now in a congregational setting instead of the village Kirchenkonvent, as they continued
to define the proper understanding and use of liberty and property.

In this urban setting, among late arrivals who lacked significant ties
to Halle but knew through family connections in Philadelphia what was
unfolding there, one glimpses the final struggle to define culturally transferred mixes of liberty and property in a North American setting. By
the 1770s, as Mühlenberg arrived in Charleston to aid the process of
definition, he was well equipped for the task. He had survived a searing
exchange over these concepts that had broken out in 1762 in the largest
German-speaking Lutheran congregation in North America. At Saint

Michael's, in Philadelphia, the final definitions of liberty and property were worked out in the presence of a German-language press, just as the struggle to defend liberty and property began to preoccupy both Britain and German-speaking Lutherans in British North America.

PART III

German-American Ideas of Liberty and Property

PART II

8

Lutherans and Property:
The Philadelphia Definition

IN 1749, seven years after his arrival in Philadelphia, Pastor Heinrich Melchior Mühlenberg tried to justify to his superiors his behavior in the ministry. (Mühlenberg had been sent by Gotthilf August Francke after Francke received in 1734 a request from three Pennsylvania congregations—at Philadelphia, New Hanover, and Providence—for a pastor.) The Halle fathers, shocked by the building costs at Saint Michael's, doubted Mühlenberg's competence. Instead of shepherding the sums painstakingly collected from benefactors, he built schools and churches with abandon. Running up shocking debts, his bricks-and-mortar ministry seemed to disregard Halle's preachings of responsible stewardship over property, especially that given by philanthropically disposed benefactors. Mühlenberg begged Ziegenhagen in London, and the Halle fathers to overlook £1,607 in costs—a good percentage of Halle's total contributions to the Pennsylvania mission field between 1735 and the Revolution. Philadelphia's Lutherans admittedly came from among artisans and the poor. Nonetheless, Mühlenberg argued, all German speakers as well as English authorities watched closely what Lutherans were doing in Philadelphia. He admitted that elders' complaints—about pastors' failure to inform laity about European collections, especially a generous one in Darmstadt—had reached Halle. He fully understood Francke's warning that contentious wrangling over the collections could only mean in the end that "the love of other charitable givers is stifled." But Mühlenberg remained adamant in his defense of pouring funds into church and school in the third largest city of the British empire: "Philadelphia can and must not be abandoned."[1]

In this episode, Mühlenberg revealed indirectly how central the issue of property became for German-speaking Lutherans in the British col-

243

onies. Far better than his superiors, he realized that the churches and schools he wanted built provided the only magnets, the only centers of sociability, for a diverse and scattered Lutheran flock. Pennsylvania, he had already warned the Halle fathers, ran riot with free-church separatist pietists. Unless he could bring Württembergers, Alsatians, Palatines, Kraichgauers, Hessians, Saxons, and Prussians together for worship with an agreeable liturgy in buildings constructed by their own labor and gifts, where German-language schools inculcated proper Lutheran doctrine, his ministry would fail. Pietist conventicles had existed in Pennsylvania before Mühlenberg arrived; the Saur press already delighted in spreading tales of immoral and irregular "Lutheran" preachers. The Kraichgauers who had arrived as long as ten years before him already had their own networks of influence. For Mühlenberg, the disputes that arose over the proper use of charitable contributions, whether from Europe or from the German speakers now in America, demanded thorough reflection on the meaning of the term property.

Saint Michael's eventually flourished because Mühlenberg wrested the congregation away from the Moravian patriarch Nicholas von Zinzendorf. Ambitious lay leaders would have forced a more respectable appearance upon the original shabby Saint Michael's, anyway. But their rise provoked bitter controversy about property. They understood that German-speaking Lutherans needed to present a public face that bespoke the order, civility, and loyalty English speakers always wanted from the continental arrivals and were never quite convinced existed in sufficient quality. The early arrivals also saw themselves representing German speakers' concerns and interests in the larger economic and social circles where they operated.

Most German-speaking arrivals, however, were marginal property owners from the southwestern territories of the Reich. Fearful of any demands (in the form of taxes and services) made upon domestic property they arrived ill-disposed toward anyone who might threaten their hard-won gains. Increasingly, by the late 1740s, these members of Saint Michael's saw the leadership as arrogant worthies who acted irresponsibly, squandering widows' mites instead of modestly responding to the congregation's needs for a place in which to worship, and occasional poor relief. This high-handedness, especially when critics began to perceive a connection to the Halle-trained pastors, awakened memories of secular officials' corruption and abuse of property in the German southwest. The tension between the domestic-pietist values of villagers from the German southwest, and the definition of property that pointed to obligations toward the broader culture, demanded, and finally received, resolution.

That process became intense and bitter at Saint Michael's Lutheran Church between 1748—the year the Ministerium of Pennsylvania was founded and the church dedicated—and 1765, the year of the Stamp Act crisis. This resolution touched definitions of liberty as well, definitions that carried beyond Philadelphia and Pennsylvania to other German-speaking Lutheran communities. In the end, German speakers connected their transferred and adapted concerns to the broader political culture and its implications. But these last developments need to be followed separately, and later. Only if one examines the socioeconomic composition of Saint Michael's, paying attention to the rise of the early arrivals from the Kraichgau; only if one notes the continuing fears of late-arriving Württembergers concerned for the integrity of their households and chary of giving to the church anyway, does Mühlenberg's solution to the property issue finally become understandable. And only then can one appreciate how a synthesis emerged between Halle's idea of property as an entity to be cared for with an eye toward public responsibility, and the familial, the domestic, village understanding of property typical of so many transplanted German speakers.

I

Variously described as a barn, a slaughterhouse, and a rundown log cabin, the original Saint Michael's Lutheran Church barely sufficed for the handful of Lutherans who worshipped there irregularly in the late 1720s and early 1730s. By the time Johann Caspar Stoever began keeping a register of communicants in 1733, Thomas Meyer, keeper of alms (Almonsenpfleger), oversaw only £2 in Pennsylvania currency. In 1735 some of the money repaired the house of worship; the average donation came to £0.7.0. By the mid-1730s the theology student Albert Langerfeld took over the ministry that Christian Schulz had started in 1732; a year later, Stoever succeeded him. From time to time a Swedish Lutheran pastor also served the German Lutherans in their ramshackle house at Mulberry (Arch) Street between Fourth and Fifth. Between 1733 and 1741 Meyer collected £0.7.0 per Sunday; the £8 per year went toward repairs, or alms of one to three shillings. Equal numbers of the forty-six men and forty-nine women received communion when they could; lacking regular pastoral care, they relied on Meyer, who functioned as both deacon and Almonsenpfleger, informing the Darmstadt Consistory in 1742 of Stoever's ordination by Christian Schulz in 1733. Meyer's career mirrored the social standing of these early German speakers: born in the Palatinate in 1709, he arrived in Philadelphia in 1732 and made his living as a fisherman until he drowned when his skiff capsized in 1763. Sent to England in 1742 to solicit funds for the struggling congregation, he met Ziegenhagen and returned in 1743, bringing his brother Mattäus to join the congregation.[2]

Ambitious post-1733 arrivals eclipsed Meyer as they began their climb in the Lutheran community and transformed this unprepossessing flock into the largest and most powerful German Lutheran congregation in the British North America. The new arrivals included the teenaged butcher and trader Heinrich Keppele, the mason Jacob Graeff, and two butchers, Johann David Säckel and Leonard Hermann. Daniel Weisiger, a native of Silesia, operated as bookseller by 1735.[3]

Early Lutheran arrivals had few possessions and settled in wood-frame houses even shabbier than the day workers' cottages some of them had left. Few examples of German speakers' domestic quarters survive from pre-1750 Philadelphia. Rural homes document that outside the town German speakers settled in one-room wooden structures. The earliest forms of domestic arts included the cast-iron stove plates which, among the more prosperous, replicated in North American form the tiled stoves of the Stube. Inventories of estates for Philadelphia Lutherans have largely vanished; many early arrivals probably escaped probate altogether. The occasional examples reveal extraordinarily meager households. Yet even in the wood-frame, one-room tenements that workers rented, most people had beds: one for parents, perhaps another for children. Saint Michael's communion register identified recently arrived members who rented, or worked in exchange for, rooms in the homes of more established parishioners. Most of the German speakers had no kitchen, and settled for cooking in the fireplace; rarely did one enjoy sleeping space separated from the common room.[4]

Philadelphia's working Lutheran's left few wills disposing of their meager worldly goods. Those who did provided for neither a religious nor an educational future. The Saxon tailor Caspar Leitbecker died in 1732, leaving the balance of his estate to his father in Kaltennorthheim, and a bequest of six pounds to his brother Andreas in London; upon his father's demise, Caspar's two younger sisters were to divide his estate equally. Peter Weiser left his worldly goods to his father and mother at Worms and to his brother and sisters, to be paid in yearly installments after his death in 1738. George Frederick Hagar exhibited singular foresight and revealed that, in his mind at least, a connection existed between religious faith and responsibility for worldly goods. After giving thanks that he had been created and sustained in "the pure and holy Evangelick Protestant religion," he created in his 1741 will a trust that provided schooling money for his four daughters and his son, Frederick Wilhelm, all of whom were to share alike, after Frederick had received a symbolic gift of two Dutch coins to avoid future challenges to the will.[5]

The successful purchase of property on the western edge of town by Leonard Hermann, Johann David Säckel, Heinrich Keppele, and Heinrich Miller transformed German Lutheran life. A five-year building project eventually costing £1,607 created a center for German-speaking Lutherans, who increasingly, because of immigration in the 1740s, emerged as the most numerous arrivals from the Reich in Penn's colony. Deaths due to the "seasoning" process may have averaged 95 per thousand by 1741 among the newly arrived, but the city continued to spread out—less rapidly after 1740, but the Northern Liberties and Southwark boomed, as German speakers settled.[6]

The population of Philadelphia grew from eight thousand in 1734, when Saint Michael's struggled, to fourteen thousand in 1751; such growth provided an expanding tax base and an apparent prosperity interrupted only by the economic slowdown of 1753–54. During these fifteen years, Saint Michael's immigrant laborers enjoyed a jump in wages that translated into three shillings a day. Moreover, the opening up of western areas for settlement funneled German speakers through Philadelphia into the twenty-five new towns in Lancaster County founded between 1730 and 1765. Before 1750, Lutheran political consciousness in Penn's city still slumbered. One incident, involving some German speakers rioting against anti-Quaker toughs around city hall, stands out because it was singular, never repeated, and atypical of the quiet, apolitical behavior of the continental settlers.

Yet the men who signed the deed of trust that secured the property purchased in 1743 on which the new Saint Michael's began to rise showed an early awareness of the broader, public world. All arrived in the 1730s; most were in their twenties or thirties, married, and skilled. Butchers, bakers, confectioners, coppersmiths, shopkeepers, masons, yeomen, they already enjoyed a measure of financial security. Their origins also bound them together.[7]

The coppersmith Johannes Sefferenz (or Zwerenz) may have come from Fellbach, a pietist center in Württemberg. Married, with his children already marrying in the late 1740s, he may have been an older early trustee. Heinrich Keppele, arriving in 1738, identified as a butcher, had been born in 1716 at Treschklingen, near Heilbronn, in the Kraichgau. Heinrich Böckele, also born in 1716, had arrived in 1732 from Schwaigern, in the Kraichgau; Jacob Graeff, a mason and bricklayer, born in 1723, arrived in 1727 as a young son of Sebastian Gräf of Hockenheim (southeast of Heidelberg and across the Rhine from Speyer), which, like both Heilbronn and Schwaigern, lay along major trade routes in the

Reich. Both Leonard and Bernhard Herrmann, who pledged security for the building of Saint Michael's, were bakers; both came from Kraichgau families. Unlike the southwesterners, the merchant Heinrich Schleydorn began his career as a confectioner, married a New York Huguenot woman with Dutch connections, and quickly became Mühlenberg's staunchest ally and friend. Perhaps his birth at Peine, not far from Mühlenberg's own Hanoverian town of Einbeck, helped. Schleydorn fell seriously ill in 1753 and lost his fortune in the Seven Years' War, weakening his steadying influence in a congregation increasingly fractious.

Johann David Säckel and Lorenz Bast stood as baptismal sponsors to each others' sons; and Säckel, with his brother Jürg David, both butchers, had leaned toward the Moravians before Mühlenberg's arrival in 1742. Bast, a yeoman married to the daughter of the wealthy farmer Peter Schneider, of Germantown, arrived in 1740, one of the latest of the original group. Marcus Kuhl and his brother Samuel, both bakers from Holstein who lived in Philadelphia's Middle Ward since the early 1740s, rounded out the list. Tantalizing but incomplete evidence suggests that the Bast family and Phillip Odenheimer, later related by marriage to Keppele, came from the Oppenheim area south of Mainz, and that Odenheimer was permitted to emigrate in 1740 because he had relatives in Pennsylvania.

Two other members of the influential early group of worthies also arrived in the 1739s, but both turned on their fellows as disputes over defining property intensified by 1762. Johannes Oswald, a tailor from the Baden village of Lichtenau, arrived on the *Snowfox* in 1738; a witness to the Declaration of Trust, he never entered the charmed circle, but his longevity made him an ideal candidate for the opposition to put forward in 1762 as a new trustee. The other man was even more formidable. Georg Hütner was born in Meckesheim, near Waldhilsbach-Neckargemünd, in the Kraichgau, and arrived in Pennsylvania at age thirty one in 1737. Marrying the sister of the powerful German Quaker Caspar Wistar, Hütner secured valuable economic connections; his stepdaughter, moreover, was to become the wife of Heinrich Keppele. A successful shopkeeper by the mid-1750s, Hütner traded with Keppele and the Kuhls, and by 1762 put his name on the deed of the parsonage and the schoolhouse conveyed in fee simple to Keppele and thence to the trustees. Yet he was deeply disaffected from the inner circle, being annoyed by a second group — clients of the original trustees — who rose to power between 1748 and 1760.

The original trustees and elders of Saint Michael's were not among the genuinely wealthy of Philadelphia. Despite being patrons of their own group of clients, these were men of comfortable means only. The

1756 tax lists, admittedly missing single men, and failing to catch wealth other than real property, overlooked mortgages, land held outside the city, bonds, specie, book debt, and investments in ships. The earliest trustees, according to this list, were worth about forty six pounds apiece. This figure placed them among holders of moderate property at a time when a ship's mate out of the port made the same in a year; when six years later a modest yearly diet cost somewhere between ten and thirteen pounds; skilled artisans paid yearly rents of twenty pounds.[8]

The controversy over property at Saint Michael's stemmed, at least in part, from the threat posed by these men to the domestic economy of poor households. That threat stemmed from the leaders' control of Nahrung—food for sustenance. Bakers, butchers, confectioners, shop-keepers, and purveyors of flour and dry goods, the worthies literally controlled the means of life among their fellow German speakers. In the city at large, only about 1.8 percent of all businesses were concerned with foodstuffs in 1756. Other tradesmen—in textiles, leather production, shipbuilding, and metalwork—were more important and more numerous in the general economy.[9] But the obsession of German-speaking villagers with Nahrung—nourishment—and the repeated references to the poor forced to support Saint Michael's out of the "widow's mite taken from that devoted to nourishment" ("*Scherflein aus der Nahrung*") revealed the basis of growing tension within a congregation that functioned, as Mühl-enberg recognized, like a village, complete with hostilities and relation-ships determined by property and its control.

Adding to the mistrust, in the 1750s the original trustees and elders began at their own discretion to appoint their clients as elders, deacons, and sextons, as well as the Vorsteher (congregational representative) and the Almosenpfleger, without consulting the congregation. These client authorities exercised extraordinary powers, no one more so than Jacob Graeff the elder, who secured absolute power over apportioning the pews sold to applicants. Not only were half of the first group of trustee-elders involved in some way with food procural or distribution, but the clients they sponsored also mastered this trade after arriving in the later 1740s, and combined it with other occupations affecting the household: they opened taverns or worked as carpenters.

The baker Martin Rau, who arrived in the late 1740s; Martin Ries, the butcher, and Daniel Grub, who both arrived in the early 1750s; and David Schäffer, who arrived in 1746, all ran taverns; Schäffer later became a shopkeeper. Andreas Boßhardt, a shoemaker who arrived in 1747, saw his sister married to the Germantown Lutheran Jacob Gensel, one of the ubiquitous Neuländer family of Matthias and the two Jacobs who plied the route between Philadelphia and villages in the German southwest.

Adam Weber, like Boßhardt, came from Rüppurr, in Baden; Adam Krebs had arrived in 1739 at age nineteen from Eggenstein, also in Baden. In the 1740s Krebs began a career in the building trades. He may not have married, and was thus missed in the 1756 assessment, but by 1771 his father, Heinrich Krebs, and Jacob Graeff and Wilhelm Hofnagel—all of Saint Michael's—were involved in building John Dickinson's new home.[10]

Mühlenberg reported that the original elders had been skilled craftsmen, shopkeepers, and innkeepers. But as immigration increased and space became ever dearer in a building seating only half of those who wanted a pew, resentments intensified.[11] Baden-Kraichgau ties in the Reich bound these men together, as did their proximity to each other in Philadelphia's wards: nearly all of them lived in Mulberry Ward, along Race and Market streets, and between Second and Fifth streets. The communicant registers at Saint Michael's, which began only in 1755, reveal also that most of the ambitious worthies refused to submit to the rigorous examination the Halle pastors insisted should precede communion. Their absence from the Lord's Supper provoked complaint by the mid-1750s, for neglect of the sacrament could be construed both as these worthies' rejection of their inferiors and as a manipulation of the sacred host similar to their control of access to daily bread.[12]

Among the original elders, Heinrich Schleydorn and Lorenz Bast communed regularly between 1755 and 1763. But Adam Krebs, Andreas Boßhardt, David Säckel, Heinrich Böckle, Marcus and Frederick Kuhl, and, most notably, Heinrich Keppele seldom or never took communion. At any given communion Sunday, forty persons received the sacrament, with the major festivals of Easter and Pentecost drawing the largest numbers. Saint Michael's, originally thought to be an extravagance by the Halle fathers, almost overnight became too small for the crowds of German speakers who wanted access to pews, which were divided in German style, with married men to the right on the main floor, married women to the left. Unmarried singles, confirmands, children, and finally servants and slaves occupied space in the rear and the balconies. By 1750, two years after its dedication, the building, which measured seventy feet by forty-five feet, overflowed: galleries had to be added on the north and south walls. The new capacity, eight hundred persons, was exceeded almost immediately. Crowds milled outside on Sunday mornings; both in the upper galleries and outside on the street, fistfights and name calling broke out, which the deacons quelled with difficulty and at the risk of personal abuse. The congregation's poverty and lack of access to another site rendered impossible the simplest solution: building another church.

The Seven Years' War also deepened the sense of apprehension and marginality that poorer Germans felt even in Philadelphia. German speakers worshipped at Saint Michael's who had formerly been on the western periphery of settlement; Johannes Miekle, who accompanied wagons to the Ohio country, left his wife, Catharina Magdalena, in the city, where she took communion regularly, he bringing back frightening tales of violence. Even more horrifying was Jacob Knodel's tale of arriving in 1754 and settling in Virginia with his wife and children: five of his children—with their mother—he had lost to hostile Native Americans. Johannes Kappel had lost his wife to an Indian attack; his two children remained captive. Four German-speaking soldiers involved in the fighting on the frontier received the sacrament at the church in 1757. Adding to the Lutherans' sense of insecurity, English speakers cast dark glances at German speakers, suspecting them of harboring a secret fondness for the French. Moravian missionaries, with their cassocks and crucifixes, looked like Jesuit agents to Britons bred on the fear of popery. In a sly preemptive strike, Conrad Weiser got up a petition against the German Catholic priest in Philadelphia who had held a Corpus Christi procession in Gossenhoppen, provoking Lutheran ire. Disappearing for weeks, the pater was rumored to have consorted with the French on the frontier.[13]

By 1757 the war had helped to focus deepening anxieties about the security of domestic property at Saint Michael's. But in the midst of war, the congregation also lost its pastors: Peter Brunnholtz, the Schleswig subject who had arrived in 1745 to act as Mühlenberg's second, and Johann Dietrich Heinzelmann, a Brandenberger who had arrived in 1751. Both men died, Heinzelmann suddenly in February 1756, Brunnholtz, never in good health, in July 1757. Despite Mühlenberg's misgivings, Pastor Johann Friedrich Handschuh, a native of Halle, had been called to Philadelphia from Germantown in 1755 to teach French at the Academy of Philadelphia and to work in the offices of the *Philadelphische Zeitung*, propaganda organ of the charity school system supported by British Presbyterians, Anglicans, and German Reformed. Handschuh's arrival precipitated the crisis over competing understandings of property.

Years later, when Mühlenberg arrived to take the parish in hand, the Catholic city constable Philip Schilling took him aside to say that already in 1753 the watchman had found Brunnholtz wandering the streets "crying out that the elders wanted to take the church away from him and take the bread out of his mouth." Schilling had seen the despairing cleric home and hushed up the scandal. For Mühlenberg, the date seemed ominous, for in 1753 he and Brunnholtz had taken the advice of English friends and drafted a Kirchenordnung for Saint Michael's.[14]

Complaints about Handschuh's high-handed behavior centered on his invasion of Württemberg congregants' domestic space and his open contempt for the Swabians of Saint Michael's. Handschuh insisted on making pastoral calls to the sick and dying with elders in tow, provoking deep resentment. At a time when one expected the comfort of scripture and perhaps the sacrament, and when one might wish to discuss putting one's worldly affairs in order, the pastor now arrived bringing elders who, for many Philadelphia Lutherans, embodied—in their business dealings, their control of foodstuffs, and their domination of the pastor—an intolerable threat to family and property. Handschuh's reputation had preceded him in Philadelphia. Saint Michael's Württembergers already knew of his undiplomatic habit—already practiced in Lancaster and Germantown between 1748 and 1755—of insulting the Swabians, who returned his dislike in kind. By early 1758, the paranoid Hallenser accused Mühlenberg of having no faith in him and the elders because of Mühlenberg's insistence on a fixed salary. Handschuh piously proclaimed himself willing to live on faith and the goodwill of his congregants. Mühlenberg left Philadelphia until contacted by the infuriated Swabians, who threatened open rebellion in 1761.

In early 1759 the elders had clearly signaled their right to control the use of church property. They spent £915 to obtain a new lot for a cemetery; and at a sheriff's sale conducted during a driving rainstorm, their most powerful member, Heinrich Keppele, purchased—without prior consultation with anyone—a lot on Fourth Street for a new schoolhouse. By February 1761, the Württembergers threatened to appeal directly to the duke of Württemberg and the consistory at Stuttgart and Tübingen, bypassing the Halle fathers.[15]

Seven leaders stood at the head of the disenchanted, 27 of whose names surfaced in the controversy. Of these 27, 11 can be identified: 6 came from the duchy of Württemberg, 2 from Baden, 1 from electoral Saxony, and 1 each from the Palatinate and the Kraichgau. Of the 27, 13 arrived in the 1750s; only 2 before 1740. Less likely in the straitened economic circumstances brought on by war to rise economically, they dwelt scattered throughout the city. The old inner circle lived in Mulberry Ward; of the latecomers whose residences can be identified, 9 lived in Mulberry. The other 18 clustered in the Northern Liberties or Dock, Upper and Lower Delaware, and Kensington. Because the latecomers had arrived in the 1750s, only 14 surfaced on the 1756 tax list. Their average taxable wealth came to seventeen pounds—a figure much less than the trustees' 46 pounds. The malcontents were no bakers, silversmiths, merchants, or butchers, instead laboring as saddlers, wheelwrights, shoemakers, and potters. The odd cabinet maker and joiner joined apothecary Hans Georg Schneider. But 5 of the group were tailors or weavers—among the most impoverished workers fleeing the German southwest.

These disaffected members of Saint Michael's represented a cross-section of the broader Württemberg emigration. Their concerns, therefore, might be taken as indicative of those of other Swabians in other congregations throughout the British colonial settlements. Among the 735 family names of the more than two thousand Swabian arrivals, 25 can be traced to Saint Michael's. Some 20 percent of the entire list were day laborers, another 14 percent weavers, a further 14 percent tailors and shoemakers. At Saint Michael's, none of the families from the more remote villages emerged among the powerful or wealthy. The Michael Pfetches, of Seißen; the Schlotterers, Steigers, and Hetzels, of Bodelshausen; the Birckenmeyers from, of Neuffen, appear on neither the 1756 nor the 1772 tax lists; the communicant list notes indicate that they apparently remained at the lower edges of Philadelphia's wording population, living in rooms rented from earlier arrivals. Neckar Valley emigrants from Grötzingen, Aich, Schlaitdorf, and Unterjesingen fared no better: the Geyers, Hermanns, and Lutzes remained people of low profile. The widow of the former Catholic Georg Ott of Würzburg struggled, selling pamphlets and books after her husband died. Ott had converted at the pietist center Reutlingen, had emigrated from Freudenstadt, in the Black Forest, to Philadelphia, and had led a mean existence plagued by alcoholism; insufficient nourishment took eight of his nine children to an early grave before his own death in 1762. Only Peter Aisenbray of Gündelbach, Johannes Fritz of Beihingen, Johann Caspar Geyer of Schlaitdorf, and Johann Michael Hess of Grötzingen—all 1750s arrivals—appear on the 1772 list as tavern keepers, a stonemason, and a watchmaker, respectively. On average their assessments came to eight pounds; three of them owned houses.

Poorer Württembergers nonetheless retained the sharpened sense of familial property rights that drove one family to plead in tears with Mühlenberg to recover an inheritance of forty Gulden and a quarter acre of mixed meadow and vineyard in Lomersheim. Arriving in either 1749 or 1750, Hans Jürg Boger insisted that he was entitled to the money despite having received a marriage present (as had the other children). He had received not forty Gulden but only a loan from his brother Adam. His father had made good the loan, but Hans Jürg wanted the balance of what his quarter acre and a child's portion were worth. In vain Mühlenberg read the court's decision that Boger's father's debts exceeded assets: Hans Jürg could expect nothing. The Bogers pleaded for their rights to an equal portion of the estate. They also promised that if justice were done to them, the Lomersheim church would profit from the village officials' rectitude.[16]

Although records suggest that the Bogers did not get their forty Gulden, the veiled attempt at bribing officials reveals Württembergers' commonplace conviction that village officials and churchmen were on the take. The charge of bribery and corruption (*Schmieren*) ran through their speech, getting many in trouble on both sides of the Atlantic, as now happened at Saint Michael's. The apothecary Hans Georg Schneider, who led the attack of the discontented Lutherans at Saint Michael's arrived in 1752 harboring dark suspicions that he could never penetrate the councils of power because of corruption and intrigue among the elders. Schneider had lent money to Christian Ruffer before both arrived in America within a year of each other. But Schneider had to plead in Saur's newspaper for a return of his money. He moved by 1755 from "the Ridge" between Germantown and the city, to Kensington, and finally settled near the Lutheran church in 1757. While in Kensington, he had poured out his frustrations to the old elder Johannes Oswald. A devoted reader of the Württemberg theologian Johann Albrecht Bengel, Schneider rejoiced to find that the wife of another Saint Michael's parishioner, Theodorus Memminger, the distiller in Second Street, was an actual blood relative of the great man.[17] In the person of Theodorus Carben, a 1751 arrival from Stuttgart, Schneider found a fellow Swabian of real means, whose Front Street silversmith's shop was already assessed at eighteen pounds in 1756. Perhaps a brother of Christian Schneider of Böblingen, a tailor who arrived on the *Edinburgh* in 1752, the Stuttgart apothecary found his ambitions blocked by the elders.

Christian Schneider brought with him the tale that part of a Stuttgart collection had not reached Germantown. Instead, Pastor Brunnholtz had secretly turned it to other, unknown purposes. The Neuländer tavern keeper Matthias Gensel repeated the story but was forced to recant by the outraged Brunnholtz. The 1753 court case *Brunholts v. Gensell,* although "not to be brot forwd," reflected Gensel's talebearing and Brunnholtz's response. Hans Georg Schneider tried to indicate his social standing and importance by giving two large communion wine flagons to Saint Michael's—only to have the elders declare them too large and ostentatious. Tobias Zimmermann, a furrier who after his arrival in 1758 lived above a sugar refinery, Mühlenberg thought a "hothead."[18] Both Zimmermann and Jacob Fuchs, who also had lived near Schneider "on the hill" but was now a wheelwright in Dock Ward, joined the disaffected.

Schneider also convinced Johannes Oswald, the tailor in Mulberry; Andreas Boßhardt; Keppele's relative George Hütner; David Shäffer the shopkeeper and tavern owner; Adam Krebs the smith; and at least temporarily, the mercurial and temperamental proprietor of the White Lamb Inn in Market Street, the Baden emigrant Jacob Barge (Bertsch). The brothers Peter and Philip Dick, both successful tailors, and members since 1749, also joined Schneider's rebellion, an important coup since Peter had acquired his own house and indentured servant since his 1756 assessment for a mere eight pounds. These wealthier, but still disgruntled or disappointed, members of the opposition pulled with them smaller bakers such as Andreas Meyer in Dies Alley, also a Württemberger. Johann Martin Trunkenmüller, a tailor and like the Bogers a 1753 arrival from Lomersheim, joined the malcontents; so did the stocking weaver Paul Kober of Lauffen am Neckar, in Württemberg, who had brothers in Schwaigern, in the Kraichgau.[19] Leonard Kessler had been influenced by the Vorsteher Johannes Kuhn, with whom he lived upon his arrival in 1754 as a twenty-two year old. Gatherings of "awakened souls" clustered around Kuhn, the joiner in Mulberry Ward, whose dwelling was home to a Württemberg conventicle and became a nucleus of discontent. The potential for full-scale disruption of Saint Michael's, complete with separatist conventicle activity, brought the alarmed Mühlenberg back to Philadelphia to sort out the competing definitions of property and its abuse.

II

If peculation and corruption accompanied disbursements of Saint Michael's funds before 1762, the extant records do not confirm it. Pastor Brunnholtz exulted when the installation of the organ in 1751 netted seventy-eight pounds, up from fifty-four pounds the previous year, perhaps because of a momentary enthusiasm stirred in music lovers. Pastor Handschuh complained in 1760 that he was beset by beggars and the needy, but provided no account of how he responded. Before his death, Brunnholtz made the deacons promise they would never "lend anyone a pence [*sic*] even for a week"; incoming money had to be locked in a chest to which only they and one elder had a key; two had to be present at the opening. Mühlenberg made vague references to bequests of three pounds from parishioners in the 1750s. By 1760, two hundred pounds in marriage and burial fees assisted the pastoral staff as between sixteen hundred and seventeen hundred persons jostled for inadequate space.[20]

Beginning in 1750 and over the next decade, Philadelphia disbursed on poor relief about £67 sterling per thousand residents. One month's bread and meat rations cost about £0.12.0 in 1751, £0.13.7 by 1761. In

1775 the city spent about £129 per one thousand persons, a sum barely adequate to cover a modest monthly food ration per indigent person. Similarly, Saint Michael's could only distribute £0.10.0 apiece to fifty-five destitute members in that year. By the latter date, pew rents were more than six years in arrears. Not until 1794 did the men of the parish found the "Society for the Assistance of Needy and Poor."[21]

Despite Mühlenberg's pleas in 1754, Halle refused to declare itself the legal authority over Pennsylvania congregations, and thus the controller of how philanthropic contributions were to be spent.[22] The reason was simple: European contributions began collapsing for both Ebenezer and Pennsylvania at midcentury, reflecting the loss of prestige Halle suffered at the accession of Frederick the Great.

The collections for Georgia averaged about 50 to 100 Reichstaler during the 1740s, and the average contribution never exceeded 30 Reichstaler. By the 1760s, however, the Ebenezer account actually was some 52 Reichstaler in arrears. By the 1770s the account had recovered enough to carry a yearly balance of 32 Reichstaler. The sole reason for the recovery, however, was the extraordinary legacy bequeathed by a Cassel nobleman Degenfeld-Schönburg. This gift of some 600 Reichstaler generated enough yearly interest to keep the account alive. By the 1760s, however, more than 12 Reichstaler was needed to purchase only £2 sterling, and £100 sterling was exchanged for £108 in Georgia currency. The Degenfeld legacy continued to generate interest into the 1820s, when the English-speaking pastor at Ebenezer closed the account, asking for the balance in medicines.[23]

Pennsylvania's account was in scarcely better condition, constantly in arrears after 1769. Halle had enjoyed steady support from friends at Wernigerode, Darmstadt, and occasionally, Stuttgart beginning in the 1730s, when the account held more than 380 Reichstaler; but expansion at Saint Michael's in the 1740s depleted the funds. From the 1740s to the 1760s, yearly contributions languished at around 60 Reichstaler, occasionally, as in 1759, reaching 145 Reichstaler. A Prussian merchant living in Venice, Sigismund Streit, promised a gift of 10,450 Reichstaler, most of which never materialized. Only in 1766 did a major gift of £231 sterling from the Count Solms-Rödelsheim correct the balance of Pennsylvania's account. These funds paid off the indebtedness for the church property at Barren Hill which Saint Michael's had assumed to avoid foreclosure in 1765. But Mühlenberg's dreams of using these grounds as an orphanage and a retirement center for Halle missionaries were never realized. More ominously, even with the Solms-Rödelsheim bequest, the Pennsylvania account was by 1771 over 437 Reichstaler in arrears. Although the fund righted itself from time to time, debits were incurred again in 1774 (196

Reichstaler), 1777 (174 Reichstaler), and 1778 (63 Reichstaler).

By the late 1760s, Mühlenberg hoped for a general collection in the Reich, an idea he had already proposed in 1752 via Fresenius in Frankfurt, with the notion that the Corpus Evangelicorum in Regensburg might authorize such a collection. Warned in 1752 that such collections were in bad odor, Mühlenberg still tried again in 1767 to approach Fresenius's successor in Frankfurt, only to have the city fathers block the attempt.[24]

The decline in European philanthropy justified for the elders their bid to shake off the remaining restrictions on their stewardship of property. For the disgruntled Württembergers, on the other hand, defending their rights in the congregation seemed to depend upon reciting the original conditions of Saint Michael's founding, in which Halle's future beneficence had rested on the assumption that "the several hundred pounds which the Reverend Fathers in England and Germany donated at our request to this church of Saint Michael's give the poorest members the right to vote." In the face of declining support from Halle, this position commanded little respect from the older Kraichgau-Palatine elders who were eager to cut their ties of dependency anyway. By 1762 the indebtedness of twenty five hundred pounds weighed heavily on the seventeen hundred members, most of whom could find no room in the church and whose children could not be added to the one hundred in the school. As Mühlenberg journeyed to Philadelphia to confront the congregation, he took refuge in Georg Honig's neutral tavern to avoid the appearance of partiality.[25]

On 18 October 1762, the men and women of Saint Michael's gathered for worship. At the conclusion of the service, Mühlenberg dismissed the women and children: men alone were invited to put their names to a new church order. The Swedish provost van Wrangel had preached after Mühlenberg led the singing of his favorite hymn, "Befiehl du deine Wege," sung at the cornerstone ceremony in 1743. Wrangel chose Philippians 2:1–4, an unsubtle text for squabbling Germans: "Be likeminded . . . being of one accord, of one mind. Let nothing be done through strife or vainglory; but in lowliness of mind let each esteem other[s] better than themselves. Look not every man on his own things, but every man also on the things of others."[26]

Over 270 members signed, although many had to return on another date, Mühlenberg adding in his hand the names of women who wished to acknowledge the authority of the new Kirchenordnung. The women's dependence on the pastor to represent their show of support underscored the power of the elders, and the fact that the fears of poorer widows and wives in the congregation could only be addressed if the pastor allied himself with them rather than with the elders. The seventeen manuscript pages of signatures seemed to signal the end of strife. In fact, the new document could not allay the distrust, the insecurity, about church property and the elders' stewardship of the mites contributed by marginal members.

The 1762 church order reads simply. Mühlenberg fought long battles to retain the current elders—who were the original elders—in office for life; opponents wanted the entire slate subjected to regular elections. Mühlenberg argued with the elders that if they submitted to reelection they would be returned to office anyway. Mutual trust had collapsed; the elders refused. Keppele in particular drew up a written stipulation that the original elders should enjoy life tenures; the congregation could elect six new elders for two-year terms. To his colleague at Lancaster, Mühlenberg explained that the three articles of the church order had been successfully put into action, and that article 1, regarding the calling, office, and duties of the pastors, had never been disputed. Neither had article 3, on membership in the congregation. But article 2, "Concerning the Visible Government of the Congregation," provoked bitter contention. By retaining the original elders as trustees, on the condition of good behavior, the congregation acknowledge the services of Keppele, Säckel, Graeff, and their colleagues. By electing six new elders and six Vorsteher, they vindicated the principle of broad congregational participation, which Halle had guaranteed by its own instructions when it funded Saint Michael's. Upon the original trustee's death or resignation, life tenures ceased. If the common law hated perpetuities, so did Philadelphia's German Lutherans.[27]

Even before Pastor Brunnholtz's death, Mühlenberg had worked on a draft church order. Between 1746 and 1750 church orders appeared in German Lutheran parishes, although in widely varying forms. Mühlenberg's own descriptions of pastoral duties in the church order for Hanover revealed his preference for keeping in pastoral hands both the spiritual duties and temporal power over buying land and acquiring proper title. Mühlenberg had assigned ultimate title in the property to Francke and Ziegenhagen, stipulating that church properties were to be used solely for the original purpose intended at purchase. Deacons and elders began to be important to his thinking during the 1740s, but he could not divorce his concept of church polity from the state church tradition. That lay deacons and elders put up bonds to secure these lands did not entitle them to a governing voice.

As funds from Halle and contributions within the colonies increased, however, Mühlenberg provided for a yearly reckoning of church properties by appointing *Aufseher,* or overseers, responsible for congregational accounts. Unlike Mühlenberg, Brunnholtz in Philadelphia and Handschuh in Lancaster never wrote down how these details should be handled.

Each of the three early church orders revealed the personality of its author, but did not clarify the relationship between authority within the church and legal responsibility for worldly goods. Just as in many Lutheran state churches, the congregation enjoyed a veto over the person suggested by pastor and elders as the Vorsteher, or representative. But Brunnholtz, like his contemporaries in the Reich, saw the twelve elders serving the congregation as advisors only. In Philadelphia, Brunnholtz met his match. Keppele and fellow Kraichgauers did not extend deference to Halle's pastors.[28]

By 1755, the Lutheran congregation at Germantown, near Philadelphia, became locked in a bitter struggle that split the congregation in two. Mühlenberg saw this situation as an opportunity to implement a novel form of church order vesting ownership of land and building in four purchaser-members; the congregation then chose nine more members in whose hand, in trust, the properties rested. But Mühlenberg's reflections on Pennsylvania's inadequate incorporation statute had begun earlier in discussions with English-speaking lawyers and advisors in both Pennsylvania and New Jersey.[29]

Mühlenberg never said when he first became aware of the 1731 Pennsylvania statute that allowed church bodies to accept donations of property and place them under the protection of incorporation. The statute could be described as quasi-corporation law, since even though religious societies were allowed organization under the statute, it did not allow them the use of corporate powers, the second constitutive requirement for a de facto corporation. Although religious societies such as the Quakers, for whom the law was intended, could acquire property under this law, this limited purpose did not settle the more vexing question of power: who held title and could control, perhaps even dispose of, a religious society's property.

The creation of a trustee corporation like the one Mühlenberg experimented with at Germantown in 1755 represented a second step in the evolution of his thinking about church properties in North America. Under a trustee corporation, however, the individual trustees might legally control their own successors, since the law tended to be vague on succession. The religious society itself was not incorporated, and hence could neither take away the original trustees' control nor transfer control to another body of trustees without the original trustees' consent. Even alienation of the property by the trustees without regard for the congregation's own expressed interests could not be prevented.

Saint Michael's operated as an unincorporated private trustee society created by deed and a declaration of trust vesting control in the original trustees—that is, Keppele and his confrères. Under such circumstances, deeds, wills, or declarations giving money or property to such a society could be challenged or revoked, leaving the congregation's future insecure. In 1748, unfamiliar with common-law procedures, the German Lutherans had failed to make out a probate to a Declaration of Trust and register it in the provincial chancery. In the absence of this sworn affidavit of the witnesses to the original declaration, Saint Michael's legal standing remained defective. Under prevailing British law, equity courts could enforce due performance of charitable bequests derived from a will, or, in this instance, the Declaration of Trust. Lacking the affidavit and registry with the provincial chancery, however, a court of equity would not enforce the intentions in the Declaration of Trust.[30]

Mühlenberg struggled to understand the implications of trusteeship, reporting his progress to Halle, never translating "ein Trusteeship" or sometimes, "ein trusteeschaft." Familiar with Halle's own legal status and with the trustees of Georgia, he had a vague sense that the "Trustees" he mentioned for the first time in 1748 were rough equivalents of the *Treuhänder* of German private law. But the notion of incorporation, and how this step could avoid the complexities of a simple charitable trust, continued to elude Mühlenberg and his German contemporaries. Not that the colonial legal precedent, or his attorney friends, who lacked a clear sense of what was allowed, gave him much help. With reference to his struggle to grapple with religious societies' control of "worldly goods"—the very subject about which pietists expressed so much unease—Mühlenberg lived in a time and place of great uncertainty.[31]

In theory, the relevant English statutes controlling charitable bequests and trusts, especially the Statute of Uses (43 Eliz. c. 4), were thought not to apply to the colonies, because these possessions had been discovered or conquered after the statute's passage. Perhaps in seventeenth-century Maryland the mortmain statutes of Henry VIII were in force, since the 1648 Conditions of Plantations explicitly accepted them. In 1753 an appeal from Antigua to the Privy Council asked whether the Statute of Uses applied to the colonies, the defendants denying its applicability because no proper officers had been appointed to enforce it. Apparently, mortmain statutes, including the most recent revisions (9 Geo. 2 c. 36), which restrained the devising of realty for charitable purposes, did not restrict colonial activities, either.[32]

The appointment of trustees for the charity school in 1754 prompted Mühlenberg to refer to the "Trustees and Menagers" of the project, signaling his growing expertise on incorporation just before the crisis at Germantown reached its nadir a year later.[33] Mühlenberg never revealed whether his marriage to Conrad Weiser's daughter gave him the opportunity to discuss with Weiser the intricacies of trusteeships. The absence of his journals and letters for the critical years 1754–59 obscures the evolution of his thinking. By 1762, Mühlenberg increasingly consulted the Berliner Ludwig Weiss, who after law studies at the cameralist center Frankfurt an der Oder had arrived in Philadelphia in 1756. Born and baptized Reformed, the Moravian attorney saw Mühlenberg regularly after his wife joined Saint Michael's. Mühlenberg knew David Henderson, author of *Des Landsmanns Advocat;* and Heinrich Krebs of Hanover, clerk to the lawyer John Ross, the attorney for the Halle partisans in the Germantown dispute. Mühlenberg's closest friend, the Swedish provost van Wrangel, had some experience comparing his own flocks to Anglican vestries, which were corporations in royal colonies, and discussed the idea with Mühlenberg.

When in October 1762 the church order failed to quiet the dispute at Saint Michael's, Mühlenberg pondered anew the idea of incorporation, just as the Germantown schism made its way to the Supreme Court of Pennsylvania. Yet Mühlenberg did not relish entrusting the property rights of his churches to the tender mercies of a colonial assembly. In an astonishing analogy, his letter to Halle in October 1763—pleading for the establishment of a college to educate Lutheran clergy in America— pointed to the College of New Jersey as an example. Such an *Anstalt* (institute) had to be grounded legally in Europe, and should under no circumstances be dependent upon "our Cromwellian Parliament" in Pennsylvania."[34]

To the pastor's sorrow, a temporary peace achieved at Saint Michael's in October shattered in January 1763, forcing him to reconsider his doubts about incorporation that depended on the act of a colonial assembly. A grueling three-hour meeting of the church council finally produced eighteen men to stand for election as the six new elders; another twelve were found as candidates for deacons. Presumably the old protesters should have been satisfied, since Johannes Kuhn, Jacob Fuchs, and Christian Dannecker all secured election as elders or deacons. Instead, congregational life degenerated over the winter, and by the summer rebellion threatened again as the discontented declared that the Kirchenordnung of 1762 had not been put into effect.

No meeting could be held in March, since the old trustees refused to come. The outraged Württemberg partisan Schneider demanded to know exactly how Heinrich Keppele had assigned an obligation for £894 executed by ten of Saint Michael's members in May 1762 to Hugh Roberts, treasurer of the Pennsylvania Hospital. Keppele had guaranteed the loan and interest on his own reputation because the hospital's Anglo-American leadership knew Keppele, not the other Saint Michael's members—a reminder of the congregation's dependence on Keppele and his connections. By June several members demanded that their signatures be removed from a constitution still in abeyance. Pews were still not reassigned but remained in Jacob Graeff's control; the new deacons could not compel the old deacons to render an account of expenditures. Mühlenberg suggested that the old trustees should keep the deeds to the church properties while the new elders retained the Declaration of Trust, symbolic of equal status.

Outraged, Keppele and David Säckel threw the keys on the church council table, claiming that their reputations were being questioned; in any event, Keppele concluded, the law required the trustees to have possession of the deeds since only they were liable. Mühlenberg responded that according to his reading, the law allowed the new elders to have the Declaration of Trust because the trustees needed only the fee-simple deeds in their possession. By September Graeff had refused to give an account of his stewardship of the deceased pastor Brunnholtz's library, bequeathed to Saint Michael's. Insisting that Mühlenberg was setting a trap for him, Graeff joined other elders in dismissing as a frivolous expense the idea of two strongboxes for documents.

Mühlenberg's depression intensified as Jacob Bertsch, the innkeeper, parted company with Schneider and his fellows. Appearing in the street outside Mühlenberg's house, where Schneider was visiting, Bertsch called Schneider out into the street to fight, much to the scandal of some who thought he meant the aged pastor. Instead of reprimanding Bertsch, however, the elders gave him a prestigious seat in one of the front pews, although Bertsch publicly declared that he could not abide the sight of Schneider; Bertsch refusing to observe the common rituals of politeness among the eminent, who rose to greet each other with a handshake as each entered his pew. The two antagonists carried private dislikes into the congregation's midst. The outbreak of Pontiac's Rebellion further alarmed Mühlenberg and directly affected his congregation, since Schneider demanded a collection for the frontier refugees. Mühlenberg regarded the appearance of a comet over Philadelphia as a sign of impending judgment, a conclusion that deepened to absolute conviction in November as the Paxton Riots broke out: "O God, what confusion everywhere!"[35]

Angered by the elders' intransigence, Mühlenberg, in a September letter to Keppele, Schäffer, and Boßhardt, threatened to flee from their parish if matters were not resolved. Shaken, the trustees caved in, agreeing to appoint one of the newly elected elders to care for the library as Brunnholtz's will had stipulated, and further agreeing to have a strongbox and two keys. But more significantly, the combatants acknowledged that a new church building, erected as common property, should rise as soon as Saint Michael's was debt free.[36] Mühlenberg's investigations of how

Brunnholtz had kept the financial records revealed extraordinary sloppiness; the elders had indeed controlled him. To Ziegenhagen and Francke, Mühlenberg wrote that the original elders continued to intimidate both the poor and the pastor at Saint Michael's through their manipulation of church property. Schneider now demanded that the Ministerium of Pennsylvania confront Handschuh and his divisive behavior in the congregation. Even Mühlenberg suggested to Halle that Handschuh be recalled to Europe. By November, Schneider threatened to lead two hundred members, largely fellow Württembergers, into schism.

A resolution appeared to be at hand at the council's meeting on 25 November. Schneider and his group wanted to know exactly how funds had been used to purchase the new schoolhouse. Keppele, perhaps sensing the impending schism, agreed to provide an account. Both factions agreed to the building of a second church. But both Mühlenberg and the elders refused to accede to Schneider's demand that communion be distributed by only one of the two pastors. Wanting to avoid communing with Bertsch and some of the elders, but refusing also to accept communion from his archenemy Handschuh, Schneider expected to be examined, receive absolution, and be given communion solely by Mühlenberg. Recognizing the significance that villagers placed on the symbolism of not eating bread with an enemy, and seeing here the potential for irreparable division at Saint Michael's should the sacrament be politicized, Mühlenberg refused. Instead, a protocol was entered into the council records declaring the old controversy settled: "no further discussion or mention of the old controversy" was to be allowed. Mühlenberg now resigned his country pastorate in Providence, Pennsylvania, retaining a purely supervisory role there as he turned to incorporating Saint Michael's.[37]

III

As long as Saint Michael's had remained the creature of a declaration of trust, the believers remained immune from the jurisdiction of secular courts, in keeping with the generally observed doctrine of the Two Kingdoms, to which most Reformation churches subscribed. Religious societies—that is, groups of persons associating themselves in the name of religion, no matter their spiritual condition or their behavior—had always existed. But with the addition of the trustees, religious societies assumed another dimension. Though it was the congregation that elected officers, the law gave legal standing to deal with issues of contract and property only to the officers. Although these trustees functioned much as they had under the deed and declaration of trust, formal incorporation bestowed upon the congregation, as the beneficiaries of trustees, a legal remedy of equity. Dissatisfied members might have regarded incorporation as a means of enforcing the stipulation that trustees for life would be retained in office only "during good behavior"—a subjective judgment, but one for whose enforcement an equity court might entertain a bill.

Externally, incorporation warned off troublemakers seeking to disturb enjoyment of title. Creditors, no matter their claim, could not recover judgment against the corporation itself, lacking means to enforce execution. The individual trustees, however, might be held liable—as Heinrich Keppele already knew, hence his alarm at the prospect of not having access to both the deeds and the declaration of trust. By September 1765 Saint Michael's had become a private corporation recognized by Pennsylvania as existing for the benefit of the incorporators, not for the public welfare, as such.[38]

Many legal experts remained convinced that the power of incorporation did not lie within the compass of a colonial assembly. Sir William Blackstone's lectures, published just a year after Saint Michael's received its charter, suggested that no secondary exercise of the power of incorporation could be made by a creature of royal prerogative. The question of legislative incorporation had been thrashed out in colonial New York during the creation of King's College and the struggle between Anglicans and Presbyterians for control of its trusteeship. New York, because of its royal status, tended to frame statutes discouraging individuals from transferring gifts in trust rather than using legislative incorporation. New York also tended to accept as its own, or "receive," all English statutes passed before 1691, when Jacob Leisler surrendered the colony to Henry Sloughter, the new royal governor. New York Lutherans wanted formal incorporation on the same basis that had been guaranteed the Dutch Reformed under the Articles of Capitulation in 1664.[39]

Mühlenberg never referred to the New York controversy and may not have been aware of it. Yet he must have known that Trinity, or "Old Dutch," pastors served as members of the board of governors for King's College according to the 1754 charter. Mühlenberg seemed more familiar with the College of New Jersey's foundation. His correspondence is filled with disapprobation for the political machinations of both Quakers and Presbyterian factions in the Pennsylvania assembly, whose stability and judgement he questioned. He linked the problems of Pennsylvania politics to the historical precedent in England during the Protectorate. His awareness of New Jersey affairs may have been strengthened by some members of Saint Michael's who came across the

Delaware from the neighboring province to worship. From contacts with Lutheran congregations at New Germantown and Bedminster, Mühlenberg knew that in 1759, both in New Jersey and in New York, concerned German Lutherans had decided to approach their respective colonial assemblies for charters.[40]

Mühlenberg reasoned that "church controversies which must be settled by the local laws are highly vexatious, costly and uncertain affairs." Legal incorporation promised an end to uncertainty. Almost simultaneously, in response to the attempt of Franklin, Joseph Galloway, and Henry Miller to lure German speakers into petitioning for a royal charter, Mühlenberg reflected upon the uncertainties and the "dark and dangerous" times unleashed in the province by attempts to deviate from "the ancient rights and freedom" granted by Penn's charter. Saint Michael's church order bound ordinary members to give offerings to support their churches and schools; a charter would secure further the right of congregational leaders to demand from members donations for the church. No one could claim that ancient custom supported this necessary practice, which recent arrivals among immigrant German speakers—especially Württembergers—found unfamiliar, and suspect.[41]

Mühlenberg never revealed the identity of those with whom he discussed incorporation. "Intermediaries" helped, possibly the Anglican commissary Richard Peters, also president of the College of Philadelphia. Mühlenberg explained to Peters in May 1764 that Lutheran pastors "have no Support for Europe, and live by charitable Subscriptions and free-willing Gifts of ye Communicating Members,"[42] underscoring the fragility of the united congregations' financial basis. Suits from disaffected members could, as the Germantown experience demonstrated, destroy even a congregation of several hundreds such as Saint Michael's. Peters, like van Wrangel, who had incorporated the Swedish Lutheran church the previous year, and perhaps Christian Lehmann or Ludwig Weiss, were the "intermediaries."

Heinrich Keppele now risked his own financial future. Perhaps paving the way for his candidacy for election to the colonial assembly in 1764, Keppele intervened in March to speed the incorporation process. Mühlenberg warned that the lack of room at Saint Michael's and the legal weaknesses of the parish caused the church "to suffer from a deficit of alms." Mühlenberg never attempted in writing to Halle to compare the terms *Treuhand* and *Fiedeicomisse* to common-law terms, but referred simply to "ein Charter" and wrote that the church had been "incorporirt."[43] Since the nearest equivalent of a charitable trust in German law would been *Stiftung,* one might have thought that Mühlenberg would attempt this translation. He may have known that Saint Michael's was a private, not a public, corporation, and that the Halle fathers, enjoying the status of a public Anstalt (institute) would have been alarmed at the secondary status of Saint Michael's. The preference for public foundations remained so central to German law that the development of charitable trusts remained weak for the next century.

Perhaps Mühlenberg believed that the elders had originally operated like Treuhänder charged with executing the purpose of a testament or a declaration of trust. Under formal incorporation, Saint Michael's would approximate the status of a *Stiftung* or *publique Anstalt*. If Mühlenberg was confused, prevailing English law on incorporation and trusts erected for charitable purposes offered little help. What today appear to be "private" corporation acts created religious societies such as the Dutch Reformed church, granted a charter of incorporation in 1696, to the dismay of Governor Bellomont. His successor, Lord Cornbury, insisted on an act of assembly confirming those rights. Although the French Huguenot chapel at New Rochelle obtained a charter of incorporation in 1762, the British government discouraged such acts, labeling them unnecessary and inexpedient. Yet in New York, New Jersey, and Pennsylvania corporate charters proliferated among religious societies or educational institutions such as the College of New Jersey.[44]

By 1775, the British government formally lifted the restriction on incorporating dissenting church bodies, but in practice the home government had not questioned either colonial assemblies' or governors' power to issue charters. Nor did British legal authorities clarify the distinction between "private" and "public" corporations—assuming, as did Mühlenberg, that the society incorporated pursued activities thought useful to society. Keppele, Dr. William Smith, the notary Peter Miller, and Jacob Graeff, Sr., helped Mühlenberg draft the petition that, despite the governor's doubts about needing the Pennsylvania proprietor's assent, produced the charter on 25 September 1765.

Incorporation fended off internal, as well as potential external, threats. Mühlenberg obliquely noted in his journal the vexing news that the wives of the original elders rejoiced that their husbands once again ruled the congregation. Grimly, the pastor noted in July 1764 that the original elders' "horns are beginning to grow again."[45] Internal dispute continued to be dictated by domestic values and transferred cultural notions exploited by self-made, ambitious leaders. The graveyard—appropriately— provided the last issue around which protests, and accusations of assaults on village values and emotions, clustered.

Folks beliefs and deep-seated feelings transferred from village life continued to swirl in the midst of urban Philadelphia. Just the rumor that the old church and graveyard would be abandoned for the new church was sufficient to provoke violent response. In reality, Saint Michael's leaders favored expanding the existing building, but alarmed dissidents believed otherwise. Tales circulated, predicting the loss of a revered, twenty-year-old site; these intensified as a scandalous riot broke out in the German Reformed graveyard in July 1763. Determined to hinder the burial of a child by a schismatic party, the elders brought constables to prevent the funeral. The riot bloodied the pastor and left the child unburied until an Anglican priest from the Philadelphia Academy slipped into the graveyard, unobserved, to perform the rites of committal. Lutheran Germans, including Saint Michael's own gravedigger and his wife, participated in the riot, further roiling troubled parish waters. By October, the apothecary Schneider formally complained to the Ministerium of Pennsylvania about the elders, making Mühlenberg fear that schism over the rumored abandonment of the graveyard now loomed. A year later, by October 1764, receiving no satisfaction, Schneider and two hundred other members left Saint Michael's. The church council immediately voted to close the graveyard to the schismatics. Those no longer subscribing to the 1762 church order were banned from the burial grounds. The last plot of earth one occupied now became "property." In Europe, baptism alone determined church membership; only suicide or apostasy could disallow burial in the village *Friedhof.* In the Philadelphia struggle, the complaints against the elders involved abuse related to three specific areas: the sanctuary, the schoolhouse, and the graveyard. Despite a reduction of debt from three thousand pounds in 1761 to thirteen hundred pounds by 1764, potential disaster still loomed.[46]

The Philadelphia Lutheran cemetery, where conflict now threatened to break out, boasted "ein Fenss," allowing those wealthy enough to have gravestones to lean them against the fence (later a wall) for lack of space. The riot in the Reformed graveyard shocked and scandalized the Swabians, in particular, since the term known to them, *Friedhof,* or *Freithof,* was an old German term for a place of peace, refuge, and sanctuary. But the appeal to household village norms by troublemakers who seized the emotional issue of the graveyard angered Mühlenberg.[47] On 12 November 1764, one of his old critics, Jacob Beyerle, articulated the protests of the Schneider group. Mühlenberg responded sharply on 28 November.[48] In this response, he put to rest once and for all a narrow definition of property as many transplanted villagers had understood it. His defense of a broader picture of the world, and of Lutherans' responsibility for it, ushered in the final stages of an understanding about property which integrated village and familial concerns with Halle's demands for stewardship.

Beyerle had been deeply involved with the Gensels, Michael Echhardt, and Georg Seyter in fomenting the Germantown unrest, and had long put himself forward as defender of his fellow southwestern compatriots against the pretensions of the Halle pastors. Dissatisfied with his limited success as a local worthy in Lancaster, he had dabbled in Moravian matters and nearly precipitated schism in the Lancaster Lutheran community. Not content with fomenting discord in Germantown, he now leaped into the fray at Saint Michael's, claiming that he had signed the 1762 church order expecting reform, only to discover continued tyranny under Halle preachers. Railing against the possible relocation of church and graveyard, Beyerle cited high costs in uncertain financial times (hinting again at conspiratorial designs on the part of clerics and council), denounced the abandonment of a place hallowed by twenty years' use, and appealed to "common sense" ("gesunde Vernunft")—an important move, since he had never been present during the elders' debates and could not rely on personal observation to back up his claims. For good measure, he invoked the Formula of Concord and the other symbolic books of the Lutheran tradition. He scorned building a large church in which an aged Mühlenberg would never be able to make his voice heard. The promised building was intended merely for appearance and as a cover ("zum Schein") and as a cover ("als eine Decke") to hide the tracks of elders and pastors from the faithful remnant of true believers ("der Hauffe der Rechtgläubigen") who stood for village domestic virtues. Beyerle slyly played upon the domestic theme, insisting that the faithful few must "begin with a new housekeeping" ("wir müßen eine neue Haußhaltung anfahen"). Otherwise, German Lutherans would be swallowed up by Anglicans, just as the poor Swedes had been—an obvious jab directed at Mühlenberg's close friend van Wrangel.

Mühlenberg's response dripped venom. The "honored friend Mr. Jacob Beyerle," had misused the Formula of Concord, which condemned assemblies of "visible saints." Schwenkfelders, Moravians, and Dunkers could exercise exclusive holiness, not Lutherans. Lutherans would protect "their costly civil liberty and freedom of conscience" in the Ministerium of Pennsylvania just as the United Provinces of the Netherlands had bound themselves together to cast off the yoke of popery. Grounding accomplishments in ancient use, Mühlenberg regretted that what older members had built over twenty years could "in one year, month, weeks, or days, be set afire or with other harmful tools, burned down, laid waste and strewn about by mischievous boys [*von bösen Buben*]."

Rejecting Beyerle's attempt to appeal to "common sense," Mühlenberg demanded to hear unimpeachable witnesses, in an open forum or court of law, testifying against Halle's missionaries. Sworn witnesses continued to be superior for Mühlenberg, suspicious of Beyerle's novel belief, coming into vogue in English "common customary law," that "common reason" "trumped" learned law or ancient custom.[49] Beyerle's appeal to public opinion anticipated the phrase German translators chose for the title of Thomas Paine's famous pamphlet. Mühlenberg, by contrast, demanded to see Beyerle's letters of appointment to be "attorney, bishop, watchman and judge of the Lutheran Congregations." Mühlenberg tossed back Beyerle's attempt to manipulate village imagery to his own advantage. This man, who could not even spell "Formula Concordiae" correctly in his letter, "was but poorly equipped to understand how to oversee the affairs of his own household."

In a torrent of scornful analogies, Mühlenberg poured out his denunciation of the limited, rural perspective on property and its responsible use which Beyerle now attempted to use against the aged pastor. Beyerle betrayed his origins as one of the "extraordinary" youths who had learned from the schoolmaster in the village how to condemn everything not customary there. From the village Schultheiß, ever on the watch for his own honor and for deference, Beyerle had learned the laws of the Reich as well as the Roman names for the months; from the master of cellars, he had learned his notions of diet and health. Punning on the word *hetzen* (to hunt down, or to foment agitation), Mühlenberg noted Beyerle's tutelage by the princely hunters; he had learned anatomy from shepherds, astronomy from cowherds, his deep sense of gravity from the village miller, and uncharitableness (*Unbarmherzigkeit*) and, in the spinning evenings, philosophy from the village beadle. When such "heroes" enter the wider world, of course, Mühlenberg concluded, they must reform both church and state using the only model they knew: the village.

As a result, Beyerle was no different than the orthodox Lutheran in New York whose idea of domestic order included beating his wife over the head with the Bible in which the symbolic books of the Lutheran confession were bound. When neighbors responded to her cries for help, the husband insisted that he had the right to discipline his wife with the Word of God, the unaltered Augsburg Confession, and the Formula of Concord. Beyerle would be better off studying his Bible and catechism to learn humility and peace of soul rather than damning himself with "his twisted understanding and foolish peasant's pride" ("verkehrten Sinn und thörigten Bauern-Stoltz"). If the English and Swedes could read Beyerle in translation, they could see for themselves "what a penetrating, sharp-thinking and learned cow's horn we German Lutherans have in our midst."

At no other time in his long ministry did Mühlenberg indulge himself in such a sarcastic denunciation of village culture as in this letter. More commonly, only oblique remarks to his Halle correspondents revealed his frustration at the grip that domestic village imagery still had on his parishioners. The pastor's vitriolic response to Beyerle reveals the depth of the frustration and fear he must have felt when, on the eve of creating both an internal order and an external, legal bulwark against future trouble, he was again set upon by an exploiter of transferred village suspicions about lay and clerical officials. Mühlenberg's attack seems to have hit home, however. Beyerle and Schneider failed in their last-ditch rebellion. By 1766 their struggle to raise money for their schismatic congregation ended and the schism collapsed, as Zion Church began to rise to accommodate the joint parish known as Saint Michael's and Zion. Zion was built just down the street from Saint Michael's; and the maintenance of the original building and graveyard ended strife over this issue, as well. Mühlenberg described Beyerle as a "63-year-old knave with a long tongue" who was now isolated, abandoned even by former friends.[50]

IV

The decision to build Zion Church ended the confrontation between the disaffected late arrivals from Württemberg and the acculturated leaders of the congregation. Grounds for distrust still existed: the enormous expenditures needed to erect Zion, and continued social distinctions and tensions within the parish, might have disturbed its peace, but they did not. Instead, the old leadership incorporated some of their opponents into the councils of power. They also belatedly showed increased sensitivity toward congregational demands for accountability in stewardship over property, and also responded, belatedly, to requests for poor relief. This development—a quasi-public accounting of stewardship—came close to acknowledging the right of ordinary worshippers to have their interests represented in the council: a notion that could, and within the decade would, be transferred outward into the broader realm of colonial political culture.

In May 1765 the parish buried one of the oldest protagonists in the struggle over competing ideas of property: the baker-merchant Marcus Kuhl of Holstein, married to a Swiss pastor's wife, had died in April, leaving an inter vivos bequest of one hundred pounds to the church, and thus helping to secure for his nephew Friedrich a leading role in the new church order and elevating him to political prominence. The younger man succeeded Heinrich Keppele in December 1766 as treasurer of Saint Michael's. As the younger Kuhl began collecting subscriptions for Zion, whose cornerstone was laid exactly a year later, in May 1766, his notations revealed that to prominent older members like Jacob Bertsch and Heinrich Keppele, a newer coterie of persons had been added. These men would figure increasingly among German speakers as political issues surfaced for the first time. Before 1766, George Laib, Michael Schubart, Friedrich Hagner, and Andrew Epley, Christopher Ludwig, and George Schlosser either had played no role in Saint Michael's affairs, or at most had appeared as witnesses at marriages or were silent signatories of the 1762 consti-tution. Yet all of these men would eventually appear as members of the Committee of Privates, the Retailers' Committee, the Mechanics' Com-mittee, and the various political tickets formed between 1770 and 1776 in the city. Their rise to prominence began only after the internal dispute over property in the Lutheran parish was put to rest.[51]

Kuhl managed to find about 50 who promised £5 or more. An initial subscription of more than 612 persons who had pledged to enlarge Saint Michael's had included himself, Keppele, Ludwig, and other eminent members who had promised between £20 and £50, a generosity now redirected toward the building of a new church. The entire subscription had produced promises of between £1,700 and £1,800. The old, estab-lished members, such as Andreas Boßhardt, Caspar Graeff, and David Schäffer, promised between £5 and £20. The committee in charge of construction was the old party: Keppele, Säckel, Schäffer, Graeff, Kuhl, and Rauh. Their connections to the eminent Quaker from the Kraichgau, Caspar Wistar, secured them the property opposite Saint Michael's school at Fourth and Cherry for £1,540.9.0.[52]

The old opposition also participated, in the person of Peter Dick, Johann Martin Truckenmüller, and Christian Dannecker. The building of Zion, which took more than three years, with many interruptions due to lack of funds and the need to repair the leaking roof at Saint Michael's, healed some of the deepest breaches caused by the strife earlier in the decade. Mühlenberg reported his own astonishment that at the dedication, three full services netted the parish £200. Yet his 1767 summary of the costs was sobering. Beginning with an indebtedness of £3,000 in 1761, the congregation had managed to liquidate most of this, reducing the debt to £1,300 by 1765, and even paying £180 per year in interest. But the rush to complete Zion nearly proved ruinous. Not only the purchase of the land, for £1,540, but also building costs and the repair to Saint Michael's had created a debt of over £4,000 by 1767. Some £8,000 would finally be spent for the new church, and a debt of £5,200 hung over the head of the parish in 1770.

Zion was erected by means of secured loans from prominent mem-bers, at the conventional rate of 6 percent interest. Over £1,250 was promised in this manner between 1766 and 1768; to this were added loans from Halle—one, for £300, in 1771, and a second, for £660, in February 1772. In its construction, Zion reflected both continued reliance on the old tie to Halle, and the importance of voluntary contributions made by property-owning German speakers in Philadelphia. And unlike Saint Michael's, Zion began under legal incorporation, with the overt statement by the elders that this building belonged to all members.

Despite the new church's capacity for between 2,500 and 3,000 persons, it proved inadequate almost at once. In assigning pews, the leaders could accommodate only half the membership; 150 "were forced to be content with places in Saint Michael's," less desirable than the spacious Zion, which was alight under a London chandelier but missing an organ the church could not afford. Again the potential for social conflict loomed, since poorer, more recent arrivals could not afford the pew rents in the larger, prestigious Zion Church. The actual pew register no longer exists; those who were seated at Saint Michael's are not always identified. But by occupation and place of residence, they include men described as "day laborer" and "poor," as well as one barber, one flour distributor, and a shoemaker; and men living "on the Neck," "on the Point," "in Camptown," or in Lancaster—that is, nonresidents or people from more distant parts of greater Philadelphia, reflecting a later time of arrival and lower socioeconomic status. None of the ruling worthies of the parish sat in Saint Michael's except for Keppele, Säckel, and Kuhl, who either out of sentiment or for political reasons rented pews in both buildings.[53]

The old building's roof leaked badly, and the organ was in such condition that David Tannenberg, the eminent Moravian organ builder from Lititz, confessed himself shocked to see how badly it had been neglected. Not only could he not promise basic repairs for less than £50 to £60 but he was committed for two years to other projects and would not delegate the task of rebuilding to apprentices. The roof could not be repaired for less than £534, since the walls threatened not to hold up if another layer of shingles was added. Churchwardens had to shore up the sagging balconies with poles. No sacramental acts were performed now in Saint Michael's, and the congregation's schoolchildren were herded over to the building to prevent their disturbing services in Zion.

The social and economic divisions within the congregation also took a linguistic turn. The council reluctantly allowed an English schoolmaster to instruct a small and restricted number of youths in that language, even while employing two German schoolmasters to perpetuate the language and culture of their past. They discovered that the wealthier were paying the English schoolmaster twelve shillings per year more than what they paid the German teachers, even though the Englishman could walk away from his charges after class, having no further responsibility for them.

Alarmed when a riot broke out between German youths attending the night school and some English toughs, the council resolved to continue the night school but to adjust salaries so that no social and economic prestige would attach itself to the English language and schoolmaster.[54]

Concerned that the young men of the parish were being lost to Philadelphia's cosmopolitan mores, the council addressed the internal social strains separating rich from poor in the two buildings. Perceiving social cleavages evident in the two buildings, the elders insisted that there was but one church corporation. In November 1772 they restored sacramental acts to Saint Michael's, ordered repairs to the sagging pews where married women sat, and assigned seats on the same basis as in Zion. Pleading with members to pay up pew rent and graveyard dues long in arrears, the council noted that open sinners — whores, adulterers, and those having bastard children and failing to bring them for baptism and instruction — would be excluded from the church, which was in desperate need of room and paying members. Acutely aware of how such a policy would appear, the council noted explicitly that they were acting for the regular membership, "be they rich or poor."[55]

The rush to finish Zion, and the attempt to obtain the chandelier for a church building designed both to quiet internal disputes and present a more respectable face to Philadelphia, also raised German Lutherans' reflections on their church property to political levels, if only briefly. The passage of the Townshend Duties, the quartering of imperial troops in Philadelphia, and the resistance movements of North American merchants all touched the German speakers and their church buildings. Since Saint Michael's had to be repaired, the six hundred subscribers to Zion first intended to take their time before plunging into further indebtedness, even though cramped quarters continued to cause discontent, especially among the poor, apprentices, and younger men and their families. Temporary quarters had been found in the chapel of the Philadelphia Academy, but the impending arrival of an Irish regiment that needed quartering forced the Lutherans out of the academy and into a headlong rush to finish Zion.

Then, since evening services in the large church had to be conducted by candlelight, two members decided to donate a chandelier. They had approached Halle and asked that an elaborate *Kronleuchter* be made in Halle, Augsburg, or Nuremberg. In the meantime, however, the effects of the Stamp Act made Michael Halling and Reinhard Uhl pause to ask whether such a chandelier would be confiscated as contraband by customs officials. Francke responded in June 1766 that if there were even the slightest danger of confiscation, the idea of a chandelier from the Reich should be abandoned; perhaps someone in London could do the work.

Mühlenberg also noted grimly that ever since the 1750s British authorities had been discussing banning the importation of German books to the colonies; he feared this discussion was being resumed in 1764.[56]

Perhaps reflecting his own growing awareness of how internal congregational affairs were connected to a widening political dispute in the colonies, Mühlenberg urged his fellow clergyman J. A. Weygand, threatened by a split in the New York Lutheran congregations, to adopt a church order. That document must, he argued, take into account North American political realities. "The English constitution, the American climate, and many other considerations, demand and exact, indeed allow nothing other, than that each member in each community must have the right to vote or at least have a hand in the voting." To the Swedish archbishop Beronius, Mühlenberg, after detailing recent events, concluded by describing his congregation as "our American-German-Lutheran Church."[57] But the hard necessity of making "the Lutheran constitution in the metropolis" work remained clear for Mühlenberg, for if it failed there, he wrote, "I would not know how it should fare in the periphery." By 1768, as he reported to Halle in London, Philadelphia's success was essential, since it was "the metropolis (midpoint) to which all poor, scattered German Lutherans in all of North America who have even a small flame of religion left direct eyes and ears after looking to God himself."[58]

The realization among German-speaking Lutherans that representation and accountability within a congregation might have implications for their assessment of political culture evolved slowly. Indeed, the potential for more bitterness within the German-speaking community, which might have turned richer and poorer German Lutherans in Philadelphia against one another in the 1770s, actually increased. Social conditions were ripe for such a development. The most recently arrived German-speaking immigrants were no longer family groups with at least some marginal property to their names; now, they were even poorer members of society. Although immigration never again approximated the heights reached in 1753, migration to Philadelphia again grew after the conclusion of the Seven Years' War, especially in 1764, 1767, and 1773. Saint Michael's was awash in more and poorer members, and almsgiving decreased in proportion to the greater needs.[59]

The downward spiral of the Philadelphia economy, especially for those in the bottom two-thirds of society, had stimulated observers in 1761–62 to create the Committee to Alleviate the Miseries of the Poor. Artisans and shopkeepers, as well as the truly indigent, were increasingly unable to make ends meet. In tax assessments during the 1750s, perhaps 6.5 percent of the city's population was excused from paying taxes. By the 1760s, the number had increased to 10 percent. Apparently, those German Lutherans who had become successful, like Keppele or the Kuhls, joined their English-speaking neighbors in acquiring more and more of the city's wealth. In 1756 the top 10 percent of the city's population controlled about 46 percent of the taxable wealth—which leaves out the considerable wealth escaping the assessors' eyes. By 1767, as the building of Zion began to stagnate, that same 10 percent controlled 65 percent of Philadelphia's wealth. It was more troubling to the German Lutherans that the people in the middling two-thirds of the population had suffered considerably in terms of taxable wealth. Whereas they had controlled about 14 percent of the city's wealth in 1756, their share had fallen to 5.5 percent in 1767. The people in the unskilled labor pool—precisely the day laborers, less-skilled artisans, tailors, and spinners of the German southwest—crowded into the Northern Liberties and the South Wards, where authorities excused the greatest number of residents from paying taxes.[60]

Among a group of sixteen emigrant families from Wertheim, on the confluence of the Main and the Tauber, who arrived at Saint Michael's from 1752 to 1773 were Michael Schubart, the future Revolutionary leader, whose family owned an inn and whose brother or cousin Johann Nicolaus was a schoolmaster. Most of the members of this group were of moderate means: millers, tailors, and musketeers in military service, but also the occasional butcher, such as Michael Hotz, or baker's apprentice, such as Daniel Frischmuth. After manumission and settlement of debts, most could not count on more than one hundred Gulden in property; after 1753 the assessment on emigrants' property was doubled to discourage sales. Among those who did leave was Zacharias Endreß, a descendant of tavern owners of Kredenbach Löwenstein-Wertheim, who arrived in 1766 to reestablish himself as a brewer. Although Endreß must have brought some funds with him, he would lose all of his warehouses and breweries in the Revolution and was forced to secure a small loan from Friedrich Kuhl, in whose account book he appears in 1778 indebted for sugar, butter, and chocolate.[61]

Nicholas Diehl, another late arrival from Frankfurt am Main, where he had been born in 1741, also managed to escape the pattern of impoverishment typical of most late arrivals. Arriving in 1761, he established himself with one hundred acres on Tinicum Island, in Chester County. By 1774, he owned over four hundred acres, and he joined the Committee of Observation in December 1774 and the Association (the voluntary boycott of British goods) in 1775, finally serving in the Chester County militia. Diehl maintained his membership at Saint Michael's and Zion long after he had moved from the city, relinquishing it only in 1806, a few years before his death. Diehl was one of those who in 1766 promised Kuhl a contribution (of £2.10.0) "on account," as was Johannes Diehl the Reformed baker, whose wife had signed the 1762 church order.[62]

A closer sense of how economic and social trends affected Saint Michael's and Zion can be obtained by comparing the worth of the property recovery attempts to the prices of basic foodstuffs in the city in the 1760s. Measuring the indebtedness of the parish against the percentage of those able to contribute to the building of Zion and the repair of Saint Michael's also reveals more when seen in the context of current food prices. If one totals the church council's expenditures for relief between 1766 and 1775, one can glimpse how competing definitions of property had been reconciled, at least to a degree, within this largest Lutheran parish in North America.

The average size of property recoveries from the Reich rarely fell below 100 Gulden, and only exceeded 300 Gulden in exceptional cases. In the absence of complete price series for the villages of the German southwest, an exact calculation of the worth of these sums in the North American economy is almost impossible. The exchange rates reflect only a select subset of the goods in trade and do not reflect purchasing-power parity across the total range of two economies. Yet calculations have been made for example, to determine on the basis of wheat prices what day laborers in Philadelphia had to pay for bread. Württemberg day laborer' yearly wages and the prices for rye bread flour provide a useful basis for comparison. The day laborers of midcentury Württemberg earned about 20 Gulden per month (the price of one cow) and spent about 24 annually for bread. By 1763, they earned about £59 in Pennsylvania currency yearly and laid out £2 per year for bread. The Reichstaler, worth about 1.5 Gulden, and £42 in Pennsylvania currency, provides another measure of comparable worth. If the late-arriving Württemberger or Wertheimer at Saint Michael's actually recovered from a village inheritance, he would have received on average about £36 in current Pennsylvania money, or enough to buy the bread he would have earned by ten months of labor; put another way, he could have purchased enough bread to last some eight years.[63]

Except for the rare instances already noted, the late-arriving Württembergers and Wertheimers did not figure in property recoveries; among the Wertheimers, of the sixteen families noted, Michael Hotz the baker returned in 1769 as attorney for the fellow Wertheimer Christian Beschler, whose unusually large inheritance of 500 Gulden came from his family's connection as masons to the local prince. But the other recoveries by Wertheimers were by earlier arrivals, and none of these individuals remained in Philadelphia.[64] These urban denizens would discover the general pattern experienced by all German speakers: the earlier one arrived and the sooner one obtained property in the rural areas or villages, the better one's chances of success if one then migrated further to Lancaster or another rural Pennsylvania community.

The earliest records of contributions to Saint Michael's that survive (for 1762) suggest that when more than one thousand persons were struggling for a place built to seat eight hundred, only seventy-five contributed regularly. Contributions for 1762 totaled £183.9.6—not even an average of £2 per giving unit; the average was much lower. The elders and trustees of the congregation, such as David Schäffer and his partner, the sugar refiner Peter Miercken, gave £6 apiece; the Kuhls, £3; Jacob Bertsch the innkeeper, £4.15.0. Most of the trustees and elders (e.g., Keppele and Graeff), contributed £0.15.0 apiece. The rising generation of figures later politically important—Friedrich Hagner, George Laib, and Michael Schubart—contributed 10 to 15 shillings apiece, although Schubart by 1763 contributed more than £1. Some gave gifts: Christian Dannecker the Vorsteher gave a communion napkin, and Christian Kopener a baptismal ewer and basin; and when Miercken finally got his pew in 1764 he was so overwhelmed that he contributed £5 "out of gratitude for a seat."[65]

When the German-speaking Lutherans decided to build Zion in 1766, about six hundred persons out of twenty-five hundred, or about one-quarter of the congregation, were able to pledge toward the £1,800 Mühlenberg mentioned. If divided by this one-quarter of the congregation, the full debt of the parish—about £8,000 in 1770— amounted to £13 per person. For the Keppeles, Kuhls, Graeffs, and that group of fifty who had pledged £5 and up, this did not prove onerous. The parish had borrowed some £1,250 from the wealthier members to start building. But those loans had been made at 6 percent interest, and the council finally asked the lenders to grant them one year of interest-free money. Their plea reflected the fact that by 1768 only £700 of the promised money was forthcoming from members squeezed by worsening economic conditions. Mühlenberg grimly noted that by 1768 no money could be borrowed anywhere.[66]

The average of £13 per person that might theoretically have been spread out among all who had promised to contribute came to one-quarter of a day laborer's yearly earnings in the city; it also represented almost all of the £12 one would have had to spend on a modest food budget by 1770. A fully employed laborer in 1762 spent perhaps £55 per year for food, rent, fuel, and clothing for self and family, leaving perhaps £5 for contributions to a church, unless his wife could work, in which case the family enjoyed perhaps another £25. By 1770, however, real wages had fallen below the 1762 level, and Philadelphians at the lower levels of society fell short of meeting a budget of basic necessities by some £14—ironically, almost exactly what the per-person debt of the church came to among those who had pledged.[67]

The surviving financial records are incomplete. Each January Keppele and Kuhl reported to the corporation on income and expenditures, reflecting a new sense of public accountability not evident in the earlier records. Yet the sums were not always recorded. From the council minutes and Mühlenberg's letters, one glimpses the general pattern of stewardship between 1762 and 1775 which shows how Halle's preaching on property finally had the desired impact. During the crisis of 1762–63, giving, like attendance at the sacrament, had declined. Neither Jacob Beyerle nor Georg Schneider contributed to the church, although other members of both parties did. The parish that took in £183 in 1762 only recorded £9.16.6 in 1763, the low figure reflecting ongoing bitterness in the congregation. The total inched upward in 1764 to £112.9.6. Only about 155 contributed during the controversy. By 1767, however, income rose to £1,000. Unfortunately, church expenditures exceeded £1,700. By 1770, giving increased to £2,083, and treasurer Kuhl was able to report that after paying £2,101 on basic needs and interest, and something on capital, a debit of only £18 remained for the year—not including the outstanding debt on the buildings and lands. By 1773 the debt still stood at £3,850. Against this debt the church took in £1,505 and in paying out £1,406 still had £99.10.3 to its name, although an error of seventeen shillings had to be deducted. That the debt had been reduced to £3,205 was noted with jubilation by council members and the treasurer. Yet by 1776 income fell to £1,050.[68]

V

On the one hand, the idea of property which Halle Pietists had urged upon their adherents showed in the increased willingness of Philadelphia's Lutherans to take up responsibility for a growing burden of poorer fellow believers. The decline in total giving reflected the general hard economic times but not a backing away from the recently acquired sense of responsibility. From 1769 to 1775, "alms" consistently made up one-third of total contributions, which also included pew rents and graveyard fees. Total collections, including those categories, fell—from £2,101 in 1770 to £1,291 in 1776; money donated for alms stayed constant at about £380, not keeping up with demand but still representing a commitment from a congregation struggling to face the socioeconomic demands of poor, recently arrived members in a major city.[69]

On the other hand, old habits of frugality and a narrow understanding of property defined in familial, domestic terms died hard. The church council confined itself to paying for basic needs such as firewood, the interest on loans, and bread and wine for communion services. They kept no record of alms disbursements, although Mühlenberg's journals and letters show alms being distributed by the pastors alone, or in conjunction with the elders and trustees, but quietly. Some hint of this practice surfaced in the question put to the council on 2 March 1774. In addition to passing collection plates on Sunday, would it not be advisable to do so at Monday evening Bible study, "to distribute with discretion among the poor, helpless members to of the congregation?" The minutes concluded, "No member had anything to say against this."[70]

Yet not until 14 January 1776 was a special collection authorized, to be taken up on 21 January and distributed the next day. The amount to be distributed—ten shillings per person—went to 55 members of a congregation numbering 3,000 persons. Perhaps the collection reflected a preference for helping one's own, and those one could vouch for because of intimate knowledge. If so, this reflected the general patterns of poor relief and the demand that the "worthy poor" be supported by contributions—patterns followed by the overseers of the poor nearly everywhere in the eighteenth-century colonies. Between 1768 and 1775, in a town of some 33,000 persons, 216 had been helped to leave the city by the overseers. Public expenditures for poor relief had increased to £135 per 1,000 inhabitants.[71]

Philadelphia's German Lutheran effort was modest, and late to develop, precisely because of the internal tension between Halle's preaching on property, with its connotations of obligation and stewardship, and transplanted villagers' narrower vision. Mühlenberg had had to struggle long and hard to advance the idea that giving of one's property in support of the less fortunate was part of the positive Christian liberty that Halle wanted its adherents to exercise. In 1766, the pastor had urged all members of the Ministerium of Pennsylvania to convey this idea to their congregations, while also urging that collections be announced and that there be strict accountability for how funds were used. "This proposal is not intended as a limitation on charity as such," he underscored. "On the contrary, it acknowledges that everyone has the Christian liberty to do good to all men, especially unto them who are of the household of faith."[72]

If, as some suggest, by 1775 one-quarter to one-third of all Philadelphians were numbered among the "lower sorts," no corresponding relief effort reached the lower one thousand congregants of Saint Michael's and Zion. The alms—amounting to two months' worth of food rations in 1775 to each of fifty-five members—reflected straitened times in a congregation more than three thousand pounds in debt, and facing declining contributions from members and from European benefactors. In fairness, one should note that those receiving relief came from both Zion and Saint Michael's, not merely from the latter. Halle's understanding of property and stewardship had made itself felt in Philadelphia but had not enjoyed an unqualified success. Support for schooling existed, not merely for the charity schools but also for Saint Michael's own parish school. The wills of some wealthy and highly skilled artisans reflected Halle's teachings about providing for education and gifts to the church. But internal difficulties stemming from late-arriving Württembergers' accusations of corruption kept alive the narrow perspective of the village attitude toward property, discouraging anything more than a "pay the bills" mentality. The more cosmopolitan visions of elders and pastors who were not from Württemberg seemed full of self-interest to the complainants, and suffered correspondingly.[73]

Among the fifty-five members who benefited from the special collection in 1775, most (thirty-two) were poor widows. Although the first names of the women are given without the first names of their husbands ("widow Krauss") one is frustrated in attempting to identify all but thirteen. Only one came from the Kraichgau in the 1730s or 40s. Late-arriving Wertheimers and Württembergers appear frequently. After Matthias Meyer drowned in the 1760s his wife Dorothea received aid; so did Elizabeth Müller, a Wertheimer whose inheritance the church had recovered for her. The widow Wohlfahrt and Sophia Fuchs, the widow of Michael, the tobacco twiner, had both married into families from Waiblingen (on the Neckar) which had arrived in the 1750s. The armorer Christian Röhr's widow was also provided for; Maria Magdalena Nagel, widow, was not cared for by the successful shoemaker Heinrich and his wife Barbara but received parish charity; Christian Bercke was poor and "a Berliner"; a "Christina in Cooms Alley" received aid, as did Maria Steber in Pewter Platter Alley. Anna Maria Schippach's husband had been ill for seven months, qualifying her for relief; also qualified was Frau Erhard, whose "husband has lost his senses."[74]

Mühlenberg's perspective on property convinced him that the impoverished and marginalized who flooded his congregation were suffering from Philadelphia's public mores and failure to take responsibility for caring for the weak and the poor. In this, he again showed, however reluctantly, the growing conviction that matters originally confined solely to the internal realm of a congregation had implications for the broader, public sphere. The need to seek incorporation for Saint Michael's in order to overcome the narrowest transferred village suspicions about how authorities abused taxes or alms drove him toward this conviction. By May 1767 he wrote on behalf of his parish against the repertory group the American Company, in an unusual foray into public affairs.

Responding to English friends, Mühlenberg insisted that they protest first, since "the Freemen and Inhabitants of the English Nation are the first born of double Britons and the German Inhabitants called foreigners and but Children of Adoption." Seizing this Biblical type of familial, domestic images he knew both German speakers and the Anglo-Americans would recognize, Mühlenberg also paid tribute to the domestic concerns of his own coreligionists. English speakers, he was sure, would take offense at German Lutherans if they protested against a theater group first, concluding that "the foreigners acted by partial Influence or Instigation and not by Sound Conscience." The Lutherans skillfully described themselves as ordinary subjects, as "Mechanicks, hav(ing) no sophistical Skill to argue about the taste, use or Abuse of plays and Games." Yet common sense made them wonder how actors could be crying "Vivant Rex et Regina, and at the same time breeding Worm-Holes and Eggs in the root of His Majestys Tender Tree and branches, so newly planted and engrafted and not yet corroborated by the principles of Christian Religion and an approved Morality reflecting from the serious practice of them." Failure to stop such "feigned higher taste of shadow" would corrupt "Mechanicks" and thus "rendre the Hospital, Bettering House and prison by far too small for the Crowd of counterfeit Moral and virtuous Inhabitants."[75]

The issue of the theater company revealed that by 1767 German speakers at Saint Michael's and Zion could conceive of a connection between a proper Christian liberty and property, and could grasp the political implications of these concepts. Should people have the liberty to corrupt public mores? Such liberty might cause poverty to deepen, especially among unwary, recently arrived immigrants. Could one divorce such developments from the impact they would have upon property—upon domestic property in the form of increased pleas for charitable giving to the hospital, and most probably in the form of higher taxes for the prisons and Bettering House?

The fact that these questions could be articulated by German-speaking Lutherans raises finally the issue of how liberty was conceived of. By the 1750s the two competing concepts transferred from Europe—positive liberty; and liberty as freedom from constraint—also had to be sorted out. German speakers now recognized that their concepts of liberty and property, once properly defined, tied them inexorably to a deepening crisis in colonial British political culture. For Lutherans, that definition was forged from the language created in the disputes in the church, using a vocabulary developed in the German-language press of Philadelphia.

9

The German-American Idea of Liberty

O N 6 JULY 1776, the first printing of the Declaration of Independence in German came from the Philadelphia press of Melchior Steiner and Charles Cist. Three days later, Henry Miller issued a second version. He had printed the first news of the Declaration's imminent appearance in *Der Wöchentliche Philadelphische Staatsbote* on 5 July, anticipating the English-language press by a day. Both translations reflected the labors of Charles Cist (Charles Jacob Sigismund Thiel), a Halle-educated pharmacist and physician who had left Saint Petersburg in 1769. It was appropriate that a translation of the Declaration issued from Miller's press which had for years adopted an urgent, political tone. The German-American language now wove domestic, familial, and religious images of liberty, long ago articulated by the Saur press, into Miller's more cosmopolitan vocabulary. German-speaking Lutherans found the mix understandable because they had had to define the term *liberty* at Saint Michael's in a way that synthesized competing interpretations of the word *Freiheit*.[1]

Part of that definition depended on German speakers' ability to develop for themselves a typology in which the history of the English in their struggle for liberty foreshadowed and explained the German speakers' own experience. In addition, the German speakers' own history had to be expanded beyond events within the Reich, to include the Swiss-German confrontation with the Habsburgs, as well. Without these crucial linkages, transferred images of liberty—either the positive liberty, implying obligation, that Halle preached; or the concept of freedom from oppression so many villagers brought with them—could not be brought to bear on issues in the realm of colonial British political culture.[2]

Yet the task of linking transferred German-language definitions of liberty to colonial political culture faced enormous obstacles. As Saur's shrewd insights had proven, most ordinary German speakers were concerned with liberty in the "negative" sense: freedom from taxation, intrusion into their domestic happiness, or claims that they should support secular or religious leaders' political adventures. The tendency toward quietism and withdrawal that Saur exploited touched even Lutherans, not just free-church German speakers. If the images conveyed in the German-language translation of the Declaration had suasive power, this was possible because they drew from readers a response that allowed identification of such "private" concerns with Halle's repeated insistence that a proper gospel liberty involved awareness of public responsibility. For Halle-educated clergy such as Mühlenberg, however, the possibility that liberty and property could justify rebellion against legitimate authority seemed utterly preposterous. For Lutherans especially, therefore, a final, proper definition of liberty proved exceedingly complex.

One can only appreciate how the term had evolved in 1776 by looking back at the early 1760s. There, both in Henry Miller's handling of political terms and in the language used by protagonists at Saint Michael's between 1762 and 1766, one finds the clues that reveal not only the linkages between competing, culturally transferred concepts of liberty, but also the new synthesis between German-Americans' concepts of liberty and property, and North American political culture.

I

The struggle by disaffected Pennsylvanians in 1764 to secure a royal charter for Pennsylvania, both to obtain royal protection for their western borders and to escape Penn family control, was followed swiftly by the passage of the Stamp Act in 1765. Henry Miller's writing changed in the wake of these events. In the midst of the Stamp Act crisis, Miller attempted for the first time to create a historic identity for German readers in America that reached back into German history, reminding readers of the oppressive taxes on printed matter common in the Reich, and recalling that their printers were strictly forbidden to meddle in political debates.[3] In the ensuing exchanges between Christopher Saur, Jr., and his supporters, who opposed changing the charter, and Miller and his sympathizers, the notion of "blessedness," or a condition of inner peace and undisturbed success, first appeared. Miller published in July 1764 a translation of an English broadside asking whether the colonial assembly had intended to send a petition to the Crown without consulting its fellow citizens ("lieben Mitbürger"), since the assembly's task was to stand before the Crown as representatives ("Vorsteher"). For German-speaking Lutherans, the term *Vorsteher* immediately brought to mind the congregation's lay representative, who spoke on behalf of the worshipping community. Miller reminded readers that no other people's "civic, inward blessedness" ("bürgerliche Glückseeligkeit") could compare with Pennsylvania's when the original charter was rigorously defended. Since disturbances were common in other colonies, blame should not be attached to Pennsylvania's proprietary charter. One wonders why Miller published this piece, which seems to argue eloquently against his own position.[4] Christopher Saur, Jr., in one of his rare instances of genuine political engagement, attacked Miller and his allies, the antiproprietary Germans centered around Market Street, in a particularly hard-hitting pamphlet that ably juxtaposed domestic images against the pretensions of innovators.

Saur's attack on Miller and Franklin pleaded for peace in the aftermath of the bloodshed on the frontier and sharp exchanges in German-language broadsides. The "inestimable justice and liberty" of old could only be retained if peace were made. Yet Saur contributed little to the restoration of peace, encouraging partisans of the proprietary party to vote "like men and not like frighted women" ("wie Männer, und nicht wie furchtsame Weiber"). Saur used the most negative domestic images, suggesting that those who sought a royal charter were *Misgeburten* (freaks, monsters) who opposed the success of men of "their own German Nation"—*Mitbürger* (fellow citizens) who supported the proprietary party. Perhaps significantly, Saur preferred the term *Mitbürger* instead of the more normal *Untertanen* (subjects) used almost interchangeably in these early disputes. Franklin, he went on, completing the imagery, has "eaten our bread" and rewarded scoundrels like Joseph Galloway with a "fat office" ("fettes Amt") while others got a few crumbs ("geringere Brocken"), leaving the province in debt, willing to see the entire house of government burn down rather than quieting the fractious relationships between governor and assembly.[5]

Although he appealed to all regardless of linguistic or religious background, Saur's German-language text took aim especially at the Lutheran and Reformed parties whom Saur feared would vote for a royal charter. Liberty, he argued, was a gift from God which he expected people to exercise. Pennsylvania's charter protected the proprietor's rights, but in practice the right to property "and your purse and all else you own" belonged to free subjects who made those rights known to the assemblymen. The defense of a local group's rights in the face of a central authority was well known to inhabitants of the Palatinate or Württemberg, whose Landtage (diets) could be presented with grievances (Gravamina) against ducal or electoral exercises of power. But in the New World, Saur warned, everyone, "by the law of the land," was free, and not a slave, all equally enjoying "all liberties of a native-born Englishmen," and all having "a share in the fundamental laws of the land."[6]

Here Saur revealed his willingness to synthesize his father's previous emphasis on freedom as the absence of constraint with a newer sense of public responsibility. He did so by tying the idea of the political to the property and purses of his readership. Saur now encouraged melding the older, quietistic definition of liberty as an inner-directed, spiritual obedience to God, bespeaking noninvolvement with worldly matters, to a more active definition. Saur, Miller, and Anthony Armbrüster published essays whose authors showed an ingenuity bordering on chicanery in their capacity for explicating the associated meanings of potentially difficult terms. The anonymous authors of the pamphlets tried their hand at explaining the appropriate German translation of Franklin's infamous remarks about the "palatine Boors." These remarks first appeared in Franklin's 1755 *Gentleman's Magazine* essay "Observations concerning the Increase of Mankind," a shorter version of which received wide redistribution via Saur's press in 1764. Franklin's supporters felt compelled to answer the incendiary paragraph in which Franklin dismissed the Germans as rude peasants, as well as the accusations that Franklin had been behind the hated double rate to be levied on foreign newspapers by the Stamp Act. Not so, this broadside—published by Anthony Armbrüster—insisted: the broadcasters of this fairytale, such as the Wistars, did not understand that Franklin had actually worked hard to prevent the proviso.[7]

The disingenuous attempt of the antiproprietary among the German speakers unconvincingly suggested that Franklin's reference to the Germans' "herding together" merely meant that such groupings "had a Tendency to exclude the English Language in a Country where men multiplied so fast." An equally dubious footnote lectured readers that " 'Tis well known that *Boor* means no more than a *Country Farmer,* and that *herding* signifies flocking or gathering together, and is applied by the best English Writers to harmless Doves, or Ladies in Distress." Franklin's defenders pretended to scoff at the notion that the Germans would have misheard the word *boors* and interpreted it as "boars" (i.e., pigs) being "herded" to the polls. In fact, as Mühlenberg had correctly divined in his explication of the lexical interference that allowed German speakers to hear "King's Attorney" as "Saturnus," German speakers did probably hear "boor" as "boar," and correctly divined Franklin's true meaning and his opinion of them. Franklin's essay, the defenders concluded, did have the virtue of illustrating why German speakers had to master political and legal language to obtain any "Office of Trust or Profit."[8]

Miller, for his part, copied English-language propaganda in counterposing "liberty" and "slavery" during the Stamp Act crisis. Shrewdly discerning the connection between the rising taxes needed to support military occupation and the tendency to override provincial assemblies, he highlighted an innovation that Great Britain had imposed during the Seven Years' War: the appointment of a British commander in chief with viceregal powers. Yet Miller did not describe as "against the constitution" (*Verfassungswidrig*) the disregard the British ministry showed for the assemblies by its imposition of the Stamp Act; instead, he used a peculiarly awkward and more cautious construction, *Unlandsverfassungsmäßig*—that is, not appropriate to, or not befitting, the constitution of the province. His choice of words revealed a disinclination, even in the midst of the crisis, to suggest actual rebellion. He settled for calling the ministry's actions "unsuitable," but also used the term *Verfassung* (constitution) at the very time when German-speaking Lutherans were debating church orders and incorporation.[9]

The refinement of terms identifying forms of taxation and specifying how taxes related to the proper definition of liberty had been largely worked out by the time of the Stamp Act crisis. Yet as late as 1773 Miller's publication of a broadside protesting the colonial assembly's decision to refuse an imposition of an excise in Pennsylvania reviewed both the terminology and the history of taxation. Excises had existed since 1700, the broadside argued, and such impositions on spirituous liquors had never been a problem for previous generations, who were just as jealous of liberty and law as the present protesters. While such excises could be used in England to oppress people, that would not happen in Pennsylvania, where, at the county level, servants of the government (*Beamten*) were controlled by the power of the people (*Volksmacht*). Assessors' appraisals of property could traditionally be appealed to the county commissioners. Against those who warned that an assessor could break down the doors of a house, cellar, or storeroom with a warrant (*Berechtigungsschreiben*), the broadside scornfully asked: "Do they understand under the word liberty to mean here the condition in which people have the right honorably or deceitfully to conduct themselves according to their own pleasure against their neighbors?"[10]

Rather, liberty was a condition in which behavior was judged against the standard of the well-being and surety of the common society ("nach der Wohlfahrt und Sicherheit der allgemeinen Gesellschaft"). Perhaps, the writer continued, they mean that it is a lesser crime to steal from the public than from a private person. In addition, it was an excise (*Akzise*) that was under discussion, not a tax on the necessities of life (*Steuer*, or

Taxen), which people would avoid paying if they could. An excise on liquors justly touched the wealthy, whose power explained why the assembly lacked the courage to adopt the measure. Is this wise, the essay concluded, "to impose yet a new burden upon moveable and immoveable property of a people already suffering under the load of heavy taxes?" This seemed especially foolish when the bill promised to bring in as much as a new tax of one penny on the pound levied against all chattels and real estate.

Miller, like Saur, showed a capacity to connect the notion that freedom was the absence of constraint to a more positive definition of liberty based on commonly shared standards of security and the need for self-defense. This appeal, in its turn, drew upon the elder Saur's 1750s definition of how German speakers should arrive at a resolution of rights or disputes among themselves—namely, according to their own thinking ("mit seinem Nachbar friedlich ausmachen . . . nach ihrem Gedancken"). Apparently not interested in commenting upon the Declaratory Act, Miller in 1767 did note the passage of the Townshend Duties, and approved of nonimportation in 1769. Shortly before this resistance took effect, Miller in 1768 again explored a typology for German speakers by relying on images from other European resistance efforts. Citing the Dutch motto "Eendracht maakt macht" ("Strength in unity"), Miller how published a pamphlet glorifying the tale of Wilhelm Tell and Swiss resistance against Habsburg tyranny.[11]

A sufficient tradition of peasant revolts existed in the German southwest, and might have provided a more familiar set of examples to arouse the political self-consciousness of German speakers in America. But the actual history of the Reich since the Thirty Years' War suggested that peasants were inclined to use cautious legal procedures to protest attacks on their rights. The use of law faculties, legal suits, and the writing of Gravamina had largely replaced resistance and uprising.[12]

By presenting Tell as the supposed founder of an association bound by an oath to protect liberties, Miller sidestepped German speakers' traditional skepticism about the possibilities of a Bündnis, or political association, not tied together by agreement in religious principles. The Tell broadside appeared only a few months before Miller offered for sale the library containing the political lexicons in which just such skepticism, reflective of the Reich's bloody past, dominated the interpretation of the term *association*. Both Miller and Saur avoided mention of the tradition of presenting Gravamina and used only the milder and more English term *Bittschrift* (petition) to describe the rights of subjects. After this initial use of the Swiss typology, Miller dropped it as tensions with Britain seemed to subside. Yet by using the Swiss model, he created for himself and perhaps for readers a role less "impartial" ("unpartheyisch") than he had, on beginning publication, originally claimed. The language of a broadside he agreed to publish in 1772 recorded this evolving identity and the manner in which liberty was increasingly tied to the public, political realm.

The broadside protested the slanders and accusations leveled against tradesmen and artisans suspected of still wanting to alter the provincial charter and the "blessed condition of our present provincial constitution and liberties" ("die Glückseeligkeit unserer jetzigen Landesverfassung und Freyheiten"). The authors described the founding of a society openly identified as a "Parthey" (party) with rules that allowed for expulsion of anyone betraying debates, or not agreeing to work against bribery and "other harmful practices." No mere private quarrel would be considered an excuse for failing to act in a patriotic manner for the best interests of the entire people; private opinions had to be subordinate. Although not precisely a society bound by an oath (*Eidgenossenschaft*) like the Swiss Confederation, the "Patriotic Society of the City and County of Philadelphia" reflected how German speakers circulated in a private sociability that now had political overtones. For most German speakers, the Lutheran church and the debates within its walls provided the only precedent and analogy for this development.[13]

In the same year that he invoked the image of Tell and exploited the Swiss image for German speakers, Miller also invited readers to contribute poetry to his paper. He began the series with an effort entitled "Das Testament." Unlike most of his pieces, this one overtly drew upon the domestic imagery favored by Saur. The poem, in which a man dies recounting his fidelity to his craft, ended with a moral lesson. In addition to leaving his son "a good book," the father observed that he had done his duty in the place God gave him, and that "true good fortune" ("Das wahre Glück") lay in being a man of clear conscience ("ein rechtschaffner Mann").[14]

By implication, Miller intended to point out how the habit of reading, with its attendant reflection, criticism, and self-conscious judgment, connected an interior liberty of clear conscience to domestic bliss, but also to duty. Miller returned in 1774 to this connection between private conscience, guarded by doing one's duty in one's station, and the broader public realm. He hinted in his essay on the utility of newspapers that the press existed to make known political developments and to reveal the secrets of ministers of state. A people in danger of losing the "priceless jewel of their liberty," Miller wrote, would find that the incomparable worth of newspapers lay in their function "as in Switzerland as watchmen on the mountains." Just as was true there, the press brought public awareness to life "like a signal fire" and warned of danger, against which only "unity and steadfastness" provided adequate defense. [15]

Yet Miller did not speak for Lutherans, directly. That his vision was not theirs was revealed by his support for the royal charter for Pennsylvania, and his brief allegiance to the Moravians. Yet in pointing to the role of a public language expressed in the press, he underscored the significance of a German-language sociability and medium of exchange that he expanded upon, one that Saur's dialogues between newcomer and experienced settler had pioneered. For Miller, a critical exchange of views on issues of common interest defined the "priceless jewel" of liberty. By the 1770s German-speaking Lutherans could understand Miller and see themselves represented in his images and typologies because of their own struggle with the concept of liberty.

II

English speakers in the 1760s, concerned about German-speaking Lutherans' political potential, had grasped immediately the utility of Luther's famous exegesis on Romans 13. That text ("Let every soul be subject unto the higher powers. For there is no power but of God: the powers that be are ordained of God") seemed unequivocally authoritative for keeping former Reich subjects obedient. The Regulators in North Carolina, of whose members perhaps a quarter were alienated German speakers, alarmed authorities nearly as much as had the rumored possibility of German-Americans allying with the French in the Seven Years' War. In North Carolina, the governor ordered a reprinting of George Micklejohn's sermon on Romans 13, "On the important duty of Subjection to the Civil Powers . . .," in which Micklejohn concluded that "for an *Englishman* to oppose the laws of his country, is an instance of the highest folly and contradiction we can conceive."[16] By implication, if German speakers wished to be considered loyal subjects, they would behave like Englishmen, remembering what Luther had already enjoined them to two centuries earlier.

But few Britons had considered well the implications of Luther's essay "The Freedom of a Christian." That treatise showed more ambivalence about liberty's proper definition than later commentators remembered. The Reformer's paradoxical statements ("A Christian is a perfectly free lord of all, subject to none. A Christian is a perfectly dutiful servant of all, subject to all"), he himself acknowledged, "seem to contradict each other." He had hinted at how property and good works might be regarded as legitimate and lawful concerns of the Christian's "freedom."

He insisted that all works and goods could be profitable only if one had accepted the definition of law as a command to discipleship, that is, service. Admittedly, most institutions and actions sprang from self-interest, not a willing submission to the law. Work "not done solely for the purpose of keeping the body under control or of serving one's neighbor . . . is not good or Christian." Refusing to condemn either work or possessions, as such, Luther nonetheless focused his attention on the problem of interior freedom. He emphasized, as had the apostle Paul (1 Cor. 4:1), Christians' roles as "stewards of the mysteries of God."[17]

In Philadelphia, however, German speakers knew this ambivalence, and its difficulties. The 1762 church order for Saint Michael's opened by citing just this passage from Corinthians, describing the pastor as the steward of God's mysteries ("geträue Haushalter über Gottes Geheim-niße"). The forceful language foreshadowed that of later political constitutions: it circumscribed power and set up barriers against possible incursions on liberty. But the description of the pastor as *Haushalter* also managed to invoke Halle's teaching about stewardship while honoring the domestic image many parishioners saw as threatened by the elders. The pastor was enjoined, on all Sundays and holy days, funerals, and "other solemnities," to proclaim the gospel according to the teachings of the apostles, the prophets, and the unaltered Augsburg Confession, "publicly, loudly, concisely, distinctly, thoroughly, and in an edifying manner" ("öffentlich, lauter, kurtz, deutlich, gründlich, und erbaulich"). He was to have "liberty" (Freiheit) to conduct additional services in church and school as his strength and demands dictated.[18]

German-speaking Lutherans had discussed these ambivalent definitions of liberty since the 1720s. Halle's representatives in London warned against the lust for worldly goods, and against those who succumbed to migration fever in 1709 to achieve freedom from legitimate authority. Pastor Boltzius had assessed liberty in North America quite positively. Unlike Berkenmeyer, in New York; or even Mühlenberg, lamenting about licentious Pennsylvania, Boltzius praised British liberty. Boltzius defined liberty as the absence of oppression, without delving deeper into consequent positive obligations. This concept of the absence of oppression and violence approximated the cornerstone English theorists founded liberty upon: certainty, the absence of power's arbitrary caprice.

On 19 April 1763, Mühlenberg described the conflicts that had torn the German Reformed in Philadelphia and the Lutherans in Germantown as struggles between the "people's party" and the "Elders, or wealthy." The latter chafed under "the Yoke" of Halle or the Synod of Holland and insisted on an "American liberty" to choose and dismiss pastors. By October 1764 those German-speaking Lutherans of Pennsylvania engaged

North American politics for the first time in a self-conscious manner. As Mühlenberg reported, there was "great rejoicing and great bitterness in the political circles of the city." Saint Michael's Heinrich Keppele had been elected to the Pennsylvania assembly by the concerted action of the Episcopal, Presbyterian, German Lutheran, and German Reformed factions, "a thing heretofore unheard of."[19]

Mühlenberg, however, omitted telling his European correspondents the manner in which his Lutherans had gone to the polls. He noted in his journal the impressive arrival on Sunday, 30 September, of "several hundred German settlers from the country . . . on account of the election of the *assembly* tomorrow." His journal entry for 1 October noted going to the schoolhouse to discuss with the congregation what the election portended. The congregation "then proceeded to the *court*house in an orderly group. It was so packed with country people, however, that our people were not able to get in until about four o'clock." In the council book Mühlenberg recorded that parishioners discussed how they should vote "for the best interests of religion and the public welfare." They then "marched in a procession to the polls, which caused a great sensation among the English. *Vis unita fortior.*"[20] Mühlenberg's choice of the Dutch motto "A unified force is the stronger," which Henry Miller also used in his publications, revealed the evolution of political consciousness among German-speaking Lutherans. During the Stamp Act crisis, Mühlenberg advised his members to stay out of the controversy and uphold the duly constituted authority of the colony and the British Empire. But to outsiders urging German Lutherans to aid Franklin's ill-fated plan to alter Pennsylvania's governmental structure, Mühlenberg also made clear in 1764 that he had come to value new definitions of American liberty.

German Lutherans' refusal to endorse changing Pennsylvania's charter did not concern Mühlenberg. According to Halle's orders, his pastoral role included staying out of politics. Perhaps he believed that he did so. To objections that the royal house was German and of potential value to Lutherans in a royal Pennsylvania, Mühlenberg replied that all were "ready to sacrifice life and property" for the king, but the "priceless religious and civil privileges" King Charles had granted William Penn ought not to be thoughtlessly discarded. Mühlenberg mischievously but half-seriously suggested that Lutheran clergy receive tithes with Anglicans in a royal Pennsylvania. The importance he placed on property and the voluntary stewardship of it became clear as he reminded his visitors that the Lutheran clergy lived on voluntary contributions and remained satisfied with "freewill gifts of love." As a "naturalized citizen and freeholder, and according to the fundamental laws of this province," Mühlenberg concluded that he and the other German Lutherans had the right to vote as they saw fit. He had endorsed a collective decision to put Heinrich Keppele into the colonial assembly. He coupled the issue of pastors' salaries being private, voluntary contributions with his own liberty as a citizen and freeholder to act in concert with other like-minded voters. Showing his own ability to invoke domestic rhetorical images, the pastor insisted that German speakers "are not bastards but his Majesty's loyal subjects and naturalized children. We have to bear taxes and *onera* just as much as the English inhabitants, and therefore we have the right and liberty to have one or more German citizens in the Assembly and to learn through them what is going on." The formula was concise: paying taxes on one's property brought privileges. More important, German speakers also began to be convinced that privileges (Freiheiten) also meant an obligation to exercise positive freedom (Freiheit) and to enter the political sphere to protect liberty. Lutherans arrived at that conclusion during the internal struggles at Saint Michael's.[21]

Mühlenberg believed that the attempt to secure a royal charter in Pennsylvania had amounted to an assault on liberty and on incorporated religious societies. He said so to Edmund Physic, in 1776. The colony's proprietors, he complained, had exhibited a rigid and ungenerous spirit in insisting on payment of five hundred pounds for a front lot on Wine Street where the Lutherans hoped to build a school and parsonage. But, although the Lutherans had always "been foremost when Necessity required to lent [*sic*] a hand and Vote against undermining Parties, as for Instance, when they were about to contrive an unhappy Change of Government," the proprietors took no notice. Those "who have been so munificent as to bestow on almost every Society Gifts and free Grants, except on the German Lutheran" should show their gratitude. For, he concluded, a "Gift for a School and Parsonage does rather encrease then hurt the Interest [of the proprietors] for I know the Custom of our well-meaning Germans by Experience. Where ever they find Churches, School- and Parsonage Houses, there they use to flock together and strife [*sic*] to settle and turn barren Deserts by Industry into fruitful Gardens."[22]

Mühlenberg's sermon rhetoric devoted to celebrating the Stamp Act's repeal in 1766 also exemplified how transferred cultural definitions of liberty now built on new experiences. Greeting the repeal with genuine relief, Mühlenberg published his fifty-nine-page sermon as an octavo pamphlet, *Ein Zeugniß von der Güte und Ernst Gottes gegen sein Bundesvolk* . . . ("A Sign of the Goodness and Earnestness of God concerning his Covenanted People").[23] The title suggests how its author had grown during the dispute in Saint Michael's to share a positive definition of liberty that included engagement and an obligation to defend this gift of God.

The pastor had remained politically aloof during the Stamp Act Crisis. He reported in November and December 1765 on the Stamp Act's passage, but briefly. Describing the decisions of the British ministry with a corporeal analogy, he suggested that the "veins of the North American Body" had been opened, but "unwittingly a nerve had also been hurt" so that the "poor lame animal" intended for stamping had broken out in "frightful convulsions." Not since the beginnings of colonization, he thought, had America suffered such poverty. In his ministry, he was besieged on all sides with appeals not for spiritual aid, but for alms.[24]

In his sermon, Mühlenberg revealed his own evolving typology, which could now see German speakers as a covenanted people, a *Bundesvolk.* He referred to his congregation as *Mitbrüder,* reinforcing the sense of communal bonds; he deferred to the English as "the first-born [*erstgeborne*] Brothers"; completing the familial and bodily analogy, describing despondent claimants in the closed courts and shattered tradesmen "making their last Wills." The Germans, or at least "the more sensible" ("Unsere verständigere Deutschen") had followed his advice and stayed out of the conflict, hoping to continue reading their Bible in German and remain loyal subjects, lest the English hear German protests and respond, "Behold, the aliens, the seditious, the ingrates who confound Israel." The pastor still regarded the German-speaking population as younger, weaker members but believed nonetheless that they possessed equal rights in the imperial North American family. Reading implied not political criticism but rather the positive liberty of self-criticism and spiritual development. Pointing out that German speakers had arrived last in city and province, he reminded listeners and readers that they had to pay the highest property taxes in the city and "nearly unbearable leases" in the country, and bear both city and provincial taxes while building schools and churches and seeking to feed their families through hard labor. Only that labor, and the charitable bequests from well-disposed patrons and benefactors in Europe, had guaranteed survival.[25]

Yet Mühlenberg obliquely revealed his respect for independence in the administration of the church. He still believed in the support of true faith by the state, reflective of his orthodox schooling in the Two Kingdoms doctrine. Although princes and nobles might not pay attention to what seemed to them small details—such as the Stamp Act—they should not think that the riches of the world were theirs to abuse at will, "as if a true, genuine Christianity were bad form in the political realm." Mühlenberg balanced the principle of proper obedience and the principle of the rightful use of positive liberty against a clear understanding of a ruling power's obligation to its people, a notion reinforced by the title's invocation of a "covenanted people." This term and concept had few antecedents in European Lutheran thought after Luther's own day, but it had become deeply rooted in Reformed theologies and carried with it explosive potential, as Luther himself recognized, if rulers ever reneged on their side of a covenanted relationship. Even though the last-born and weaker in the American family, Mühlenberg hinted, German speakers had at last arrived as full participants in the political liberties of North America, with responsibilities for those liberties.

In the Reich, later critics of America, like Schlözer, from Hanover, continued to miss the typology German speakers had built for themselves by the 1760s. In 1823 there appeared a searing indictment of republican licentiousness, and of Americans' inherent contempt for authority and the public welfare. Johann Georg Hülsemann's history of democracy in America lamented that Lafayette and other European sympathizers had not stayed in America rather than bringing American republicanism back to Europe. Americans were either religious fanatics, or people of the third estate whose brutish behavior threatened civilization. It was a pity that the original vision of Washington, Jay, and Hamilton had not succeeded, but the inevitable corrupting force of democratic notions had done its work. The German-speaking population in America, Hülsemann dismissed; from Jacob Leisler on, German-speaking leaders had been "drawn out of the common people"; and the immigrants came from the lowest classes of Europe. The most unenlightened and oppressed there, the Germans' "sole inclination . . . was their own self-interest which they ever bequeathed to their descendants, compounded with frugality, whenever these were not infected with the luxuries of the other colonists, or corrupted by the dissipation of the Irish riff-raff [*von der Lüderlichkeit des Irrländischen Gesindels verderbt*]."[26]

Hülsemann's comments, admittedly based on later developments, nonetheless reveal much about the gulf that by the 1760s began to separate German speakers in North America from the positive, European definition of liberty. It was precisely their capacity to reflect upon self-interest "compounded with frugality" that allowed them to debate, in the context of the German-language congregations, exactly what a property liberty consisted of. Had Mühlenberg's sermon language merely reflected a personal odyssey, and Hülsemann's censures an attack on German-speaking leaders, both would have had limited significance. But the pastor also recorded the exchanges of the discontented critics at Saint Michael's in detail. In this unpublished history of the disturbances, one can see the combatants employing a rhetoric that combined the culturally transferred definitions of liberty as well as concerns over property abuse. But the argument reflects an adopted British history, replete with its legal and political terms. This new language possessed a pliancy suited for constructing a mythic identity that seamlessly wove together English history and German definitions of liberty, making a defense of liberty and property possible. These arguments and the identity German speakers created for themselves began by extension to point toward a public, political realm in which they had to take an active interest.[27]

The first half of the history reviewed Mühlenberg's relationship to the Philadelphia community. The English had been hearing rumors of strife among the German speakers. Mühlenberg identified Philadelphia's problem as identical to that of Ephesus in Saint Paul's time: greed and too much concern for worldly affairs. In 1745 he had found a "poor, scattered bunch of sinners and tax collectors" whom Brunnholtz served. Mühlenberg blamed the irregularity of Handschuh's call by Saint Michael's elders to serve in Philadelphia for precipitating the crisis. A formal call should have been written into the church protocols and signed; and since Mühlenberg's own call included a ministry to Saint Michael's which he had never resigned, the elders should have asked him about this. To his inquiries, they had responded with "undeserved insults" that they needed a preacher, not Mühlenberg presuming to play the role of bishop.

The crux of the dispute, however, lay not with Mühlenberg's role but with the elders' abuse of donated alms, and their contempt for the liberty of the entire congregation. All had to contribute out of their meager worldly goods to build the church, but they had been denied the liberty of voting to call Handschuh, and had been doubly insulted when Heinrich Keppele had gotten the ground for the new schoolhouse at public sale, deepening parish debt without authorization from the congregation. Ordinary poor people had contributed "their mite out of their subsistence" ("ihr Scherflein aus der Nahrung"), a phrase that appears time and time again in the protesters' account and in Mühlenberg's letters describing the affair for Halle.[28]

By September 1761, as Mühlenberg moved back into the city under the watchful eyes of the elders, his visitors were spied on and feared to be seen, "like a Jew in olden days going to see a pagan or tax collector." In the popular slang of the day, Mühlenberg became the "Swabians' Pastor." By January 1762, Mühlenberg believed that the attacks by both parties could not have been found aboard a privateer "or among a drunken company in the Bush." Never in all of America, and certainly not among the Native Americans, could he imagine such insulting and violent language. The only analogy that fit was the image of the victorious party in the old Reich bringing the ringleaders of opposition to the public square for execution, muffling the condemned men's speeches with the roll of drums out of fear the assembled might hear the truth.

The protesters based their claims on the fact that "all protestant churches and congregations under the crown of England . . . from God and the Laws have the Right and Liberty through majority voice vote to elect their congregational servants [*Beamten*] and to set them in office." The elders insisted on maintaining "old custom as long as it pleased them." Without using the term, the protesters demanded representation, on the basis of their labors, and by the clear intent of the Halle fathers who had sent them Mühlenberg in 1742. Mühlenberg himself pondered how to move from the old to the new order without disadvantages and insults. He appealed to *Patrioten* (patriots) to sacrifice for the good of the congregation. To oppose the new order because malcontents wanted it was absurd. The right of free election "was not discovered yesterday or two years ago in the German apothecary," he concluded, rejecting the elders' claims that the Württemberg pharmacist Georg Schneider and the Swabians had invented the idea. Rather, wherever people lived under the "blessed English laws" such rights were guaranteed. If the "creatures" of ill-disposed persons continued to publish broadsides deepening the split in the congregation, Mühlenberg warned, he would proceed against them "according to the sharpness of the laws."

Mühlenberg's own reliance on English political terms and privileges of the law reflected his growing conviction, shared with the protesters, that the congregation's having donated their property gave them the liberty of voting for representatives. He had come to appreciate the perspective of the malcontents, whose somewhat reluctant spokesperson he became. Greeting the "revered elders and spokesman," the protesters themselves denied that they were guilty of hatred and vengefulness. But the response of the elders reminded the protesters of the "Spanish Inquisition." They lived, "after God himself, under Great Britain's certain, sure privileges [*Freiheiten*]." The elders professed to be ignorant of the cause of the problems cast by the malcontents' use of a "dark lantern and a useless light." To this the protesters responded with their own counterimage of fire: the elders should confess that they were human and that in haste they had "helped to carry wood and straw to the fire of contention," with the help of Handschuh, the man "who in L[ancaster] and G[ermantown] had already done the same there."

Elders, "the dear brothers," erred in thinking that only a few fomented rebellion. Rather, "the members who have contributed their mite from their substance"—especially the widows and orphans of the poor—received scorn and abuse when trying to bring complaints to the lawful authority of the elders. "Thus the sighing [sufferers] received [scorn] through the clouds." German pietists had long used this imagery of the "sighing" of the innocent, which should shame the mighty who did not condescend to listen to the groanings from beneath the clouds. The elders, stung by these charges, hurled them back at the malcontents, accusing them of insubordination. More telling, the elders, using the domestic imagery of the villagers, charged that the protesters were guilty of irresponsible management of their means of subsistence ("untüchtig in Handel der Nahrung"), a charge reminiscent of Reich authorities who had always dismissed unwanted immigrants as poor stewards ("schlechte Haushalter"). The Württemberg protesters retorted in a classic prefigurement of later declarations of no faith which would be advanced in secular politics. They demanded written guarantees defining the boundaries demarcating the duties of congregational officers according to "common consent." While using the German to express "boundaries" (*Grentzen Ihrer Pflichten*) protesters referred to common consent as "gemeine Consent," not "Zustimmung," "Mitstimmung," or "Zugeben," or even Saur's phrase, "ausgemacht nach ihrem Gedancken."

Reaching into an imaginatively constructed history, the protesters warned that public opinion would be outraged by elders who disregarded the petitions of the poor. Other Lutherans in North America were looking to Philadelphia. Censure of those who protested, they insisted, was comparable "almost to the court proceeding against witches [*Hexen-Proceß*] in Germany." Even the elders must recognize that if the churches' debt was to be relieved, they could not afford to drive members away. Reflecting the North American concern for securing contributions, the protesters pointed out that under the elders' "tyranny," last wills and testaments would never contain charitable gifts. All members, and not merely those elders who had become trustees, had to bear the burden of incurred expenses. Graphically belittling the elders' social pretensions, the protesters invoked the image of the hallowed property around which controversy had swirled: how would the graveyard testify if it could speak? Equality in sin and death was its answer: "Soon, I will receive you all into my lap," warned the cemetery, which the elders tried too hard to control.

Rather than responding in a Christian manner, the elders had arrogantly answered Mühlenberg "in a lawyer-like fashion" and thought of malcontents as dogs to whom they, like the English, said, "Come in or come out." Continuing to mix English customs and German images, the protesters had accused the elders of not understanding the parable of the vineyard, in which those who had borne the heat of the day and its burdens were nonetheless paid according to God's justice, not that of the world. If such stubbornness continued, Saint Michael's could only resemble the "proverbial Polish Parliament," where disorder reigned. Rather, under the English right of religious liberty, Germans in America would decide their future in common, with no visible leader in spiritual matters to make arbitrary laws out of a protocol book as the elders did.

Those same elders, so many of whom had gotten their start in life by controlling foodstuffs, had too often tried to control and intimidate the poorer members. They acted too much like a private club in which decisions were made by friends around the supper table (*Tischfreunde*) who scorned the "God-given Liberty" of the people and attempted to "impose a forced peace." The protesters showed here a striking awareness of how private sociability could work against, as well as for, a broader, common interest. Rather than using the forum of the entire congregation to discuss how German Lutherans should relate to the wider world, the elders had instead created an even more private club that smacked of secret, conspiratorial doings. They would discover, however, that the "new patch will not take the stitches needed to hold it to the old suit." Even though the protesters knew no Latin, the impenetrable language of the educated elite, "we nonetheless can see to a degree into the political machinations" of the elders. Other congregations (such as the Reformed), the protesters insisted, received a detailed, public account of incoming and outgoing sums and thus contributed "their gifts and mites with pleasure." Lutherans, they warned, would not see themselves treated "like children under the care of a court-appointed guardian [*Vormund*]."

For their closing image the protesters chose the practice, followed in all Philadelphia congregations, of laying aside alms in collection boxes. Just so should elders fill the church with patience and gentleness. But in a world that was turned away (*verkehrt*) from God, some, instead of being converted to him, put the alms boxes behind the door, ashamed of the poor. At Saint Michael's, elders were guilty of "unconverted" behavior. Only the unconverted would have tried to bribe Mühlenberg with a gift from the almsbox, like "ravens." The protesters at this point sharpened their rhetoric by using the image of carrion birds associated with the gallows. Nor did they risk having the elders miss the point. They cited directly the key passage on stewardship: "Render unto Caesar that which is Caesar's and to God that which is God's." They finished with the even more shameful image of public execution. But the metaphor was not the protesters' invention; it had been created by one of the elders' partisans, Jacob Bertsch, who had turned on the malcontents, saying that if they sought a church, they could erect one under the common gallows.

The protesters' final appeal was grounded in a mythic British past that the dissenting members claimed as their own. To the elders' query as to whether the protesters thought that God and the king gave them the right of annual election, they replied affirmatively. All Protestant churches under the laws of England, in all parts of the world under the sway of English law, enjoyed "this inalienable right [*unwidersprechliches Recht*] to liberty of conscience and the exercise of religion freely to elect church servants whether they be called elders or spokesmen." Millions enjoy this right "as a precious jewel" ("als ein edles Kleinod") of their liberty.

III

These extraordinary images, which mixed English with German historic fact, derived their power from both, in part because the term *liberty* had such a rich and diverse history. Here, the "precious jewel" of English liberty—identified by Henderson's treatise of 1761 as the jury trial, by Miller as public information and exchange of opinion—appears as the liberty to elect representative officers in a German Lutheran congregation. This definition depended on a creative reading of the Toleration Act of 1689, and of Pennsylvania's *Landrecht*—the Charter of 1681. The Toleration Act had—even in colonies such as New York by 1709, when Presbyterians and the royal governor disputed its application—simply lifted penalties from dissenters who wished to organize congregations and to preach. Penn's charter said nothing about internal, representative elections within congregations. But Penn's charter *did* reflect upon the problematic definition of liberty. On the one hand, "any government is free to the people under it . . . where the laws rule, and the people are a party to those laws." But the elders at Saint Michael's could just as easily read Penn to their advantage by pointing out, "that, therefore, which makes a good constitution, must keep it, viz., men of wisdom and virtue." In short, Penn also had acknowledged the proper definition of liberty, and liberty's double-edged quality, which the German speakers knew from their own heritage: "Liberty without obedience is confusion, and obedience without liberty is slavery."[29]

German-speaking Lutherans, most of whom had emigrated from the Kraichgau or the Palatinate (many of these were from Swiss backgrounds), or from Württemberg, Ulm, Hesse-Darmstadt, or Baden-Durlach, were able not only to comprehend these British analogies but now also to read Miller and his use of Swiss political and religious history and of domestic moral values, and recognize themselves. Miller encouraged the identity further by publishing an essay by the Swiss Reformed pastor Johann Joachim Zubly, from Savannah. Thereafter, in relatively quick succession, he printed Zubly's sermon *The Law of Liberty* together with an English version of the Swiss fight for freedom; and in July 1776 in the *Staatsbote* he included Salomon Geßner's poem "Das hölzener Bein: Ein Schweitzer Hirten-Gedict von Getzner," recounting the 1386 battle of Näfels in Glarus, where Albert III of Austria had been defeated. In this mawkish piece, the wounded veteran recounting his story to a young shepherd reveals that an unknown hero bore him out of battle; in tears the shepherd recognized his own dead father as the hero who after his heroic act had returned to the battle for liberty. The tale ends with the marriage of the shepherd and the veteran's daughter, affirming the importance of family and inheritance and defining the defense of liberty as risking all to protect individual and private interests, and domestic bliss. German-speaking Lutherans recognized this fusion of competing definitions of liberty and property, both positive and negative, as theirs.[30]

Zubly's handling of the issues surrounding liberty and tyranny emanated from pure Swiss Reformed doctrine. His Zwinglian view of the relationship between politics and faith summarized Miller's own, although Miller would remain loyal to the Revolution, whereas Zubly was unable to compromise his oath of obedience to the king. Zubly's *The Law of Liberty,* a composite sketch of Swiss Reformed theology, contained political principles, theological orientation, and the mythic-historical allegory to the Swiss struggle for liberty. The inscription on the title page ("Ephraim shall not envy Judah, and Judah shall not vex Ephraim" [Isa. 11:13]) suggested both the unity of the colonies with the British Empire, and the impossibility of divorcing politics from religious conviction. Zubly, like Zwingli before him, took for granted the unity of the political and the religious world, and was, oddly enough, more medieval in this respect than Luther, who concluded that although the church needed the protection of princes, the latter were not to be trusted; and that the church was essentially invisible, its true members known only to God.

Zubly's account of the Swiss struggle also assumed that while liberty had been banished from nearly all the world, including perhaps Great Britain, it had been preserved in Switzerland. Yet the active resistance of the peasants in Uri, Schwyz, and Unterwalden, which finally spread to thirteen cantons, had ramifications beyond the borders of Switzerland. It had been, after all, Zwingli's purpose to include the German southwest in the confederation plans, and that relationship had never been totally forgotten in the Reich. More importantly, Zubly insisted that Christians had a theological obligation to resist acts of tyranny, perhaps by disrupting trade. His citation of Paul's Letter to the Galatians ("Stand fast therefore in the liberty wherewith Christ hath made us free" [5:1]) was classically Reformed, not Lutheran. Zubly, like Zwingli, interpreted this text as a command to resist tyranny in a world that refused to distinguish sacred from secular. This reading of the relationship between power and liberty did not abandon the doctrine of the Two Kingdoms, but it gave a novel turn to that tradition by locating authority in the independent local congregation, rejecting a state-supported episcopate, and using dialectic argument—another form of the political "conversation"—as a form of biblical exegesis in which revelation was related to contemporary political events. Lutherans could never perform this exegesis, for the wider context of this text commanded them to do good to fellow members of the household of faith.

Zubly's analysis of the imperial crisis, though penetrating, finally prevented him from endorsing the severing of imperial bonds. For just as he saw a unity between the sacred and secular aspects of liberty, so too he believed that the political bonds of empire had a divinely blessed component within which liberty had to be defended, just as Zwingli had insisted that liberty within the bounds of the Swiss Confederation had to influence the politics of all Europe.[31]

Miller, on the other hand, and the German-speaking Lutherans, could connect an ethic of political resistance to private, domestic, and sectarian privilege which the printers' first groping citations of the Wilhelm Tell legend pointed toward in 1768. By early 1775, alarmed about rumors that German speakers in the isolated regions of New York and North Carolina, were indifferent to the impending crisis, Miller and the Lutheran and Reformed leaders of Philadelphia addressed those whose transferred ideas of liberty and property—isolated from the exchanges about these concepts among a readership Miller had carefully cultivated and nurtured—threatened to undermine resistance. The pamphlet aimed at bringing into line the uninformed who lived outside the networks of trade, religious, and linguistic exchanges.

The *Schreiben des evangelisch-lutherisch und reformierten Kirchen-raths . . . in der Stadt Philadelphia* addressed the lack of information that hampered isolated Lutheran and Reformed German speakers from seeing how dire was their peril.[32] Their reliance on inherited ideas of positive liberty— defined as obedience, personal ties to wealthy patrons and families, or even adherence to religious doctrines that seemed to support "positive liberty"—needed exploding. For Miller, a lack of access to the printed word explained North Carolina and New York Germans' remaining outside the readership that since the 1750s had evolved in those places linked by religious and agent networks. Miller found it pathetic that New York Germans still referred to Sir William Johnson as their "father-in-law," perhaps because of Johnson's first common-law wife, a former Palatine indentured servant. Rejecting domestic analogies, Miller pointed out the extraordinary difference separating an American farmer from an

English one, claiming (with little regard for accuracy) that the latter was forbidden to carry a loaded musket over his own fields or garden, and that the former was unable to imagine not hunting game over hundreds of miles and was certain of his rights to do so.[33]

Miller must have been gratified to learn in early 1776 that his old nemesis Saur had offered customers a piece affirming Miller's own Swiss heritage. The essay, entitled "Der Tod Abels in fünf Gesängen," by "Herr Getzner of Zürich," had been so popular "among the Germans that it was republished three times in one year"; perhaps less impressive or appropriate to a revolutionary generation, the essay had also enjoyed a British translation with a dedication to Queen Charlotte of England.[34] By the winter of 1776, the German speakers most closely attuned to the publications of the German presses in Philadelphia had added to their domestic and religious definitions of liberty and property an identity that located them firmly in an English libertarian past. This German rhetoric created over the past decade contained a mix of culturally transferred elements and North American experience which was different from that found in the rhetoric of English neighbors. That fact did not make the two discourses mutually unintelligible.[35] If knowledge constituted power for those determined to resist British policy, Philadelphia Germans were armed, and ready. They understood something that would not have been clear at the start of the great German migration in 1727: namely, as Joseph Butler had written in 1729, "every man is to be considered in two Capacities [i.e., capabilities], the private and public."[36]

As the violence with Great Britain erupted, Miller seized his readers' attention by appealing to "You Germans, especially in Pennsylvania"— making explicit the parallels between British taxation policies and feudal obligations, chattel slavery, forced labor, crops being ruined by hunts, the costs of court appeals, and the threat that male children would be marked with a red throat band for future service as British soldiers like those now quartered among the people. The British threat was aimed equally at the transferred definitions of domestic property and liberty, and the recently discovered public weal of North America, which German speakers recognized as their responsibility.[37]

Mühlenberg moved swiftly to protect his congregation, hoping to preserve the liberties only recently secured by incorporation. The pastor and the council, using Friedrich Kuhl, as a member of the Pennsylvania Constitutional Convention, as their mouthpiece, continued to interpret both internal difficulties and external turmoil in the same manner. Fearful that church order and incorporation now were in jeopardy, the Lutherans appealed to the "Laws for the Encouragement of Virtue" and asked that additional words be inserted into section 47: "that all religious Societies and Bodies of Men here to fore united and incorporated for the Advancement of Virtue and Learning and for other pious and charitable Purposes Shall be encouraged and protected in the Enjoyment of the Privileges, Immunities and Estate, which they were accustomed to enjoy and might or could of Right have enjoyed under the Laws and former Constitution of this State."[38]

On 25 August 1775, Pastor J. H. C. Helmuth wrote from Lancaster to the Halle fathers about the deepening political crisis. By the time they received his letter on 26 November, the actions taken by the Second Continental Congress anticipated independence. Helmuth exhibited for the American cause an enthusiasm that Mühlenberg, senior Lutheran pastor in America, could not. Mühlenberg would agonize for two years over the moral dilemma posed by revolution against a Christian monarch. Helmuth saw the deepening crisis differently. Describing General Gage's destruction of Charlestown, Massachusetts, and the bravery of the provincial forces, Helmuth noted that the latter "up to the present time have enjoyed all manner of advantage." Royal troops could not match the enthusiasm of the volunteers who were flocking to the defense of liberty in such numbers that they could not all be used, to their great disappointment. "My own small knowledge of history affords me no other comparable situation in which one could have believed that a people would freely stand to arms for more than a year, as soon as the news reached them of the first encounter near Lexington in New England." Even Mennonites and Quakers, who otherwise shunned all appearances of warfare, joined in these military exercises, Helmuth reported. Now, "the raw rumors of the war one hears continually in the streets."[39]

"England," Helmuth believed, "has admittedly deserved such a situation in which God has allowed such a rupture to occur; this land, however, has also earned [this state of affairs] as it only belatedly sought refuge in God." From a pastoral perspective, he predicted grimly that defense of America's "previously enjoyed Liberties under which the Land had been so happily ruled" would close the people's hearts to hunger for the gospel. Vengeance and bitterness would be unavoidable. In a not-too-veiled reference to Pastor Mühlenberg's son Peter, in Virginia, Helmuth concluded, "There are in the American Army many preachers who clothe the function of a teacher with that of an officer of war at the same time." Marveling at the unanimity of the colonists' defense of "Liberties," Helmuth noted that anyone who dissented dared not say so openly for fear of losing his life.

Even Mühlenberg, a loyalist when independence was declared, eventually saw the defense of property as justification for rebellion. Defense against warfare and against economic upheaval that endangered property—familiar themes in the German speakers' past—trumped the legal argument in support of obedience. Angered by the ravaging of New Jersey by Hessian soldiers, whose "robbing" and "plundering" he denounced, the aged pastor struggled with the injunction of Romans 13 to be obedient to authority. His solution was classically Lutheran: both prudence and the previous passage, Romans 12, counseled using active judgment to discern where legitimate government lay.[40]

Luther's 1531 "Warning to His Dear German People" rejected his earlier doctrine of unconditional obedience to authority. Rulers failing to protect subjects who were bound to them violated "a baptismal pledge and Christian covenant." When this happened, Luther concluded, "the doctrine regarding government, regarding worldly peace, worldly estates" collapsed. To support such rulers was to defend "thieves and robbers." Mühlenberg concurred, noting in June 1775 that "every right-minded housefather should protect his house and property against thieves who may be presumed to come not only to steal but also to slay and destroy." The dilemma stemmed from "the abuse of noble freedom, a carnal security, and the sins and evils which arise therefrom." Mühlenberg, belatedly, found his own way of synthesizing positive and negative definitions of liberty and property, both those he had inherited and those currently in dispute between colonials and Britons. In 1772 he had approved of Pastor Friedrich Schultz's building a new rectory as the decrepit Tulpehocken church threatened to collapse. Mühlenberg reasoned, "Charity begins at home . . . . they were not building the house for him alone, but for their own and their children's benefit." By 1777 he worked through the dilemma surrounding Romans 13 by noting that one should "be subject to that power which rules . . . and offers protection, or, as it is put, which has the strongest arm and longest sword." His own 1766 musings on the notion of a covenanted people had made it possible, eleven years later, to see that Britain's failure to uphold its contractual responsibilities to defend property against thieves and brigands cancelled the obligation of loyalty.[41]

In Philadelphia, both English and German students formed companies of volunteers, wore livery, and exercised as regular soldiers. "What the father does, the child mimics as well." For preachers like Helmuth, the charge to preach repentance remained unchanged. Anticipating a negative judgment of the patriot cause by superiors who had cultivated their network with Britain, Helmuth demurred at preaching against Revolution. "I at least for my own small part, cannot determine whether America is justified in the matter or not."[42]

Lutheran and Reformed congregants in Philadelphia harbored no such doubts. Members of Saint Michael's and Zion served on various committees in the city; companies of German Lutheran and German Reformed soldiers organized; and the field officers elected in May 1775 included Francis Hasenclever, George Laib, Heinrich Keppele's son, John Keppele. By 4 July 1776, other members of Saint Michael's, such as Johannes Lautenburger, were recommended to the Committee of Safety for officers' commissions in the German Forces by Jacob Bertsch and Peter Dick, the former an innkeeper, and a bitter enemy of the protesting Württembergers, the latter one of those successful tailors who had arrived in the 1750s, a staunch opponent to the old trustees and elders. Those animosities had been dampened in the 1770s through more sensitive responses to the needs of the poor, and played no part in the political consciousness of the largest German Lutheran congregation in North America. On Sundays, companies of German speakers, both Lutherans and Reformed, formed and marched accompanied by fife and drum to their respective churches, the Lutherans proceeding on the left down Ray Street to leave the double formation to enter Zion, and the smaller, Reformed regiment continuing to the Hexagon Church at Sassafras and Fourth. The accompanying music was deemed so execrable that the fifers and drummers were ordered to practice more diligently.[43]

The British occupiers expected that the younger Saur's willingness to publish for them would help with their military plans. Three loyalist regiments—one of Catholics, another of Maryland refugees, and a third of mixed German-English loyalists—never materialized, however. Some five hundred German-speaking women left town in June 1778, one hundred said to have been married to German mercenaries by a Hessian chaplain. This incident, an instance of loyalism nearly unique among German speakers sprang from the hope of social and economic betterment among Philadelphia's poor. As such, perhaps it, too, should be regarded as a political statement on liberty and property, and on the absence of both among those women at the lowest end of Pennsylvania society. The Saur almanac, which had run a series of biographical sketches of the British monarchs during the past several years, ended, appropriately enough, in 1776 with a biography of Oliver Cromwell. British authorities identified Lutheran and Reformed churches as hotbeds of patriot sympathy.[44]

The German mercenaries employed by Britain concurred. The surgeon Julius Friedrich Wasmus, serving with a Braunschweig regiment, noted, "The German inhabitants of North America have . . . treated most of us quite shamefully in their utterances, even refused us entrance into their homes and closed their doors." Another German-American, a "Saxon by birth and probably a Rebel," "was quite indifferent about seeing his countrymen and spoke with contempt of the German nation and of Germany." Wasmus puzzled over the inexplicable phenomenon of "all these Germans [meeting] their countrymen with so much contempt." Unable to penetrate the mysteries of what property and liberty now meant to German-Americans, Wasmus concluded, with most European observers, that only someone who had "perhaps . . . committed many crimes and [whom] the fear of punishment might have driven . . . to the desperate decision of going to America," could harbor such attitudes.[45]

In a distinctly Palatine accent, an elderly Germantown woman asked Johann Ewald, a Hessian mercenary, "What harm have we people done to you, that you Germans come over here to suck us dry and drive us out of house and home?" Astonished to hear himself addressed as a foreigner in a regional dialect of his own language, Ewald, too, marveled how "these people, who only two years before were hunters, lawyers, physicians, clergymen, tradesmen, innkeepers, shoemakers, and tailors," could fight so staunchly for liberty. Ewald released from British captivity the Reformed pastor Dr. Caspar Dietrich Weyberg, whose sermons at the Hexagon Church for the German Reformed exposed him as "a very fiery rebel . . . [who] had defamed the King, and everyone well disposed to him, by inciting feelings of revolt in his sermons."[46]

Ewald showed some shrewdness in his guess that German-Americans' distance from the networks of trade and communication around their largest centers played a key role in predicting their response to the revolt. While he met with uniform hostility in eastern Pennsylvania, he thought the case otherwise among the Germans who came "especially from the area of the Main and Rhine," now settled in the Shenandoah Valley of Virginia and taken prisoner near Spencer's Ordinary. Marveling at the privations the American soldiers would endure, Ewald believed them all to be "true slaves of the Congress . . . for in no monarchy in the world is levying done more forcibly than in this country, where it is said without distinction of position, 'Serve or provide your man, else you lose your goods and chattels.'" Recognizing his countrymen's proclivity to defend households from the threats of forced labor or taxes, Ewald believed that "these people [German speakers] lived at their happiest, since the tyranny of Congress has not yet been able to penetrate beyond a distance of a hundred miles into the mountains. Should one demand a certain number of these people to bear arms, only as many would come as have a mind to procure booty or to derive profit from the wretched evils of war, which means plundering the loyalists."[47]

Ewald and other German observers of German-Americans dismissed political consciousness as "enthusiasm" or opportunism. Ewald rightly guessed that for those at a distance from the developed centers of German-speaking culture, liberty still meant the absence of government, of obligations. He could not imagine that other German speakers had constructed, in debate with one another, more integrated ideas of liberty and property.

Johann Carl Buettner, born in 1754 in Lauta, Senftenberg, in Saxony, told a similar tale, although homesickness drove him to desert to the British in hopes of returning home. Buettner, arriving in Philadelphia in the 1770s, described it as "very beautiful and built with nearly the same regularity as Mannheim; but . . . much larger." Market Street he compared to "the Muehlendamm in Berlin. On both sides of this thoroughfare carriages can be driven without hitting each other, and during rainy weather it is possible to walk past the houses on dry cobble stones, under balconies." But he also recalled having been stripped naked for examination before being bound out to pay the costs of his transportation by working first for a Quaker in New Jersey, and later, after a foiled attempt to escape to Virginia, for Abraham Eldrige, a militia lieutenant and innkeeper outside Philadelphia. Hessian mercenaries deserting to the Americans gave him the information he needed to find the British force "and to return with it, after the war was over, to my fatherland, for which I grew constantly more homesick." Buettner freely admitted, "I was less concerned about the freedom of North America than about my own," but he too caught the contagion of liberty "when [he] saw the great enthusiasm for the cause of freedom manifested in Philadelphia." Six months of service in the American cause, however, did not cure homesickness.[48]

Buettner also confessed a lack of understanding about the terms *liberty* and *property*. At Princeton, his conversation with an American prisoner rehearsed the history of unjust taxation beginning in 1765 and ended with an assessment of American advantages in the struggle. "Even if the English have more experienced soldiers and officers . . . our commanders and soldiers will shortly learn the trade of war from our enemies, just as the Russians did from the Swedes some time ago . . . and we have the advantage of greater numbers and knowledge of the territory." Even for Germany, "your mistreated Fatherland," the Revolution portended "better times and . . . a higher political and moral life." Although Buettner laughed, he later concluded that the prisoner's assessment, "which I did not wholly understand," was correct. After seeing the effects of the French Revolution, Buettner recalled the American's domestic and sylvan images: "Just as once Asiatic and Egyptian culture, transplanted to the woody shores of Italy and Greece, put forth new blossoms, in the same manner European culture will burst into flower in the forest of America, and the well developed youth will cease to fear the rod of the father but will dwell here, independent and strong for himself." It was not until years later that Buettner recognized an ability of German speakers who had been in America longer than he had—the capacity to see themselves as individuals capable of making choices and defining liberty accordingly.

Buettner revealed that at Saint Michael's, where he had been given permission to worship, he had met a group of German servants who had decided to desert their masters and hazard the desperate escape to Virginia. For at least some German speakers trapped in the lower orders of North American life, liberty still meant freedom from constraint; perhaps it even meant being *Vogelfrei*—free as the birds and beasts, as the German lexicons defined the word. More isolated German speakers, and perhaps some among the lower urban orders, remained untouched by the newer, more complex definitions, having no property and absent from the discussions about it that had swirled in the German churches. For many servants, the term *Freiheit* still lacked the capacity to evoke a political consciousness that tied property and liberty together, the lesson Buettner only learned under the prisoner's tutelage. The artisans and agricultural laborers who remained unpropertied and marginal perhaps saw little difference between their situation in the New World and in the Old. If so, they did not respond as loyalists. Among the five hundred suspects proclaimed to be enemies to Pennsylvania and America by the Pennsylvania assembly and the state's executive council, only six had German surnames. Nor did the activities of the government in this heavily German-speaking state reveal any special concern over German speakers as potential traitors. Given the suspicion in which German speakers were held during the Seven Years' War, the absence of such accusations by 1776 must have been gratifying, another confirmation that the American public realm was undeniably the German-Americans' own.[49]

A German-American community made up of a reading public and attentive listeners had been fashioned in the debates over family property and church trustees and emerged forty seven years later to provide German speakers with the ability to interpret alarming developments emanating from the British ministry. One can finally see why German speakers could understand and affirm the Cist translation of the Declaration of Independence despite their unfamiliarity with the arguments that lay behind Thomas Jefferson's use of the triad "life, liberty, and the pursuit of happiness." Cist had exercised his abilities a few months earlier in providing the translation for Tom Paine's *Common Sense*. Cist's translation of the title meant "healthy reason," or "sound reason." It used the same term that Miller had employed since the 1760s and that Pastor Berkenmeyer had used as early as the 1730s. Whatever Cist's intention in using this term, however, German speakers very likely read it and thought of images associated with sound bodily health. What Paine meant, however, could not have differed more from the way Pastor Berkenmeyer had written of "Gesunde Vernunft" in the 1730s. Berkenmeyer had meant an informed reason that would keep those using it in a positive, inner liberty, obedient to God's laws and to legitimate authority. German-American readers now had no trouble understanding Paine's argument that society existed because of humans' needs (*Bedürfnissen*) and government because of their wickedness (*Bosheit*); government existed to ensure *Glückseligkeit* and to ensure the security of citizens' property. In Paine's argument against "regency" in a monarchy, German readers saw *regency* translated as *Vormundschaft*—the term used to describe guardianship over property for the dependents in the domestic economy: minors and women.[50]

German speakers could read Cist's translation without necessarily sharing Jefferson's understanding of Locke. For Locke, liberty had been connected to the individual's power to choose. The untranslatable term *happiness* was the object of the individual will, a will that like a coiled spring lay behind the impulse of desire, which in turn directed the individual's hands to pursue happiness, endlessly and restlessly. Whether German speakers saw this in Cist's translation, one doubts. But enough had happened in their own debates and exchanges on concepts of liberty and property for German-American Lutherans to grasp that definitions in North America were worked out in public exchanges, exactly as Sauer had said: "ausgemacht nach ihrem Gedanken." For German-Americans in Philadelphia and elsewhere, happiness had, as a result of struggles within the churches, where they had insisted on their liberty to choose those to represent their deepest needs and desires, become associated with freedom of choice. Alexander Graydon had been partly right: the German-Americans, "extremely tenacious of property," now understood the connection between private property and political liberty. The deeper consequences and conclusions that flowed from that connection, however, remained hidden.[51]

10

Piety and Bürgertum in the New Republic

THE PHILADELPHIA Lutherans' refinement of the concepts of *liberty* and *property* did not receive universal endorsement. Loyalist coreligionists in some isolated districts of New York and North Carolina rejected both concepts. The elaborate exchanges that had been necessary to sort out both transferred definitions and the uses of these terms by English speakers could not reach into all corners of German-American Lutheran settlement. Each colonial Lutheran group adapted and applied what it had learned in the process of redefinition, with widely differing results. In the end, however, no matter how diverse, those results tended to encourage German-American Lutherans to accept without much debate the prevailing, English-language public opinion that now shaped political culture in the new states.

I

The Salzburger settlement in Ebenezer, Georgia, riven by the conflicts between entrepreneurial late arrivals bent on individual choice and old settlers who heeded Halle's call to stewardship, did not survive the Revolution's destructive redefinition of liberty and property. No acculturated "charter group" had emerged on the Savannah River, partly due to the appallingly high death rates. Providing an ironically appropriate image, observers foretold the eclipse of Ebenezer by economic liberty: the success of the sericulture experiment by the 1760s was noted by a visitor who described mulberry trees so thick that one could no longer see the dozen or so houses and the church.[1]

At first, as Ebenezer adopted a church order written by Boltzius's

311

successor, Pastor Triebner, building upon the customs and practices in place since 1733, all had seemed well. With suggestions added by Mühlenberg and perhaps the justice of the peace Johann Adam Treutlen, the document promised reconciliation between the Swabians in outlying Goshen and the older settlers over the difficult questions of property use and liberty to settle where one wished.

The language of the Kirchenordnung appears unexceptional at first glance. Like Saint Michael's church order, it describes pastors as "loyal servants and esteemed managers of God's house" in this "American desert." Unlike Saint Michael's church order, however, Triebner's document defined the Jerusalem and Zion churches as daughter churches of the Lutheran church in Augsburg, reflecting the dependent character that, he believed, legally described the relationship. That conviction also informed his sense of his own trusteeship over properties developed with European philanthropy. Nevertheless, like the Philadelphia document, this one could not disguise the American conditions that created a novel role for property in defining congregational membership. For in the chapter describing the role, privileges, and duties of members (Chap. 7), the church order, after demanding that members be baptized and make use of the Lord's Supper and attend to preaching of the Word, insisted that each "must according to his property [*Vermögen*] freely contribute his worldly goods and mite [*leibliche Gaben und Scherflein*] toward the maintenance and spread of evangelical worship." This entry underscored what had become customary since the 1760s: pews in the settlement churches were assigned on the basis of ability to pay; at the death of the holder, the pew reverted to the congregation. To retain the pew in the family, one made a small donation. Here, as in Philadelphia, property defined the quality of membership.[2]

Deep fissures lay beneath the apparent agreement. Boltzius, even with his access to the SPCK and Halle, had failed to get the legal complexities of trusteeship right. This failure triggered the split in the settlement between Triebner's followers and Rabenhorst's adherents. As Mühlenberg reviewed the complicated history of the properties, not only that on which Jerusalem Church stood but especially the mill lands, he discovered how defective had been the legal safeguards erected to protect both liberties and property. Admittedly, "we poor preachers are too far away from our reverend constituents and best advisers . . . moreover, we are not masters of English constitution and laws and cannot foresee many consequences. In the beginning and as time went on, it would have been easy to establish a church and congregational constitution and to obtain a *charter* [in English in the German entry in the journal], etc. But who knows and sees all things in advance?" The failure to enter a declaration of trust meant that the Jerusalem Church at Ebenezer lawfully belonged to the Church of England. Out of naiveté, Boltzius had even had the Vorsteher and the deacons sworn to their office using the Anglican terms "wardens" and "vestrymen." This, Mühlenberg noted, gave the established church grounds to claim possession of the church—regardless of forty years of Lutheran use. Partisan quarrels between the Swabian party and Triebner prevented a rational solution. "These stubborn Germans will not, and some of them cannot, understand and recognize the laws of this country," Mühlenberg complained; the lust for dominance over the congregation now threatened to ruin the settlement.[3]

Not only had Boltzius failed to enter a declaration of trust but, in the attempt to make the mills at Ebenezer profitable, he had asked his colleague Lemke to oversee them. When Pastor Rabenhorst arrived, he too was asked to help, and leased the mills to a private tenant. Triebner contested Rabenhorst's role as trustee, claiming for himself the title, on the basis of the unfortunate ignorance of the Halle fathers, who had, without clarifying his role as first or second preacher, allowed him to believe that he was Rabenhorst's superior. Since the mills had been built partly with the proceeds from the old mill and partly with money from collections taken up at Augsburg and by Halle, the mixing of types of property—invested labor and philanthropic donations—created an impossible stew of counterclaims. Because of SPCK involvement, Halle and London insisted that monies from the mills remain under European control. The "third minister's plantation" was supposed to be used to provide a retirement center for aged pastors and their widows, a project dear to the hearts not only of Ebenezer's pastors but also of Halle and Mühlenberg. But the one hundred acres proved inadequate. To further this project, Boltzius instructed Rabenhorst to apply for his five hundred-acre headright, with the understanding that the one hundred acres would be included in the grant. But Rabenhorst could not actually regard the total of five hundred acres as personal property. Rather, he had agreed to hold the one hundred acres in trust; but if he ever resigned as pastor he would have to pay the Ebenezer congregation £649.16.5, the amount that covered expenses and investments made on the property before its sale in trust to him. Only Rabenhorst's own labor, his wife's shrewdness, and her inheritance from her first husband, Kraft, enabled them to take on the obligation, in Mühlenberg's opinion.

This tortured mix of the public and the private forced German speakers to make choices about what they valued most. Not only German speakers but also English speakers had never been clear about such semiprivate trusts, which were not genuinely public trusts. British law remained vague about this distinction. Mühlenberg understood that such ambiguities could no longer be tolerated; instead, papers must be "drawn up in English, and in the old-fashioned English legal style, otherwise they are not valid."[4]

Georgia disputes over property did not end on the nebulous border between private and public interests in church lands and plantations. Another lengthy provision of the new church constitution reflected Ebenezer's wives' deep concern about privileges that they saw as being in grave danger. In January 1773 part of the Degenfeld legacy, the last of any significance Ebenezer received, partially met their demands. The Triebner party, led by Johann Wertsch and Johannes Flörl, drew a bond against the legacy ordering that "the Interest arising from the remaining two Hundred Pounds of the said Legacy shall be yearly paid towards Support of a pious and virtuous School-Mistress of our Profession, which is able and Skilful to instruct and teach our young Girls in Spelling and Reading, in Needle Work, Knitting and other Branches, necessary for Compleating our femal Sex in the Fear and Nurture of the Lord." The liberty to enjoy the fruits of one's labors to best advantage now extended to women's education, advanced by the conservative faction.[5]

Triebner, deeply committed to the original communal vision of Halle and its pedagogical definition of philanthropy, worked devotedly among the pietist women. Seeking to make unassailable his pastoral authority, he bought in London and now donned a surplice with lawn sleeves, giving the aura of public, Anglican authority to his services. Rabenhorst wore civilian dress but in response took on the black Luther gown (*Talar*) that Boltzius had used, assuming the mantle of that departed Elijah. But these outward appearances deceived. Rabenhorst favored the private property innovations of Treutlen. He remained indifferent to Halle's insistence on rigid moral standards and the definition of property as a trust, to be stewarded. Triebner, however, in examining parishioners for communion, perpetuated the rigorous questioning that Boltzius and Mühlenberg had practiced. Even a rumor of scandal could be grounds for refusing a potential communicant. Pietist wives supported Triebner, perhaps seeing here a pale version of what the consistory courts of the Swabian villages had helped them accomplish—discipline and order within the household. They recoiled in horror when Rabenhorst communed a transvestite who had been tolerated in the settlement but not allowed access to the sacrament. Rabenhorst had signaled indifference to good order by holding services in civilian dress, and he had dispensed with rigorous precommunion examination. Influenced by his liberal Halle professor Siegmund Jacob Baumgarten, Rabenhorst had assimilated Enlightenment principles on religious doctrine which Baumgarten himself had learned from studying, with his brother Alexander Gottlieb, under Christian Wolff.[6]

But Triebner's insecurity and rigor overreached themselves in 1774, destroying his support among the married women. Perhaps out of genuine conviction, perhaps out of spite because one of Treutlen's supporters, Jacob Waldhauer, was now deacon of the opposing party and justice of the peace, Triebner excluded Waldhauer's wife from communion. To the horror of the congregation, Triebner seized upon the mere rumor that Frau Waldhauer had been playing cards as sufficient grounds to embarrass her publicly. Unaware of Triebner's advance warning to the woman, Rabenhorst gave her the consecrated wafer, only to have Triebner refuse her the cup before the assembled worshippers. The shock waves of the scandal reverberated far and wide, creating, as Mühlenberg reported, "a great sensation, not only in Georgia, for I had already heard of it in Carolina." Triebner justified his action as discipline intended to prevent scandal from sullying Waldhauer's office; Waldhauer was one of the king's justices for Effingham County. Triebner's refusal to consult with his associate smacked of a high-handedness exceeding the authoritarian tradition Boltzius had admittedly pioneered. Triebner's stock with the women of the parish now began to fall.[7]

This incident created in the final version of the church order a lengthy section (chap. 6, para. 2) obligating pastors to consult carefully before excluding anyone from communion, and placing the ban only upon extreme, public sinners. A victory for Rabenhorst's liberalized approach to admitting members to the sacrament, the change signaled a further erosion of Halle's primitive rigor that Boltzius, Lemke, and Gronau exercised.[8] The new document also reflected Mühlenberg's conviction that majority decisions alone could control questions of money, the mills, and the schools. Congregants were to be given a full week's notice of pending issues to prevent resolutions from passing without their knowledge and full debate (chap. 3, para. 11).

Mühlenberg departed in December 1774, confident that his ministrations and mediation between October and December had saved Halle's oldest experiment in North America. But he was soon disillusioned. Five weeks later, Triebner made various excuses to inquiring parishioners and left on a long journey, taking with him Johanna Lemke, the younger daughter of the deceased pastor. (Triebner had married the widow Gronau and was the father of two children.) Johanna's brother Timothy went on the trip, a hard horseback ride to the Congarees, in South Carolina, and thence to Charleston. By spring, outraged wives in Ebenezer knew why. Johanna Lemke was delivered of an illegitimate son, and suspicion immediately fell upon Triebner—since, the women insisted, no other man had ever been near her, but Triebner had regularly visited her at Urban Buntz's plantation. The hard ride, the women went on, had been intended to induce an abortion, or, failing this, to cause the birth in godless Carolina, where it could be hidden. By the time eleven parishioners had notified Mühlenberg of these events in June 1775, all hopes of reconciling the disputing parties had been destroyed.[9]

When news of the scandal reached London, Ziegenhagen ordered an investigation, to which Triebner refused to submit. Removed from office, Triebner stayed on in Ebenezer, but the settlement struggled without pastoral aid when Rabenhorst died suddenly in 1776. Desperate to salvage their outpost, now caught in the throes of war as well, the Halle fathers, after a meeting lasting several days in August 1778, empowered Mühlenberg via a letter of attorney to assume control in their name. Acknowledging Triebner's refusal to cooperate, they begged Mühlenberg to send his son Friedrich Augustus Conrad, who had fled New York before the British troops, to assume the pastorate of desolated Ebenezer. Unaware of the younger Mühlenberg's political leanings, which later would carry him to the speaker's chair of the national House of Representatives, the Halle fathers begged Pennsylvania to keep the network with Ebenezer intact. But in a bow toward Triebner's perspective, they gave the elder Mühlenberg an impossible task. He was ordered to protest against those who wished "to make themselves in church affairs independent from Europe."[10]

The outbreak of the war focused conflicting definitions of liberty and property at Ebenezer which had been in conflict for at least a decade. Upon Rabenhorst's death, shortly before the Revolution assumed its violent, military character, Treutlen had approached Triebner intending to uncouple the mixed public and private properties, asking the republican government to assume control. Upon vesting them permanently in the hands of the congregation as church property, the assembly would then statutorily empower the congregation to reimburse Triebner (on behalf of Halle) for that portion that had come from European contributions. The attempt to resolve the property issue in favor of private property and lay trustees became a moot point once hostilities began.[11]

A petition of Ebenezer residents against the resolution of August 1774 protesting the Boston Port Bill revealed the gulf separating two notions of liberty and property. These German signatories claimed they had been deceived into thinking the petition had been intended to beg relief for the Bostonians "as a child begs a father, when he expects correction." Instead, they discovered that the resolutions would displease the king, "so as to prevent us from having soldiers to help us in case of an Indian war." The royal governor's admonition to the colonial assembly expressed their own beliefs, namely, that they were for liberty, "but in a constitutional and legal way . . . and . . . where there *is no law there can be no liberty.*" The Ebenezer signatories, all of whom were members of Triebner's faction, saw no merit in defining liberty otherwise, and certainly not in the fashion Treutlen and Rabenhorst represented, a libertarian preference for "private" opinion over public considerations. The forty signatories comprised eleven old Salzburger and Ulmer heads of families who had settled in the 1730s and 1740s. The patriots, fifteen German speakers who were active republican leaders, six of whom had attended the Provincial Congress at Savannah in July 1774 as delegates, included only three persons from the older group—Johann Flörl, Ernst Zittrauer, and Jacob Waldhauer. Among the republican leadership of fifteen, half wrote wills leaving significant amounts of land to descendants. Among the forty opponents, only eleven wrote wills bequeathing property; the rest died intestate.[12]

Smallholdings, fear of Indian attack, recognition of dependence on London and Halle—such realities still guided one party's understanding of both liberty and property. Theirs remained the guarded, conservative attitude of exiles who had absorbed both Halle's teaching on the need for careful stewardship of property, and the centrality of an inward, spiritual liberty. Treutlen and Rabenhorst had jettisoned such notions. Caught between opposing visions that tore at its churches, mills, and farms, the Salzburger settlement split apart, and vanished. Given the fractious debates within the settlement over worldly goods, many of these pietist Lutherans took refuge in the inward-directed liberty of their faith, hoping to ride out uncertain times. Members of the Eppinger family and other Ebenezer residents became militia members and fought for independence. Only Triebner; Wertsch's daughter, who was Triebner's niece by marriage; and the innkeeper Jacob Bühler suffered confiscation and exclusion from pardon. But German speakers did not profit from Triebner's departure. Elizabeth Mohn was allowed twenty pounds against Triebner's estate; but German speakers did not acquire his lands and cattle near Ebenezer. John Lucas, Charles Adingsell, Lewis Cope, and Richard Wylly did.[13]

II

South Carolina Lutherans, connected to Halle's network late enough to benefit from Mühlenberg's visit, tied to Philadelphia by family relations and, in some cases, by personal prior residence there, avoided such internal agonies. The oft-cited remark made by Charles Drayton upon his return to Charleston—"The Dutch are not with us"—reflected his frustrating trip to the isolated Dutch Fork.[14] But Lexington County, Saxe-Gotha, and Orangeburg German speakers connected to Charleston exhibited less reluctance to endorse the republican cause. No loyalists surfaced at Saint John's in Charleston; Kalteisen, May, Gillon, and other members were ardent patriots. Some of the Saxe-Gotha, Lexington County, and Orangeburg settlers traced from the German southwest to these areas later sought compensation for revolutionary service. Yet Jacob Lohrmann, Conrad Hungerbieler, Nicholas Dorn, and Walter Jacob, among others, only petitioned for services rendered in 1781 or 1782, but not earlier. Some actually served, usually for a period of two or three months; others provided fodder or cattle. Although their petitions were honored, English speakers like Drayton tended to interpret such documents as evidence that "the Dutch" lacked enthusiasm for liberty.[15]

The former Württemberg resident Friedrich Claß explained events differently. Claß's petition, filed by a poor and aged man in 1823, reviewed events. Called to defend Charleston, he had served in the militia until the city fell; unscrupulous neighbors made off with his horses; he was then paroled. Forced again into service by loyalist officers who imprisoned him in the fort on the Congarees he had refused to fight for the British. Claß was obliged to labor as secretary for the loyalists. He inadvertently revealed how important connections to the Charleston network were to the creation of informed German Lutherans. He had been pressed into service as amanuensis because the loyalist officers were illiterate backcountrymen. When the fort fell to the patriot forces, Claß and a group of other German speakers were wrongfully labeled Tories and given the choice of imprisonment or service to the American cause. Claß ended his war duties as a tailor, an ironic return to the occupation so many marginalized southwestern Germans had followed before emigrating. People who knew him before the war testified he was "a good Whig," and he received compensation.[16]

Yet Claß's story also reveals how German speakers in Carolina had synthesized both transferred and North American understandings of liberty and property. Originally Claß was to have been compensated by receipt of a slave. Later a justice of the peace for the Orangeburg district, he informed his daughter in 1806 from Charleston that prices for slaves were high: "a Negro about the Size of Ben & Hannah, 255$ I am afraid I Cannot purchase without Destroying myself." Passed over once, he insisted upon a slave in his petition of 1823.[17] For him, the active defense of property included the freedom of choice to defend slavery, exactly as Halle had feared when it opposed the institution in early Georgia. Engagement with the political culture of Carolina had certainly occurred among German speakers; the idea of property which included stewardship and public trust had never been strong in Carolina; neither had the inward, passive, gospel liberty of Pietism shaped the final definitions of the terms as much as the view that liberty was freedom from interference with the right to choose—including the liberty to defend slavery.

South Carolina's chancery court had to settle a number of pleas from the Hoffmans, the Strohmans and the Giessendanners, sorting out partitions of slaves and other property. That a false definition of liberty would lead to licentiousness, pietists had never doubted. The South Carolina court expressed revulsion at what had happened in the Danztler family. Heinrich Dantzler, given to drink and "a very weak & illiterate man; not an Idiot or natural fool, But of a very inferior understanding and hardly capable of managing any important affairs," died in April 1821. In an agreement reminiscent of the village practice of *Vermögensübergabe*, the giving of property to one's heirs in exchange for an annuity, he had promised his lands to his two nephews in exchange for care. Two months before his death, he married. The court could not forebear noting, "This case exhibits a most disgusting Case of depravity." While her husband was still living, Dantzler's wife, Maria, took a slave lover, giving birth to a mulatto child. Abhorring "the prostitution of this miserable Creature to a black man," the court managed to control its contempt for licentious Germans and Africans to conclude that the wife's behavior could not "take away or diminish her rights derived from the marriage." Yet the deed made to the nephews remained in force, the court refusing to apply equitable relief to Maria's petition for "a moiety of the real & personal estate." The "monstrous sins" of which Halle had warned, and the increasing harshness of private contract law, left married German speaking women perhaps worse off than they had been in the villages, where consistory and village courts could be used to great effect. The court's refusal to interpret broadly the Strohman family's will designating grandchildren as "heirs" had the same effect. Because, according to the letter of the law, only "children" could benefit from the provisions of deeds and a will, the law may have been a dubious ally for married German-American women who were bent on exercising a maximum of liberty and control over property.[18]

A late arrival, Wilhelm Stein of Lübeck settled in Carolina in 1773 after a sojourn in England working for the leather dressers Meares and Shepley. Stein found that he misjudged the political meaning of property and liberty just as the Strohmans found the application of these concepts to family wishes frustrated. For his loyalty to the Crown, Stein lost his Newberry plantation in Dutch Fork, having served in the South Carolina

Royalists as "one of the Men in the Ebenezer Redoubt at Savanna." He paid with "his Property consisting of Cattle Crops Implements of Husbandry and for three years the total loss of his Farm or Plantation." Stein later returned to England for compensation (£220 sterling), perhaps contemplating his mother's advice. Writing in 1757, Frau Stein had advised against going to America, pleading that a future still could be had in Kiel. At the least, she advised, "go to France, Germany, and other such places where you will be able to turn a profit as a propertied man."[19] Stein had expected to enjoy the "famous English Liberty" of which Pastor Boltzius had boasted, "the absence of difficulty, oppression, and violence." Instead of living "comfortable and happy under the British Government," he found "truly Shocking . . . [the] striping [sic] of . . . all . . . Property," whereon he had "raised as fine Vegetables and roots as cou'd be seen in any market in the old Country." Excluded from the exchanges in the German-language churches, Stein and other loyal German-speaking British-Americans found that the prevailing understanding of the vexing terms *liberty* and *property* continued to elude them.[20]

III

In Virginia, German speakers managed to avoid internal divisions, although some were like Adam Crum, a later petitioner for a pension who confessed that while serving with the revolutionary forces he had understood almost no English. His discharge papers he had lost, thinking them "dead, useless papers."[21] Hebron Lutherans had strengthened their ties to Philadelphia, obtaining a pastor and a schoolteacher. Mühlenberg concluded in 1768 that these Virginia Lutherans long ago should have "applied to the government for a *charter* while it was still possible to obtain it." Freed from the county parish tax, members of Hebron congregation would have been able to "retain their dear German mother tongue as long as it may be necessary."[22] By 1775 Pastor Jacob Frank of the Ministerium of Pennsylvania bound Virginia Lutherans solidly to Pennsylvania affairs. His congregation's delight in his voice matched his own homesickness upon hearing them sing familiar German hymns. His leadership lasted from 1775 to 1778, long enough to allow him to use his experience as a teacher to reopen the Hebron school, build a new parsonage, and catechize Hebron's slaves and the far-flung congregations in Augusta and Dunmore counties.[23] Under his leadership, Hebron moved ahead of all other religious groups in Virginia to protect its liberty and property. Its 22 October 1776 petition to the House of Delegates was the first to ask that body to release the Lutherans from paying the assessment for the Protestant Episcopal Church. Its definition of property built upon what had been transferred, too. Stewardship had been weak at Hebron; by the younger generation's own admission, the founding generation had mismanaged European charity gifts and resources. What Hebron petitioned for in 1776 was liberty in a "negative" sense, freedom from an obligation to support a public faith. The settlement's residents chose instead to endorse what would increasingly typify the new republic: a freedom of religious conscience that by 1786 would allow Virginia to define religion as a matter of "private opinion."[24]

A few of the clergy hoped for a more aggressive, publicly engaged German Lutheran identity to help save the virtue of the new republic. The Henkels, from their press at New Market, Virginia, labored long and hard to preserve both the German language and Lutheran adherence to the Augsburg Confession. Too much Americanization had happened already, but they clung to hope. By 1810, Paul Henkel wrote of the Virginia and North Carolina Germans that "superstition and unbelief is still very dominant. . . . besides that, very little religious practices are observed in the homes . . . since the climate is so hot, it is impossible for teachers that come from other countries to go there and remain any length of time." The Reverend Robert J. Miller suggested that Virginia Lutherans "loose [*sic*] their Religion with the German Language." Warning their charges against intermarriage with the Irish or the English, North Carolina pastors asserted: "It is very seldom that German and English blood is happily united in wedlock. Dissensions and feeble children are often the result. The English wife will not permit her husband to be master in his household, and when he likewise insists upon his rights crime and murder ensue. In the third place, the English of this region do not adhere to any definite religion. . . . We owe it to our native country to do our part that German blood and the German language be preserved and more and more disseminated in America, for which the present indications in these regions are very favorable."[25]

In fact, little distinguished German Lutherans in postrevolutionary Virginia from their neighbors. The last known legal opinion Thomas Jefferson drafted had its origin in a complex petition in chancery stemming from an inheritance dispute among the Hebron Lutherans. A contemporary attorney believed that the case employed the talents of the best legal minds of Virginia for more than a generation. *Wayland* v. *Utz* began over a contested 1776 will; it ended in 1822, easily qualifying for comparison with the notorious chancery cause Charles Dickens memorialized in *Bleak House*. Yet the case was not unique. A number of unrecorded chancery causes retained by the clerk of Madison County, reflected similar disputes, in which custom gave way to more systematic and regular treatments of familial property law.[26]

Adam Wayland had written a will in 1775, before the death of his first wife, directing that she receive her dower and that his estate be equally divided among his children. But his wife died, and Wayland remarried. His second wife was Maria Finks, who bore him two children. Wayland died without revoking or altering the will. Did the younger children enjoy a right to the estate? and what of the second wife's rights? Jefferson wrote that the children were entitled, but not the second wife. Like the South Carolina chancery decision, his decision recognized only her dower in one-third of the lands and slaves and one-ninth of the personal estate.[27]

Within a generation, the streamlined resolution of disputes through equity bills erased any distinction between German speakers' and other Virginians' handling of disputed property matters. Madison residents petitioned between 1776 and 1816 for a variety of causes, including the readjustment of tax rates, changing the day of court, lowering the amount of money to be paid to obtain a substitute for military service, and incorporating the town of Madison. The Lutherans were interested in almost none of these, save the 1785 petition to have the day of court sitting changed — about 40 of the 282 signatures were German.[28]

Instead, German speakers, like their English-speaking neighbors, contented themselves with mundane, local privileges. In October 1778, ninety persons petitioned the House of Delegates to compel millowners on the Rapidan and Robinson runs to open the dams between 1 April and the end of May to allow the passage of fish. As early as 1759, an ineffectual law had been attempted which millowners resisted, pointing out that tearing down their milldams injured their livelihood. But the petitioners of 1778 argued that they had "formerly Catched Large quantities of Fish in the Rivers . . . to the Great Relief & Satisfaction of Themselves & Families." Of the ninety signatories, eighteen were Germans. The entrepreneurial millowners' interference with fishing may have struck the petitioners as redolent of aristocratic hunting privileges from their past; perhaps they resented the wealthier few who demanded protection for their mills. Personal property tax lists for the period reveal that despite their long residence in the county, these signatories were still not assessed for "wheels" or other signs of gentry status; most were farmers of modest means. As late as 1816 when the justices signed the petition to alter the court day to the Thursday after the second Monday of the month, German names were still missing. The Madison County Court — on which no Germans sat as justices — held its first session at the home of John Yaeger, Jr., in May 1773. Henry Wayland had become surveyor of the county by 1798, but German public profile remained modest in the new county. Their property disputes settled in chancery, Virginia's oldest German speaking citizens retained a low local profile. Their sense of responsibility for, and participation in, a public arena remained correspondingly modest. They became almost archetypal Jeffersonians, supporters of minimal government, content to practice the private virtues of domesticity, frugality, and hard work.[29]

IV

For Germans in the Reich who had toiled in secular networks, the American Revolution signaled the end of these connections. Not only did correspondence and funds from Halle disappear in the course of the war; Jacob Geiger of Ittlingen also moved to cut his losses in the face of potential disaster for the rebels. On 9 April 1778, at Karlsruhe, Augustus Ruppele sold his interest and share in the lands "of Godfrey Theil of Germantown" that Ruppele had "purchased . . . in Company with Jacob Geiger Junior of Ittlingen" and Johann Adam Seitz, the master miller of that town, having acquired power to dispose of them as he saw fit.[30] As late as 1808 Valentin Geiger returned from South Carolina to his old village to attempt a property recovery via Hamburg through C. L. Leopoldt and Company for his Charleston neighbor Bernhardt Preusch, originally from Eppingen, a few kilometers to the south of Ittlingen. But recovery efforts dwindled. Ernst Ludwig Baisch made a few recoveries in the 1790s, but his activities declined and never again reached the record levels of the prewar years.[31]

Networks binding Virginia German speakers to Britain and the Reich had barely existed; and now those that had existed, collapsed. When George Christoph Voigt died in Amelia County's Raleigh parish, he ordered his executors to empower the firm of Balfour and Barraud in Norfolk to convey his property to a niece in Ruppin. The Norfolk merchants used contacts in Hamburg, Ruppin, and the London branch of the Splittgerber firm of Berlin to fulfil his wishes. Benjamin Ward, one of the executors, asked Friedrich Kühn in Neu-Ruppin to come to Virginia to obtain the bequest in 1772. Explaining to the Norfolk merchants in August 1773 that a shortage of currency prevented his paying the bonds required to fulfil his duties, Ward confidently predicted that when the House of Burgesses met in April 1774, he would be able to complete the business. News of the Boston Port Bill brought the burgesses into conflict with Governor Dunmore, and in the ensuing uproar, the Fee Bill that guaranteed operation of the courts failed to be renewed. The courts closed, and Ward never got his money. In 1793, the Prussian consul general Carl Gottfried Paleske, a former Königsberg merchant, intervened on the niece's behalf at Philadelphia, but as late as 1816, this was to no avail.[32]

Seen from the perspective of Halle or the secular traders, the Revolution may have been a colonial rebellion that severed imperial ties. But it proved to be far more than that. It proved so disruptive that many of the components that had contributed to the eventual definitions of liberty and property so painfully arrived at by German speakers before 1776 vanished from memory. For later German-American Lutherans, this fact caused separation from, not connection with, the German-speaking colonial world.[33] Few, save clergy such as Pastor Helmuth in Philadelphia, attempted to maintain Halle's definition of property as a trust held for the sake of a larger, public good. And Helmuth's frustrated preaching both on that theme and on his abhorrence of Jeffersonian libertarianism indicated how quickly a sense of the public realm and a disinterested obligation toward it—virtue, as English-speaking republicans called it— vanished. Embittered at Jeffersonian Enlightenment thinking that lured his congregation away from support of a Federalist public good to support the Fries rebellion in 1799, Helmuth attacked libertarian definitions of liberty and property. To a European correspondent in 1800 he wrote, "the present so-called Enlightenment has in my experience destroyed much happiness and blessedness and in their place installed a careless abandon with its sorry results—the common man has, at least, won nothing therefrom."[34] But Helmuth could not stem the tide of sympathy for Fries, which German-American women dramatically underscored by pouring scalding water on tax collectors, those enemies of the domestic hearth who presumed to count the house windows. The desire for freedom from assaults on the household merged with a conscious, confident self-concept that defined American liberty as freedom from Federalist taxes and tyranny.

German-speaking Lutherans did not possess a very strong sense of confessional or cultural identity when they arrived from disparate parts of the Reich. Nor did they construct a typology of persecution or an Old Testament identity of the faithful remnant for themselves, except briefly, among the earliest Salzburgers. Mühlenberg might invoke the identity of pietist heroes such as Arndt, Spener, and Francke privately— but not for the members of his congregations. By the 1770s, German-American Lutherans connected themselves to the political history and definitions of property and liberty they selectively heard and read from the British past, as well as to Swiss and, less often, Dutch, or southwest

German episodes. Never particularly interested in "ethnic" identity, in "Germanness," or even in "Lutheranism," the emigrants from the south-western territories of the Reich seemed unconcerned as after 1776 the rising generation abandoned the German language—even pressing for church services in English—and left German to women. The wives and mothers maintained this domestic voice somewhat longer, but it, too, grew more silent except in isolated rural settlements. Postwar German-language newspapers became more provincial and scattered in Maryland, in rural Pennsylvania, and in Virginia, reflecting the diminished role of Philadelphia, now no longer the center of networks that bound German-speaking Lutherans together. Pastor Helmuth could not even tell Halle the name of the pastor at Ebenezer when queried; by the early 1800s pastors on the Savannah could not write to Halle in German; as synodal organizations in various states were founded, North American Lutheranism became highly provincial and fragmented. Not even the tercentenary of the Reformation in 1817 received any significant attention as a unifying event among these German-Americans. Helmuth failed in his elaborate attempts to erect educational institutions instilling Halle's tradition of public obligation among the defenders of liberty and property. From time to time, a pastor or schoolmaster would argue for the idea that a responsible liberty had to be schooled and guided in reasoned religious sentiment and good will. Most German-American Lutherans, like their English-speaking neighbors, were not convinced.[35]

The upheaval of 1776–83 created new variations on the synthesized definitions of liberty and property. To some degree, Halle's original vision—encouraging the stewardship of "worldly goods" to support pedagogy that would train self-sufficient believers whose industry would transform society—did survive in novel form. In England and in Calvinist circles, writers concurred that the worthiness of the recipient should be examined when charity was dispensed. Work furthered betterment, hence the "hopes for better times"—one of Halle's favorite slogans. The support of orphanages and printing, milling, and farming enterprises both at Halle and on the Savannah had reflected this understanding of the stewardship of property. But Halle, like its English contemporaries, retained the conviction that philanthropy was tied to public agendas and interests. Among German speakers in North America, this idea could hardly flourish in a Pennsylvania founded to avoid state involvement in matters of religious and social policy, and to prevent non-Quakers from bringing about such intrusion. Revolution guaranteed the collapse of Halle's experiment on the Savannah. Instead, philanthropy became limited to the care of one's own, defined by voluntary membership in a particular denomination. German-American Lutherans did not create the North

American preference for "private" charity and benevolence. But with the attenuation of ties to Halle, discussion of the public implications of philanthropy declined. Voluntarism succeeded, as Alexis de Tocqueville noted. The French observer erroneously believed that philanthropy would fall under state control even in a democracy, since "in a democracy only the state inspires confidence in private persons, for it alone seems to them to have some force and permanence." Germans in Europe agreed; German-Americans did not.[36]

The Alemannic and broadly "Swiss" definition of liberty which envisioned political activity to defend essentially medieval privileges of peasants and *Bürger* against the state also survived in North America; again, in new guise.[37] That definition had much to offer in its insistence on broad participation in discussions about property and its use, and in its sharpening of awareness of the need for vigilance against wealth and power exercised by government. Less attractive aspects survived too— a petty litigiousness and legalism, an inability to see far beyond local and short-term horizons, a quick retreat from engagement with public affairs except in time of military threat, with a growing conviction of the superiority of the *commercium* to issues of the *res publica*. The entrepreneurs and traders who had constructed the networks of communication and regional markets, especially the intrepid Swiss-Kraichgauers, survived transatlantic migration to ensure their definition's triumph.[38]

German Americans believed with other new republicans that property provided an absolute bulwark against government intrusion. Both the domestic hearth and the German-speaking church rested secure from state interference.[39] This conviction had not come for German speakers from translations of John Locke. They would readily have agreed with him that language is "the great bond and common tye of society."[40] Increasingly, therefore, the ambitious leadership also moved to abandon the German language after the Revolution, even within the churches. Rhetorical forms can both bind and liberate. The ambitious German-American lay leaders had instinctively reached for a borrowed or "stolen" rhetoric to explain how they fit into the English-speaking world, whose language of hearth and faith only partly represented their own, and whose emotional content different terms conveyed differently.[41] By the 1760s, as Blackstone summarized a new wisdom defining the rights of property in terms of prior possession, the German speakers of North America, never clear what the term *possession* meant, and consistently leaving it untranslated, put their faith instead in the notion of use and privilege— exactly as they had in their ancestral villages—and claimed that no one had ever thought otherwise.[42] German speakers had managed to synthesize parts of their own inherited definitions of liberty and property in shared conversations within the sociability offered by German-language congregations. Out of those exchanges came a construction and reinterpretation of self, a typology that bound English history to them, and an identity that English speakers' revolutionary rhetoric, once translated, brought into focus. That construction made a distinction between private and public interests possible, bestowing upon the private a status only the public sphere enjoyed in Europe.[43]

German speakers gave little thought to the fact that the borrowed or "stolen" rhetoric by which they redefined ideas of property and liberty dispossessed them of part of their past. Inhabitants of a "minimalist" culture shaped by generations of warfare, opposed to expansive states, exposed to vagaries of weather and markets, and forced always to balance resources and needs, German speakers opted for liberation from a heritage of perilous dependency.[44] The German-language press had created the vocabulary, and provided a medium of exchange for this process. The congregations functioned as ersatz village forums.[45] The German speakers' language was neither irrational nor simply representational. The rhetoric that aided German-Americans to liberate themselves from Halle, Augsburg, or London also imposed cloture on ongoing redefinitions of property and liberty. What remained of the pietist legacy tended to devalue reasoned reflection about hard choices, preferring instead a subjective, emotional language of private sentiment, safe from governmental or clerical dictates. And because by 1776 the final arbiters of the new synthetic vocabulary were exclusively male, the German-speaking wives, whose concerns had lain behind so many of the lively exchanges defining liberty and property before, found their voices stilled even more as sons came of age uninterested in the language of the hearth.[46]

Mühlenberg glimpsed this development, although he could make little sense of it. In 1774 he rejoiced in the publication of Johann Joachim Spalding's essays on religious feelings. But among Americans, Mühlenberg concluded, the requirement to distinguish nature from grace was ignored. Particularly among free-church sectarians, but also among some Lutherans, feelings justified religious belief; Americans tended to "set forth their wild feelings and concrete sensations as extraordinary and immediate operations and tokens of conversion."[47] Objective truths drawn from scripture, the sacraments as objective means of grace, Americans dismissed in favor of private opinion.

Such tendencies found their full expression in postrevolutionary America, giving birth to a bewildering diversity and subjectivity in religious experiment. Unwittingly, German Lutherans contributed to both the riot of private opinion in matters religious, and the gradual decay of politics, to the dismay of those republicans who treasured the public realm.[48] Lutheran Pietism in North America quickly retreated from engagement with the public sphere, where informed and cultivated leaders shaped and guided opinion. Helmuth pursued the ideal of such engagement in Philadelphia, finding that he and other Halle-trained pastors shared the same intellectual world as their contemporary Scottish Common Sense brethren.[49] Among German-American Lutherans, Pietism never quite became the exclusive preserve of women and the clergy. But the cultural brokers among the laity found in the new, revolutionary definition of liberty and property justification enough for keeping gospel liberty within the confines of home and church. Gospel liberty had little part in their broader connections to an increasingly diverse social and religious order, and certainly did not play a critical, judgmental role. Encomiums from republicans such as Benjamin Rush cemented these patterns in place.[50]

German-American Lutherans' satisfaction with definitions of liberty and property selectively detached from European roots received added support from the Continent itself. Events there continued to sweep away the villages and relationships German-Americans had once known. The French Revolution and its Napoleonic aftermath, too, disrupted and finally destroyed the last commercial and religious networks, ended the old Reich itself, closed the Francke Foundations at Halle, and gave birth at Vienna to a political order in which Pietism would be as irrelevant as republicanism.

The swift finality of these events on both sides of the Atlantic goes some distance in explaining why the "German idea of freedom" that developed in the later nineteenth-century European context did so in isolation from what had happened among German speakers who had emigrated from the old Reich. The gulf that opened between German speakers in the new republic and their former homeland had its parallel in the gulf separating prerevolutionary from postrevolutionary German-speaking America. Together, these breaches have made exceedingly difficult the task of deconstructing the resultant mythology that there had been rapid and simple "acculturation" and "adaptation" of a diverse people who carried conflicting definitions of liberty and property with them.[51] The myth has fitted neatly into the general claims for American uniqueness, opportunity, and progress—a story that German speakers, as uncertain citizens in an anxiety-ridden new nation, clasped to their bosoms and made their own. What has often been said of the Saxons, the German Auswanderer in general prided themselves on: they have always been highly adaptable.[52]

From the postrevolutionary perspective, the picture of total adaptation looks unconvincing, but nineteenth-century German speakers also seem to have had little sense of connection to the prerevolutionary experience. Scholars studying Butler County, Ohio, in the early nineteenth century identified the persistence of stereotypic behavior surrounding land and family. There, German-speaking parents did hang on to the "home place" and made aggressive bequests of land while still living, following partible inheritance customs that guaranteed land for sons and made roughly equivalent settlements for all children. Legal historians long ago identified odd customs such as the "Dutch Contract." These informal verbal contractual agreements about land and inheritance arrangements point to a marked tendency for keeping the "home place," and put a high priority on settling children in proximity to parents. They resemble what in Germany in the eighteenth century was known as the bäuerliches Testament or the testamentum rusticum. Nineteenth-century residents of New Ulm, Minnesota, while changing and being changed in some ways, persisted in some behaviors and values remarkably similar to those of their predecessors in British North America, although the colonial experience was wholly unknown to those midwestern transplants.[53] Well into the nineteenth century, German-language congregations argued bitterly and split repeatedly over the language issue and subscription to European confessional standards. Yet later arrivals knew almost nothing of the process we have reconstructed here.[54]

Perhaps for German speakers on both sides of the Atlantic, their difficult relationship with political history has meant that a cultural nation alone—defined almost exclusively by language, music, and literature—existed to define what was most dearly valued. German speakers in Europe had for centuries valued domestic peace, reflection, inward liberty, and a certain skeptical detachment from the state. The state is thus regarded on one side of the Atlantic as essential for the order that is the precondition of liberty; on the other as an entity best kept weak. Yet forms of private sociability—clubs and reading societies, or conventicles and congregations on both sides of the Atlantic—made possible engagement with political culture, an engagement dictated by deeply held emotional attachments defined increasingly by the late eighteenth century as "private."

German-speaking Lutherans of North America were not conscious of how their redefinitions prefigured and contributed to the "transformation" of American law and society. The creation of the "private sphere," the preference for private philanthropy, the later paeans to a "cult of domesticity" that some historians believe arose after 1790—these were all familiar to the German-American Lutherans by 1776, though expressed in terms of Freiheit and Eigentum. Whatever else the Revolution was about, it operated to integrate smaller, local aspects of life into a larger whole. So successful, so complete did that integration become that the German speakers, diverse in origin and scattered in settlements throughout North America, were swallowed by the event. Their "mother tongue" had absorbed enough of the broader, male-dominated, English political vocabulary to allow them definition of self and let them absorb the political terms of the eighteenth-century British world. When that world was swept away in North American by the transforming event they participated in, much of what had gone into the definition vanished from their memory, and their descendants became nearly indistinguishable from the many other private groups of the nineteenth-century American version of democracy.[55]

Serious consequences flowed from this lapse of cultural memory. In writing their own history, most German-American Lutherans have since the 1790s seized erroneously on the supposed error of clinging to the German language as the explanation for the decline and lack of transforming energy in their tradition. Few have recognized that men such as Lancaster's Pastor Helmuth and his New York contemporary Johann Christoph Kunze sensed the weakness of attachments to Lutheran confessional symbols, and fell back upon the German language as a defense against liberal Deism and Calvinist-tinged evangelicalism.[56]

Both Helmuth and Kunze knew that no help could be expected from the German states, now served by a clergy thoroughly imbued with liberal, anticonfessional principles. But neither the teaching office of a pastor, Kunze wrote dispiritedly to his brother, nor the critical norms German-Americans might have employed to discern what was right or wrong in the broader political and social realm would arise in America. "There is not much fruit here from the preaching office . . . what hinders it is that the people here are completely English." By this, Kunze did not mean that things German were superior; on the contrary, in 1804 he wrote to the Pennsylvania synod that denial of the divinity of Christ was precisely what "men are at present doing boldly in Germany through pulpit, life, and pen — and who eat the bread of the Church. God preserve us, my dear brethren, in this sad time, from apostles coming from there!"[57]

Instead, a few discerning clerics perceived the subtle manner in which the new vocabulary fashioned in German had incorporated English political and legal concepts that required ongoing examination within the context of Lutheran theology. They knew that their people possessed no very strong cultural identity save their language. The pastors did not express well what bothered them and were dismissed as ethnic cranks for their insistence that this debate ought to be carried out in German, the theological language that provided a framework for a confessional identity. A serious consequence of their being disregarded manifested itself in the hesitancy among German-American Lutherans to ask what, if anything, it meant to be an Evangelical Lutheran in North America now that the terms *liberty* and *property* seemed to be safely defined. The most searing critique of this complacency, this willingness to be dictated to by conventional wisdom, has been issued against German Christians in Europe. A type of person emerged there whose *Spießer-ideologie,* or middling, petit-bourgeois culture, dominated religious life, preventing the emergence in the state church of a critical vocabulary by which believers could continue to examine self and society. Instead, "caught in the midst of rapid change . . . lacking the leisure, education and often the perception to make the cultural heritage of mankind part of his own life, he substituted nationalist catch-phrases made readily available by the advocates of 'national culture,' the modern apostles of mediocrity."[58]

German speakers' eagerness to adapt to prevailing British-American concepts of liberty and property which they made resemble their own transferred ideas seems innocent and understandable. But when German-American Lutherans got around to contemplating what, if anything, now defined them in the United States of America, much had been forgotten, or rejected. Those among them who insisted upon confessional standards or the German language hoped to perpetuate the engagement with crucial issues they knew had flourished within the congregations before the Revolution. Yet as Alexis de Toqueville later recognized and as these critics did not, public opinion in the new political order would not look kindly on criticism of itself. Perhaps especially when such criticism emanated from a non-English-speaking group, "the slightest sting of truth turns [public opinion] fierce; and one must praise everything, from the turn of its phrases to its most robust virtues. No writer . . . can escape from this obligation to sprinkle incense over his fellow citizens. Hence the majority lives in a state of perpetual self-adoration; only strangers or experience may be able to bring certain truths to the Americans' attention."[59]

Pietism in the old Reich ended by encouraging passivity and a sentimental obedience to state authority. Yet German-American Lutherans' concepts of liberty and property became in the end no less problematic. The very success of their adapting these key political concepts to their own emotional and political needs and values discouraged continued reflection and criticism about self and society. Their own insecure identities had been successfully submerged in that of a broader people, which after 1776 seemed none too sure of its own identity. Once the gulf opened separating colonial from national culture, German-speaking Lutherans rested content in their wider, recently acquired identity as Americans.[60]

For generations to come, continued waves of migration piled even more complicated layers of adjustment upon German-American Lutherans only partly aware of what they had wrought, of what they had chosen. More than two centuries later, we—and perhaps their descendants—are just beginning to understand both that process and them.

APPENDIX

Measures and Currency Conversion

TABLE 1
Units of Measure, and Coinage

Land
  1 Morgen = 0.78 acre = 0.32 hectare
  1 Jauchert = 1.5 Morgen = 0.47 hectare
  1 Viertel = 0.25 Morgen

Coinage
  1 Gulden = 60 Kreutzer (German southwest)
  1 Reichstaler = 1.5 Gulden
  1 Taler = 1.5 Reichstaler
  1 Pfund vlamische = 2.5 Reichstaler
  1 Pfund = 20 Schilling vlamische
  1 £ sterling = 35 Schilling 6.66 Grote = 4.44 Reichstaler

TABLE 2

Equivalents of £100 Sterling in the Currency of Five Colonies and in Five Currencies of the Reich, 1765–75

Currency	Equivalent of £100 Sterling (current)
New York £	176
Pennsylvania £	163
Virginia £	128
South Carolina £	706
Georgia £	109
Hamburg Reichstaler (banco)	437
Hamburg Reichstaler (current)	536
Hamburg Taler (current)	805
Frankfurt Reichstaler (account)	647
Frankfurt Gulden (account)	971

SOURCE: Figures taken from John J. McCusker, *Money and Exchange in Europe and America, 1600–1775: A Handbook* (Chapel Hill, 1978), 61–79, 156–229; and supplemented or revised by McCusker's ongoing research communicated to the author. The par of exchange between Hamburg and Frankfurt, 1765–75, 148 Frankfurt Reichstaler (account) was the equivalent of 100 Hamburg Reichstaler (banco). The value of the inherited property that German speakers in the British colonies recovered in their native land generally ranged between 100 and 300 Gulden, or £10 and £30 sterling.

TABLE 3
**The Equivalent of £100 of the Currency of Five Colonies in Sterling
and in Hamburg and Frankfurt Currency, 1765–1775**

| | *Colonies* | | | | |
Currency	New York	Pennsylvania	Virginia	S.C.	Ga.
£ Sterling	57	61	78	14	92
Hamburg Reichstaler (banco)	248	267	342	61	403
Hamburg Reichstaler (current)	304	328	420	76	495
Hamburg taler (current)	457	492	630	114	742
Frankfurt Reichstaler (account)	367	396	506	92	596
Frankfurt Gulden (account)	551	593	759	138	895

SOURCE: Figures taken from John J. McCusker, *Money and Exchange in Europe and America, 1600–1775: A Handbook* (Chapel Hill, 1978), 61–79, 156–229; and supplemented or revised by McCusker's ongoing research communicated to the author. The par of exchange between Hamburg and Frankfurt, 1765–75, 148 Frankfurt Reichstaler (account) was the equivalent of 100 Hamburg Reichstaler (banco). The value of the inherited property that German speakers in the British colonies recovered in their native land generally ranged between 100 and 300 Gulden, or between £10 and £30 sterling. For discussion of the terms *banco, current,* and *account,* refer to McCusker's book.

NOTES

Abbreviations

Abbreviations for the most frequently cited archives and journals in the notes, and abbreviations for terms that appear in German archive citations, are as follows:

Archives

AFSt   Archiv der Franckeschen Stiftungen, Universität Halle–Wittenberg, Halle/Saale
GDAH   Georgia Department of Archives and History, Atlanta
GLAK   Generallandesarchiv Karlsruhe
HHStAW   Hessisches Hauptstaatsarchiv Wiesbaden
HSP   Historical Society of Pennsylvania, Philadelphia
HStASt   Hauptstaatsarchiv Stuttgart
LAS   Landesarchiv Speyer
LC   Library of Congress, Manuscripts Division, Washington, D.C.
LCP   Library Company of Philadelphia
LTSA   Lutheran Theological Seminary Archives, Philadelphia
NStA   Nürtingen Stadtarchiv
PrGStA   Preußisches Geheimes Staatsarchiv, Berlin-Dahlem
SArS   Stadtarchiv Sinsheim
SCDAH   South Carolina Department of Archives and History, Columbia
StAl   Staatsarchiv Ludwigsburg
VSLAD   Virginia State Library, Archives Division, Richmond

Journals

BWK   *Blätter für württembergische Kirchengeschichte*
PMHB   *Pennsylvania Magazine of History and Biography*
PN   *Pietismus und Neuzeit*

SCHM *South Carolina Historical Magazine*
VMHB *Virginia Magazine of History and Biography*
WMQ *The William and Mary Quarterly*
ZGO *Zeitschrift für die Geschichte des Oberrheins*
ZWL *Zeitschrift für württembergische Landesgeschichte*

German Archival Terms

Abt. Abteilung
Best. Bestand
Bü. Büschel
Kirchenkonvent Kirchenkonventcensurprotokoll
Rep. Repertorium
R.u.I. Realteilungen und Inventuren
T.u.I. Teilungen und Inventuren

Preface and Acknowledgments

1. Willi Paul Adams, "The Colonial German-Language Press and the American Revolution," in Bernard Bailyn and John B. Hench, eds., *The Press and the American Revolution* (Worcester, Mass., 1980), 151–228, quotation at 182.

2. For a bibliography of and introduction to the "Pennsylvania Dutch," see Don Yoder's essay "Pennsylvania Germans," in Stephan Thernstrom et al., eds. *The Harvard Encyclopedia of American Ethnic Groups* (Cambridge, Mass., 1980), 770–72. Also see Kathleen Neils Conzen, "Germans," in ibid., 405–25; and idem, "The Writing of German-American History," *Immigration History Newsletter* 12 (1980), 1–14; A. G. Roeber, "In German Ways? Problems and Potentials of Eighteenth-Century German Social and Emigration History," *WMQ*, 3d ser., 44 (1987), 750–774; idem, "German Speakers," in Peter Williams and Mary Kupiec Cayton, eds., *Encyclopedia of American Social History* (New York, forthcoming).

3. Stephanie Grauman Wolf, *Urban Village: Population, Community, and Family Structure in Germantown, Pennsylvania, 1683–1800* (Princeton, 1976); James T. Lemon, *The Best Poor Man's Country: A Geographical Study of Early Southeastern Pennsylvania* (Baltimore, 1972). Lemon's first attack on the claims of German-American uniqueness appeared in idem, "The Agricultural Practices of National Groups in Eighteenth-Century Southeastern Pennsylvania," *Geographical Review* 56 (1966), 467–96.

4. David Hackett Fischer, *Albion's Seed: Four British Folkways in America* (New York, 1989), 816–17; see also 512–13 and throughout to 613. Fischer concedes significant cultural differences elsewhere among German speakers, whom he carelessly lumps together under the never-defined apellation "German pietists." For responses, see 'Forum," *WMQ*, 3d ser., 48 (1991), 223–308.

Chapter 1   New York: Theme and Variations

1. Giles Jacob, *A New Law-Dictionary* (London, 1729), 132; Richard Price, *Observations of the Nature of Civil Liberty . . .* (London, 1776). For commentary, see Bernard Bailyn, "1776 in Britain and America: A Year of Challenge—A World Transformed," in idem, *Faces of Revolution: Personalities and Themes in the Struggle for American Independence* (New York, 1990); 155–56; for the quotation on property, see idem, "The Central Themes of the American Revolution," in ibid., 206.

Throughout the notes that follow, when an archive's name indicates that the archive belongs to a particular German city, town, or village (e.g., Oberboihingen Parish Archive), the archive is located in that city, town, or village unless otherwise indicated. In addition, all translations are mine unless otherwise indicated. I have given the full names of German-speaking men and have not dripped the initial "Johannes" or "Hans" as they themselves often did, except in the cases of Johann Henirich Keppele, Hans Jacob Sailer, and Hans Jacob Beyerle. These three men are mentioned once in full, and are thereafter referred to by the commonly used second name. I have also silently standardized spellings of German proper names to match modern usage so as to avoid retaining myriad variants that would confuse readers and make use of the index next to impossible. A table of units of measure and currency conversions is given in the Appendix.

2. Alexander Graydon, *Memoirs of a Life, Chiefly Passed in Pennsylvania within the Last Sixty Years . . .* (Harrisburg, Pa., 1811), 121–22.

3. Leonard Krieger, *The German Idea of Freedom: The History of a Political Tradition from the Reformation to 1871* (Chicago, 1960); see 3–10 on the late development of the word *Libertät*. See also the essays in Alan Ryan, ed., *The Idea of Freedom: Essays in Honour of Isaiah Berlin* (Oxford, 1979); David Calleo, *The German Problem Reconsidered: Germany and the World Order, 1870 to the Present* (Cambridge, 1978), 146–59. Even Michael Kammen, *Spheres of Liberty: Changing Perceptions of Liberty in American Culture* (Madison, Wis., 1986), a masterful survey of American uses of the term *liberty,* does not illuminate German speakers' thinking about the concept. The richness and complexity of the term in German thought and experience have not yet been appropriated in the English-language literature. See Diethelm Klippel, "The True Concept of Liberty: Political Theory in Germany in the Second Half of the Eighteenth Century," in Eckhart Hellmuth, ed., *The Transformation of Political Culture: England and Germany in the Late Eighteenth Century* (London, 1990), 447–66; Diethelm Klippel and Rudolph Vierhaus, "The Revolutionizing of Consciousness: A German Utopia?" in ibid., 561–77. On the struggle against the pretensions of centralizing powers in sixteenth-century states, see Gerald Strauss, *Law, Resistance, and the State: The Opposition to Roman Law in Reformation Germany* (Princeton, 1986), 240–96.

4. Thomas A. Brady, Jr., *Turning Swiss: Cities and Empire, 1450–1550* (New York, 1985). Brady suggests that neither city *Bürger* nor princes wished to see Swiss communalism extended into the Reich. For a critical assessment

of the thesis, see Steven E. Ozment's review in *Journal of Interdisciplinary History* 18 (1987), 367–69.

5. The notion of "key words" is borrowed from Raymond Williams, *Keywords: A Vocabulary of Culture and Society* (New York, 1976). General surveys of the problem of language and discourse are Francis P. Dineen, *An Introduction to General Linguistics* (New York, 1967); Emile Benveniste, *Problems in General Linguistics,* trans. Mary Elizabeth Meek (Coral Gables, Fl., 1971). On the concepts of "discourse" and "sub-languages," see J. G. A. Pocock, "The State of the Art," in idem, ed., *Virtue, Commerce, and History: Essays on Political Thought and History, Chiefly in the Eighteenth Century* (Cambridge, 1985), 29–31. For a broader survey of the issue of language and historical writing, see John E. Toews, "Intellectual History after the Linguistic Turn: The Autonomy of Meaning and the Irreducibility of Experience," *American Historical Review* 92 (1987), 891–93. On the problem of lexical transference and interference, see Uriel Weinreich, *Languages in Contact* (The Hague: 1979), 47–51.

6. Hans Medick and David Warren Sabean, "Interest and Emotion in Family and Kinship Studies: A Critique of Social History and Anthropology," in Hans Medick and David Warren Sabean, eds., *Interest and Emotion: Essays on the Study of Family and Kinship* (Cambridge, 1984), 9–27. The term *property* is especially vexing since Germans tended to use the term *Vermögen* to describe total wealth or value but *Eigentum* to describe property held with absolute authority (e.g., *Eigentumsvorbehalt, Eigentumsrecht*). See A. G. Roeber, "The Origins of German-American Concepts of Property and Inheritance in Village Transactions," *Perspectives in American History,* n.s., 3 (1987), 115–71; John Phillip Reid, *The Concept of Liberty in the Age of the American Revolution* (Chicago, 1988), 5–23.

7. I do not suggest that the tradition is irrelevant for Anglo-American politics in general. See A. G. Roeber, *Faithful Magistrates and Republican Lawyers: Creators of Virginia Legal Culture, 1680–1810* (Chapel Hill, 1981).

8. Richard T. Ely, *Property and Contract in Their Relations to the Distribution of Wealth,* 2 vols. (1914; reprint, Port Washington, N.Y., 1971), 1:429, 126–28, quotation at 126.

9. For an introduction to the topic of Pietism, see F. Ernst Stoeffler, *German Pietism during the Eighteenth Century* (Leiden, 1973); idem, ed., *Continental Pietism and Early American Christianity* (Grand Rapids, Mich., 1976); A. G. Roeber, "Germans, Property, and the First Great Awakening: Rehearsal for a Revolution?" in Winfried Herget and Karl Ortseifen, eds., *The Transit of Civilization from Europe to America: Essays in Honor of Hans Galinsky* (Tübingen, 1986), 169–92; Günter Birtsch, "The Christian as Subject: The Worldly Mind of Prussian Protestant Theologians in the Late Enlightenment Period," in Hellmuth, ed., *Transformation of Political Culture,* 309–26.

10. *The Oxford Universal Dictionary on Historical Principles* (Oxford, 1955), 1586–87. On the later evolution of this idea in German, British, and American contexts, see Herbert J. Spiro, "Privacy in Comparative Perspective," *Nomos:*

Yearbook of the American Society for Political and Legal Philosophy 13 (1970), 121–48.

11. Erich Angermann, "Das 'Auseinandertreten von Staat und Gesellschaft' im Denken des 18. Jahrhunderts," *Zeitschrift für Politik,* n.s., 10 (1963), 89–101.

12. Bernard Bailyn, *The Origin of American Politics* (New York, 1968), 76–78; Gordon S. Wood, *The Creation of the American Republic, 1776–1787* (Chapel Hill, 1969), 191, 214–22, 265–69, 404–11, 503–4. The lack of extended treatment of the distinction between public and private may account for later attacks on the notion of "republicanism" or "whig thought" by critics who could not see a believable scenario in which private cupidity and concern for the general welfare were never mutually exclusive. On the supposedly later rise of "private" categories, see Richard Sennett, *The Fall of Public Man* (New York, 1977).

13. My assumption is just the opposite of David H. Flaherty's in *Privacy in Colonial New England* (Charlottesville, 1972).

14. Manfred Herrmann, *Der Schutz der Persönlichkeit in der Rechtslehre des 16–18. Jahrhunderts,* vol. 2, *Beiträge zur neueren Privatrechtsgeschichte* (Stuttgart, 1968); Franz Wieacker, *Privatrechtsgeschichte der Neuzeit* (Göttingen, 1952), 201; Hermann Conrad, *Individuum und Gemeinschaft in der Privatrechtsordnung des 18. und beginnenden 19. Jahrhunderts* (Karlsruhe, 1956).

15. Jürgen Habermas, *Strukturwandel der Öffentlichkeit* (Neuwied, 1962); Barrington Moore, Jr., *Privacy: Studies in Social and Cultural History* (Armonk, N.Y., 1984); Phillipe Ariès and George Duby, eds., *A History of Private Life,* 4 vols. (Cambridge, Mass., 1987–90) originally published as *Histoire de la vie privée*; Norbert Elias, *The Civilizing Process: The History of Manners,* trans. E. Jephcott (New York, 1918).

16. For a useful overview, see Margaret C. Jacob, "The Enlightenment Redefined: The Formation of Modern Civil Society," *Social Research* 58 (1991), 475–95. The term *private sociability* seems almost oxymoronic but demonstrates exactly the middle ground between the purely personal and the broader, "public" realm being fashioned in the eighteenth century.

17. Jon Elster, *The Cement of Society: A Study of Social Order* (Cambridge, 1991). For an Anglo-American example of authoritative cultural values, see Aviam Soifer, "Assaying Communities: Notes from *The Tempest,*" *Connecticut Law Review* 21 (1989), 871–97. I wish to thank David Konig for the latter reference.

18. On the terms *cultural crystallization* and *brokers,* see George M. Foster, *Culture and Conquest: America's Spanish Heritage* (New York, 1960), 28–31; T. H. Breen, "Creative Adaptations: People and Cultures," in Jack P. Greene and J. R. Pole, eds., *Colonial British America: Essays in the New History of the Early Modern Era* (Baltimore, 1984), 221–23.

19. Ralph C. Wood and Fritz Braun, comps., *PennsilfaanischDeitsch: Erzählungen und Gedichte der Pennsilvaniadeutschen* (Kaiserslautern, 1966), 18–20; Lester W. J. Seifert, "The Word Geography of Pennsylvania German:

Extent and Causes," in Glenn G. Gilbert, ed., *The German Language in America: A Symposium* (Austin, Tex., 1971), 14–42.

20. Edmund S. Morgan, *Inventing the People: The Rise of Popular Sovereignty in England and America* (New York, 1988).

21. See Jack P. Greene and J. R. Pole, "Reconstructing British-American Colonial History: An Introduction," in Greene and Pole, eds., *Colonial British America,* 1–17. For some comparisons of German-speaking centers and networks to Dutch-speaking ones, see A. G. Roeber, " 'The Origin of Whatever Is Not English among Us': The Dutch-speaking and the German-speaking Peoples of Colonial British America," in Bernard Bailyn and Philip D. Morgan, eds., *Strangers within the Realm: Cultural Margins of the First British Empire* (Chapel Hill, 1991), 220–83. On the notion of "convergence," see Jack P. Greene, *Pursuits of Happiness: The Social Development of Early Modern British Colonies and the Formation of American Culture* (Chapel Hill, 1988).

22. J. H. Plumb, *Georgian Delights: The Pursuit of Happiness* (New York, 1980); Ragnhild Hatton, *George the First, Elector and King* (Cambridge, Mass., 1978). Royal connections that meant relatively little to the peoples of the Reich or of England extended back into the seventeenth century. See Alan Palmer, *Crowned Cousins: The Anglo-German Royal Connection* (London, 1985). The political and military relationship with Hanover, on the other hand, was quite complex until the middle of George II's reign. See Gert Brauer, *Die hannoverisch-englischen Subsidienverträge, 1702–1748* (Aalen, 1962). George III's speech on ascending the throne was widely hailed as a sign of his "English" inclinations, as opposed to those of his predecessors, who were still regarded by many Britons as foreign princes. See James L. McKelvy, *George III and Lord Bute: The Leicester House Years* (Durham, N.C., 1973).

23. Total figures for German migration to the colonies in the eighteenth century remain uncertain; perhaps 120,000 persons arrived between 1683 and 1783. See Lowell C. Bennion, "Flight from the Reich: A Geographic Exposition of Southwest German Emigration, 1683–1815" (Ph.D. diss., Syracuse University, 1971), who estimates (pp. 177–97) that about 12,000 German speakers reached Philadelphia before 1727. On migration patterns, see below chap. 4.

24. On the proverb, see *Oxford English Dictionary* 2 vols. (Oxford, 1971), 1572, entry 78 c.

25. *The Palatines Catechism . . . in a Pleasant Dialogue between an English Tradesman and a High Dutchman . . .* (London, 1709), reprinted in Hugh Hastings, comp., *Ecclesiastical Records of the State of New York,* 7 vols. (Albany, 1900–1916), 3:1817–20.

26. On the difference between "freedom" and "liberty and property," see the discussion in Reid, *Concept of Liberty,* 21, 27–31. Genuine liberty, even "natural," liberty, was tied to constitutional rights and when invoked referred to property.

27. Order of Council for Naturalizing and Sending Certain Palatines to New York, [written at] Kensington, 10 May 1708, in Edward O'Callaghan, ed., *Documentary History of the State of New York* (Albany, 1849–51), 3:541–

42. (*Documentary History of the State of New York* is hereafter cited as *Doc. Hist.*)

28. Clarendon to Dartmouth, 8 March 1710/11, in *Doc. Hist.* 3:656–57; also see ibid., 3:546–48, 551–67; and Livingston's contract to victual the Palatines, in ibid., 3:653–55. See also Walter Allen Knittle, *Early Eighteenth Century Palatine Emigration* (Philadelphia, 1937; reprint, Baltimore, 1970). Knittle's version of both Hunter and Livingston reflects the "imperial" history of a half century ago; both protagonists are portrayed as conscientious builders of empire. For a still sympathetic but more critical view, see Lawrence H. Leder, *Robert Livingston, 1654–1728, and the Politics of Colonial New York* (Chapel Hill, 1961), 211–26.

29. For the orphans bound out, see *Doc. Hist.* 3:566–68; on cost cutting, see Hunter to Livingston, 30 July 1712, in ibid., 3:682–83.

30. Cast to Hunter, 27 March 1711, in *Doc. Hist.* 3:658–59.

31. "The Condition, Grievances, and Oppressions . . . ," in *Doc. Hist.* 3:658–59, 708. The Germans' own characterization of the ground as "bare rock," and their general pattern of resistance, matches peasant resistance charted in other cultures. See James C. Scott, *The Moral Economy of the Peasant: Rebellion and Subsistence in Southeast Asia* (New Haven, 1976). Scott suggests that in a subsistence economy the "safety first" principle demands preservation of the household, and acquiescence to authority's demands for taxes, service, and loyalty. The disruption of household economy by unreasonable demands leads to revolt. For a critique, see Michael G. Peletz, "Moral and Political Economies in Rural Southeast Asia: A Review Article," *Comparative Studies in Society and History* 25 (1983), 731–39.

32. Hunter to Cast, 6 September 1712, in *Doc. Hist.* 3:683–84; quotation from "Condition, Grievances, and Oppressions," 710.

33. Knittle, *Palatine Emigration,* 200–202.

34. From the Latin, *scultetus,* the public authority in the village. Representing the prince or duke, the Schultheiß was elected by the village Bürger (persons holding full rights), and confirmed by the regional authority *(Vogt; Stabsbeamter)* at the district center *(Amt).* The most powerful and important local authority, he presided over the local court, or *Gericht,* composed of between three and seven leading town fathers, which acted as the community court; it had powers over petty misdemeanors *(Frevel)* although its main duties were administrative and advisory. The Schultheiß was also a leading figure in the smaller *Rat,* or local town council. The Rat also elected each year two *Bürgermeister,* or *Heimbürgen,* one from the Gericht, the other from their own number; one was responsible for keeping the books of the village in order, the other for submitting the accounts to the regional officials who appeared twice yearly in the village to inspect them. For details, see David Warren Sabean, *Property, Production, and Family in Neckarhausen, 1700–1870* (Cambridge, 1990), 66–87. I leave German titles untranslated to avoid the easy and misleading assumption that there is a simple English equivalent. Weiser was never a Schultheiß, since his brothers had already occupied the position during his stint in the military. His father and grandfather held the

office, and an uncle was *Stadtschreiber* in neighboring Großgartach. I am indebted to the Reverend Frederick Weiser for lengthy discussions of the family background; see also P. A. Wallace, *Conrad Weiser, 1696–1760: Friend of Colonist and Mohawk* (Philadelphia, 1945).

35. Vrooman to Governor Hunter, 9 July 1715, in *Doc. Hist.* 3:687; Friedrich Kapp, *Geschichte der Deutschen im Staate New York* (New York, 1869), 128–29; Knittle, *Palatine Emigration,* 202–3. The original story was told by Adams to Judge J. M. Brown, who recounts it in *Brief Sketch of the First Settlement of the County of Schoharie by the Germans* (Schoharie, N.Y., 1823), 13.

36. Why Magdalena Zeh emerged as the leader remains a mystery: she had lost no children to indentured servitude and had neither marital, baptismal, nor blood ties to Weiser. She seems to have been acting to defend customary law, the set of norms that "actors in a social situation abstract from practice and . . . invest with binding authority" (Ian Hammett, *Chieftainship and Legitimacy* [London, 1975], 9–23, 107–15, quotation at 14).

Knittle, obviously embarrassed by the event, presents a sanitized version of it and dismisses Magdalena Zeh and the other women as possessing "Amazonian strength" (*Palatine Emigration,* 203). On the calibrated manner in which insults and depredations could be revenged, see David Warren Sabean, *Power in the Blood: Popular Culture and Village Discourse in Early Modern Germany* (Cambridge, 1984). The difficulties involved in comparing ethnographic differences across legal systems has received considerable attention from scholars of non-European cultures. See Ian Hammett, *Social Anthropology and Law* (London, 1977); Leopold Pospisil, *Anthropology of Law: A Comparative Theory* (New York, 1971); Mary Douglas, *Implicit Meanings: Essays in Anthropology* (London, 1975); Laura Nader, ed., "The Ethnography of Law" (special publication), *American Anthropologist* 67 (1965); idem, ed., *Law in Culture and Society* (Chicago, 1969).

37. *Doc. Hist.* 3:712–13.

38. Ulrich Simmendinger, *True and Authentic Register . . . ,* trans. Hermann F. Vesper (Baltimore, 1978), viii.

39. Knittle, *Palatine Emigration,* 150–53, 203–4.

40. The document discussed here if "The Condition, Grievances, and Oppressions of the Germans in His Majesty's Province of New York in America" (see n. 31, above). My interpretation of the document has been influenced especially by Elizabeth Mensch, "The Colonial Origins of Liberal Property Rights," *Buffalo Law Review* (31 (1982), 635–735, at 683–88; and Carol M. Rose, "Possession as the Origin of Property," *University of Chicago Law Review* 52 (1985), 75–89.

41. Knittle, *Palatine Emigration,* 150–51, disproved the claim but does not clarify why the account arose in the first place.

42. Hastings, comp., *Ecclesiastical Records,* 3:1813, 1816, 1861–63, 1871, 1880; Charles H. Glatfelter, *Pastors and People: German Lutheran and Reformed Churches in the Pennsylvania Field, 1717–93* (Breinigsville, Pa., 1980), 30. On Böhme, see R. Barry Lewis, "The Failure of the Anglican-Prussian Ecu-

menical Effort of 1710–1714," *Church History* 47 (1978), 381–99; Arno Sames, *Anton Wilhelm Böhme, 1673–1722: Studien zum ökomenischen Denken und Handeln eines halleschen Pietisten* (Göttingen, 1990).

43. Rudolf Schomerus, *Die verfassungsrechtliche Entwicklung der lutherischen Kirche in Nordamerika von 1638 bis 1792* (Göttingen, 1965), 44–46.

44. Ibid.

45. Berkenmeyer's fellow Hamburger Pastor Johann August Wolf had split with the congregation over his dissolute life. Berkenmeyer sided with Wolf in defense of the ministry, though disgusted with Wolf's behavior. After years of court disputes and acrimony, Mühlenberg was asked to intervene. He disparaged going to law, insisting that the original agreement between pastor and congregation was actually a "call," although it had been turned by the disputants into a secular contract. Berkenmeyer accused some Germans of using *Freiheiten* as an excuse to act licentiously against sound reason *(gesunde Vernunft)*—words that by 1775 would be used to translate Thomas Paine's *Common Sense* (see chap. 9). Arbitrators informed the Hamburg Consistory that the reputation of Lutheranism was being damaged. The references to *Freiheiten* are to acts of Parliament giving "Privilegien" for Lutheran pastors. See *Die Korrespondenz Heinrich Melchior Mühlenbergs* . . . , ed. Kurt Aland (Berlin, 1986–   ), 1:168–91, esp. at 169–70, quotation at 180.

46. Simon Hart and Harry J. Kreider, trans., *Protocol of the Lutheran Church in New York City, 1702–1750* (New York, 1958), 187.

47. This paragraph and the next depend on Harry J. Kreider, *Lutheranism in Colonial New York* (New York, 1942), 3–5, 21–48; Glatfelter, *Pastors and People,* 215–21.

48. *The Journals of Henry Melchior Muhlenberg,* trans. and ed. Theodore G. Tappert and John W. Doberstein, 3 vols. (Philadelphia, 1942–58), 1:337–38, quotation at 339; *Doc. Hist.* 590–603.

49. Mühlenberg's relationships with the New Yorkers, his disgust over the brewery, and his annoyance with the High Germans' insistence on services in German can be followed in his letters: Mühlenberg to Johann Martin Boltzius, in Ebenezer, Georgia, 23 November 1751; Mühlenberg to C. R. Herttel, 9 January 1752, in *Korrespondenz Mühlenbergs* 1:380–473, 458, 470–71, quotations at 441–42.

50. Pastor Wernig to Classics of Amsterdam, 14 September 1752, in Hastings, comp., *Ecclesiastical Records* 5:3285.

51. *Journals of Muhlenberg* 1:281, 254.

52. Alexander Murray to Rev. Dr. Burton, 26 March 1772 and 25 January 1764, in "Papers Relating to the Founding of the 'Society for the Propagation of the Gospels in Foreign Parts,' " *PMHB* 25 (1901), 380, 542.

53. Niedersächsiche Universitäts- und Landesbibliothek Göttingen, "Nachrichten aus Pennsylvania" Cod. Ms. Hist. 821; Staatsarchiv Wertheim, BR 387h, Johannes Schlessman, letters of 26 November 1753, 27 November 1769, quotation from letter of 1753.

54. *Catalogus von mehr als 700 meist Deutschen Büchern* . . . (Philadelphia,

1769). The catalog was probably part of a library purchased for sale.

55. This offering was not the exclusive source for such political or legal treatises. Other booksellers advertised works such as the Basel resident Christopher Lochner's offerings, including the laws of Württemberg; Moser's *Grundsätze des Völker-Rechts,* on international law; copies of the *Policey-und Cameral Magazin,* and Würffel's *Jurisprudentz*—all treaties that shed no light on Anglo-American practices. See Lochner's advertisement, HSP, Broadsides, AbG. (1760–68).

I have checked the political and legal titles in the *Catalogue* against the *Allgemeines Verzeichniß derer Bücher, welche in der Frankfurter und Leipziger Ostermeße* . . . , published at Leipzig for the years 1760–70, a catalog that covers all titles sold in Frankfurt and Leipzig at the biannual book fairs. None of the political and legal titles in the former catalog appear in the latter. Nor do these titles reappear in North America; see Karl J. R. Arndt et al., eds., *The First Century of German Language Printing in the U.S.A.,* 2 vols. (Göttingen, 1989).

The titles include *Doctoris Nicolai Vigelii, Bornehmen Jurisconsulti zu Marpurg Sel. Gerichtsbüchlein, sampt dem Zusaß von ungewissen Rechten* . . . (Jena, 1635); Christoph Lehman, *Floregium Politicum auctum, Das ist, Erneuerter Politischer Blumen-Garten* (Frankfurt, 1662); Justus Abele, *Wohlgelaunter Doctor Juris* . . . (Augsburg, 1715); Johann Martin Hübner, *Neuvermehrter politischer Nach-Tisch* (Leipzig 1613); Johann Caspar Schade, *Bedencks Berlin* . . . (Leipzig, 1696). Despite a thorough search of all titles cited in the National Union Catalogue and in Hilmar Schmuck and Willi Gorzny, *Gesamtverzeichnis des deutschsprachigen Schrifttums (G.V.), 1700–1910* (Munich, 1987), 160 vols. and suppl. some titles remain mysterious. These include *Schmiede des Politischen Glücks, Crausers Jurament oder Eydbüchlein,* possibly written by Johann Gottfried Krause, the Saxon law professor; *Sechste Unterredung zwischen einem Politico und Theologo von Welthändeln,* possibly by Johann Gottlob Rothen of Copenhagen (in a 1767 printing it was titled *Unterredung zwischen einem Hofmanne und einem Geistlichen* . . .); *Wohlgegründete Remonstration an alle höhe und niedere Obrigkeiten, in Puncto des Gewissenszwangs; Freud's Warnung an die Obrigkeiten, um sich vor aller Alienation geistlich Güter zu hüten,* possibly by Michael Freud, author of other essays on sumptuary laws, such as the 1682 *Almode-Teufel: oder Gewissensfragen von der heutigen Tracht u. Kleiderpracht);* and *Mosemans Politische Kaiser-Chronik,* which looks like the 1765 fragment contained in the *Monumenta Germanicae Historica . . . Deutsche Chroniken . . . Kaiserchronik eines regensburger Geistlichen,* ed. Edward Schröder (Dublin, 1969), whose first edition was 1892. Hans Ferdinand Massmann also had published an early edition, but not until the early nineteenth century. The 1765 fragment was published at Passau, but this title is as mysterious as the other four.

56. Philip Jakob Spener had published an edition of Schade's *Christliches Eheren-Bedächtnuß;* the pamphlet is bound with ten others, including August Hermann Francke's *Die wahre Glaubens-Grundung* (Berlin, 1691). On Schade (1666–98), see Stoeffler, *German Pietism,* 72. Schade's main attack was against

the misuse of the private confessional; on that controversy (1695–98) in Berlin, see Johannes Wallmann, "Philipp Jakob Spener," in Martin Greschat, ed., *Orthodoxie und Pietismus* (Stuttgart, 1982), 220; and Helmut Obst, *Der Berliner Beichtstuhlstreit* (Witten, 1972).

57. The context of Freud's essay is known only through the title; I have been unable to find a copy. Freud is presumably the same man as the author of the *Almode-Teufel,* a condemnation of sumptuous dress and worldly vanities.

58. Vigelius, *Gerichtsbüchlein.*

59. Johann Hübner, *Kurze Fragen aus der politischen Historia* (Hamburg, 1721), 974–77.

60. Lehman, *Florilegium Politicum auctum.* The next paragraphs summarize Lehman; see 17–22, 225–28, 273–75, 584–98, quotations at 225, 18, 588.

61. Ibid., 125–31, 186–88, quotations at 186, 126, 334–38, 580, Heinrich of Nassau case at 19; Vigelius, *Gerichtsbüchlein,* 62–63.

62. Conrad, *Individuum und Gemeinschaft,* 7–16; Helmut Coing, "Der Rechtsbegriff des menschlichen Person und die Theorien der Menschenrechte," *Beiträge zur Rechtsforschung: Sonderveröffentlichungen der Zeitschrift für ausländisches und internationales Privatrecht* (Berlin, 1950), 191–225; Hermann, *Schutz der Persönlichkeit,* vol. 2. Also see the exhaustive review of the literature for the medieval period and the analysis of the terms *Recht* and *Freiheit* in Alexander Ignor, *Über das allegemeine Rechtsdenken Eikes von Repgow* (Paderborn, 1984), chap. 11, esp. 227–51.

63. Smith to Secker, 13 October 1756, Lambeth Palace Documents, in E. B. O'Callaghan, ed., *Documents Relative to the Colonial History of the State of New-York,* 11 vols. (Albany, 1856–61), 7:165–68, quotation at 166.

64. William Smith, Jr., *The History of the Province of New-York,* edited with an introduction by Michael Kammen, 2 vols. (Cambridge, Mass., 1972), 138, quotation at 219. Fewer than one out of every hundred left wills that would have protected their property in a manner consistent with village practice. See the raw data in Henry Z. Jones, Jr., *A Study of the German Immigrants Who Arrived in Colonial New York in 1710,* 2 vols. (Universal City, Calif., 1985).

65. *Journals of Muhlenberg* 1:282.

66. HSP, Penn Correspondence, Hamilton to Penn, 18 November 1750; also cited in Dietmar Rothermund, *The Layman's Progress: Religious and Political Experience in Colonial Pennsylvania, 1740–1770* (Philadelphia, 1961), 165.

67. Minutes of the Board of Property, 25 January 1771, in Charles F. Hoban, ed., *Pennsylvania Archives,* 8th ser., vol. 8 (Harrisburg, 1935), 6610–11. Miercken's petition, however, touched off considerable controversy, because it was unclear whether the right to trade should be extended to someone not a natural-born subject of the empire. On the debate, which followed by only a few years the 1764 opinion of the British attorney general that aliens not naturalized under the naturalization act 13 Geo. 2 (1740), c. 7, were ineligible to acquire property, see James H. Kettner, *The Development of*

American Citizenship, 1608–1870 (Chapel Hill, 1978), 104–5.

68. *Korrespondenz Mühlenbergs* 1:470–71, 461.

69. Charleston Historical Society (Charleston, S.C.), acc. no. 34/97, Commonplace Book (no name), 1760. This text was copied from the third English edition of Johann Georg Keyssler, *Travels Through Germany . . .* (London, 1760). The original German edition appeared in 1740.

70. SCDAH, Transcripts of British Public Record Office, 30:248–55, Lt. Gov. William Bull to Board of Trade, Charlestown, 15 March 1765.

71. See Leo Schelbert and Hedwig Rappolt, *Alles ist ganz anders hier: Auswandererschicksale in Briefen aus zwei Jahrhunderten* (Olten, 1977), 34–144. Hansmartin Schwarzmaier, "Auswandererbriefe aus Nordamerika: Quellen im Grenzbereich von Geschichtlicher Landeskunde, Wanderungsforschung und Literatursoziologie," *ZGO,* (n.s., 87 (1978), 303–70, contains nineteenth-century examples but reflects the same concerns. Also see Otto Brunner, "Das ganze Haus," in idem, *Neue Wege der Sozial- und Verfassungsgeschicte,* 2d ed. (Göttingen, 1960), 103–27.

72. John Phillip Reid, *A Constitutional History of the American Revolution: The Authority of Rights* (Madison, Wis., 1986), 99.

73. K. G. Davies, comp., *Documents of the American Revolution, 1770–1783,* Colonial Office Series, vol. 1 (Shannon, Ireland, 1972), 29–30; vol. 3 (Shannon Ireland, 1973), 49 (CO 5/1102, FO).

74. LCP, Broadsides, Sm. Am. 1769.

Chapter 2   Liberties and Households: The Village

1. Oberboihingen Parish Archives, Oberboihingen Kirchenkonvent, 1732–59, 22 May 1740. The records for Oberboihingen, Reudern, and Sachsenhausen were kept in the same book by the pastor and Schultheiß of Oberboihingen; they will be cited hereafter without the archive name.

Meetings of the court and other public gatherings were announced by bell ringing; within three-quarters of an hour, villagers were to attend. See Fritz Reiff, *Neckartenzlingen einst und jezt* (Neckartenzlingen, 1972), 76.

2. Oberboihingen Kirchenkonvent, 6 June 1740, 11 May 1741.

3. Ibid., 23 January 1743.

4. G. C. Seybold, "Von Hebammen," in idem, *Ordnung für die Communen, auch deren Vorstehere und Bediente in dem Herzogthum Württemberg* (Ludwigsburg, 1750), 21–22.

5. Oberboihingen Kirchenkonvent, 14th Sunday after Trinity (June) 1759.

6. Jeffrey M. Diefendorf, "Soziale Mobilität im Rheinland im 18. Jahrhundert," *Scripta Mercaturae* 19 (1985), 88–112; Christopher R. Friederichs, "Capitalism, Mobility, and Class Formation in the Early Modern German City," *Past and Present* 69 (1975), 24–49.

7. Brady, *Turning Swiss,* 38–42, 223–30, identifies the latter two as the "Austrian" and "Saxon" options. Brady suggests that neither city Bürger

nor princes wished to see Swiss communalism extended into the Reich. On protoindustrialization, see Peter Kriedte et al., *Industrialisierung vor der Industrialisierung: Gewerbliche Warenproduktion auf dem Land in der Formationsperiode des Kapitalismus* (Göttingen, 1977).

8. Hermann Rebel, *Peasant Classes: The Bureaucratization of Property and Family Relations under Early Habsburg Absolutism, 1511–1636* (Princeton, 1983), 33.

9. Bodelshausen Village Archives, R.u.I. 557:605–8, Testamentliche Disposition Johannes Hauser, 5 December 1766. For 1690–1790 fewer than fifteen wills exist, compared to more than nine hundred surviving inventories; this compares well with Sabean's findings in Neckarhausen (Sabean, *Property, Production,* 203, table 7.1).

10. Joachim von Zimmerman, "Bodelshausen: Ein Gemeindeporträt," *Tübinger Blätter* 69 (1982), 26–28. Württemberg and the Palatinate experienced few peasant uprisings by comparison with Switzerland and north-central Reich territories (Winfried Schultze, *Bäuerlicher Widerstand und feudale Herrschaft in der frühen Neuzeit* [Stuttgart, 1980], 49–61). This should not, however, be read as evidence that there was little tension in these societies. Schultze estimates that 70–80 percent of the peasant families lived on the precarious edge of economic ruin (p. 72). See also Peter Blickle, "Bauer und Statt in Oberschwaben," *ZWL* 31 (1972), 104–20. Peasants from nearby Hohenzollern villages did revolt, and approached the university at Tübingen for legal advice on their rights (pp. 103–4) during the Peasant Revolt of 1525. For further comparisons, see the essays in Winfried Schultze, ed., *Aufstände, Revolten, Prozesse: Beiträge zu baüerlichen Widerstandsbewegungen in frühneuzeitlichen Europa* (Stuttgart, 1983); Volker Press, "Von den Bauernrevolten des 16. zur Konstitutionellen Verfassung des 19. Jahrhunderts: Die Untertanenkonflikte in Hohenzollern-Hechingen und ihre Lösungen," in Hermann Weber, ed., *Politische Ordnungen und soziale Kräfte im alten Reich* (Wiesbaden, 1980), 85–112.

11. "Reise nach Constanz am Bodensee und nach Schaffhausen . . . 1781 von Herrn Prof. Sander in Carlsruhe . . . ," in *Johann Bernoulli's Sammlung kurzer Reisebeschreibungen* (Berlin, 1781–82), 3:207–84, at 229.

12. Lauffen/Eyach Village Archives, *Ruggerichtsprotokolle,* 10 May 1762. On the marginal districts, see James Allen Vann, *Württemberg: The Making of a State, 1593–1793* (Ithaca, N.Y., 1984), 39, 249.

13. Angelika Bischoff-Luithlen, *Der Schwabe und die Obrigkeit* (Stuttgart, 1978), 181–87. Herders and peasants periodically quarreled with the aristocracy in the Black Forest area and the Alb over the conflict between their rights and the claims of the lords for services during the hunt, and over attempts to convert forest land and some meadows into hunting preserves. For details, see Ursula L. Neugebauer, *Die Siedlungsformen im nordöstlichen Schwarzwald und ihr Wandel seit dem 17. Jahrhundert* (Tübingen, 1969), 117–18. The ducal handbook prescribed the oath to be taken by herders. It treats the offices of herders and field and vineyard warders as lesser offices, subsidiary to those of Schultheiß, village scribe, Bürgermeister, and midwife,

all of which are treated first (Seybold, *Ordnung für die Commumen,* 23).

14. Karl-Heinrich Bieritz, *Das Kirchenjahr: Feste, Gedenk- und Feiertage in Geschichte und Gegenwart* (Munich, 1987), 211–13; Oswald A. Erich and Richard Beitl, *Wörterbuch der deutschen Volkskunde* (Stuttgart, 1974), 372–73, 411–15, 695–97.

15. See George M. Foster, "Peasant Society and the Image of Limited Good," *American Anthropologist* 67 (1965), 293–315.

16. Lauffen/Eyach Village Archives, Ruggerichtsprotokolle, 1762–81. For similar beliefs on the properties of quicksilver, and casting spells against enemies on St. John's Eve, in the Salzburg region see Nora Wattech, "Abergläubisches und Magisches für den Hausgebrauch und zum Erzsuchen," *Mitteilungen der Gesellschaft für salzburger Landeskunde* 110–111 (1970–71), 367–69.

17. M. Jeremias Höslin, *Beschreibung der Wirtembergischen Alp . . .* (Tübingen, 1798), 235–41; Otto Strübel, "Seißen-Dorf und Flur und ihre Entwicklung seit dem ausgehenden Mittelalter," typescript, (copy in my possession), initially prepared as a seminar paper for Hermann Grees; see also Otto Strübel, "Entwicklung von Dorf und Flur seit dem ausgehenden Mittelalter," in Wilhelm Arnold Ruopp and Otto Strübel, eds., *900 Jahre Seißen glei bei Blaubeura: Beiträge zur Heimatskunde eines Albdorfes* (Sigmaringen, 1985), 48–81.

18. Johann Freidrich Eisenhart, *Grundsätze der deutschen Rechte in Sprüchwörtern durch Anmerkungen erläütert,* 3d ed., expanded (Leipzig, 1823), pt. 3, "On Property and Its Acquisition," no. 3; Hermann Grees, "Sozialgenetisch bedingte Dorfelemente im ostschwäbischen Altsiedland," in idem, ed., *Die europäische Kulturlandschaft im Wandel: Festschrift für Karl Heinz Schröder* (Kiel, 1974), 41–68.

19. Hans Ammerich, *Landesherr und Landesverwaltung: Beiträge zur Regierung von Pfalz-Zweibrücken am Ende des alten Reiches* (Saarbrücken, 1981), 79–93; Werner Habicht, *Dorf und Bauernhaus im deutschsprachigen Lothringen und im Saarland* (Saarbrücken, 1980), 225–34.

20. Peter-Per Krebs, *Die Stellung der Handwerkerswitwe in der Zunft vom Spätmittelalter bis zum 18. Jahrhundert* (Regensburg, 1974), 21–43, 91–100; Gerhard Deter, *Handwerksgerichtsbarkeit zwischen Absolutismus und Liberalismus: Zur Geschichte der genossenschaftlichen Jurisdiktion in Westfalen im 18. und 19. Jahrhundert* (Berlin, 1987), 22–25, 65–89; Peter Schichtel, *Das Recht des zünftigen Handwerks im Herzogtum Pfalz-Zweibrücken während des 18. Jahrhunderts* (Berlin, 1986), 31–49, 55–58, 186–89; Otto Könnecke, *Rechtsgeschichte des Gesindes in West- und Süddeutschland* (Marburg, 1912), 220–29.

21. Rudolf Eickemeyer, *Über die Erbauung der Dörfer . . .* (Frankfurt am Main, 1787), 1–2, 6–11.

22. On viticulture in a later political context, see Wolfgang von Hippel, *Die Bauernbefreiung in Königreich Württemberg: Darstellung und Quellen,* 2 vols. (Boppard am Rhein, 1977), 1:64–71; for Baden, see Albrecht Strobel, *Agrarverfassung im Übergang: Studien zur Agrargeschichte des Badischen Breisgaus vom Beginn des 16. bis zum Ausgang des 18. Jahrhunderts* (Freiburg, 1972).

23. "Erste Reise in Westphalen und angränzenden Provinzen in Jahre 1764 . . . ," in *Bernoulli's Sammlung* 2:210–15.

24. Wolfgang Hartwich, "Speyer vom 30jährigen Krieg bis zum Ende der Napoleonischen Zeit," in Wolfgang Eger, ed., *Geschichte der Stadt Speyer,* 2 vols. (Stuttgart, 1982), 2:1–114; "Hrr Prof. Sanders Lustreise von Carlsruhe nach Speyer am Rhein im Jahre 1781 . . . ," in *Bernoulli's Sammlung* 5:223–64. On Mainz, which unfortunately as a Catholic bishopric produced negligible numbers of emigrants, see Walter Rödel, *Mainz und seine Bevölkerung im 17. und 18. Jahrhundert* (Stuttgart, 1985), 298–335, on emigration within the Reich. On the centrality of wine and the resulting trade connections, see F. Meyer, *Weinbau und Weinhandel an Mosel, Saar und Ruwer* (Koblenz, 1976).

25. See, for example, C. Meiners, *Beschreibung einer Reise nach Stuttgart und Strasburg im Herbst . . .* (Göttingen, 1803), 16–18, 51–52; "Reise nach Constanz von Herrn Prof Sander," quotation at 3:215–16.

26. The separate development of the villages in the Schwäbische Alb after the Thirty Years' War stemmed from the destruction of vineyards that were planted even in these unpromising areas. Local village records hint that the delectable Würtemberg Trollinger was cultivated and bottled in these hills until the 1640s. See Angelika Bischoff-Luithlen, "Trollinger aus Schwäbisch Sibirien," in idem, *Der Schwabe und die Obrigkeit,* 146–50. To keep tax rates high, even marginal wine-producing villages such as Neckarhausen were forbidden to cease cultivation until the nineteenth century (Sabean, *Property, Production,* 43–44, 53–54).

27. Werner Fleischhauer, *Barock im Herzogtum Württemberg,* 2d ed. (Stuttgart, 1981); *Journals of Muhlenberg* 1:678; on Württemberg religious life see Martin Brecht and Hermann Ehmer, *Südwestdeutsche Reformationsgeschichte* (Stuttgart, 1981); Heinrich Bornkamm et al., eds., *Der Pietismus in Gestalten und Wirkungen: Festschrift für Martin Schmidt zum 65. Geburtstag* (Bielefeld, 1975); Martin Greschat, ed., *Zur neueren Pietismusforschung* (Darmstadt, 1977); Martin Hasselhorn, *Die altwürttembergische Pfarrstand im 18. Jahrhundert* (Stuttgart, 1958).

28. This area produced large numbers of migrants to both Pennsylvania and South Carolina and has been unusually well documented. See Annette Kunselman Burgert, *Eighteenth Century Emigrants from German-speaking Lands to North America.* vol. 1, *The Northern Kraichgau* (Breinigsville, Pa., 1983); Werner Hacker, *Kurpfälzische Auswanderer vom Unteren Neckar* (Stuttgart, 1983). On the Reichsritterschaften, see Volker Press, "Reichsritterschaften," in Kurt G. A. Jeserich et al., eds., *Deutsche Verwaltungsgeschichte: Vom Spätmittelatter bis zum Ende des Reiches* (Stuttgart, 1983), 1:679–89.

29. Karl J. Svoboda, "Aus der Verfassung des Kantons Kraichgau der unmittelbaren freien Reichsritterschaft in Schwaben unter besonderer Berücksichtigung des territorialen Elements," *ZGO,* n.s., 77 (1968), 253–89; Volker Press, "Die Ritterschaft im Kraichgau zwischen Reich und Territorium, 1500–1623," ibid., 83 (1974), 35–98; Harold H. Kehrer, "Die Familie von Sickingen und die deutschen Fürsten, 1263–1523," ibid. 88 (1979), 71–158; Alfred Caroli, "Aus der Stüber Cent-Zerissene Bande," in Adam Schlitt, ed., *Kraichgau:*

Heimatforschung im Landkreis Sinsheim unter Berücksichtigung seiner unmittelbaren Nachbargebiete, Pts. 1, 2 (Sisheim, 1968, 1970), 100–104.

30. GLAK A 229/50209, Ittlingen, Kirchendienst, 1718.

31. Meinrad Schaab, "Die Wiederherstellung des Katholizismus in der Kurpfalz im 17. und 18. Jahrhundert," *ZGO,* n.s., 75 (1966), 147–205.

32. SArS, Beilagen zum Raths-Protocoll, 18 April 1764.

33. *Die Stadt und die Landkreise Heidelberg und Mannheim: Amtliche Kreisbeschreibung,* vol. 2, *Die Stadt Heidelberg und die Gemeinden des Landkreises Heidelberg* (Karlsruhe, 1970), 442–66.

34. GLAK 229/19981 171, Dossenheim, 1749.

35. Ibid. 229/19980 170, 1748–91; 229/19951 139, 1749; 229/19970 160, p.23, 1769, query no. 67: "Ob er nicht mit einigen Pfarrkindern oder protestanten in unfrieden und process lebe? (A) Wisse nichts besonders jedoch gienge es ihm wie allen pfarren wie in Parocho duodenario."

36. Ibid. 229/50205; for a similar quarrel, see 229/118 893, 894, 895, involving the Venningen family's claims on serfs' dues (*Leibeigenschaft*) in Zuzenhausen, and the electoral counterclaims.

37. Volker Press, *Calvinismus und Territorialstaat: Regierung und Zentralbehörden der Kurpfalz, 1559–1619* (Stuttgart, 1970), 78–96; Georg Droege, "Gemeindliche Selbstverwaltung und Grundherrschaft"; in Jeserich et al., eds., *Deutsche Verwaltungsgeschichte* 1:193–213; Volker Press, "Die Wittelsbachischen Territorien: Die pfälzischen Lande und Bayern," in ibid., 552–99; Fritz Zimmermann, *Die Weistümer und der Ausbau der Landeshoheit in der Kurpfalz* (Berlin, 1937), 52–53, 86–87; Karl Kollnig, *Die Weistümer der Zent Schriesheim: Badische Weistümer und Dorfordnungen* (Stuttgart, 1968); idem, *Die Zent Schriesheim: Ein Beitrag zur Geschichte der Zentverfassung in Kurpfalz* (Heidelberg, 1933); Walter Grube, *Vogteien, Ämter, Landkreise in Baden-Württemberg,* vol. 1, *Geschichtliche Grundlagen* (Stuttgart, 1975), 56–66; Dieter Werkmüller, *Über Aufkommen und Verbreitung der Weistümer nach der Sammlung von Jacob Grimm* (Berlin, 1972), 97.

38. On the Swiss in the Kraichgau, see Kunselmann Burgert, *Eighteenth Century Emigrants* 1:419–32; and on the many publications documenting Swiss migration into the Palatinate, see Leo Schelbert, *Einführung in die schweizerische Auswanderungsgeschichte der Neuzeit* (Zürich, 1976), 201 n. 39.

39. Walter Grube, *Der Stuttgarter Landtag, 1457–1957: Von den Landständen zum demokratischen Parlament* (Stuttgart, 1957); the discussion in this paragraph relies on an examination of the surviving outlines of the Gravamina, in HstASt A9 47–115. The originals and contents were destroyed in 1943.

40. For Ulm, see Gerold Neusser, *Das Territorium der Reichsstadt Ulm im 18. Jahrhundert: Verwaltungsgeschichtliche Forschungen* (Ulm, 1964), 152–74; for Baden, see Wolfgang Leiser, *Der gemeine Zivilprozess in den badischen Markgrafschaften* (Stuttgart, 1961), 6–19, 72–83.

41. Benedict Anderson, *Imagined Communities: Reflections on the Origin and Spread of Nationalism* (London, 1983), 66–79; see also Ernest Gellner, *Thought and Change* (London, 1964).

42. See J. A. Sharpe, " 'Such Disagreement betwyx Neighbours': Liti-

gation and Human Relations in Early Modern England" in John Bossy, ed., *Disputes and Settlements: The Law and Human Relations in the West* (Cambridge, 1983), 167–87; James Casey, "Household Disputes and the Law in Early Modern Andalusia, in ibid., 189–217; Nicole Castan, "The Arbitration of Disputes under the 'Ancien Régime,'" in ibid., 219–60; and John Bossy, "Postscript," in ibid., 287–93. See also John L. Comaroff and Simon Roberts, *Rules and Processes: The Cultural Logic of Dispute in an African Context* (Chicago, 1981), 175–215.

43. Sabean, *Property, Production,* 183–207; on the general literature regarding inheritance, see Lutz Berkner, "Inheritance, Land Tenure, and Peasant Family Structure: A German Regional Comparison," in Jack Goody et al., eds., *Family and Inheritance: Rural Society in Western Europe, 1200–1800* (Cambridge, 1976), 71–95; Alan Mayhew, *Rural Settlement and Farming in Germany* (London, 1973), 123–30, 178–83; John W. Cole and Eric R. Wolf, *The Hidden Frontier: Ecology and Ethnicity in an Alpine Valley* (New York, 1974); Robert McC. Netting, *Balancing on an Alp: Ecological Change and Continuity in a Swiss Mountain Village* (Cambridge, 1981); Günter Golde, *Catholics and Protestants: Agricultural Modernization in Two German Villages* (New York, 1975), 14–16. My thinking about the various sources of law reflects Martin Chanock, *Law, Custom, and Social Order: The Colonial Experience in Malawi and Zambia* (Cambridge, 1985).

44. Wilhelm Brauneder, "Historical Introduction: The Development of Estate and Property Law," in Arthur K. Marshall, ed., *International Academy of Estate and Trust Law: Seminars in Vienna and Munich on Austrian and German Law* (Los Angeles, 1979), 4–22. German law does not define an "estate"; rather, it defines differing categories under which lands and chattels are grouped. *Nachlaß* I translate as "residue"; *Errungenschaft,* as "acquest property"; *Vermächtniß,* as "bequest"; and *Erbteil,* as "inheritance portion."

45. John P. Dawson, *The Oracles of the Law* (Ann Arbor, Mich., 1968), 154; Paul Gehring, "Weistümer und schwäbische Dorfordnungen," in Peter Blickle, ed., *Deutsche ländliche Rechtsquellen: Probleme und Wege der Weistumsforschung* (Stuttgart, 1977), 41–51; Rudolf Endres, "Ländliche Rechtsquellen als sozialgeschichtliche Quellen," in ibid., 164–84; Werkmüller, 93–97; Karl Kollnig, ed., *Die Weistümer der Zenten Eberbach und Mosbach* (Stuttgart, 1985), 423–27. Few Weistümer survive for Ulm and eastern Swabia; for the sayings, see Eisenhart, *Grundsätze der deutschen Rechte in Sprüchwortern.* For the citations, see third section; the comment on sustenance is also sometimes "Guter Will ist kein Erbe" ("Goodwill is no inheritance").

46. Sabean, *Property, Production,* 335–70; Johannes W. Pichler, *Die ältere ländliche Salzburger Eigentumsordnung* (Salzburg, 1979), 44; see also Bischoff-Luithlen, *Schwabe und die Obrigkeit,* 62–64; A. L. Reyscher, *Beiträge zur Kunde des deutschen Rechts: Erster Beitrag. Über die Symbolik des germanischen Rechts* (Tübingen, 1833), 35–36.

47. See K. Krafft, *Anerbensitte und Anerbenrecht in Württemberg: Unter besonderer Berücksichtigung von Württembergisch-Franken* (Stuttgart, 1930). For the areas with nonpartible inheritance, see Hermann Grees, *Ländliche Untersichten*

und ländliche Siedlung in Ostschwaben (Tübingen, 1975); idem, "Sozialgenetisch bedingte Dorfelemente," 41–68; Neusser, *Territorium der Reichsstadt Ulm.*

48. On feudal village customs and laws, see Karl S. Bader, *Das Mittelalterliche Dorf als Friedens- und Rechtsbereich* (Weimar, 1957); idem, *Dorfgemeinschaft und Dorfgemeinde* (Cologne, 1962); idem, *Rechtsformen und Schichten der Liegenschaftsnutzung im mittelaterlichen Dorf* (Vienna, 1973). On the Württemberg revisal, see Helmut Röhm, *Die Vererbung des landwirtschaftlichen Grundeigentums in Baden-Württemberg* (Remagen, 1957); Rolf-Dieter Hess, *Familien- und Erbrecht in württembergischen Landrecht von 1555 unter besonderer Berücksichtigung des älteren württembergischen Rechts* (Stuttgart, 1968); Ludwig Friedrich Griesenger, *Commentar über das herzoglich württembergische Landrecht,* 5 vols. (Frankfurt, 1795); Christopher H. Riecke, *Das württembergische Landrecht vom 1. Juni 1610* (Stuttgart, 1842), 221–23; Edward Faber and A. Schlossberger, eds., *Die Vorarbeiten zum Württembergischen Land-Rechte vom 1. Juni 1610 im Auftrage des königl. Württemb. Justiz-Ministerium aus Archival-Urkunden* (Stuttgart, 1859); Georg von Wächter, *Quellen und Literatur des württembergischen Privatrechts,* 2 vols. (Stuttgart, 1839–42, 1851), 1:189–459. No complete collection of these *Rescripten* (princely written orders) exists for the Palatinate; I rely on those at the GLAK and those I found in local records. See also Fritz Zimmermann, *Weistümer in der Kurpfalz,* 86–95; Press, *Calvinismus und Territorialstaat,* 78–96; Harold H. Kehrer, "Die Familie von Sickingen und die deutschen Fürsten, 1262–1523," *ZGO,* 88 (1979), 71–158; Kollnig, *Die Zent Schriesheim,* 71–77. For the area of the Palatinate not observing equal partition, see Walter Braun, *Die Entwicklungstendenzen der Vererbung des landwirtschaftlichen Grundeigentums in Rheinland-Pfalz und dem Saarland* (Hohenheim-Stuttgart, 1961); Otto Müller, *Gerhardsbrunn, ein Dorf der Sickinger Höhe,* Ortskroniken des Landeskreises Kaiserslautern, no. 5 (Otterbach, 1977), 137–82.

49. Sabean, *Property, Production,* 55–60; Hans-Volkmar Findeisen, *Pietismus in Fellbach, 1750–1820: Zwischen sozialem Protest und bürgerlicher Anpassung* (Tübingen, 1985), 78; Heinrich Höhn, *Geschichte der württembergischen Stadt Grötzingen unter Berücksichtigung der Ämter Nürtingen und Neuffen bis 1700* (Stuttgart, 1907); Strübel, "Entwicklung von Dorf," 48–81.

50. Ahasver von Brandt, *Mittlelalterliche Bürgertestamente: Neuerschlossene Quellen zur Geschichte der materiellen und geistigen Kultur* (Heidelberg, 1973); Gabriele Schulz, *Testamente des späten Mittelalters aus dem Mittelrheingebiet: Eine Untersuchung in rechts- und kulturgeschichtlicher Hinsicht* (Mainz, 1976); Gustav Klemens Schmelzeisen, *Polizeiordungen und Privatrecht* (Münster, 1955).

51. Antonie Kraut, *Die Stellung der Frau im württembergischen Privatrecht: Eine Untersuchung über Geschlechtsvormundschaft und Interzessionsfrage* (Tübingen, 1934); Hess, *Familien- und Erbrecht,* 120–43.

52. For the 1567 statute, see August Ludwig Reyscher, ed., *Vollständige, historisch und kritisch bearbeitete Sammlung der württembergischen Gesetze,* 19 vols. (Stuttgart, 1828–51), 4:376, specifying that inventory be taken to clarify inheritances and avoid cheating; the district Amtsmann appointed the assessor in the presence of the interested parties. See also A. R. Frischlin, *Instruction*

und Bericht (Tübingen, 1679); A. I. Röslin, *Abhandlung von Inventuren und Abtheilung . . .* (Stuttgart, 1761); Friedrich Ludwig Hochstetter, *Anleitung für angehende Witembergische Stat- und Amtsschreiberei-Scribenten zu Inventur- und Theilungs- auch Steuer-Geschäften* (Stuttgart, 1780); Röslin includes references to ducal orders about deductions to be taken not from the residual property of the deceased but from the inheritance portions of emigrants who had already received money or goods. The instructions reflect officials' concern about property being taken out of the duchy by emigrants to North America.

53. Seißen Village Archives, R.u.I., vol. 13, 26 March 1794, Catharina Class; quotation from vol. 3, 3 December 1733, Anna Kiefer.

54. Tax lists were constructed using the inventories; a 1735 ducal rescript demanding yearly assessments indicates widespread noncompliance. Such assessments hit day laborers and the marginal property-holders hardest; see Joachim Mantel, *Wildberg: Eine Studie zur wirtschaftlichen und sozialem Entwicklung der Stadt von der Mitte des sechzehnten bis zur Mitte des achtzehnten Jahrhunderts* (Stuttgart, 1974), 36–37, 133–38; Sabean, *Property, Production,* 70–75.

55. The biblical source is Psalms 90:10; see Ludwig Julius Friedrich Höpfner, "De Hereditatis Petitione et Divisione," in idem, *Theoretisch-prachtischer Commentar über die heineccischen Institutionen nach deren neuesten Ausgabe,* 8th ed., (Frankfurt am Main, 1818), 544–46.

56. The formulas cited here and throughout this section can be found in Frischlin, *Instruction*; Röslin, *Abhandlung*; the variations here I find in the various village R.u.I..

57. GLAK 229/85386, Reihen Village, R.u.I., Johann Valentin Schuch.

58. For a mother engaging in this practice, see Bodelshausen Village Archive, R.u.I., no. 37, 9 February 1736. On the subsistence economy, see Hans Medick, "Teurung, Hunger und 'moralische Ökonomie von oben': Die Hungerkrise der Jahre 1816–17 in Württemberg," *Beiträge zur historischen Sozialkunde* 2 (1985), 39–44; Hans Jänichen, *Beiträge zur Wirtschaftsgeschichte des schwäbischen Dorfes* (Stuttgart, 1970).

59. Seißen Village Archives, R.u.I., 6:245–52, 2 October 1749; 2:632–36, 27 May 1728; 4:83 (misnumbered 82), 22 [March?] 1734, quotation at 85.

60. Wolfgang Schmild, *Alte Gerichtsbarkeit: Vom Gottesurteil bis zum Beginn der modernen Rechtsprechung* (Munich, 1980), 125–52; Karl Frölich, *Rechtsdenkmäler des deutschen Dorfs* (Giessen, 1947); Reyscher, *Sammlung* 4:330–44, 353–58; Theodore Knapp, *Gesammelte Beiträge zur Rechts- und Wirtschaftsgeschichte vornehmlich des deutschen Bauernstandes* (Tübingen, 1902); idem, *Neue Beiträge* (Aalen, 1964); Grötzingen Village Archives, R.u.I., no. 542, 3 March 1738; no. 570, 9 November 1739, quotation at 542r, 18v.

61. On the Kraichgau custom, see Reyscher, *Beiträge zur Kunde des deutschen Rechts,* 53; on Hildenbrand, GLAK 229/11194, Weiler R.u.I., p. 195, 1750–51. Marriage contracts were used throughout the southwest, more commonly in eastern Württemberg and in neighboring Ulm, Bavaria, and Salzburg. On the Salzburg customs, see Heinrich Siegel, *Das Güterrecht der Ehegatten in Stiftslande Salzburg: Ein Beitrag zur Geschichte des deutschen ehelichen Güterrechtes* (Vienna, 1882). The tendency toward mutual covenants if no

children came of the marriage came under attack in the seventeenth century for failing to respect the rights of more distant family members; see Johannes W. Pichler, *Die ältere ländliche Salzburger Eigentumsordnung* (Salzburg, 1979); Heinrich Siegel and Karl Tomaschek, eds., *Die salzburgische Taidinge* (Vienna, 1870), 217.

62. Seißen Village Archives, R.u.I., 11:456–66, 9 November 1796.

63. Bodelshausen Village Archives, R.u.I., 541:102–10, 5 December 1747; in this case, no escape from encumbered lands was intended; the siblings did receive equal portions, the daughter receiving more linens, the Bible, and domestic utensils, i.e., what was most useful to her.

64. On the sanctity of custom and old sayings, see Eisenhart, *Grundsätze der deutschen Rechte in Sprüchwörtern*. The founding of the "Königlich-groß-britanische kurfürslich-braunschweigisch-lünebürgische Landwirtschaftsgesellschaft" at Celle in 1664 constitutes the earliest adoption by northern German towns (influenced by Hanover and the connection to London via Hamburg) of English agrarian reform techniques. Reforms did not penetrate the southwest until the very late eighteenth century. See A. J. Bourde, *The Influence of England on the French Agronomes, 1750–1789* (Cambridge, 1953); and G. Schröder-Lembke, "Englische Einflüße auf die deutsche Gutwirtschaft im 18. Jht.," *Zeitschrift für Agrargeschichte und Agrarsoziologie* 12 (1964), 29–36.

65. Albert Eßer, "Die Lohn-Preis-Entwicklung für landwirtschaftliche Arbeiter in Deutschland, England und Nordamerika im 18. Jahrhundert," in Klaus Tenfelde, ed., "Arbeiter und Arbeiterbewegung im Vergleich" (special issue no. 15), *Historische Zeitschrift* (Munich), 238 (1986), 100–136.

66. Staatsarchiv Wertheim, Rep. BR 387 F, Hans Jörg Spatz of Dietenhaam, 16 May 1760.

67. Bischoff-Luithlen, *Schwabe und die Obrigkeit,* 132–35, 239–41.

68. *The Papers of Thomas Jefferson,* ed. Julian Boyd et al. (Princeton, 1955), 13:18, 27, 48.

Chapter 3   Pietism, Christian Liberty, and the Problem of "Worldly Goods"

1. [Johann Heinrich Jung], *Heinrich Stillings Jugend, Eine Wahrhafte Geschichte: Jung-Stillings Lebensgeschichte, von ihm selbst erzählt,* 15th ed. (Konstanz, 1929), 32–33.

2. Ibid. The prevalence of locks on every room and receptacle may explain in part why theft appears so rarely as a misdemeanor in the village court records. Sabean also found no significant instances of theft before 1800 (*Property, Production,* 452–53).

3. Erich Auerbach, *Mimesis: The Representation of Reality in Western Literature,* trans. Willard R. Trask (Princeton, 1953), 434–60; Arthur W. McCardle, *Friedrich Schiller and Swabian Pietism* (New York, 1986); Gerhard

Kaiser, *Pietismus und Patriotismus im literarischen Deutschland* (Wiesbaden, 1961).

4. No scholarly study, not even Rosemary Radford Ruether and Rosemary Skinner Keller, eds., *Women and Religion in America,* vol. 1, *The Colonial and Revolutionary Periods* (San Francisco, 1983), examines German Lutheran or Reformed women and Pietism in the New World.

5. The conventicle was not unique to Württemberg. But actions taken by orthodox régimes in Hamburg, Baden-Durlach, Electoral Saxony, and Braunschweig left Württemberg for much of the eighteenth century ruled by a Catholic duke, as the southwest pietist epicenter. See Klaus Deppermann, *Der hallesche Pietismus und der preußische Staat unter Friedrich III. (I.)* (Göttingen, 1961), 62–63.

6. On Spener, an introduction in English is K. James Stein, *Philipp Jakob Spener and the Renewal of the Church* (Chicago, 1985). See also Carter Lindberg, *The Third Reformation? Charismatic Movements and the Lutheran Tradition* (Macon, Ga., 1983), 143–50; Kurt Aland, "Philipp Jakob Spener: Sein Lebensweg von Frankfurt nach Berlin (1666–1705), dargestellt an Hand seiner Briefe nach Frankfurt," in idem, ed., *Kirchengeschichtliche Entwürfe* (Gütersloh, 1960); Paul Grünberg, *Philipp Jakob Spener,* 3 vols. (Göttingen, 1893–1906). Throughout, I use *philanthropy,* a word appearing after 1650 in English, to describe Protestant response to the command to care for others. *Charity,* although sometimes used interchangeably, conveyed a theology of medieval, Catholic, "works" that pietists rejected.

7. For the conventional view, see Stoeffler, *German Pietism;* for a criticism of the propietist interpretation, see Lowell C. Green, "Duke Ernest the Pious of Saxe-Gotha and His Relationship to Pietism," in Bornkamm et al., eds., *Pietismus in Gestalten und Wirkungen,* 179–91. On Leipzig and orthodox piety, see Christian Mahrenholz, *Johann Sebastien Bach und der Gottesdienst seiner Zeit* (Kassel, 1950); Gunter Stiller, *Johann Sebastian Bach and Liturgical Life in Leipzig,* trans. Robin Leaver (St. Louis, Mo., 1970); Martin Petzoldt, *Bach als Ausleger der Bibel* (Berlin, 1985). For the same corrective for Hanover and Hamburg, see Martin Schmidt and Dietrich Blaufuß, eds., *Orthodoxie und Pietismus: Gesammelte Studien von Hans Leube* (Bitterfeld, 1975).

8. Dietrich Blaufuß, "Bürgerschaft und Kirche im Pietismus," in Jürgen Sydow, eds., *Bürgerschaft und Kirche* (Sigmaringen, 1980), 113–29; Carl Hinrichs, *Preußentum und Pietismus* (Göttingen, 1971), 11–17.

9. Johannes Weigelt, "Gedanken zur Universitätsgeschichte," in *250 Jahre Universität Halle: Streifzüge durch Ihre Geschichte in Forschung und Lehre,* (Halle, 1944), 1–47, quotation at 13. Despite National Socialist taints, this is still a valuable collection.

10. The next two paragraphs summarize Heinrich Muth, "Der pfälzische Kalvinismus und die brandenburgische Geheimratsordnung von 1604," *ZGO,* n.s., 68 (1959), 400–67; Volker Press, "Die 'Zweite Reformation' in der Kurpfalz," in Heinz Schilling, ed., *Die reformierte Konfessionalisierung in Deutschland: Das Problem der "Zweiten Reformation"* (Gütersloh, 1986), 104–29; and Rudolf von Thadden, "Die Fortsetzung des 'Reformationswerks' in

Brandenburg-Preußen," in ibid., 233–50; Mary Fulbrook, *Piety and Politics: Religion and the Rise of Absolutism in England, Württemberg, and Prussia* (Cambridge, 1983), 153–73.

11. Fulbrook, *Piety and Politics,* 154–55; Deppermann, *Pietismus,* 24–25, 71–72.

12. PrGStA, Rep. 148; on the orphanage founding, see August Hermann Francke, *Segens-volle Fußtapfen . . . Wahrhafte und umständliche Nachricht von dem Wäysen-hause . . .* (Halle, 1709).

13. PrGStA, Rep. 4A, Kammergericht. Only summaries of the cases survive. See also Fulbrook, *Piety and Politics,* 50–52.

14. Deppermann, *Pietismus,* 88–90.

15. Ibid., 100–108. About £1,406 sterling by 1720.

16. See the entries and discussion in August Langen, *Der Wortschatz des deutschen Pietismus* (Tübingen, [1954]; reprint, Tübingen, 1968).

17. The relationship of Pietism to capitalism has been much debated. For summaries of the conflicts, see Deppermann, *Pietismus,* 176–79, on the assessments by Max Weber and Carl Hinrichs; see also the disagreements between Carl Hinrichs, "Der Hallische Pietismus als politisch-soziale Reformbewegung des 18. Jahrhunderts," in Greschat, ed., *Zur neueren Pietismusforschung,* 243–58; and Gerhard Bondi, "Der Beitrag des Hallischen Pietismus zur Entwicklung des ökonomischen Denkens in Deutschland," in ibid., 259–93.

18. I have compared the pericopes to *The Interpreter's Dictionary of the Bible: An Illustrated Encyclopedia* (Nashville, Tenn., 1980); and to the sixty-four authors and their texts taken from Gottfried Mälzer, *Die Werke der württembergischen Pietisten des 17. und 18. Jahrhunderts: Verzeichnis der bis 1968 erschienenen Literatur* (Berlin, 1972). See Spener's somewhat vaguely formulated thoughts on a society where everyone fulfils his duty in his station and where Christian charity would redistribute goods to the needy, in Philipp Jakob Spener, *Pia Desideria . . . ,* ed. Kurt Aland (Leipzig, 1955), 30.

19. Gustav Clemens Schmelzeisen, "Polizeiordnungen," in Adalbert Erler and Ekkehard Kaufmann, eds., *Handwörterbuch zur deutschen Rechtsgeschichte,* (Berlin, 1971–   ), 3:1803–7, argues that "police" ordinances crossed willy-nilly into areas that were theoretically "Privatrecht."

20. On disagreements over how Halle's social reforms compared to other pietist experiments, see Udo Sträter and Friedrich de Boor's positions, which are given in Kurt Aland, "Der Pietismus und die soziale Frage," in idem, ed., *Pietismus und moderne Welt* (Witten, 1974), 99–137; Udo Sträter, "Pietismus und Sozialtätigkeit: Zur Frage nach der Wirkungsgeschichte des 'Waisenhauses' in Halle und des Frankfurter Armen-, Waisen- und Arbeitshauses," *PN* 8 (1982), 201–30. The term *privat Anstalt* (private institute) did not receive final definition in German discourse until the early nineteenth century. See Helmut Coing, *Europäisches Privatrecht,* vol. 1, Älteres Gemeines Recht (1500 bis 1800) (Munich, 1985), 265–68, and literature cited there.

21. See the accessible but somewhat one-sided view of Elaine Pagels, *Adam, Eve, and the Serpent* (New York, 1987), 98–126.

22. Gottfried Wilhelm Locher, *Der Eigentumsbegriff als Problem evangelischer Theologie* (Zürich, 1954), 22–31; Dieter Schwab, "Eigentum," in Otto Brunner et al., eds., *Geschichtliche Grundbegriffe: Historisches Lexikon zur politisch-sozialen Sprache in Deutschland* (Stuttgart, 1975), 3:65–115; Richard Schlatter, *Private Property: The History of an Idea* (New Brunswick, N.J., 1951), 77–123.

23. Edward A. Dowey, "Law in Luther and Calvin," *Theology Today* 41 (1984), 146–53.

24. The "busy Martha of Halle" is a reference to the incident in which the two sisters Mary and Martha received Jesus, Mary quitting her work to listen to his teaching, Martha indignant that she had to do the housework alone, only to be told that she should put aside worldly cares enough to listen while she had the chance (Luke 10:41–42). See Deppermann, *Pietismus,* 145–46 nn. 17–19, for further literature on mercantilism and manufactures at Halle.

25. Martin Schmidt, "Spener's Wiedergeburtslehre," in idem, *Wiedergeburt und Neuer Mensch: Gesammelte Studien zur Geschichte des Pietismus* (Witten, 1969), 168–70, 185; and idem, "August Hermann Francke's Stellung in der pietistischen Bewegung," in ibid. See also Lindberg's *Third Reformation,* 149–50, 153–54.

26. August Nebe, "Thomasius in seinem Verhältnis zu A. H. Francke," in Max Fleischman, ed., *Christian Thomasius Leben und Lebenswerk: Beiträge zur Geschichte der Universität Halle-Wittenberg* (Halle, 1931; reprint, Aalen, 1979), 383–420, quotation at 399; Hans Leube, *Orthodoxie und Pietismus: Gesammelte Studien* (Bielefeld, 1975), 122–23.

27. For Pastorius's connection to Spener and Straßburg, see Marion Dexter Learned, *The Life of Francis Daniel Pastorius: The Founder of Germantown* (Philadelphia, 1908), 85–90; see also Julius Friedrich Sachse, *The German Pietists of Provincial Pennyslvania* (Philadelphia, 1895); Elizabeth W. Fisher, " 'Prophesies and Revelations': German Cabbalists in Early Pennsylvania," *PMHB* 109 (1985), 299–333; Frankfurt Stadtarchiv, Sammlungen S 2/1516, Hiob Ludolff.

28. Johann Jakob Moser, *Rechtliches Bedenken von Privat-Versammlungen der Kinder Gottes . . .* [Legal reflection on the private meetings of God's children] (Tübingen, 1734).

29. "Eine heimliche Zusammenkunfft, unerlaubte Congregation, wird allzeit im bösen Verstand gebraucht" (Johann Heinrich Zedler, *Großes Vollständiges Universal-Lexikon,* vol. 6 [Halle, 1733], 1167.

30. As a jurist, Moser probably intended the first reading; however, in common usage the phrase "wenn man es so recht bedenkt," or "when one comes to think of it," implies that one is having second thoughts, and probably was read this way by nonjurists.

31. Reinhard Rürup, *Johann Jacob Moser: Pietismus und Reform* (Wiesbaden, 1963), 17–18, 32–51. See Mack Walker, *Johann Jakob Moser and the Holy Roman Empire of the German Nation* (Chapel Hill, 1981), 73–74, 124–25, on the distinctions between Württemberg Pietism and Prussian Pietism.

32. Robert Uhland, *Geschichte der Hohen Karlsschule in Stuttgart* (Stuttgart, 1953), 48–52.

33. Otto Borst, "Pietismus und Industrie," in Martin Blümcke, ed., *Abschied von der Dorfidylle? Ein Lesebuch vom Leben und Arbeiten im deutschen Südwesten in den letzten 200 Jahren* (Stuttgart, 1982), 186–95; Christoph Carl Ludwig von Pfeil, *Evangelische Herzensgesänge,* ed. Gustav Knack, 3 vols. (Berlin, 1856, 1858), 1:vii–xvii, 2:300–301; on the orphanage at Stuttgart, see Eduard Lempp, *Geschichte des Stuttgarter Waisenhauses* (Stuttgart, 1910); Gerhard Schäfer, " 'Das Gute bewahren, Abwege aber verhüten': Zur Geschichte des württembergischen Pietismus," *BWK* 82 (1982), 218–35, quotation at 223–24.

34. For the text of the Rescript, see Reyscher, ed., *Sammlung,* 14:641–52.

35. F. A. Weckherlin, *Wirtemberg. Pietismus. Schreiber. Schule. Und Erziehung und Aufklärung Überhaupt* (n.p., 1787), 13–14; also cited in Fulbrook, *Piety and Politics,* 149 n. 45.

36. Hasselhorn, *Altwürttembergische Pfarrstand.*

37. Martin Brecht, ed., *Kirchenordnung und Kirchenzucht in Württemberg vom 16. bis zum 18. Jahrhundert* (Stuttgart, 1967), 36–38; Heinrich Hermelink, *Geschichte der evangelischen Kirche in Württemberg von der Reformation bis zur Gegenwart* (Stuttgart, 1949), 153–70.

38. Heinrich Bechtel, *Wirtschaftsgeschichte Deutschlands,* vol. 2, *Vom Beginn des 16. biz zum Ende des 18. Jahrhunderts* (München, 1952), 28; Grube, *Stuttgarter Landtag,* chap. 9; Hartmut Lehmann, *Pietismus und weltliche Ordnung in Württemberg vom 17. bis zum 20. Jahrhundert* (Stuttgart, 1969), chap. 1; Martin Brecht, "Philip Jakob Spener und die Württembergische Kirche," in H. Liebing and K. Scholder, eds., *Geist und Geschichte der Reformation: Festgabe Hanns Rückert* (Berlin, 1966); Heinrich Fausel, "Von altlutherischer Orthodoxie zum Frühpietismus in Württemberg," *ZWL* 24 (1965), 309–28.

39. Fulbrook, *Piety and Politics,* 150–52; Sabean, *Property, Production,* 46–47, 68–70; Medick, "Teurung," 20.

40. Moser's essay, "Von Anwendung des Vermögens," is in Friedrich Carl von Moser, *Gesammelte Moralische und Politische Schriften,* 2 vols. (Frankfurt, 1763), 235–84, quotation at 264.

41. Georg Conrad Rieger, *Herzens-Postille: Predigten über alle Fest-, Sonn- und Feiertags-Evangelien,* 2d ed. (Beilefeld, 1843), quotations at 531, 170, 514, and 719–42; 936 for further examples. Also see idem, *Richtiger und leichter Weg zum Himmel,* 1st ed. (Stuttgart, 1744), 514; and, for a more detailed examination, Roeber, "Germans, Property, and the First Great Awakening."

42. Lehmann, *Pietismus und weltliche Ordnung,* 28–47, 68–125; Friedrich Fritz, "Konventikel in Württemberg von der Reformationszeit bis zum Edikt von 1743," *BWK* 49 (1949), 99–154; 50 (1950), 65–121; 51 (1951), 78–137; 52 (1952), 28–65; 53 (1953), 82–130; 54 (1954), 75–119; Hartmut Lehmann, "Pietismus und Wirtschaft in Calw am Anfang des 18. Jahrhunderts," *ZWL* 31 (1972), 249–77; Martin Brecht, "Philipp Matthäus Hahn und der Pietismus im mittleren Neckarraum," *BWK* 77 (1977), 101–31, at 103–5.

43. Lehmann, *Pietismus und weltliche Ordnung,* 15–17.

44. Lehmann has suggested that deep anxiety and group identity theory may account for seventeenth-century conventicles. My research in middle Neckar villages found no provisions in wills or estate partitions providing for even small bequests to keep such pietist groups going. Group identity theory seems not to explain much in the eighteenth century. See Hartmut Lehmann, " 'Absonderung' und 'Gemeinschaft' im frühen Pietismus: Allgemeinhistorische und sozialpsychologische Überlegungen zur Entstehung und Entwicklung des Pietismus," *PN* 4 (1977–78), 54–82, at 65, 68. Sabean found nothing on Pietism and property in Neckarhausen until the nineteenth century (*Property, Production,* 427–29).

45. For a use of social marginality and crisis theory to study a pietist community, see Findeisen, *Pietismus in Fellbach;* for doubts on the applicability of such theories to early Christianity and later renewal movements, see Bernard McGuinn, ed. and trans., *Apocalyptic Spirituality* (New York, 1979), 7, which suggests that the invocation of crisis theory is a "roadblock to further thought"; Kenelm Burridge, "Reflections on Prophecy and Prophetic Groups," *Semeia* 21 (1982), 99–102; Abraham J. Malherbe, *Social Aspects of Early Christianity* (Baton Rouge, 1977); Kilian McDonnell, *Charismatic Renewal and the Churches* (New York, 1976), 17–40.

46. Fulbrook, *Piety and Politics,* 68–69.

47. The 1781 visit was described in "Reise nach Constanz, von Herrn Prof Sander," 3:217–19; and the earlier visit (1764) in "Erste Reise in Westphalen," Meiners, *Beschriebung einer Reise nach Stuttgart,* 35, 59–66.

48. For distinctions within Württemberg, see the initial surveys of housing types in *Referatsammlung: Heimattage Baden-Württemberg. Bäuerliche Freilichtmuseen in Baden-Württemberg* (Eßlingen, 1980); Hermann Kolesch, *Das altoberschwäbische Bauernhaus* (Tübingen, 1967); Max Lohse, *Vom Bauernhaus in Württemberg und angrenzenden Gebieten* (Heidelberg, 1932). For adjoining regions, see Habicht, *Dorf und Bauernhaus,* 173–301; Heinrich Schneider, *Das Baugesicht in sechs Dörfern der Pfalz* (Marburg, 1971); Helmut Weyand, *Untersuchungen zur Entwicklung saarländischer Dörfer und ihrer Fluren* (Saarbrücken, 1970), 130–33. The emergence of divided rooms in more elaborate structures occurred earlier on the lower Rhine and in lower Saxony; see Adelhart Zippelius, *Das Bauernhaus am unteren deutschen Niederheim* (Wuppertal, 1957); Wilhelm Brednich, *Haus und Hof: Westfälischer Bauern* (Münster, 1980).

49. Eickemeyer, *Über die Erbauung der Dörfer,* table 3, and fig. 6.

50. For examples of more elaborate houses of the wealthy, see the texts and photographs in Erwin Huxhold, *Das Bürgerhause zwischen Schwarzwald und Odenwald* (Tübingen, 1980). On the important distinction between "personal" space (surrounding both the body and one's possessions) and "privacy" (in contrast to a public realm), see George Duby and Philippe Braunstein, "The Emergence of the Individual," in Ariès and Duby, eds., *History of Private Life,* 2:509–630; Alain Collomp, "Families: Habitations and Cohabitations," in ibid., 3:493–529.

51. Ernst Christmann and Julius Krämer, eds., *Pfälzisches Wörterbuch,* 4

vols. (Wiesbaden, 1965–86), 1:1235. See also, on the irrelevance of the term in eighteenth-century usage, Ernst Ochs et al., eds., *Badisches Wörterbuch,* 2 vols. (Lahr, 1925–40, 1942–74), 1:329.

52. Adelbert von Keller, *Schwäbisches Wörterbuch,* [founded by Hermann Fischer], 6 vols. (Tübingen, 1904–36), 1:1426; for an example of the written use of the term, see Moser's pamphlet, *Rechtliches Bedencken,* or Oberboihingen Kirchenkonvent, 17 April 1739, investigation of premarital pregnancy of Barbara Hausmann by Catholic dayworker of Eßlingen.

53. Oberboihingen Kirchenkonvent, 20 January 1737.

54. Friedrich Heinz Schmidt-Ebhausen, "Kirchenkonvents-Protokolle und ihre Auswertung für die Ortsgeschichte," in *Württembergisches Jahrbuch für Volkskunde, 1965–69* (Stuttgart, 1969), 94–98.

55. This summarizes the conclusions of Kirchenkonvent activities in Derendingen, just outside Tübingen (Martin Brecht, "Die Kirchengemeinde Derendingen im 17. und 18. Jahrhundert," in idem, ed., *Kirchenordnung und Kirchenzucht,* 83–104); see also Sabean, *Property, Production,* 68–69, 102–3, 428–30.

56. Seißen Village Archive, Seißen Kirchenkonvent, 1729, May 1738.

57. Ibid., 1731.

58. This conclusion and the next paragraph are drawn from my reading of the Seißen, Oberboihingen, and Reudern Kirchenkonvent proceedings from the 1730s to the 1760s, along with Brecht, "Kirchengemeinde Derendingen"; for Grötzingen, see the summary of church court activities in Otto Schuster, *Heimatgeschichte der Stadt Grötzingen* (Nürtingen, 1929), 160–65.

59. Seißen Village Archive, Seißen Lichtstubenordung, 4 June 1727. These rules were repeated again or added to in 1774, 1789, 1791, and 1802; similar rules, and offenses against them, can be found in other villages.

60. For many instances, see Sabean, *Property, Production,* 329–34.

61. Oberboihingen Kirchenkonvent, 31 March 1749.

62. Ibid. The outcome of the case is not clear from surviving records. For an example of blaming a Catholic offender, see ibid., 16 March 1749, investigation against Catharine Sommerin.

63. NStA, Gerichts-(Amts)- u. Gemeinderatsprotokolle, Kasten 23, Fach 3–5, 1586–1925, 27 October 1753, with continuations to November. Because of an open wound on his foot, and sickness, Manhardt was taken out of the tower near the city baths and allowed the comforts of the citizen's tower (*Bürger-Thurm*). Manhardt and Braunlen were residents but not citizens; the younger mischief maker, Solomon Schmolen, seems to have worked in, or been from, Neckarhausen.

64. This summarizes Carsten Küther, *Räuber und Gauner in Deutschland: Das organisierte Bandenwesen im 18. und frühen 19. Jahrhundert,* 2d ed. (Göttingen, 1986).

65. Gerhard Florey, "Bericht über die Mission die im Pfleggericht Goldegg vom 3. September bis zum 27. Oktober 1733 gehalten wurde," *Mitteilungen der Gesellschaft für Salzburger Landeskunde* 124 (1984), 489–97; Friederike

Zaisberger, "Der Salzburger Bauer und die Reformation," ibid., at 393–94, on book culture among the Salzburgers who sold property in order to buy Lutheran books secretly before the 1731–32 exile.

66. Johannes Stegmaier, *Schultheiß in Magenheim: Ein biographischer Beitrag zur Sitten und Rechtsgeschichte des schwäbischen Volkes* (Stuttgart, 1840), 5–6.

67. Hildegard Neumann, *Der Bücherbesitz der Tübinger Bürger von 1750 bis 1850: Ein Beitrag zur Bildungsgeschichte des Kleinbürgertums; Die Bücherverzeichnisse in den Vermögensinventaren und Erbteilungen der Tübinger Bürger aus den Jahren 1750–60, 1800–10, 1840–50* (Munich, 1978).

68. This paragraph summarizes Angela Bischoff-Luithlen's compilation of all inventories for Feldstetten bei Münsingen from 1650 to 1850, "Auszüge aus den Inventur- und Teilungsakten der Gemeinde Feldstetten Kreis Münsingen," typescript, in Universität Tübingen (Tübingen, Germany), Ludwig-Uhland-Institut.

69. This summarizes my reading of inventories for 1720–60 in the village archives of Seißen, Bodelshausen, Lauffen/Eyach, Schlaitdorf, Grötzingen, and Freudenstadt (all of these villages are in Württemberg). Full runs of inventories seldom exist; the books inventoried do not reveal those already given to children or relatives as predeath gifts. I believe the above to be a reasonably accurate summary of the typical household for this area at mid-century. Unless one can find the descriptions of estate at first marriage (*Eventual-Abteilungen*), one cannot be sure what was in the household. I have tried to search out the inventories at first marriage where possible.

70. I have tested some three hundred surviving inventories for this village for 1758–84: LAS F 11/1211–14, 1187–92, 1204–10. The Ausfautheiakten are now ordered alphabetically by family name, one hundred inventories to each box. In the Kraichgau villages nearest to Württemberg, pietist tracts are more numerous and common—as they also are in Schwaigern, within Württemberg and on the border with the Kraichgau. Titles match the lists from deeper within Württemberg.

71. HHStAW, Abt. 179.2038, Nassauer Ämter, Inventare, Nachläße, Bü 17, Camberg, 1765–67, no. 467, Dietz, 1769; nos. 467, 570, citation of Maria Elizabeth, widow Seybert, estate at remarriage. These large libraries were calculated to be worth some seven to ten Gulden, nearly half the value of a small acreage at this date. I have read all inventories under this heading as well as those contained in HHStAW, Abt. 132, no. 11, 1711–42, for Burgschwandbach; and no. 193a, 1 to 194 for Odenbach, with identical results. Unfortunately, the inventories for this region were not as carefully written up as those for Württemberg; prices and even titles are sometimes missing. Nonetheless, the total absence of books in the most humble estates is striking by comparison with the Württemberg villages or the Kraichgau.

72. Heiner Faulenbach, "Die Anfänge des Pietismus bei den Reformierten in Deutchland," *PN* 4 (1977–78), 190–233.

73. J. Wallmann, "Labadismus und Pietismus: Die Einflüsse des niederländischen Pietismus auf die Entstehung des Pietismus in Deutchland," in J. Van den Berg and J. P. van Dooren, eds., *Pietismus und Reveil: Referate der*

internationalen Tagung: Der Pietismus in der Niederlanden und seine internationalen Beziehungen (Leiden, 1978), 141–68.

74. *Reichs-Post-Amts-Zeitung,* 13 May 1741 for quotation; 4 December 1741. Except where otherwise indicated, this paragraph and the three that follow summarize my reading of all issues from 1740–41, 1743, 1744–48, 1760–62, 1764, and 1768–69 from the most complete files of the paper, in Thurn und Taxis Fürstliche Bibliothek (Regensburg). The advertisements usually occur on the final page; by the mid-1740s they ran two full pages; after 1750, more. Besides political and trade news, the paper printed inheritance notices, advertisements for property sales, and requests for news of disappeared or deserted soldiers or tradesmen.

75. AFSt, Haupt Abt. C 788 43, 20 August 1717. Whether this Gentzell of Ingelfingen was related to the Gensels (two Jacobs, one Matthias) in North America who came from Ebingen, I cannot determine. The Halle factor makes no reference in surviving letters to North America or relatives there.

76. Lehmann, *Pietismus,* 17–19, suggests the two types of pietist for this period.

77. Immanuel Gottlob Brastberger, *Evangelische Zeugnisse der Wahrheit* . . . (Reutlingen, 1758; reprint, Stuttgart, 1762) Brastberger was not only popular among pietists along the middle Neckar: copies of his sermons also came to America with the Lohrmann family of South Carolina. I wish to thank them and Brent Holcomb for alerting me to the family copy. Brastberger's sermons were reprinted in the Pennsylvania area; see, for the 1834 and 1854 editions of *Evangelische Zeugnisse,* nos. 183 and 184 in the catalog *Keystone Ten: Die Alte Zeit. German Americana and Classics of the Reformation* (Glen Rock, Pa., 1989).

78. Brastberger, *Evangelische Zeugnisse,* quotation at 282.

79. Ibid.; see introduction, vii; then especially his sermons for Holy Thursday (Matt. 26:26–28), 394–96; for Second Advent (Luke 21:23–26), 18–20; on stewardship for the Ninth Sunday after Trinity, 685–702; quotation at 394.

80. Philipp Mattäus Hahn, *Die Kornwestheimer Tagebücher, 1772–1777,* ed. Martin Brecht and Rudolf F. Paulus (Berlin, 1979), 136–37. Cf. Brastberger's treatment in *Evangelische Zeugnisse,* 204–7.

Chapter 4   Marginal Property-Holders, Brokers of Liberty

1. Alsheim Magistrate to Electoral Government at Heidelberg, 8 December 1685, reprinted in George Frederick Newman et al., comps., *Letters from Our Palatine Ancestors, 1644–1689* (Hershey, Pa., 1984), 110.

2. W. H. Quarrell and Margaret More, trans. and eds., *London in 1710 from the Travels of Zacharias Conrad von Uffenbach* (London, 1934), 27–28.

3. See David Cressy, *Coming over: Migration and Communication between England and New England in the Seventeenth Century* (Cambridge, 1987), 144–48; on the symbolic significance of journeys, see Victor W. Turner, *The Ritual*

Process: Structure and Anti-Structure (Chicago, 1969), 94–130; idem, *Dramas, Fields, and Metaphors: Symbolic Action in Human Society* (Ithaca, N.Y., 1974), 166–69, 200–204, 321–33. Cressy suggests (drawing upon Turner) that ships became special communities freed of conventional social considerations. Whatever truth the insight holds for the English migration, the voyage did not make this impression on the Germans.

4. *Journals of Muhlenberg* 2:564, 565.

5. For the forty-three hundred migrants from the Rheinpfalz, Saarland, Baden, and Breisach, see Werner Hacker, *Auswanderungen aus Baden und dem Breisgau: Obere und mittlere rechtsseitige Oberrheinlande im 18. Jahrhundert archivalisch dokumentiert* (Stuttgart, 1980); idem, *Auswanderungen aus der Rheinpfalz und dem Saarland im 18. Jahrhundert* (Sigmaringen, 1987). The same pattern applies to the Kraichgau: the five hundred-plus emigrants documented are also overwhelmingly family members related to each other (Hacker, *Kurpfälzische Auswanderer*). See also Farley Grubb, "German Immigration to Pennsylvania, 1709 to 1820," *Journal of Interdisciplinary History* 20 (1990), 417–36. Before 1760 most German (in contrast to English), migration was in family groups; even for the more than half who entered some form of servitude, family bonds remained largely intact. Migration siphoned off about 20 percent of population increase in southwest Germany. See Wolfgang von Hippel, *Auswanderung aus Südwestdeutschland: Studien zur württembergischen Auswanderung und Auswanderungspolitik im 18. und 19. Jahrhundert* (Stuttgart, 1984), 27–33.

6. Farley Grubb, "The Market Structure of Shipping German Immigrants to Colonial America," *PMHB* 111 (1987), 27–48.

7. Niedersächsische Universitäts- und Staatsbibliothek Göttingen, Cod. Ms. Hist. 821, "Wohlmeinende Nachricht, wie sich die Teutsche, die nach Pensilvanien reisen wollen, zu verhalten haben," 19 October 1749, "L.M." The duke of Württemberg ordered copies of this document spread over his entire duchy in 1750 to discourage emigration. The pamphlet is reprinted in its entirety in von Hippel, *Auswanderung,* 294–99.

8. *Korrespondenz Mühlenbergs* 1:235; AFSt, 4 G 6, letter of van den Smithen Söhne, 19 August 1774; Johann Reinhardt Maurenbrecher to Halle, "Onkost-Reekening . . . ," 8 August 1774.

9. Marianne S. Wokeck, "Promoters and Passengers: The German Immigrant Trade, 1683–1775," in Richard S. Dunn and Mary Maples Dunn, eds., *The World of William Penn* (Philadelphia, 1986), 259–78; Abbot Emerson Smith, *Colonists in Bondage: White Servitude and Convict Labor in America, 1607–1776* (Chapel Hill, 1947), 3–25, 50–52; David W. Galenson, *White Servitude in Colonial America: An Economic Analysis* (Cambridge, 1981), 13–15, 233; Hans-Jürgen Grabbe, "Das Ende des Redemptioner-Systems in den Vereinigten Staaten," *Amerikastudien/American Studies* 29 (1984), 277–96; Farley Grubb, "The Incidence of Servitude in Trans-Atlantic Migration, 1771–1804," *Explorations in Economic History* 22 (1985), 316–39; idem, "Redemptioner Immigration to Pennsylvania; Evidence on Contract Choice and Profitability," *Journal of Economic History* 46 (1986), 407–18.

10. This simplifies Bennion, "Flight from the Reich"; Marianne S. Wokeck, "A Tide of Alien Tongues: The Flow and Ebb of German Immigration to Pennsylvania, 1683–1776" (Ph.D. diss., Temple University, 1982); William I. Hull, *William Penn and the Dutch Quaker Migration to Pennsylvania* (Swarthmore, 1935); and Marianne S. Wokeck, "Harnessing the Lure of the 'Best Poor Man's Country'": The Dynamics of German-Speaking Immigration to British North America, 1683–1783," in Ida Altman and James Horn, eds., *To Make America: European Emigration in the Early Modern Period* (Berkeley, Calif., 1991), 204–43. The migration of the first families from Krefeld to North America was part of an older, internal migration back and forth from the country of Mörs, with Hollanders settling in the Palatinate around Kriegsheim, near Worms. See both Samuel Whitaker Pennypacker, *The Settlement of Germantown, Pennsylvania, and the Beginning of German Immigration to North America* (Lancaster, Pa., 1899); and Wolf, *Urban Village.*

11. On the debate over population estimates and ethnic percentages, see Thomas L. Purvis et al., "The Population of the United States, 1790: A Symposium," *WMQ*, 3d ser., 41 (1984), 85–135; Grubb's estimates (in "German Immigration") placing Pennsylvania's German-speaking population at nearly 50 percent seem more plausible. See also Georg Fertig, "Migration from the German-speaking Parts of Central Europe, 1600–1800: Estimates and Explanations" (John F. Kennedy Institute for North American Studies Working Paper no. 38, 1991), 9–11, which reviews various means of estimating gross numbers for the German-speaking migration to North America. I find an estimate of 100,000 immigrants in 1683–1800 too low and think that 114,000 to 120,000 is more likely. For the purpose of comparing attempted inheritance recovery to total numbers of immigrants (below), I have accepted the more conservative estimates.

12. Benjamin Franklin, "Observations concerning the Increase of Mankind," in *The Papers of Benjamin Franklin,* ed. Leonard W. Labaree, 28 vols. (New Haven, 1959–90), 4:234.

13. Halle authorities engaged Daniel Falckner to write the first guide to North American settlement, the *Curieuse Nachricht von Pennsylvania,* in 1702; Falckner's brother had contributed to the Halle hymnal of 1697, perhaps bringing the two to Francke's attention. Harrsch's role as a publicist encouraging emigration so alarmed Halle that they engaged their nonordained preacher in London, Anton Wilhelm Böhme, to write *Das verlangte, nicht erlangte Canaan* (Frankfurt, 1711) to counter Kocherthal's *Ausführlich und umständlicher Bericht von der berühmten Landschafft Carolina* (Frankfurt, 1709).

14. This paragraph and the two that follow are based on von Hippel, *Auswanderung,* 94–101; Hacker, *Auswanderungen aus Rheinpfalz,* 31–35, 45–49, 83–86; Hacker, *Kurpfälzische Auswanderer,* 19–27.

15. Klaus Wust, "Palatines and Switzers for Virginia, 1705–1738: Costly Lessons for Promoters and Emigrants," *Yearbook of German-American Studies* 19 (1984), 43–55.

16. This paragraph and the two that follow are based on the following sources: Martina Sprengel, "Studien zur Nordamerikaauswanderung in der

ersten Hälfte des 18. Jahrhunderts: Nassau-Oranien" (M.A. thesis, Universität Köln, 1984), 12–14, 45–47, 104–20, 132–35; and on the miners, B. C. Holtzclaw, *Ancestry and Descendants of the Nassau-Siegen Immigrants to Virginia, 1714–1750* (Orange, Va., 1978). For the Lutherans, initial patents of land on Robinson Run averaged about four hundred acres; for the Siegeners, between four hundred and one thousand acres (Eugene M. Scheel, *Culpeper: A Virginia County's History through 1920* [Culpeper, Va., 1982], 17–23).

17. Joseph Friedrich Abert, "Die Vorschläge Karl Theodor von Dalbergs zur Verbesserung der Armenpolizei im Hochstift Würzburg, 1779," *Archiv des historischen Vereins für Unterfranken und Aschaffenburg* 54 (1912), 198.

18. Montague Spencer Ginseppi, "Naturalizations," *Publications of the Huguenot Society of London* 24 (1921), 8–9; Erich Keyser, ed., *Deutsches Städtebuch Rheinland-Pfalz und Saarland*, vol. 4, *Südwest Deutschland* (Stuttgart, 1964), chap. 4.3.

19. Mack Walker, *The German Home Towns: Community, State, and General Estate, 1648–1871* (Ithaca, N.Y., 1971), 116.

20. Robert Selig, *Räutige Schafe und geizige Hirten: Studien zur Auswanderung aus dem Hochstift Würzburg im 18. Jahrhundert und ihre Ursachen* (Würzburg, 1988), 161–62.

21. Ibid., pp. 114–18, 165–71.

22. The conclusions come from my study of R.u.I. and Ausfautheiakten in LAS and GLAK. Other early Virginia arrivals, the Lotspeichs from Frankenthal, between Worms and Mannheim, also fit the general pattern: members of a tailor's family, several emigrated, following the example of their father, who had emigrated to Frankenthal from Mahlberg, in Baden. See Don Yoder, ed., *Rheinland Emigrants: Lists of German Settles in Colonial America* (Baltimore, 1981), 61.

23. GLAK, 229/85386, Reihen, Johann Valentin Schuch; 229/11195, Weiler, Conrad Hildebrand; 229/118807, Zuzenhausen, Johann Georg Kirsch; also 229/118815, Zuzenhausen, Johann Dietrich Kirsch; 229/118823, Zuzenhausen, Hans Georg Koberstein; Stadtarchiv Schwaigern, R.u.I., 15 March 1757, Johan Georg Hölle, 21 March–18 April 1757, Johannes Lober; 10 April 1749, Christian Abendschön; 11 July 1746, Rosina Abendschön; 7 January 1754, Conrad Ofner; 17 December 1755, Johan Georg Luttmann; 19 January 1750, Peter Lohrman, letter in testament of Friedrich Brettgauer; 21 March 1749, Jacob Baumgärtner's widow; the partition and recovery of inheritance of Gottlieb Böckle's father is missing from the records although indicated in the index for folio 30 A 872, 1790. My survey of the inventories began with those for the 1720s and continued through those for 1791–92.

24. SArS B5, Gewährbuch, 1720–30, 26 August 1729, 11 November 1729; B6, Gewährbuch, 1730–35, 17 March 1730, 14 April 1730.

25. *Die Stadt und die Landkreise Heidelberg und Mannheim, Amtliche Kreisbeschreibung*, vol. 3, *Die Stadt Mannheim und die Gemeinden des Landkreises Mannheim* (Mannheim, 1970), 442–66; Gabriel Hartmann, "Emigrants from Dossenheim in the 18th Century," trans. Don Yoder, in Yoder, ed., *Rhineland Emigrants*, 63–65.

26. GLAK 229/19936, Dossenheimer Acta, 1–29.

27. Ittlingen Village Archives, Bürgerbuch 2. (Book 1 is missing, book 2 is incomplete, with letters A and B missing; assessments are for an unspecified date; on the basis of internal evidence, they are most likely for 1740.) A later 1759 assessment (Ittlingen Zinß und Fleisch Buch über alle zur Pfarr-Competenth gehörige gefälle . . .) reveals the extensive holdings of Jacob Geiger, but in the absence of the partitions of estate, all that is clear is that Geiger was taxed on lands in fruit, cereal, and vineyards some distance from Ittlingen. Like Johann Georg Hoffmann, the innkeeper, Geiger owned his own house; most of the emigrants from Ittlingen were renters, though the Grobs, the Kilians, and some other families were the children of persons who owned half a house or were tenants on one of the *Höfe.*

28. Mark Häberlein, "Vom Oberrheim zum Susquehanna: Studien zur badischen Auswanderung nach Pennsylvania im 18. Jahrhundert" (Ph.D. diss., Universität Augsburg, 1990), 61, table 9; 62–64.

29. Ittlingen Village Archive, Verwaltungs-Sachen Generalia: Anschlag und Resolvierung bey der Ittlinger Schatzungs Renovation; Bürgerbuch 2.

30. Josef Brettenthaler, "Die Wiederbesiedlung," *Reformation, Emigration: Protestanten in Salzburg* (Salzburg, 1981), 172–79; Gerhard Florey, *Geschichte der Salzburger Protestanten und ihrer Emigration 1731/32* (Vienna, 1977), 166–67.

31. See Theodor Mayer, ed., *Beiträge zur Siedlungs-, Verfassungs- und Wirtschaftsgeschichte von Salzburg: Festschrift zum 65. Geburtstag von Herbert Klein* (Salzburg, 1965); Wilhelm Brauneder, "Die Entwicklung des bäuerlichen Erbrechtes," in Alfons Dworsky and Hartmut Schider, eds., *Der ehre Erbhof: Analyse einer jungen Tradition* (Salzburg, 1980), 55–65.

32. Heinrich Siegel, *Das Güterrecht der Ehegatten in Stiftslande Salzburg: Ein Beitrag zur Geschichte des deutschen ehelichen Güterrechtes* (Vienna, 1882); Johannes W. Pichler, *Die ältere ländliche salzburger Eigentumsordnung* (Salzburg, 1979); Heinrich Siegel and Karl Tomaschek, eds., *Die salzburgische Taidinge* (Vienna, 1870), 217.

33. Renate Wilson, "Halle and Ebenezer: Pietism, Agriculture, and Commerce in Colonial Georgia" (Ph.D. diss., University of Maryland, 1988), 12, 99–100, 143–49.

34. Lonsee Village Archive, Gemeinde Rechnungen, 1705–54.

35. Altheim Village Archives, Steur-Beschreibung Söglingen und Zähringen, 1750. No records survive for Langenau, which sent some thirty-one emigrants to America between 1750 and 1754; no records of partitions of estate survive for Lonsee or Bernstadt, and in the villages where partitions do survive, they are fragmentary and mostly unordered and unindexed. The choice of the villages was determined by counting the emigrants listed in Werner Hacker, "Auswanderung aus dem Territorium der Reichsstadt Ulm," *Ulm und Oberschwaben* 42–43 (1977–78), 161–257; most of the total of fifty-seven given in Hacker's paper came from Langenau, Weidenstetten, and neighboring villages.

36. Friederich Krebs, "New Materials on 18th Century Emigration from

Württemberg," ed. Don Yoder, in Don Yoder, ed., *Rhineland Emigrants, 43–44.* I have checked the *Pflegschaftsrechnungen* (records of estates under guardianship) for Iflingen (just outside Freudenstadt) and the partitions of estate for fifteen of these emigrants. At marriage, most brought between 300 and 600 Gulden into the common property holdings; after payment of dues and debts, little was left.

37. Lauffen/Eyach Village Archive, Grundstücksbeschreibung, 1714, 1737; Teilungsakten, 1689–1817, 20 September 1731, Bitzer-Treuckin; 10 May 1734, Philip Rominger. Compilations for the area are from Don Yoder, ed., "Emigrants from Wuerttembertg: The Adolf Gerber Lists," in idem, ed., *Pennsylvania German Immigrants, 1709–1786: Lists Consolidated from Yearbooks of the Pennsylvania German Folklore Society* (Baltimore, 1980), 1–137.

38. Seißen Village Archive, Teilungen, 4 February 1766, 13 March 1792. Seißen produced the largest number (27) of the 45 emigrants from Württemberg's eastern Swabian towns who chose America. The balance of the 1,436 left for Hungary, Prussia, Russia, or other lands within the Reich (Werner Hacker, *Auswanderungen aus Oberschwaben im 17. und 18. Jahrhundert archivalisch dokumentiert* [Stuttgart, 1977]).

39. My selection of local archives is based on the survey by von Hippel, *Auswanderung,* 47 n. 112. The 385 persons emigrating between 1746 and 1773 came from Grötzingen, Neckartenzlingen, Neuffen, and Oberboihingen. As von Hippel notes, most (some 69 percent) of the Württemberg emigrants were handworkers; many of these were also marginal property holders. See also, on average property holdings, Sabean, *Property, Production,* 7 n. 7.

40. Schuster, *Heimatsgeschichte der Stadt Grötzingen,* 161–68.

41. Grötzingen Village Archives, Teilungen, Elizabeth Jäcklen, 1762; see Yoder, ed., "Emigrants from Wuerttemberg," 71.

42. Reiff, *Neckartenzlingen,* 93, 120–25; of the documented seventeen Grötzingers in the Gerber lists arriving in Pennsylvania, ten were householders listed in the 1721 assessments, indicating their original status as householders, and gradual improverishment over the period 1721–49; Grötzingen Village Archives, Teilungen, 12 February 1740, 27 April 1753; on Neckarhausen, see Neckarhausen Village Archives, Teilungen, 19 August 1746, Johann Jacob Thumm. The evaluation at the time of Thumm's emigration is missing from the Teilungen. I have consulted archives in selected villages of the Palatinate with identical results. For Mußbach, Lachen, Weissenheim, and Mühlhoffen-Billigheim, I have surveyed several hundred partitions of estate at LAS and find no significant difference in the standing of emigrants from what is described above for the Neckar or Kraichgau emigrants (LAS A 2 1432/1433; A 2 309; A 2/1674, pp. 1745–55; F 11/1211–14 and 1192–10).

43. HStASt a 211, Bü. 673, 30 September 1750, query 19.

44. NStA, Gerichts-(Amts)- u. Gemeinderatsprotokolle, Kasten 23, Fach 3–5, 1586–1925, 208r, February 1755; 215b; 259b–260. Other poor persons became the object of charity: e.g., Paul Wittib, the gravedigger whose sons left for Pennsylvania, was by 1755 receiving four Kreuzer and one loaf of bread per week in charity (Bürgerrechtsverzichten, 1700–1769, Kasten 24,

no. 64, 25 May 1753). For the deaths of children, see Oberboihingen Parish Archives, Kirchenbücher, Totenbuch, 1688–1779, entries for March–June 1751; the families who later emigrated—the Haussmanns, Schmids, and Fromms—were among those who lost children (Yoder, ed., "Emigrants from Wuerttemberg," 3–137).

45. Braun, *Entwicklungstendenzen in Rheinland-Pfalz,* 36–40, 86–98.

46. Willi Alter, ed., *Pfalzatlas: Im Auftrag der pfälzischen Gesellschaft zur förderung der Wissenschaften* (Speyer, 1963), maps 9, 58, 86. Few records exist for Oppenheim, none for Oberamt Alzey; Mannheim's archives were destroyed, leaving what remains at LAS for the area around Neustadt as the basis for analyses. For emigration figures, see Annette Kunselman Burgert, *Eighteenth Century Emigrants from German-Speaking Lands to North America,* vol. 2, *The Western Palatinate* (Birdsboro, Pa., 1985), 12–22, 348–60.

47. LAS F 11/1187–1209, Mühlhoffen and Billingheim Ausfautheiakten; the inventories are boxed (about one hundred to the box) alphabetically; my conclusions are based on reading them for the period 1720–80.

48. Samuel Urlsperger, comp., *Detailed Reports . . . ,* ed. and trans. George Fenwick Jones (Athens, Ga., 1972–   ), 7:159, 9:64, 10:85, 11:104; Hacker, "Auswanderer aus Ulm," 231.

49. Urlsperger, comp., *Detailed Reports,* 11:39, 109; 9:27.

50. Wilson, "Halle and Ebenezer," 26–65; 334–54; Urlsperger, comp., *Detailed Reports,* 7:116, 228; 8:140–41, 191, 199, 212–13, 285, 459, 494; 9:29, 64; 10:28, 51; 11:101, 20.

51. Frankfurt Stadtarchiv, Kal.15/Handelsadreßbuch; no earlier copies of the city directory survive; this copy is for 1773. Advertisements from *Ordentliche wochentliche Kaiserliche Reichs-Post-Amts-Zeitung* (hereafter cited as *Reichs-Post-Amts-Zeitung*), 1740–85.

52. Stoever details these exchanges in his will, probated both in Philadelphia and again in 1739 after the pastor's death at sea. See the copy made first in Philadelphia on 20 March 1738/9 and then entered again in Orange County on 24 May 1739, in VSLAD, Orange County Will Book A, 83–89.

53. Hacker, *Auswanderungen aus Rheinpfalz,* 242, 565; LAS A 2 1309, Verlassenschaften, Inventare, 28. Lachen lay on an advantageous route; the objections here seemed to stem from the use of the booksellers themselves.

54. Weidenstetten Village Archive, Teilungen, with extracts from the *Amtsprotocollbücher* (district minute books), letters from Sailer enclosed.

55. The Edenkoben conclusions are drawn from the lists of emigrants in the card catalog at the Center for the History of the Palatinate (Kaiserslautern, Germany); the various villages mentioned occur repeatedly in the lists already mentioned above.

56. Darmstadt's records for the eighteenth century were destroyed in World War II; for a surviving instance of an interest in inheritance, see the letter of Georg Müller of Madenheid, Berks County, 18 April 1792, nearly twenty years after his emigration in 1773 (Hessisches Staatsarchiv Darmstadt, G 28 Groß-Umstadt F 276). I wish to thank Dr. Jürgen Rainer Wolf for his aid. On Halle's relationship with Darmstadt and the extensive collections

(sixty-three pounds sterling) taken up in Darmstadt on behalf of Pennsylvania, see AFSt 4 F 10, 1744. As late as 1792 Pastor J. H. C. Helmuth of Philadelphia inquired on behalf of his parishioner Andreas Braun for an inheritance in Darmstadt, asking the city recorder to investigate (AFSt 4 G 9, pp. 167–70, 20 July 1792, 31 December 1792).

57. Hacker, *Auswanderungen aus Rheinpfalz,* 209.

58. Wokeck, "Tide of Alien Tongues," 91 n. 94.

59. These figures draw on all of Hacker's published lists, my own surveys of the village archives, and the surviving cases in the archives at Speyer, Karslruhe, Stuttgart, Ludwigsburg, Wertheim, Wiesbaden, Koblenz, Darmstadt, Hamburg, and Halle. For 170, more or less, complete documentation exists; for the balance, reference to the recovery in a letter or a mention by a court officer provides the only clue. An exhaustive search is beyond any single researcher's capacity; no one, for example, has yet read through all the Ausfautheiakten for the Pfalz at LAS.

60. For details, see Roeber, "Origins of German-American Concepts of Property," 147–48.

61. A. L. Schlözer, *Briefwechsel* (Göttingen, 1777), pt. 2, Heft 8, p. 112. On Schlözer, see Hermann Wellenreuther, "Mutmaßungen über ein Defizit Göttingens Geschichtswissenschaft und die angelsächsische Welt," in idem and Hartmut Boockmann, eds., *Geschichtswissenschaft in Göttingen: Eine Vorlesungsreihe* (Göttingen, 1987), 261–86, at 263–64.

62. The classic attempt at distinguishing between "push" and "pull" factors among German emigrants is Hans Fenske, "International Migration: Germany in the Eighteenth Century," *Central European History* 13 (1980), 332–47. Until a systematic survey of eighteenth-century circulars and pamphlets that encouraged emigration, is done in all major German repositories, no real estimate of the impact such literature had can be hazarded. See also the confirmation of the general pattern of marginalization and repeated waves of migration in Hans Ulrich Pfister, *Die Auswanderung aus dem Knonauer Amt, 1648–1750: Ihr Ausmass, ihre Strukturen und ihre Bedingungen* (Zürich, 1987).

63. Hacker, *Kurpfälzische Auswanderer,* 169.

64. Wilhelm Störmer, "Ländliche Betriebsgrößen in der Grafschaft Wertheim II: Die Orte Kreuzwertheim, Oberwittbach, Altfeld, Glasofen, Eichenfürst und Steinmark in den wertheimischen Lagerbüchern um 1710," *Wertheimer Jahrbuch* n.s., 36 (1986), 133–48; Yoder, ed., *Pennsylvania German Immigrants,* 214, 276–82.

65. Heilbronn Stadtarchiv, Raths-Protocoll, 1740–57, RP 143–68, p. 279, 1754.

66. HStASt A 211, Bü. 673, A.2; Koch may have been the son of the Swedish merchant Peter Koch, who died in 1749 after a long career as *Vorsteher* of the Swedish Lutherans in New York. On Peter, see *Korrespondenz Mühlenbergs,* vol. 1.

67. HStASt A 211, Bü. 673, p. 26, query 7.

68. For an example, see the receipt signed by Christian Martins in 1759 acknowledging Halle's role in recovering the inheritance of four hundred

Gulden for his wife (*Korrespondenz Mühlenbergs* 2:362 n. 20). Many variants of the Gensels' family name (e.g., Gensel, Genßell, Gänsel) appear in documents. For the sake of simplicity, I have used "Gensel" throughout.

69. Ibid., 2:299.

70. AFSt 4 F 5, Pastor Brunnholtz to Halle authorities, 3 March 1752, details Landenberger's ties to Heilbronn, where the Schmal family who built the Philadelphia organ had also built one in 1726 for Reutlingen, the imperial city not far from Balingen in Landenberger's Württemberg. Mittelberger was paid four Gulden for sending to the city of Heilbronn twenty-four copies of his famous *Reise nach Pennsylvania* in 1756 (Heilbronn Stadtarchiv, Raths-Protocoll, 1740–1757, RP 1756, p. 131). Partitions of estate and other local documents perished in the archives in the 1940s.

71. HStASt A 211, Bü. 673, 27 December 1751, query 26; LAS B 2, 1346/7; *Reichs-Post-Amts-Zeitung,* 9 January 1740.

72. *Korrespondenz Mühlenbergs* 1:312 n. 7. On the Gensels' later competition with Mühlenberg and the clerical network, see below, chap. 8.

73. Lauffen/Eyach Village Archives, Realteilungen, 6 March 1762, 14 July 1762, 31 August 1762; HStASt A 213, Bü. 9426.

74. HSP Amf. 893, John Potts's Ledger, 1744–49.

75. On the Hillegas family, see Kunselman Burgert, *Eighteenth Century Emigrants,* 1:165–68; Yoder, *Rhineland Emigrants,* 11; HSP, Philadelphia Orphans' Court Records (microfilm), 15 February 1749/50; LTSA, St. Michael's Lutheran Church, Baptismal Records.

76. Grubb, "Market Structure," 43, table 3; Keppele detailed his own earnings and outlays (without ever mentioning his involvement in the immigrant trade) in his "Arithmatic Book," which also includes tables for converting currency from the Reich into pounds sterling and Pennsylvania currency; Keppele indicated that he had over twelve hundred pounds in ready money, as well as linens, shares in ships, and outstanding debts due him in excess of another one thousand pounds; his debts totaled only two hundred to three hundred pounds (HSP Am. 867, entries for 1761). A record of Keppele's prosecuting a debtor can be found in Lancaster Historical Society (Lancaster, Pa.), Court of Common Pleas Appearance Dockets, May 1751, *Keppele v. Jacob Klyne*; in this instance the defendant acknowledged his debt of twenty-seven pounds.

77. Despite Keppele's eminence, there is no collection of his papers. The above summarizes a wide variety of receipts and miscellaneous information in the HSP collections, among which see Stauffer Collection, Keppele to Yeates, 13 December 1771, 30 December 1772; Society Collection, box 1 B, Receipts; Penn Physick Papers, 4:25; Gratz Collection, case 1, box 2; Weiser Papers, Correspondence, Receipt 17, February 1756. See also Jerome H. Wood, Jr., *Conestoga Crossroads: Lancaster, Pennsylvania, 1730–1790* (Harrisburg, Pa., 1979), 103.

78. HSP AC 981, Cassel Collection, Christian Lehmann MSS, Stam Register derer Voreltern.

79. HSP F 4, Lehmann Legal Papers, box 1, D 60; Lehmann Papers, F

11, Notebooks, D 61; F 14, Germantown Land Surveys; F 24, Philadelphia City Land Surveys.

80. HSP F 4, Lehmann Legal Papers, box 1, D 60; Philadelphia Orphans' Court Records (microfilm), book 3, 1756–52, 31 March 1752; Lehmann Papers, F 14, Germantown Land Surveys, 8 May 1761; *Korrespondenz Mühlenbergs* 2:562 n. 5.

81. HSP, Lehmann Papers, F 14, Germantown Land Surveys, [undated], "The late Jacob Gensell's Land"; Philadelphia Orphans' Court Records (microfilm), 7 March 1761, 16 March 1761, 6 June 1761; Am. 0803, Letterbook of Michael Hillegas, 1757–60, Hillegas to Peter Clopper, July 1759. As indicated above, there were two Jacob Gensels: the other was a Lutheran member of the Germantown parish and died in 1763. How either was related to Matthias, also involved in these recovery attempts, I have been unable to determine.

82. SArS B 5, Gewährbuch, 1720–30, 11 November 1729.

83. Hacker, *Kurpfälzische Auswanderer,* 76; Kunselman Burgert, *Eighteenth Century Emigrants* 2:57–59; GLAK 61/5552, Amts-Kellerei Protocoll, 15 April 1737.

84. Lancaster County Historical Society (Lancaster, Pa.), V-103-A, "Extracts from the Records, Minute Books, Miscellaneous of Trinity Lutheran Church," 24 February 1743.

85. HSP, "Licenses for Marriages, Taverns, and Peddlars," 2 vols.

86. Glatfelter, *Pastors and People,* 100–101.

87. *Korrespondenz Mühlenbergs* 2:38, 41; HSP, Weiser Correspondence, Weiser to Peters, 8 March 1755.

88. HSP, Edward Carey Gardiner Collection, Philadelphia Court of Common Pleas, extract.

89. Archiv Hornberg, 11, Fach 9, fasc. 19, Ittlingen Amts-Protocollen, 1760–81. I wish to thank Hans Wolf Freiherr von Gemmingen for his permission to use the family archives, and Dr. Wolfgang Angebaur, Kreisarchivar Heilbronn, for arranging the visit. The Geiger family's activities are reconstructed from these sources and the other sources cited below in the next six notes.

90. Ibid., 11, Fach 8, fasc. 18, Ittlingen Amts-Protokollen, 1756–59; 11, Fach 8, fasc. 15, Ittlingen Gerichtsprotokolle . . . Akten von 1769.

91. Gustav Neuwirth, *Geschichte der Gemeinde Ittlingen* (Karlsruhe, 1981), 89–95, 177; see further details in section 4 of this chapter.

92. Hacker, *Kurpfälzische Auswanderer,* 136–37, provides many of the details for the following four paragraphs.

93. Yoder, ed., "Emigrants from Wuerttemberg," 57.

94. SCDAH, Miscellaneous Records of Bills of Sale, 7:21, 1729–1825; Percy L. Geiger, *The Geigers of South Carolina* (n.p., n.d.), 128.

95. Charleston Historical Society, "The First Consistory Book of the German Evangelical Lutheran Church of St. John's [*sic*] the Baptist" trans. Gertha Reinert (1981), 58–60, power of attorney, 10 January 1789; quotations are from 61–62, Jacob Geiger to Heinrich Geiger, 2 July 1789.

96. HStASt A 213, Bü. 9414; Häberlein, "Vom Oberrhein zum Suse-quehanna," 120–24; on Bertsch at St. Michael's, see below, chap. 8.

97. HSP, Papers of Dr. Jonathan Potts, vol. 1, 1766–76, nos. 53, 54.

98. Winthrop Bell, *The "Foreign Protestants" and the Settlement of Nova Scotia* (Toronto, 1961), 126–29, 171.

99. Johann Georg Keyßler, *Fortzetzung neuster Reisen durch Teutschland, Böhmen, Hungarn, etc.* (Hanover, 1741).

100. *Papers of Thomas Jefferson* 13:20, 266.

Chapter 5   Liberty and Property in the Early Lutheran Settlements

1. On the petitions and the eventual report to the House of Burgesses, see Henry M. McIlwaine, ed., *Executive Journals of the Council of Colonial Virginia,* vol. 6, *1754–1755,* ed. Benjamin J. Hillman (Richmond, 1966), 688 n. 300.

2. Scheel, *Culpeper,* 42, 44; G. M. Brydon, "The Clergy of the Established Church in Virginia and the Revolution," *VMHB* 41 (1933), 234; for quotation, see Henry M. McIlwaine, ed., *Executive Journals of the Council of Colonial Virginia,* vol. 5, *1739–1754* (Richmond, Va., 1949), 385, 16 April 1752.

3. HSP, Etting Collection, copy of report to House of Burgesses; Glat-felter, *Pastors and People,* 71. The standard histories of the congregation include William P. Huddle, *History of the Hebron Lutheran Church, Madison County, Virginia, from 1717 to 1907* (New Market, Va., 1908), 31–38; William Edward Eisenberg *The Lutheran Church in Virginia, 1717–1962* (Roanoke, Va., 1967), 5–18.

4. Glatfelter, *Pastors and People,* 138–39; Johann Caspar Stoever, *Kurze Nachricht von einer Evangelisch-Lutherischen Deutschen Gemeinde in dem Amer-icanischen Virginien . . .* (Hanover, 1737); HSP, Correspondence of Samuel Wolspurger [*sic*] with Fresenius.

5. Glatfelter, *Pastors and People,* 126, 139–43; AFSt 4 F 7, Rechnungen über die milden Verehrungen . . . ; 4 F 5, Pennsyl. Kirchenrechnung, 1743–53.

6. AFSt 4 F 10, Darmstadt. Kollekte für die Pensyl. Gemeinden, 1744–49; this totaled 579 Gulden. Europeans continued to hear occasionally of the Virginia settlement; see, e.g., *Acta-Historico-Ecclesiastica,* vol. 18 (Weimar, 1755), 612, which depends upon Halle for its source, reporting Klug's 1749 visit to Philadelphia and his complaint of loneliness.

7. *Korrespondenz Mühlenbergs* 1:346, 349 n. 25, 488, 493–94 n. 34; 2:89. Mühlenberg mentions Klug only once more during the latter's lifetime, to report via the traveling Reformed minister Johann Joachim Zubly of Savannah in 1754 that Klug had "given himself over unreservedly to drink" and was neglecting his ministry (*Korrespondenz Mühlenbergs* 2:145).

8. *Journals of Muhlenberg* 2:374. The Greek term *adiaphoron* (indifferent matter) Mühlenberg employs to refer to social customs, which, as Luther

suggested, were bound to be different in various places and cultures. Lutheran theologians disagreed on the tension between the demands of the law and the freedom of the gospel, and considerable debate has always raged over exactly what *adiaphora* covers. Pietists tended toward the most legalistic interpretation, condemning drinking, card playing, and theater going.

9. William Hinke and Charles Hemper, eds., "Moravian Diaries of Travels through Virginia," *VMHB* 11 (1903), 113–31, 225–42, 370–93; 12 (1904), 55–82, 134–53, 271–84; 12 (1904), 70. Given Klug's known hostility to itinerants, it is not unreasonable to suppose he may have been among those urging Gooch to issue the proclamation.

10. Ibid. 12 (1904), 71–72; on von Mosheim and his influence in North America, see A. G. Roeber, "Citizens or Subjects? German-Lutherans and the Federal Constitution in Pennsylvania, 1789–1800," *Amerikastudien/American Studies* 34 (1989), 49–68.

11. Hinke and Hemper, eds., "Moravian Diaries," 11 (1903), 230; Eisenberg, *Lutheran Church,* 8, 13–14.

12. VSLAD, Orange County Will Book 1, 1735–43, treasurer's report of the congregation for 1733–34, reported 24 August 1738, translated from German by James Porteus, presented by John Carpenter on behalf of the deceased Andrew Kercher, churchwarden. In addition to being available at VSLAD, some county records have also been published: see John Frederick Dorman, comp., *Orange County, Virginia, Deed Books 1 and 2 (1735–1738); Judgments, 1735* (Washington, D.C., 1961); idem, comp., *Orange County Deed Books 3 and 4 and Judgments 1736* (Washington, D.C., 1966).

13. Ibid., Orange County Orders, Commission of the Peace, 21 January 1734; see also Orange County Judgments, letter of Borden to the Court, 15 November 1745, in which Borden begged to be excused because he needed to sell several properties in Jersey "which I left honsole [*sic*]" and asked the court's indulgence to "consider the grate vantage [*sic*] of moving so far with a grate famaly and settling all a new." The Hebron settlement was originally located in Spotsylvania County. Changes in county borders later placed it in Orange, Culpeper, and finally Madison counties.

14. I am indebted to Klaus Wust for correspondence and information on the Shenandoah settlers and their relationship to the public institutions in those counties.

15. I rely both on VSLAD, films of county court Order Books for Spotslvania, Orange, and Culpeper counties for 1726–76; and on prosopography contained in the *Germanna Record* publications.

16. VSLAD, Orange County Will Book 1, pp. 83–89, Stoever's will, probated first at Philadelphia in 1739 and recorded again in Orange in May 1739; J. D. F. Smyth, *A Tour through the United States of America,* 2 vols. (London, 1784; reprint, New York, 1968), 1:226–29.

17. Dorman, ed., *Orange County Deed Books 3 and 4,* 71–101; VSLAD, Orange County Order Book 1, 1734–39, 26 April 1738, 22 February 1738/9; Orange County Order Book 4, pp. 74, 149, 279.

18. *Germanna Record No. 3* (Culpeper, Va., 1963), 5–11.

19. *Germanna Record No. 10* (Culpeper, Va., 1967), 4–8.

20. VSLAD, Orange County Order Book 1, 1734–39, 23 March 1738.

21. Gooch to Board of Trade, Colonial Records Project, Colonial Williamsburg Foundation, PRO: CO 5/1327, see 10 May 1750, observation 7. On the 1748 revisal, see Roeber, *Faithful Magistrates,* 102–11; William Walter Hening, *The Statutes at Large: Being a Collection of All the Laws of Virginia, From the First Session of the Legislature, in the Year 1619,* 13 vols. (Richmond, 1809–23), 6:140–43.

22. *Germanna Record No. 6* (Culpeper, Va., 1965), 40–44, 66–68, 34–40.

23. Ibid., 14–16, 23–25, 40.

24. Prosopography on these families can be traced in the *Germanna Record.* Among settlers' names, I cannot identify Henry Boikman [Beekman?], Jacob Burrnur, Stefan Suel, or John Ralschback, a very late arrival (1764) in Hebron; Abraham Major may be a descendant of George Majer noted above; Paul Le[derer?] possibly the 1733 arrival, married Margarete Clore, daughter of the 1717 settler Michael.

25. Hinke and Hemper, eds., "Moravian Diaries," 233. On types of village settlement patterns, see, e.g., in addition to the literature cited in chapter 3, Glenn T. Trewartha, "Types of Rural Settlement in Colonial America," *Geographical Review* 36 (1946), 568–96.

26. H. C. Groome, *Fauquier during the Proprietorship* (Richmond, Va., 1927), 129–30.

27. Stephen Baring-Gould, *Germany Present and Past,* 2 vols. (London, 1879), 1:98–129, "Peasant Proprietors"; esp. 107–11.

28. Claude Lindsay Howell, *A History of Madison County, Virginia* (Strasburg, Va., 1926), 29–45, 138–39; Margaret G. Davis, *Madison County, Virginia: A Revised History* (Ephrata, Pa., 1977), 24–32.

29. H. R. McIlwaine et al., eds., *Journals of the Virginia House of Burgesses, 1619–1776,* 13 vols. (Richmond, Va., 1905–16), pp. 377–78, 21 April 1756.

30. VSLAD, Archives, Culpeper County Personal Property Tax Lists, 1782–89; tithables and other figures taken from the Order Books for 1749–76; land prices and surveys of patents are summarized in Scheel, *Culpeper,* 24–38.

31. I am indebted to Dr. Klaus Wust for sharing with me the results of his many years of research in the archives in Koblenz and other archives relative to both the Nassau-Siegen group and the Lutherans, mainly from the Kraichgau. This also confirms my own failure to find any mention of the settlement in village archives.

32. VSLAD, Culpeper County Will Book C, 4 February 1773.

33. County Clerk's Office, Bourbon County (Kentucky), Indentures, Deeds, and Releases, book C, 317–22, Indenture of Bargain and Sale, November 1795.

34. On this family's history, see Yoder, ed., *Rhineland Emigrants,* 61. Unaccountably, Hacker, *Auswanderungen aus Rheinpfalz,* which covers Frankenthal, misses these families. Why the nephew Johann Wilhelm is not named in the bequest is not clear, although he may have died by this time. Although

the Lotspeich name surfaces in the Virginia records, Johann Wilhelm's activities in the Hebron community remain a mystery. He and his wife deeded land away in 1774 and 1775, and his wife was a daughter of Pastor Klug. See *Germanna Record No. 6* (Culpeper, 1965), 87–88.

35. VSLAD, Spotsylvania County Will Book A, 7 March 1732, Michael Holt and Nicholas Blankenbecker, witnesses, proven 5 February 1734.

36. For an example of such self-help books in Germany, see the Ulm bookseller Johann Conrad Wohler's advertisement in the 20 October 1770 issue of the Frankfurt *Reichs-Post-Amts-Zeitung* for the *Sicherer Testament-Macher, d.i., kurze doch gründliche Anweisung, wie eine jede Gattung von Testamenten in der Schnelle nach den allgemeinen Rechten gemacht werden könne.* For examples of Klug's work on the Virginia wills, see Johann Schneider's 17 April 1760 will (VSLAD, Culpeper County Will Book A, 214–15), or the will of Heinrich Hoffmann, written in December 1763, probated 19 June 1766 and "translated from the German Tongue as Literal as the Idoim [*sic*] of that Language would permit by Saml Klug" (pp. 419–21). If one looks beyond this "charter group," another half-dozen examples of the German pietist redemptive language appear in second-generation wills from 1760 to 1800.

37. For an examination of testation patterns in nearby Albermarle which reveals among English speakers a tendency toward equal division of property among both sons and daughters, but with realty going largely to sons, see Daniel Blake Smith, *Inside the Great House: Planter Family Life in Eighteenth-Century Chesapeake Society* (Ithaca, N.Y., 1980), 231–48.

38. VSLAD, Culpeper County Will Book B, pp. 422–23, 28 March 1781, probated 18 June 1781.

39. For the Clore, Wilheit, and Weber family practices, see *Germanna Record No. 6*, 20–29, 68–69, 94–95. For a brief discussion and further literature, see Wilhelm Brauneder, "Jüngstenrecht," in Erler and Kaufmann, eds., *Handwörterbuch zur deutschen Rechtsgeschichte*, 10:467. Despite these cautions, it may be significant that the Wilheits and the Webers came, respectively, from Catholic territories of Mainz, and from Eisern, the Catholic part of Siegen; the origins of the Clores remain a mystery. There is at least some evidence that *Minoratsuccesionsrecht*, also known as *Jüngstenrecht*, was more common in Catholic areas.

40. VSLAD, Orange County Will Book 2, 1744–48, pp. 106–7; Culpeper County Will Book B, p. 243, 25 February 1760; Culpeper County Deed Book 1, p. 89. For a full discussion of the English practices regulating trusts, and uses, and a comparison with German private law, see Hein Kötz, *Trust und Treuhand: Eine rechtsvergleichende Darstellung des angloamerikanischen trust und funktionsverwandter Institute des deutschen Rechts* (Göttingen, 1963). It is only important here to note that, while the English common law often vests legal title in the trustee to ensure that he carry out the wishes of the testator, German law retains completely the heir's rights over the "estate"; the person designated to ensure that the will is executed has only administrative powers, and legal title never is vested in him (pp. 98–99). No provisions in the Hebron

wills implied more than administrative power, and none suggests protective trusts.

41. See Marylynn Salmon, *Women and the Law of Property in Early America* (Chapel Hill, 1986), 325–30, on Maryland and South Carolina similarities. For Virginia, Hening, *Statutes at Large* 1:405, 2:212 (1664), seems to suggest that thirds can be taken in real or personal property; and 2:303 (1693) elaborates on this. The 1705 Revisal of the Laws 3:371–76), however, establishes dower in realty only. Later clarifications (4:222–28) require a bill in equity to obtain dower in slaves; and under the Revisal of 1748 (5:444–45), the possibility of the widow taking one-third of slaves in dower upon petitioning the court to grant administration of estate to the widow was allowed. Many of the Hebron wills seem to ignore the 1705 provisions and continue to give dower in realty or personalty. Whether such provisions were allowed in the courts, the surviving evidence does not clarify.

42. VSLAD, Culpeper County, Deed Book 5, p. 158; the will of 1757 is in Will Book A, 158.

43. The estate was not settled until 1795 (ibid., Madison County Will Book 1, pp. 221–26. Contrary to the opinion of *Germanna Record No. 3* (Culpeper, Va., 1963), 9–10, the law of primogeniture was probably not the problem here, since that provision seems to have been ignored regularly by colonial Virginians.

44. Huddle, *Hebron Lutheran Church,* 510, discusses this singular instance; the deed is in VSLAD, Culpeper County, Deed Book H, p. 339–40, 18 November 1776.

45. My account of the dispute over the will is drawn from VSLAD, Culpeper County, Will Book B, 95–97.

46. Ibid., Will Book B, p. 524, 16 September 1782.

47. Ibid., Will Book A, 419–20. On the Hoffmanns, see *Germanna Record No. 3* (Culpeper, Va., 1963). See also the order of the court in the case of John Schneider's will on 17 April 1760, after Klug's translation was received, that the "said Copy be Recorded in Lieu of the said Will" (VSLAD, Culpeper County, Will Book A, 215).

48. VSLAD, Culpeper County, Will Book A, pp. 309–10, 13 November 1762, probated 17 March 1763.

49. Ibid., 369, 17 May 1764.

50. Glatfelter, *Pastors and People,* 129.

51. *Journals of Muhlenberg* 2:311, 373.

52. On Virginia's treatment of naturalization, see Kettner, *American Citizenship,* 83–99; on the naturalization of several Hebron church members, see Ginseppi, "Naturalizations," 8–9.

53. For my elaboration of Gooch's basic disinclination to confront the "country," see Roeber, *Faithful Magistrates,* chap. 2. For a contrasting view of Gooch as a frustrated and inept court politician, see Karl Tilman Winkler, "'The Art of Governing Well': Virginias Gouverneur William Gooch, die Rolle der kolonialen Exekutive und das Tabakinspectionsgesetz von 1730," *Amerikastudien/American Studies* 29 (1984), 233–75.

54. Klaus G. Loewald et al., eds. and trans., "Johann Martin Bolzius Answers a Questionnaire on Carolina and Georgia," *WMQ*, 3d ser., 14 (1957), 226.

55. Böhme, *Das verlangte, nicht erlangte Canaan*, 44, 63.

56. Gerhard Florey, "Die schwarzacher Versammlungen der Salzburger Protestanten im Jahre 1731," *Aus Mitteilungen der Gesellschaft für Salzburger Landeskunde* 114 (1974), 243–70.

57. See Kettner, *American Citizenship*, 101 n. 138, 102–3.

58. See Allen D. Candler, comp., *The Colonial Records of the State of Georgia* (Atlanta, 1904–16), 18:464–72, 659, for the statutes. Boltzius' opinion is in his answer to a questionnaire; see Loewald et al., eds. and trans., "Boltzius Answers a Questionnaire," 254. It may be that the 1765 statute was inspired by the 1764 opinion of the attorney general that aliens not naturalized under the 1740 act had no rights to property, but no solid evidence links the colonial statute to the British opinion.

59. *Henry Newman's Salzburger Letterbooks*, edited and transcribed by George Fenwick Jones (Athens, Ga., 1966), 35–37, 42–46.

60. Phinizy Spalding, *Oglethrope in America* (Chicago, 1977), 61–65; Amos Aschbach Ettinger, *Oglethorpe: A Brief Biography,* ed. Phinizy Spalding (Mercer, Ga., 1984), 34–73, on the philanthropic theories of the trustees; Urlsperger, comp., *Detailed Reports* 3:100, 117. Boltzius informed Augsburg in February of several Lutherans from Purrysburg desiring to move, but on learning "that the land that was to be given to them could be held only by a man and that the female sex was excluded from inheriting it after the death of the husband or father . . . they wished to request Mr. Oglethorpe to remit this hard stipulation before they should resolve to move here" (3:54).

61. Mortality figures for the entire period of settlement remain inexact, as do population figures for the Ebenezer community and its environs. Boltzius reported that more than one-quarter of the adults and one-third of the children of his congregation were dead after the first three years in Georgia. According to Wilson, "Halle and Ebenezer," 160–61, the mortality rate for children may have approached 80 percent for the period up to 1738; adult mortality is harder to establish, and improved steadily after the 1740s, although no exact population figures for the 1750s and 60s for Ebenezer and the settlements at Abercorn and Goshen have been established; by the 1750s, when Ebenezer boasted perhaps 1,500 people, the new settlement at Bethany numbered about 160 persons.

62. Urlsperger, comp., *Detailed Reports* 12:67.

63. Wilson, "Halle and Ebenezer," 18–17, citing AFSt A 10 117, for the Francke citation; also see 18–25, discussion of the early objectives and mixture of public and private enterprises; 94–96, on relations with the Indians; and 99–118, on the orphanage and labor problems. Also see James Ethridge Callaway, *The Early Settlement of Georgia* (Athens, Ga., 1948), 36–41, table 2A; esp. p. 39, on land applications.

64. The quotation from Boltzius is in Urlsperger, comp., *Detailed Reports* 5:172.

65. For the English description of the ministers' role, see Benjamin Martyn, *An Impartial Enquiry into the State and Utility of the Province of Georgia* (London, 1741), 47; see also AFSt AG 3, 16 February 1755, three eminent citizens who aided in a court of conscience (equity) as Schöffen. For the quotation, see Urlsperger, comp., *Detailed Reports* 3:190.

66. Ibid. 191.

67. Wilson, "Halle and Ebenezer," 334–67. I have searched AFSt in vain for evidence that Halle was informed of what von Münch intended; Wilson also believes that Halle was bypassed by von Münch but also has not located evidence, which may lie in SPCK or Augsburg sources.

68. Herrmann Winde, "Die Frühgeschichte der lutherischen Kirche in Georgia . . ." (Ph.D. diss., Halle/Zalle, 1960), 47–52, 106–9, 184–90; Wilson, "Halle and Ebenezer," 396–420.

69. These stories, possibly circulated by Rabenhorst's enemies, are contradicted by Mühlenberg, who asserted that despite Rabenhorst's vast ownings, he was so much in debt that selling all he had would still have left his widow encumbered. Rabenhorst died intestate in 1776; his wife died three years later, leaving a will that does not clarify Mühlenberg's statement. For Mühlenberg's report, see *Journals of Muhlenberg* 2:649. Frau Rabenhorst's straitened circumstances she reported to Mühlenberg in 1777 (LTSA PM 95 G 17, 20 February 1777). According to the Halle records, Frau Rabenhorst was left everything, and she in her turn left forty pounds to the orphanage at Halle; the proviso that no paper money but only gold or silver would be accepted caused considerable problems. Other beneficiaries included Rabenhorst's sisters in Berlin and the missions in the East Indies; attempts to invoke John Adams's aid through Ghent and the Prussian government were rejected since this was a private matter. As late as 1799 the impoverished sisters were still waiting in Berlin for their pastor, Johann Lüdeke at the Petrikirche, to obtain their legacy, which the warfare since 1789 had made irrecoverable (AFSt 5 E 6, Erbschaft u. Legat Rabenhorst).

70. Exactly who funded this retirement plantation remains unclear; it was not either of two patrons who gave to the American missions, Sigismund Streit or the Count Solms-Rödelsheim, the former of whom explicitly excluded Ebenezer from his bequest. The person is simply described as someone of high birth and position (AFSt 4 E 53).

71. William Wright Abbot, *The Royal Governors of Georgia, 1754–1775* (Chapel Hill, 1959), 15–17; Wilson, "Halle and Ebenezer," 103–6, 141–49.

72. George Fenwick Jones, "John Martin Boltzius' Trip to Charleston, October 1742," *SCHM* 82 (1981), 87–110; Henning Cohen, "Four Letters from Peter Timothy, 1755, 1768, 1771," ibid. 55 (1954), 160–65; Wilson, "Halle and Ebenezer," 351–52. See also Urlsperger, comp., *Detailed Reports* 7:212–13, 8:459; chests were apparently sent from Halle via London to Charleston, where thirty shillings sterling paid for forwarding to Savannah and Ebenezer; even news from London apparently traveled to Charleston from London and thence to Savannah and the Hallensians at Ebenezer (11:96–97).

73. Urlsperger, comp., *Detailed Reports* 11:8–9.

74. Ibid. 7:159; 8:87–88, 191, 212–13, 520; 9:30, 64; 10:28, 51, 99; 11:104. Riesch did not pursue legacies in Salzburg alone. Schmidt also sent his request for the legacy nominally to his brother, a day laborer in Regensburg, the seat of the imperial Protestant Council, the Corpus Evangelicorum; but to secure the matter the request went via Ziegenhagen in London, where it was forwarded to Urlsperger, then to Francke at Halle, and then to the privy councilor Walbaum at Saalfeld, who pursued the matter with the archbishop's court.

75. On the 16,000 Salzburgers who made their way from Berlin via Königsberg in 1733, see Wolfgang Menger, "Die Salzburger Emigration nach Ostpreußen 1731/2: Ein medizinisch-geschichtlicher Beitrag zum Umsiedlungsproblem," *Aus Mitteilungen der Gesellschaft für Salzburger Landeskunde* 98 (1958), 115.

76. AFSt 5 E 1, 1741, p. 31; another trader in Prussian Pomerania obtained a description of the new settlement and became a contributor (p. 96, 29 December 1741). In surveying the fascicles through 5 E 7, it appears that small gifts of between one and ten Reichstaler were common, as were larger contributions from merchants and members of the aristocracy.

77. Urlsperger, comp., *Detailed Reports* 8:237, 10:83, 11:34, 40.

78. AFSt 5 A 11, pp. 124–26, 9 July 1745.

79. Urlsperger, comp., *Detailed Reports* 12:30.

80. To these instances, add Bacher, a Swabian on the fourth transport, who donated fifty Gulden to the orphanage (ibid. 9:142). The notation of so many bequests in 1742 may reflect either Boltzius's particular concern to report such charity, or the mortality rate; Boltzius noted a year later that there were 279 persons—81 men, 70 wives, 6 widows, 52 boys, 59 girls, and 11 serving girls in the community—but that few of the children born in Ebenezer had survived the previous decade (9:104). See 9:92, 101, 148–50, 163–64, 165, 186; and 10:99, 107, noting a gift of the Duchess of Kendal in London for the orphanage. Boltzius records an anonymous gift of sixty pounds sterling in 1741 (8:71).

81. GDAH, Will Books A and AA; and the copies made from British sources. These wills are now available at GDAH on microfilm under "Colonial Wills," RH 5-006 and 007, and RH I and RH II 40/29 and 30/30. In citing these wills below, I include only the testator's name and the date of the will; interested readers can find the documents easily because each of the film rolls is indexed. In addition to Boltzius's notes, there are several instances in the record of wills that were recorded but are now noted as "missing." My calculation is that before 1777 approximately fifty-six German testators left wills, of which forty-one examples survive (excluding those mentioned by Boltzius).

82. GDAH, Johannes Alther, Will, 5 April 1755; Amelia Alther, Will, 25 December 1770; Bartholomew Zouberbühler, Will, 5 November 1766; Conveyances, book C-1, p. 733, 9 July 1763.

83. Altheim Village Archive, T.u.I., 5 May 1769, 17 June 1768, 3 June

1755, 29 December 1745; excerpts from the Herrschaftliche Pflegamt Austrag, 25 January 1767 and 19 August 1768. The yearly taxes levied on the day laborers, weavers, blacksmiths, and widows who left for Georgia and South Carolina averaged one Gulden on various sorts of rented properties. See Altheim Village Archive, *Altheim, Söglingen und Zähringen Renovirte Steur Beschreibung, 1750* for Bauer, Bensel, Erhardt, Glöckler, Hellman, Lohrman, Usenberg, and Weber. Despite their intentions to settle at Ebenezer, many of these emigrants eventually went to South Carolina.

84. GDAH, Bonds, Bills of Sale, book D, pp. 300–302, 3 April 1765.

85. Based on my reading of all conveyances, bonds, bills of sales, indentures that survive in GDAH for the period to 1776, available on film as Bonds, books HH, JJ, KK; Miscellaneous Bonds and Store Accounts; Miscellaneous Bonds, books Y1 and Y2; Bonds, Bills of Sale, books J and D, 1755–65; and book R, covering to 1772; Conveyances, books C-1 and C-2, 1750–1766; books S, 1766–69; books U and V, 1768–71; and books X-1 and X-2, 1771–74.

86. Theobald Kieffer, Will, 27 February 1767; Urlsperger, comp., *Detailed Reports* 8:324.

87. GDAH, Anna Steinhebel, Will, 17 May 1748; George Maurer, Will, 5 April 1775.

88. Ibid., Thomas Schwieghofer, Will, 26 November 1772, probated 10 December 1772. The original German reads: "Meine durch Christum Theure erkaufte Seele . . . von diesem Jammerthal zu sich nehmen in sein Ewiges Freuden-Reich der Leibe aber in sanfter Ruhe bis zur frölichen Auferstehung."

89. Wilson, "Halle and Ebenezer," 411–16; the evidence concerning these courts comes from AFSt AG 3, *Nebendiarium* kept by Boltzius for 6 June 1759; see also 16 February 1755. No diaries survive for the years 1754–59 and for the 1760s; the account in which supplementary or extra diaries were kept is the four-part series edited by Samuel Urlsperger and his son, Samuel, Jr., entitled the *Americanisches Ackerwerk Gottes* . . . (Augsburg, 1753, 1755, 1765, 1766). See Wilson, "Halle and Ebenezer," 430–32.

90. This conveyance, dated 15 April 1757, was followed by another, dated 10 October 1763, in which Boltzius, with John Flörl and Johann Caspar Wertsch, conveyed to Lemke for five shillings the public lot in Ebenezer originally designed for an orphan house for a rent of one penny for six months in order to qualify the pastor for full possession (GDAH, Conveyances, books C-1 and C-2, 1750–66, pp. 1032–35). This was defective, as Mühlenberg pointed out later in trying to settle a dispute over the mills. A counter deed or declaration of trust should have been filed stating the specific purpose and use intended by the trust, vesting it in Ziegenhagen, in London, and Urlsperger, in Augsburg, as members of the SPCK, who would then name the Georgia pastors as their agents. Lacking the specific declaration, the original intent ad pias causas could be disputed by later heirs of the original owners. For the dispute, see chapter 8, below; for Mühlenberg's observation, see *Journals of Muhlenberg* 2:602–3.

91. George Fenwick Jones, "The Salzburger Mills: Georgia's First Suc-

cessful Enterprises," *Yearbook of German-American Studies* 23 (1988), 105–17, at 114–15.

92. See Marion R. Hemperley, *English Crown Grants in St. Matthew Parish in Georgia, 1755–1775* (Atlanta, 1974).

93. GDAH, Bonds, Bills of Sale, book R, 1765–72, pp. 143–45.

94. Boltzius's will is in ibid., Will Book A, 1 June 1763, probated 8 July 1766; the power of attorney made out on 23 March 1770 before the local court at Halle is in Bonds, Bills of Sale, book R, 1765–72, pp. 437–38.

95. Ibid., Bonds, Bills of Sale, book D, Colonial Inventories, 107–8, 214–15, 253–56, 272–37, 309–10, 327, 493–95.

96. Ibid., book J, p. 69, 7 April 1754; book R, pp. 545–46; 18 May 1772.

97. Bartholemew Zouberbühler, Will, 5 November 1766. No manumission orders occur either in the trust provisions of the 41 wills, or in the conveyances.

98. AFSt C 532, 19 February 1746, 19 May 1752, 19 July 1752. For further discussion, see Karl Zehrer, "Die Beziehungen zwischen dem hallischen Pietismus und dem frühen Methodismus," *PN* 2 (1975), 43–56; for Boltzius' negative reports, Urlsperger, comp., *Detailed Reports* 8:378–80, 412–13; Betty Wood, *Slavery in Colonial Georgia* (Athens, Ga., 1985), 59–73.

Chapter 6   The Early Language of Liberty and Property in Pennsylvania

1. On the function of printed forms of language, see Jack Goody, "Literacy, Criticism, and the Growth of Knowledge," in Joseph Ben-David and Terry Nichols Clark, *Culture and Its Creators: Essays in Honor of Edward Shils* (Chicago, 1977), 226–43; Michael M. J. Fischer, "Ethnicity and the Post-Modern Arts of Memory," in James Clifford and George E. Marcus, *Writing Culture: The Poetics and Politics of Ethnography* (Berkeley, 1986), 194–233.

2. Anita L. Eyster, "Notices by German and Swiss Families . . . ," *Yearbook of the Pennsylvania German Folklore Society* 3 (1938), 3–41.

3. No copies of the Stuttgart paper survive for this period; I have checked the notices for the *Reichs-Post-Amts-Zeitung* for the period from 1740 through the 1770s; most of the notices seem to come from the Palatinate, Baden-Durlach, or one of the other territories affected by emigration. On the *Ediktalzitation*, see Erler and Kaufmann, eds., *Handwörterbuch zur deutschen Rechtsgeschichte*, 1:803–6. The decision of where and how to print such notices was left to regional custom and did not find statutory definition in imperial law. Copies of almanacs from the Palatinate also were sent to Pennsylvania. These carried the names of court officials whom agents would have to contact to have their powers validated, as well as the table of court days and holidays, and the venues of the local and regional courts, in addition to the schedules of the post wagons. See LCP, *Chur-Pfälzischer Hoff- und Staats-Calendar* (Mannheim, 1767).

4. Alan Tully, "Literacy Levels and Educational Development in Rural

Pennsylvania, 1729–1775," *Pennsylvania History* 39 (1972), 301–12; Farley Grubb, "Colonial Immigrant Literacy: An Economic Analysis of Pennsylvania-German Evidence, 1727–1775," *Explorations in Economic History* 24 (1987), 63–76; idem, "German Immigration," 417–36.

5. See Paul Wernle, *Der schweizerische Protestantismus im 18. Jahrhundert,* vol. 1 (Tübingen, 1922), 111–356; Rudolph Dellsperger, "Kirchengemeinschaft und Gewissensfreiheit: Samuel Güldins Einspruch gegen Zinzendorfs Unionstätigkeit in Pennsylvania, 1742," *PN* 11 (1985), 40–58.

6. For the North American context, see references and discussion in Harry S. Stout, *The New England Soul: Preaching and Religious Culture in Colonial New England* (New York, 1986), under index heading "Liberty."

7. The quotation is from the subtitle of Saur's paper.

8. The acts of 10 Anne c. 19 (1711) and the renewal, 16 Geo. 2, c. 2, did not affect devotional sermons published singly, or pamphlets, but did control political pamphlets; under the expanded form of the law, the tax was assessed on the numbers of columns laid out in newspapers. Thus a paper able to sustain such a tax was likely to be owned not only by wealthier printers but also by those politically careful not to risk censorship; hence, such a paper would present an "official face" of truth. For details, see the exhaustive and exemplary study by Karl Tilman Winkler, "Tagesschriftum und Politik in der Ära Walpole" (Habilitationsschrift, Universität Göttingen, 1989), 46–65.

9. Joseph Stoudt, *Pennsylvania German Poetry, 1685–1830* (Allentown, Pa., 1956), suggests a schematic breakdown of Pennsylvania German poetic efforts into mystical religious poetry, folk literature and mysticism, mystical love poetry, and dialect verse dedicated to romantic nostalgia.

10. See the editions of the almanac, *Der Hoch-Deutsch Americanische Calender . . .* (Germantown, Pa.), for the years 1741–44 for these examples; quotation from 1741 almanac. (In subsequent citations the almanac's title is shortened to *Calender.*) Hochman von Hochenau's (1670–1721) confession of faith was printed at Lippe-Detmold in 1702, reprinted in 1703, and advertised by Saur in 1744.

11. LCP, Broadsides, *Gründliche Anweisung zu einem Heiligen Leben . . . ,* published in 1748 (Saur had translated this a year earlier and noted it as the work of a deceased cleric); HSP, Broadsides, Heinrich Melchior Mühlenberg, *Unpartheische Gedancken in Reimen . . . ,* 1 October 1752.

12. Weiser's poem is reprinted in Stoudt, *Pennsylvania German Poetry,* 93–95. Luther's substitution of *testament* for *covenant* is well-known among Luther scholars. The Old Testament Hebrew *b'rith* suggests covenant, alliance, or agreement. The New Testament Greek *diatheke* means will, or testament. Even when Luther had, in his Old Testament translation, rendered the Hebrew as *covenant,* in translating those same passages when cited in the New Testament he systematically alters *covenant* to read *testament* whenever he seeks to highlight the radical difference between the old relationship of God with Israel, and the absolute, one-sided posture of reception appropriate to God's people in the New Testament. (see, e.g., Rom. 11:26–27 and its quo-

tation of Jer. 31:33). See also Walter Bauer, *A Greek-English Lexicon of the New Testament . . . ,* translated and revised by Frederick W. Danker, et al. (Chicago, 1979).

13. Niedersächsische Universitäts- und Landesbibliothek Göttingen, Cod. Ms. Hist 821, Mathias Otte, letter from Philadelphia, 1725.

14. Stadtarchiv Schwaigern, A 1246.

15. See R. S. White, "The Birth of the Reader," in Graham McGregor and R. S. White, eds., *Reception and Response: Hearer Creativity and the Analysis of Spoken and Written Texts* (London and New York, 1990), 242–259; Cathy N. Davidson, *Revolution and the Word: The Rise of the Novel in America* (New York, 1986), 38–54; and Rolf Engelsing, *Analphabetentum und Lektüre: Zur Sozialgeschichte des Lesens in Deutschland zwischen feudaler und industrieller Gesellschaft* (Stuttgart, 1973), which probably overemphasizes the intensive re-reading of a very few pieces in silence. In fact, such pieces had a shared and lively social function, emphasized by Reinhart Siegert in *Aufklärung und Volkslektüre exemplarisch dargestellet an Rudolph Zacharias Becker und seinem 'Noth- und Hülfsbüchlein' mit einer Bibliographie zum Gesamtthema* (Frankfurt am Main, 1978). Cathy Davidson, in her "Toward a History of Books and Readers," in idem, ed., *Reading in America: Literature and Social History* (Baltimore, 1989), 1–26, appropriately warns against the notion of passive "consumerism" and passive reception and recommends a focus on what people made of what they read.

16. The distribution of the *Gebetbücher* of Starck and Habermann can be followed in Arndt et al., eds., *First Century of German Language Printing,* as well as in the advertisements of imported books by Armbrüster, Saur, Reinholdt, and Geyer. For background, see Karl Dienst, "Johann Friedrich Starcks Tägliches Handbuch in Guten und Bösen Tagen: Ein Geschenk des Pietismus an die Volkskirche," *Jahrbuch für hessische Kirchengeschichte* 32 (1981), 67–91; Hans Medick, "Buchkultur auf dem Lande: Laichingen 1748–1820: Ein Beitrag zur Geschichte der protestantischen Volksfrömmigkeit in Altwürttemberg," in *Glaube, Welt und Kirche im Evangelischen Württemberg* (Stuttgart, 1984), 46–68.

17. I borrow from Günter Grass's *Headbirths, or the Germans are Dying Out,* trans. Ralph Manheim (New York, 1982), 20. Manheim translates Grass as using the phrase "the narrows of German life" to convey the thrust of this meditation/fantasy on the obsession with childbirth and overpopulation, and the problem of separating private concerns from public issues.

18. Starck's *Tägliches Handbuch in guten und bösen Tagen* (Frankfurt, 1724), is still in print; quotations here are from the modern edition (Neuendettelsau, 1990), 12, 45, 89, 68–70, 125. The schema for both Starck and Habermann is roughly similar, covering the same areas: inner spiritual development; crises due to natural disasters, warfare, sickness, and aging; and festivals of the church year.

19. Thomas R. Brendle and William S. Troxell, collectors, trans., and eds., "Pennsylvania German Folk Tales, Legends, Once-upon-a-Time

Satires, Maxims, and Sayings Spoken in the Dialect popularly known as Pennsylvania Dutch," *Pennsylvania German Society Proceedings and Addresses* 50 (1944), 72–73; 150–51.

20. On the complex story of the legend, see Elisabeth Frenzel, *Stoffe der Weltliteratur* (Stuttgart, 1970), 235–38; *Keystone Ten*, entries 400–402; *Eine schöne anmüthige und lesenswürdige History von der unschuldig-bedrängten heiligen Pfaltz Gräfin Genovefa* . . . (Philadelphia, 1762); another edition appeared in 1772 at Lancaster, a third in 1790.

21. For extended comment on the literature for heads of family (*Hausvaterliteratur*), and Otto Brunner's concept of "das ganze Haus," see Sabean, *Property, Production,* 90–101.

22. Quotations are from HSP, Weiser Correspondence, box 1, 20 September 1741. Despite some earlier studies on Weiser, a reassessment of him is badly needed in light of new work both on Native American-European relations and on the role German speakers played in shaping Pennsylvania's frontier concerns beginning in the 1740s. For the older literature, see Arthur D. Graeff, *Conrad Weiser: Pennsylvania Peacemaker* (Allentown, Pa., 1945); Joseph S. Walton, *Conrad Weiser and the Indian Policy of Colonial Pennsylvania* (1900; reprint, New York, 1971).

23. The only other hint of early German-American political activity came in an unusual battle between seamen and a small group of Germans in Philadelphia during the election of 1742; see Alan W. Tully, "Ethnicity, Religion, and Politics in Early America," *PMHB* 107 (1983), 491–536; Saur's address to his readers has been published in *PMHB* 23 (1899), 516–21. See also Sally Schwartz, *"A Mixed Multitude": The Struggle for Toleration in Colonial Pennsylvania* (New York, 1987), 174–75.

24. LCP, Broadsides, *A Copy of Verses* . . . (1747); the reference is to 1 Kings 17:3–6.

25. German speakers actually had three forms of speech: that which was used at home and in conversation, dominated by the Palatinate and Swiss dialects; High German, in church and in written communication; and English, in contact with non-Germans. The interlarding of these to form an "interlanguage" affected both written and dialect German usage. For a close examination of how these three languages evolved among the Amish, see Werner Enninger, "The Ethnolinguistic Profile of the Old Order Amish in Transit and Transition," in Herget and Ortseifen, eds., *Transit of Civilization,* 197–216. The problems created by overlapping languages being employed to describe perceptions of the human condition have been surveyed in Harold R. Isaacs, *Idols of the Tribe: Group Identity and Political Change* (New York, 1975), 93–114; William F. Hanks, "Discourse Genres in a Theory of Practice," *American Ethnologist* 14 (1987), 668–92.

26. *Schule der Weisheit* . . . (Germantown, 1750), begins with "Abendmahl" (Lord's Supper), but under "J" it lists "Juristen-Krieg" (lawyers' war). In 1748 Saur had already published an edition of Theodore Arnold's *Grammatica Anglicana Concentrata, Oder, Kurtz-gefaßte Englische Grammatica* . . . (Germantown, 1748). Records of the books ordered from Halle also reflected

the upsurge in interest in English dictionaries by the 1760s: a two-volume set of Ludwig's *English Lexicon* was included in a shipment in 1765 (AFSt 4 F 6/2, Rechnungen, 1746/7–1768, p. 297).

27. *Eine Nützliche Anweisung . . .* (Germantown, 1751). On Mühlenberg's attempt to explain the term *freeholder* to his superiors, see *Journals of Muhlenberg* 2:192; the original in the Halle Reports, *Nachrichten von den vereinigten Deutschen Evangelisch- Lutherischen Gemeinden in Nord-America, absonderlich in Pennsylvanien. Mit einer Vorrede von D. Johann Ludewig Schulze* (Halle, 1787), copy in LTSA 4, 3447, reads "Wir könnten von den rechten Eigenthumsherrn noch ein besser Recht, nemlich als Erbe und Eigen bekommen welcher aber unmöglich war" I thank Dr. Helmut Lehmann for his aid in locating Mühlenberg's original language rendered misleadingly simple by the translation as "freeholder" and "fee-simple." He describes the use of the two languages in a letter (*Korrespondenz Mühlenbergs* 1:353–54). Technical discussions of this pattern of lexical borrowing can be found in the following: Suzanne Romaine, *Pidgin and Creole Languages* (London, 1988), 206–10, 312–34; Uriel Weinreich, *Languages in Contact* (The Hague, 1979), 47–51; Marion Lois Huffines, "Language Contact across Generations: The English of the Pennsylvania Germans," in Wolfgang Noelleken, ed., *Dialectology, Linguistics, Literature: Festschrift for Carroll E. Reed* (Cöppingen, 1984), 93–103. On the concept of absolute property ownership (Eigentum), see Dietmar Willoweit, "Dominium und Proprietas: Zur Entwicklung des Eigentumsbegriffs in der mittelalterlichen und neuzeitlichen Rechtswissenschaft," *Historisches Jahrbuch* 94 (1974), 131–56; Gerhard Köbler, "Eigen und Eigentum," *Zeitschrift der Savigny-Stiftung für Rechtsgeschichte (Germanistische Abteilung)* 95 (1978), 1–33; and Otto Brunner et al., eds., *Geschichtliche Grundbegriffe: Historisches Lexikon zur politische-sozialen Sprache in Deutschland* (Stuttgart, 1970–84), s.v. "Eigentum."

28. See Roeber, "German-American Concept of Property," 148–49.

29. Two men of this name, one born at Assenheim, near Ludwigsburg, the other at Dürkheim, were active in Pennsylvania, the one returning finally to Germany in the late 1760s, the other dying in Berks County in 1767; (Center for the History of the Palatinate, Auswanderer Karteienkatalog).

30. The above descriptions rely on advertisements in Saur's newspaper and various incidental allusions in village archival sources too numerous to cite here. For Saur's distribution network, see Adams, "Colonial German-Language Press," 166–69; on Marie Catharine Andrein, see LAS A 2/924, 1556.

31. *Pennsylvanische Berichte . . .*, 1 April 1753; Keppele continued running the ad into early 1754 (I consulted this issue and the others cited below in HSP, bound volume, 1754 [*sic*] to 1761. Saur changed his newspaper's name in 1746 from the *Hoch-Deutsch Pennsylvanischer Geschichts-Schreiber* to the *Pennsylvanische Berichte*. His son changed it again in 1763 to the *Germantowner Zeitung*. See Adams, "Colonial German-Language Press," 157 n. 18, for further details on the renaming; 166–72, for information on circulation and prices. On the latter topic see also Alexander Waldenrath, "The Pennsylvania-

Germans: Development of Their Printing and Their Newspress in the War for American Independence," in Gerhard K. Friesen and Walter Schatzberg, eds., *The German Contribution to the Building of the Americas: Studies in Honor of Karl J. R. Arndt* (Hanover, N.H., 1977), 47–74 at 53–55.

32. On the creation of a public discourse and public opinion by a self-conscious set of cultural brokers, see Habermas, *Strukturwandel der Öffentlichkeit;* also idem, *Theorie und Praxis,* published in English as *Theory and Practice,* trans. John Viertel (Boston, 1971), 4, 77–78, 281–82. See also Winkler, "*Tagesschriftum,*" 46 n. 2, 1168–69. The quotation about the almanac is from the description that follows the title.

33. Except where otherwise indicated, the remainder of this section is based on my reading of all the extant almanacs between 1739 and 1776, including Saur's; the few numbers of Franklin and Armbrüster's *Neu-Eingerichteter Amerikanischer Geschichts-Kalender* (Philadelphia, 1747–61, 1765, 1767–68); and Miller's *Neueste, Verbessert- und Zuverläßige Amerikanische Calendar* (Philadelphia, 1763–1775); only Saur's almanacs contain such advisory essays. Because the almanacs are not consistently paginated, citations of them will refer only to the year of publication.

34. *Pennsylvanische Berichte,* 16 January 1756; this is a translation of Franklin's dialogue in the *Pennsylvania Gazette,* 18 December 1755.

35. Among a vast literature on this topic, see, e.g., Dieter Berger, *Konversationskunst in England, 1660–1740: ein Sprechphänemen und seine literarische Gestaltung* (Munich, 1978); Michael Harris, *London Newspapers in the Age of Walpole: A Study of the Origins of the Modern English Press* (Rutherford, N.J., 1987), 169–71; Winkler, "*Tagesschriftum,*" 1184–94.

36. For the literature on the transformation of the German almanacs, especially during the eighteenth century, see Jan Knopf, *Die deutsche Kalendargeschichte* (Frankfurt am Main, 1983), 104–47.

37. Gotthard Armbrüster, "Ein Gespräch zwischen einem ehrlichen Neuländer aus Pennsylvania, und einem Teutschen Bauer, von dem Natur- und Kirchen-reich in America überhaupt, und besonders in Pennsylvania," in *Neu-Eingerichteter Amerikanischer Geschichts-Kalender* (Philadelphia, 1749). Both of the Armbrüsters were members of St. Michael's Lutheran Church in Philadelphia, where they were identified as having converted from the Dunkers ("Dunker heraus").

38. For further details on naturalization, see Schwartz, "*A Mixed Multitude,*" 160–64.

39. *Korrespondenz Mühlenbergs,* 1:354, 410.

40. *Pennsylvanische Berichte,* 16 May 1755.

41. Given Saur's famous opposition to the charity school project of the 1750s, one can assume that much of the 1752 Gespräch was motivated by his opposition to this plan, which, he believed, was intended to eliminate the use of the German language. For details, see Samuel Edwin Weber, *The Charity School Movement in Colonial Pennsylvania* (Philadelphia, 1905).

42. The quotations from Saur in this paragraph and the remainder of this section are from the *Calender;* the years of publication are given in the text.

43. This word means in this context "surety," or bond, and not a land warrant, which apparently was never translated into German since no rough equivalent exists. This fact also suggests why disputes over unwarranted lands could so easily break out among Germans, who could not understand what this legal term referred to.

44. "O Mein Lieber! Hüte dich vor Schulden! Lass keinen Hunger leiden wan du Brod hast, und wan du einem Betrieger borgen solst, so nimm dich in acht oder sogleich verlohren, so macht dirs hernach keine Gedanken noch Rühe, wan du es nicht wieder bekommst" (*Calender* [1754]).

45. *Calender* (1763). Benjamin Franklin confirmed Saur's suspicions about the German readiness to employ attorneys in suits in a letter to a friend written in London three years later. To Rudolph Erich Raspe, Franklin suggested in 1766, "If you think you could seriously apply yourself to this Profession, I believe America would do well for you, especially as your Knowledge of the German Language would qualify you particularly to do the Business of those People" (*Papers of Franklin* 13:408).

46. The almanacs between 1760 and 1775 rarely missed printing anti-lawyer squibbs, but the younger Saur did not continue the practice of using the political conversation for instruction. The 1775 almanac, however, does provide the form of a testament, and the assignation of a bond. Saur seems also to have abandoned genuine research on current political and social detail by the 1760s. In explaining Georgia and its people to his readers in the 1760s, he erroneously copied the old reports on Georgians and South Carolinians' dependence on Pennsylvania for wheat and mills, stories taken from the Halle Reports of the 1730s (see n. 27, above) but long since out of date given the accomplishments on the Savannah. See *Pennsylvanische Berichte,* 28 March 1760.

47. LAS A 2 1029; B 2 1331/2.

48. *Calender* (1754).

49. *Journals of Muhlenberg,* 2:515.

50. David Henderson, *Des Landsmanns Advocat, Das ist: Kurzer Abzug aus solchen Gesetzen von Pennsylvania und England, welche daselbst in völliger Kraft, und einem freyen Einwohner auf dem Land höchst nötig und nützlich zu wissen sind . . .* ["The fellow countryman's advocate, that is, a short extract of such laws of Pennsylvania and England which are in full effect, and which are highly necessary and useful to know for the free farmer . . ."] (Philadelphia, 1761).

51. Ibid., vii; see 110–23, 144–54, for the sections on wills, property, and naturalization. See the dedication and introduction for Henderson's account of how he wrote the book

52. Saur's definition is in his *Nützliche Anweisung,* beginning at 61.

53. Henderson, *Des Landsmanns Advocat,* vii; see also viii, references to "ein Jury Trial"; 28–36, "Concerning the Jury."

54. Boltzius's letters, Mühlenberg's journals and correspondence, and, for Nova Scotia, documents reprinted in Bell, *"Foreign Protestants,"* 584–85, all confirm the universal use of the term *Fensen.*

55. This paragraph is based on a comparison of the language in Henderson's volume with Saur's almanac, his newspaper, and his *Nützliche Anweisung.*

56. Henderson, *Des Landsmanns Advocat,* ii, iii–iv.

57. Ibid., viii.

58. Adams, "Colonial German-Language Press," 162–64.

59. HSP, Broadsides, Henry Miller, *Geistlicher Irrgarten.* . . . Miller attached himself to no religious group until the Moravians persuaded him to rejoin them in 1773; see Adams, "Colonial German-Language Press," 164.

60. *Der Wöchentliche Pennsylvanische Staatsbote* . . . 14 August 1770 (hereafter cited as *Staatsbote*).

61. Harold James, *A German Identity, 1770–1790* (London, 1989), 11–33; on the relevance of the Swiss model, see Brady, *Turning Swiss;* on the eventual use of the United States as a model for German identity, see Horst Dippel, *Germany and the American Revolution, 1770–1800: A Sociohistorical Investigation of Late Eighteenth-Century Political Thinking,* trans. Bernard A. Uhlendorf (Chapel Hill, 1977).

62. *Staatsbote,* 18 January 1762, 22 March 1762. Only two incomplete copies of the almanac survive for 1763, and through 1774 Miller showed no interest in devoting himself to the type of explanatory essays that the elder Saur had printed.

63. *Staatsbote,* 22 March 1762, 19 April 1762. Miller also identifies Dresden and Hamburg in a similar manner.

64. Ibid., 16 September 1765; the emphasis is Miller's; Adams, "Colonial German-Language Press," 183.

65. Donald June Lineback, "An Annotated Edition of the Diary of Johann Heinrich Miller (1702–1782), Pietist and Printer of the American Revolution" (Ph.D. diss., University of North Carolina, Chapel Hill, 1975), 145.

66. Adams, "Colonial German-Language Press," 176. Three months after its appearance in the *Gentleman's Magazine,* Miller finally printed Franklin's satire in which Prussian policy was identified as ruinous, "How a Great Empire may be Reduced to a Small One," *Staatsbote,* 21 December 1773.

Chapter 7   Carolina Liberty and Property, and "Such Monstrous Sins"

1. Urlsperger, comp., *Detailed Reports,* 2:193.

2. AFSt 5 E 4 Lit. C, Pasche to Francke, 15 June 1762: "die Schiffe nach Ost-Indien hatten fast die ganze Reise hindurch gute Conovoye, die nach America aber wären mehr der Gefahr blos gestellt."

3. *Journals of Mühlenberg* 1:58, Charlestown, 23 September 1742. Despite the eighteenth-century designation of the place as "Charles Town," I use the post-revolutionary conventional spelling throughout.

4. "First Consistory Book of Church of St. John," art. 25. (For complete information on this source, see chap. 4, n. 95, above).

5. *Journals of Muhlenberg,* 2:513.

6. Leo Schelbert, "Schweizer Auswanderung in das Gebiet der Vereinigten Staaten von Nordamerika" in *Handbuch der schweizerischen Volkskunde* (forthcoming); idem, *Einführung in die schweizerische Auswanderungsgeschichte der Neuzeit* (Zürich, 1976), 230, 233; Charles G. Cordle, ed., "The John Tobler Manuscripts: An Account of German-Swiss Emigrants in South Carolina," *Journal of Southern History* 5 (1939), 83–97; Walter L. Robbins, ed. and trans., "John Tobler's Description of South Carolina (1753) and (1754)," *SCHM* 71 (1970), 141–61; 257–65; Paul Wernle, *Der schweizerische Protestantismus im 18. Jahrhundert* (Tübingen, 1922), 1:11–356; Wilhelm Hadorn, *Kirchengeschichte der reformierten Schweiz* (Zürich, 1907), 208–26.

7. The above simplifies the argument of Arlin Charles Migliazzo, "Ethnic Diversity on the Southern Frontier: A Social History of Purrysburgh, South Carolina, 1732–1792" (Ph.D. diss., Washington State University, 1982); see also Florence Janson Sherriff, "The Saltzburgers and Purrysburg," *Proceedings of the South Carolina Historical Association* (Charleston), 1963, pp. 12–22.

8. GLAK, Extractus Geheimen Raths-Protocolli de dato Carlsruhe den 9ten Dezember 1737, no. 9847, letter of Durs Thommen to Meister Fischer, 11 November 1736. On Thommen, see Leo Schelbert, "On the Power of Pietism: A Documentary of the Thommens of Schaefferstown," *Historic Schaefferstown Record* 17 (1983), 43–78.

9. A. S. Salley, Jr., *The History of Orangeburg County, South Carolina* (Orangeburg, S.C., 1898), 59–71; Paul G. McCullough et al., *History of the Lutheran Church in South Carolina* (Columbia, S.C., 1971), 21–24; 46–55; 58–63.

10. Nancy Fox et al., comp., *Newberry Co., S.C., Historic Resource Survey Report* (Columbia, S.C., 1985); John Biveus, Jr., "Fraktur in the South: An Itinerant Artist," *MESDA: Journal of Early Southern Decorative Arts* 1 (1975), 1–23; Christian Kolbe and Brent Holcomb, "Fraktur in the 'Dutch Fork' Area of South Carolina," ibid. 5 (1979), 36–51.

11. On the land policies and naturalization, see Kettner, *American Citizenship,* 102, 123; Janie Revill, comp., *A Compilation of the Original Lists of Protestant Immigrants to South Carolina, 1763–1773* (Baltimore, 1974), 1–5; Robert C. Ackerman, *South Carolina Colonial Land Policies* (Columbia, 1977).

12. In what follows, the composite of land acquisitions is compiled from the records of land surveys, plats, memorials, and warrants that can be obtained from SCDAH, Combined Alphabetical Index. For the sake of economy, I do not attempt to list in each instance the plat, memorial, survey, or will where the names of some of these settlers appear.

13. See Hacker, *Kurpfälzische Auswanderer,* 158; McCullough et al., *Lutheran Church in South Carolina,* 27–29; the Riemenspergers are another family that, like the Geigers, had branches in Carolina as well as Switzerland and the Kraichgau-Heidelberg area.

14. See Brent H. Holcomb, *South Carolina Marriages, 1688–1799* (Baltimore, 1980), 279.

15. On the Charleston group, see section 2, below; SCDAH, letters of

administration on Ehney's estate, 2 October 1767, granted to his widow Christina; Journal of the Court of Ordinary, 1767–71.

16. Ibid., South Carolina Court of Common Pleas, Judgment Rolls, box 70A, no. 210 A, 1767.

17. Ibid., Quit Rent Rolls, 1760–74; local tax records for the counties do not exist for this period; earlier quit rent rolls exist for the 1740s, but not the 1750s.

18. South Caroliniana Library, University of South Carolina (Columbia, S.C.), Knotts-Scott Family Papers, 10048/9844, Genealogy.

19. GLAK 229/188807; 118/815, Zuzenhausen; Hacker, *Kurpfälzische Auswanderer,* 125.

20. C. Dixon Hollingsworth, Jr., *The Bethany Colony* (Sylvania, Ga., 1974), 7–9; George Fenwick Jones, *The Salzbuger Saga: Religious Exiles and Other Germans along the Savannah* (Athens, Ga., 1984), 94–100.

21. For Bozenhard after his return from Georgia, see Langenau Village Archive, Gemeind-Buch über Langenau und Dellingen . . . , 1 September 1755; the key book of sales for 1743–53 is missing, as are all partitions of estate. The *Pflegschaftsaketen* after 1781 contained an extensive case in 1786 regarding quarrels over the care of the emigrant Johannes Remshard, which has since been lost. (I thank the village archivist Hans Bühler for his aid in clarifying these sources.) Presumably this is the same as the recovery of property now belonging to Christian Remshard in America being recovered by the agent Baisch (StAL, Best. 209 a, 117; 556–557). The letters of the Bozenhard brothers were published originally in the newspaper *Der Ulmer Ordentliche-Wöchentliche Anzeigszettel,* no. 69 (9 February 1754), and reprinted in the *Ulmer Albzeitung* 2, no. 269 (1935), copy in my possession.

22. Hacker, "Auswanderer aus Ulm," 225; McCullough et al., *Lutheran Church in South Carolina,* 29.

23. Lohrmann, along with Sailer, a fellow emigrant, was among the petitioners in 1788 along Sandy Run hoping to organize Salem Church. See McCullough et al., *Lutheran Church in South Carolina,* 133 n. 225.

24. Upon the death of Löcher's father, the farrier Abraham, in 1775, Löcher, his brother Johann, and his sister Agnes divided the estate; each received 102 Gulden, although authorities noted that Jacob "had cost his blessed father much [no exact figure is given] in clothing" (Weidenstetten Village Archives, Teilungen, 21 October 1775).

25. Ibid., fasc. 1, no. 70, 19 January 1787.

26. Upon the final partition of their mother's estate (ibid., 2 November 1782), the five Sailer children each were to receive 177 Gulden; Jacob had already invested the 100 Gulden in books noted above and had taken with him another 30 Gulden of his own property in 1752. This indicates the prosperity of the family from which he came. The Sailers were related by marriage in Weidenstetten and nearby villages not only to the Lohrmanns but also to the Tausendwalds, Stumpfs, Kassbergers, and Baders, all of whom sent family members to South Carolina in the 1750s and 60s. By the time of his mother's death, Jacob was also dead, and David renounced his twin

claims in favor of their sister Barbara, the wife of Georg Lohrmann, in Weidenstetten. The document of renunciation, in German and English, was prepared at St. John's in Charleston, witnessed by the pastor and vestry, notarized, and sent with a terra-cotta seal of the State of South Carolina attached (fasc. 1).

27. Ibid., T.u.I., with extracts from the letters of the brothers from Heidelberg, 3 September 1765, 9 January 1770, 16 February 1775. Jacob Sailer had attempted to avoid paying manumission taxes for his brothers by donating 1 Gulden 24 Kreuzer to the orphanage at Weidenstetten. The attempt failed and his father was told to pay the 2 Gulden 10 Kreuzer owed (StAL, Best. 209 1, 117:258b, 17 December 1765). The three younger brothers left after paying the Nachsteuer on 400 Gulden (p. 327r). For David Sailer's later success, see South Carolina Historical Society (Charleston, S.C.), David Saylor Receipt Book, 1784–87.

28. Salley, *History of Orangeburg County,* 275, list of civic officers.

29. "Report of Mr. Ettwein's Journey to Georgia and South Carolina, 1765," ed. George F. Jones, *SCHM* 91 (1990), 247–260.

30. Except where otherwise noted, the rest of this paragraph is based on Weidenstetten Village Archives, Weidenstetten und Schechstetten Protocollum Aller Vorganener Contract und Handlungen . . . , 1761, alphabetically arranged showing the buying and selling or the administration of property.

31. Ibid., Teilungen, 24 July 1782, Johannes Bader.

32. The Swiss and southwest German term *Juchert* derives from the "yoke" of oxen, and refers to the amount of land one could plow in one day—hence, between 34 and 47 hectares, or 85 and 118 acres. One or two quarters would total 21 to 59 acres, worth between 110 and 220 Gulden at current village prices.

33. I have been unable to prove arrival for all of these figures, but the family names, in addition to Junginger of the Ulm village cluster, occur not only in the Charleston records but also in the petition of the Lutherans at Orangeburg District for a Church of St. Martin, most of them on the north side of the Saluda near the lower end of the Broad and Saluda Forks. See McCullough et al., *Lutheran Church in South Carolina,* 138.

34. The sources of this paragraph and the two subsequent ones are as follows: on freemasonry, Albert G. Mackey, *The History of Freemasonry in South Carolina from its Origin in the Year 1736 to the Present Time* (Columbia, S.C., 1861), 27 (no German names are mentioned in the early descriptions of the Charleston Lodge); on St. John's day and Swabian customs and songs, Erich and Beitl, eds., *Wörterbuch der deutschen Volkskunde,* 410–16; and Bieritz, *Kirchenjahr,* 211–13; on Friederichs, McCullough et al., *Lutheran Church in South Carolina,* 74–77. (See also Steven C. Bullock, "The Revolutionary Transformation of American Freemasonry, 1752–1792," *WMQ,* 3d ser., 47 [1990], 347–69, for comparisons to the Boston and Philadelphia lodges.) The congregation worshipped in the Huguenot church until the cornerstone was laid in 1759 for a church; by this time Friederichs had left for St. Matthew's, in Amelia township. Mühlenberg seems not to have heard of Friederichs

before when he received a letter from him while visiting Charleston in 1774 (*Journals of Muhlenberg,* 2:589); but see *Korrespondenz Mühlenbergs,* 2:255 for a 1755 letter to Thomas Krone, pastor at Einbeck, Mühlenberg's hometown, deploring the enthusiasm among Hanoverians for Carolina; the four letters of Krone to Mühlenberg have been lost, but Krone might well have known of Friederichs's acceptance of a pastorate in South Carolina.

35. Terry W. Lipscomb, ed., *The Journal of the Commons House of Assembly,* vol. 13, *1754–1755* (Columbia, S.C., 1986), quotations at 34–35; 49, 179. Kogar is almost certainly Jacob Joseph Kochert of Ratzweiler, a Palatine emigrant of 1739 (Hacker, *Auswanderungen aus Rheinpfalz,* 485; Kunselman Burgert, *Eighteenth Century Emigrants,* 2:296, 369).

36. J. H. Easterby et al., eds., *The Journal of the Commons House of Assembly,* vol. 9 *1749–1750* (Columbia, S.C., 1962), 369, 399, 408; vol. 11, *1751–1752,* (Columbia, S.C., 1977), 37; vol. 12, *1752–1754* (Columbia, S.C., 1983), xvi–xvii, 142, quotation at 347, 412, 423; by March the Commons House agreed in principle to a fund of £250 per year to aid in poor relief but refused the committee's recommendation that masters of vessels be obligated under penalty to give security for indigent and lame imported immigrants or to remove them. The bounty provisions were restored under an immigration act of 1761, which expired again in late 1764; but the Commons House did vote in 1765 to pay the bounty to "Palatine" immigrants. See Alexander S. Salley, ed., *Journals of the Commons House of Assembly for South Carolina for the Year 1765* (Columbia, S.C., 1949), 9. By the 1760s bounty money came to £3 for adults and for children between 2 and 12 (Robert Selig, "Emigration, Fraud, Humanitarianism, and the Founding of Londondery, South Carolina, 1763–1765," *Eighteenth-Century Studies* 23 (1989), 1–23).

37. Peter A. Coclanis, *The Shadow of a Dream: Economic Life and Death in the South Carolina Low Country, 1679–1920* (New York, 1989), 75–86; Robert M. Weir, *Colonial South Carolina: A History* (New York, 1983), 171, 218–230; Richard Walsh, *Charleston's Sons of Liberty: A Study of the Artisans, 1763–1789* (Columbia, S.C., 1959), 29–65; Stephen Edward Wiberley, Jr., "Four Cities: Public Poor Relief in Urban America, 1700–1775," (Ph.D. diss., Yale University, 1975), 36–48.

38. Jeanne A. Calhoun et al., *A Survey of Economic Activity in Charleston, 1732–1770* (Charleston, 1982), 34–40; 53–54; 62–63; George C. Rogers, *Charleston in the Age of the Pinckneys* (Norman, Okla., 1969), 12–13, 56–73.

39. *Korrespondenz Mühlenbergs* 2:256.

40. Neuffen Village Archives, Index to Realteilungen; only the index survives in the attic of the current *Bürgermeisteramt.* Michael Muckenfuß, a blacksmith, expanded his holdings beyond Charleston, where with his wife Catherine he sold for £1,250 to the Charleston baker Nicholas Fiddey [*sic;* the name was actually Fittig] part of a lot on King Street which Muckenfuß had bought in 1761 (Clara A. Langley, ed., *South Carolina Deed Abstracts, 1719–1772* (Columbia, S.C., 1974), book I-3, p. 149, 13 and 14 May 1766. With part of this money he probably purchased five hundred acres of swamp

near Pine Island in St. Mathew's Parish (GDAH, Georgia Plats, n. 930, p. 271).

41. SCDAH, Court of Common Pleas, Judgment Book, 1770–71, pp. 220–22; the two German speaking plaintiffs recovered both the debt and damages in the suit.

42. SCDAH, Shipping Manifests: Holland Trade, details May's Amsterdam-Charleston activities and an occasional import from Bremen, a connection he developed extensively after 1787. May only rarely appears in the minutes of St. John's in Charleston. On Francis Hasenclever's Dutch trade, see LCP, Broadsides, the *Beylage* to Miller's *Staatsbote,* 18 January 1774. On the Hasenclever family, see Bennion, "Flight from the Reich," 241–42.

43. Philadelphia City Archives (Philadelpha, Pa.), Letters of Attorney 1408/1, pp. 464–65, on May's connection to Nixon; *Journals of Muhlenberg* 2:570–80.

44. Hacker, *Auswanderungen aus Rheinpfalz,* 283; "First Consistory Book of Church of St. John," 28, South Caroliniana Library, Hennig Cohen, "Index of Personal Names for the South Carolina Gazette 1732–38," typescript; Mary Bondurant Warren, *South Carolina Jury Lists, 1718 through 1783* (Danielsville, Ga., 1977); SCDAH, Court of Common Pleas, Journals and Judgment Books; Langley, ed., *South Carolina Deed Abstracts.*

45. SCDAH, Court of Common Pleas, Journals, 2:187.

46. This paragraph and the next are based on ibid., Charleston County MS Wills, 1740–47, pp. 39, 482; 1747–52, p. 320. I have surveyed all the surviving lists and common pleas records, 1713–73.

47. J. E. Crowley, "The Importance of Kinship: Testamentary Evidence from South Carolina," *Journal of Interdisciplinary History* 16 (1986), 559–77; and idem, "Family Relations and Inheritance in Early South Carolina," *Histoire Sociale/Social History* 17 (1984), 35–57.

48. Marylynn Salmon, "Women and Property in South Carolina: The Evidence from Marriage Settlements, 1730–1830," *WMQ,* 3d ser., 39 (1982), 655–85; idem, *Women and the Law of Property,* 9, 156–60; M. Leigh Harrison, "A Study of the Earliest Reported Decisions of the South Carolina Courts of Law," *American Journal of Legal History* 16 (1972), 70; Herbert A. Johnson, "The Palmetto and the Oak: Law and Constitution in Early South Carolina, 1670–1800," in Kermit L. Hall and James W. Ely, Jr., eds., *An Uncertain Tradition: Constitutionalism and the History of the South* (Athens, Ga., 1989), 92–94; Jack P. Greene, "South Carolina and the Caribbean Connection," *SCHM* 88 (1987), 207; M. Eugene Sirmans, "Legal Status of the Slave in South Carolina, 1670–1775," *Journal of Southern History* 28 (1962), 462–73.

49. SCDAH, Miscellaneous Records, vol. OO, pp. 480–82, 30 January 1771.

50. Except where otherwise indicated, the rest of this section is based on the surviving wills in SCDAH, with occasional reference to wills in the South Caroliniana Library, Leonardo Andreas Collection; the occasional German-language will seems to have been written and not recorded. These figures

do not include the wills left by the French-surnamed Purrysburg settlers noted above, some of whom were also fluent in German.

51. SCDAH, Wills, 1767–71, pp. 180–82, 28 December 1765; pp. 465–66, June 1771; pp. 208–9, 15 April 1768; quotations from 1774–78, pp. 503–4; 1780–83, pp. 268–73. On Goette, see *Journals of Muhlenberg* 2:382.

52. SCDAH, Wills, 1776–84, pp. 83–84; 1767–71, pp. 357–58. The original Geiger conveyance has disappeared; the bond is in Records of the Secretary of State, Miscellaneous Records II P, pp. 590–92, 1773.

53. "First Consistory Book of Church of St. John," p. 40, 9 June 1768.

54. Ibid., p. 57, 7 September 1769.

55. SCDAH, Wills, 1780–83, pp. 249–51; 1774–78, 120, 568–69; Inventories, vol. 17, 1772–76, pp. 399–400; Plats, Memorials, 6:314.

56. Ibid., Wills, 1760–67, 16 February 1764; 1780–83, pp. 167–68, April 1779, Johann Ernst, blacksmith in Ansonborough. My check of the Pflugfeld records reveals the marriage of Johann Georg Claß and Anna Margaretha Raff on 15 October 1748, but no evidence that her orders to recover property under village administration with Jakob Raff were carried out (StAL, Pflugfeld Eheregister). See also Hacker, *Auswanderungen aus Baden,* 306–7.

57. SCDAH, Wills, 1757–61, p. 231, 16 October 1759.

58. All examples taken from "Consistory Book of Church of St. John"; to these gifts Jacob Williman's loan of one thousand pounds should be added.

59. I have attempted to check variant spellings of names against all extant inventories for this period; only a handful of the Charleston congregants can be identified. I am grateful to my student Thomas Price for providing the computerized lists of the inventories with which the register of St. John's was then compared.

60. A check of all surviving inventories (in SCDAH) from 1783 to 1810 against the names of the founding families produces the following list of the wealthiest leaders' descendants, who served as vestrymen, wardens, and owners of pews: Minzing, Speidel, Kalteisen, Schütterling, Muckenfuß, Ehney, Werner, Birckenmeyer, Hoff, Bomer, Eberle, Wehrle.

61. For details on Anglican poor relief in the city, and the statistics, see Wiberley, "Four Cities," 69–75, 110–56. The German Friendly Society records suggest that small loans (between £50 and £200 were extended to members; by 1773 restrictions were imposed so that only members in good standing could apply for relief of £7 per year for three years. Long-term charity cases were taken on for a maximum of seven years at no more than £60 per year for the last four years. Such sums obviously would have been barely sufficient to sustain anyone: at that time, wages for common laborers in Charleston averaged about 9 shillings per day, or perhaps £117 per year, in South Carolina currency, while Philadelphia laborers averaged about £60 per year.

62. "First Consistory Book of Church of St. John," 20, 23.

63. Ibid., 23, 24.

64. SCDAH, Wills, 1761–67, pp. 358–62, 2 May 1764, Friedrich Strouble, bricklayer with house and lot on King Street, and slaves; 1771–74, pp. 231–

32, 7 August 1772, Johann Gotsman, tavern keeper; p. 285, 23 September 1772, Conrad Kysell, tavern keeper; pp. 19–20, 4 August 1773, Samuel Lieber, chapman, owner of Horse Swamp in Charleston; 1776–84, pp. 568–69, 10 October 1777, Henry Metzger; 1774–78, pp. 6–7, 8 November 1776. Johann Kirchner, carter and drayman; 1776–84, pp. 115–16, 7 October 1774, Bernard Leitz, tailor, Charleston Neck; 1776–84, pp. 162–63, 5 April 1781, Philip Mintzing. In locating the streets and "Dutch Town," I have referred to South Caroliniana Library, map 2–1790–1, the "Ichnography of Charleston," done at London.

65. George J. Gongaware, *The History of the German Friendly Society of Charleston, South Carolina, 1766–1916* (Richmond, Va., 1935), 1–22; "First Consistory Book of Church of St. John," 32–34.

66. "First Consistory Book of Church of St. John," 32–34; SCDAH, Wills, 1760–67, pp. 397–98, 3 November 1764.

67. "First Consistory Book of Church of St. John," 21.

68. Yoder, ed., *Pennsylvania German Immigrants,* 47; Volker Schäfer and Uwe Jens Wandel, eds., *USA-Universität Tübingen: Die Amerika-Beziehungen der schwäbischen Landesuniversität im Kaleidoskop* (Tübingen, 1976), 62, gives his name as Ludwig Friedrich and his matriculation date as 1739—clearly impossible unless they are referring to a different individual or unless Daser's date of birth is mistakenly given as his matriculation date. No other record of a Daser at Tübingen exists for this period, however. The suggestion that the pastor was the son of Paulus Achatius (McCullough et al., eds., *Lutheran Church in South Carolina,* 83 n. 161) seems implausible. Daser was ordained by Pastor Hahnbaum in Charleston after the latter examined him, leading one to suspect that perhaps he did have university training.

69. *Journals of Muhlenberg* 2:580–82; Wachsel had been pastor since 1763 in London, and worked in conjunction with the Halle pastors Ziegenhagen and Pasche in responding to pleas from the colonies for pastoral assistance. The vestry noted on 10 June 1771 that "the whole congregation has been appreciating so far the way in which the minister Friedrich Daser labored as pastor" ("First Consistory Book of Church of St. John," 64).

70. This paragraph and the two that follow are based on "First Consistory Book of Church of St. John," 65–67; McCullough et al., *Lutheran Church in South Carolina,* 82–83. Wage estimates are drawn from the tables in Walsh, *Sons of Liberty,* 143–45.

71. Vielhaur was probably originally from the Huguenot family Vielfaure; the South Carolinian had a relative at Versailles as well. See Hacker, *Kurpfälzische Auswanderer,* 182; *Journals of Muhlenberg* 2:572. The next paragraph is based on "First Consistory Book of St. John."

72. *Journals of Muhlenberg* 2:574, quotation at 582; The Greek translates as "avocation." Mühlenberg also noted conversations with the wife of Johannes Delger, the tanner; she was a sister of Conrad Kiemle's wife, recently arrived from Philadelphia (p. 584).

73. Ibid., 582.

74. "First Consistory Book of Church of St. John," 30, 53, 55, 74, 120.

75. *Journals of Muhlenberg,* 575–76.

76. *Documentary History of the Evangelical Lutheran Ministerium of Penn-sylvania and Adjacent States* (Philadelphia, 1898), 91.

77. George Fenwick Jones, "The 1780 Siege of Charleston as Experienced by a Hessian Officer," *SCHM* 88 (1987), 23–33, 63–75, at 71; Raymond A. Mohl, ed., " 'The Grand Fabric of Republicanism': A Scotsman Describes South Carolina, 1810–1811," ibid. 71 (1970), 170–188.

78. For details on Indian affairs in South Carolina, see William L. Mc-Dowell, Jr., ed., *Documents Relating to Indian Affairs, May 21, 1750-August 7, 1954,* Colonial Records of South Carolina, ser. 2 (Columbia, S.C., 1958), 372–75; see also Easterby et al., eds., *Journal of Commons House* 10:xix–xxxiv; Lipscomb, ed., *Journal of Commons House* 12:172. The reference to "northern" Indians is obscure but might refer to Hurons active in the Mississippi Valley and against the Chickasaw. See Theodore Calvin Pease and Ernestine Jenison, eds., *Illinois on the Eve of the Seven Years' War, 1747–1755,* French Series, vol. 3 (Springfield, Ill., 1940), 817, 851.

79. Murti June Clark, *Colonial Soldiers of the South, 1732–1774* (Baltimore, 1983), 881–946; Kalteisen's observations are in *Journals of Muhlenberg* 2:572–73.

Chapter 8   Lutherans and Property: The Philadelphia Definition

1. *Korrespondenz Mühlenbergs* 1:332, 344.

2. On Meyer's life, see *Journals of Muhlenberg* 1:618–19. Meyer was pos-sibly the brother of Mathäus Mayer of Waldhilsbach-Neckargemünd arriving on the *Robert and Alice,* 1743? (Kunselman Burgert, *Eighteenth Century Emi-grants,* 253); if so, Meyer was also a Kraichgauer. The financial details about the church are from HSP, Communicants' Register of St. Michael's Lutheran Church. In this chapter, unless otherwise noted, references to "St. Michael's" are to the Philadelphia congregation and not to the Germantown parish of the same name.

3. Glatfelter, *Pastors and People,* 411–20; *Journals of Muhlenberg* 1:68; AFSt 4 F 7, pp. 24–25.

4. The above summarizes Billy G. Smith, *The "Lower Sort": Philadelphia's Laboring People, 1750–1800* (Ithaca, N.Y., 1990), 158–65; LTSA, St. Michael and Zion Communion Register, marginal notations; John Joseph Stoudt, *Sunbonnets and Shoofly Pies: A Pennsylvania Dutch Cultural History* (New York, 1973), 95–102, on broader patterns of housing and domestic furnishings; Scott T. Swank, "Henry Francis du Pont and Pennsylvania German Folk Art," in idem et al., eds., *Arts of the Pennsylvania Germans* (New York, 1983), 77–101 at 97–98; idem, "The Architectural Landscape," in ibid., 20–34, I concur with Swank that although most folk art forms are rural and pragmatic in nature, Philadelphia acted as the stimulus that sustained those artifacts that are not direct cultural transfers from specific regions of the Reich. Most

domestic arts were created by village and town artisans, not rural farmers.

5. Philadelphia City Archives, Philadelphia Wills, GA 262-2, books F-H, 1736–47, 10 March 1732, Caspar Leitbecker; 18 January 1738, Peter Weiser; 11 January 1741, George Frederick Hagar. After a brief initial attempt, I refrained from attempting to use the surviving inventories now housed in the new city archives repository. So poor is the condition of these documents that until extensive preservation work can be done on them, the removal of the inventories from their envelopes will result in their destruction.

6. This paragraph and the next are based on Tully, "Ethnicity, Religion, and Politics," which comments on the election incident; Susan E. Klepp, "Demography in Early Philadelphia, 1690–1860," in idem, ed., "The Demographic History of the Philadelphia Region, 1600–1860" (special issue), *Proceedings of the American Philosophical Society* 133 (1989), 85–111; P. M. G. Harris, "The Demographic Development of Colonial Philadelphia in Some Comparative Perspective," in ibid., 262–304; Gary B. Nash, *The Urban Crucible: Social Change, Political Consciousness, and the Origins of the American Revolution* (Cambridge, Mass., 1979), 179–80, 412–13; Schwartz, *Mixed Multitude,* 181–83; Joseph E. Illick, *Colonial Pennsylvania: A History* (New York, 1976), 173–78.

7. Unless other sources are cited, all prosopographies and descriptions of church affairs in section 1 of this chapter are taken from the baptismal, death, and communicant registers of St. Michael's; the tax lists of 1756 and 1772; the constables' reports for the city of Philadelphia; comments or advertisements in the German almanacs and newspapers; records of deeds and wills; and various business papers—mainly housed at the HSP or in German archival repositories—and the various immigrant lists and genealogical sources already referred to many times in the above chapters. For the names on the Declaration of Trust, see LTSA H 10 P5 M6 C 3, 5.

8. I cannot identify among the early elders, in addition to the dozen noted above, Valentin Unstatt and Georg Jacob Burckhardt; Unstatt seems to have come from Mannheim and may have been descended from Germantown's Hans Peter. The Heinrich Müller identified as "yeoman" remains obscure. Figures on wealth rely upon my examination of the 1756 tax lists, published as Hannah Benner Roach, "Taxables in the City of Philadelphia, 1756," *Pennsylvania Genealogical Magazine* 22 (1961), 3–41; and calculations in Smith, "*Lower Sort,*" 84–106, 110, 129–41.

9. Smith, "*Lower Sort,*" 213–15, table C.1. One other index of the status of these families can be found in members of the Graeff and Säckel families who purchased policies from the Mutual Assurance Company beginning in 1784 (Anthony N. B. Garvan et al., *The Architectural Surveys, 1784–1794,* vol. 1 [Philadelphia, 1976], 95, 124, 129, 219–20).

10. Despite considerable effort, I have failed to identify among the second tier of clients Adam Weber; Michael Kuntz, who arrived in 1747; Johannes Lampeter, who arrived in 1753, a client of Martin Ries; and Philip Lehrer, who arrived in 1752 and lived with Heinrich Böckle in Frankfurt. These details come from the St. Michael's communicant lists. Ries, the butcher,

arrived in 1752, aged twenty-one, from Massenbach, in the Kraichgau; Schäffer also seems to have come from Schriesheim, in the Kraichgau.

11. See, e.g., *Journals of Muhlenberg* 2:457.

12. The original Communion Register (Name der Abendmahl-Gäste . . . 1755–1763), in LTSA fH10/ P5 M6, 1755–64, contains information on how long the communicant lived in North America, the number of children he or she had, his or her place of residence, and "other things to be noted." The register first records, through 1762, communicants who are Lutheran married couples, then returns to record mixed marriages, then widows, then free single persons. The figures below compile all these lists to give a simplified sense of communicant patterns. On the village habit of refraining from communing with enemies, see Sabean, *Power in the Blood,* 37–60.

13. The descriptions are taken from LTSA H10 P5 M6 L2, pp. 14–29, Carl F. Hausmann, "History of St. Michael's and Zion Congregation" (typescript) the various notes made by the pastors in the margins of the Communion Register (LTSA fH10/ P5 M6, 1755–64) for the years 1755–58. On the anti-German and anti-Catholic fears, see Lambert Schrott, *Pioneer German Catholics in the American Colonies, 1734–1784* (New York, 1933), 43–50, 100–101; Arthur D. Graeff, *The Relations between the Pennsylvania Germans and the British Authorities (1750–1776)* (Norristown, Pa., 1934), 40.

14. This paragraph and the next are based on *Korrespondenz Mühlenbergs* 2:325–38; for the quotation see *Journals of Muhlenberg* 1:565.

15. *Korrespondenz Mühlenbergs* 2:447–50, Mühlenberg's summary of the complaints in his letter to Handschuh and the church council 6 February 1761; as a result of the two new land purchases, St. Michael's indebtedness was about twenty-five hundred pounds by the time of the uprising. I collated the names of the discontented, discussed below, from *Journals of Muhlenberg* and *Korrespondenz Mühlenbergs.*

16. *Korrespondenz Mühlenbergs* 2:13–14; see also the arrival of Joseph Boger from Lomersheim in 1754 in the Gerber lists (Yoder, ed., *Pennsylvania German Immigrants,* 40). Whether this is a brother or cousin of Hans Jürg cannot now be determined.

17. For examples of charges of bribery and corruption, see Sabean, *Power in the Blood,* 206–13; also, for examples in sermons and court prosecutions, see Peter Lahnstein, *Schwäbisches Leben in alter Zeit: Ein Kapitel deutscher Kulturgeschichte, 1580–1800* (Munich, 1983), 317–19. On Bengel, see Gottfried Mälzer, *Johann Albrecht Bengel: Leben und Werk* (Stuttgart, 1970).

18. HSP, Am. 3036, Philadelphia Court Dockets, June 1753; *Korrespondenz Muhlenbergs* 2:20–25, 48 n. 33. Mühlenberg's description of Zimmermann is in *Journals of Muhlenberg* 1:511.

19. By the 1790s Kober's familial connections were revealed in his attempt to recover a fifty-pound inheritance to be shared with his brothers Johannes, in Lauffen, and Elias, a tailor, in Schwaigern, as well as the children of the deceased Kilian, also from Schwaigern. (AFSt 4G9, Lieferungen, 1790–94).

20. Hausmann, "History of St. Michael's," 30, citing Brunnholtz's 1757 address to the congregation.

21. In section 2 of this chapter, except where I cite other sources, I am drawing upon, for the period after 1762, LTSA, St. Michael-Zion German Lutheran Church, Philadelphia, Council Minutes, microfilm by Presbyterian Historical Society, 1990 (hereafter cited as LTSA, St. Michael-Zion Council Minutes), vol. 1, 1763–77, entries for 5 January 1776; for the earlier data, see AFSt 4F5, Brunnholtz's letter of 3 March 1752; Wiberly, "Four Cities," 69–75, 142, 155; *Journals of Muhlenberg* 1:216, 266, 433; Smith, *"Lower Sort"*, 98–107; Nash, *Urban Crucible*, 402, table 10; LTSA, P5 M6 H10 F6, "Hilfskraft zur Unterstützungen der Hilfsbedürftiger und Hausarmen." The treasurer's accounts for this men's society begin in 1795; a women's society for poor relief was not founded until 1884, suggesting that philanthropic work was long considered the province of the male membership in this congregation.

22. *Korrespondenz Mühlenbergs* 2:126–27.

23. This discussion of Halle's funding summarizes yearly accounts kept at Halle (AFSt 5 D 5; 5 E 1–7); rates of conversion are taken either from Halle's own computations or from John J. McCusker, *Money and Exchange in Europe and America, 1600–1775: A Handbook* (Chapel Hill, 1978).

24. On the 1767–68 attempt, see *Korrespondenz Mühlenbergs,* vol. 3, no. 403; when citing the page proofs for the forthcoming vol. 3, I give the letter number rather than the page number. For the refusal, see Frankfurt Stadtarchiv, Bü. B 1768, Protocollus 1768, 226: "Auf eingerichte Bittschrift der evangelischen Prediger Mühlenberg und Schultze samt einiger Gemeindevorsteher zu Philadelphia in der amerikanischen Provintz Pensilvania um Verwilligung einer Collecte zur Erbauung der dortigen St. Michaels-Kirche: Solle man das Gesuch abschlagen." On the 1752 proposal, see Francke to Mühlenberg 13 September in *Korrespondenz Mühlenbergs* 1:531; 1752, the summary of Halle's expenditures for Pennsylvania is taken from AFSt 4 F 4–10; 4 G 3–9. The Sigismund Streit legacy, announced by a Venetian merchant formerly of Berlin, excluded the Salzburgers, who were patronized by the Venetians Schalkhauser, Flügel, and Jastrum. Despite long negotiations that eventually put the 10,450 Reichstaler in the hands of Ziegenhagen in 1769 as trustee, the American missions received little (AFSt 4 F 6; 4 F 9). The Solms- Rödelsheim legacy, on the other hand, generated real money for the North American missions.

25. *Journals of Muhlenberg* 2:453, 503, quotation at 515; see also the letters beginning in January 1761, *Korrespondenz Mühlenbergs* 2:445–50, 454–56, 458–60, 469–71, 524–26.

26. Mühlenberg describes the events in *Journals of Muhlenberg* 1:561–62; see also *Korrespondenz Mühlenbergs* 1:573–76, 578–85.

27. *Journals of Muhlenberg* 1:556–60; *Korrespondenz Mühlenbergs* 2:573–76. The Württemberg apothecary Schneider and two hundred others as late as 1763 threatened separation over Handschuh's insistence that Holy Communion be distributed jointly by himself and Mühlenberg; Schneider and

others insisted that this was not specified in the church order and that they would leave if forced to receive communion from the hands of their enemy Handschuh (see *Korrespondenz Mühlenbergs,* vol. 3, no. 282 n. 4). The original manuscript with signatures is in LTSA.

28. Schomerus, *Verfassungsrechtliche Entwicklung,* 80–93; Thomas Jakob Müller, "Die evangelische Obrigkeitsproblematik bei Heinrich Melchior Mühlenberg: Der Aufbau der lutherischen Kirche in Pennsylvania" (M.A. thesis, University of Göttingen, 1988), 194–204.

29. The details of the Germantown controversy, which centered more on personalities and differing customs and not particularly on the issue of property, can be followed in Müller, "Evangelische Obrigkeitsproblematik," 98–121; for more socioeconomic details, see Elizabeth Fisher, "A God of Order: The German Lutheran Controversies in Germantown, Pennsylvania, 1750–1765" (Ph.D. diss., Harvard University, in progress).

30. James T. Mitchell and Henry Flanders, eds., *Statutes at Large of Pennsylvania, 1682 to 1801* (Harrisburg, Pa., 1896–1911), 4:113; Carl Zollmann, *American Civil Church Law* (1917; reprint, New York, 1969), 38–79; Dallin H. Oaks, *Trust Doctrines in Church Controversies* (Macon, Ga., 1984), 11–34; Gareth Jones, *History of the Law of Charity, 1532–1827* (Cambridge, 1969), 3–23, 72–115; William Blackstone, *Commentaries on the Laws of England: A Facsimile of the First Edition of 1765–1769,* with intro. by A. W. Brian Simpson (Chicago, 1979), 273–74; *Journals of Muhlenberg* 1:201–2, 390, 453, 727–28.

31. *Journals of Muhlenberg* 1:220; see also his struggle to describe conveyancing and the dangers of defects in 1753. Significantly, however, Mühlenberg did not realize that proper vesting of title in the persons of trustees, and the registry of a declaration of trust in chancery, would have solved the problem in New Jersey, where an English justice of the peace explained the defect to him (pp. 361–62). See his explanation to Halle of the procedure of finding trustees (described as "Eigenthums Herren") and a "Declaration" in *Korrespondenz Mühlenbergs* 1:485.

32. Joseph Henry Smith, *Appeals to the Privy Council from the American Plantations,* with intro. by Julius Goebel, Jr. (New York, 1965), 466–89, on the general problem of the extension of parliamentary law, and on the particular case *Dunbar* v. *Webb.* On the general hostility of the legal profession and the judiciary to death-bed gifts to churches or foundations which jeopardized the heir, see Jones, *History of the Law of Charity,* 106–16.

33. *Korrespondenz Mühlenbergs* 2:152.

34. Ibid., vol. 3, no. 275. The next three paragraphs are based on *Journals of Muhlenberg* 1:583–679.

35. *Journals of Muhlenberg* 1:597–98, 605, 637–42, 647–57, quotation at 679; see also 693–94; 2:26–29; and *Korrespondenz Mühlenbergs,* vol. 3, no. 280. The appearance of the comet prompted the publication of the pamphlet *A Remarkable Relation of a Visionary Sight* . . . (Philadelphia, 1763); the German press published two years later a related account of sightings at Riga and Kirschberg, near Danzig, of heavenly portents including crossed swords, coffins, deaths-heads, an hourglass, and a serpent entwined around a pyramid,

all interpreted as signs of imminent warfare and death in the absence of repentance (*Zwey wahrhafte von gantz besondern Himmels-Zeichen* . . . , LCP, Broadsides, 1765 8336.F). Mühlenberg noted as well an apparent meteorite shower on 2 February 1765 over Philadelphia (*Journals of Muhlenberg* 2:174).

36. Mühlenberg believed the decision to build Zion only two blocks away from Saint Michael's to be shortsighted, preferring one large new building that could house the entire congregation and school. He was overruled, however, and after 1766 the parish and congregation became known as St. Michael's and Zion. See *Journals of Muhlenberg* 2:297; *Korrespondenz Mühlenbergs,* vol. 3, no. 355.

37. *Journals of Muhlenberg* 1:656–59, 669–71, 679, 689, 710–16, quotation at 712; *Korrespondenz Mühlenbergs,* vol. 3, nos. 268, 275, 276.

38. Zollmann, *American Civil Church Law,* 52–79.

39. On Blackstone, n. 30, see above. Whether New York "received" all such statutes is debatable. See Herbert Alan Johnson, "The Advent of Common Law in Colonial New York," in George Athan Billias, ed., *Law and Authority in Colonial America* (Barre, 1964), 74–87; Herbert Alan Johnson, "English Statutes in Colonial New York," *New York History* 57 (1977), 277–96; Johnson concludes that in practice, despite lawyers' opinions of total "reception," usage in the courts was more uncertain until the failed attempt to pass a reception statute in 1767 drove New York toward acts of assembly to specify what had been received.

40. The New Jersey incorporation did not occur until 1767 and was modeled on that of St. Michael's in Philadelphia; New York Lutherans and Presbyterians were denied their petitions. See Glatfelter, *Pastors and People,* 207–10, 215–19.

41. *Journals of Muhlenberg* 2:101–3.

42. *Korrespondenz Mühlenbergs,* vol. 3, no. 303 for quotation.

43. See ibid., no. 302, for quotation about lack of alms; see also nos. 323, 339. For examples of Mühlenberg's untranslated terms, see nos. 312, 346. See also Kötz, *Trust und Treuhand,* 65–72, 119–25.

44. The paragraph and the next summarizes Joseph Stancliffe Davis, *Essays in the Earlier History of American Corporations,* 2 vols. (Cambridge, 1917; reprinted New York, 1965), 1:49–107; ibid., 65–68; Erler et al., eds., *Handwörterbuch zur deutschen Rechtsgeschichte,* 1:1071–73, s.v. "Familienfideikomiß"; *Journals of Muhlenberg* 2:257, 259–60, 271.

45. *Journals of Muhlenberg* 1:563; quotation at 2:94.

46. Ibid., 1:650–52; LTSA, St. Michael Zion Council Minutes, 310.

47. For details on graveyard culture and its significance, see Bischoff-Luithlen, *Der Schwabe und die Obrigkeit,* 242–46; Erich and Beitl, *Wörterbuch der deutschen Volkskunde,* 237–38, 298–302; P. A. Barba, *Pennsylvania-German Tombstones: A Study in Folk-Art* (Philadelphia, 1954); Donald A. Shelley, *The Fraktur-Writings or Illuminated Manuscripts of the Pennsylvania Germans* (Allentown, Pa., 1961); Frederick S. Weiser, "Piety and Protocol in Folk Art: Pennsylvania German Fraktur Birth and Baptismal Certificates," *Winterthur Portfolio* 8 (1973), 19–43; and idem, "His Deed Followed Him: The Fraktur

of John Conrad Gilbert," *Der Reggeboge (The Rainbow): Quarterly of the Pennsylvania German Society* 16 (1982), 33–45. I am indebted to Pastor Weiser for extended conversations about Pennsylvania German funerary customs and rituals.

48. Except where otherwise noted, the remainder of this section is based on Beyerle's protest and Mühlenberg's response, both in *Korrespondenz Mühlenbergs,* vol. 3, no. 317.

49. James Whitman, "Why Did Early Modern Lawyers Confuse Custom and Reason?" *University of Chicago Law Review* 31 (1991), 1–48. On the English changes, see Barbara Shapiro, *Probability and Certainty in Seventeenth-Century England: A Study of the Relationship between Natural Science, Religion, History, Law, and Literature* (Princeton, 1983), 163–93.

50. See *Korrespondenz Mühlenbergs,* vol. 3, nos. 372, 373, 396, quotation from no. 372. The negative effect of Beyerle and Schneider's attempts, however, was to further discourage Europeans from sending monetary aid to the North American congregations; see nos. 383, 396.

51. For details, see Richard Alan Ryerson, *The Revolution Is Now Begun: The Radical Committees of Philadelphia, 1765–1776* (Philadelphia, 1978), 264–74. As Ryerson notes, however, most of these men achieved prominence only in 1774, and later served as militia officers and as members of the Sixty-Six and the Council of Safety, although the Stamp Act crisis began their rise to political activity. See also Steven Rosswurm, *Arms, Country, and Class: The Philadelphia Militia and the "Lower Sort" during the American Revolution, 1775–1783* (New Brunswick, N.J., 1987), 18–100, 260, table A.2; Schwartz, *Mixed Multitude,* 276–80.

52. This paragraph and the next are based on *Korrespondenz Mühlenbergs,* vol. 3, no. 415; LTSA, St. Michael-Zion Council Minutes, entries for 1767–70.

53. LTSA, St. Michael-Zion Council Minutes, pp. 161–62, 16 September 1769. The surviving pew index does not reveal where people sat; by matching pew rentals in each building with the protagonists taken from the communion registers and Mühlenberg's writings, however, I arrive at the above conclusion. See Clements Library (Ann Arbor, Mich.), MS Department, St. Michael's and Zion Pew Register Index (c. 1770). Five pages are missing, out of about forty-seven; some names are reduplicated in the index.

54. LTSA, St. Michael-Zion Council Minutes, p. 170, 12 March 1770; pp. 254–55, 17 February 1773. In fact, the altercations between German and English youths finally resulted in the stabbing death of a German Lutheran night watchman, who was eulogized at Zion in 1773. The incident was but one of several about which the pastors agonized, believing that the youth of the parish were being irretrievably corrupted. For details, see the 16 May 1773 letter of Kunze to Halle, in AFSt 4 C 17, in which Kunze noted that all night watchmen were German speakers, since "the English are much too ashamed to be involved in such a job."

55. LTSA, St. Michael-Zion Council Minutes, pp. 161–62, 10 September 1769; p. 195, 15 April 1771; p. 199, 3 September 1771; pp. 201–7, 18–23

November 1771; p. 219, 13 January 1772; quotation is from 23 November 1771 meeting.

56. See *Korrespondenz Mühlenbergs,* vol. 3, nos. 311, 331, 338, 374.

57. Ibid., no. 383.

58. Ibid., nos. 415, 447. Mühlenberg actually uses the term *Verfassung* (constitution) and not simply *Kirchenordnung,* indicating a deepening awareness of the political implications of adopting such instruments in a "private" religious context.

59. For Mühlenberg's comments, see *Korrespondenz Mühlenbergs,* vol. 3, nos. 381, 321, 351, which cover 1764–65; for details on the later migration, see Wokeck, "Tide of Alien Tongues," 260–64.

60. This summarizes Nash, *Urban Crucible,* 250–60, 316–31; Rosswurm, *Arms, Country, and Class,* 18–24; Smith, "*Lower Sort,*" 84–91.

61. HSP, Wastebook of Friedrich Kuhl, 10 October 1778. On the Wertheimers, see Yoder, ed., *Pennsylvania German Immigrants,* 139–287; I have checked these entries against the archives in Wertheim and against St. Michael's records. The original inventories of estate, and recovery attempts, were destroyed by water damage or reused to make new paper in the nineteenth century. I am indebted to the archivist Erich Langguth for aid in checking the work of his father, Otto Langguth.

62. John W. Jordan, ed., *Colonial Families of Philadelphia,* 2 vols. (New York, 1911), 1:1229–59; HSP, Wastebook of Friedrich Kuhl, Zion Contributors (entered at end of Wastebook accounts).

63. See chapter 3, above, on village prices; and von Hippel, *Auswanderung,* 65 n. 16; Smith, "*Lower Sort,*" 95–105.

64. Based on my examination of archives in Wertheim and Yoder, ed., *Pennsylvania German Immigrants.* Hotz appears as "Hutz" in the 1772 tax list and was appraised for three pounds; he owned his own house by this date.

65. LTSA, Receipts and Expenditures (which follow St. Michael-Zion Council Minutes and are bound in the same volume). The initial notes indicate that a collection for church bells was begun in March, although the record claims that the accounts begin on 26 April 1762; for entry on Miercken, see 1764 account.

66. *Korrespondenz Mühlenbergs,* vol. 3, no. 447.

67. Smith, "*Lower Sort*", 107–12.

68. LTSA, St. Michael-Zion Council Minutes, 1767–68, 1770–76; annual financial report, January of each year. (No meetings of the council were held between September 1768 and January 1769 because Mühlenberg was gone; according to the recently acquired charter, no resolutions could lawfully be made in council in the rector's absence).

69. Ibid., annual financial reports.

70. Ibid., p. 283, 2 March 1774.

71. Ibid., pp. 321–23, 14 January 1776; Wiberley, "Four Cities," 48, 63, 75, 155–56.

72. *Journals of Muhlenberg* 2:309. The scriptural reference is to Gal. 6:10. In classic Lutheran understanding, however, "liberty" here means "obli-

gation," especially since St. Paul opens this chapter with the admonition "Bear ye one another's burdens, and so fulfill the law of Christ"; the preceding chapter makes the connection clear with its exhortation to "stand fast therefore in the liberty wherewith Christ hath made us free."

73. John K. Alexander, *Render Them Submissive: Responses to Poverty in Philadelphia, 1760–1800* (Amherst, Mass., 1980), 11–25; Rosswurm, *Arms, Country, and Class,* 22–24; Smith, *"Lower Sort",* 174–75, 187–88. For wills, see HSP, Will Book T, p. 1703, Catherine Hillegas, 1770; p. 1608, barber Michael Zeh, 1767; Will Book X, pp. 463–64, shoemaker Heinrich Nagel; shoemaker Will Book U, pp. 129–31, shoemaker Peter Sefferenz.

74. Anomalies also exist: why Thomas Lutz, the Wertheim arrival of 1755, listed as carpenter in Mulberry Ward on the tax list, appears here remains unclear, unless another man of the same name is indicated. The names are taken from LTSA, St. Michael-Zion Council Minutes, 14 January 1776.

75. Mühlenberg's letter is in ibid., 98; see 99–100 for the petition of the congregation, undated but roughly May 1767. The strictures on the theater fit Halle's general disapprobation of such attractions.

Chapter 9   The German-American Idea of Liberty

1. Karl J. R. Arndt, "The First Translation and Printing in German of the American Declaration of Independence," *Monatshefte* 77 (1985), 138–42.

2. On the tradition of typology (i.e., symbolic signification), see Ursula Brumm, *American Thought and Religious Typology,* trans. Joan Hoaglund (New Brunswick, N.J., 1970); Sacvan Bercovitch, ed., *Typology and Early American Literature* (Amherst, Mass., 1972); Barbara Kiefer Lewalski, *Protestant Poetics and the Seventeenth-Century Religious Lyric* (Princeton, 1979). No systematic work on German speakers' use of this mechanism exists for North America.

3. For general background on Pennsylvania politics, see James H. Hutson, *Pennsylvania Politics, 1746–1770: The Movement for Royal Government and Its Consequences* (Princeton, 1972), 162–74; Schwartz, *"A Mixed Multitude,"* 229–36.

4. HSP, *Die Rede, Herrn Joseph Galloways . . . ,* 24 July 1764 (possibly not Miller's press, but attributed to him).

5. For Saur's anti-Franklin pamphlet, see ibid., *Höret ihr deutsche Bürger in Philadelphia, daß euch Gott auch höre!*; original in the Royal Swedish Academy of Science. A petition in favor of royalization was circulated among Philadelphia citizens. I have checked the names on it against both St. Michael's communicant and baptismal lists. Although some signatures are illegible, I could find no correlation between the two lists, indicating that Miller's position found little positive response among Philadelphia Lutherans. For the petition, see HSP, Franklin MSS, Petitions, Photostats, PRO London Privy Council 1, bundle 50. The translation of "Privileges granted them by Your Majesty's Predecessors" reads "verliehene Freyheiten," i.e., privileges granted, bestowed, or conferred, but not necessarily guaranteed. For the

second Saur pamphlet, see LCP, Broadsides, undated and unsigned broadside *Eine zu dieser Zeit höchstnöthige Warnung und Erinnerung an die freye Einwohner der Provintz Pennsylvanien* [Germantown? 1764?].

6. For Adams's different reading of the *Warnung,* see his "Colonial German-Language Press," 180.

7. LCP, Broadsides, *An die Freyhalter und Einwohner der Stadt und County Philadelphia, deutscher Nation* [Philadelphia, 1764], contained the reminder of Franklin's 1755 essay; *An die Deutschen, vornehmlich die zum Wählen berechtigten in Philadelphia-Bucks-und Berks Caunty* (Philadelphia, 1765), contains the accusation against the Wistars.

8. LCP, Broadsides, *To the Freeholders and Other Electors . . . of Pennsylvania* (Philadelphia, 1765).

9. *Staatsbote,* 7 October 1765.

10. The quotations in this paragraph and the next are drawn from LCP, Broadsides, *An die guten Einwohner in Pennsylvanien . . .* (Philadelphia, 1773).

11. *Ein schön Lied von dem Schweizerischen Erz-Freyheitssohn Wilhelm Thellen, dem Urheber der Löbl. Eydgenossenschaft . . .* (Philadelphia, 1768). Miller published the essay and song on Wilhelm Tell at the same time that he reprinted the Massachusetts Circular Letter in April and reported on the nonimportation movement and the decision by students at Harvard to wear homespun as a form of nonviolent protest; see Adams, "Colonial German-Language Press, 194–95. Although some scholars suggest that the Wilhelm Tell legend may have parallels in the story of Henning Wulff or a Norwegian "Ur-story," Miller drew on his own Swiss background and experiences in deciding to use the story. On the legend, see, e.g., M. Wehrli, ed., *Das Lied von der Entstehung der Eidgenossenschaft: Das Urner Tellenspiel,* in *Quellenwerk zur Entstehung der schweizerischen Eidgenossenschaft,* Abt. III, vols. 1, 2 (Zürich, 1947–52).

12. For a summary of the approach emphasizing peasant resistance, see Schultze, ed., *Aufstände, Revolten, Prozesse.* The best argument against this perspective, especially Peter Blickle's work on the southwest, is Dietmar Willoweit, "Genossenschaftsprinzip und altständische Entscheidungsstrukturen in der frühneuzeitlichen Staatsentwicklung: Ein Diskussionsbeitrag," in Gerhard Dilcher and Bernhard Diestlekamp, eds., *Recht, Gericht, Genossenschaft und Policey: Studien zu Grundbegriffen der germanistischen Rechtshistorie. Symposion für Adalbert Erler* (Frankfurt, 1987), 126–38.

13. LCP, Broadsides, *Die Artikel der Patriotischen Gesellschaft der Stadt und Caunty Philadelphia* (Philadelphia, 1772).

14. *Staatsbote,* 12 April 1768.

15. *Staatsbote,* 31 May 1774.

16. William S. Powell et al., comps. and eds., *The Regulators in North Carolina: A Documentary History, 1759–1776* (Raleigh, N.C., 1971), 179. See, for further details, A. G. Roeber, " 'He Read It to Me from a Book of English Law': Germans, Bench, and Bar in the Colonial South, 1715–1770," in David Bodenhamer and James Ely, eds., *Ambivalent Legacy: A Legal History of the South* (Jackson, Miss., 1984), 215.

17. The English translation cited here is by W. A. Lambert, with revisions by Harold J. Grimm, taken from *Luther's Works,* ed. Jaroslav Pelikan et al., 54 vols., vol. 44, ed. Helmut T. Lehmann (Philadelphia, 1957); also published separately as Martin Luther, *Three Treatises* (Philadelphia, 1982), quotations at 227, 292, 308.

18. LTSA, f H10 P5 M6 E v.1 contains the 1762 Kirchenordnung (bound together with the Building Committee Report).

19. *Korrespondenz Mühlenbergs,* vol. 3, no. 254; quotations from LTSA, St. Michael-Zion Council Minutes, 1 October 1764.

20. *Journals of Muhlenberg* 2:122; LTSA, St. Michael-Zion Council Minutes, 1 October 1764.

21. *Journals of Muhlenberg* 2:190–92.

22. LTSA, PM 95, Mühlenberg to Physic, 10 March 1776.

23. Heinrich Melchior Mühlenberg, *Ein Zeugniß von der Güte und Ernst Gottes gegen sein Bundesvolk . . .* (Philadelphia, 1766); the original is archived at Gettysburg College Archives (Gettysburg, Pa.), uncataloged, item #2713; photocopy at LCP. Henry Miller published the sermon for Mühlenberg.

24. *Korrespondenz Mühlenbergs,* vol. 3, no. 348.

25. This paragraph and the next are based on Mühlenberg, *Zeugniß,* 40, 41, 42, 31–32. In general, Mühlenberg and the German-language press continued to speak of German speakers as loyal "subjects" until 1775; the invocation of citizenship, or the use of the term *Mitbürger* (fellow citizens) by Miller and other writers came only as reconciliation with the Crown seemed impossible.

26. Johann Georg Hülsemann, *Geschichte der Demokratie in den vereinigten Staaten von Nord-Amerika* (Göttingen, 1823), xx–xxii, 66, 133.

27. Unless otherwise noted, all quotations in the remainder of this section are from Mühlenberg's history, "Zeruttung der Philadelphischen Gemeinde . . . ," in LTSA, PM 95 Z 27, 1762.

28. *Korrespondenz Mühlenbergs* 2:402; and vol. 3, no. 260, where Mühlenberg refers again to the "Scherflein der Witwe"; the term *Scherflein* comes from *Scherf,* the German name for the half-penny derived from the Roman *serratus*; in combination with the word *Nahrung,* the expression conveyed the smallest amount of income necessary to sustain life. On the cultural significance of food and village bonds, see Sabean, *Power in the Blood,* 97–110.

29. On the Toleration Act, the disputes in New York, and Penn's 1681 charter, see the documents and commentary in H. Shelton Smith et al., eds., *American Christianity: An Historical Interpretation with Representative Documents,* vol. 1, *1607–1820* (New York, 1960), 231–61, quotations at 238, 239.

30. This paragraph and the two subsequent ones are based on Johann Joachim Zubly, *Eine Kurzgefaßte Historische Nachricht von den Kämpfen der Schweitzer für die Freyheit* (Philadelphia, 1775); idem, *The Law of Liberty* (Philadelphia, 1775); Salomon Geßner, "Das hölzener Bein: Ein Schweitzer Hirten-Gedicht von Getzner," *Staatsbote,* 26 July 1776.

31. My reading of Zwingli and Zubly relies on many conversations with my colleague Leo Schelbert and on his important unpublished essay, "The

Contest between Power and Liberty: John J. Zubly's Swiss Perspective of America's Revolutionary Struggle" (Paper given at the German-American Symposium, University of Wisconsin, Madison, 14 October 1983).

32. *Schreiben des evangelisch-lutherisch und reformierte Kirchenraths . . . in der Stadt Philadelphia* (Philadelphia, 1775); the account begins by reminding German readers that the ministries had been against America since 1763 and vindicates the North American position by pointing to the repeal of the Stamp Act (3).

33. On Johnson, see Bernard Bailyn, *Voyagers to the West: A Passage in the Peopling of America on the Eve of the Revolution* (New York, 1986), 576–82.

34. *Staatsbote,* 19 March 1776.

35. Donald Davidson, "On the Very Idea of a Conceptual Scheme," in Michael Krausz and Jack W. Meiland, eds., *Relativism: Cognitive and Moral* (Notre Dame, Ind., 1982), 68–80; Richard Rorty, *Philosophy and the Mirror of Nature* (Princeton, 1976), 316.

36. Joseph Butler, *Fifteen Sermons Preached at the Rolls Chapel . . . ,* ed. W. R. Mathews (London, 1969), 83; see Richard D. Brown, *Knowledge Is Power: The Diffusion of Information in Early America, 1700–1865* (New York, 1989), which, however, does not treat the German-language information systems.

37. *Staatsbote,* 19 March 1776. The last moral tale that Miller reprinted ("Ein Märchen") appears on the front page on 16 April; it recounts the injustice of an older brother robbing his younger sibling of his freedom and inherited property.

38. LTSA, St. Michael-Zion Council Minutes, 98–100, May 1767; quotation at 329, September 1776; no meetings of the council were held between April and September 1776.

39. This paragraph and the next are based on AFSt 4 C 17, J. H. C. Helmuth, "Briefe aus Philadelphia," 1773–75, quotations from letter of 25 August 1775.

40. *Journals of Muhlenberg* 2:765.

41. Ibid., 2:518, 700; 3:55, 123–25. For Luther's essay and commentary on it, see Quentin Skinner, *The Foundations of Modern Political Thought* (Cambridge, 1978), 2 vols., 2:12–19, 74–81, 196–206; *Luther's Works,* ed. Jaroslav Pelikan et al., 54 vols. (St. Louis, 1955–67), 47:5–55. For a Maryland German's outrage over the actions of "British thieves," see Smyth, *Tour through the United States* 2:258, 274–75.

42. AFSt 4 C 17, J. H. C. Helmuth, "Briefe aus Philadelphia," 1773–75, quotation from letter of 25 August 1725.

43. HSP, Gratz MSS, case 1, box 20; Peters Papers, 8:44, 56; the description of the respective religious groups marching is in Orderly Book of German Battalion of Continentals, January 1777–16 June 1781 (vol. 1 actually begins with 17 September 1776); see entries for 26 October 1776, 4 June 1777.

44. John W. Jackson, *With the British Army in Philadelphia, 1777–1778* (San Rafael, Calif., 1979), 83, 100, 266; less useful, but still informative, is George

Washington Greene, *The German Element in the War of American Independence*
(Philadelphia, 1876); Henry Melchior Mulenberg Richards, *The Pennsylvania-
German in the Revolutionary War, 1775–1783* (Lancaster, Pa., 1908; Baltimore,
1978), 190–231.

45. *An Eyewitness Account of the American Revolution and New England Life:
The Journal of J. F. Wasmus, German Company Surgeon, 1776–1783,* trans.
Helga Doblin, ed. Mary C. Lynn (New York, 1990), 94–95, 56.

46. Captain Johann Ewald, *Diary of the American War: A Hessian Journal,*
trans. and ed. Joseph P. Tustin (New Haven, Conn., 1979), 91, 108, 119.

47. Ibid., 341–42. Yet Hessian regulars apparently recognized immediately the value of staying in America to avoid returning to a principality
where recent reforms of inheritance law had driven younger sons into the
military. For details, see Charles Ingrao, *Hesse: The Making of a Military State,
1730–1775* (Cambridge, 1986).

48. This paragraph and the next are based on *Narrative of Johann Carl
Buettner in the American Revolution,* translated and published for Charles Fred-
rick Heartman (New York, n.d.), 25, 39–42, 55–56; the original is *Buettner,
der Amerikaner: eine Selbtsbiographie Johann Carl Buettners, ehemaligen nordamerikanischen Kriegers* (Camenz, 1828). For an instance of a similar cause—
homesickness, and incomprehension of the American officers' prohibition
against frequent bathing—creating a minor mutiny, see HSP, "Order Book
of the German Regiment, Lt. Col. Hubley Commanding, at Wyoming, from
July 19, 1779 to July 30th, 1779 [Lt. John Weidman, Adjt.]," 6, 24, 27 July
1779.

49. Anne M. Ousterhout, "Controlling the Opposition in Pennsylvania
during the American Revolution," *PMHB* 105 (1981), 3–34; Wallace Brown,
"Viewpoints of a Pennsylvania Loyalist," ibid. 91 (1967), 428. Enoch Story
estimated that three-quarters of Pennsylvanians were loyalists, a supposition
historians now discount; see also Wallace Brown, *The King's Friends: The
Composition and Motives of the American Loyalist Claimants* (Providence, R.I.,
1965), 85–105, 142–49; Brown finds 23 German claims among the 149 claims
for Pennsylvania and also confirms the geographic pattern: individuals far
from the networks of trade and communication among German speakers
(i.e., in upper New York in the Mohawk Valley, or in North Carolina's
backcountry) had a greater tendency toward loyalism.

50. Thomas Paine, *Gesunde Vernunft an die Einwohner von Amerika
. . . ,* trans. Charles Cist (Philadelphia, 1776); compare this German version
of *Common Sense,* which was delayed until the latest English edition arrived
to be the basis for translation, with the critical edition in Thomas Paine,
Political Writings, ed. Bruce Kuklick (Cambridge, 1989), 3–38. Miller's advertisement for *Gesunde Vernuft* appeared on 23 January 1776. According to
one observer, the German translation enjoyed great success among its readers;
see HSP, Shippen Papers, 7:161, E. Burd to [?], 15 March 1776. There is no
exact German translation for *happiness.* In the context of both Paine's and
Jefferson's use of the term, I infer that German speakers understood *Glückseeligkeit* to refer to security or certainty in property, since the term means

generally an inner state of repose, serenity, and blessedness.

51. On the vexing term *happiness,* I am indebted to Professor Frank Shuffleton for allowing me to read his unpublished essay "Thomas Jefferson and the Pursuit of Happiness." See Adrienne Koch, *Power, Morals, and the Founding Fathers: Essays in the Interpretation of the American Enlightenment* (Ithaca, N.Y., 1961), 29–30; John Locke, *Essay concerning the Human Understanding,* ed. Alexander Campbell Fraser (New York, 1959), 1:298–303, 316.

Chapter 10   Piety and Bürgertum in the New Republic

1. "Ettwein's Journey to Georgia," 254.

2. In the text of this chapter, parenthetical citations of chapter and paragraph numbers refer to the Jerusalem and Zion Kirchenordnung. The handwritten copy of the document which Mühlenberg apparently took back with him is at LTSA, PM 95/ Z 13; unfortunately, it is not complete. Chap. 3 of the Kirchenordnung also reflects upon Halle's and Augsburg's generosity, which supplemented the congregation's "mite."

3. This paragraph and the next are based on *Journals of Muhlenberg* 2:550–85; Mühlenberg's rehearsal of the tangled property relationships; quotations at 600, 598.

4. Ibid., 558, 598, 602–3, 614–25, quotation at 661.

5. LC, Records of the Lutheran Church at New Ebenezer, Ga., 1754–1820, box 628, 13 January 1773.

6. Winde, "Frühgeschichte," 54, 181–86; Baumgarten's work exemplifies the growing influence of Enlightenment thinking at Halle, of which older missionaries such as Mühlenberg were unaware; see Siegmund Baumgarten, *Evangelische Glaubenslehre,* 3 vols. (Halle, 1759).

7. For Mühlenberg's quotation, see *Journal of Muhlenberg* 2:637.

8. Most of the sections into which paragraphs are divided are one page in length; this one is over two pages long.

9. The events are detailed in a fragmentary letter from Rabenhorst, Treutlen, and nine others (Johannes Gugel, Joseph Schubdrein, Christian Steiner, Johannes Hangleiter, Simon Reuter, Ulrich Neidlinger, Jacob Waldhauer, Sigmund Ott, and Conrad Rahn)—the same men who had complained about Triebner to Ziegenhagen in London in 1771. The letter is at LTSA, PM 95 D8. Mühlenberg acknowledged receipt of the letter, as well as a letter from Triebner, without noting the contents; see *Journals of Muhlenberg* 2:704–9.

10. LTSA, PM 95 Z 6, copy in Mühlenberg's hand with accompanying copies of letters to Pasche in London and to Ebenezer, received by him in February 1779.

11. The Halle archives do not reveal how Triebner responded. For further details, see Winde, "Frühgeschichte," 65–67.

12. Allen D. Candler, ed., *The Revolutionary Records of the State of Georgia,* 3 vols. (Atlanta, 1908), 1:32–35, quotations at 35; also see 35 for a list of those belonging to the republican faction: Johann Adam Treutlen, William

Holsendorf, Johann Stirk, Samuel Stirk, Johann Schneider, Rudolph Stro-
haker, Jonathan Schneider, Johann Gottlieb Schneider, Jonathan Rahn, Ernest
Zittrauer, Joshua Helfenstein, Jacob Helfenstein, and Jacob Waldhauer; to
these one should add the eminent Savannah Lutheran Stephan Millen.

13. GDAH, Executive Department, Incoming Correspondence, 202/67,
1754–1800, Justus Scheuber to Colonel Fishbourn, 29 May 1789; Executive
Orders for Military Commissions, box 1, 1787–93, 14 October 1790, lists
commissions for nine companies of Effingham County Militia; Executive
Department Confiscated Estate Sales, 1782–85, MS vol.; and Reports of
Commissioners, 1783, 1 vol. The statutes governing confiscation are in H.
Marbury and W. H. Crawford, *Digest of the Laws of the State of Georgia
. . .* (Savannah, 1802), 82–90.

14. The most recent assessment of South Carolina repeats this impression;
see Rachel N. Klein, *The Unification of a Slave State: The Rise of the Planter
Class in the South Carolina Backcountry, 1760–1808* (Chapel Hill, 1989), 50,
81, 86. Klein omits any genuine discussion of German-language settlement
or activity beyond these traditional impressions. For Drayton's remark, see
Richard J. Hooker, ed., *The Carolina Backcountry on the Eve of the Revolution:
The Journal and Other Writings of Charles Woodmason, Anglican Itinerant* (Chapel
Hill, 1953), 189.

15. SCDAH, Comptroller General Records, Petitions for Compensation,
AA 3877A, roll 76; Aa 7774, roll 146; AA 8162, roll 152.

16. Ibid., AA 2886-B, nos. 1, 2, 3. Claß's companions were Georg,
Friedrich, and Heinrich Slappey (Schleppi); Johann Adam Minick, Jacob
Koyley (Köhle), Simeon Theus, Martin Hittle, Johann and Peter Foust, Hein-
rich Senn, Johann Goßert, and three English speakers, James Mashborn,
Oliver Legran, and Edward Wells. The Saxe-Gotha officials who received
the original petition in February 1783 included Jacob Geiger.

17. South Caroliniana Library, Claß MSS, 1805–10, P/1987, letter to Ann
Class, 30 April 1806.

18. Brent Holcomb, ed., *Orangeburgh District South Carolina Returns in
Partition from the Court of Equity, 1824–1837* (Greenville, S.C., 1982), 35–41,
62–63, 71–79.

19. This paragraph summarizes letters, wills, claims, and genealogy in
South Caroliniana Library, P/ 7849, Stone Family MSS.

20. For further examples, see SDCAH, Confiscated Estates, Loyalist
Petitions Loose MS File, claim of Adam Bauer, and fourteen others. I discover
no loyalist petitions for the Charleston German Lutherans; almost all surviving evidence points exclusively to the late-arriving, Londonborough group
and the isolated Dutch Fork or '96 area—i.e., the far western South Carolina
frontier.

21. SCDAH, Revolutionary War Pensions and Bounty Land Warrants,
roll 705, 172/M 804. Other Hebron veterans also were pensioned—Jacob
Aylor, for instance (Secretary of War Pension Reports, vol. 2, 1835). But
Christopher Tanner, Jr., who died at the siege of Yorktown, left a widow
who unsuccessfully petitioned for pension and relief in 1795; for details, see

Germanna Record No. 6 (1965), 64–65; and *German Record No. 12* (1970), 8.

22. *Journals of Muhlenberg* 2:375.

23. On Frank, see Glatfelter, *Pastors and People,* 40; on the signing, see LTSA, PM 95 1, Frank's journal for 20 October 1775–28 November 1776, entry of 29 October 1776; for his letter of call, see *Journals of Muhlenberg* 2:705–6.

24. VSLAD, Virginia Legislative Petitions, Culpeper County, 22 October 1776.

25. Earl Gregg Swem Library Archives, College of William and Mary (Williamsburg, Va.), Henkel to unknown correspondent, 8 January 1810; "The Journals of the Reverend Robert J. Miller, Lutheran Missionary in Virginia, 1811–1813," ed. Willard E. Wright, *VHMB* 61 (1953), 141–66; William K. Boyd and Charles A. Krummel, "German Tracts concerning the Lutheran Church in North Carolina during the Eighteenth Century," *North Carolina Historical Review* 7 (1930), 245.

26. John Cook Wyllie, "The Second Mrs. Wayland: An Unpublished Jefferson Opinion on a Case in Equity," *American Journal of Legal History* 9 (1965), 64–68; Madison County, Virginia, County Clerk's Office (Madison, Va.), Old Chancery Causes, boxes 3-A to 7-A; I count thirteen such causes involving German family disputes over land titles and inheritance problems.

27. See in Madison County Clerk's Office, "Attorney's Opinion"; deposition of John Walker, 28 November 1811.

28. VSLAD, Virginia Legislative Petitions, Orange County, 1777–94; Culpeper County Legislative Petitions, box 1, 1776–90; Madison County Petitions, 1795–1825.

29. Ibid., Madison County Order Book 1, 1793–98, 23 May 1793, 22 August 1798. The conversion of German speakers from Federalism to Jeffersonian Republicanism has been most extensively traced by Kenneth W. Keller, "Rural Politics and the Collapse of Pennsylvania Federalism," *Transactions of the American Philosophical Society* 72 (1982), 1–73.

30. Philadelphia City Archives, Letters of Attorney 1408/1, p. 326.

31. Ittlingen Village Archive, Pfandbuch-Beilagen zum Band 0; B1. Go 18/ p. 80, r and v. My survey of surviving recovery attempts in various archives suggests not only that numbers of attempts declined but also that local and regional officials in the Reich, distrustful of the legitimacy of the new states, tended to refuse to process such applications.

32. LC, copies of German archival material, original now in Merseburg, originally Berlin, PrGStA, Rep. 11, 21 a, Bü. 2, 1780–1817. On the Boston Port Bill, see Roeber, *Faithful Magistrates,* 160–61.

33. For the most recent treatment of the Revolution from this perspective, see Jeremy Black, *War for America: The Fight for Independence, 1775–1783* (London, 1991).

34. AFSt 4 D 5, Phila. Schriftwechsel, 1800–1804, pp. 24–26, Helmuth to Knapp, 28 July 1800, on Pennsylvania Germans and politics, Owen F. Ireland, "The Crux of Politics: Religion and Party in Pennsylvania, 1778–1789," *WMQ,* 3d ser., 42 (1985), 453–75; Jürgen Heideking, "Die geschicht-

liche Bedeutung der amerikanischen Verfassungstdebatte von 1787 bis 1791," *Amerikastudien/American Studies* 34 (1989), 33–48; see also Roeber, "Citizens or Subjects?"

35. On this repeated theme, see Don Yoder, "The 'Dutchman' and the *'Deitschlenner':* The New World Confronts the Old," *Yearbook of German-American Studies* 23 (1988), 1–17. I comment on Helmuth's struggles over education and virtue in "The von Mosheim Society and the Preservation of German Education and Culture in the New Republic, 1789–1813," in Hartmut Lehmann and Kenneth F. Ledford, eds., *German Influence on Education in the United States to 1917* (Cambridge, forthcoming).

36. Donna T. Andrew, *Philanthropy and Police: London Charity in the Eighteenth Century* (Princeton, 1989), 3–43, 197–202. Alexis de Tocqueville, *Democracy in America,* trans. George Lawrence, ed. J. P. Mayer (New York, 1969), 680–83. As late as 1991, Robert Wuthenow estimated that 55 percent of all volunteer work in the United States, most of it done for some charitable cause, occurs within the churches; see his *Acts of Compassion: Caring for Others and Helping Ourselves* (Princeton, 1991). I have investigated the growing crisis in financing such private philanthropy in one German-Lutheran institution; see A. G. Roeber, *Good and Faithful Servants: A Centennial History of the Lutheran Home and Services for the Aged* (Arlington Heights, Ill., 1991).

37. Brady, *Turning Swiss,* chap. 2; on German nineteenth-century developments, see James Q. Whitman, *The Legacy of Roman Law in the German Romantic Era: Historical Vision and Legal Change* (Princeton, 1990); Kötz, *Trust and Treuhand,* 117–27.

38. Both the Franconian and the Alemannic areas of the southwest, by 1750, were capable of creating vigorous middle-class public consciousness and boasted communications and trading networks. The later history of Germany, however, demonstrated that these were relatively weak and disorganized circles. See, e.g., Andrea Hofmeister-Hunger, "Provincial Political Culture in the Holy Roman Empire: The Franconian Margravates of Ansbach and Bayreuth," in Hellmuth, ed., *Transformation of Political Culture,* 146–64.

39. On this mythic dimension of property, see Jennifer Nadelsky, *Private Property and the Limits of American Constitutionalism: The Madisonian Framework and Its Legacy* (Chicago, 1990), 246–54; for a more balanced and sympathetic view of British notions of property and social responsibility, see Thomas A. Horne, *Property Rights and Poverty: Political Argument in Britain, 1605–1834* (Chapel Hill, 1990).

40. John Locke, *An Essay concerning Human Understanding,* ed. Peter H. Nidditch (Oxford, 1975), book 3, chap. 1, p. 402.

41. Mary Douglas, "Notes and Queries about Analysis of Cultural Bias," cited in Michael Thompson et al., *Cultural Theory* (Boulder, Colo., 1990), 263–65. See also Gerald Stourtz, " *'Constitution':* Changing Meanings of the Term from the Early Seventeenth to the Late Eighteenth Century," in Terence Ball and J. G. A. Pocock, eds., *Conceptual Change and the Constitution* (Lawrence, Kans., 1988), 13–34; and J. G. A. Pocock, "States, Republics,

and Empires: The American Founding in Early Modern Perspective," in ibid., 55–57.

42. Blackstone, *Commentaries* 2:8; William B. Scott, *In Pursuit of Happiness: American Concepts of Property from the Seventeenth to the Twentieth Century* (Bloomington, Ind., 1977), 5–23.

43. See the comments and literature in John M. Murrin, "Self-Interest Conquers Patriotism: Republicans, Liberals, and Indians Reshape the Nation," in Jack P. Greene, ed., *The American Revolution: Its Character and Limits* (New York, 1987), 224–29; and Gordon S. Wood, "Illusions and Disillusions in the American Revolution," in ibid., 355–61.

44. Foster, "Peasant Society"; Thompson et al., *Cultural Theory,* 39–43; the limited horizons or "minimalist" expectations held by German speakers were probably shared by many other groups in the colonies as well. On the liberating possibilities that come from forgetting parts of one's history, see Friedrich Nietzsche's *The Use and Abuse of History,* trans. Adrian Collins (New York, 1957), 5–8.

45. Despite its somewhat tortured approach, see Michael Warner, *The Letters of the Republic: Publication and the Public Sphere in Eighteenth-Century America* (Cambridge, Mass., 1989); for a useful caveat, see Gordon S. Wood, "The Liberation of Print," *New Republic* 76, no. 3956 (1990), 40–44.

46. Bailyn's and Wood's explorations of the rhetoric of the period overstated the gap between experience and expression, leaving little room for religious sentiment and emotion, and tended to portray the rhetoric as irrational. See Bernard Bailyn, *The Ideological Origins of the American Revolution* (Cambridge, Mass., 1967); idem, "The Ideological Fulfillment of the American Revolution: A Commentary on the Constitution," in idem, *Faces of Revolution: Personalities and Themes in the Struggle for American Independence* (New York, 1990), 225–78; Gordon S. Wood, "Rhetoric and Reality in the American Revolution," *WMQ,* 3d ser., 23 (1966), 2–32.

47. Johann Joachim Spalding, *Gedancken über den Werth der Gefühle in dem Christenthum* (Leipzig, 1773); see *Journals of Muhlenberg* 2:683–84, quotation at 645.

48. Despite dubious assumptions about the insignificance of the growth of institutions among German speakers in the 1740s, see Jon Butler, *Awash in a Sea of Faith: Christianizing the American People* (Cambridge, Mass., 1990), 124–27, 190–270; more generally, see Nathan O. Hatch, *The Democratization of American Christianity* (New Haven, 1989); neither work integrates German Pietism into its overall interpretation.

49. Habermas, *Theory and Practice,* 77–81; on the Scottish school and its implications in North America, see Mark Noll, *Princeton and the Republic, 1768–1822: The Search for a Christian Enlightenment in the Era of Samuel Stanhope Smith* (Princeton, 1989).

50. Robert Lawson-Peebles, *Landscape and Written Expression in Revolutionary America: The World Turned Upside Down* (Cambridge, 1988), 84–99.

51. A few recent works have suggested the contrary, i.e., that the Ger-

mans may have held fast to as many aspects of their culture as possible. For arguments in favor of cultural persistence, see Elizabeth Augusta Kessel, "Germans on the Maryland Frontier: A Social History of Frederick County, Maryland, 1730–1800" (Ph.D. diss., Rice University, 1981), 395–447; Tully, "Ethnicity, Religion, and Politics"; Hermann Wellenreuther, "Image and Counterimage, Tradition and Expectation: The German Immigrants in English Colonial Society in Pennsylvania, 1700–1765," in Frank Trommler and James McVeigh, eds., *America and the Germans,* 2 vols. (Philadelphia, 1985), 1:85–105. Wellenreuther has ironically noted that where political or public ideas are concerned, research so far has "proceeded on the assumption that the political notions of the immigrants radically altered in the instant they kissed the ground of the glorified new world" (*Der Aufstieg des ersten Britischen Weltreiches: England und seine nordamerikanischen Kolonien, 1660–1763* [Düsseldorf, 1987], 161).

52. "Die Sachsen sind Hell"; a more unsavory version, "Die Sachsen sind die Musterschüler" (i.e., they are the star pupils of whoever is in power) suggests that they (and perhaps other Germans) are unprincipled.

53. Kathleen Neils Conzen, "Peasant Pioneers: Generational Succession among German Farmers in Frontier Minnesota," in Steven Hahn and Jonathan Prude, eds., *The Countryside in the Age of Capitalist Transformation: Essays in the Social History of Rural America* (Chapel Hill, 1985), 259–92; Kathleen Neils Conzen, "Making Their Own America: Assimilation Theory and the German Peasant Pioneer," *German Historical Institute Annual Lecture Series,* no. 3 (New York, 1990), 1–33.

54. William H. Newell, "Inheritance on the Maturing Frontier: Butler County, Ohio, 1803–1865," in Stanley L. Engerman and Robert E. Gallmann, eds., *Long-Term Factors in American Economic Growth* (Chicago, 1986), 261–303. On the "Dutch contract," see August G. Eckhardt, "The Support Contract," in *Wisconsin Law Review* (1951), 577–622. I am indebted to Professor Karl Kroeschell of the law faculty at the Albert-Ludwig Universität, Freiburg im Breisgau, for information on the "Dutch contract."

55. Morton J. Horwitz, "The Legacy of 1776 in Legal and Economic Thought," *Journal of Law and Economics* 19 (1976), 467–88; idem, "The History of the Public/Private Distinction," *University of Pennsylvania Law Review* 130 (1982), 1423–28; and idem, *The Transformation of American Law, 1790–1860* (Cambridge, Mass., 1977). On the "integrative" function of the Revolution, see Clifford Geertz, "Integrative Revolution: Primordial Sentiments and Civil Politics in New States," in idem, ed., *Old Societies and New States* (New York, 1963), 154–55. On "mother tongues" and "distancing languages," see Walter J. Ong, "Transformations of the Word and Alienation," in idem, *Interfaces of the Word: Studies in the Evolution of Consciousness and Culture* (Ithaca, N.Y., 1977), 22–34.

56. For the conventional views, see Helen E. Pfatteicher, *The Ministerium of Pennsylvania: Oldest Lutheran Synod in America Founded in Colony Days* (Philadelphia, 1938), 40–54, under the significantly worded subhead "Re-

tarded Growth"; also E. Clifford Nelson, *The Lutherans in North America* (Philadelphia, 1975), 83–101.

57. AFSt 4 D 2, Kunze to Halle, 27 October 1789; 4 D 2, Kunze to Johann Carl Kunze, 18 July 1796; Kunze to Pennsylvania Synod, cited in Pfatteicher, *Ministerium,* 41.

58. Hermann Glaser, *The Cultural Roots of National Socialism (Spießer-ideologie),* trans. Ernest A. Menze (Austin, Tex., 1978), 18. On nineteenth-century "middling" culture, see Jürgen Kocka, ed., *Bürgertum im 19. Jahrhundert: Deutschland im europäischen Vergleich* (Munich, 1988); Lothar Gall, *Bürgertum in Deutschland* (Berlin, 1989).

59. De Tocqueville, *Democracy,* 256.

60. On German Pietism's inadequacy to provide a language for social or political criticism, see Kaiser, *Pietismus und Patriotismus*; on public opinion, see Daniel Gordon, " 'Public Opinion' and the Civilizing Process in France: The Example of Morellet," *Eighteenth Century Studies* 22 (1989), 302–28. For a misguided attempt to claim Halle Pietism as the inspiration for a small antislavery perspective among New York Lutherans, see Paul P. Kuenning, *The Rise and Fall of American Lutheran Pietism: The Rejection of an Activist Heritage* (Mercer, Ga., 1989); and my review in *Christian Century* 106 (1989), 600–602.

BIBLIOGRAPHIC NOTE

A COMPLETE bibliography of the primary and secondary sources consulted and used would make this book affordable only to libraries; readers are referred to both the list of abbreviations of archives and secondary journals and to the notes for each chapter. I have elsewhere discussed in some detail the problems surrounding local archives in Germany; the interested reader should refer to my " 'Origins of German-American Concepts of Property and Inheritance in Village Transactions," *Perspectives in American History,* n.s., 3 (1987), 750–74, part of which is reproduced with permission in chapters 2 and 3. For further details on immigration, see my " 'The Origin of Whatever Is Not English among Us': The Dutch-speaking and the German-speaking Peoples of Colonial British America," in Bernard Bailyn and Philip D. Morgan, eds., *Strangers within the Realm: Cultural Margins of the First British Empire* (Chapel Hill, 1991), 220–83, also reprinted in part, with permission, in chapter 4; as well as my essay "In German Ways? Problems and Potentials of Eighteenth-Century German Social and Emigration History," *William and Mary Quarterly,* 3d ser., 44 (1987), 750–74. I have also omitted some details of Württemberg church history which the reader can consult in my "Germans, Property, and the First Great Awakening: Rehearsal for a Revolution?" in Winfried Herget and Karl Ortseifen, eds., *The Transit of Civilization from Europe to America: Essays in Honor of Hans Galinsky* (Tübingen, 1986), 169–92. Also reproduced in part here with permission, chapter 4. The analysis of Miller's use of the Swiss past originally appeared in more expanded form as "Henry Miller's *Staatsbote*: A Revolutionary Journalist's Use of the Swiss Past," *Yearbook for German-American Studies* 25 (1990), 57–76, and is reproduced here in chapter 9 with permission.

The present study rests in part on an examination of local estate inventories, tax books, sales books, court records, and church parish registers, in varying states of completeness, for the German villages listed below. The choice of villages was made largely by reading Werner Hacker's many lists of emigrants and attempting to identify by region what villages produced the largest number of emigrants. These were, for Württemberg, Bebenhausen, Bodelshausen, Seißen, Lauffen an der Eyach, Freudenstadt, Neckartenzlingen, Neuffen, Oberboihingen, Reudern, Gingen-Fils, Neckartailfingen,

Neckarhausen, Grötzingen, Schlaitdorf, and Schwaigern; for the Kraichgau, Ittlingen, Michelfeld, Zuzenhausen, Sinsheim, Dühren, Weiler, and Rohrbach; for the Palatinate, Dossenheim, Edenkoben, and Mühlhofen; for Hesse, Burgschwandbach, Odenbach, and Camberg; and for Ulm, Weidenstetten, Altheim, Langenau, Geislingen, Holzkirch, Lonsee, Bernstadt, and Nerenstetten.

As I explain at various points in the text, the destruction of large portions of the archives in Stuttgart, in Mannheim, and in Darmstadt render accurate re-creations of emigration or property relationships impossible for much of these areas. For the Kraichgau and some of the Palatinate, the as yet undocumented and uncataloged village materials that probably do exist at the Generallandesarchiv Karlsruhe may at some future date provide a more accurate picture of the patterns sketched here. The new archival facilities in Speyer make them an unusually pleasant environment in which to work for the Palatinate proper; the general archives at Stuttgart and Ludwigsburg, and regional archival centers such as the ones at Eßlingen and Nürtingen, are well organized—though understaffed, especially the regional centers. The Center for the History of the Palatinate (formerly the Heimatstelle Pfalz), at Kaiserslautern, remains an invaluable starting point for tracing families from this region because of the card file compiled there. Nothing quite like this exists for the other regions.

Both lack of space in this volume and the ongoing work of a promising group of younger scholars led me to drop from the essay analyses on families done in Lancaster, Reading, and York, Pennsylvania. Rural Pennsylvania German speakers are now being investigated by Mark Häberlein, at Freiberg am Breisgau; Aaron Fogleman, at the University of South Alabama ("Hopeful Journeys: German Immigration and Settlement in Greater Pennsylvania, 1717–1775" [Ph.D. diss., University of Michigan, 1991]); Georg Fertig, at the Free University of Berlin; and Rosalind Beiler, at the University of Pennsylvania. We badly need a study of German speakers in colonial New York City from its role in the colony of New Netherland onward; backcountry settlements in North Carolina, including those populated by German speakers, are beginning to receive attention from Jim Whittenburg, at the College of William and Mary, and Joshua McKaughan, at the University of North Carolina-Greensboro. Both Elizabeth Lewis, at Northwestern University, and Paul Baglyos, at the University of Chicago Divinity School, are investigating the later eighteenth-century German speakers. For the Philadelphia German Lutherans, I have relied on the 1756 tax lists, and the 1772 tax lists matched with the 1775 City Constable Returns as prepared by Billy G. Smith of Montana State University. To this I have added other materials from both the Philadelphia City Archives and the Lutheran Theological Seminary Archives to reconstruct the outlines of Saint Michael's and Zion Church.

On the topic of networks and the construction of "private sociability," in addition to the literature cited in Margaret C. Jacob's essay "The Enlightenment Redefined: The Formation of Modern Civil Society," *Social Research*

58 (1991), 475–95, I have found the work of David S. Shields to be informative: see his *Oracles of Empire: Poetry, Politics, and Commerce in British America, 1690–1750* (Chicago, 1990); Jeremy Boissevain, *Friends of Friends: Networks, Manipulators, and Coalitions* (New York, 1974); and idem and J. Clyde Mitchell, eds., *Network Analysis: Studies in Human Interaction* (The Hague, 1973). Mitchell explains his own perspectives in "Social Networks," *American Review of Anthropology* 3 (1974), 279–99.

This book has focused on the intersection of social and material conditions with the values, ideas, and emotions that German speakers, living in two languages, relied on, to interpret their lives. Some will recognize here my indebtedness to Bernard Bailyn's point that historians need to show how the "latent" (here, the "private") and the "manifest" (public activity and language) interact (Bernard Bailyn, "The Challenge of Modern Historiography," *American Historical Review* 87 [1982], 1–24.) An extended comment on the vast literatures I have used to probe the central question of the book seems superfluous, as well as nearly impossible to bring off gracefully. As much as possible, I have buried any apparatus in the notes and the texture of the argument. Most readers will see where my sympathies and biases lie; should it be necessary to point out, I do retain the conviction that despite the problems of contextualism, one can relocate reasonably well the more and the less probable intentions, meanings, and choices of humans in a given time. Although I am deeply sympathetic to the "relational" approach to cultural studies which David Sabean's work represents (*Property, Production, and Family in Neckarhausen, 1700–1870* [Cambridge, 1990], 7–22), my own concerns here have been different. Although the individual conscience is not the focus of this essay, inevitably, my tracing the emergence of an individual and confessional identity and its relationship to both religious rhetoric and the politics of a public arena distinguishes my own efforts from Sabean's. The fact that I examine German speakers' conventions and their creation of a rhetoric to describe themselves and their place in North America, makes it obvious that I believe that it is possible to trace the evolution of a religious or political discourse over time, and that to a limited degree, one can "get at" what was being passed on in what some scholars like to call "traditionary discursive speech acts."

Those who find this approach naive or insufficiently sensitive to cultural relativism should follow the arguments noted in the following essays: Quentin Skinner, " 'Social Meaning' and the Explanation of Social Action," in Patrick Gardiner, ed., *The Philosophy of History* (Oxford, 1974), 102–26; idem, "Conventions and the Understanding of Speech Acts," *Philosophical Quarterly* 20 (1970), 118–38; idem, "Motives, Intentions and the Interpretation of Texts," *New Literary History* 3 (1972), 393–408; idem, "Meaning and Understanding in the History of Ideas," *History and Theory* 8 (1969), 3–53; C. Tarlton, "Historicity, Meaning, and Revisionism in the Study of Political Thought," ibid. 12 (1973), 307–28; Bhikhu Parekh and R. N. Berki, "The History of Political Ideas: A Critique of Q. Skinner's Methodology," *Journal of the History of Ideas* 34 (1983), 163–84; Gordon J. Schochet, "Quentin Skinner's Method,"

Political Theory 2 (1974), 261–76; Peter L. Janssen, "Political Thought as Traditionary Action: The Critical Response to Skinner and Pocock," *History and Theory* 26 (1986), 115–46. I still find considerable value in E. D. Hirsch's observation that scholars have made too much of the split between "autonomous meanings" and "intended meanings" *Validity in Interpretation* [New Haven, 1967]; see also idem, *The Aims of Interpretation* [Chicago, 1976]). For a useful but sometimes erroneous reading both of "intentionalists" and of Wittgenstein, see David C. Hoy, *The Critical Circle* (Berkeley, 1978), 1–40; see also Dominick La Capra, *History and Criticism* (Ithaca, N.Y., 1985), 115–42; and the essays in Dominick La Capra and Steven L. Kaplan, eds., *Modern European Intellectual History: Reappraisals and New Perspectives* (Ithaca, N.Y., 1982). For one historian's wry observations about the difficulties involved in following Skinner's approach, see J. A. W. Gunn, *Beyond Liberty and Property: The Process of Self-Recognition in Eighteenth-Century Political Thought* (Kingston, Ont., 1983), 2–4. Readers must judge for themselves whether we can now move beyond liberty and property in understanding Lutheran German speakers in British North America, and the early republic.

INDEX